The Coon-Sanders Nighthawks

The Coon-Sanders Nighthawks

"The Band That Made Radio Famous"

Fred W. Edmiston

McFarland & Company, Inc., Publishers
Jefferson, North Carolina, and London

The present work is a reprint of the illustrated case bound edition of The Coon-Sanders Nighthawks: The Band That Made Radio Famous, *first published in 2003 by McFarland.*

LIBRARY OF CONGRESS CATALOGUING-IN-PUBLICATION DATA

Edmiston, Fred W., 1930–
    The Coon-Sanders Nighthawks : the band that made radio famous / Fred W. Edmiston.
       p.   cm.
    Includes bibliographical references and index.

    ISBN 978-0-7864-4327-7
    softcover : 50# alkaline paper ∞

    1. Coon-Sanders Nighthawks (Musical group)   2. Dance orchestras—Missouri—Kansas City.   3. Jazz musicians—Missouri—Biography.   I. Title.
ML3518.E35   2009
784.4'8165'0922—dc21   2002011779

British Library cataloguing data are available

©2003 Fred W. Edmiston. All rights reserved

No part of this book may be reproduced or transmitted in any form or by any means, electronic or mechanical, including photocopying or recording, or by any information storage and retrieval system, without permission in writing from the publisher.

Manufactured in the United States of America

On the cover (left to right): Elmer Krebs, Joe Sanders, Carleton Coon, Russell Stout, Joe Richolson, Harold Thiell, Robert Pope, Floyd Estep, Rex Downing, John Thiell (photograph by Maurice Seymour, courtesy Harvey C. Rettberg)

McFarland & Company, Inc., Publishers
  Box 611, Jefferson, North Carolina 28640
    www.mcfarlandpub.com

To Harvey Clark Rettberg
Pickens, South Carolina,
who helped me gather much of my material

and to the memory of
Douglas Edward Mitchell (1903–1968)
Mobile, Alabama,
who heightened my interest in the music of the Twenties
and in the Coon-Sanders Nighthawks

and John Allyn Coon (1913–1999)
Prairie Village, Kansas,
who persuaded me to write the story of his father's orchestra
and gave me valuable information about the Nighthawks

Acknowledgments

I wish to express my gratitude to the following individuals for their valuable help during work on this book:

C. Van Akin, Claude and Ruth Anderson (Floyd Estep's brother-in-law), Pamela Barta-Kacena, Rachell Bateman, Linda Begue, Joy Bevan, Leah Ann Bezin, David Birge (Dewey Birge's son), Joan Boeck, Sherri Bonham, Les Brown, Jr., Gregg J. Buttermore, Katheryn Carrier, Kristi Chapman, Sylom M. Coast, Suzanne Colin, Carleton Allyn Coon, Jr., John Allyn Coon (deceased), Carolyn Cottrell, Judie Christensen, Matthew L. Daley, Thomas A. DeLong, Dan Doty, Shirley Dressler, Sherry and Steve Drummond, John Emory, Linda Fairchild, David Free, Vicky Frey, Roger Gambrel, Jill Gardner, Carol Genova, Molly Gibson, Mark Guyer, Stuart Hinds, Lynn Hobbs, Alice Faye Hubbard, Diane B. Jacob, Dale Jones, Pam Kacena, Michael Keepper, Angie Kindig, Erik D. Larsen, Kevin B. Leonard, David N. Lewis, Clinton Lowell, Mary Lyons, Curtis R. Mann, Shirley Mann, Norma Maring, James C. Marshall, Marian McPartland, Mary Jane Sanders Meyer (Joe Sanders' niece), Janet K. Miller (Joe Sanders' great-niece), Max Morath, Willis Morrisette, Denise Morrison, Nancy Neumann, Melinda Nunn, Sara J. Nyman, Kelly Pigott, Mary Ann Pirone, Michael R. Pitts, LeeAnn Platner, Robin Rader, Margaret Remy, Harvey Clark Rettberg, Jimmy Sandifer, Nina Sappington, Bernie Schermetzler, Charles Sengstock, Janine Shilling, Gretel Smith, Brian Spangle, Vaughan Stanley, Nate Stoller, Connie Sutton, Shannon Swain, Ralph Waite, Marilyn Wilkerson, Cathy Birge Williams (Dewey Birge's granddaughter), Dan Wingate.

I would also like to thank the following institutions for their assistance:

Akron-Summit County Public Library, Akron, Ohio; Allen County Historical Society, Lima, Ohio; Allen County Public Library, Fort Wayne, Ind.; Anderson Public Library, Anderson, Ind.; Ann Arbor District Library, Ann Arbor, Mich.; Appleton Public Library, Appleton, Wisc.; Atlanta Public Library, Atlanta, Ga.; Auburn Cord Duesenberg Museum, Auburn, Ind.; Auburn University, Ralph Brown Draughon Library, Auburn, Ala.; Aurora Public Library, Aurora, Ill.; Bloomington Public Library, Bloomington, Ill.; Bowling Green Public Library, Bowling Green, Ky.; Buffalo and Erie

County Public Library, Special Collections, Buffalo, N.Y.; Cabell County Public Library, Huntington, W. Va.; Cadillac-Wexford Public Library, Cadillac, Mich.; Capital Area District Library, Lansing, Mich.; Carnegie Library of Pittsburgh, Pittsburgh, Penn.; Carnegie-Stout Public Library, Dubuque, Iowa; Champaign Public Library, Champaign, Ill.; Chattanooga-Hamilton County Bicentennial Library, Chattanooga, Tenn.; Chillicothe & Ross County Public Library, Chillicothe, Ohio; Cleveland Public Library, Cleveland, Ohio; Columbus Metropolitan Library, Columbus, Ohio; Daniel Boone Regional Library, Columbia, Mo.; Dayton & Montgomery County Public Library, Dayton, Ohio; Davenport Public Library, Davenport, Iowa; Detroit Public Library, Detroit, Mich.; Eckhart Public Library, Auburn, Ind.; Erie County Public Library, Erie, Penn.; Evansville-Vanderburgh County Public Library, Evansville, Ind.; Fairfield County District Library, Lancaster, Ohio; Fond du Lac Public Library, Fond du Lac, Wisc.; Fort Dodge Public Library, Fort Dodge, Iowa; Franklin Public Library, Franklin, Penn.; Freeborn County Historical Society Library, Albert Lea, Minn.; Galena Public Library, Galena, Ill.; Grand Rapids Public Library, Grand Rapids, Mich.; Herrin City Library, Herrin, Ill.; Hopkins County Genealogical Society, Madisonville, Ky.; Huntington City-Township Public Library, Huntington, Ind.; Indiana State Library, Indianapolis; Indianapolis-Marion County Public Library, Indianapolis, Ind.; Iowa City Public Library, Iowa City, Iowa; Jackson District Library, Jackson, Mich.; Johnsonburg Public Library, Johnsonburg, Pa.; Joliet Public Library, Joliet, Ill.; Kansas City Public Library, Special Collections, Kansas City, Mo.; Keyser-Mineral County Library, Keyser, W. Va.; Knox County Public Library, Vincennes, Ind.; La Crosse Public Library, La Crosse, Wisc.; La Salle Public Library, La Salle, Ill.; Lexington Public Library, Lexington, Ky.; Lima Public Library, Lima, Ohio; Lincoln Library, Springfield, Ill.; Marathon County Public Library, Wausau, Wisc.; Marion Public Library, Marion, Ind.; Marion Public Library, Marion, Ohio; Marshfield Public Library, Marshfield, Wisc.; Memphis Public Library, Memphis, Tenn.; Meridian Community College, L. O. Todd Library, Meridian, Miss.; Meridian-Lauderdale County Public Library, Meridian, Miss.; Metropolitan Library System in Oklahoma, Oklahoma City; Milwaukee Public Library, Milwaukee, Wisc.; Monroe Public Library, Monroe, La.; Morrison-Reeves Library, Richmond, Ind.; Mt. Carmel Public Library, Mt. Carmel, Ill.; Museum of Broadcast Communications, Chicago, Ill.; Nashville and Davidson County, Public Library of, Nashville, Tenn.; Nebraska State Historical Society, Lincoln; New Orleans Public Library, New Orleans, La.; Norelius Community Library, Denison, Iowa; Northwestern University Library, Evanston, Ill.; Oklahoma Dept. of Libraries, Oklahoma City, Okla.; Omaha Public Library, Omaha, Neb.; Past & Present Research, Cadillac, Mich.; Pollard Memorial Library, Lowell, Mass.; Portsmouth Public Library, Portsmouth, Ohio; Potomac State College, Mary Shipper Library, Keyser, W. Va.; Public Library of Nashville, Nashville, Tenn.; Quincy Public Library, Quincy, Ill.; Racine Public Library, Racine, Wisc.; Reuben McMillan Free Library Association, Youngstown, Ohio; Ritter Public Library, Vermilion, Ohio; St. Louis Public Library, St. Louis, Mo.; Saint Louis University, Pius XII Memorial Library, St. Louis, Mo.; Sioux City Public Library, Sioux City, Iowa; Stark County District Library, Canton, Ohio; State Historical Society of Missouri, Columbia; State Historical Society of Wisconsin, Madison; Streator Public Library, Streator, Ill.; Tippecanoe County Public Library, Lafayette, Ind.; Toledo-Lucas County Public Library, Toledo, Ohio; Traverse Area District Library, Traverse City, Mich.; Union City Public Library, Union City, Penn.; University of Detroit Mercy Libraries, Detroit, Mich.; University of Illinois Library, Urbana; University of Iowa Libraries, Iowa City; University of Kansas Alumni Association, Lawrence; University of Michigan, Bentley

Historical Library, Ann Arbor; University of Notre Dame, Hesburgh Library's Archives, South Bend, Ind.; University of Wisconsin Library, Madison; Vigo County Public Library, Terre Haute, Ind.; Virginia Military Institute, Preston Library, Lexington, Va.; Waltham Public Library, Waltham, Mass.; Warren-Trumbull County Public Library, Warren, Ohio; Washington and Lee University, Leyburn Library, Lexington, Va.; Wayne Township Library, Richmond, Ind.; Wentworth Military Academy, Lexington, Mo.; Willard Library, Battle Creek, Mich.; Youngstown and Mahoning County, Public Library of, Youngstown, Ohio.

Contents

Acknowledgments	vii
Preface	1
One. Joe and Coonie	5
Two. Postwar Kansas City	21
Three. Coon-Sanders Novelty Orchestra	57
Four. The Nighthawks	83
Five. Chicago's Congress Hotel	116
Six. The Blackhawk Years	186
Seven. The Final Year	250
Epilogue	291
Notes	297
Appendix A: The Band's Personnel	321
Appendix B: Nighthawks and Their Associates	324
Appendix C: Coon-Sanders' Schedule of Road Tours	334
Appendix D: Songs Composed by Joe Sanders and Carleton Coon	339
Bibliography	343
Index	353

Preface

Once upon a time there was an orchestra — a dance orchestra whose music gladdened and quickened its audiences, whether they danced or merely listened, and whether they heard it in person, on radio, or on phonograph recordings. That the band achieved great popularity and success was the result of a fortuitous set of circumstances. Its two leaders, with very dissimilar personalities, tended to complement each other as managers and as musicians. They were singularly adept at attracting excellent players, and they chose songs and created arrangements that carried popular music to new heights.

But for all their talent, their orchestra might have gone largely unnoticed and unappreciated but for the advent of radio, which occurred at just the right time to carry this new music all over the United States and far beyond.

This band, perhaps more than any other of its time, symbolized the era. Its music was gay, saucy, and bustling; its musicians were carefree and extravagant. Furthermore, its existence was almost exactly contemporaneous with the delightfully mad period between the First World War and the onset of the Great Depression.

One might well wonder whether the band was a product of the Twenties, or whether it helped to generate that remarkable era.

It has been great fun to work on this history. My only regret is that I know so little about the band members other than Sanders and Coon. I know, for instance, that banjoist Russ Stout kept a scrapbook, for Harvey Rettberg borrowed it and apparently had it with him when he visited Joe Sanders in July 1961. But where is it today? I've been unable to answer that, and my attempts to contact members of Stout's family have been unsuccessful. Perhaps other band members, too, had similar relics of the Nighthawk days; but if so, I've not heard of them.

All of my life I have enjoyed popular music from before my time. The earliest music I can recall hearing, starting about 1934, was from old phonograph recordings played on a Victrola that my parents bought at that time, a year or so before we got our first radio (a little battery-operated Crosley). I enjoyed those recordings, all of which were from the middle or late 1920s. Perhaps this is the reason that my favorite popular music was, and still is, that of my parents' era. The music of my teenage years, the 1940s, always took second place. It is not surprising, therefore, that I began at an early age to collect both 78s and cylinder recordings, as well as machines to play them. In 1948 a schoolmate gave me some old popular records she had acquired from our Latin teacher, and one of them was Coon-Sanders' recording of "Nighthawk Blues" and "Red Hot Mama." It did seem somehow to have more charm than many of the other recordings, though I knew nothing of the orchestra. Fortunately my brother-in-law, Douglas Edward Mitchell (1903–1968), was quite familiar with them. When I asked him which other Coon-Sanders recordings he advised me to get, he replied, "*All* of them."

When in 1965 RCA Victor brought out, as part of their "Vintage Series," a choice collection of Nighthawk records, it sparked a deeper interest for me in that band's work. For a number of years thereafter I pondered the information noted on the album that there was a new Nighthawk fan club, begun in 1959 by Clyde Hahn and Harvey Rettberg. However, almost thirty years went by before I was moved to try to contact them. By then, Hahn had died, but Rettberg was still very much alive. And as Harvey had done for scores of others, he taped for me copies of all Coon-Sanders recordings that he had, as well as many by other bands from the Twenties. I visited him in Pickens, S.C., and taped much of our conversation. He also let me borrow his very considerable collection of jazz materials, correspondence, and other items of interest, and finally told me to keep it. It has been valuable for work on this book.

Harvey also put me in contact with several other persons, one of whom was John A. Coon, oldest child of Carleton A. Coon, Sr. When I telephoned Johnny, he told me that he had long thought the story of the Nighthawks would make an excellent book. In fact, he said that he had often tried to imagine his writing one and beginning with "Once upon a time there was an orchestra." But, said he, he wouldn't have known how to take it beyond that.

In the course of two or three telephone calls to Johnny in Prairie Village, Kansas, he persuaded me to try to write something that would keep the Nighthawks from slipping further into obscurity. Many of their well-known contemporaries—Paul Whiteman, Guy Lombardo, Ted Lewis, Ted Weems, and others—lasted well into the 1940s and beyond and so had managed more or less to fix their accomplishments in the history of popular music.

I suspect that I almost waited too long to tell the Coon-Sanders story, and it is my regret that I did not become interested in undertaking this book until almost everyone with firsthand information had passed from the scene. Had I started even ten years sooner, for instance, I might have met Floyd Estep and Nick Musolino, both of whom lived to be nearly 100. What stories those two could have told!

But Harvey Rettberg knew personally several members of the old band. He became acquainted with Joe Sanders, Harold Thiell, Rex Downing, Joe Richolson, and Russ Stout. He talked and corresponded frequently with all of these, as well as with many others who knew something of Coon-Sanders. Sometimes he recorded his conversations with them on tape. He met and corresponded with John Coon, who, nineteen when his father died in 1932, recalled much about the Nighthawks. Thanks to Harvey's excellent memory and long life, I have had the benefit of all of his contacts and research.

In addition to Harvey Rettberg's valuable help, there have been two other important and complementary sources: Johnny Coon's recollections and family records and the Joe Sanders Collection in the Kansas City Public Library. Johnny visited me in January of 1995 when I was a librarian at Auburn University, Auburn, Alabama. He stayed three days, during which time we had many conversations and tapings of conversations. A drive one afternoon over to Warm Springs, Georgia, gave us a good chance to trade chitchat about his father's band, while Johnny enjoyed seeing that famous retreat to which Franklin Delano Roosevelt, one of Johnny's favorite politicians, enjoyed escaping occasionally. We subsequently kept in contact by telephone and correspondence, and I saw Johnny again in Kansas City in the fall of 1997. During that visit to Kansas City I also delved heavily into the public library's Joe Sanders Collection. Those records are kept in the library's Special Collections, and my work was made easy and pleasant by that department's excellent librarians.

It was on my third trip to Kansas City, in 2001, that I had the pleasure of meeting several others who have been very helpful: Joe Sanders' niece Mary Jane Sanders Meyer and her daughter Janet K. Miller, and Sherry and Steve Drummond, both of whom were Johnny Coon's friends.

Dale Jones, head of the New Nighthawk Club, Huntington, West Virginia, has been helpful, especially by suggesting to me persons I might contact. He has also passed on to me inquiries from others, including Cathy Birge Williams, granddaughter of banjoist Dewey Birge. She has given me good information and put me in contact with her father, David Birge.

Thus, though I started this endeavor rather late, I have still managed to collect much information. In the past there have been articles about the Nighthawks, as well as a few books that have dealt with them briefly and in passing; but so far as I know, this is the first book solely about them. Moreover, the band seemed to generate and to encourage myths about its members, and some articles about the band have tended to accept these stories uncritically. Though I have attempted to stick to facts, I can't help suspecting that I, too, may be ensnared in a few Coon-Sanders myths. But in the long run, perhaps even myths can be instructive in understanding human activities. My intention has been to present enough material to give some impression of the various persons who played in the Coon-Sanders Nighthawks, particularly those in the later band, the best-remembered one. I have tried also to describe the band's famous tours, those hard-driving, often protracted series of one-nighters that helped spread their fame throughout much of the nation. Above all, I hope I have done justice to the memory of every band member of whom I have information.

I hope the reader will find here an account that, though obviously incomplete, still captures enough of the Nighthawks' story and spirit to be interesting. I have gone into some detail about American society during those years when the Nighthawks regaled dance halls and college campuses. And in all of this I have tried studiously to avoid an overly formal narrative, for that would certainly *not* be appropriate in an account of those wonderful zanies. Perhaps in the coming years someone else can add to this history and tell it better. But I'm certain that the Nighthawk story is so charmingly human that it deserves to be remembered.

CHAPTER ONE

Joe and Coonie

Except that both were bibulous, improvident, and musically very talented, it would be difficult to think of a more unlikely pairing than that of Carleton Coon and Joe Sanders. Especially after they became famous and appeared before many audiences, the contrast in personality must have been striking, and in physical stature they probably reminded many of Mutt and Jeff, two popular comic strip characters of the day.

Coonie was an outgoing, generous, inveterate clown, as well as a natural musician with little if any formal training. Johnny Coon told me that his father's height was about 5'10", though photos somehow suggest he was shorter. His weight fluctuated between 180 and 250 pounds, usually closer to the latter figure. But it was his good nature, more than his physical appearance, that impressed others; he seemed as prodigal with his cordiality as he was with his money. Unusually generous, he dispensed legal tender as nonchalantly as one deals playing cards, and on those occasions when he had to borrow from others, Coonie's fellow band members said he could be just as carefree about repayment.[1] He regarded money as nothing more than a charming convenience, if kept in circulation. In fact, Coonie doubtless agreed with a popular saying of that day: "Money was made round so that it would roll."[2]

Johnny Coon thought the word *mischievous* a very fitting adjective for his father and called him "a practical joker of the first water," one who was ever the zany. Coonie told engaging and whopping lies about himself, cultivated audiences, ribbed his fellow musicians, and generally endeared himself to those he met. Though he apparently drank little beer or wine, he was on the best of terms with distilled liquors. Johnny Coon recalled that even in an era when it seemed that almost everyone drank some kind of alcoholic beverage, Coonie stood out as a remarkable imbiber, especially of Scotch and cognac. And as Johnny added, "You can get fat drinking Scotch." Coonie, especially toward the end of his life, was fat.[3] Drinking was simply a part of his convivial nature, though the habit eventually took on a darker aspect. Whenever Joe's volatile personality created a public relations shambles, as it sometimes did, Coonie was often able to straighten out the situation. In fact, Coonie came to have but two really serious enemies, alcohol and improvidence.

What a contrast Sanders was! Joe was physically a fine, athletic specimen. At his prime in 1926, age thirty, he stood six-feet-one and weighed a trim 195 pounds. He had a 15½–inch neck and wore 9½ shoes. He was highly trained as a musician and was outstanding as both a vocalist and a pianist. Moreover, he learned to create excellent musical arrangements, some of them demonstrating interesting innovations. According to John Coon, Joe took this work very seriously and apparently never hired a copier. Instead, he carefully and clearly wrote out each band member's part. It took a great amount of his time, but if Joe resented doing it, I've seen no indication of it in the records.[4]

But though talented as a musician, Joe sometimes was inept at public relations. While Coonie was usually voluble, affable and sociable, Joe could be taciturn, solitary, and moody. Though Coonie seemed to have a good word for everyone, Joe was occasionally acerbic and temperamental. His competititve instinct, while it led to his marvelous achievements in music and sports, sometimes expressed itself also in something like jealousy of other orchestras. For example, when keeping a record in his personal journal of the Nighthawks' engagements, Joe often wrote comments that reveal a very competitive and sometimes caustic attitude toward other bands that had played the same locations. Vincent Lopez, especially, seemed to bring out Joe's sharpest comments.[5] In fine, it might be said that Joe was the brains of the Nighthawks and Coonie the heart.

But instead of unduly dwelling on the shortcomings of the two men, let us merely note those traits, when pertinent, as part of their human makeup. By their characters and abilities they had as good a claim to a favorable estimation as the rest of us. I shall endeavor, therefore, to accentuate their strengths and to say how fortunate we are that Coon and Sanders met and produced one of the best and most interesting aggregations in the history of popular music.

Claude and Henrietta (Nettie) Jacks Coon moved from northeastern Nebraska to Rochester, Minn., where on 5 February 1893 (often misstated as 1894) Dr. Charles Mayo* delivered Carleton Allyn Coon.[6] From then on, Coonie would often see his first name denied its *e*.

In 1898 Claude took young Carleton to live in Lexington, Mo., which has led some to believe mistakenly that the family lived in Lexington, *Kentucky*. Just why Carleton's parents separated is still a mystery; and as Johnny Coon later stated, Coonie spent years looking for his mother. He found her in Minnesota in 1925 and brought her to live with him in Kansas City.[7]

Coonie's father bought a hotel that, while not the largest, was perhaps the best in Lexington. It was popular with traveling salesmen, or what were then called drummers. He became active in business circles and was one of the founders of the local chapter of Rotary. In his spare time Claude attended Shrine meetings and played the cornet in their band. Joe Popper, writing years later for the Kansas City *Star*, described Claude as "an attractive man, and something of a roué." He must have had a touch of vanity, as well, for he forbade young Carleton to call him "Dad" in public. "Uncle Claude," however, was acceptable.[8]

Claude was married twice more. Johnny couldn't remember the name of his father's first step-mother, but she and Claude had a daughter named Corona, who later moved to California and married a movie director. Claude's third wife was Gertrude, and they too eventually moved to California where they lived until their deaths.[9]

Claude Coon sold a beverage called Allen's Red Tame Cherry, and even near the end of his life Johnny Coon could still exclaim, "Boy, was it good!" Later the company

---

*William James Mayo (1861–1939) and his brother Charles Horace Mayo (1865–1939) founded the Mayo Clinic in Rochester, Minn.

went into partnership with Coca-Cola, but by that time Claude was no longer with the enterprise.[10]

In Lexington, Carleton had an interesting, if sometimes unhappy, life. Johnny Coon thought his father led a somewhat "protected" early life and that his paternal grandmother "Dada," whom Johnny remembered as staid and prim, tried to keep the young Coonie under her control. In fact, Johnny quoted his sister Nancy as saying that Dada's control was so effective that Coonie could scarcely get out of his grandmother's sight. Johnny was dubious about that, however, and thought his father got out pretty often. Moreover, Johnny believed that his father got into some kind of scrape during his Lexington days but doubted that it was serious.[11]

Johnny heard from an early friend of Coonie's, Pete Nane, later a livestock broker, that the two boys often went down to the wharves along the Missouri River to hobnob with the stevedores. From them Coonie learned the fascinating art of shooting craps and such skills as African-American dances and playing the bones. Johnny thought that his father was "probably the only really modern-day musician who knew how to play the bones," though he doubted that Coonie ever used them when playing with the Coon-Sanders Orchestra. Coonie learned also many African-American songs and how to harmonize in singing. Said Johnny, "My dad picked up a lot ... of his know-how in the music field by observing the blacks down on the wharf at Lexington, Missouri."[12]

At about twelve or thirteen years of age Coonie, probably only briefly, went to Wentworth Military Academy, in Lexington, Mo.; but when I checked with Wentworth, their records revealed no such student. John Coon said that his father was constantly getting into mischief, committing such pranks as putting Limburger cheese on banisters or introducing pepper into the ventilation system. Once, at Hallowe'en, he disassembled a wagon and deposited the components on a church roof. Coonie's son suspected that this sort of misbehavior perhaps accounts for the absence of any such name in the school's records. Even Wentworth's *X File*, names of problem students, contains no one named Carleton Coon.[13] So, either the school, no longer able to abide Coonie's pranks, completely erased all traces of his attendance, or else this was simply one of the earliest of many such legends that Coonie seemed to encourage.

After the family moved to Kansas City, Kans., and he was in his teens, Coonie put his natural musical talents to work in the Electric Theater by singing during the projection of illustrated songs. His was a very pleasing tenor voice that encouraged audiences to sing along with him.[14]

Coonie finished high school in Kansas City, Kans., where he met his future wife, Virginia Eula Jenkins, who was about two years older than he and a native of the town. (Johnny said that she practically dropped her first name and used only her middle, but she hated the name *Eula*, as well.) They were married 20 May 1911 at a church that stood where the Hotel Muehlebach is now. In later years both were associated with Christian Science, of which Eula was a member.* Four children were born to them, John first, in 1913, followed by Nancy, Jennie, and Carleton, Jr., in that order.[15] Some found it confusing that it was the younger son who carried the father's name; and in later years when John had his own band, he usually was known as Carleton A. Coon, Jr.[16]

A growing family required a steady income, so about 1911 Coonie began playing with bands, one of which was apparently that led by Jack Riley, often dubbed "the father of Kansas City orchestras." Johnny Coon recalled that in those days his father had at least one group of his own in Kansas City and played occasionally in nearby towns. In

---

*Johnny Coon wasn't certain that his father ever joined a Christian Science group and said that though neither son followed that denomination, both of Coonie's daughters did.

addition, at some point during this period he began operating a booking agency for bands, or as his son Johnny later observed with a laugh,

> whatever they were in these days—little combos of some kind. And now we're talking about times when there were not sections ... as there are now. They had maybe one trumpet and one violin and a banjo player and a drummer, a piano player, and a bass player, and everyone was fighting to ... be heard. And they weren't playing necessarily arrangements; they were just playing stuff that came into their heads, I suppose.... But none of them sounded too good because they didn't have any sections.[17]

Coonie's office was in the Gayety Theater Building at Twelfth and Wyandott. How successful it was is difficult to ascertain, but Johnny Coon said his father did find some business.[18]

When the United States entered the First World War in April of 1917, Coonie became a civilian inspector in the Federal Dairy Inspection Department, with the nominal rank of Army captain, stationed possibly first in Kansas City, Kans., but later at Jefferson Barracks near St. Louis. Exclaimed Johnny Coon: "Milk inspector! He went around and checked the dairies, I guess. He didn't have much expertise in being a milk inspector, and I don't even know what his duties were ... and how long he did it." Well, he did it for the duration of the war and, in fact, had just been released, though still in uniform, when he and Sanders met just before Christmas of 1918.[19]

Coonie always liked to say that he had gone to the University of Kansas, but Johnny Coon said that was just more of his father's benign buncombe. The University of Kansas Alumni Association agrees, for it has no such name in its records. Coonie probably wished he had gone to college and medical school. Nevertheless, though the future Nighthawk did seem to have a natural inclination for medicine, he never studied it, despite reports to the contrary and that little black satchel of medical instruments he sometimes carried with him. Johnny Coon said: "All my father's best friends were top surgeons and physicians—all of them. That's all he ran around with.... And they loved to be around him. Of course—naturally, he was a big celebrity and they liked to be seen with him, and he ... picked up a lot of things from them."[20] Some of those things he picked up were probably food and beverage tabs, for Coonie enjoyed treating his friends.

Coonie was somewhat liberal in outlook, though this did not produce any strong interest in politics. He was vaguely Democratic, but about the only politician for whom his oldest son recalled Coonie's expressing any great liking was Missouri's maverick Democratic senator, James Alexander Reed. Johnny Coon believed his father would have liked Franklin Delano Roosevelt and Harry S Truman, both of whom were about to arrive on the national scene when Coonie died. When he could find the time, Coonie liked to read, especially Sinclair Lewis's iconoclastic fiction.[21]

Though he was very generous with money, Coonie told his wife he did not wish to set up trust funds for his children, and that they should make it on their own. But as Johnny Coon wryly remarked, it hardly mattered anyway, because his father couldn't hold onto money. His generosity often turned into pure wastefulness. His eldest son recalled seeing his father tip waiters fifty dollars for a cup of coffee, and lend as much to practically anyone who asked. And money thus lightly lent was as lightly owed, nor did Coonie seem to expect it to be repaid.[22] Trust funds, indeed!

Carleton had the traditional attitude toward what was proper entertainment for one's children, especially one's daughter. Johnny, who as the oldest child was the one who more often accompanied his father, remembered one time when he and his sister Nancy were visiting their father in Chicago and were at the famous Blackhawk Restaurant where the Nighthawks were playing. John and Nancy stayed until the band finished at 1 a.m., and someone suggested to Coonie that they take Nancy out to a club which featured the promising, but not-yet-famous, Benny Goodman. Coonie thought it an unsuitable place for his daughter and vetoed the idea.[23]

After Coonie joined the Masons, he took a great interest in that society and was instrumental in the rest of the band's joining as well. This was the Chicago body, and he also helped Charles Correll and Freeman Gosden,* of Amos 'n' Andy fame, become members.[24]

Joe Sanders' grandparents were Isaac and Lavinia Pickerill Sanders, the latter a direct descendant of Sir Thomas West, Lord De la Warr, first governor of Virginia. Joseph Harrison Sanders, Joe's father, was born in Cicero, Ind., in 1858, and his mother Helena Soice on 8 May 1873, in Topeka, Kans. Helena's parents were John and Mary Steffenhaugen Soice, both of whom came from Germany after the American Civil War. John Soice, a stonemason, was working on a church in Stafford, Kans., when his daughter Helena met Joseph H. Sanders. They were married in Stafford on Christmas Day 1890. After Isaac Sanders' death, Lavinia and her daughters operated, in Thayer, Kans., a "hotel" that was really more like a boarding house.[25]

Joe and his partner Coonie apparently believed they had American Indian ancestry, and they are probably the ones who gave this "information" to Jerry Wald in December 1931. "Both boys," wrote Wald, "arc part Indian; they love the romance of 'feathered gear' but they have as yet to wear the 'high hat.'" Janet K. Miller is reasonably certain that her great-uncle was simply pulling Wald's leg. She has traced the family's genealogy back to at least the sixteenth and seventeenth centuries and says that she finds nothing to corroborate Joe's claim. She believes that the myth may have had its genesis in the possibility that John Sanders (born 1702), Joe's great-great-great-great-great-grandfather, had siblings who either married or adopted American Indians, probably Cherokee.[26]

Joseph LaCeil Sanders was born 15 October 1896 in Thayer, Kansas, in his grandmother's hotel, or boarding house, that Joe later described as "famous for wonderful food." (The few sources giving Joe's middle name provide at least three versions. I've chosen the one that I suspect is correct.) Like his partner Coonie, Joe was apparently not above embroidering his early life. In fact, his great-niece takes considerable exception to her great-uncle's account of his tender years. But for what it's worth, the following is taken from what Joe had to say about his childhood; and if there is any stretching of the facts, that very embroidering is interesting and perhaps instructive as to Joe's personality.

Joe described his father as a "pioneer of the plains, driving cattle up from Texas and Oklahoma into Kansas in the wild and wooly days." The elder Sanders, according to his younger son, was not especially prosperous—"Misfortune seemed his lot," as Joe later wrote, adding:

> At one time, he traded a herd ... for 5,000 acres of what is now fabulous citrus fruit land on the Rio Grande acreage. Hold it! I have that just backwards. He traded the land, acre for acre, for cows—and then lost the entire herd when it contracted blackleg. At another time, he owned part of what later was gusher oil land. In those days, neither the to-be-citrus fruit land nor the oil land was thought to be of any value except for grazing.[27]

The Sanders family, which included also Joe's older brother Roy Garvin Sanders, moved several times. Joe's first year in school, or rather kindergarten, was in Indian Territory, soon to be Oklahoma, at a little place in Craig County called Centralia. His father ran a store, and in his home had

---

*Correll (1890–1972) and Gosden (1899–1982), famous black-face comics on radio, 1926–1928 as Sam 'n' Henry, and thereafter as Amos 'n' Andy.

The Sanders family about 1907, probably in Belton, Missouri. From left: Joseph H. Sanders, Joe, Helena Soice Sanders, and Joe's brother Roy. (Courtesy Mary Jane Sanders Meyer.)

a phonograph that fascinated Joe's playmates and others in the area. The community was twenty-seven miles from the nearest railroad and was surrounded by small mountains. Since Joe and his brother Roy were two of only four Caucasian children in the place, most of their playmates were American Indians.[28]

The rest of Joe's elementary and high school education was at Belton, Mo., a town south of Kansas City. His final year in high school was at Westport High School in Kansas City, where he was graduated in 1914. Describing the move from Belton to Kansas City, he said: "When we moved to K.C., I, my dog, a cat and a parrot were all in the back of a wagon that took us away from Belton and my friends and kid sweetheart. With legs dangling from the tailgate, I waved to my girl until a turn in the street brought a misty-eyed finale to the parting."[29]

Sanders later said that in Belton when he was about nine, he began to study piano under a Professor Ware, and a year or so later he added voice study under Lillian Kreiser, who came over from Kansas City once a week to meet with several pupils in Belton. A piano teacher, Virginia Tisdale, also made weekly visits from Kansas City to give lessons to Joe and several others. Free rooms at the small hotel that Joe's parents operated paid both teachers for the young boy's lessons. Joe's musical training — piano for six years, voice for five — continued after the move to Kansas City. There he was able to study voice under the rather accomplished baritone David Grosch. He also was lead tenor and accompanist in the Kansas City Oratorio Society and for one season sang in the male chorus of the Kansas City Grand Opera Company. He sang also tenor or high baritone in the choir of the Linwood Methodist Church. Years later Joe described his progress in music:

> I was, at first, a boy soprano and when I sang a high C in a clear soprano, behind sliding doors in a parlor back of the hotel office, traveling salesmen thought surely a big luscious bosomy blond[e] must be caroling. My vocal teacher brought a wealthy widow to hear me and she, in turn, arranged for me to sing, as a boy soprano, at the Grand Avenue Temple, a prosperous congregation of Methodists. I played and sang in local recitals and, later, made a solo piano and singing concert appearance in K.C. If I recall correctly, my gate receipts for memorizing almost two hours of concert efforts was a thumping big sixteen dollars.[30]

Of his music training in general and its bearing on his later career, he said many years later:

> David Grosch, my coach, organized and taught and directed the K. C. Oratorio Society and I got my lessons free in return for playing the piano accompaniments at both choir and oratorio rehearsals. This was an invaluable and very lasting musical education for me. In picking out the several voices in the oratorio scores—tenors, bassos, sopranos, altos, etc., some times [sic] as many as eight parts at one time — I established training for my male quartet and orchestral arranging in later years (I was one of the very first arrangers to *spread* the saxophone section voicing). It was just such voicing that made Glenn Gray's sax section so distinctive.[31]

From as early as his twelfth year, Sanders' name appeared increasingly on programs for local musical events. He was clearly a youngster with unusual musical promise. On 17 November 1908, for example, he appeared at the City Hall in Virginia Tisdale's recital. "Master Joe Sanders" was third on the program with "The Pilgrim," by a composer named Speaks. On April 6 and June 29 of the next year, Joe performed in concerts by the Schumann Choral Club. On 4 November 1910 he sang a solo at the Grand Avenue Methodist Episcopal Church, and the following December 17 he was featured at Virginia Tisdale's recital as "Joe Sanders, Boy Soprano." He was back at the Grand Avenue Methodist Episcopal Church on 3 September 1911 to sing "The Better Land," by one Cowan.[32] A week later the minister of that church, the Rev. Edwin B. Olmstead, wrote to Joe, enclosing a letter testifying to the youngster's musical talent but failing to say why Joe needed such a recommendation. The clergyman misstated Joe's middle initial, not an encouraging lapse in a testimonial. Olmstead's statement was as follows:

> Master Joe S. [sic] Sanders is a truly remarkable boy singer. He has a high order of musical ability and a phenomenal voice which he uses with fine effect. He has sung a number of times at public services and social functions at Grand Avenue Church,

Joe Sanders' photograph in his high school annual, *Westport High School Herald*, 1914. (Courtesy Special Collections, Kansas City [Mo.] Public Library.)

Kansas City, and always delighted the people. We have found that his name is an attraction on any program. Those who hear him once invariably want to hear him again. I have confidence in his ability to please any music-loving audience.[33]

During his mid- and late teens and up to about the time the United States entered the First World War, young Joe was very busy in local musical circles. He sang often in churches in the Kansas City area, and he appeared in recitals, both as soloist and with other performers. Perhaps about 1912, while still described as a "boy," he appeared in recital with an apparently older friend named Novus Reed, who billed himself as "Novus Homo Est Reed,* Eccentric concert Entertainer," and adding, "Assisted by Joseph La Seile Saunders [*sic*], Kansas City's Greatest Boy Pianist." The program bulletin, a mixture of the facetious and the serious, contained one violin number by Reed and titled "The Country Violeeniste."[34]

In 1912 and 1913 Joe's public appearances were even more ambitious than previous ones. For example, on 4 May 1912 Sanders was first on a program called an "Invitational Piano Recital." He played several pieces that included Ludwig van Beethoven's sonata, opus 13; "Shadow Dance," by Edward MacDowell; and Franz Schubert's "Hark, Hark, the Lark." On 17 March 1913, at another recital by Virginia Tisdale's pupils, he played the first movement of another Beethoven sonata, opus 27; Antonín Dvořák's "Humoresque"; and an arrangement of selections from Giuseppe Verdi's *Rigoletto*. The following June 26, at the Densmore Hotel, he offered pieces by Mac-Dowell and Franz Liszt, performing them on a Steinway grand furnished by the J. W. Jenkins' Sons Music Company. The following New Year's Eve, at the St. Francis Hotel, Joe was reported in the local press as being at the piano "when he was not singing himself, and sometimes could not keep from joining in a catchy chorus, when playing for the Warren sisters and Helen Reid."[35]

"Yes," wrote Sanders many years later, "I did entertain in one of the toughest dives in town, the Blue Goose Cafe. I played piano and accompanied the singers—no wages, just my share of tips that were split at the end of each night." This activity came in the evening while he was in his senior year at Westport High, 1913–1914. As Joe later put it, "I went to my classes in the day and played in a honky-tonk at night." His brother Roy, living with his parents at 3425 Michigan Avenue and pitching for the Kansas City Blues, was puzzled to see Joe go out for mysterious evenings and return with extra money. He worried, as Joe put it, that "I had fallen in with a gambling gang and was going down 'Wrong Street.'" Joe belonged to no union and was strictly on his own, though he said

---

*Thus making a pun in Latin on his name to mean "The new man is Reed."

later that it might be called his first professional engagement.[36]

Even as the spring of 1914 brought the threat of war in Europe, it also witnessed Joe's high school graduation and his most ambitious musical activities yet. On March 3 he sang in the Orpheus Quartette at the Scottish Rite Temple. And on June 19, in the clubhouse ballroom of the Knights of Columbus, Sanders gave what was probably the premiere of his own composition, "The Debutante Waltz." Said the local press, "Mr. Sanders is only 18 years old, but is making a mark as a musician." About a week later, only three days before the assassination of Archduke Franz Ferdinand, at Sarajevo, Bosnia, Joe played a recital at the Densmore Hotel, and offered MacDowell's "Shadow Dance" and a piano arrangement of the "Quartette" from *Rigoletto*. There were several other appearances of a lighter nature, such as recitals and more programs with the Orpheus Quartette.[37]

But he was no longer in school and was no longer *Master* Joe Sanders. He had to find steady work, and it was probably as a result of this need that a friend of his from Belton, J. A. Lewis, manager of Fowler-Jones Coal Company, of Kansas City, wrote to Georgia Murphy: "This will introduce you to one of my Belton friends, Mr. Joe Sanders. 'Some pianist.' Sing! *Yes*. Play — Just listen. In case you can make a deal with Mr. Sanders, do so. Their people will talk about your show. Hire him, Georgia."[38]

Sometime about 1916 or 1917 Sanders had the lead male's role, as Jack Churchill, in a musical titled *The Girl from Frisco*, written and produced by Mr. and Mrs. Lucien Denni, and performed at the Garden Theater as charity work for the Minute Circle. Mary Bainbridge was the female lead. A local reporter said: "An unusually good vocal showing was made by both principals and chorus. 'Everyone I Know Loves You,' 'Safety First,' 'The Nightingale Love Song' and 'What Is Love without a Quarrel?' were some of the decided hits of the evening."[39]

In 1915 there was the usual number of minor appearances — here a church service, there a "junior-senior musicale," and somewhere else Joe as accompanying pianist for a chorus. On June 19 he played at a rather prestigious program for the Knights of Columbus, and at the bottom of the program there was a note, "Mr. Sanders prefers the Mason and Hamlin piano from Wunderlich's The Music Center, 1015 Grand." Well, perhaps so, but in later years Sanders seemed to prefer Baldwin products.* He made some appearances as a vocalist with such friends as Walter Ehrnmann, Bill Chase, and Novus Reed.[40]

At about this time Joe was accompanist and director for the Builders Club Minstrel Show, at the Linwood Boulevard Methodist Episcopal Church. Said one critic:

> That was some show! Yes, you turn the Builder's [*sic*] Club loose and they give you something to think about. In this case you probably ask, "Where did they learn all that?" Well, that makes no difference just now, they learned it just the same, and altho' I never did see a minstrel show by professional players, I would like to see one just to satisfy myself that they are not as good as our own boys.[41]

But in 1917, while America was preparing to help save the world's democracy, Joe was finally getting paid adequately for his music. In those days male vocal ensembles, especially duets and quartets, were very highly esteemed. Such groups as the Peerless Quartette, the American Quartette, and the Avon Comedy Four enjoyed great popularity both in vaudeville and on phonograph records. Joe joined the U.S. Four, a quartet consisting of Marion Fosdick (first tenor), Bobby Owens (second tenor), Sanders (baritone), and Walter Wood (bass). The group went on tour, probably as a Chautauqua feature, through the Midwest and got good re-

---

*Even his future wife's maiden name was Baldwin, though she was apparently unrelated to the piano makers.

Joe Sanders (front row, dark uniform) on baseball team, probably in Kansas City, date unknown but perhaps about 1916. (Courtesy Special Collections, Kansas City [Mo.] Public Library.)

views. Sanders later said that at the Liberty Theatre in Cleveland, Ohio, they had the "honor position." Assuming that Joe was not being ironic, I would guess that he meant by "honor position" that they sang just before intermission or were the next-to-last act on the program. If there were two headliners, the latter spot was thought preferable. At any rate, the first and final places were to be shunned, for at those times the theater was often filling or emptying.

In the latter part of the year the four men appeared in a "Stag Vaudeville" presented by the Western Vaudeville Managers' Association. Their act was described as "high class cabaret" and "the biggest hit of the '1918' season." Joe also toured for the Ridpath Company, and he was doing some tours, sometimes with Walter Ehrnmann, on the Chautauqua Circuit. One such tour took him through the North for ten weeks, and another engagement was for a twenty-five-week tour of the West. This may have been with a group calling themselves The Collegians, of William Jewell College, Liberty, Missouri. Their singers were Sanders, Ehrnmann, W. A. Hill, W. J. Chase, and N. H. C. Reed, the latter apparently the same as Novus Reed, the close friend with whom Joe had been associated for several years. Said a critic: "The concert consisted of instrumental music, solos, duets, etc., etc., and was of a high class character." Some of Joe's appearances were under the aegis of the Burgess Dramatic company, though, despite the name, Joe's participation apparently was only musical. One wonders how the others in the company reacted to an article in one local paper that said, "Mr. Sanders was a favorite however with his beautiful tenor voice and in his excellent piano numbers." One Frank McCourt heard Sanders' quartet in Saginaw, Mich., and declared them one of the best musical organizations he had heard in quite a while. So, now Joe was making money! He could feed himself, have his laundry done, and send a little money back home.[42]

The U.S. Four Quartette was very active during 1917 and 1918. They appeared for twelve weeks at the Edelweiss Winter Garden, Chicago, and proved popular with that city's theater crowd. Following that, they played a long engagement at the Winton in Cleveland, Ohio. Among the audience one evening was the famous and popular actor De Wolf Hopper. He was so impressed by what he heard that he contacted the Keith Circuit in New York, and forty-eight hours later the U.S. Four had a contract for a tour.[43]

But in April of 1917 the United States entered the war, and everything for Joe and all other Americans became tentative. Though the war offered new opportunities for music and entertainment that would rally the nation for its unpleasant but exciting task, travel might not be quite so easy to arrange; and there were those "meatless," "heatless," and "wheatless" days. There was also sometimes a disturbing tendency by the federal government to use questionable propaganda, and, more troubling, some high-handed attacks on personal liberties. And above all, there was no certainty about when one's draft number might be called. The first number was drawn in July; and while civilians were being pressured to buy Liberty Bonds and to listen to the "Four Minute Men" give out their propaganda in cinemas and other public places in the country, boys in khaki were drilling, marching and, in many cases, enjoying their first taste of freedom from the restraints of home.[44] It seemed, at least in the early part of the war, a good opportunity for men to get into uniform and validate their masculine credentials. The war presented opportunities also for Tin Pan Alley, some of whose songs were calculated to stir the blood of lusty youth, as well as others that suggested that military service wasn't all glamorous. As Emil Brietenfeld's song "The Last, Long Mile"* put it,

> They put me in the Army
>   and they handed me a pack,
> They took away my nice new clothes
>   and dressed me up in khak;
> They marched me twenty miles a day
>   to fit me for the war,
> I didn't mind the first nineteen —
>   but the last one made me sore....
> And it's not the hike on the
>   hard turnpike that wipes away your smile,
> Nor the socks of sisters
>   that raise the blooming blisters,
> It's the last, long mile.[45]

On the lighter side were such songs as the 1917 hit by H. Johnson and Harry Pease, "I Don't Want to Get Well." It tells of a soldier lucky enough to get shot and end up in a hospital that employed one very fetching nurse. Gus Van and Joe Schenck made a popular recording of it, doing their usual two-part harmony on such lines as the following:

> I don't want to get well!
> I don't want to get well!
> I'm in love with a beautiful nurse....
> She holds my hand and begs me not to leave her,
> And all at once I get an awful fever....[46]

The next year Irving Berlin's output included one to bring a big smile, "They Were All out of Step but Jim," a little ditty that showed that though Jimmy couldn't march, it wasn't obvious to his doting Irish-American mother:

> There was Jimmy just as stiff as starch,
> Just like his daddy on the seventeenth of March....
> Sure it made me glad to gaze at the lad,
> And the Devil'll take the Kaiser if he's like his dad.
> Were you there and, tell me, did you notice?
> They were all out of step but Jim.[47]

Of course Joe heard many such songs, and it probably wasn't long before he decided to try his own hand at one. What was probably his first effort was a rather generic one that, like many others of the time, relied on ethnic humor. And the most serviceable ethnic groups in Tin Pan Alley were the Irish, Jews, Italians, and African-Americans. It was called "Patrick Shay," subtitled "novelty war song"; and though today it certainly doesn't seem memorable, it was no worse than a lot of others that somehow managed to have some popularity. That Joe's song apparently did not "take off" is probably a matter of circumstance. Here it is:

> Patrick Shay marched away, over
>   to France with the rest,
> With never a fear, a brave
>   volunteer, to do his fighting best.
> And when he got there and killed his share
> Of Huns on the fighting line,
> He wrote a letter to Mary Malone,

---

*"The Last Long Mile," from the 1917 musical *Toot, Toot*, became the marching song of Upstate New York's Camp Plattsburg.

And said "I'm feeling fine":

Chorus:

It won't be long 'til I'm home, Mary darlin',
For the war will soon be over over here.
We've got the Kaiser's army running
    back to where they came from
And they'll never cross the Rhine again, my dear.
You know it takes the Irish to beat the dirty Hun,
And with the Tommies and
    Yankees and fighting French,
We've got them on the run.
And we'll go thru that Von Hindenburg line
And get the Kaiser, too.
I guess that's all, good-bye, my dear,
I'll soon be home to you.[48]

Well, there are hints in it of such other songs on that subject as "Long Boy" and "I Don't Want to Get Well"; and the phrase "over here," with its counterpart "over there," saw a lot of use after George M. Cohan's "Over There" was first performed publicly in the fall of 1917. It quickly caught the nation's attention, and apparently Joe's, as well. But I am too charitable to suppose that "that Von Hindenburg line" was suggested by a similar phrase in the almost incredibly bad "We Don't Want the Bacon, What We Want Is a Piece of the Rhine." This howler, according to Max Morath, the ragtime artist, was reputedly General John J. Pershing's favorite war song.[49] At least Joe's ditty isn't *that* bad, and its music, which I haven't seen, was perhaps superior to the lyrics.

Another opportunity for Joe to see what he could do musically for the war effort came with the Fourth Liberty Loan in July of 1918. He concocted a number titled "Kick In," which was chosen as Kansas City's official song for the new loan campaign. It was sung for the first time at Kansas City's Convention Hall on October 3, before an audience of 13,000, one of whom was Theodore Roosevelt, the orator for the occasion. (It was probably one of Roosevelt's last public acts, for he died the following January 6.) Joe wrote friends back in Belton that his song would perhaps be a "restorative" to Kansas City's "lagging sense of duty."[50]

The U.S. Army was getting close to Joe, but the death of his mother made him request, and receive, a deferment. On 6 August 1918 Helena (or Lena) Sanders, who had just had an operation at Grace Hospital, died at the tragically early age of forty-five, having lived in Kansas City for the past several years. Her older son Roy at the time was playing with the Pittsburgh Pirates. Joe's father later remarried and was survived by his second wife.[51]

During the period prior to his leaving for camp, Joe had been doing some amateur pitching for the Belton baseball team, but now there was another team that called for his service. After the lapse of the deferment granted because of his mother's death, Uncle Sam's famous greeting reached him on 15 October 1918. The influenza epidemic, which made travel problematic, apparently delayed his departure. Eventually, however, Joe and a group of other men were sworn in at a local warehouse and put on a train for Ft. Worth, Texas, and Camp Bowie. They were off, as he later expressed it, "to fight the battle of Bowie." That Joe was in charge of his group suggests that he was the oldest, and the crown of command seldom rests easy. "En route," he complained, "a conscientious objector tried to throw himself under a passing freight. Another locked himself in a rest room and was missing until the train pulled into the Ft. Worth yards." The cars that carried the fledgling doughboys were taken by sidetrack into Camp Bowie, where Joe feared he might be court-martialed for any missing soldiers under his supervision. But all were accounted for, so Joe made his "little speech to the C.O." and, as would be expected of the "Old Lefthander," he saluted with his left hand. Apparently accustomed to such boners, the officer merely smiled and returned the salute.[52] There would be plenty of time later to iron out such kinks.

Company B were given the necessary shots—"several big strong guys couldn't take it," sneered Joe. A little later they were herded into what Sanders, recalling his baseball games, referred to as the Bull Pen, an enclosure surrounded by high wire. There

Joe Sanders in minimal Army uniform, Camp Benton, Texas, late 1918 or early 1919. (Courtesy Special Collections, Kansas City [Mo.] Public Library.)

the men beheld a crude stage on which they were subjected nightly to what Joe called "very bad amateur talent." It was not, he said, "conducive to a cheerful frame of mind." So one night when the camp entertainment director, Sam Harris—not *the* Sam Harris of Cohan and Harris fame—asked anyone with talent to volunteer, Joe did so, allowing that he could "sing and play the piano." Harris invited him to the platform, whereupon Joe gave them some ragtime and vocalizing. It went over well, and the next morning the company commander, Lt. Cyrus Q. Speck, sent for Joe and told him he was being transferred to Headquarters Company. Furthermore, by military magic he would be turned into a corporal so that he could organize a small jazz band to entertain at the officers' mess—apparently Joe Sanders was regarded as too good to waste on the enlisted men.[53]

This wasn't good news to Joe, who later wrote, "I was heart-broken, for HDQ Co. was a bunch of misfits, not capable of rigorous drilling and marching. In addition I had to leave my gang in Co. B...." But orders were just that, so Joe proceeded to organize what he termed "an every-man-for-himself combo," with Joe as leader, pianist, and vocalist. The other members were Owen Hitchler, drums; Karl Weihe, tenor sax; and Freddy Hamm, trumpet. Hamm, Joe later said, "played a beautiful horn" and in later years had his own successful band. The group was known as the Camp Bowie Jazz Hounds, and they played for the officers' mess, or dining hall. "We four were compensated for amusing the big shots," said Joe, "by being privileged to partake of the same mess after the officers had eaten...." Furthermore, said Joe, the camp commander, Col. Cleveland Sammons, told Lt. Speck to keep the band always on call "for little private parties to provide dance music for him and his subalterns." The small upright piano that Joe used was often seen being shoved into and out of many private homes in the area. But Sanders was not impressed with Colonel Sammons, who, so Joe later recalled,

fancied himself quite a gay blade and a devil with the ladies.... Sporting tremendous feet, he was just about as graceful as a galloping ox [and] as feathery and graceful as a berzerk [*sic*] Mack truck sans driver.... Although we played these little extra-curricular parties for Mr. Big until almost dawn, we were nevertheless made to stand reveille. The four of us would stumble out of our tent, dressing on our way to a very groggy inspection. After this farce, we were permitted to grab a bit of shuteye before being roused by the top kicker with orders to furl our tent and police up [i.e., clean] the company street. It was quite a war I had inadvertently gotten myself embroiled in![54]

Several local young women, whom Sanders referred to as "society debs," had persuaded the base commander to help put on an entertainment "extravaganza." Colonel Sammons, flattered by their request, called on the camp jazz band—"and an excellent one it was," added Joe. "We four were to be on stage, throughout, doing ragtime specialties and I was to dream up a novel act of some sort." Three of the "debs" were fairly good pianists, so Joe employed them in a special four-piano act, all playing simultaneously. According to Joe, "It was the smash hit of the show and my debs came through with flying colors." Joe used his previous musical training and "scratched off my *first* effort at arranging," adding, "The debs could read, their doting maws having given them a bit of culture in the nature of piano lessons." It was a great success and reminded Sanders of what Irving Berlin had recently done in his show *Yip, Yip, Yaphank*, though Berlin had used six grand pianos, not four battered, badly-out-of-tune uprights. But that wasn't the end of it: "The success of the entire show led to even more musical duties we couldn't seem to duck. The Jazz Hounds were widely discussed in the city of Ft. Worth and society balls and pompous military balls at the camp became yet another routine succession of extracurricular jobs that we four didn't want nor care for."[55]

Around the Clock with the Debutantes, or *Midnight Frolic*, was staged at Ft. Worth's

Savoy Theater on the fourth through the sixth of February, 1919. What the local press called the "Missouri 'Jazz' Hounds" proved to be the hit of the show. They appeared in a "jazz scene" in the second act.[56]

In the meantime Joe and several of his fellows continued to live in a tent and to put up with the heavy rains that turned the entire camp into a swamp, and since it was late fall, a *chilly* swamp. The fighting in Europe had ended with an armistice on November 11, and some men were already being released; but the Battle of Camp Bowie continued. Thus, Joe and his comrades pondered their situation. It was at this time that Camp Bowie's brass pulled a fast one in an effort to keep their Jazz Hounds around a little longer. The four men were told that they were being given Christmas furloughs. It sounded pretty good, so about a week before Christmas, 1918, Joe made his way to Kansas City.[57]

And now we find ourselves at a dramatic point in this story for all those who like good jazz.

Back in Kansas City, Joe sought to get some sheet music to take back to camp for the Jazz Hounds, so he dropped into Jenkins Music Store. In his own reminiscences about the event, Joe never named any of the pieces he examined, but they might well have included such as "I'll Say She Does" and a new piece of jibberish titled "Ja-da." Even with the Armistice just signed, there were still war songs coming out, amusing ones such as "Good Morning, Mr. Zip-Zip-Zip!" "If He Can Fight Like He Can Love, Good Night, Germany!" and "Would You Rather Be a Colonel with an Eagle on Your Shoulder or a Private with a Chicken on Your Knee?" Whatever he picked would have been chosen with an eye for what the guys back in camp would like. He sat down at a piano and proceeded to try several pieces, occasionally humming softly as he played. "I suddenly heard a voice join me," he later recalled. "A lovely tenor quality proved to be possessed by Carleton A. Coon, a handsome and extremely personable man." Coonie was still in his uniform as a nominal captain, and Joe was dressed in his corporal's uniform. The two men found many common interests, one of which was the possibility that Joe might be useful in Coonie's little band that was supposed to play on New Year's Eve. But would the musicians' union allow it? Coonie promised to look into it.[58]

That Coonie was in uniform when he and Joe met has led many to assume that he was fully in the Army. As we have already seen, however, his duties as milk inspector had given him only a quasi-military status. His oldest child assured me that his father *never* saw actual military service.[59]

Since Carleton had already been released from duty, he no longer could count on his government pay and was having to find gigs to support his growing family. But could he count on Sanders? Many musicians were still in the military, so the union gave its permission for Sanders to join. As Joe later put it, "I played my first professional engagement on that New Year's Eve [*i.e.*, 31 December 1918]"; and during the next few days the two men met several times and discussed how they might most effectively work together. Since Joe was still in the Army, they agreed to form a partnership as soon as Joe was released. Jack Riley, not only a band leader but also a very successful booking agent in Kansas City, invited Coonie and Joe to come into partnership with him; but the two decided instead to form their own agency, as well as (to use Joe's phrase) "an official Coon-Sanders orchestra."[60]

The rest of Joe's enlistment was extremely irritating and anticlimactic. When he returned to Camp Bowie, he found that almost all of his division had been discharged. There were few officers and noncommissioned men left, and no provision had been made for Joe's billeting. He spent his first night sleeping atop a mound of army clothing and blankets. The next morning he and his Jazz Hound buddies were rounded up and put back into a tent. It was at this time that the four discovered that they apparently had been given furloughs merely to keep them from being discharged with the others, thus assuring the remaining officers good musical entertainment. Perhaps sensing the four men's disgust, their commanding officer arranged for all four to be promoted to sergeant; and there is a photograph showing Joe wearing his new stripes, and a dour expression. In disgust, Joe wrote to Coonie to do anything he could to help him get a discharge; and by return mail Coonie promised to do so. "It was three long months later," wrote Sanders long after the event, "that Lt. Speck told us the camp was to be abandoned now and all the officers and non-coms returned to civilian life or transferred if desirous of remaining in the service. We four were given our transfer papers and, in due time, received our honorable discharges at Camp Funston, Kansas."[61] Disgusted with the Army, Joe returned to Kansas City, but his brief stint in it would allow him access, in his last days, to a veterans' hospital.

CHAPTER TWO

Postwar Kansas City

When World War I ended, Kansas City, Missouri, was a vital city of over 300,000 inhabitants and was growing rapidly. By July of 1924 its estimated population was 359,650.[1] Situated on important routes of rail and river transportation, it was far more cosmopolitan than were many other cities of similar size in the United States. Persons from the Northeast possibly found it vaguely Southern, but many Southern visitors probably thought it dizzily sophisticated and pleasantly sinful, though in that respect perhaps still a notch or two below New Orleans. Those from places in New England, the Middle Atlantic area, and even elsewhere in the Midwest would not have been discomfited by the heterogeneous population, but many of them almost certainly were often reminded that much of the city's population had family and sentimental ties to the late Southern Confederacy. There was a considerable black population who were little if any freer here than were those in Dixie,* and this part of the nation had a very visible Ku Klux Klan that threatened not only black Americans but other groups as well. The Klan was ultra-conservative in everything except bigotry, and that it dished out liberally. One finds in files of the city's newspapers for this era many accounts of lynchings, in Missouri as well as in other parts of the nation, though mostly in the South. Neighboring Oklahoma, for example, had a particularly large Klan. So did such other states as Indiana and Illinois.

But Kansas Citians apparently found these terrorist activities far less interesting than they did such entertainments as music, vaudeville, and legitimate theater. Lovers of classical music and opera were accustomed to visits by an array of luminaries including Ignace Paderewski, John McCormack, Sergei Rachmaninoff, and Josef Casimir Hofmann. Stars of lighter material and top vaudevillians made Kansas City a regular place on their circuits. There was also quite a lot of

---

*But at least African-Americans in Kansas City were better off than those in some other non–Southern places. For instance, in September of 1923 the mayor of Johnstown, Pa., ordered all blacks resident in the city for fewer than seven years to leave. The American Civil Liberties Union filed a protest (Kansas City Star, 14 September 1923).

local dramatic and musical talent, and a number of excellent music teachers.

In the field of popular music there was so much local talent that Kansas City was about to take its place in the jazz world with New Orleans, Memphis, and Chicago. And when jazz began to intrude on the public scene, it found many willing ears in Kansas City, and a good number of musicians who saw the possibilities of the raw, new music. But jazz didn't come easily to Kansas City or the nation.

Everywhere there were many who refused to regard jazz as music. Many probably agreed with the "lowbrow acquaintance" whom the *Kansas City Star's* staff-member quoted as saying, "Popular music is that which you tire of in a week. Classical is that which you tire of at once."[2] As far as the nation's General Federation of Women's Clubs was concerned, popular songs such as were coming out of Tin Pan Alley were outrageous and were having a dangerous influence on the youngsters. The group favored proscribing them. They wished to encourage such older songs as "There's a Long, Long, Trail" and "Keep the Home Fires Burning" that were popular during the late war.[3]

It would probably be impossible to agree on a time when the era began that was to take its name from this new music. Some might say, with F. Scott Fitzgerald, that the Jazz Age began in 1919 with the May Day riots in such cities as New York, Chicago, and Cleveland.[4] Another plausible starting point might be April of that same year, when some thirty-seven bombs were mailed in packages, one of which exploded at a senator's home in Atlanta, Ga. (The others were intercepted.) For those whose pocketbooks are their most vital organs, the Wall Street bombing on 16 September 1920 might seem a good candidate. For the many Americans who had come to think of baseball as almost on a level with Holy Scripture, the disillusioning "throwing" of that game's World Series in 1919 — the so-called "Black Sox" Scandal — was enough to turn one into a cynic. A great many of us might say that the Jazz Age began when Americans lost their innocence in the World War, though this assumes there had been much to lose. And there is, of course, the start of Prohibition, along with other possible choices. What seems to be true, however, is that the Jazz Age, and all that it suggests, began as a protest against social, political, and economic systems that many considered stifling, bigoted, uncharitable, and hypocritical. Was the protest excessive? Well, so are most other protests. But it was so silly! So? When are humans *not* at least a little silly? And they seem to be silliest when they are most serious.

And now, instead of discussing the origins of jazz and the various ethnic contributions to its development, or whether it brought on the era, or the era brought it on, or whether any other interesting theories may be valid, I shall merely try to describe Kansas City in the years immediately after the First World War, especially the various influences on the development of popular music. It will be useful also to examine the attitudes of its population on such matters as politics and social issues, and see how the city as a whole reacted to the great changes going on in it and in the nation. Most of all, we'll see what role the new music played in these changes and how that music generated numerous popular orchestras, several of which eventually made a great contribution to American popular music, and one of which we shall chronicle in more detail than has yet been done. For about a decade the Coon-Sanders Nighthawks were one of about a half-dozen of the most popular orchestras in the nation. For my money, they were the most entertaining and vital of all.

Kansas City and the nation had survived what was frequently being called "The Great War," an ironic term that might more appropriately be altered to the *Great Obscenity*. Perhaps at first glance everything seemed intact, and everyone was elated that the war was over. There was a general admiration of those who had participated in it, and much public discussion about what to do with those who had not. One case in

Sgt. Joe Sanders, Camp Benton, Texas, early 1919. His third stripe was intended to help ease disappointment at delay in discharge. (Courtesy Special Collections, Kansas City [Mo.] Public Library.)

particular exercised the city and the nation for a while, that of the champion boxer Jack Dempsey, who never seemed to come up with a good reason for not having offered himself for target practice overseas. Whatever his reason, his lack of service caused a lot of sneering comment. And when Dempsey went to Europe after the war's end, a member of the staff of the *Kansas City Star* tartly observed, "It must be true, then, that the war is over."[5]

But of course the city's problems didn't end with the Armistice. The years 1918 and 1919 have passed into history as the time of the great Spanish influenza epidemic. Soldiers in Europe, most of whom had managed to dodge the Kaiser's bullets and were now waiting to come home, contracted it; many of them died. In the United States there was scarcely anyone who did not get the flu or know someone who did. By the beginning of February 1919, Kansas City had lost 1,823 persons to the disease; and the Chamber of Commerce estimated that each death had cost the city about $3,000.[6] (Putting things into monetary terms always makes them easier to assess.) In late 1921 a smallpox epidemic struck. By late November, while city officials debated whether to have compulsory vaccination, there had been at least 263 cases and 93 deaths. Then, in early December, Dr. J. P. Leake, from the United States Public Health Service, visited Kansas City and proclaimed the city's epidemic at an end.[7]

There were even some amusing, if slightly disconcerting, problems in the war's wake. One, discussed in an article in the *Star*, told of a Mlle. Susanne Boitard, a Frenchwoman who was now in the United States to look for twenty American officers who had proposed marriage to her in France. She was here, she said, "to investigate their records," and had put "eight into the discard already." She was working her way westward from New York, a trip that by March of 1920 had carried her to Louisville, Kentucky. Her next target was St. Louis, uncomfortably close to Kansas City, though whether she ever got to the latter doesn't seem to have been recorded.[8] Nevertheless, there may have been at least one or two nervous males in Jackson County and environs.

There were economic problems, too. In 1919 prices rose, but a buyers' strike helped lessen the effect somewhat. Some Democrats perhaps thought it might give them another issue for the 1920 elections, and with President Wilson's growing unpopularity, they were going to need some good ones. Agricultural industry was important in the areas around Kansas City, but the farmers, almost always flirting with financial difficulty, were entering a decade that would see them, as a group, fail to share the prosperity that many others in the nation would enjoy. In 1920 the average annual income for a farmer was only $830, as compared with $1,428 for a clergyman, $1,375 for a Federal employee, and $1,924 for a construction worker. By 1924 the average clergyman's salary had risen 13 percent and the federal employee 10 percent, while the average annual incomes of the construction worker and farmer had fallen 5 percent and 26 percent respectively.[9] There was a recession in 1921–1922, partly as a result of decreased demand for products in peacetime and the sudden dumping of the veterans into the work force. As Elizabeth Stevenson observes, the condition of the nation's business was going to be greatly influenced by Andrew W. Mellon, President Harding's very wealthy secretary of the treasury. He was, she writes, "much admired by his age" and "was the pivot from which the curiously negative, shallow, but determinative policy of the [next] three administrations was exercised." "Mellon's principles," says Stevenson, "were two: that wealth should be encouraged to pursue its own ends; and that government, except for its usefulness in helping to promote these ends, should retire into as small a compass of activity as possible."[10] In other words, let government stay the hell out of business. After 1920, and especially after about 1924, American business and the federal government proceeded wholeheartedly to act on those principles.

The average American now seemed to hope that everything might return to the way it had been before 1917. In other words, it was hoped that there would be a return to normality, or perhaps one should say to *normalcy*.

Normalcy! Whatever President Warren Gamaliel Harding may have had to do with that word's etymology, he certainly seemed the personification of it. One would have been hard pressed to find a more average American in looks, ability, and interests. The Baltimore *Evening Sun's* Henry L. Mencken described him as "simply a third-rate political wheel-horse, with the face of a moving-picture actor, the intelligence of a respectable agricultural implement dealer, and the imagination of a lodge joiner."[11] In Harding's own appraisal of the nation's needs, he seemed determined to exhaust the possibilities of antonyms and alliteration — Americans needed "not nostrums but normalcy," "not experiment but equipoise," "not heroics but healing," "not revolution but restoration," "not surgery but serenity," etc.[12]

And as for Harding's critic, Henry Louis Mencken (1880–1956), this gadfly was having the same effect on American political, social, and literary traditions that jazz was having on American music, and then some. That is to say, Mencken was turning orthodoxy upside down; and not content with that, he was giving it a good shaking. The "Sage of Baltimore" wrote books and journalistic pieces that ripped into almost every aspect of the "genteel tradition." From his entry into journalism in 1899 until his stroke in 1948, Mencken's columns were carried in newspapers all over the nation. But it was the Twenties that produced the Mencken that is best remembered. His many books gave his rollicking views permanence beyond his journalistic essays, and his literary criticism and encouragement of young, daring authors made him, in the opinion of many, the single most influential individual in American intellectual life. Something of an heir to Ambrose Bierce's mantle, Mencken carried that bitter, witty writer's jihads much further. If Bierce wrote in acid, Mencken wrote in *sulphuric* acid. And while Bierce often seemed personally outraged by what he saw as idiocy in the general population, Mencken almost always gave the impression of rather enjoying the ridiculous, gaudy show. Here, observed Mencken,

> the unending procession of governmental extortions and chicaneries, of commercial brigandages and throat-slittings, of theological buffooneries, of aesthetic ribaldries, of legal swindles and harlotries, of miscellaneous rogueries, villainies, imbecilities, grotesqueries, and extravangances — is so inordinately gross and preposterous, so perfectly brought up to the highest conceivable amperage, so steadily enriched with an almost fabulous daring and originality, that only the man who was born with a petrified diaphragm can fail to laugh himself to sleep every night, and to awake every morning with all the eager, unflagging expectation of a Sunday-school superintendent touring the Paris peepshows.[13]

This amused, detached type of attack only made Mencken more infuriating to his detractors. H. L. Mencken was definitely an important part of the Jazz Age, though he disliked the music for which it was named.

Today, "return to normalcy," the catchphrase given by historians to the Harding administration, seems extremely ironic. Nothing was going to be the same again. In fact, many adults at the time began to fear that their world was falling apart, and a large number of youngsters apparently hoped fervently that it was. Youth! To the restless that seemed the most valuable commodity. Who cared how it had been *before* the war? Besides, the war had been to make the world safe for democracy, hadn't it? Well, it was time for the youngsters to express their democratic aspirations! And to the horror of the more sober citizens, those aspirations seemed to center on booze, sex, and jazz, with the automobile as a vital accessory to all of them. And bobbed hair.

Bobbed hair? But what about more important matters such as the Ku Klux Klan, inflation, or the immigration question? James J. Montague explained to the *Star's* readers how such matters were ranked:

> "Bailiff," I asked of the long-faced man
> Who stood so erect and proud,
> "What is the case that has filled the place
> With this vast and curious crowd?
> A murder, perhaps, or a swell divorce?...."
> "You got it wrong," said the long-faced man
> With the pitying type of sneer,
> "We ain't got time for the trial of crime
> In a law mill like this here....
> We are all about to hear the case
> Of one Annice Bedella Gee,
> An atrocious flirt who has worn her skirt
> Two inches below her knee."[14]

Indeed, first things first. And lest one laugh at any supposed exaggeration in Montague's poem, let it be known that how far down the hem of a woman's dress happened to reach, and whether that same woman had decided to rid herself of excessive hair, were matters that caused more than raised eyebrows or clearing of throats.

The flapper! If the pages of the Kansas City press are any indication, a good share of the public couldn't weary of talking about her, making jokes at her expense, or just shaking the head at her fancied depravity. Many municipal and state politicians doubtless hoped to get some good mileage out of the issue, while some Kansas Citians probably agreed with their own Ed Howe, who laughed it off with a "Most people nowadays are disgracefully young." (He was 69.) And the *Star*, usually inclined to keep a level head, could mildly observe that a flapper was "a small bundle of femininity entirely surrounded by cosmetics," and paraphrase Rudyard Kipling by describing a female as "A rag, a bone — and *less* than a hank of hair."[15]

By the spring of 1922 women's fashions seemed headed into chaos. Kansas Citians, at least those who had nothing better to do, were clucking over a fad among many young females which involved leaving galoshes open, thus allowing them to flap ostentatiously.[16] (Though the practice seems a good candidate, it was apparently not the origin of *flapper*.) And with the radical new fashions at that time, such flapping would have been ostentatious indeed; for women's dresses were almost to mid-calf, even higher for a more daring minority. Over the next several years those skirts would gradually rise until by 1929 they were at the knee. (There has always been a temptation to try to relate them somehow to stock prices.) And with this shortening of dresses came the inevitable jokes, such as one about a policeman who told a lost youngster that he ought to have held onto his mother's skirt. The little fellow sobbed that he couldn't reach it.[17]

Those flapping galoshes, by the way, seemed to be a national craze, with some special refinements added by New Yorkers. In mid–February of 1926 the city experienced snow, and the flappers in the Times Square area left their galoshes unbuttoned in such a way as to announce their status with the opposite sex. One button undone indicated that the young woman was spoken for, two buttons indicated an engagement, and three buttons signified marriage. What if *all* buttons were left undone? Well, explained one flapper, that would allow the observer to guess.[18] It might also have indicated absent-mindedness.

Among the conservative dressers, however, the "tailored" look for suits was popular, with jacket lapels plunging and buttoning rather low. Large, bulging front pockets were common. For the well-dressed woman in public, hats were still *de rigueur* and rather large, often crossing the brow in a sort of arc that gave the face a slightly wistful appearance — or sophisticated if one worked it right. The cloche hat was still off-stage but being cued. An ad for Vanitisilk described a new article of women's underwear as a "double-back knicker," a somewhat dainty version of the older bloomers, with an extra thickness of glove silk; because, said the ad, "a knicker has always worn through first in the back where the corset rubs." Well, then, so much for corsets! They'd have to go, along with a number of other items of lingerie. The *teddy*, a one-piece undergarment with a T-shirt-like top and loose-fitting bottom, was about to enter the picture. The song "Roll 'em, Girls" advised females not only to roll their hose below the knee but also not to wear anything they regarded as superfluous.[19]

Someone who signed himself "C.T.B." wrote a protesting letter to the *Star*, not against the new feminine fashions but rather complaining of what he regarded as the inappropriateness of having "some small salaried girl trying to ape the manners and dress of society girls." "In these days ... it is becoming difficult to distinguish between the appearance of the working woman and that of the woman of wealth and position."[20] It was a pretty good re-statement of the old sumptuary laws of previous centuries.

Male fashions, aside from those affected by the *cake eaters** and the soon-to-arrive *sheiks*, were much less radical than those worn by the females. Men's street fashions around 1920, except for such accessories as hats and spats, would not cause undue notice today, though suits were fairly close fitting and trousers narrow and shortened to the ankle, especially if spats were worn. Dress shirts often still had the higher, detachable collar; but an increasing number of men were buying the new lower, more-comfortable collar. A well-dressed man *had* to wear a hat, perhaps a fedora or the golfing-type cap (with a metal snap on the bill) though just as likely a derby or, in warm weather, a hard, flat-topped, straight-brimmed straw hat called a *sailor*, *bouter*, or *cady*. Adolescent males' wardrobes included the popular knee-length knickerbockers (a term often shortened to knickers), a large golfer's-type cap, and a coat with belt and prominent front pockets, two breast pockets and two corresponding lower ones. Long socks usually were worn with knickers. In the spring of 1922 such an ensemble was prominently advertised at twenty dollars by Gordon & Koppel, 1005-1007 Walnut.

Many females resented attacks on the new styles and often used the press to say so. Alice Cole, in a letter to the *Star's* editor, defended females against smug males who criticized bobbed hair. "Many [women]," she informed the *Star's* readers, "have added about thirty minutes to each working day by removing, in some cases, veritable mops of uncomfortable insanitary 'tresses'; in other cases, a few poor, scorched, faded, pathetic looking hairs." She said she expressed the righteous indignation of many women "who refuse to remain martyrs to weekly 'marcels,' curl papers, rats, false curls and 'permanent waves.'"[21]

At about this same time Margaret Rohe was telling women in Kansas City that the new fashions were not for the buxom maid, and that

> The spring styles all for slim folks are,
> And so to get more thin,
> The fatties, dieting and stunts,
> Do desperately begin.[22]

"Yet," she said, "the fat female *must* wear something, and when she is panting to be smart as well as panting *embonpoint* [plumpness], it is cruel fate that fashion should design exclusively for willow wand figures this spring."[23] It's interesting that at about this time two vaudeville stars, Gus Van and Joe Schenck, both of whom visited Kansas City on their circuits, had recorded the song "Dance and Grow Thin," in which they recommended, in good syncopated rhythm, vigorous dancing for those overweight.[24]

In August 1921 the *Kansas City Star*, in a reprint from the *New York Times*, gave the city's females more to worry about than how they were dressed, or even how many extra pounds they might be carrying. They now were advised to avoid being too intelligent, that is, if they wished to attract the males.[25] After all, what male likes to be shown up?

Nor was the liberated young male let off entirely. Often the attitude was the familiar

---

**Webster's* Third International Dictionary *defines cake-eater as "an effeminate party-going dandy," which does not seem to fit precisely the term as used in the* Kansas City Star.

one of, well, they're males; what can you expect? But not always. In the early 1920s, before Rudolph Valentino's film brought the word *sheik* into common if mispronounced usage, the flapper's male counterpart in the Kansas City area was known as a *cake-eater* or *cookie-pusher*, or sometimes just *cake*.[26] He was a fellow who affected all the latest jargon, and the *Star* occasionally published glossaries to help troubled parents interpret the talk of the city's cliques, including its puzzling youth. Some of the terms still have some currency, those such as *gold digger*, meaning a mercenary female; or *dogs*, for feet (any larger than size nine were *airedales*); or the word *knockout*, which according to the *Star* referred to a flapper who was so attractive "as to make all the cake-eaters drop their cake...." Some of the other terms, however, seem to have been lost with all that Wall Street stock in 1929, such words as the following:

Berries—Indicates surprise and approval, as "Isn't that the berries!"
Tomato—Nice, as in "That's very tomato." Later this seems to have been used mainly to describe a fetching young woman.
Tin can—Something truly delightful and exciting.
Slick—An adjective that came into use shortly after boys began using bear grease or brilliantine on their hair. A slick date was a young man who was good looking, cynical, and sophisticated, and gave the impression of having been very successful in college love affairs.
Sad—An adjective that referred to a poor but honest girl who powdered moderately, but did not use paint or lipstick. She made a favorable impression on people who were looking for somebody with sense—never a very large percentage of the "slick" males.
Seraph—A young lady who liked to be kissed with lots of repression, as in the good old-fashioned days. She was not in great demand among males of the Lost Generation.

Wrestle—A dance engaged in by a flapper and a cake-eater or cookie-pusher. Almost any dance could become a wrestle, and often did.[27]

The *Star* turned its lexicographic attention also to Twelfth Street, a lively midway that gave rise not only to "The Twelfth Street Rag" but also to a reputation for raciness and crime. The paper's interest was spurred by a civic desire to show "how Twelfth Street 'slings' its argot." How would a law-abiding citizen otherwise interpret such as the following: "I was putting in the works when a buzz flashed the pan. I took it on the lam. He might have turned the heat on, but I didn't want to be sneezed in that store, so I dogged* it."[28] Thus a list of the following forty-three terms:

- Turn the heat on—to discharge firearms.
- Flash the pan—to display a police star.
- On the hoist—a bandit.
- A screw—a turnkey or prison guard.
- Putting in the works—using crooked dice or cards.
- Store—a gambling house.
- Buzz—a detective.
- Cinder dick—a railway special officer.
- Take on the lam—to flee arrest.
- Lamster—an escaped convict or bond jumper.
- Short con—any petty confidence game other than politics.
- Sneeze—arrest.
- Get settled—to receive a penitentiary sentence.
- On the haul—transporting whiskey in motor cars.
- Kick the log around—to Smoke opium.
- Paperhanger—a writer of bad checks.
- Rap—identification.
- Kiester—a suitcase.
- Hot—stolen.
- Cuter—a prosecuting attorney.
- Jack's house—penitentiary.
- Racket—any illegal occupation.

*The Star's *list omitted this term but one can make a good guess as to its meaning.*

- Cool off in a refrigerator — hide stolen property.
- Monkey — a victim of a swindle.
- Jug — a safe.
- Peteman — a safe blower or yegg.
- Steerer — the person who lures a victim to a gang of confidence men.
- Cannon — a pickpocket.
- Poke — a pocketbook.
- Shieve [sic] — a knife.
- Big mitt egg — a member of a gang of confidence men.
- Riding the shorts — a pickpocket's operations on a streetcar.
- Tog — a light topcoat carried over the arm of a pickpocket to hide the movements of his fingers.
- Mouthpiece — a defense attorney.
- Harness bull — a uniformed patrolman.
- Make — to understand.
- Booster — a shoplifter.
- Fall money — funds crooks hold in reserve for bonds and attorney fees.
- Stiff reader — a worthless check.
- Mix mud — prepare opium for smoking.
- Do a jolt in a stir — serve a penitentiary sentence.
- Door shaker — a private watchman.
- Shade the duke — conceal one's hand before picking a pocket.[29]

In mid–April of 1922, while in Kansas City to appear in Vicente Blasco Ibañez's *Blood and Sand*, the actor Otis Skinner complained of American slang, especially as modern writers were using it. Playwrights, he said, wrote "impossible English"; and he added, "How are we going to keep the English language from being constantly defiled? Slang, careless speaking, and careless writing each is putting our language in the gutter."[30]

In traditional and more judgmental circles the cake-eater, as well as his preposterous garb, was regarded as a contemptible, perhaps even unmanly person. In fact, the *Star* carried an article about a group of college students in Chicago who had formed a Five-Minute Club, so named because a five-minute egg is hard-boiled. It was with disgust that such males regarded the somewhat foppish fellow, a pipe in his hand, with hair neatly combed and heavily coated with some kind of oil, trousers loose and bell-bottomed, and a very form-fitting coat. Another article from Chicago, and also reprinted in the *Star*, said that the Rev. George H. Stewart, rector of Chicago's St. Luke's Episcopal Church, had asked females to give wholehearted support to university athletes and, furthermore, to use their influence over male students to "enforce" interest in sports.[31]

In Kansas City the attitude toward these "wayward" males seems to have been a more tolerant and amused one. Bell-bottoms, some of them reaching a yard in circumference at the bottom of each leg, were a greatly exaggerated adaptation of a Navy seaman's pants; though the ones worn by the cake-eaters were often made of corduroy and sometimes elaborately decorated. There might, for instance, be rows of yellow or blue buttons, about five inches apart, all the way down the side of each leg. Ask a Kansas City high school student why he wore them, observed a *Star* reporter, and the answer would probably be something along the line of "Because — well, the other fellows wear them."[32] If an ad by the Doric Theater was correct, they wore them also because "Bell bottom pants, they flop in the breeze, and, oh! My goodness! How they torment the 'shes.'"[33] As we've seen, they tormented a lot of the *hes*, too.

As I have suggested above, the term "cake-eater" was perhaps an early term for what became better known as a "sheik." However, I have seen some evidence that, in the minds of some observers of the popular scene, the two terms were not quite synonymous. As late, for instance, as December of 1925, long after the term *sheik* had become current, the Palace Theater in Cleveland, Ohio, held a "new box office stunt" of "selecting the best dressed 'caker' (boy) and flapper (girl) walking through the door." The boy would be judged by the width of his trousers and the girl "as a regulation flapper."[34]

But it was the flapper who received the brunt of the reaction against the liberated youngsters, and some of them fought back. One of them, who signed her letter to the *Star* as "P.S.," flatly said that "those who criticize the flapper are simply older people who are sore because they are getting old and are jealous of youth and the spirit of unusual pep which seems to predominate in the young people of today." Furthermore, she couldn't see that "the young girls of today look any more silly, idiotic or ridiculous than our mothers or grandmothers did when they were in their teens." She found an inconsistency in meddling with a woman's right to choose her own grooming and clothing. Why was it, she demanded, "anybody's business if a girl wants to bob her hair in order to be more comfortable? When we wore high heels and tight corsets[,] they said we were ruining our health as well as the future generation — now, when we wear sensible low heels, no corsets and bob our hair, they say we look sloppy and all that."[35]

This concern about the flapper was an aspect of the general realization, in Kansas City and elsewhere, that females were showing independence. And though Kansas City in November 1922 elected the state's first female member to the legislature, there was still a strong prejudice against those women who appeared to be stepping out of their traditional roles. There are many illustrations of this, one of the most interesting being the handling, in February 1920, by the Athenaeum of a presentation of the opera *The Secret of Suzanne*. Suzanne's secret is that she enjoys smoking; but her furtive actions to prevent her husband's knowing makes him suspect that she is seeing another man. He is greatly relieved to learn the truth, and the opera ends as the two relax with cigarettes. That is, in the *opera* they do, but not in Kansas City, where for Suzanne to smoke on stage would have been "too naughty."[36]

There was a general assumption by many — mostly males — that the female mind was well adapted for domestic matters but not for those things regarded as in the male's domain, in other words, such weighty matters as boozing, sports, and cars. But the women were quickly learning. An article from the *New York Times*, and reprinted in August 1921 in the *Star*, was titled "A Woman Driver Ahead." It said that despite familiar disparaging remarks about women drivers, "Habitual indulgence in outdoor sports has instilled in many women drivers a self[-]reliance and mental poise that proves invaluable when piloting the car through traffic."[37]

Since it was obvious that the female had started to think for herself, manufacturers and retailers were not slow to anticipate a new market. And who could tell? The bobbed-hair craze just might cause a rise in the cost of haircuts, and that might fuel inflation and thus give the Democrats a badly needed issue. Undaunted by all the bobbed-hair pishposh, ads for Danderine assured the girls that "Danderine grows hair" and that they should "beautify" their hair with it. And taking a cue from popular jargon, Robinson's Shoe Company advertised a "Flapper" shoe for five dollars. A junior style and size was termed the "Kewpie-Twin" and sold for between $2.25 and $3.50.[38]

For men wishing to look like other than simian rustics, and willing to risk being labeled *powder-puffs* or perhaps *jelly beans*, there were on the local market a flood of cosmetics and items of clothing. Hair Groom said that its use kept hair combed and glossy, that it was a "greaseless combing cream ... not sticky, smelly."[39] Hanes advertised for a dollar a very popular one-piece "summer union suit,"* that offered an athletic top and short legs that reached to just above the knees.[40] It looked somewhat like a male version of the female teddy, and may have suggested the latter for those women wishing to ape the male's "freedom." Arrow Collars were already on the scene and becoming so

---

*Has anyone discovered whether there was any objection to the term union suit among diehard ex–Confederates?

popular that within a few years Cole Porter, in his song "You're the Top," would salute them, along with such other new items as cellophane and the chic pants on an usher at New York's Roxy Theater.[41]

Other products bid for public patronage. There was Wrigley's chewing gum, sold in four flavors: juicy fruit, spearmint, double-mint, and a new flavor called P-K, described as "the new sugar-coated peppermint gum." Arctic Dairy Products produced ice cream that made "life sweeter." Also making life sweeter was "The original Cake-eater candy bar," selling for a nickel and consisting of "butter cream center covered with caramel, peanuts and chocolate." There was a logo of a young man in bell-bottoms. Pepsodent toothpaste had arrived, as had Luden's menthol cough drops. Vacuum cleaners such as the Premier were not greatly different in appearance from those of today. There were Skylark gasoline, Crême Elcaya to "look as young as you feel," Whip-o to make cream easier to whip, Bluehill pimento cheese, and Instant Postum as a coffee substitute.[42]

For a quarter, one might avail oneself of the delightful effects of Vivaudou's Mavis Talcum Powder.[43] That product, however, was intended primarily for women; its use by males was still problematic. Many of the city's and the nation's males would have regarded even the suggestion that they use talcum as a *casus belli* and the suggester as probably a former saboteur for the late Kaiser. This super-male reaction found expression in the song "Masculine Women! Feminine Men!" by Monaco and Leslie, and recorded by Irving Kaufman.[44] Poor Rudolph Valentino, of filmdom's sheik and toreodor fame, ran willy-nilly into the issue. Having arrived in America only recently, Valentino was unfamiliar with national mores; and in the mid–Twenties he found himself quite unwittingly standing athwart the national canon that an American male, if he was indeed *all* male, had to approximate the "missing link" of Evolutionism. Most American men probably thought Valentino, at least in his films, looked too damned suave and sophisticated. What was worse, too many women seemed to like the image. An enterprising reporter in Chicago happened to mention in one of his columns that he had seen, in the men's room of a fine local hotel, a dispenser for talcum powder, and *pink* talcum powder, at that. Subsequently, an editorial in the paper lightly picked up the story and suggested that perhaps Valentino and his films were effeminizing the American male. Valentino was furious and challenged the writer to a duel, or at least fisticuffs; but the matter stumbled on into absurdity. The movie idol's last days were embittered by the flap, a silly trifle he should have laughed off.[45]

Despite an earlier impression by many Americans that cigarettes were unmanly, by the time of the First World War they were regarded as a common item of bona fide male paraphernalia. When the early Twenties arrived, there was a large selection of cigarettes available in Kansas City. Herbert Tareyton London Cigarettes, selling for a quarter, promised the public that "There's something about them you'll like." Booher's Drug Stores, 1300 Grand and 401 E. Tenth, advertised Chesterfields, Spurs, Piedmonts, Favorites, Lucky Strikes, Beechnuts, Home Runs, and Clowns for about twenty cents; while Fatimas (the name accented on the second syllable) and Omars cost about three cents more. Earlier prejudice was evaporating, and already cigarettes were taking on the aura of sophistication, not only for men but for women as well. And while ads were still hesitant to show women as cigarette smokers — though some women were indeed smoking them — a few commercials toyed with the idea. In one advertisement the woman, indicating to her escort that she enjoys the aroma of the smoke, says, "Blow some my way." Those persons fighting bulging waistlines could ponder the advice in a Lucky Strike ad, "Reach for a Lucky instead of a sweet."[46]

Just one more type of ad and we'll make an end: "Regularity" was already something of an obsession with many Americans. In former times there had been such grim laxatives or "physics" as croton and castor oils, as well as the fearsome calomel. There were probably not many in Kansas City who had not heard the joke about the druggist who, needing to be away for a few minutes, asked a friend to mind his shop. Upon his return the druggist asked whether any customers had come by.

> "Just one."
> "What did he want?"
> "Cough syrup."
> "What did you sell him?"
> "Croton oil."
> "Croton oil!" yelled the druggist; "That won't stop coughs!"
> "You think not?" laughed the helpful friend. "See that guy out there?"
> "Yeah."
> "He's afraid to cough."[47]

By the early Twenties more seemly cathartics were on the market. As early as 1920 Carter's Little Liver Pills were working their magic on Kansas City. Another, Pluto Water, promised that "When nature won't, Pluto will." And for children, there were Cascarets and Syrup of Figs, as well as Castoria, a liquid advertised as "a harmless substitute for castor oil, paregoric, drops and soothing syrups."[48] Anyone who remembers castor oil would regard almost anything else as preferable.

Lest one assume that in Kansas City it was mainly the young who sought diversion or were likely to err during the "return to normalcy," we need to take a quick look at their parents, and even their grandparents.

To begin, even a cursory examination of the local press in Kansas City, during the postwar years, indicates that the entire concept of the family, including such factors as idealized courtship, marital fidelity, permanence of marriage, and rearing of children, was undergoing a very considerable change. The practice of making jokes about courtship and the husband-wife relationship is an old one; many a vaudeville star owed much of his humor to it. Such a joke as "You stole my wife, you horse thief" probably always got a good response. In fact, that particular gag was turned into a song by Frank Clark, Lester Lee, and Billy Glason.[49] And though it would be easy to exaggerate the popularity of such humor in the Twenties, by the early part of the decade negative "family" witticisms seemed much more prevalent, with the jokes taking on a sharper edge. And in British music halls and variety, America's attitude toward marriage came in for a good bit of ribbing: "I say," went one part of a routine, "I understand that she was married three times." "Yes," was the reply, "twice in America and once in earnest." A little later in the decade, an advertisement for the film *The Private Life of Helen of Troy* offered several wittily sardonic aphorisms on male-female relations: "If a strange woman dresses attractively, she's stylish; if it's your wife, she's indecent!" "Marriage is only exchanging the attentions of a dozen men for the inattention of one." "The human knee used to be a joint; now it's an entertainment!"[50]

One comic strip based on marital problems, *Bringing Up Father*, and better known as Maggie and Jiggs, was older than the Twenties. But by the time of our story it had been joined by several others, one of which, *Mr. and Mrs.*, greeted Kansas Citians each weekday. There was hardly an episode in which bickering and shouting matches were not the theme. "Mr." was a man of prosaic instincts whose days seemed to be spent doing little else than going to his office and using his free time to indulge his interests, or lack of them. His wife was a simple soul who should have married a man with more imagination and consideration, as well as one willing to tolerate a certain amount of feminine logic. Usually, after a particularly violent argument, the last frame of the strip showed their little boy, asking one or the other, "Mama love Papa?" or "Papa love Mama?" (This perhaps suggested the song in 1923 "Mamma Loves Papa," by Cliff Friend and Abel Baer.)

The pages of the *Star* were filled with amusing anecdotes, single-frame comic strips, and jokes, many of which indicated that the originator had a somewhat wry view of romance and marriage. One reprinted from the *London Mail* featured two women, one of whom shows her new engagement ring to her friend and asks, "Have you seen the ring he has given me?" to which the other replies, "Not for a long time."[51] Another cartoon shows a young suitor with his girlfriend: "That young brother of yours saw me kiss you just now. What ought I to give him to shut him up?" "He usually gets half a dollar," is her disturbing reply.[52] And another cartoon showed how divorce was getting to be a very familiar fact of married life:

> FIRST WOMAN: I'm giving a party for the anniversary of my divorce.
> SECOND WOMAN: Which one, dear?
> FIRST WOMAN: I forget whether it's the second anniversary of my first or the first of my second.[53]

Hardly anyone at the time took a more cavalier view of marriage and divorce than Peggy Hopkins Joyce, a famous and much-married chorus girl and actress on the national scene. Her name, often seen in the Kansas City press, was a byword for marital shallowness. The *Star* reported in December of 1921 that she had just returned from Europe and that a rumor suggested that she was about to take on yet another husband. Was it true? the reporters asked as she disembarked. "No — not soon, anyway. Too much is enough."[54] Most people in the United States at this time, especially those outside the larger metropolitan areas, were still conservative in their attitudes on this subject and probably regarded divorce, and especially remarriage, as disreputable, something to be hushed up.

But ironically, many of these same Americans who took a disapproving view of such a relatively minor matter as divorce were not equally shocked by extreme bigotry, especially that marshaled so forcefully — and often forcibly — by the Ku Klux Klan. There was at this time a very strong Klan in the United States, and it certainly wasn't limited to the South. And though Missouri had a large number of the robed philanthropists, such nearby states as Oklahoma and Texas seemed to have more vocal and bumptious ones. Despite the Triple-K's many supporters in the Kansas City area, Mayor Harry B. Burton was strongly opposed to the bilious group. With great theatricality Klan members occasionally — in a group, of course — made great shows of piety by parading silently into local churches and walking down to the front of the congregations, where they left monetary offerings. Sometimes the Klan rented local auditoriums and held conventions that attracted thousands. For example, on Saturday, 29 October 1922, 14,000 Klan members and supporters met at Convention Hall. At about the same time, Kansas Governor Henry J. Allen told the Klan that they were un–American, cowards, and false to Christianity. The *Kansas City Star*, which also had no use for the Klan, added with relish, "That was not all the governor said and doesn't half tell the emphases which he put into his remarks."[55]

For several years after William J. Simmons formed the new Ku Klux Klan in 1915 at Atlanta, Ga., the group failed to excite much interest. Then, when the postwar unrest began to challenge traditional attitudes, there was a great surge in membership. In those days Klan members, despite their clear hostility to various minorities, pretended to be great paladins of morality and traditional American values; and in that guise the group became a potent political force in a number of areas, especially the South and the Midwest. The hooded organization was tapping into what is unfortunately the human tendency to fear what appears alien. Those in the Twenties who preyed on this fear had quite a cheering section that included such luminaries as the Rev. Billy Sunday, among whose choice assertions was, "America is not a country for dissenters to live in."[56]

In 1924 the Klan, in open competition with the Chautauqua Circuit, even began what it termed the Klantauqua. At first it enjoyed considerable success and was much written about in such entertainment journals as *Variety*. The plan was to form Klantauqua groups in every state by 1925. They promised to pay entertainers better salaries, and would get some of the money for higher pay by having local Klan members prepare auditoriums and thus lessen overhead. In that first year they did pretty well, especially in Illinois, Iowa, and Indiana. The Klan ordered a large number of tents and fixed upon an admission charge of one dollar. Said *Variety*, "They are offering their audience a number of high-priced and entertaining acts, in most cases, considerably more than the Chautauquas offer. They can do this because of the small expense." It was, said the entertainment weekly, the first time that the Chautauqua had been threatened with serious competition, and simultaneously all over the nation. The Klan even asked its members already in the Chautauqua Circuit not to sign on in the future. When, in a typical situation, Klantauqua shows began to attract as many as three or four thousand, Chautauquans' fears seemed well founded.[57]

One Klan member who was a star performer for the Klantauqua was S. Glenn Young, a Klan leader from Herrin, Ill., one of the places on the Nighthawks' several road tours. According to one source, he traveled through Illinois "as though it were all Herrin" and as though he and his group had a "divine right to ignore such laws of America as they disapprove." On one occasion Young was stopped as his bullet-ridden car went through Champaign, Ill. A group of local right-thinkers clustered about the vehicle to protect its patriotic passenger, though the sheriff learned that the car carried an impressive armory, from automatics to machine guns. Said the reporter, "If a tire had blown out, it is likely the hair-trigger hooded knights would have blown up the town before a spare could have been put in place."[58]

The Klan's invasion of the entertainment world, coupled perhaps with a house manager's carelessness, caused a very embarrassing *faux pas* in a theater of the Keith-Albee Circuit. From time to time it was the custom to offer all-comedy programs and to call them "Keith Komedy Karnivals. One house manager, thinking perhaps to save electricity, and otherwise *not* thinking, put on his marquee "K. K. K. Vaudeville."[59] It must have been difficult to explain.

But 1925 proved a difficult year for the white knights. There was a series of scandals in Indiana, where the grand dragon raped a woman and then beat and even bit her so badly that she soon died. When the accused Klansman got no help from several state officials, he revealed information about their own corrupt practices and helped convict them.[60] From headquarters in Chicago, the managers announced in February that, despite previous success and nearly $500,000 spent on the project, it might be necessary to close all Klantauquas. That previous success had caused the Klan to expend a lot of money, but now everything was threatened by internal dissension.[61]

After that fateful sixteenth of January, 1920, it was illegal for Kansas Citians and other Americans to make, sell, or transport alcoholic beverages.* And though Rhode Island and other litigants brought suit in the Supreme Court to declare the new amendment unconstitutional, Prohibition, that demonstration of misguided altruism, would last for thirteen years and would reap its harvest of victims to some of the most lethal junk imbibed by a theoretically civilized nation. Following that date there were many articles in the local press discussing the demise of John Barleycorn, and one church in the city, anticipating the Eighteenth Amendment by several months, even held a funeral service for that convivial, if unlamented, fellow.[62] (Such obsequies quickly proved premature.) The majority of local residents seemed to face the "Noble

---

The Volstead Act was the enabling legislation for the 18th Amendment. President Woodrow Wilson had vetoed the Volstead Act, but Congress passed it over his veto.

Experiment" with skepticism, hostility, or ribald humor. They probably agreed with Fiorello H. La Guardia, a young Republican congressman from New York City, when he sneeringly said that Prohibition would succeed only when Congress could stop fermentation and repeal the law of gravitation.[63]

At first, those who avoided alcoholic beverages no doubt regarded the success of the Prohibition movement as ushering in a new and glorious era, while the other side's thinking probably ranged from those who wondered, gosh! can they really get rid of booze? to those who said, *no way!* And the song writers saw the matter as another subject for lyrical treatment. There was the "Alcoholic Blues" by Edward Laska and Albert von Tilzer—"I've got the blues! I've got the blues, since they amputated my booze!" Silvertone Records appropriately put it out on a disc, the other side of which expressed the opposite attitude in H. E. Rogers and Harry Akst's saucy "You Don't Need the Wine to Have a Wonderful Time While They Still Make Those Beautiful Girls":

> Adam and Eve never tasted champagne
> Still they were able to go out and raise Cain.
> For a sweet little miss who
>   knows the right way to kiss,
> Can set any brain in a whirl....
> Lots of people like a cordial after dessert,
> But give me something cordial that
>   is wrapped in a skirt....[64]

Harry Ruby came up with "What'll We Do on a Saturday Night When the Town Goes Dry?" M. K. Jerome and Harry von Tilzer were threatening in "If I Meet the Guy Who Made This Country Dry," and William Tracey and Halsey K. Mohr reminded those who could afford the trip that "It Will Never Be Dry Down in Havana." Irving Berlin addressed that same idea with "I'll See You in C-U-B-A." The popular singer Frank Crumit* recorded his own song that offered another solution to the problem of Prohibition, "I Married the Bootlegger's Daughter."[65]

Thus, it was inevitable that Joe Sanders would get into the great topic of the day with a number that apparently had too much good competition to endure, "What Were All the Wild Wild Women Like?" The lyrics, not exactly deathless but with an interesting rhythm, are as follows:

> The other day I chanced to
>   see a book on ancient history
> And something there attracted my attention.
> Way back in nineteen seventeen,† the
>   wise men of the land convened
> And passed a law that called for the prevention
> Of the sale of fiery stuff
>   they called intoxicating liquor
> That made the pulse beat quick
>   and the head a little thicker.
> They said "Good-bye, wild women, we
>   have seen the last of you."
> And that's the thing that puzzles
>   me and if it's really true,
> Oh! What, tell me what, were
>   all the wild, wild women like?
> I just can't keep from thinking that
>   they got that way from drinking
> That fiery stuff called liquor that
>   filled 'em full of vigor.
> Did they wear the skins of
>   animals and live in rocky caves?
> And tell me is it really true
>   that men were all their slaves?
> Did they woo them with sentimental stuff
> Or subdue them with clubs and treat
>   'em rough? Oh![66]

A typical local news item on the "Noble Experiment" described the hammy display put on by deputy federal marshals, on 22 February 1922, when, in a type of bust that was becoming routine and laughable, they poured out 200 barrels of liquor and wine. Calling it a "little show," the *Star* deliberately edged close to purple prose in its reporting of the event: "Rivulets of homemade wine and whisky raced over a bed of grape skins and corn mash to a swollen stream of contraband joy water, the fumes of which per-

---

*Frank Crumit (1889–1943), a popular singer and recording artist, was married to Julia Sanderson (1887–1975), who was herself a very popular singer. The two often sang duets.
†Joe was referring to the 1917 passage by Congress of a proposed amendment to outlaw liquor.

meated the foggy atmosphere in the vicinity of 2619 Grand avenue yesterday afternoon."[67] Earlier that year the *Star* matter-of-factly described the status of Prohibition in Kansas City:

> Safe, bottled-in-bond whisky is scarce in Kansas City and higher in price. Bootleggers are quoting $155 a case, an advance of $40 to $50 over two months ago. The supply of imported stock is limited because of the bad conditions of country roads, over which bootleggers must motor. The present supply here was accumulated last fall. [It is possible to get] liberal quantities of homemade whisky, but demand for it is small [because of the injurious quality of the product]. Saloon men report poor business in sales of whisky by the glass, due to the activity of the police patrol system.[68]

A watchful group of plainclothes police made saloon activity so risky that few proprietors kept their beverages on the premises but rather hid them somewhere outside and fetched them for customers' orders. Furthermore, customers who were unfamiliar to proprietors had a difficult time slaking their thirst.

> Whisky [continued the *Star*] in case lots is delivered direct to consumers in motor cars, usually at night. There are a half dozen Kansas Citians who have become rich from this traffic.
>
> Most of the good whisky here is from Pittsburgh or Canada. Old-fashioned beer has disappeared from Kansas City. Many saloons, however, handle a brand known as "hypo" or "sprayed" beer. [Apparently the same as what some called "needle beer."] This variety is near-beer into which a quantity of alcohol has been injected. "Hypo" beer retails for 25 cents a bottle. While tasting somewhat "flat," this beer carries a lusty "wallop," and consumption is generous.
>
> Home brew is not made so abundantly as it was a year ago, due to an indifferent demand. Much of the home brew was made by inexperienced persons and the quality of the product was generally poor.
>
> Real champagne and "honest-to-goodness" gin are practically impossible to obtain here, but home-made gin is available in liberal quantities at low prices.
>
> Jamaica ginger and grain alcohol diluted with water and fruit flavoring are popular drinks at certain drug stores. Physicians assert that such drinks are highly injurious. One physician today, by way of illustration, poured a small quantity of grain alcohol on a piece of raw beefsteak. The meat turned black.[69]

There are those who swear that consumption of alcohol increased as a result of Prohibition. Whatever the truth of that may be, many Americans during that era did consume a tremendous quantity of various kinds and qualities of alcoholic beverages; there is plenty of evidence that Kansas City held its own with verve and distinction in this regard. Even the government must have come around to the reality of it, for Noah Crooks, local collector of revenue for the U.S. Internal Revenue Service, announced in May of 1923 that he was beginning a campaign to collect the income tax on bootleggers' profits.* He was cautious enough, though, to say that at the moment he was unsure just how that might be done.[70] But it was an admission that no one, not even the federal government, could put Americans on the water wagon.

And they certainly were not going to stop the Kansas City musicians, especially the Kansas City Nighthawks, who successfully upheld the reputation that musicians, by and large, are omnibibulous. Johnny Coon said that both his father and Joe Sanders were marvelous drinkers. And in reply to my question whether Coonie drank more than he should have, Johnny replied, "They both did."[71] But from all that I've read and heard—and some of the evidence is from Johnny Coon himself—my guess is that Coonie's beverage capacity made Sanders and the rest of the band, by comparison, almost qualified candidates for Sunday school superintendents.

The city never seemed to lose its sense

---

*And you probably thought that the black market tax was exclusively a Mississippi device.

of humor over Prohibition; at least the *Star* didn't. Just before Christmas of 1921 the "Starbeams" column, in one issue of the paper, commented ironically: "Jazz is dead, says a writer. And buried. Like John Barleycorn."[72] A typical reaction to the national idiocy was expressed in a cartoon in the *Star* in which two businessmen were discussing important matters of the day:

> 1ST MAN: There's an awful lot of guys dying on account of bad hooch.
> 2ND MAN: Yeh — I notice.
> 1ST MAN: I was reading just the other day about a guy going stone blind — rotten hooch.
> 2ND MAN: A guy can't be too careful.
> 1ST MAN: Just think of the chances a guy takes for one shot of bootleg — it doesn't pay.
> 2ND MAN: Of course it doesn't pay. (Gets up and rummages in a clothes closet to retrieve a bottle.) Well, I guess I got a coupla shots left. Whaddya say?
> 1ST MAN: That won't go so bad on a chilly morning like this. (Looks at label.) I never heard of that brand. Where'd you get it?
> 2ND MAN: Oh, a guy comes around once in a while. I don't know his name. I give him 12 bucks for it. Not bad — eh?
> 1ST MAN: Well, here's how!
> 2ND MAN: Happy days![73]

And why so much space given to Prohibition in this history? For the simple reason that during the Twenties alcohol seemed to affect everything in Kansas City and the nation, almost to the point of defining the era. And for another reason, the Coon-Sanders band seemed to run on it as surely as their Hudsons, Maxwells, Buicks, Cords and Auburns ran on gasoline. Well, if the Nighthawks hit the bottle rather heavily, and still managed to remain sufficiently vertical to play their excellent music, then some of those other bands might well have tried to find out what brands the Nighthawks preferred. But who ever heard of jazz musicians who didn't know good liquor and how to find it?

The Nighthawks, once they moved to Chicago, and after they had begun playing those exhausting one-night stands, doubtless found liquor a familiar, comforting fact of life. And once they had begun to make good money, they could afford the best brands, not that "needle beer" or such potentially lethal stuff as "Jamaica ginger." They got the choice items that made it through the meager blockade operated by the U.S. Coast Guard, or that were spirited across the Great Lakes from Canada.

In the dozen years that the band existed, Coon-Sanders must have seen many raids, such as the one that targeted the New Year's Eve celebration for which they played at the Hotel Muehlebach's Plantation Grill in December of 1922. The federal Prohibition agents were out in force in the city that evening, concentrating especially on hotels and restaurants. The city was far from dry and just about everyone knew it; but the agents were impressed that on the whole everything seemed comparatively quiet.[74]

At the Plantation Grill, Frank Cunningham and two assistant agents casually joined the celebrants who were enjoying and dancing to music by the Nighthawks. That the agents were dressed in business suits, instead of formal attire, apparently raised no suspicions. Casually the three men moved about the large room, all the while apparently unmoved by some of the best dance music to be heard anywhere. One agent meandered into the kitchen where he discovered a man with four pints of champagne — it wouldn't have been a New Year's party without it. The agent simply made a mental note of it and kept observing. In the main part of the Grill, there wasn't a lot of booze, at least not on the tables. As the *Star* described it, "Usually the diners would leave the tables as unostentatiously as possible and return rejoicing." Often, some diner might drop a napkin and in picking it up, use the napkin for cover while someone recharged the diner's glass. After the agents had seen enough, Cunningham saw a man carefully hand a bottle to a woman with a party of eight. As she rose to leave the table, the agent walked over to her, identified himself, and asked for the bottle. The woman tossed her head impatiently and handed it over. Eight persons were arrested at the Plantation Grill that night.[75]

Elsewhere in the Muehlebach, over in the Trianon Room, several men added charades to their celebration. Realizing that Prohibition agents were the only ones who could legally take possession of liquor, they posed as feds and "confiscated" several bottles for themselves.[76]

There were others high on the agents' list of suspicious places. One was the Muehlebach's sister hotel, the Baltimore, where three were arrested. Ernie Young's Marigold Revue was featured at the Baltimore's Pompeiian Room, recently redecorated, and Louis Forbstein's Pompeiian Terrace Players furnished the music.[77] But it was obvious that "How Dry I Am" was not the theme song in either hotel.

There apparently was a good bit of conviviality also at what were called, in somewhat tongue-in-cheek phrasing, "chicken-dinner farms" or just "chicken farms." The Edgewood and the White City Gardens were perhaps typical. These and others had become important places of entertainment in some of the outlying areas, and they were almost constantly in trouble with the police, not only for selling booze but perhaps for prostitution as well.[78] But they did serve chicken — apparently pretty good chicken, too. The term perhaps had a double meaning — both fair and fowl.

A staff member, identified only as "E.S.D.," told the *Star's* readers in November of 1922 of the problems he faced when looking for "night life" in Kansas City:

> Night life in Kansas City now-a-days is confined rather closely to restaurants. Some time ago I accompanied a number of my friends on a search for a "live wire" cafe. They have practically disappeared from the city. We rode up and down Fifteenth street — and then along Kansas City's overrated "gay white way." It was a series of restaurants, mostly of the stool-counter variety. The only music to be heard floated out as the final stanzas of a burlesque show. There are a number of places that furnish music for their diners, but the orchestra makes an early exit to fill an engagement at a picture show. There are no more places of the old-fashioned cabaret variety — none where one may pay a "cover" charge and witness an entertainment — dancing between the acts, if he chooses.
>
> We soon gave up the idea of anything more varied than straight dancing. At the hotels one hears merely the efforts of a jazz orchestra. There is no pretence at anything more varied. You may dance if you choose. The crowds there consist in the main of the town's debutantes and their escorts.[79]

For those who admire the Nighthawks, the above statement, "At the hotels one hears merely the efforts of a jazz orchestra," must sound strange, especially if the critic was talking about the Plantation Grill. One might as well imagine Adam complaining that "in Eden all we have is perfection!"

In the early Twenties many in Kansas City enjoyed going down to the Union Station after dances. By, say, Saturday midnight there usually was a crowd ambling about, lingering over their food in the restaurant, and sociably shouting back and forth across tables. The depot's restaurant was almost the only place open all night and capable of accommodating large numbers. Many of the customers were waiting for the Sunday papers, whose arrival helped to thin out the crowd. There was always considerable interest in the engagements announced in the paper, or the results of the ball games and prize fights. One observer said that these Union Station gatherings had been a popular form of entertainment ever since the depot was built.[80]

The city certainly offered a great variety of entertainment, not the least of which was provided by the cinemas and vaudeville houses. The vaudeville season did not start officially until about the beginning of autumn. Kansas City had sufficient patronage of its theaters to draw such top stars as Eddie Cantor (whose humor and double meanings before local audiences disturbed a few sensitive ears), the Scotsman Sir Harry Lauder (said to be unable to entertain without a good quantity of rye under his kilt), Fannie Brice, the Marx Brothers, Jack Benny, and of course the famous "I Don't Care Girl," Eva Tanguay. Tanguay, by now in her forties, was perhaps more suited to the Twenties' rebellious atmosphere than she had been back in 1915, when a New York critic said her act reminded him of a German zeppelin dropping bombs on London.[81]

Among the best vaudeville theaters were the Globe, Shubert, Grand, Loew's Empress, Orpheum ("The Best of Vaudeville"), and Century. Another, the Gayety, was actually a burlesque house that phrased its ads so as to leave no one in doubt about the show. One ad promised "20 beautiful girls de looks all under 20."[82] The acts offered by the Gayety in the early Twenties perhaps included the Nighthawks on one occasion. This was at a time when gigs perhaps weren't very plentiful and the band had to take whatever they could get. For that matter, it probably wasn't necessary to twist the arms of Coon-Sanders to get them to play at the Gayety, anyway.

In March of 1920, while the Gayety's customers were enjoying "a real Girlesque show,"[83] Adolf Hitler, in Munich, Germany, had just received his membership card in the German Workers Party and was busily designing a flag. He also changed the group's name to the National Socialist German Workers Party. Somewhere between the Gayety Theater and a Munich beerhall is a story of ironic, willful fate.

Listed under the heading "photoplays" were such theaters as the Newman, Liberty, and Royal. They offered stage shows, but these, less of the typical vaudeville type, were only part of a program that included feature motion pictures. Indeed, it was the Newman that gave Coon-Sanders one of their first big, extended, and highly popular engagements. Most of the better theaters had permanent "house orchestras" that appeared on the same billing with whatever temporary bands a program might feature. The Newman was proud of its Concert Orchestra, led by Leo F. Forbstein, who later did important work for films in Hollywood. The director of the Orpheum Orchestra was Michelino Angelo Lenge, who had come to Kansas City about 1884 to direct the orchestra at the Gillis Opera House, and in 1897 went to the Orpheum. Milo Finley was director of the Royal's symphony orchestra. Frederick J. Curth was at the Liberty.[84]

Probably at least as early as 1922, several theaters featured pipe organs specially designed for popular music, the so-called *theater organ*. For instance, the Globe in January of that year advertised its new Robert Morton organ that had cost $20,000.[85] The Newman's theater organ had already been entertaining audiences for some time and was soon being heard frequently over WDAF in conjunction with the Nighthawks' program.

The city had an impressive group of good dining places, some of which offered the best dinner orchestras that this musical city afforded. Perhaps at the top of this category were the Hotels Muehlebach and Baltimore. By the fall of 1923 the Baltimore's Pompeiian Room was featuring special daily menus of meals "served in washed air," an early type of air cooling system. For seventy-five cents one could get a choice of broiled lake trout, fried breaded oysters, Hungarian goulash, fried turkey steak, or roast prime rib, followed by raisin pudding or orange ice. At the Muehlebach's Plantation Grill a "special plate luncheon" was available at sixty cents and included "chicken patty *a la reine*." Both hotels had popular coffee shops. In the evening each hotel featured one or more of the city's better popular bands.[86] In early 1920 the Baltimore promised "a swing, a dash and a plenty of color in the 'Summerland Revue,'" with Duke Yellman's Dance Orchestra. At the same time the Muehlebach offered Riley's Dance Orchestra in its Cafe Trianon.[87]

Kansas City had at least twenty-four good restaurants—cafes, tea rooms, cafeterias, etc.—that advertised in the local press.[88] There were, for instance, the Blue Ridge Inn, east of Swope Park on Blue Ridge Boulevard ("dining and dancing and 'home cooked chicken dinners'"); the Interstate Cafe, 313 East 12th ("free — a superb cup of coffee with each meat order"); the Peking Cafe, 214 East 12th; El Rigoletto, Eighth and Walnut; Café de la Louisiana, 1211 Baltimore ("the only real French cafe in Kansas City"); and many others. Those who liked cafeterias could go to such as the Forum, which had two locations, and the Bliss. Templeton's Harmony Cafeteria, in the basement of a building at Twelfth and Walnut, offered breakfast, lunch, and dinner. On each table a diner found, according to an ad, "Silver rolled in a clean napkin; ice water served with plenty of ice in the glass; water bottles, Heinz Tomato Catsup and Lea & Perrin's Sauce on tables that are covered with clean linen. All without extra charge."[89] And, as we have already seen, back in 1913 and 1914 at one called The Blue Goose Cafe, which offered both dining and dancing, a young high school senior named Joe Sanders helped support himself by playing the piano, five years before he had ever heard of Carleton A. Coon.

Out at Electric Park, which described itself as "Kansas City's Coney Island," one could be amused by an array of shows ranging from, say, "Talk of the Town Ice Follies" to a "Cake-eater and Flapper contest." The latter was so popular that it was repeated. Girls with bobbed hair were admitted free, and the spectator saw a throng of young women striving to approximate the flapper image, as well as a lot of bell-bottomed young males trying equally hard to look sophisticated. As the flapper and cake-eater contestants paraded across the stage, one spectator, who wore a Sunday school convention badge, was heard to murmur, "Solomon, in all his glory, was not arrayed like one of these!" On another occasion Electric Park featured a band under the direction of Roy Mack, who, styling himself "King of Jazz," perhaps anticipated Paul Whiteman, though the phrase must have occurred to many band leaders almost simultaneously.[90]

Most Americans by the early Twenties were accustomed to dancing and, perhaps with reservations, approved of it. In addition to such staid older dances as the schottische, minuet, quadrille, and polka, "proper" dances were limited to such as the square dance, waltz and, in a bit more daring places, the one-step (or fast foxtrot) and the two-step. Older, more-traditional persons might have recalled feeling a pang of regret back in 1907 when a song appeared with the title "I'd Rather Two-Step Than Waltz, Bill." They probably recalled also the shock they had felt when ragtime roared upon the scene and brought a herd of so-called "animal dances" to accompany the fast, syncopated music. There were the bunny hug, fox trot, horse trot, crab step, kangaroo dip, camel walk, fish walk, chicken scratch, lame duck, snake, grizzly bear, and, as Mark Sullivan puts it, "especially common, in both senses of the word — the turkey trot." Sullivan's *Our Times* printed an illustration of a couple dancing the grizzly bear, and with the caption, "But, in heaven's name, what kind of conversation goes with this?" When the grizzly bear helped spawn a song titled "Everybody's Doin' It," a parody followed right on its heels, "Everybody's Overdoin' It."[91] It really ought to have made the parents of the Twenties' flaming youth a little more restrained in their criticism. As "Starbeams" reminded Kansas City: "How time does fly! There are flappers foxtrotting at the country clubs now who were babes in arms when the uplifters first started out to reform the tango."[92]

Jazz could be expected to produce its own dances, but by 1920 and 1921 there weren't many, at least not many with names or that were widely known. Certainly there must have been ancestors of such dances as the Charleston and the black bottom, especially among the black population. When the tango reached America, about 1915, it quickly became identified with a somewhat "fast" life style. But the dance that seemed to draw the most fire in 1920 was the very new shimmy, a word coined from the expression "to shake one's chemise," and sometimes called the "shimmy-shake."[93] (In no time at all the term was applied humorously to the violent shaking that often characterized cars of that day.) As early as February of 1919 the *Star* informed its readers of a tongue-in-cheek report from Newark, N.J., about how that city's government had banned the shimmy:

> And it came to pass that in the year of our Lord MCMXIX, the pure in heart of the city called Newark did promulgate an eleventh commandment, to wit:
> Thou shalt dance only with thy feet; verily the shimmy shiver is a thing of evil and shall be cast out beyond the pale of society.
> This great movement (reform) was builded upon the desire of the city patriarchs that the youths and maidens should confine their gambols to the innocent pleasures which are termed trotting the fox and stepping but once.[94]

And about two years later the *Star* reported a scandal in Paris that involved a French duke and his duchess and the breakdown of their marriage. Their divorce trial revealed her association with forty-three men. Reported the article, "She became so enamored of the [shimmy] dance that she began to patronize all-night resorts in which the world and half world rub shoulders."[95]

There is every indication that the national dance craze had arrived in Kansas City. At least six schools of dance advertised in the local press, one of them directed by Professor B. Feri, who taught "European dancing." There were no fewer than ten dance halls, two of which — The New Casino, 1023 Broadway, and the Ararat Temple, 12th and Prospect — employed "Deveney's celebrated orchestra."[96]

Many dancers preferred the non-commercial dance floor, usually at someone's home. Here they shook their feet to the brimstone sounds of jazz phonograph records. Already such companies as Victor, Columbia, and Vocalion were turning out great quantities of discs of popular music and comic novelties. At the Grafonola Shop, 1112 Grand Avenue, the public were invited to buy, for example, vaudevillian Bert Williams' amusing recording of "When the Moon Shines on the Moonshine," as well as current numbers by the Ted Lewis and Art Hickman orchestras. And Boice Voice Shop advertised new recordings by Paul Boice's Novelty Orchestra. Among other popular bands featured on phonograph records were those led by Isham Jones, Carl Fenton, Vincent Lopez, and Paul Whiteman. There were other music stores where the sale of sheet music and dance records fed a seemingly insatiable public appetite. One such store was the Jenkins Sons Music Company, so important, as we have seen, in the Nighthawk story.[97]

When some of the public complained about the jazz records being sold by local music stores, the latter defended themselves by saying that jazz simply wouldn't die, despite all their efforts. "Pretty tough," laughed "Starbeams" at the *Kansas City Star*. "We remember when the liquor traffic wouldn't die, either, in spite of the best efforts of the saloon keepers."[98] The catch in "Starbeam's" humor, however, was that the liquor traffic *hadn't* died.

While private dancing was popular, by far the more spectacular demonstrations by terpsichoreans were at public dance halls where a very considerable number of orchestras, some of them probably very competent, found steady employment.

In addition to the Nighthawks, among the many popular bands in Kansas City in the early 1920s were those in the following list, compiled after an issue-by-issue examination of the *Kansas City Star* from 1919 to 1924. When known, I have indicated both the players and their instruments. There was a great amount of moving about, so some names appear in more than one band; and all players listed for an orchestra were not necessarily employed at the same time. Italicized names are of those known to have played at one time or another with the Nighthawks.[99]

Brown Brothers Saxophone Sextette — Tom Brown, director.

Johnnie Campbell's Society Orchestra.

Jack Chapman's Chaquette Saxophone Band.

Emil Chaquette's Kansas City Club Orchestra.

Leo R. Davis's Orchestra — Davis (violin), Harold E. Harlow (saxophone), Joe W. Reardon (saxophone), Ted Williams (piano), *Clarence Russell "Russ" Stout* (banjo), Z. I. Smith (flute), Ed Huckett (cornet), Charley Wagner (xylophone), Sam Pusatari (drums), Harold Johns (violin), Paul Bell (drums), Frank Manning (banjo), Harold Nordberg (saxophone), Eddie Werner (piano), Arthur Ogden Winter* (cornet), James Sell† (trombone), *Orville Knapp* (saxophone), Perry Gay (trombone), John De Feo (cornet), J. W. Hardin (saxophone), Sam Murphy (drums).

Deep River Orchestra — Eddie Kuhn (director), Willard Robison (piano), Arthur Bonger. Kuhn also led a group called Harmony Artists, or possibly Harmony Boys. In March of 1922, when playing over the *Star's* early radio station, Kuhn was reported in the press as saying that he had eliminated jazz from their wireless broadcasts.

Devenney's Orchestra. Played at The New Casino dance hall.

Milo Finley's Orchestra.

Charles Gray's Campbell Society Orchestra, sometimes called the Radio Orchestra — Gray (piano), John McClure (violin), *Orville Knapp* (saxophone), Eddie Kaelin‡ (saxophone), Frank Manning (banjo), Edwin Huckett (cornet), Jimmie Sell (trombone), Billy Mountain (drums).

D. Ambert Haley's Orchestra — Haley (piano), Leo R. Davis (violin), Ralph Stevens ('cello), Lawrence Parrish (cornet), Sterling Croft (clarinet), Paul Bell (drums), Sam Pusatari, George Parrish (piano), *Nick Musolino*, *Robert Pope*, Bodo Kamman, *Robert Norfleet*, Paul Desser, Sam Pushtart, Lyle Bevansee, *Harold Thiell*, Elmer Erdman, *Floyd Estep*.

Fritz Hanlein and his Trianon Ensemble (Hotel Muehlebach) — Hanlein ('cello), Erling Knutsen (violin), Myron Johnson (violin), Michael Russo (harp), Fritz Hartwitt (bass), William Ganz (piano).

Mel Hoffman's Orchestra.

Ben Kendrick's Orchestra.

Frank B. Marks' Orchestra — Marks (leader), Morris Bransohn (violin), E. R. Black (saxophone), Floyd Taylor (banjo), Numa Lane (cornet), Paul Bush (trombone), Glenn Daniels (drums). (This band played over WDAF earlier on the evening that Coon-Sanders played their first Midnight Frolic from the Plantation Grill.)

Moonlight Novelty Orchestra.

Pompeiian Terrace Players, of the Hotel Baltimore.

Jack Riley–Ted Williams Orchestra. Johnny Coon believed that his father played with Jack Riley about the year 1911.

Riley-Ehrhart Orchestra. This band was the first to play on WDAF.

Ray Stinson's Orchestra. Stinson (leader and violin), Edward Kaelin (saxophone) *Robert Pope* (cornet), Phil Palmesana (cornet), C. Peters (banjo), Earl Riley (drums). This band played on the *Star's* early, experimental (pre–WDAF) radio station.

Edward Werner's Orchestra — Werner, Leo R. Davis, Frank Harris, Arthur Ogden Winter, *Orville Knapp*, Frank Manning, Oliver Benedict.

Sweeney Orchestra, of the Sweeney Radio Station WHB — Louis Forbstein (director and violin), Paul Tremaine (alto saxophone), Glen Werner (cornet), *Nick Musolino* (trombone), George Parrish (piano), Charles Wagner (drums), Gilbert Dutton (saxophone), *Frank M. Estep* (bass).

Duke Yellman's Kansas Citians — Yellman, Herbert Baldwin, Murray Fitzgerald, Harry Adkins, and one name imperfectly printed in the *Kansas City Star* as Thurlow [?]-rans.

Though next to nothing appeared in the

---

*Or possibly Winters.
†Or possibly Bell.
‡Sometimes given as Kaeling. I am unsure which is correct but have dropped the g.

Kansas City press about black orchestras, there were some very good ones. One of the best was that led by Bennie Moten, who played piano. His other players in 1923 were Lamar Wright (cornet), Thamon Hayes (trombone), Woody Walder (clarinet), Sam Tall (banjo), Willie Hall (drums), Harry Cooper (cornet), and Harlan Leonard (clarinet). Between 1923 and 1932 Moten's band made a good number of recordings for Okeh and Victor companies. Among his players at one time or another were William "Count" Basie, Jimmy Rushing, Ben Webster, Oran P. "Hot Lips" Page, and Walter Page.[100]

At least as early as the fall of 1921, the Kansas City Board of Public Welfare made certain rulings as to what constituted permissible dancing in public places.[101] A little later the Board vetoed what they called "extreme" dancing.[102] This included anything regarded as salacious, such as the tango, and obviously anything even remotely resembling the shimmy, whether rendered solo or with a partner. There were probably several other rather rococo steps that were already surfacing from time to time but that weren't yet fully developed and identified by precise names. In addition, the Board placed restrictions on where dance halls might be established in the city. Dance hall proprietors often complained that such rules and restrictions were arbitrary and unreasonable, and they were not inclined to accept them tamely.[103]

In what was perhaps a typical confrontation, H. P. Strahan in January of 1922 faced about fifty persons, most of them hostile, when he appeared before the Board of Public Welfare, presided over by Board President M. V. Watson. Strahan wished permission to open a dance hall at Twelfth Street and Monroe Avenue, on property owned by F. L. Hairgrove. The latter's cousin and counsel, E. L. Hairgrove, began by asking the protesters to put aside religious prejudice and to understand that Strahan had gone to considerable expense to outfit the hall. Alderman William A. Finucane objected that the area was residential and would be damaged by the proximity. Dr. C. A. Arnold elicited murmurs of approval when he said, "I have seen figures showing that 75 per cent of girls who go wrong start in public dance halls." A supporting statement by Rose Wickey, principal of Whittier School, initiated a sharp exchange. "On behalf of the thousand children who attend the Whittier school," she said, "I wish to protest against the dance hall. It is a menace to the community."[104] This provoked the following dialog, which, for ease of reading, has been edited slightly:

> HAIRGROVE: Were you at the Whittier school when my two daughters attended?
> WICKEY: Yes, I was a teacher then.
> HAIRGROVE: Well, I want to inform you the first step in dancing that my children learned was at the Whittier school. They teach it in all the public schools and then want to close the door to others who desire to teach it. [general whispering] I have paid admission to entertainments at public schools where they had dances similar to those one sees at burlesque theaters. [hisses that Watson rapped to order]
> E. R. DURHAM: They don't teach the camel walk at the school, do they?
> WICKEY: No, they don't.
> WATSON: I believe the statement that seventy-five per cent of the girls who go wrong start in public dance halls is a little broad. I do believe, however, that eighty-five per cent start in the movie theaters and in motor cars.

The Board voted unanimously against allowing the dance hall to open.[105]

Superintendent of Schools I. I. Cammack spoke before more than a thousand teachers in February of 1922. He compared what he regarded as the problem of jazz with that of the Prohibition movement:

> The nation has been fighting booze a long time. It is incorporated into state and national laws; it is one of the greatest questions we have to deal with, and I am just wondering if this jazz, which [Henry] Van

Dyke defines as "an invention of demons, for the persecution of imbeciles," isn't going to have to be legislated against as well?

It seems to me that where it gets into the blood of some of our young folk, and I might add older folk, too, it serves them just about as a good stiff drink of booze would. We know that it goes hand in hand with the objectionable forms of dancing among young folks that are being decride [sic] the world over. I think the time has come when teachers should assume a militant attitude toward all forms of this debasing and degrading music.[106]

In October 1923 the Kansas City Board of Public Welfare met with about thirty managers of dance halls, hotels, and cafes to give them the Board's new dance regulations, which included the following:

- No cheek-to-cheek dancing.
- No rocking back and forth on the feet.
- Lady's hand should rest on partner's shoulder, and should not encircle his neck.
- The proper position for the gentleman's hand is in the center of the lady's back.
- No stiff-arm dancing.
- Dancers' hands should be above waistlines at all times.
- There should be a reasonable "daylight" space between dancers.
- No gliding or extreme dancing.[107]

About a year before the Kansas City Board of Public Welfare took this action, just over the state line in Kansas City, Kan., the school system banned jazz. Ostensibly, this decision was not prompted by any reform group but rather by a statement from the music company that rented pianos to the schools. Said the company officials to the school adminstrators, "Jazz is too hard on the instruments. Some of our pianos that have gone through sieges of jazz look and sound as if someone had been jumping up and down on the keyboards." The city's school officials had neither sanctioned nor proscribed jazz officially, but teachers admitted that occasionally "many spare moments have been spent with the strains of the newest foxtrots."[108] One might suspect that the school officials had been looking for a plausible excuse that would look more practical than moralistic.

Such proceedings and regulations, seen through more modern eyes as prudish and unrealistic, were so regarded by some even at that time; and there were ingenious ways to circumvent them. The *Star* in October of 1921 described one such method:

> Dance hall proprietors generally took advantage of technicalities and jazz music last night to circumvent the order of the board of welfare, issued Friday, banishing the one step.
>
> "This dance will be a foxtrot," the announcer would proclaim, and the orchestra would begin. Couples danced whatever step they pleased and each couple, dancing something different, found rhythm in the jazz notes.
>
> The order of the board suggested a return to some of the old-style dances. It did not meet with favor among some proprietors.
>
> "There's too much regulation, that's the trouble," one complained. As he talked[,] the dance ended. "Play a waltz," he directed the orchestra leader.
>
> A jazz tune ensued which could not be distinguished from the preceding one. The dancers all had different conceptions of the waltz.[109]

Public attitudes would gradually change, more rapidly in some areas of the country than in others. In Massachusetts in 1924, for instance, the Methodists at a general conference in Springfield heard its bishop urge the changing of the church's rules of discipline. He reminded the group that for fifty-two years their rules had forbade dancing, gambling, attending theaters and horse races, and other similar activities. Some of these objections, he suggested, had become "embarrassing."[110]

But dancing and listening to popular orchestras were certainly not the only activities available in a city of well over 300,000 inhabitants. For example, since 1887 there had been the annual Priests of Pallas Festivals. President Grover Cleveland had attended that first one; and no doubt His Excellency, already a year into his marriage and thus no longer the nation's most eligible bachelor, took a great interest in the young woman chosen as queen. By 1922 the festival was an important social and fashion extravaganza, and that year Ada Belle Files, of Fort Scott, Kansas, reigned over the affair as Queen Pallas.[111]

The newly formed American Legion picked Kansas City for its annual convention in late 1921. The city was fully aware that this was going to be a great civic and economic coup, not only because of the thousands of visiting Legionnaires but also because there would be present such World War heroes as France's Marshal Ferdinand Foch, General John J. Pershing, and Britain's Admiral David, Lord Beatty, to say nothing of a host of lesser lights that included Vice President Calvin Coolidge. "City's Dress Suit Ready," as the Kansas City *Star* put it. The city really was elaborately prepared with much colorful bunting, thousands of flags of the various nations represented by the prestigious visitors, and many signs greeting all the guests. "Welcome, boys, the place is yours," proclaimed an advertisement by the Doric Theater, which represented itself as "The official photoplay [*i.e*, cinema] of the American Legion." And all the decoration was intended to be the best within the city's abilities. To make sure of this, there was a Decoration Committee, headed by a rather obscure Great War veteran from Independence, Harry S Truman.* "Tag your home with a flag," he urged, with the advice not to "wait until the eleventh hour." The police weren't waiting until the eleventh hour either. "Police Ready for Crooks," said the *Star*, which told its readers, "The jail at headquarters is rapidly filling with pickpockets, women of the street, and liquor sellers."[112]

When the Legion's executive committee announced a contest for an official convention song, Joe L. Sanders and Carleton A. Coon thought it a good opportunity to advertise themselves and jumped in with a musical candidate titled "Old Legion Buddy of Mine." It had a good deal of competition, too much in fact — one competitor was Victor Herbert. Here's the product of Joe and Coonie's labor:

Hey there! Say, there! Old
   Legion Buddy of mine —
Gee! I'm glad to meet you! Seems
like old times to greet you!
I'll tell the world you're lookin' fine.
It seems a long, long time since we were together
In the days of 1–2–3–4– count
   off in all kinds of weather.
Remember how the old "top kicker"
   used to make us hike it
For miles and miles and miles! I'll
   say he made us like it.
Old Legion Buddy of mine.[113]

Not exactly immortal lyrics, and the sentiments were certainly artificial. After all, Coonie had never served in the military, and Joe's few months at Camp Bowie had not been such as to make him particularly eager to see any of *those* old buddies. Not surprisingly, their song didn't win, nor apparently did Victor Herbert's.

Those in Kansas City who wished to learn to ice skate could go to such places as Coliseum Rink, at Thirty-ninth and Main, which advertised that it was the "Largest roller rink west of Chicago." In addition to skating lessons and uniformed attendants, there was even a jazz band. "The craze is here," said the ad. "Everybody's skating. Let's go."[114]

In September of 1922 the "motor car" enthusiasts of the area were treated to a contest of racers at the city's mile-and-a-quarter speedway. It was to have been on the sixteenth, a Saturday, but heavy rains forced a cancellation until the next day, Sunday, when there was a favorable change in the weather. After impressive dedication ceremonies, the fifty-mile race began amid cheers and great excitement — and then turned ugly. There were several accidents and one fatality. But

---

*Truman had no middle name, so the S is not an abbreviation.

there was also a winner, Tommy Milton. The *Star* received several letters critical of holding such races on Sunday, and one of them suggested the propriety of outlawing races on that day.[115]

Probably a majority of Kansas Citians saw nothing very wrong with races on Sunday, for the automobile in any form was as popular here as anywhere else in the nation. The local press was filled with advertisements of the latest brands and models, and frequently published special magazine sections dedicated to automobile shows. Not only were more persons able to afford cars now than ever before, but also the price of gas fluctuated slightly around a modest 20 cents a gallon.[116] And was gasoline selling! In 1922 drivers in Kansas City bought thirty-five million gallons of gasoline at 504 fuel pumps. But an inspection in the fall of 1921 revealed that over half of the city's service stations were cheating customers with "short measures" of oil and gasoline.[117]

Usually, when a company brought out its latest model, there was much hoopla accompanying its arrival in town. In early 1920, for instance, Kansas City eagerly awaited a new open-air touring car made by the Re-Vere Company. It had a four-cylinder Duesenberg engine which, the makers assured the public, would allow the vehicle to attain a speed of eighty-five miles an hour.[118] That a driver of such an automobile in 1920 would have had difficulty finding a road to accommodate such speed apparently was beside the point. There were somewhat more modest vehicles such as a new Oldsmobile touring car for $1,395.[119] In addition to Oldsmobile and other names, better known today, such as Buick and Packard, there was also an array of other brands, most of them largely unknown today — Jordan, Pierce-Arrow, Hupmobile, Jewett, National, Essex, Reo, Maxwell, Chandler, and yet others. And if one simply wanted an automobile that was, though plain, very dependable and cheap, why there were such as those put out by the Ford Company and that sold for not more than about $600.[120] At a price of only $890, Hathaway Motor Company, 1727-35 McGee, advertised their new Durant four-cylinder touring car. There were even electric starters on many brands, an innovation that held out hope that the unpredictable hand crank might soon stop breaking arms.[121]

The Lyons & Conland Motor Company, 3113 Gilham Road, touted their new Stanley steam automobile. Simplicity was its salient characteristic — "The car has but thirty-seven moving parts," said the advertisement. There were "No gears to shift, no clutch to slip, no starter to balk, no cranking to do." And in a statement that may throw some light upon all the city's traffic mayhem that the *Star* often complained about, the ad boasted, "Requires no experience — a child can operate it."[122]

As has often been stated about the years following the First World War, the automobile was changing the face of the nation. It was changing the face of Kansas City, too, which was beginning to experience traffic congestion, drunken drivers, wrecks, ill-mannered drivers, and recreational use of cars. Every week one could find in the *Star* a suggested auto tour to a nearby place, even providing detailed maps. At a time before the publication of good road maps and the systematic numbering of highways, such aids doubtless were useful. There were other "recreational" uses of the auto that met with less approbation by the majority, the increasingly-popular "petting" parties by the young.

As scarcely any other innovation had in as brief a time, the automobile's popularity was revealing aspects of the American character that were not attractive. Even as the last boys were returning from Europe, the streets and roads in and around Kansas City seemed to have become speedways. There were only rudimentary traffic regulations and, before mid–October 1922, no traffic lights within the city. On about the fifteenth of that month the local automobile club installed in Penn Valley Park, at Twenty-sixth Street, the city's first "signal light." It was an experiment and, if successful, would be the first of a number of others. The club was also placing warning signs in various sites about the county.[123]

For a while, therefore, it seemed worth one's life to travel on the highways, or what passed for highways in the early Twenties, in and around Kansas City or almost anywhere else. "A Fool and His Car Are Soon Busted" proclaimed an article in the *Star*.[124] And as though bodily endangerment were not bad enough, many feared that the soul was right behind it. In August of 1921 there was probably much sympathy for the citizens of Dodson, just south of Kansas City, when they asked the county court for a "road orgy ban" to stop persons from using automobiles on country roads for "drunken revels." The effort apparently was no more successful than one might have predicted, so in May of 1923 the county marshal vowed to "make war on country road spooners and motorists who loiter along the rural highways."[125] But here, as elsewhere in the nation, the attitude seemed to be that of, Yes, we'll reform, but not just yet.

Even though cars were becoming very popular in the Kansas City area, there were those who had none and who, along with even many who did, found very agreeable an excursion trip on the Kansas City, Clay County & St. Joseph trolley line. Running from Kansas City to St. Joseph, Excelsior Springs, Liberty, and other places, it offered parlor and observations cars that appealed both to individuals and to clubs. There were special facilities for groups wishing to hold business meetings while traveling.[126] Probably to many it seemed a chaste alternative to the wicked automobile and the mayhem it created.

Events in Hollywood heaped more fuel on the pietistic fire in and around Kansas City. To those easily shocked, as well as perhaps some who wished to appear so, many of the films being produced were troubling. The "vamp" image, the obvious sensuality displayed by such actors as Rudolph Valentino and Theda Bara, the suggestive phrasing of advertisements—all of this seemed to confirm the worst of the critics' suspicions. Although Kansas City apparently took such matters more calmly than did many other places in the nation, just next door the reaction was quite different. In November of 1921, the state of Kansas banned Rudolph Valentino's film *The Sheik*.[127] And several deaths, made more titillating by lurid details, allegations, or rumors, occurred within the film colony.[128] At about this time Will Hays resigned from the Harding cabinet to head a group designed ostensibly to clean up films, but it soon was obvious that the panel was little more than a placebo. Nor did it help quiet the critics when such a director as Cecil B. DeMille suggested the seriousness of his efforts to clean up his films by observing that one of them began with a woman in her bathtub.[129]

Both sides of the morality issue were disturbed. The conservatives predicted a total breakdown of American morality, while their counterparts feared a national inquisition. The successful effort to ban alcoholic beverages had already demonstrated what a really dedicated crusade could accomplish, even when supported by what many wet opponents believed were only a minority. On the heels of this successful effort, at the end of the World War there came the now-notorious effort by such federal officials as Attorney General A. Mitchell Palmer to inflame the nation against "reds" and radicals. The Socialist leader Eugene V. Debs had leisure in Atlanta Penitentiary to ponder what could happen to anyone, however gentle and well-intentioned, who had not supported the late war, one that many regarded as a great blunder. And this same harsh spirit expressed itself in many other ways, not the least of them the questionable trial in Massachusetts of two radicals, Nicola Sacco and Bartolomeo Vanzetti.*

All of it was simply another expression

---

*Sacco and Vanzetti, two Italian immigrants, were arrested on 5 May 1920 for a payroll robbery and the deaths of two officials, in South Braintree, Mass. The sensational trial was held amid the national "Red Scare" of the early postwar period, and many believed them innocent. They were executed by Massachusetts on 23 August 1927.

of the too-human tendency to fear the unfamiliar. One manifestation of this xenophobia occurred just after the Armistice, by which time any fear of Germans ought to have vanished. Yet, the *Kansas City Star* was moved, in February 1919, to publish an editorial titled "Spy Hunting in Kansas City," in which the writer deprecated the recent hysteria which pretended to see German spies and saboteurs as still threatening. They were allegedly either lacing the city's water supply with germs, or putting ground glass into bakery products, or doing who-knew-what-else. Even after the Armistice, many with German names continued to be harassed.[130]

The situation caused the *Star*, in an editorial in July of 1922, to ask, "Have We Lost Control of Civilization Forces?" It quoted Professor Frederick Soddy, of Oxford, who said that he hoped the discovery of how to use atomic energy would not come until the human race was considerably fitter to understand its potential and consequences. The following November, in commenting on the fourth anniversary of the Armistice, another *Star* editorial suggested that the lofty goals and deeds of the war were being abandoned.[131]

This was not the first occasion when the *Kansas City Star* was willing to state unpopular opinions. In the midst of the oppressive laws and attitudes during the late war, the paper published a letter from a Socialist who had criticized wartime profiteers. The reaction by governmental officials to this and other *seditious* actions moved the *Star* to publish an editorial that said, "We must make the world safe for democracy even if we have to 'bean' the Goddess of Liberty to do it." Both the Socialist and the editor were punished.[132]

So, what might be the next target of the puritans? Kansas Citians read about those in the New York theatrical world who feared that the attack on liquor would be followed by one on the stage. Said the Actors' Equity Association's publication, *Equity*: "'The lottery evil' had to go; horse racing faces the prospect of being suppressed completely; dancing in public places has been interfered with as a reputed evil; the evil of smoking is being made much of, and the theater must be prepared to be singled out as the next on the list of 'social excrescences' to be attacked."[133] They feared another such onslaught as that carried out in the seventeenth century by the original Puritans.

As it turned out, the new decade brought such a plethora of challenges to orthodoxy that the forces of repression seemed no longer able to concentrate on a single target. But if there was one that stood out in conservative enmity, it was probably jazz music. The stuff was everywhere, and the new radio stations were so powerful that the new music's sulphurous strains were carried to every part of the nation and even beyond. And it didn't help jazz's reputation among its enemies when statements such as one in January of 1922 arrived from New York: "If you don't like the sermon, tune out the preacher and tune in the jazz," and adding, "New York is enjoying a virulent attack of radiomania." The local clergy must have been upset especially by a statement in "Starbeams" in the *Kansas City Star*: "A Kansas editor wonders how a man whose bedsprings* are in tune with a nearby radio ever gets any sleep. Well, he sleeps when the music stops and the sermons begin."[134]

The whole nation was experiencing radiomania. According to the *Star* there were in the nation but three licensed "wireless telephone" stations in mid-1921. By February 1922 the number had risen to twenty-one, then eighty-seven by April, 212 by May, and 542 by October. An ad by the Midwest Radio Company, a retailer of sets at 1232 Main Street, informed the public that it was forced to move to larger quarters in order to keep up with demand. In January 1923 the *Star* reported at least one station in every

---

Radio owners were beginning to learn that ordinary bedsprings, not covered in those days, made a good aerial.

state except Mississippi, and the U.S. Department of Commerce estimated that by the middle of 1922 there were 600,000 radio sets in the country. Other well-informed sources set the number at about a million.[135] *Radio Digest Illustrated*, available for ten cents on newsstands, was popular in Kansas City.

Record companies quickly began to issue recordings of both songs and dialog that celebrated this popular novelty. For instance, apparently sometime in 1924 Paul Whiteman recorded "Mr. Radio Man," a number which today suggests that he still needed to work on his arranging. Somewhat later in the decade, and after the advent of electronic recording, Victor issued a double-sided, twelve-inch record, titled "Twisting the Dials." Employing something similar to what, in television of the future, would be called "channel surfing," Billy Jones and Ernest Hare, Radio's Happiness Boys (early in their careers they were sponsored by Happiness Candies) caricatured a radio fan's playing with a radio tuner and bringing in a mishmash of news, how-to commentary, opera, hillbilly music, etc. But what its efforts at humor suggest is that already radio's offerings were being examined critically and often found wanting.[136] Jones and Hare, with their excellent harmonizing and witty dialog, were themselves among the most successful persons in early radio. They offered good singing and amusing chatter.

With somewhat more success at humor, Joe Hayman, better known for his comic monolog recording of "Cohen on the Telephone," made a disc titled "Cohen Buys a Wireless Set." In the Jewish accent that Hayman employed on his "Cohen" records, he showed how his struggling hero's problems with the English language could make it difficult to communicate with others, especially in such an arcane field as radiotelephony. Cohen, puzzled when asked whether he would like a "crystal set," exclaims, "Vat do you mean 'a crystal set'? Can you tell fortunes with it?" When the salesman says that Cohen would need an aerial wire, the latter exclaims that a "vireless" should need no wires. And worse follows:

> SALESMAN: This set has three tubes, tuner, and loud talker, complete. It uses four watts.
> COHEN: Vat?
> SALESMAN: Yes, four watts.
> COHEN: Four vich?
> SALESMAN: Watts.
> COHEN: (Exasperated) *Vat's dis vat?*[137]

The year 1922 brought radiotelephony to Kansas City. The *Kansas City Star*, on Thursday evening, February 16, was first with an experimental station whose range was an estimated 100 to 150 miles, if there was no static and if "the amateur sender at Independence [Mo.] will refrain from broadcasting phonograph records during the concert." The program, which featured such musical groups as the Deep River Jazz Orchestra, seems to have been received as far away as the state of Washington and even beyond the Rio Grande in Central Mexico.[138] The *Kansas City Post* experimented with the new medium on 19 May and featured the Coon-Sanders Band. On Monday, 5 June, and amid much hoopla and expectation, the *Star* inaugurated its new station, WDAF. It boasted the latest and most powerful equipment manufactured in America, powered at 500 watts, and designed especially for entertainment. According to the *Star*, there was only one other station like it in the nation, that at Detroit, though WDAF, so the *Star* averred, radiated an even greater amperage than Detroit's. And when the Sweeney School of Auto-Tractor-Aviation, on Tuesday, 15 August, introduced its new 500-watt station WHB, Kansas City could feel pride in its powerful stations.[139]

The new pastime spawned the expected sallies of wit, many of them duly reported by the *Star*. In March 1922, in "The Ravings of a Radio-Maniac," there was an addition to Mother Goose with "To market, to market, to buy a radio-phone set — Home again, home again, there ain't enough yet." And with cavalier reference to Longfellow and

Wordsworth, there were "I shot a song into the air; it fell to earth 'most everywhere," and, "My heart leaps up when I behold an aerial in the sky." Secretary of Commerce Herbert Hoover's new motto allegedly was "An amateur is known by the wave lengths he keeps." And one with somewhat less wattage: "It looks as if the wireless affairs of the universe soon may be in the hands of a receiver."[140]

As with the later practice by some parents of letting television serve as a baby sitter, at least some parents in the early Twenties perhaps saw such possibilities for radio. The *Star* reprinted an item from the Birmingham *Age-Herald* about a father who became increasingly embarrassed by his little son's questions:

> BOY: Pa, who was Hercules?
> FATHER: Why — er — a mighty man, son.
> BOY: But what did he do?
> FATHER: Well, he carried a club, for one thing.
> BOY: Was he a policeman, Pa?
> FATHER: Son, I'll rejoice exceedingly when you are old enough to get interested in a radio outfit.[141]

The *Star*, even before it entered the broadcasting field, offered numerous articles on the new field of radio. Over a period of many months it published an ever-growing list of the licensed stations in the United States, advising its readers, "If you receive strange 'call letters' while listening in, consult the [*Star's*] list and you will know the source of the message." And despite shaky proofreading, another list gave forty-three "Q" signals that were in use, because "The air is full of their jargon and the conservation [*sic*] of the amateur unconsciously drops into technicalities strange to the uni[ni]tiated." "QRA," for instance, indicated "What ship or station is that?" and "QRS" meant "Shall I send slower?" The same issue that published these lists contained also a column of questions and answers about radio. There was even a warning that borrowed a term from Prohibition: "A 'bootlegger' is a vacuum tube that is manufactured illegally. There are many on the market. Some will work. Some won't. Some will light and will seem all right except that they won't pass any signals."[142]

Some businesses in the city were discovering the advantage of the radio as an attraction to potential customers. In February of 1922, O. E. McGinnis, proprietor of a barbershop at Fifteenth Street and Kensington Avenue, installed a radio and thus "eliminated the tedium of getting a shave." His son Kenneth had come up with the idea, and the elder McGinnis admitted that the radio made it no longer necessary "to indulge in the customary hackneyed persiflage to entertain customers." And the following June at his soda pop stand at Sixty-first and Oak Streets, ten-year-old Angus McCallum solved his problem of slow business by installing a radio to pick up the *Star's* new station, WDAF. In addition to a big sign "Ice Cold Soda Pop, 5 cents," he had another, "Hear the WDAF Radio Ball Scores."[143]

Somewhat more offbeat applications of that same idea included one employed by what the *Star* wryly termed a "radio shop" at 220 West Twelfth Street. The gambling establishment was raided in early December 1922 when four "radio enthusiasts" were indicted and sent to the North Side court. The police, familiar with such enterprises, knew also the difficulty of getting solid evidence. They reported that though "Radio Shop" was inscribed on the front windows, the only visible implements of trade were dice, money, and cards, which, it was averred, were "broadcast nightly." The following exchange ensued at the examination:

> SGT. BOYCE: We went into the room and found these four men seated about a table — they must have destroyed all evidence of gambling, for we found none.
> JUDGE KILROY: No evidence?
> SGT. BOYCE: No evidence.
> JUDGE KILROY (turning to the prisoners): What about it?
> ONE DEFENDANT: We were just listening to a radio concert.
> JUDGE KILROY: Discharged.

It was the second effort in a week by the police to stop this particular operation. The first had occurred the previous Sunday when the police found them with only a deck of cards, hardly sufficient evidence. The police knew who ran the operation and cited a report along Twelfth Street that the owner's bank deposits "were lowered $4,500 at one of the 'concerts' last week."[144]

It was music, however, that seemed to endear the radio to most listeners in Kansas City, and the *Star's* announcements of radio programs gave comprehensive coverage of musical offerings. With both WDAF and WHB broadcasting liberal quantities of jazz, the tastes of many of the city's population must have undergone almost a revolution. It is obvious that many in the area were becoming convinced that jazz might not be so bad after all.

What one must remember is that often the term "jazz," as used in those and later times, was not precise. To some it meant almost any music played by popular bands. Many professional musicians, however, eventually used the term only for music played in a free style first developed by black ensembles and afterward employed in varying degrees by many white groups. By the latter definition, true jazz avoided formal arrangements. Thus, many of the popular groups that were developed in Kansas City, including the Nighthawks, played music that contained elements of jazz but wasn't jazz by classic definition.

"There Is Jazz — and Jazz," concluded an article in the *Kansas City Star* on Wednesday, 15 March 1922. Earlier that day a group of Kansas Citians at the Athenaeum attended a program in which James D. Kemper, former vaudeville singer and dancer, spoke on jazz and demonstrated it. The *Star* almost incredulously described his appearance before a typically "staid, conservative [group], devoted to the study and criticism of history, literature and kindred subjects, [that] listened and found it good." First, Kemper explained what jazz was. Then, he sang "I'm Just a Carolina Rollin' Stone," quietly, just to bring out what the *Star* said was "the best of the not exceptionally worthwhile words." The audience applauded. Then Kemper sang it the way he said he had heard it sung in New York by a youngster "in very — well, 'jazzy' clothes." The *Star* described the reaction:

> His audience applauded. The most impartial of judges would have had to admit the applause the second time was noticeably longer and louder than the first. It might have been in appreciation of Mr. Kemper's versatility. It might have been in sudden realization of just what constitutes the difference between jazz and "better class" music. Anyway, the audience applauded.
> "I like jazz [said Kemper]. As one who tries to write, I find inspiration in the better class music. It uplifts me. But as an eccentric dancer, I find it hard to keep my feet still when the cowbells and the sleighbells jangle and the dishpans bang."[145]

Kemper's demonstration at the Athenaeum illustrated an important truth about jazz, namely, that the new music was not so much a matter of *what* one played as of *how*.* A cartoon in the *New Yorker* at this time illustrated the point. The picture showed a typical popular orchestra, such as the Nighthawks, whose director announced the next number: "Let's have the Schubert Serenade and get some dirt into it."[146] As Mark Sullivan observed, the term *jazz* became also a verb, often used with *up*, meaning to put life and excitement into something otherwise a little boring. What were these elements that many saw as "dirty" by its detractors, or "swell" or "mean" by its aficionados? They included exaggerated syncopation and what Sullivan calls "brazen defiance of accepted rules." He adds:

> Jazz never made the apology of the reproved member of an orchestra who explained that he had "played the fly-specks." The unusualness of notation was deliberately

---

*As Mae West, at about this same time explained, "It's not what I do but the way that I do it."

sought, and attainment of the most outré of cacaphonic combinations was the jazz composer's triumph. Erratic syncopation, eccentricity deliberately planned, was only one of the characteristics of jazz. It was rapid, feverish, excited, and exciting.[147]

Among the Kansas City public there seemed to be little ambivalence about jazz. Its effect on devotees was powerful and immediate, especially when the orchestra played standard songs liberally sprinkled with jazzy elements. Those who disliked it perhaps felt strongest about its tempo and volume, both of which to them suggested barely controlled emotion. A popular song of the day, "Crazy Rhythm," described how one listener, unable to resist the charm of the lascivious music, had to keep away from it.[148]

There were others who, though they might not like jazz, could at least see it as funny rather than threatening. Furthermore, as a cartoon in the *Kansas City Star* illustrated, perhaps jazz might even have its practical applications:

> FIRST MAN: How is the music in the Jazz-Razz Cafe?
> SECOND MAN: Great! I was there with my wife last night and couldn't hear a word she said.[149]

Kansas Citians on both sides of the state line were warned about the new music. Over in Kansas City, Kans., Bessie Miller, music supervisor in the smaller city's public schools, had declared war on it. There would be a drive in 1922 from January 29 through February 4, and during this period "racy airs" would find the city an unfriendly place. A few days later, on the Missouri side, there was a meeting at the junior college, where one of the discussion topics was jazz. The *Star's* announcement of the meeting quoted Walter Damrosch as saying that "Jazz is inspired noise." Superintendent I. I. Cammack confessed, "I cannot say too much against jazz music." He doubted that it could be called real music, for it appealed "to the lowest elements in emotional life, more to the animal than the aesthetic nature." At about the same time the *Star's* column "Starbeams" cited without comment a new ordinance in Savannah, Ga., that forbade the playing of jazz on stages and at all public dances, declaring it to be "indecent and injurious to public morals."[150] And as though harming the moral sense weren't bad enough to merit censure, the *Star* carried an item from Chicago about an alleged "jazz disease":

> Flappers now find a new worry confronting them. It is "diarthrositis," a permanent affliction of the diarthrosis joints, which makes it impossible for Miss Marie Ehlers, a dancer, to sit still when there is any jazz music about. At least that is what appears from a declaration in a suit filed in the superior court by an attorney asking $10,000 damages for Miss Ehlers from Ernie Young, theatrical agent for a North Side cafe.[151]

Ehlers' problem reminds one of a song, wonderfully recorded by Elsie Janis about 1911, in which a young woman complains that she can't restrain a mad desire to dance when the band plays such irresistible ragtime as the "Grizzly Bear." On those critical occasions, she is obliged to yell, "For de Lawd's Sake Play a Waltz!"[152]

And film star Mary Pickford, "America's Sweetheart," informed the public that she didn't "jazz." "I'm not a prude," she declared, "and I'm not censuring other folks' activities." However, her husband, the actor Douglas Fairbanks, didn't "think it the right thing" for her to dance to jazz pieces with other men. She limited her dancing to "small at-homes" with six or eight persons, and even then only to waltzes or two-steps.[153] That should have helped continue her status as "America's Sweetheart," at least until she eventually divorced Fairbanks.

In the late fall of 1921, the *Star* ran an ad for the *Ladies' Home Journal* that called attention to a current article titled "Jazz Must Go." "Is America dancing hellward? Is jazz madness drawing us to ruin?" asked the ad. It excoriated "[p]resent-day indecencies of dress, of talk, of manners," and urged a return to "Pre-War Morals." "These questions," it continued, "are asked not by prudes, but by seriously thinking people who are concerned for the future of our boys and girls."[154]

Star readers were almost inundated by advice from many persons distant from Kansas City on the subject. Wisdom arrived from Thomas Tynan, warden of the Colorado State Penitentiary: "Jazz parties and joyriding bring more hardened criminals to this institution than any other factor of modern life." Furthermore, said he, "the new criminal is very smooth, sometimes highly educated young fellows [sic] whom you might expect to see at gatherings of respectable people."[155] The Rev. Phillip Yarrow, superintendent of the Illinois Vigilance Association declared jazz a "menace," adding, "Moral disaster is coming to hundreds of young American girls [apparently boys were already hopelessly lost] through the pathological, nerve-irritating, sex-exciting music of jazz orchestras." He had gone to a dance in Chicago's Second Ward, and "Mid the distracting notes of the saxophone and the weird beat of the tom-tom lights were lowered, and actions that are indescribable took place."[156]

Not everyone who commented publicly took so humorless or hostile a view of the new music. Even among those who regarded jazz as a noisy, overly animated exercise, some could nevertheless see it as something silly rather than sinister. In April 1922 the *Star* carried a cartoon in which a couple are passing a restaurant when the wife, hearing what she believes to be a jazz band, says she'd like to go in to listen, but in another part of the drawing we see that the noise she had heard was only a waiter dropping a tray of dishes. And another cartoon, joshing the vigorous playing of a jazz band, shows a typical ensemble watching while the leader interviews a new candidate:

> "Have you had much experience in a jazz orchestra?"
> "Have I? Why, five years ago I was a physical weakling."
> "Well?" replies the puzzled leader.
> "Feel my muscle now!"[157]

The *Star's* regular column "Starbeams" reported that composers of popular songs on Broadway insisted that they had quit writing jazz but that it didn't seem to matter. Why? Well, band members, undeterred, took their saxophones and trombones and perversely made jazz "from their simple, proper melodies." "Starbeams" agreed that jazz was mainly a matter of rendition, though at the same time insisting that this did not "exonerate them from the blame for writing music that invites jazz treatment." But the Kansas City journalist confessed to being mystified about the "longevity" of jazz saxophonists. It was this instrument that symbolized for many the whole jazz problem, and "Starbeams" observed, "Probably there is not a professional reformer in the world who would not like to witness the extermination of the tin-tone tribe...."[158]

But however that might have been, Hollywood, fearful that they were being singled out for the blame of "all modern humanity's depravity," could have found some solace in the opinion by the *Star's* critic that they did not really carry all the blame but only half of it—"The jazz producers will carry the other half." Speaking with the leader of one of Kansas City's dance orchestras, "Starbeams" listened to his opinion that the new medium, radio, would spell the end of jazz music, "because cowbells and other appurtenances of the jazz orchestra don't take on the radio." The *Star's* reporter might have been otherwise encouraged by that statement except that, so he observed, "phonographic reproduction meets many of the same difficulties as are met by radio, but jazz always seemed to get over on the phonograph."[159]

But as "Starbeams" says above, it was definitely the "tin-tone" saxophone that came in for most of the blame from critics of jazz. Earl Fuller, who appeared at Kansas City's Pantages Theater in January of 1923, claimed that he had introduced the *lascivious* saxophone to Broadway. After two years as a drummer for the first orchestra at New York's Rector's Restaurant, he reorganized the band, introduced the saxophone, and then proceeded to make other innovations. Up to that time scarcely more than violins, flutes, and pianos had been used in such groups as were at that time termed "novelty." His group, consisting of drum, saxophone, and banjo, had been playing for a year when the first jazz orchestra appeared in New York at Riesenweber's Cafe. It was the Original Dixieland Jazz Band, using five instruments—trombone, clarinet, cornet, piano, and drum. His competitive spirit thus aroused, Fuller sought out two more players, one of whom was Ted Lewis, who would soon have his own band. This competition led also to recording sessions, the New Orleans group making their first recording in January of 1917 and Fuller's the following June. It was apparently shortly after this time that Fuller introduced the saxophone. And for a while he actually conducted two groups at Rector's Restaurant, only one of which was "novelty."[160]

What did recognized classical musicians think of jazz? There was a considerable difference of opinion among them. When Anna Millar, manager of the Kansas City Symphony Association, returned in November of 1921 from St. Louis, she was full of admiration for the way Maestro Rudolph Ganz had "controlled that orchestra as if it were a piano." The previous day he had presented a "pop" concert that included a fox trot, one written by Hugo Frey, "the best," said Ganz, "of the composers of so-called bad music and therefore preferable to the bad composers of so-called good music." Having delivered himself of that aphorism, he enlarged on this theme:

> The piece is not for use in the ballroom. I offered it on its merits as a musical composition.... No doubt ... Haydn, when he first introduced the minuet into the symphony, was reproached by his contemporaries with vulgarity and shamelessness. And what are the gigues, courantes, chaconnes and passepieds which have come down to us from the classic composers? Simply dances of the time to which the greatest musicians did not disdain to turn their hands.[161]

In July of 1922 there arrived in Kansas City the Latin American Alfonzo Zelaya, well-known pianist and son of an ex-president of Nicaragua. Just before his appearance at the Mainstreet Theater, he was interviewed by the *Star*. Zelaya was certain that jazz would disappear eventually "because it is injurious to the physical and moral sense of each individual who takes decided interest in it." Moreover, "There is only one kind of music, and that is good music." Kansas City, he said flatly, did not encourage good music as it ought. Why wasn't there, for instance, a municipal opera house? St. Louis was having great success with such a project. And why not a municipal theater to offer plays in the summer months? The idea was proving very successful in Indianapolis, which had two.[162]

In February 1920, Josef Casimir Hofmann (1876–1957), Polish-American composer and one of the greatest pianists of his time, visited Kansas City and was interviewed at his hotel. Something about Hofmann's pleasant manner emboldened a *Star* reporter to raise the subject of jazz music "which may not stir the soul, but cause thousands to shake a wicked foot." "Jazz?" responded Hofmann. "Why, I think it's very good, very electrifying—if well done. If not, it's just noise and annoyance. Cowbells, for instance, as music, are just vulgar. But otherwise, no. The modern orchestra, you know, with all its percussion instruments, is close to jazz." And when, asked the interviewer, was jazz well done? "When it is not overdone," answered Hofmann. He explained:

> Jazz [heard] all the time is too exciting, too nerve wracking; it wears one down fast. One's musical meal, you know, must be well balanced. We must not have all stimulant—shall I say coffee? We must have beefsteak, too. [And what was "beefsteak"?] Beethoven. So filling, so satisfying. [Did Hofmann play jazz?] No, I don't. A piano alone is hardly enough. [Laughing] One must have dish pans, and tin cans and china to break. No, no, I do not play it myself. It is very difficult and one must make a special study of it.[163]

Well, jazz was in its infancy, though some critics might have thought "colic phase" more appropriate. And many, including those who saw possibilities in the new music, agreed that it often lacked form and flirted with unbridled improvisation. There were also those who suggested that various new combinations of instruments might be advantageous. By the early Twenties, there were already important efforts to tame the scruffy urchin, and the *Kansas City Star*, in its "Starbeams" in January of 1922, discussed some of them. Anti-jazz critics, said the article, could be credited with having forced an improvement upon jazz dance music:

> Whether the dancing that it accompanies is any better is another matter. But there is no doubt that the music value of dance music, as put out this winter by phonograph record manufacturers, is of a much higher grade than that of two years ago. The reformers may never be able to abolish the jazz element from dance music, but they may be able to improve it to respectability. Several of the new dance records out this month contain more musical art than is contained in band records of the "Poet and Peasant" type familiar to phonograph players before the "curse" of jazz descended upon us.[164]

"Starbeams" was referring to the dreary plethora, in the early years of the phonograph, of discs and cylinders by so-called bands and orchestras, honking away at marches and snippets of classical music. In those days there was a good market for almost any reproduced sound. Looking for quality in such products perhaps seemed irrelevant.

The *Star* published some excellent articles on jazz. In February of 1922, for example, that paper reprinted an article by Helen Hullitt Lowry, in New York City, titled "New York Is Taking the Gymnastics out of Jazz." "Don't for an instant think," she wrote, "that jazz has been reformed by earnest missionaries in the Broadway field. Jazz music is passing because something better is happening...from the inside...," that is, the "new trick" of "orchestrating syncopation by the rules of harmony." She declared that Paul Whiteman, having seen possibilities in the new music, was the one to thank for these developments. Whiteman himself, on one occasion in early 1924 said that what he played was "syncopated rhythm" rather than jazz.[165] In October of 1923 the *Star* published another article that elaborated on Whiteman's role in making jazz more "respectable" and interesting. Observing that the original jazz band contained but five instruments — piano, clarinet, trombone, cornet, and drum — the article continued:

> The piano, which kept the rhythm, provided nothing particularly new. It played four beats to the measure, but the clarinet added a touch that was completely foreign. It was an E flat clarinet called, in the vernacular, "corn fed." It emitted tones as shrill and as weird as a woman under the lash. It was the first instrument ever "jazzed." This was done by a blending and blurring of tones with "off" notes to slide into pitch. All this was merely a manipulation of air pressure, but such a strange manipulation that the legitimate clarinetist found it impossible to do.
> Gradually, the other instruments came to be played in the same fashion, but not without much work, for it was difficult, indeed. And the result was the wildest, most blatant, most sensuous music that the nation ever has known.[166]

One may assume that most of the jazz musicians in Kansas City saw the article, or at least heard about it. If by some strange oversight any of them did not, they most assuredly heard about Whiteman's famous concert four months later, "An Experiment in Modern Music," on 12 February 1924, at New York City's Aeolian Hall. The program offered such popular numbers as "Livery Stable Blues," "Mama Loves Papa," a comical explanation of the origins of "Yes, We Have No Bananas," and several popular pieces by Irving Berlin. Edward E. "Zez" Confrey entertained with a popular medley, and then astounded the audience with his "Kitten on the Keys," composed in 1921. Featured in the second half of the concert were a jazz composition by Victor Herbert and, as perhaps the program's highlight, the first public performance of George Gershwin's *Rhapsody in Blue*, with the composer at the piano. It was a remarkable occasion, regarded as such even at the time. And those otherwise inclined to sneer were perhaps wobbled by the presence at the concert of such musical figures as Igor Stravinsky, John McCormack, Victor Herbert, Leopold Stokowski, Sergei Rachmaninoff, Walter Damrosch, Jascha Heifetz, Fritz Kreisler, Amelita Galli-Curci, and Alma Gluck.[167] Regardless of whether all of these persons of recognized musical attainments were unanimous in considering jazz a legitimate form of music, their very willingness to listen was almost an imprimatur. Though many jazz purists perhaps thought Whiteman was damaging a good thing, he had made a great contribution toward legitimizing the music that had been more often associated with dives and brothels than concert halls. Most important, no longer could jazz be easily dismissed as mere katzenjammer.

But when Coon-Sanders made its debut in Kansas City, all of this was in the future. In the years 1919 to 1923 the new music was trying to prove itself, even to many who, though not yet fans, would become such. Meanwhile, rebellious youth, eager to do almost anything, so long as it irritated their elders, accepted jazz uncritically — just as it was — unadorned by fine points of music theory, and without regard to whether it sounded to some like the smashing of crockery. Its merest shriek would be their anthem. They would flaunt all its trappings — bell-bottoms, short skirts, minimal lingerie, bobbed hair, booze — whatever they understood they were *supposed* to adopt, as members in good standing of the "Lost Generation." And many of their elders would continue, just as adamantly and thoughtlessly, to condemn what they did not understand, and therefore saw as sinister.

CHAPTER THREE

Coon-Sanders Novelty Orchestra

The first full year of peace began with President Wilson in Paris for the peace conference, the first American chief executive thus to absent himself from the nation while in office. Prohibition was now assured by the ratification of the Eighteenth Amendment in 1919, though it would not go into effect until early the following year. It was a cause of great concern for many Americans. Prices were rising, and that was a cause for concern by almost everyone. Those who read the sports page were noticing such names as Ty Cobb, Bobby Jones, and Bill Tilden, II. If the sports enthusiast read carefully, he might see even a slight mention of a young Boston Red Sox player named Ruth, though in April the future "Babe" would hit only one home run, and only two in May. A new song, "How Ya Gonna Keep 'Em Down on the Farm," anticipated some changed attitudes in the returning soldiers. Among more serious songs, "The World Is Waiting for the Sunrise" offered a somewhat optimistic mood, while "I'm Always Chasing Rainbows" did not. Irving Berlin, usually good for coming up with a popular melody, produced one of his best in "A Pretty Girl Is Like a Melody," which Ziegfeld used in his Follies for 1919.

By the time Joe Sanders returned to Kansas City, probably in early April, Coonie had already prepared him for getting his union membership. The two immediately began to develop their plans. They formed a band and set up their own booking office in what Joe described as the old Victor Building at Tenth and Main streets. A newspaper article of about the same time, however, identified the address as room 230 of the Federal Reserve Bank Building.[1] At any rate, it was at Tenth and Main. Joe, highly trained in music theory, attended to musical arrangements. Since Coonie was older and more experienced, and since he knew more musicians and potential clients in the city, he handled that aspect of the new enterprise. He contacted several of the best available players, enough to form several small groups that could be used simultaneously in different gigs at clubs, weddings, and other functions. "In those days," wrote Joe forty years later, "a four-piece outfit was considered a big band."[2]

In these early days Floyd Estep, a very talented musician not yet twenty years old, worked for a while with Joe and Coonie, though at about this same time Estep played also with D. Ambert Haley's Orchestra. Floyd's and Joe's personalities apparently clashed, so Floyd left Coon-Sanders. Very quickly the new agency attracted what Joe termed "the two top dancing clubs in town"; and whenever the Raven Club and the Tiger Club needed a band, they went to the little agency at Tenth and Main. Such events as the Raven's annual Sunrise Dance were especially good publicity for the new enterprise. The dance began at midnight and continued until six, and was followed by a sumptuous breakfast. The location for these dances was Electric Park Pavilion, a popular entertainment center in Kansas City. Joe nostalgically recalled it many years later and regretted that it had been destroyed by fire. The Coon-Sanders Agency grew so rapidly that it had to seek new quarters, so Joe and Coonie moved to an office in the Gayety Theatre Building.[3]

Johnny Coon said it was while Coonie and Joe had an office at this address that Coonie decided they needed a safe. Though it was delivered while Coonie was out of the office, he had told others where to put it. Coonie already had the combination, but unknown to him another copy of the combination was delivered with the safe. Coonie returned to the office with a bottle of liquor, which he proudly showed to the others. "See what I have? I'm putting this in the safe where no one can get to it. How do you like *those* apples?" Then, under the impression that his immediate future was secure, Coonie left for the day. The others opened the safe, removed the liquor for subsequent purposes, and in its place put a quantity of horse manure that they had collected on the street and boxed to express to Coonie their gratitude.[4] It was a churlish trick that surprised Coonie and hit him where it hurt most. He was learning that there are those to whom nothing is sacred.

In the course of playing for various country clubs, the two men became acquainted with Billy Maxwell, whom Sanders described as "a bon vivant" and one "known for his social activities," whatever that meant. Maxwell took a personal liking for Coonie and Joe and for the music they were playing. Sometimes, after the men's regular engagements, Maxwell asked just the two to play for his own private parties at his palatial home. Observed Joe, "These informal gatherings became the talk of the town and the upper crust fought to secure invitations to the soirees." Sometimes the parties lasted until dawn, the guests enjoying nothing but drums and piano and the two musicians' vocal solos and duets.[5] This personal contact led to an adventure that became one of the favorite parts of the Coon-Sanders legend, though it has generally been assigned to a much later date.

One day, probably sometime during 1919, Maxwell asked the two men whether they might be interested in going to Tulsa, Oklahoma, to play at a big society bash at Earl Sinclair's estate, he of the famous Sinclair oil family. The price offered was "juicy," as Joe put it, so he and Coonie jumped at the chance. A short time later the two men, and three other players, arrived in Tulsa where they were met by one Mr. Lockhart, who represented himself as Earl Sinclair's personal secretary. He escorted them to one of the city's best hotels where rooms had been reserved for them. A little later, while the five men were stripped down to their underwear and were playing cards on a bed, there was a knock. Someone opened the door, and Lockhart entered. "Gentlemen," he asked, "how soon can you dress and be ready? Mr. Sinclair wants you to play at dinner at a country club prior to the dance at his home." Entirely willing to show every courtesy, the quintet dressed, gathered their instruments, and hopped into a limousine that took them to the railroad station. Lockhart explained that they would take the train, because the country club was some miles from the city and a train was the best way to get

Mianos Jazz Band, Kansas City, Missouri, about 1918. Saxophonist is Floyd Eugene Estep, who later played with Coon-Sanders; others unidentified. (Courtesy Claude and Ruth Anderson.)

there. After a considerable wait, a train arrived with an elegant Pullman car attached at the rear. The five men were told to leave their instruments on the car's observation platform and then were invited into a very luxurious lounge of the private car. Two men greeted them.[6]

Lockhart introduced one simply as Mr. Sinclair, a man whom Joe later described as a "rugged, pompous man" and yet "affability personified." The other was Archibald Roosevelt, son of the late president. Sinclair asked everyone to be seated and rang for his black servant Tom, a polished man who inquired after each guest's favorite beverage. While Sinclair and Roosevelt were keeping up a steady stream of conversation, the drinks arrived and the train sped on. "We were so flattered that these three great men sounded us out on our views," wrote Joe, "that we forgot the world and time." And the five musicians were so mellowed by the drinks and so awed by their luxurious surroundings that it was not until Tom brought out a dinner menu for Sinclair's inspection that Joe, Coonie, and their companions began to sense something fishy that wasn't on the menu. If they were supposed to play for Earl Sinclair's party, which was also a dinner occasion, why would they be having dinner on the train? Their present host sensed this wonderment and smiled. "Gentlemen," he began, "I see that I cannot longer withold the truth from you. I am *not* Earl Sinclair. I am his brother Harry." Well, Joe and the others knew that Harry F. Sinclair was one of the richest men in the country and head of the Mammoth Oil Company.

Joe Sanders (left) and Carleton Coon, about 1919, probably Kansas City. (Courtesy Kansas City [Mo.] Museum.)

Sinclair continued his explanation: "This afternoon I was at my brother's house. Earl was busy preparing the mansion and grounds for the big society event of the Tulsa season. Acting upon impulse, I said to Earl, 'I think I'll kidnap your band and take them with me to New York, as it is impossible for me to attend the party tonight.'" Earl was so preoccupied that either he didn't fully comprehend what his brother Harry had said, or else he didn't take it seriously. So he said simply, "Sure, Harry, go ahead." "Well, boys," said Harry to his nervous musical guests, "having always been a gambler, I accepted the challenge. I gambled with the earth and made my millions from oil. I gambled this afternoon that you boys might accept my little joke on Earl and be my guests for a week in New York. Are you with me?"[7]

They were, with scarcely any urging, on the understanding that Harry Sinclair would pay the fines the union would impose on Coon-Sanders for failing to show for an engagement. In addition, Sinclair promised plenty of spending money and the services of Mr. Lockhart as host. But since their luggage had been left at the hotel, the five had not even a toothbrush. During the night, Lockhart ascertained the men's semi-vital statistics and wired them ahead. The next morning, at St. Louis, a redcap came aboard with an armload of articles for each man. In addition, Sinclair gave Lockhart $500 to purchase clothing, new luggage, and other supplies to be used in New York. As the train neared New York, Sinclair met with the five men and told them they would be quartered at the Waldorf Hotel. They would have individual credit cards, and they would be free to come and go as they wished. He gave them only one bit of admonition: "Gentlemen, you are Harry Sinclair's personal guests for a week. All I ask of you is that you do nothing to reflect upon my name or standing." In light of Sinclair's immediate future, this sounds ironic, but Joe, Coonie, and the other three men vowed to be upright citizens.[8]

As for Sinclair's subsequent history, he mauled his own reputation sufficiently to qualify for Spartan accomodations at Leavenworth, and he might have gone to that institution had he not been wealthy and, hence, widely regarded as an exemplary businessman. Even still, he was called before the congressional committee investigating the illegal leasing of oil reserves at Elk Hills, California, and Teapot Dome, Wyoming. When Sinclair refused, "on advice of counsel," to answer a number of questions, Senator Thomas Walsh declared him in contempt, and the Senate upheld the charge with a lopsided vote of 72 to 1. He was then convicted in criminal court. After much argument and several appeals, Sinclair was fined $1,000 and sentenced to three months in jail in the District of Columbia. He spent his time filling medical prescriptions and ingratiating himself with other prisoners. There were those who argued that when Secretary of the Interior Albert B. Fall, without competitive bidding, granted leases on federal oil reserves to Harry F. Sinclair and Edward L. Doheny, the action was not against national interest. The argument was that no illegal profits would have accrued to either Sinclair or Doheny, even had the transactions not been voided and declared "illegal and fraudulent." And some argued that the leases had been quasi-military matters and that the security of the nation would have been harmed by making the matter public. Whatever one might think of those fanciful arguments, it nevertheless was a fact that for authorizing the transfers, Fall received about $260,000 in Liberty Bonds from Sinclair, as well as a "loan" of $100,000 from Doheny, with neither security nor interest.[9]

But that was several years later. At present, Sinclair was merely the very rich head of the Mammoth Oil Company and a very generous host. As Sanders later put it, "Finally, after two weeks [elsewhere he said *one* week] of gorgeous hospitality, we had to tear ourselves away, but we had seen New York City from Rip Van Winkle's bowling alley to Tex Guinan's penny arcade."[10]

"Tex Guinan's penny arcade," indeed! Mary Louise Cecilia "Texas" Guinan (1884–1933) was probably the most famous speakeasy proprietor in New York. It is entirely possible that, at some later time, Joe met her at Larry Fay's El Fay Club, or Club Moritz, or perhaps the Three Hundred Club. But that Sanders and the other band members saw her on this early trip to New York is unlikely, for at that time she was almost certainly still heavily involved with making moving pictures in California. Earlier, she had had a career in rodeo, operetta, and vaudeville. It was probably during these earlier years that she began to use her well-known phrase "Give the little girl a big hand" when introducing the club's performers, though Anthony Slide suggests that she probably got that expression from Jack Osterman.[11] Here's how *Variety* described one of Texas' typical introductions:

> "Here's Dottie Wilson," says Miss Guinan, as she leads forward a demure young thing who took no chances on the heat by taking off almost all of her clothes. "You know Miss Wilson, don't you? Give her a hand. Encourage the girls. That's right, give her another hand. She's a great star, aren't you, Dottie?" After the miss had done her dance, Texas got right to work again with the "hand stuff." Texas and her "hands" are almost enough to have any of the girls demand more money nightly from Larry Fay for the "hit" they are making.[12]

Well, the young lady already had two hands but could perhaps have used more clothes. Guinan's other famous phrase, "Hello, sucker!" was more to the point; and she often used it as a robust greeting to customers as they entered her speakeasy. Despite the greeting's association with Guinan, it probably originated not with her but with Harry H. Tammen, a circus man and newspaper figure, originally from Denver, Colorado. Guinan perhaps started using the phrase when she read in various publications about the recently deceased playboy, whom *Variety* described as "revered showman, editor, millionaire, philanthropist and good scout." Tammen good-naturedly shouted "Hello, Sucker" at almost everyone he met. He used to say, "And if I ever got to Heaven's gate — though I don't know how or why I should — I'll walk up to St. Peter and say — 'Hello, Sucker!'"[13] By the time Texas had appropriated the salutation and made it even more famous, Tammen and St. Peter were perhaps old friends.

All his life Joe Sanders enjoyed sports and as a young man played basketball and baseball with great zest and skill, especially excelling in baseball, which he learned from his brother Roy. Joe's desire for a brief time was to be a professional baseball pitcher, and though he had been too young to play with the "big tough Belton [baseball] team," he did play basketball there. While a senior at Kansas City's Westport High, he pitched and helped that school's team to an undefeated season.[14] After leaving high school and while he was making the Chautauqua circuits with the Burgess Dramatic Company, Joe occasionally pitched in games along the route. On one occasion in Davenport, Iowa, an observer remarked, "Joe Sanders ... gave one of the nicest exhibitions of the twirling art as one cares to see. This young man made a decided hit on the platform, but he equally distinguished himself as a ball player." Not only as a pitcher did he shine, for in that game Joe batted four times and got two homers.[15]

Joe's pride in those days, and throughout his life, was his older brother Roy, who had some success in major league baseball. In games at Kansas City's old Association Park, Joe liked to sit in the grandstand and, in his stentorian voice, yell, "Come on, Roy!" As someone commented, "You could hear him a block away." Roy starred in football and baseball at William Jewell College, though he apparently quit college in 1913 to join the Muskogee, Oklahoma, baseball club of the Western Association. The league disbanded and Roy had to pawn his overcoat for train fare to get back to Belton, Missouri.

While working in Omaha, Nebraska, he pitched in home games for the Western League, and did so well that he had an offer from the Kansas City Blues in the American Association. The Blues sold him to the Cincinnati Reds where he played one season; and then, after a short return to Kansas City, he went to the Pittsburgh Pirates. On 2 February 1920 the University of Kansas announced that they had hired Roy as a baseball coach.[16]

It seems strange that Joe Sanders, even after he had definitely decided to make his living in the music field as a pianist, continued to play baseball occasionally. Anyone involved in such games as baseball or football is always risking physical injury, especially one to the hand; and that would have been disastrous for someone in Joe's situation. As a matter of fact, in conversation years later with Anne Steward, on the staff of *Radio Digest*, Joe proudly held up a crooked third finger on his left hand as proof that he had been, as he put it, pretty badly "knocked around" in a baseball game.[17] Joe may have been exaggerating, but the possibility of debilitating injury was always real.

Despite the risks, Joe did play baseball and enjoyed an achievement that many Coon-Sanders fans have wondered whether to take seriously. But on 1 July 1922 Joe really did strike out twenty-seven batters in nine innings of a semi-professional game for the Kansas City Athletic Club. Joe was pitching for the Craddocks against the Lowe-Campbells. As one reporter wrote after the game: "Sanders had everything a pitcher could expect. His fast ball was a trifle faster than usual and his curve was breaking over a foot." But as this reporter went on to explain, Joe's victory was not the no-hit variety. Actually, his opponents got several good hits and managed to end the game with four runs. This, however, was not good enough to defeat Joe's Craddocks, who got seven runs. But that Joe managed to strike out twenty-seven batters was, said the reporter, "deserving of far more credit than even a no-hit, no-run game." Robert Ripley, in his column

"Believe It or Not" on 3 June 1923, reported the feat.[18]

While this was Joe's most spectacular achievement in baseball, his playing in earlier years was not much less so. In his teens, when he played for Belton, Mo., he established a record number of strikeouts in a game against the Kansas City White Sox. Sanders allowed only three hits and "whiffed" twenty-three batters, only four fewer than he would strike out a bit later in Kansas City. Belton won 2 to 1. In another game Belton won 8 to 1 against the Aines Dairy team of Kansas City. In that game Joe fanned fourteen batters, and got a home run with two on base. In yet another game, against Kansas City's Produce Merchants, Joe struck out fifteen batters in what was described as "a fast 2 to 1 exhibition." Both Belton runs were Joe's.[19] There probably were a lot of other games in which Joe did nearly, if not quite, as well.

Joe's proficiency in baseball was such that he might have gone far with it. He was, all his life, highly competitive; this trait, coupled with his obvious athletic talents, could well have taken him into baseball's major leagues. Apparently, however, all his family discouraged this, perhaps because they knew his musical ability was even greater. His driving creativeness and competitive instinct doubtless had both positive and negative effects on his musical career.

Carleton and Joe, both of them excellent self-advertisers, set out to make the city very much aware of them, and they were tremendously successful and well received. There were in the city other orchestras with good musicians, but Coon-Sanders had something more — a band that was entertaining both aurally and visually. Their shenanigans were as eagerly anticipated as their music. What was more, both Joe and Coonie were singers, *good* singers, individually and as a duet. Male duos such as Gus Van and Joe Schenck had long been a popular feature of vaudeville, but they seem to have been a rarity in dance orchestras in the early years. (Most musicians perhaps thought they were doing quite enough just playing their instruments.) In fact, duets by Coon and Sanders were sufficiently distinctive for the orchestra often to be designated as a *singing* orchestra.

One of the most promising possibilities for Coon-Sanders was to be hired for a regular run at a local theater, and by 1919 several theaters had orchestras of one kind or another. The Regent, for example, offered Forbstein's Royal Orchestra. Other theaters that advertised bands included the Liberty, which had Frederick J. Curth's Orchestra; the New Diamond, with Moreman's Orchestra; the Isis, with Stalling's Orchestra; the Maywood, with Werner's Orchestra; and perhaps most prestigious, the Newman, that offered the "Newman Concert Orchestra of Forty," under the direction of Leo F. Forbstein.[20]

But theaters would have to wait a bit. Another, and perhaps equally advantageous possibility, was an engagement at one of the city's best hotels. It was probably sometime in the late summer of 1919 that Carleton and Joe began a stint with the Muehlebach, the start of an association that was to have positive and far-reaching significance for the band. It would give Coon-Sanders some excellent advertisement, for the Muehlebach played an important part in the city's business and social life. Johnny Coon, Carleton's oldest child, recalled in 1995 that the Muehlebach was a good, popular place to take a date to dine for about $1.50 each, and then to dance to a good band.[21]

The hotel needed a band for its Cafe Trianon and had engaged a group named the Hawaiian Quintet, recently featured at New York's Biltmore Hotel. Two of its members became ill, however, and the group had to cancel. Joe and Coonie, already well known for their appearances at golf and country clubs and other social affairs, readily agreed to fill in. The engagement would include both lunch and dinner periods, as well as what the Muehlebach referred to as its Saturday afternoon "Tea Dansants." The engagement of the Coon-Sanders band was met with great approval. Jimmie Selby, in his

"News and Gossip of the Hotel Muehlebach," for the *Kansas City Star*, had this to say about the new band:

> Mr. Coon and Mr. Sanders, together with their artists, are well known to Kansas City as a result of their engagements at the golf and country clubs and many social affairs. Mr. Sanders, at the piano, is formerly of the Orpheum [Vaudeville] Circuit, and Mr. Coon enjoys an enviable reputation with his "traps" [drums]. But that isn't all. Both possess excellent "harmony" voices and are capable of putting over some great song numbers as they play for dancing. And they've proved favorites because they seem to know just what the public wants…. Mr. Sanders and Mr. Coon also "put over" several song numbers as the hotel's patrons danced which proved a great novelty.[22]

And also in 1919, on the occasion of the opening of the Liberty Memorial Campaign, the Coon-Sanders band was entertaining during a Trianon lunch period when several military men were present. The band was playing some of the recent war songs in its program and eliciting considerable enthusiasm. A captain in the audience spoke to Joe and suggested that an appropriate song for the memorial drive would be very useful, because many workers in the drive often had lunch or dinner at the Trianon. Joe pondered the suggestion; and after the band stopped playing at 2 p.m., he and Coonie went to the music room on the mezzanine and set to work. An hour later they had finished both words and music of a song and probably introduced it that evening. Apparently the song was a cooperative product, especially the lyrics. Though Jimmie Selby, in his "News and Gossip of the Hotel Muehlebach," gives the title as "Lest the Ages Forget," I suspect the correct title is "Let's Not Forget."[23]

Coonie sang the words, apparently as a solo. As Selby later put it, "Every evening it has been used with great success and it is not exaggeration to say it has brought tears to several guests each time." It is impossible now to know its melody, apparently in waltz time, or just how it might have sounded on that occasion; but today the bare lyrics do not seem remarkable. The first line suggests John McCrae's famous, and earlier, poem, "In Flanders Fields." Though I have seen two slightly different versions of Joe and Coonie's lyrics, I believe the following is the correct one:

"Let's Not Forget"
Poppies are blooming in Flanders fields,
Many a grave they cover;
Plunged into depths of despair and grief
Is many a brave lad's mother.
Victory is ours—but oh, the price!
Somebody had to pay—
But sacrifices were never in vain
When remembered from day to day.

Chorus

Let's not forget what they did for us—
Those brave lads who gave their all;
They paid the price, shall we help them now?
Hear their call.
They fought for us, our homes, our lives,
Many a boy in Flanders lies—
Oh, let's not forget they are not all home yet,
Let's not forget.[24]

Among those who heard the song were William Gibbs McAdoo, a former secretary of the treasury under President Woodrow Wilson and the latter's son-in-law, and Charles Evans Hughes, associate justice of the Supreme Court and Republican candidate for the presidency in 1916. They were in Kansas City to attend the local Federal Court during aruguments as to the constitutionality of the Federal Farm Loan Act of 1916. With them were George W. Wickersham, attorney general under President Taft, and William Marshall Bullitt, an attorney who would figure prominently in Franklin Delano Roosevelt's presidency. Jimmie Selby reported, "Every evening it [the song] has been used with great success and … has brought tears to several guests each time. Mr. McAdoo and Mr. Hughes were two of those who were so affected."[25] At least the "washed air" in the hotel must have helped its reception.

Coon-Sanders continued to delight diners and dancers at both the Muehlebach and Baltimore hotels, as well as to make numerous other appearances. Occasionally they did charitable programs, such as a Christmas party at the County Home. George Birmingham, who directed the affair, impersonated Santa Claus, and, as the local press somewhat insensitively put it, "spread amusement and cheer in a manner foreign to most of the tottering old persons who gathered in the auditorium." After the group sang "My Old Kentucky Home," the Coon-Sanders band "struck up a jazz tune and canes and softshoes beat accompaniment to the airs." At one point, a gray-haired resident climbed onto the stage and executed a dance; then another elderly woman, with sparkling eyes and her silver hair done into a tight knot above her face, accepted an offer from Birmingham, and the two waltzed about the hall.[26]

I have seen no records of the names of players that Coonie and Joe employed during the first two years of the band's existence, that is, up to the early spring of 1921. My suspicion is that Coonie and Joe went through a considerable number of musicians. On the basis of what Harold Thiell often said in later years, he apparently was with them from the very start, or at least from a very early date, and until the band broke up following Coonie's death. Earlier, Thiell had played with D. Ambert Haley's group. As has already been mentioned, Floyd Estep, too, played briefly with the early Coon-Sanders.

In the spring of 1921 the Coon-Sanders Novelty Orchestra had achieved sufficient fame to bring an offer from Columbia Records for a recording session. This in itself would have been of sufficient pride to Kansas City, but there was the additional honor of having the company send technicians to Kansas City to do the recording there, apparently the first time for commercial recording locally. Thus, on 24 March 1921 the band's eight members crowded around recording equipment and made four records, namely, "Some Little Bird," "Hindu Dream Man," "Learning," and "Treasure." "Hindu Dream Man" was a Sanders composition. The only recording that seems to have survived is "Some Little Bird," which when issued additionally on a related label called Regal, identified Coon-Sanders as the Regal Novelty Orchestra. In addition to Coon on drums and Sanders on piano, the band consisted of the following personnel: Clyde Hendrix, trumpet; Carl Nordberg, trombone; Harold Thiell and Hal McLean, clarinet and alto saxophone; Harry Silverstone, violin; and, on banjo, Bob Norfleet, who had until just recently played with D. Ambert Haley's band.[27]

"Some Little Bird" sounds unremarkable today, totally unlike anything the band recorded thereafter. But it was done at a time when the jazz orchestra, especially the jazz dance orchestra, was still in its very early, experimental stage. If one listens to any of the orchestras of that date, including such well-known ones as Paul Whiteman's and Isham Jones's, one is usually struck by the flatness and banality of the music, its monotony, and above all, the almost total absence of anything justifying the term *arrangement*. That those early recordings were acoustical had little to do with it. Listen to Coon-Sanders' recordings of "Red Hot Mama" and "Nighthawk Blues," both of them done acoustically just three years later, and the contrast with the band's first recording is striking. What was needed was what other bands needed as well—good arranging, voicing, etc., all of which came only with experience, and no one had much in 1921. Of course, I have heard only this one example of the band's early music, and I suspect that it isn't representative. Perhaps Columbia Phonograph Company also found it unremarkable, for I've seen nothing to suggest that they approached the band about additional recordings. By the time Coon-Sanders had improved to a point at which Columbia might have been interested in further efforts, the band was under contract with the Victor Company.

Nevertheless, whatever the merit of their first recording, the band was certainly getting a lot of mileage out of it in advertisements.

Coon-Sanders Novelty Orchestra, Kansas City, Missouri, about 1920. From left: Hendrix, Nordberg, Norfleet, Silverstone, H. Thiell, McLean, Sanders and Coon. (Courtesy Kansas City [Mo.] Museum.)

That it had been done locally would, of course, account for some of this interest. The ad run by the Doric Theater, where the band was playing, made a point of referring to the new Columbia recording. The Grafonola Shop, at 1120 Grand, placed ads in local newspapers advising the public, "Do not be disappointed. Get yours today." One of the store's ads assured their patrons, "We know all the boys personally — they are O. K., so are their records." (The plural form of the noun "records" was stretching the point a bit.) The Paul Talking Machine Shop, 1112 Main Street, placed an ad that shouted, "Oh, Jazz! Where IS thy sting? Tomorrow at 2 o'clock the Coon-Sanders Novelty orchestra, famous Columbia record artists, will play a concert featuring their latest hit, *Some Little Bird*. You should see these boys perform. If movements could be recorded, this record would be a tornado."[28]

Joe and Coonie began to get offers from several of the city's theaters. Which offer came first is difficult to say, though it is possible that they had already played at the Gayety sometime in 1920. If not, then their offer from the Doric, in March of 1921, was most likely the first. The band was so popular that the theater had to issue the following ad: "We're sorry! that the Doric has been unable to accommodate the tremendous crowds that are flocking to this great program. Take our advice — attend the early shows. TRY THE MATINEE!" The Doric offered both a film and a stage show, and the film on this occasion was "The County Fair." The Coon-Sanders group used a device that would almost become a trademark in their future appearances in theaters. That is, they concocted a skit suggested by the film and called it the County Fair Jazz Band. For this presentation, Joe and Coonie seem to have arranged some sort of cooperative effort with Emil Chaquette and his "Syncopated Soloists."[29]

The Doric's advertisements featured Coon-Sanders prominently. Al Jolson* had

---

*At left: *Al Jolson (1886–1950), prominent in revue, musical comedy, film, and radio, starred in 1927 in* The Jazz Singer, *the first major film to contain dialog.*

Carleton Coon, about 1920, probably Kansas City, Missouri. (Courtesy Harvey C. Rettberg.)

apparently seen the band either at the Muehlebach or possibly after they had begun playing at the Doric, and that theater quoted him indirectly as saying that "those boys are the greatest he ever heard," to which the theater's ad, perhaps referring to the band's recent recording session, affixed the comment "he spoke a—RECORD FULL!!"[30] And not just the Doric, but also a local critic had praise for the act:

There is probably no entertainment in the amusement week in Kansas City causing more favorable comment than the performance offered by the Coon Saunders [sic] orchestra at the Doric theater in conjunction with "The County Fair," the Doric's film for the week.

The jazzy, swaying music of this group of musicians is causing a riot and is the talk of theater row. All members of the orchestra are Kansas City boys who make their own records right in Kansas City....

Sanders is the featured pianist of the outfit and this week is singing "Yiddisha [sic] Vamp," his own number, to the repeated encores of the Doric audiences. This is a jazz classic.

The Coon-Sanders orchestra is proving itself a worthy Kansas City institution.[31]

Joe's composition "Sadie, That Yiddisher Vamp" was receiving some favorable comment. Rae Samuels* was reported using the song in New York and to have secured exclusive rights to it for sixty days. She was known as "the Blue Streak of Vaudeville" because of the vigor of her presentations and her way of often ending her act by punching the scenery.[32]

With regard to Jolson's having said (as we've just seen) that Coon-Sanders was "the greatest," it might be in order at this point to mention that Jolson's reaction, whatever it was, seems to have started speculation on the subject. One report represented Jolson, perhaps the best-known entertainer in the nation at the time, as indeed believing "that Coon-Sanders Plantation Grill Orchestra is the best dance orchestra in the United States." Another report, however, said that Jolson had pronounced it second best. The Columbia Phonograph Company, at about the time of their recording the band's "Some Little Bird," thought Coon-Sanders the third best.[33] Columbia, which had already been recording such other bands as Ted Lewis's, might have been a little reluctant to risk offending them. But whatever Jolson or anyone else might have said or opined, Coon-Sanders could be pleased that, within so short a time, they had become the subject of such speculation.

On Saturday evening, 29 October 1921, Joe and Coonie's band began playing at the Hotel Baltimore's Pompeiian Room and would continue through the following week. It was a strategic time to be playing in such a popular hotel, because the American Legion would be holding their annual convention and could be expected to patronize the city's better hotels. Jenkins' Sons Music Company and several other businesses were noising it abroad that one of the pieces Coon-Sanders would play was "She's a Mean Job," which was, said the ads, "The jazziest, most tantalizing song and dance number of the year." One wonders how the song, and the band, went over with some very prominent guests on Tuesday evening, All Saints Day. There were the Governor of Missouri, France's Marshal Ferdinand Foch, Italy's General Armando Vittorio Diaz, Britain's Admiral Sir David Beatty, and Belgium's Lt. General Baron Jacques.[34] All that brass must have felt quite at home with Coon-Sanders!

The Coon-Sanders band also may have been the jazz ensemble featured in the Pompeiian Room, Wednesday evening, 25 January 1922, for what was termed a "jazz bandwagon." Said the *Star*: "Now enters the dinner dance into politics. The erstwhile instrument of the social dowager is to be used to bend the haughty necks of the political bosses and to win votes." The social-political event was known as the "young men's booster banquet and dance," and the "debutant" was Judge Edward J. Fleming, founder and president of the "Forget-It Club," and Democratic candidate for mayor. But though of their party, Fleming was not a particular favorite of the city's two Democratic bosses, Tom Pendergast and Joe Shannon. The *Star* suggested that Fleming was "bringing gray hairs to Tom and Joe" and was "the closest thing to a revolt of the workers and Democratic voters that the bosses have faced in all their life."[35]

After hearing the band on one occasion at the Pompeiian Room, a guest commented, "When Coon and Sanders sing — there's a hush over the Pompeiian Room with only the sounds of their voices, the soft music of the orchestra and the rhythmical steps of the dancers." This charmed guest thought the band "one of the few singing orchestras of

---

*Rae Samuels' first major appearance was for the Ziegfeld Follies of 1912. She died, at age 93, in New York City on 24 October 1979.

the country...."[36] Singing orchestra, indeed! In these early, experimental days of popular jazz, almost everything was new, and most bands, and especially most leaders, were content just to play their instruments. Any vocalizing that was attempted was usually mediocre and even bizarre, but both Joe and Coonie sang well. In more recent years, Joe Popper, of the staff of the *Kansas City Star*, has given a vivid description of how Joe and Coonie might have rendered "The Nighthawk Blues," composed by Joe in late 1922 and used as their theme song:

> The Nighthawk theme was one of the band's first big hits. It started off with a long rinky-tink introduction in Charleston tempo. Then Joe Sanders stepped to the microphone and sang the opening vocal in a smooth tenor as the band began to swing out with an intricate syncopated arrangement. Coon smiled behind the drums, twirling the sticks like a magician. And then something happened. Coon was beside Sanders, singing — shouting — harmonizing as the gang seemed to explode with pent-up energy. The trumpet took off. The clarinet played joyous riffs. Sanders banged the piano top in driving rhythm.[37]

In the latter days of 1921 Kansas City enjoyed some of the best and most famous vaudeville entertainers of all time. Eddie Cantor appeared in late November at the Shubert in a skit called "The Midnight Rounders," which suggests a line from what would soon be the Nighthawks' theme song—"Started with a bunch of midnight rounders...." At the Mainstreet Theater there were the Four Marx Brothers, and Victor Herbert was at the Newman. A week after the Marxes, the Mainstreet offered two blackface comedians, George Moran and Charles Mack, both of them native Kansans, and in the Twenties one of the most successful comedy teams of stage, phonograph recording, and film.[38]

Meanwhile, during this period the Coon-Sanders band was making changes to form an organization that in the next year would make musical history. The violin was dropped and the sousaphone added. Harry Williams replaced Bob Norfleet on the banjo. And in the *Kansas City Star* the column "Starbeams" carried the following item about a future member. Reprinted from "Society Personals" in the *Wichita Beacon*, it said, "Mr. And Mrs. Fred Leu announce the marriage of their daughter, Gladys, to Nicholas L. Musolino of Quincy, Ill., which took place on November 29 in Kansas City, the Reverend Casimir J. Welch performing the marriage ceremony."[39] Musolino, who with several others of the band had to contend with having his name regularly mangled, would join Coon-Sanders in late summer, 1923.

In January of 1922 the *Star* published a feature article that asked the question, "Is [the] Traffic Cop Doomed?" Kansas City and other cities about the nation were familiar with and comforted by the traffic cop. He stood athwart the Tin Lizzies, Franklins, Locomobiles, Jordans, and the many other brands of cars, as well as wagons and pedestrians, trying to bring some order to the novel confusion created by road hogs and green drivers. But now the best information had it that this noble figure was doomed, that there soon would be mechanical lights to do his work.[40]

But how could one relate to a machine? More important, how could one play a trick on a machine, as Carleton Coon did once to a policeman? Once? Well, once that we know about. It involved one "Darby Hicks," a fictitious person apparently invented by the Nighthawks. Johnny Coon said that the band's members employed his name as a facetious scapegoat, or as an imaginary boon companion, or perhaps for a prank on some unsuspecting victim. It was a pastime for these loony tuners, and just mentioning his name could send them into almost disabling laughter.[41]

One day when a harried policeman was directing traffic near the Muehlebach, at the busy intersection of Twelfth and Baltimore, Coonie recognized him, walked over to him, and in a confidential manner, told him that

Front cover of Sanders' composition "The Nighthawk Blues," the band's theme song during earlier years. (Courtesy Special Collections, Kansas City [Mo.] Public Library.)

a fellow back at the hotel had just been saying that the policeman fancied men rather more than he did women. "What the hell!" yelled the shocked lawman. "Where is this [deleted expletive]?" Coonie said that he had seen him in the men's room at the hotel. "Do you know his name?" asked the angry cop. "Yeah," said Coonie, "Darby Hicks, I think." And since, as has already been stated, the brave new world in Kansas City did not yet include traffic lights, transportation in that area was, for upwards of an hour, much the worse for it. Coonie's victim searched the hotel to mop up the floor with the misbegotten Mr. Hicks.[42]

In addition to "Darby Hicks," there was another name involved in a running joke, but Joe later cloaked it in mystery. Said he, "There is a story connected with the name 'Elmer.' Ask any of the boys. Thereby hangs a tale — give a guess." Did it perhaps have something to do with Elmer Krebs, or — more likely — with Elmer Kohlman? Another possibility is that it was Joe himself; for in the days of the early Nighthawk broadcasts on WDAF, Joe was often referred to either as "Professor" or, for some reason, "Elmer."[43] Too bad Joe left the matter hanging.

For those in Kansas City who didn't view life as a prison sentence, and who considered legal bans an iffy approach to moral problems, these times must have been especially difficult. The protracted Arbuckle prosecution in California was greatly exercising the community, and on top of that came several other events, especially the murder in Hollywood, in early 1922, of William Desmond Taylor, a film director. Said an unsigned article in the *Star*: "The murder of William Desmond Taylor has had a fearsome effect upon the movies. It has threatened the reputations of some of the brightest names in the film world, it is exposing debauches, the looseness, the rottenness of Hollywood. It may cost the producers hundreds of thousands of dollars."*

---

*The moralizing over Taylor's murder would have been even greater, had it been generally known at the time that he was homosexual.

Late 1923, Kansas City, Missouri. Sanders at piano; others (from left): Musolino, J. Thiell, H. Thiell, Knapp, Estep, Richolson, Beckham, and Coon. (Courtesy Harvey C. Rettberg.)

And on February 9 the *Star* carried an extraordinary article titled "Into Mystic Love Cult," that tut-tutted about the Taylor case and smacked its lips over alleged "oriental mysticism, weird philosophies of the Far East, and strange teachings in the realms of the psychic and supernatural."[44] "Oriental mysticism!" What that meant is anyone's guess, but perhaps someone had been caught reading Confucius. Small wonder that in 1924 Congress passed a very restrictive immigration law aimed especially at Far Easterners.

But in Kansas City there seemed to be less of the xenophobia that, in many parts of America, was bringing out some of the worst traits in human nature. No doubt Kansas City had its Tartuffes and Torquemadas, but these apparently were more than matched by the Falstaffs and Franklins. Also, there seemed to be at least some civilized instinct in most of those who ran the city's government. Extraordinary alarms were usually met with skepticism, and patently absurd ideas were often given the horselaugh. Not least among the debunkers was the Kansas City press. It is inescapable that among a community's most valuable assets are good newspapers and restaurants.

We are fortunate in this. The development of popular jazz groups and orchestras probably could not have happened in Kansas City without a considerable amount of tolerance of new ideas. So, when that new medium radiotelegraphy (mercifully shortened to radio) suddenly appeared to put the new music into the air, there were plenty of potential fans waiting. They didn't have long to wait.

In February of 1922 radio still was in its larval stage in Kansas City and almost everywhere else. The Western Radio Company, at

Carleton Coon, place and date unknown, but probably Kansas City in early '20s. (Courtesy Kansas City [Mo.] Museum.)

Fourteenth and Main, announced on the sixth that it needed to ask amateur senders between the city and Manhattan, Kansas, to "keep out of the air" Tuesday evening. The company intended to "lease the air" to the Co-operative Club of Manhattan for a one-hour program of its annual "Women's Night." In addition to an address by J. P. Somerville, of Kansas City, there would be some local musical talent.[45]

Well, today it all sounds quaint and dull, but in 1922 almost *anything* coming from a radio seemed worth hearing. It was even more exciting than watching an airplane go overhead or witnessing an arrest on Twelfth Street. In a few months, however, there would be so many sounds coming over local radio stations—*real* stations—that listeners would become discriminating and critical. But not just yet.

One of the first serious efforts to broadcast in Kansas City came just a few days after the above event, when on February 16 the *Kansas City Star*, in its own offices, broadcast an experimental program by means of the Western Radio Company's wires and sending apparatus. The newspaper informed the public that the music used would be of varied types, from jazz to grand opera. And though the distance that the signal would carry was estimated at from 100 to 150 miles, actually it was heard as far away as the state of Washington and Central Mexico. It seemed miraculous, and when next day it was reported that President Warren Harding had installed a receiver in his study, the writer of "Starbeams" said, "All right, Mr. Harding, the Star's next radio concert is Wednesday night."[46] These were not very sophisticated broadcasts, even by the meager standards of that day; but they represented great progress and were exciting enough to generate ambitious plans.

At the Ashland cinema about two thousand persons listened to this broadcast of the *Star's* radio station. A single amplifier on the theater's stage was so audible, and carried the music and voices so clearly, that the theater's regular orchestra was dismissed for the entire hour and the radio broadcast allowed to serve as accompaniment for the film. The Ashland was one of the city's largest, but Richard Steadman, the theater's manager, said that even in the rear, 150 feet from the speaker, the broadcast was quite clear. Most in the audience were fascinated by the experiment, but there were some who either were puzzled by the demonstration or else were "from Missouri." One woman went up to the stage after the show, took a good look at the speaker, and exclaimed, "Why, that's nothing but an old phonograph." She was quite sure that it was all a hoax. Nevertheless, W. L. Shelton, the owner of the Ashland, ordered a larger and better sound system, with speakers in several parts of the theater.[47]

Residents in the Kansas City area were responding enthusiastically to the new sounds that they drew, as though by magic, from the air. By early March everyone seemed obsessed with radio, experiencing, as did the proverbial hare, a bit of madness. The *Star*, of course, was delighted and reported it all with relish: "In many homes in Kansas City youngsters, parents and neighbors gathered around makeshift home-made apparatus. Those who were fortunate in having amplifiers 'hooked on' and danced to real dance music." The sounds emanating from the *Star's* studio were being broadcast by a large antenna above the Western Radio Company's building, from where they were "sent out into the ether."[48]

The excitement of radio's arrival caught the imagination of the city's merchants and songwriters. For instance, an ad by Satterlee Electric Company, 22 E. Ninth, announced, "We have the supplies for those who desire to make their own wireless telephone receiving sets and become familiar with the basic principles of the radio telephone." Radio Supply Company, 1600 Grand Avenue, had just received radio sets, with which anyone could "get market and weather reports, etc., out of the air." Robinson Shoe Company, 1016-1018 Main, had an ad for "Radio" shoes for men "that broadcast style — tune in at $11.50." And J. W. Jenkins' Sons Music Company advertised the sheet music for "Kiss Me by Wireless," subtitled "a radio fox trot."[49]

It was on Saturday, 4 March 1922, that the *Star* began its second, more elaborate experimental radio station — "Tune in at 360 [meters] tonight," said an item in that day's issue. The broadcast would be a result of a contract between the *Star* and the Western Radio Company, an association that had "shown the possibilities of wireless telephony and ... that entire programs may be broadcast many miles with accuracy." As befitted a city which would eventually take its place with New Orleans and a few other cities in the development of jazz, the first broadcast would feature the Duke Yellman Jazz Orchestra, one of whose pieces would be "Lonesome Mama Blues." Commented "Starbeams" elsewhere in the same issue: "Dancing to absent music will be general in Kansas City tonight during the *Star's* radio dance, but probably science will not perfect a contactless cheek-to-cheek dance for a good many years." Two days later the station began broadcasting every evening starting at 7:45 and included what the *Star* represented as the first broadcast from the city's vaudeville houses. It was obvious that the station was going to be heavily dependent upon popular entertainment, for the public were informed that "[a]rrangements have been made by the Star and the managers of the various higher class theaters for the exclusive broadcasting of the acts appearing at the theaters." Now there would be things worth listening to, that is, if there were not too much interference from the weather and amateur senders.[50]

Indeed, amateur senders were especially annoying, and irritated listeners had little redress. A. G. Clark's "The Tuning Troubles of Messrs. Gallagher and Shean," a poetic take-off on those popular gentlemen's musical act, grew lyrical about these pests of the airways:

Oh Mister Gallagher, Oh Mister Gallagher,
I was listening on the radio last night,
But an amateur quite near
   seemed to like to interfere,
So I'm going to kick and have him closed up tight.

Oh Mister Shean, Oh Mister Shean,
In the radio game I see you're pretty green;
As they say in gay Paree,
   what an animal you'd be—
What, an air-hog, Mister Gallagher?
No, a jackass, Mister Shean![51]

One of the earliest bands to play over the new station was Eddie Kuhn's Harmony Boys. On Monday, March 6, while William Jennings Bryan was assuring an audience in Philadelphia, Pa., that the evolutionists would never make a monkey out of him, Kuhn introduced a series of *Forty Minutes of Music*, short nightly concerts of a half-hour or so to enable listeners, if they wished, to tune in from time to time to other stations. He promised a "medley of popular tunes," but by Friday, Kuhn oddly announced that he "had eliminated jazz from [his] wireless music." Perhaps it seemed like a good idea at the time, but he no doubt came to regret the promise. At that time Kuhn was playing at the Hotel Muehlebach's Plantation Grill and was attracting some attention with a euphonium, described as being a cross between an alto horn and a trombone.[52]

But even this second *Star* station was obviously limited in its abilities, nowhere near so powerful as that in, say, Detroit, Michigan. Why shouldn't Kansas City have something just as grand, something that would befit a city of its size and vitality? Thanking the Western Radio Company for the use of its facilities, the *Star* on May 7 announced plans to install "the latest and most powerful radio telephone broadcasting set manufactured in America." It would have a power of 500 watts, with a broadcast radius of about 2,000 miles, and would be designed especially for entertainment. There would have to be new microphones—present ones were merely telephone mouthpieces with small megaphones attached—which would eliminate the problem of overtones from voice and musical instruments "in volume." Also, such microphones would eliminate the need to stand directly before the receiver. It would look like the old microphone but would be twice as large and could be placed anywhere in the room. A speaker or player could move about and still be quite audible.[53]

At that time, according to the *Star*, no station of more than 500 watts existed in the United States, and only five or six were that powerful. (This could be the basis of the misconception held by many, including Joe Sanders as late as 1961, that at this time there were only about a half-dozen radio stations in the nation.) Westinghouse had the three in Pittsburgh, Newark, and Chicago; General Electric had one in Schenectady; and the *Detroit News* had one. The *Star* believed that only Detroit's had the efficiency of the one planned for Kansas City.[54]

Meanwhile, the *Star*'s competitor, the *Kansas City Post*, let it be known that they, too, would go on the air. On Friday evening, 19 May 1922, at 7:45, station WRW broadcast using the facilities of the station owned by the Sweeney Automobile, Tractor and Radio School. It was an engaging program that, though nearly ignored by the *Star*, fascinated the public. And for readers of this book, the interesting fact is that it was the Coon-Sanders Band's introduction to radio. On the Wednesday before the broadcast, Sanders put in a long-distance phone call to old friends in Belton, Mo., as well as that town's local paper, and told them to be sure to listen to the broadcast. The Belton press lived up to Joe's expectations and gave him quite a pre-broadcast puff, including the inaccurate statement that "Coon-Sanders orchestra will be the only broadcasting artists on Friday night." In fact, there would be several, including one other band. The Belton newspaper stated also that only urgent business would be able to interfere with the broadcast, "so Belton people should be able to catch every note distinctly." No doubt at 9:15, Belton, as well as a lot of other places, were listening and heard the Coon-Sanders Orchestra, in what was probably their first radio appearance, give delightful renditions of such numbers as "The Sheik," "Three o'-Clock in the Morning," Joe's composition "Martha," "Teasin'," "Ty-Tee," "Just a Little Love Song," "Cutie," and "Rosy Posy."[55] Though this broadcast occurred while the Coon-Sanders Orchestra was employed by the Hotel Baltimore, it is unclear where it broadcast from, whether from that location, or perhaps from the radio station. Speaking later about this introduction to radio broadcasting, Joe said that the band were a little cowed by "that black thing hanging down." After the program someone called all the way from Liberty, Missouri, ten or fifteen miles away, to say how good the band had sounded. Can you beat that! mused Joe.[56]

The *Post* was extremely glowing in its comments about the various members of the band. Of Coonie and Joe, the paper said, "They stand high in the musical world as exponents of both the jazz and 'straight' music." As for Harold Thiell and Hal McLean, "The croonin', moanin' tones of the saxophone are made realistic by [these] two real artists.... For those who love the 'sax,' the work of these boys will be a revelation." "Clyde Hendrix, cornetist, and Carl Nordberg, trombone player," continued the paper, "have gained favorable comment wherever they have played, while the work of Harry Silverstone, violinist, and Harry Williams, banjo player, is known throughout this section." Williams had taken over the place that had been filled earlier by Bob Norfleet. Of Sanders and Coon, both of whom were "well known in Kansas City and throughout Missouri," the *Post* observed that they needed no introduction. It spoke of Coonie, by the way, as "drummer and general manager," and of Joe as "pianist and conductor."[57]

Another report had special praise for Hal McLean and his playing of "Aunt Hagar's Children's Blues." Said the item, "His 'sax' fairly crooned itself into the hearts of Post radio fans," and Harold Thiell "pushed some mean keys, jazzically speaking," especially with the foxtrot "Jimmy." Harry Williams "starred in every number but was especially good in 'The Sheik,' when he trummed [sic] the minds of his listeners back to Arabian courts."[58]

Also making the broadcast were the Blue Crescent Entertainers from the Peking Cafe; the Witmark Trio (Hal King, Frankie Watkins, and Bert Beuder); Helen Sullivan and Marcella Gillespie, local vocalists; and Tony Denocenzo, described as a "concertinist."[59]

On the day of the broadcast, J. W. Jenkins' Sons Music Company, 1015 Walnut, advertised Joe's song and said: "'Martha'— Joe Sander's [sic] New Song Hit, Listen in Tonight at 9:15, Meter 360, Broadcasted [sic] nationally by the Sweeney station." Exactly what the term "nationally" meant is unclear, for there were as yet no networks. Perhaps it meant merely that the fairly powerful station would send the station's signal a long distance. On Saturday morning after the broadcast, Joe went to Belton, where in Kreigh's Restaurant, he sold autographed copies of his song for a dollar each. Said the Belton newspaper, "Joe is a former Belton boy and his friends will be glad to greet him on this occasion."[60]

Meanwhile, the *Star*, on the heels of much publicity about what its new station proposed to do, how it would do it, and how radio broadcasting in general worked, used its paper of Monday, June 5, to prepare its listeners. In the same issue that carried news of Lillian Russell's death, an article titled "WDAF Will Talk Tonight" informed the public: "Barring accidents, the Star expects to deliver. There will be thousands of radio listeners. It is to be hoped the summer static will be no stronger than usual tonight." The next day in St. Louis, the *Post-Dispatch*'s station notified its listeners that it would close down at 9 p.m., and requested them to try to pick up WDAF, and, if successful, to let the *Post-Dispatch* know. Said the St. Louis paper, "There were many reports of getting WDAF in the St. Louis area [last evening], and one in which WDAF was received by using only a bedspring aerial and a detector." WDAF broadcast on 360 meters.[61]

An interesting detail about these early wireless efforts was the first broadcast over WDAF by the Follies Company at Electric Park at 11:45 p.m. on Friday, 23 June 1922, and ending at 1 a.m. Roy Mack, the park's director, announced the program as the Midnight Frolic, which the *Star* grandly proclaimed as "the first midnight frolic by radio in the history of the world." Ben Kendrick's Orchestra was part of the group. It was so popular that a second frolic was broadcast on July 21, and yet another at the end of July.[62] The name of these programs perhaps suggested the use of the term when Coon-Sanders started broadcasting the Nighthawk "frolics" from the Plantation Grill a few months later, and in the same time slot.

In light of the close association that later developed between the *Kansas City Star* and the Coon-Sanders Orchestra, it seems remarkable that the paper's new station, WDAF, when it made its first official broadcast, by-passed Coon-Sanders in favor of the Riley-Ehrhart Orchestra.[63] In fact, WDAF waited well over three months before having them play; and even then, on September 22, it was only a brief spot in a program that aired several of the stage acts at the Newman Theater.[64] Perhaps there was a little sensitiveness about Coon-Sanders' having been featured so prominently in that broadcast by the *Post*. Before the first appearance of Coon-Sanders, at least eleven other popular bands played over WDAF, including the Duke Yellman Orchestra, which played seven times. The others that played included the following: William R. Green, Elms Hotel, Marks, Stinson-Wheeler, Ben Kendrick, Kansas City Florist Club, Hammontree, Bert Phelps Royal Garden, and Leo Davis.

Duke Yellman's orchestra, in particular, seemed to occupy a very conspicuous place with WDAF. On July 10, for instance, the radio station offered what it described as a "novel feature." "WDAF will inaugurate real musical comedy tomorrow night," said the *Star*, "when a production, especially written for The Star, will be broadcast for the first time from The Star's station." It was a musical comedy, whose book was written by James D. Kemper and whose music was arranged by Duke Yellman. The *Star* explained that the two-act production, titled *Jazz vs. Classics*, would "introduce notable figures of royalty in a radio setting." It added, "The King of Jazz will be on the job and he will be surrounded by his satellites, every one of whom, it is guaranteed by Mr. Yellman, knows how to entertain." The cast were as follows:[65]

The King of Jazzland	Duke Yellman
The Queen of Jazzland	Mrs. Duke Yellman
A Page	Master Seymore Silverberg
A Court Dancer	Dolores Farris
Prince Violin	Sam Lighter
Baron (Bear on) Saxophone	Herbert Baldwin
Prince Cornet	Jack Bradley
Earl Banjo	Clarence Herron
Duke Saxo	Roy Morton
The Duke of Drums	John Mountain
The Stranger, a Reformer	James D. Kemper
Stage managers	B. Howard Smith and Nell Adamson

The musical contained such numbers as Yellman's arrangement of "The Jazzing Fool," as an overture; the popular pieces "Stumbling" and "There's Sunlight in Your Eyes"; and arrangements of two operatic pieces, the Sextet from *Lucia di Lammermoor* and the Quartet from *Rigoletto*. In act 2, there were "Swing Me," a popular medley, several other numbers apparently written especially for the program, and two novelty items, one of which was titled "Grand Opera Burlesque." The story is that Yellman and his "court" of jazz musicians have arrived on an island that they declare to be the new kingdom of Jazzland, a place where they will be free from the criticism of those advocating "better" music. But there arrives a Stranger, someone who is trying to spread the "gospel" of classical music among jazz heathens.⁶⁶

When the musical begins, the King (Yellman, on piano) and his court have just finished several jazz pieces:

> KING: Thank heavens we are in a land where we can have our own way. There is no one here to stop us. From now on, this, our new island, shall be known as the Isle of Jazz and the natives under our rule shall be called Jazzimites. I am no longer duke [a pun on his first name], but the king of this Isle of Jazz. I have been decorated with the WDAF by the famous Stargazer of the spiritual world. Let there be a feast of happiness tonight. Do you hear my command?
> ALL THE COURTIERS: Yes, your highness. Jazz, Jazz, JAZZ. (The jazz orchestra follows with music, but before they finish, there is a loud noise outside. The music stops.)
> KING: What is that noise?
> PAGE (enters): Oh, King, a stranger has arrived in our Jazzland.
> KING: Who is he?
> PAGE: He refuses to tell me and only asks to see you. He looks foreign to me. I fear he is no member of our Jazzimite tribe.
> KING: We shall soon see. Bring him to me. (To court) Let our guest have a royal welcome. Lift your voices to greet him. (There follows a greeting of jazz music.)
> STRANGER (bows to King): Please, sir, tell me what was that terrible noise?
> COURTIERS: What!
> STRANGER That noise.
> KING: That was music.
> STRANGER: Music? Ye gods. Where am I?
> KING: In the Land of Jazz.
> STRANGER: Oh, Mercy!
> KING: Where did you come from?
> STRANGER: I have been seeking you. I am from the land of good music. I come here as a missionary and to save the natives from your power. Many have died from those horrible diseases, Shimmi-eptics and Hula-huch-tics. I came to save them and I command you to play for me good music as I deliver my word to your heathens.⁶⁷

At this point the various members of the orchestra, refusing to cooperate with Stranger, start leaving. Stranger begs them to stay: "I've got to have some support." Prince Violin blithely replies, "Go back home and get it. Ta, Ta." And Duke Banjo says, "I'll say 'Good night.' Our motto is 'Give the natives what they want.' You'll come around." The King (piano) starts to leave. "What are you going to do?" asks Stranger. "Why, they have all left," replies the King. "Why should I stay. I have no one to direct. I'm closing my box until you are starved out." This brings a wailing protest:

> STRANGER: You — you — you can't leave me. That box you call the piano is my best friend. Without you now I cannot live. I am before my Judges. You must be my support. Show the world you can be as happy in the Classics as in your Jazz. I come from a land with a new art. There the natives declare me different from all others. I have a message. Without you I cannot deliver it.
> KING: Oh, very well. I'll do it because I feel sorry for you. I play in only one key and that is four flats, WDAF.
> STRANGER: Good, all my messages are written in WDAF.
> KING: I'll play a classic or two for you. Just [to] show you I can. [Plays them] Now, I'll play two more songs. What are they [to be]?
> STRANGER: Two Negro Spirituals as my great master David Bispham might have sung them.
> KING: [Plays the spirituals] There, I'm through now. You'll have to buy a Duo-Art [i.e., player piano]. Either that or sing jazz.
> STRANGER: No, I'll stay here and teach these people the right.
> KING: You'll starve to death. So long. [door slams]⁶⁸

In the second act, the Stranger has fared badly and, looking like a beggar, returns to the Jazzimites. He tells them of his missionary travels and all the reverses he has suffered, and ends with, "I am in the land of Jazz. I'll never leave you." "You have done well," says the King, "and I will do you great honor. You may sing a song with my wife, the

Queen." The musical ends with all preaching the same faith and shouting "Jazz, Jazz, Jazz!"[69]

Yellman, by the mid–Twenties, was in New York City and doing well. His band recorded a number of sides for the Edison and Gennett companies, and he also was employed by Samuel L. "Roxy" Rothafel, while the latter was building his great Roxy Theater.[70]

While WDAF was groping its way into radio and trying to find a practical broadcasting schedule, the local citizens were struggling with yet another aspect of "progress." According to the *Star*, some customers reacted to the new automatic telephone service "with wailings and gnashing of teeth." Phone customers were skeptical when the company advised them that "You can't get a wrong number, if you work the dial right." The "Starbeams" column in the *Star* reminded the phone company "of the average person's capacity for making mistakes."[71]

At first WDAF broadcast only on Mondays, Wednesdays, and Fridays, and for only one to two hours each day. Mondays and Fridays featured popular bands, while on Wednesdays there usually was classical music, or at least somewhat graver music than jazz. The station gave baseball scores at 3 p.m. and at half-hour intervals thereafter, and sporadically on Sunday evenings.

Music definitely was the most prominent feature of these early broadcasts, though it was almost with a little shrug of regret that the *Star's* columnist who wrote "Starbeams" spoke of the changed atmosphere in the newspaper's plant. The number of listeners would never have been so large had popular music not been prominent. "Since radio took such a prominent role in modern journalism," said the paper's columnist, "the big news office still looks the same, but the sounds heard throughout the building remind one more of a conservatory of music."[72] "Starbeams" always tended to take a wry view of everyday events. Its writer was Kansas City's milder version of Baltimore's H. L. Mencken. So, while the city's residents struggled with the new telephone system and awaited the fruition of all those plans for the new wireless medium, they could smile at the column's good-natured wit. Very soon, concluded "Starbeams," the novelty of radio would wear off and then singers would have to sing well and lecturers would be obliged to have something worth hearing.[73]

Into the business of making broadcasting stations came the Sweeney Automobile, Tractor and Radio School, no longer willing simply to do others' broadcasting but determined to pursue in earnest its own claim of the airways, under the designation WHB.* A 500-watt Western Electric transmitter would supplant the weaker equipment the school had been using during the last few months. On the evening of Tueday, 15 August 1923, the new station went on the air at 8 p.m. It featured the Sweeney Orchestra under leader Louis Forbstein, formerly musical director of the Royal Theater. WHB was proud of this orchestra and informed the public, "We have the finest orchestra in America. These men are employed by us and paid straight salaries so that they can devote all their time to practice, so that when we broadcast a concert you will have real music by the best artists obtainable — all professionals." There would be music at the noon hour "so the farmer can have music with his meals." At 2:30 p.m. there would be a "ladies' hour," and at 7 p.m. the "kiddies' hour." And three days a week — Tuesday, Thursday, and Sunday — there would be "popular concerts and educational numbers." The members of the orchestra were as follows: Forbstein, the director, played violin; Paul Tremaine, alto saxophone; Glen Werner, cornet; Nick Musolino, trombone; George Parrish, piano;

---

*In later years call letters for stations west of the Mississippi River generally began with K, while those to the east started with W. In the early days, however, this was not yet standard. Thus, all three of the early stations in Kansas City started with W, and the nation's pioneer station, in Pittsburgh, Pa., was KDKA.

Charles Wagner, drums; Gilbert Dutton, saxophone; and Frank M. Estep, bass.[74] Two of them, Musolino and Estep, would soon play with Coon-Sanders.

Although the exact date is elusive, it was possibly sometime in mid–1922 that Coon-Sanders broadcast a special program described by one source as "the first time that any orchestra west of Chicago has broadcast nationally and ... only the third time that any orchestra in the country has attempted the feat." In the Joe Sanders Collection at the Kansas City Public Library, there is an undated and unidentified newspaper clipping that states that Coon-Sanders would share a nationwide broadcast with the Isham Jones Orchestra, in Chicago. It was the second of what the Conn Band Instrument Company, of New York, intended as a series of programs. The two orchestras alternated the playing of numbers, and Joe sang his "latest composition, 'Martha.'"[75]

This summer of 1922 was proving to be a turning point, not only for Kansas City but also for the Coon-Sanders Orchestra. The new broadcasting stations would carry the city's name and fame all over the nation and beyond, and one of those stations would assure the orchestra's fame. There was also a greater interest in the city's appearance and amenities. Local gadflies looked about for what were often called "uglies," a term that referred to buildings, places, or activities that ignored aesthetics. One such was a lean-to at the side of the Federal Building. Another was the Blue River, which in late August Alderman John J. Manning described as filthy and "a menace to the health of the entire eastern part of the city ... and worse than an open sewer." And when the thermometer atop the Scarritt Building recorded 103 degrees, the open sewer became a malodorous one. (Nearby Emporia, Kansas, recorded 111!)[76] But shacks and putrid streams weren't the only things to report. And when public buildings started receiving more than casual attention, someone discovered that the Telephone Building at Eleventh and Oak, with its "gingerbread kings and queens and at their sides the pawns and castles of lesser import," reminded one of a divine chessboard. Among buildings being razed was the Electric Theater, 646 Minnesota Avenue, which would be replaced by a new theater in Spanish Renaissance style. With political implications for the nation and the world, it was announced on August 2 that Major Harry S Truman, of Independence, had won the Democratic nomination of judge of the county court's eastern district. And Coon-Sanders, in early September, began an engagement with the Newman Theatre that would be scarcely less valuable to them than the broadcasts for WDAF later this year.[77]

This is perhaps the place to record another important event this summer. I say perhaps, for there is uncertainty about when Joe Sanders and Madeline Esther Baldwin were married. Janet K. Miller, Joe's great-niece, tells me that the marriage license at the Jackson County Courthouse gives the date as 18 January 1922, which would seem to settle the matter. In addition, a retrospective article in the *Kansas City Star-Times*, using material from the paper's files, agrees with Miller's findings. However, the two principals in the matter, in extant written records from 1931, state that August 23 of that year was their ninth wedding anniversary.[78] One would suppose that Joe and Madeline certainly knew when they took that very considerable step, but one would suppose also that such a public record as a marriage license may be trusted. It remains a mystery for which I've seen no accounting. Perhaps it is yet another item in the mythology that seems to characterize Joe's and Coonie's careers.

Coon-Sanders had already made some brief appearances at local theaters. That at the Doric Theater has already been described. If, as I suspect, they played one engagement at the Gayety Theater, it probably was not one that boosted their image particularly, because the Gayety was actually more of a burlesque house. But employment of any sort was not to be too readily spurned in the band's early days. Somewhat more advantageous was their appearance at the Twelfth Street Theater. There, on 4 September 1921, Coon-Sanders began an engagement that lasted through the seventeenth. The re-opened theater prefixed its name with "New" for the first several weeks of the season. The first film shown during their engagement there was *Crazy to Marry* with Fatty Arbuckle. Less than a week later the actor's prosecution began in connection with Virginia Rappe's death,* and two days after that the Arbuckle film was replaced by *Snowbound*, starring Mary Alden, Cullen Landis, Pauline Starke, and Russell Simpson. Coon-Sanders was billed as "Feature No. 3 — Kansas City's Most Popular Entertainers — Offering a selection of popular song hits." The ad, with a photograph of the entire band, represented an important step up for Coon-Sanders.[79]

On September 3rd the "Coon-Sanders Novelty Singing Orchestra" started a thirty-eight week engagement at the Newman Theatre, one that would last through the following May 26th, when they closed to prepare for their first road trip. Sometimes Joe exaggerated the length of the Newman engagement, but thirty-eight weeks was sufficiently impressive to need no embellishment. Actually, this was not the first contact Joe Sanders had had with the Newman. At a previous time, probably about 1918 when he was simply "a Kansas City pianist," he wrote a song titled "No One Just Like You" that was sung at the theater by Lloyd Garrett.[80]

But now Sanders, along with the rest of his group, could be said to have *arrived*. Ever after, the band would list their long engagement at the Newman very prominently among their credits. There is a bit of irony in that the film shown during their first appearance at the Newman was *Nice People*, with the explanation "jazz life exposed." It starred Wallace Reid, Bebe Daniels, Conrad Nagel, and Julia Faye.[81]

This contract with the Newman led almost immediately to what was apparently the first Coon-Sanders broadcasts over WDAF. The *Star's* new radio station was constantly trying to think of novel entertainment to put into the air, and they hit upon the idea of broadcasting occasionally from the city's theaters. The program on Friday, 22 September 1922, was not the first one aired over WDAF from a theater, but it probably was the first that included Coon-Sanders. What the band played is not stated, but one number may have been "Stories," with a vocal by both Coonie and Joe.[82] While the band was enjoying this very important boost to its fame, the nation was gossiping about a double murder that had just been discovered near New Brunswick, N. J., that of the Rev. Edward W. Hall and his parishioner, Mrs. Elinor Mills. The Hall-Mills case became one of the events of the Twenties.

On Sunday afternoon, October 1, there was another broadcast from the Newman Theatre over WDAF, and again, in addition to music by Leo Forbstein and the Newman Concert Orchestra and by the theater's pipe organ, Coon-Sanders was featured, probably in a skit titled "Making a Jazz Band." The band was now being billed by the Newman as a "Novelty Singing Orchestra," and it seems that the solos and duets by the two leaders always went over well with the audiences.[83]

Male duos, with one singing lead and the other tenor harmony, had long been a familiar and very popular entertainment, both in vaudeville and on phonograph records. Collins and Harlan, for instance, made many recordings in the years before 1920. But singers of that type, as well as the songs they sang, were featured on such recordings and

---

*Roscoe C. "Fatty" Arbuckle (1887–1933), who spent his childhood in Smith Center, Kansas, was one of filmdom's most popular comedians. Charged in the death in 1921 of actress Virginia Rappe, he was finally exonerated, but his film acting career was ended.

the musical accompaniments were almost always secondary and usually unremarkable. Later, during the Twenties, such duos as Gus Van (real name August van Glone) and Joseph T. Schenck, whose partnership had achieved stardom before 1920, were still very popular throughout the Twenties both on recordings and in vaudeville.[84] There were others such as Billy Murray, Ed Smalle, Aileen Stanley, Irving Kaufman, Ada Jones, Johnny Marvin, and Walter Scanlan who, in various combinations, made a great number of popular discs. But these later singers and their songs, as with the earlier ones, were the main attraction, not the accompaniment, which was usually a small ensemble or even perhaps just a piano. This was a time when bands, if they employed vocalists at all, did so almost as an afterthought. As often as not, the vocalists sounded, by later standards, eccentric and even unintentionally comical. It was unusual, therefore, that when Coon-Sanders began to perform, the band offered two good vocalists. Duets by Coonie and Joe were often the highlight of the band's appearance. In these duets Joe usually carried the melody and Coonie the tenor harmony, and their voices blended unusually well. What's more, their vocals often were more than simply singing, for they also performed and clowned. It is therefore not surprising that the band was often listed as the Coon-Sanders Novelty *Singing* Orchestra.

On 18 October 1922 the *Star* announced that WDAF had been granted a wavelength of 400 meters instead of the 360 that it had used and that many smaller stations used. This meant that WDAF's concerts would experience less interference from smaller stations and thus would provide better reception. This put the station into very exclusive company of not more than about a half-dozen in the nation. But there were stipulations, one of which was that no "mechanical" music could be broadcast, including not only phonographs but also such equipment as player pianos. Only concerts by artists in person would be permitted. It was also necessary that the station's transmitting apparatus deliver 500 watts to the antenna, and that the acoustics of the studio "be as near perfect as possible." Moreover, there had to be an electrical signaling system between the studio and the operating rooms, and no harmonics on that wavelength. It was another important development with important implications for Coon-Sanders about a month and a half later.[85]

Joe, Coonie, and the boys would continue to do their skits for the Newman, perform their hotel obligations, and try to avoid driving on Grand Avenue, between Eighteenth and Twenty-fifth streets, especially between 4:30 and 6 p.m. Traffic there and at other similar points was becoming a matter of great concern to the city. The presence of "vigilance cars" apparently had little effect. Complained the *Star*, "This stretch is a challenge even to the careful driver, but scores of careless and reckless driving instances were noted the other afternoon...." The paper said that at the rush hour, probably fifty motor vehicles passed a given point in one minute. Trucks, roadsters, and touring cars "twist and dodge in the heavy traffic." To make matters worse, many cars had blinding headlights and no taillights. The mayor believed that making many streets one-way would be an improvement. The *Star* published several fanciful cartoons suggesting how to curb what it termed "speederinos," one of which was to let pedestrians walk under an aluminum, turtle-like protective cover, whose spikes on top flattened the cars' tires.[86]

While Leo R. Davis and his orchestra prepared their program of popular music over WDAF for Monday, November 5, with a promise to promote better dance music, Joe and Coonie cooked up a skit for the Newman titled "Desert Jazz," suggested by the feature film *Burning Sands*, described as "A man's flaming answer to 'The Sheik!'" The next week the boys came up with a "blues program," in which the two men sang solos. On Christmas Eve at the Newman, the band presented a special jazz arrangement titled "The Night before Christmas."[87] The topical skit was becoming one of their regular specialties in stage shows at cinemas.

Sometimes the other actors on a program worked with Coon-Sanders in their skits, and occasionally some of the band members helped other acts. At times even members of the audience participated. Johnny Coon said that when he was about nine years old, his father called him down to the Newman Theater to meet someone on the show with them. It was Harry Houdini, famous magician and escape artist. Coonie told Houdini that Johnny would be in the audience and asked the magician to give his son some part in the act. Houdini obliged by inviting Johnny to go onto the stage to corroborate the magician's claim of authenticity of some contraption used in the act. Johnny duly went up, made the inspection, and declared it bona fide. He was quite a celebrity next day among his playmates.[88]

Perhaps the *Star's* radio station was starting to hear some favorable comments concerning the last time WDAF broadcast from the Newman and caught a little of Coon-Sanders' act. And doubtless the thousands who had heard the band at the Newman for the past several weeks were making the station take a good look. At any rate, at 4 p.m. on Sunday, 26 November, WDAF again broadcast from the Newman Theatre, and this time Coon-Sanders was prominently mentioned.[89] But by this time, WDAF was getting ideas about a plan that would involve the band much more deeply. Clearly, this orchestra had qualities not found in the others in town.

CHAPTER FOUR

The Nighthawks

With regular engagements at the Muehlebach and at the Newman Theatre, the Coon-Sanders Novelty Singing Orchestra would have been entirely justified in thinking that they had reached an imposing plateau, if not a summit. They were getting more attention than any other band in town, their engagements were with two of the city's most prestigious employers, and both places were close enough to allow the band's members to get back and forth easily. They played at the Newman in the afternoon and for the dinner dance session at the Plantation Grill, then went back to the theater at about 9 p.m. Following all that, they played for the late crowd at the Plantation Grill. Thus, they had busy days and evenings; but for young, eager musicians such as they, it must not have been a difficult schedule. Besides, the band's members obviously enjoyed what they were doing.

The *Star's* radio station apparently reached the conclusion that since their license allowed them to have only live music in their broadcasts, they were obliged to try to get the best bands available. The station had been regularly using such other good orchestras as those led by Duke Yellman, Ben Kendrick, and Bert Phelps. But now they wanted one other, considered by many the best. Thus it was that WDAF approached Coonie and Joe about setting up a microphone in the Muehlebach's Plantation Grill. It might seem that both men would have been delighted by the suggestion, simply for the publicity, but such was not the case. In June 1926, and apparently in a reference to Coon-Sanders' earlier program for the Kansas City *Post*, Coonie described how he had reacted to the *Star's* request:

> We had a pretty fair, eight-piece band when somebody happened to hire us to play a radio concert. We didn't like it at all and when the Kansas City Star later asked us to play for nothing, I took great pleasure in insulting one of that good paper's chief executives. But the Star stuck a microphone in the Muehlebach anyhow and sent over a cub police reporter named Leo Fitzpatrick to run the show.[1]

Since the *Star* wasn't going to put Coon-Sanders on salary, it wasn't taking any great risk. In those days almost everything radio did was an experiment, but many assumed that most "listeners-in" simply would not last beyond about eleven o'clock, whatever the attraction. Yet, entertaining such nightowls—I know! I know! But we'll get to that word shortly—was exactly what the newspaper's station was proposing. Coon-Sanders was being well received at the Newman Theatre, as well as when that theater broadcast its programs, or parts of its programs. And the band's other location, the Muehlebach's Plantation Grill, had them playing with great acclaim to an audience of late diners. And yet, while the hotel probably had nothing to lose from having its late evenings broadcast, would there be—well, anyone "out there" to hear them? No one really knew.

The plan was for the broadcast to begin at 11:45 p.m. and end at 1 a.m. Thus it was that late in the evening of Monday, 4 December 1922, WDAF employees set up their equipment, including a microphone about the size of a dinner plate. Over the following weeks and months, various different physical arrangements were made for the broadcasting and announcing. But from the very beginning it was obviously necessary to make provision not only for Leo J. Fitzpatrick, until now a police reporter, to perform his engaging chatter, but also for Coonie and Joe to be close enough to be heard when they sang or, on occasion, spoke. No doubt the arrangement changed considerably after the broadcasts became routine, but at first Fitzpatrick probably had little other than a table, chair, and microphone. From the few photographs I've seen of the broadcasting area in the Plantation Grill, it would appear that Fitzpatrick quickly added several other items for his desk, including the famous cowbell whose clatter ceremoniously inaugurated members into the new radio club. Eventually, Fitzpatrick's desk held a second microphone for Joe and Coonie to use on occasion; but at first they most likely simply moved as close to the one microphone as possible or perhaps made some use of the small megaphones that they often used, especially in later years, not only on radio but also on their tours.

The day before the first broadcast, the Newman Theatre's ad put the Coon-Sanders act in first place and in bold type. About the broadcast the *Star* had this to say: "An hour's program [actually it would be one-and-a-quarter hours] will be broadcast, interspersed with the reading of communications from listeners[-]in. A special microphone will be installed near the orchestra in the Plantation grill and will 'pick up' the strains of music, the 'atmosphere' of the dance floor and the vocal solos by Carlton [*sic*] Coon and Joseph Sanders." For the benefit of the public to whom radio was still arcane, the paper explained some of the technical aspects of the procedure: "An amplifier has been installed in the hotel and will amplify the sound currents before they are sent over a special telephone cable to The Star's station. In the broadcasting station the sound currents will again be amplified before being sent to the radio transmitter to be converted into radio energy."[2]

Apparently no one now knows precisely when Coonie's famous remark gave the band its new name, but my guess is that it occurred on the very first evening, certainly by the second or third. At any rate, here is how he described it:

> Fitz [i.e., Leo Fitzpatrick] knew less about radio than we did and one night he left the microphone turned on when we thought it was off and an impromptu conversation got out. During the chatter I happened to mention that anybody idiotic enough to stay up that late to hear radio must be a real nighthawk. The next day we got about two tons of telegrams from people who claimed they were nighthawks and always would be. They liked the chatter and wanted more. They got it. From then on the WDAF Nighthawks hawked nightly.[3]

Since this was the first broadcast, there probably were few telegrams or phone calls from fans to read or acknowledge, except perhaps from local well-wishers, but in future programs there would be plenty. Exactly how many songs the band played on this first night and just what sort of chatter filled the pauses do not appear in anything I've seen. And exactly how Fitzpatrick, who soon would become known as the "Merry Old Chief" and the "Chief Hawk," introduced and closed the program seem also lost to history.

But within a very few days, responses began pouring in, and very quickly there was an effort to acknowledge as many fans as possible between numbers by the band. By the tenth of the month, less than a week after the first broadcast, over 60,000 letters had arrived from eager listeners in thirty-one states and the two closest foreign neighbors. The *Star* printed the following commentary:

> It's an informal gathering, the crowd of "Nighthawks" that gather around receiving sets and tune into the Star's midnight dance programs. Already the organization embraces three nations—United States, Canada and Mexico…. Promptly at 11:45 o'clock, the "Chief Hawk" rings a cowbell in front of the microphone in the Plantation grill and calls his flock together. The diners peer curiously at the announcer sitting at a table and talking into a small wooden box. Over in a corner an operator cuts in a switch and the meeting of "Nighthawks" is on…. When the Star's radio editor reads the names of some of the applicants and the telegrams received[,] a charter is granted the applicants. The initiation consists of a ring of the cowbell. Even the dancers have entered into the spirit of good fellowship. They gather around the microphone eager to hear the names of the new members. The election of new members is made during the intermission. Then the Coon-Sanders Orchestra star[t]s to play. The meeting is immediately converted into a dance.[4]

As did other early radio announcers, Fitzpatrick urged those listening over their radios to phone, wire, or otherwise let the station know about the reception. At some very early time, possibly in the first program, the possibility of a club was broached. Fitzpatrick jokingly observed that the organization intended to declare war on sleep and against the manufacturers of mattresses and bed springs, even though many of those listening had probably attached their aerial wires to their bedsprings, a common practice in radio's early days. In fact, "Enemies of Sleep" was quickly adopted as one of the band's aliases.[5] And during each program, said the *Star*, "The atmosphere of the grill room is broadcast. The applause of the dancers, the clinking of dishes, the shuffling of feet and the by-play of the orchestra, all go into the ether to entertain the whole crowd of 'Nighthawks.'" And when the end of a program arrived, Fitzpatrick, the Merry Old Chief, made some appropriate farewell remarks.

Within the first week one listener, C. D. Botts, of Minneapolis, Minn., submitted a drawing that he recommended as an official emblem for the Nighthawks. It showed a very stylized bird-like creature, in profile, with folded wings and tail suggestive of a cutaway coat. Under the right wing was a staff from which hung a cowbell labeled "charter." The "hawk" wore something similar to an ancient Roman soldier's helmet, encompassed by earphones, and had on its forehead some sort of transmitter from which radio waves emanated. The bird stood upon a platform, labeled "Night Hawks," that topped a globe of the world. The day that the suggested emblem arrived saw more than 1,100 new members added.[6] Coonie and Joe liked Botts's drawing so much that they adopted it and used it for the rest of the band's existence. It would appear on advertisements that preceded their arrival at towns on their tours and long engagements about the country.

Though it's daunting today for one to imagine how it could have been done, there was an effort, apparently successful, to grant memberships, or "charters," to all who wrote or wired. There were other necessary tasks as well. Joe Sanders, already quite busy with his arranging, somehow during that first week tossed off a theme song that caught everyone's imagination and that in a little over a year would be one of the band's first two recordings for Victor. It was so popular, in fact, that it was often requested and was played on most evenings at some point in the program. On the recording Joe sings the verse, and he and Coonie sing harmony on the chorus. Here are the words:

A "Nighthawk" Emblem Suggested.

C. D. Botts of Minneapolis, Minn., one of the charter members of The Star's radio "Nighthawks," has submitted the above drawing as the official emblem of the organization. The "Nighthawk" is carrying his charter membership (a cowbell) and standing on "top of the world." More than eleven hundred members were added to the organization today.

Stylized "hawk" designed by C.D. Botts, Minneapolis, Minnesota; adopted as band's logo. (From *Kansas City Star*, 12 December 1922, page 4.)

"Nighthawk Blues"

Have you heard the very latest news?
All about the very latest blues?
Originated just the other day
In a most peculiar way.
Started with a bunch of midnight rounders,
Who never sleep, they are the founders
Of the Nighthawk Club, you know,
Listen in on the radio.

Chorus

When Coon and Sanders start to play
Those Nighthawk Blues, you'll start to sway;
Tune right in on the radio,
Grab a telegram and say "Hello."
From coast to coast and back again
You can hear that syncopated strain;
It's a bear, you'll declare!
Listen to the Nighthawk blues—tune in!
Listen to the Nighthawk blues![7]

In addition to "The Nighthawk Blues," another song that the band, and Joe and Coonie in particular, derived quite a bit of mileage out of was "Mister Gallagher and Mister Shean," whose title is sometimes given as "Positively, Mister Gallagher? Absolutely, Mister Shean." The history of the song is a little cloudy, but it appears that Bryan Foy, one of Eddie Foy's* sons, wrote the number in 1921 for Ed Gallagher and Al Shean,[†] the two comedians who popularized it. The song grew out of an original act that Gallagher and Shean had done titled "Mr. Gallagher and Mr. Shean in Egypt." And since in that skit Gallagher had worn a straw sailor hat and Shean a fez, they used that same headgear when singing the song. They are said to have paid Foy fifty dollars for it, a price very acceptable to Foy at the time. The publishers thought so little of it that they let Gallagher and Shean have, in addition to royalties, all "mechanical" royalties it might garner. Subsequently, phonograph recordings could scarcely keep up with the demand. Bryan Foy was heartbroken and filed suit saying that he had sold only the performing

---

*Eddie Foy (1856–1928), variety and vaudeville star, died in Kansas City while appearing on the Orpheum Circuit.
†Ed Gallagher (1873–1929) and Al Shean (1868–1949) disagreed in 1925 and ended their successful partnership. Shean's sister was Minnie, mother of the Marx Brothers.

rights. At the time that Gallagher and Shean bought the song, they were getting less than $500 a week for their "talking act"; but when they used Foy's song, they were suddenly a real commodity. They became instant stars and got top prices. Ziegfeld hired them and paid them $1,500 a week for his *Follies*. The two men added more words, sang-talked them for several years, and became a vaudeville legend.[8]

Coonie and Joe quickly took the song and adapted it for their purposes so successfully that it became almost as closely associated with them as was "The Nighthawk Blues." The simple melody of "Mister Gallagher and Mister Shean" and the trick of dialog made the song perfect for almost any kind of occasion that invited comedy—a convention, an election campaign, a vaudeville theater, etc.—and many comedy teams about the nation concocted new lyrics to match whatever the occasion demanded. Joe and Coonie found it very effective on their broadcasts and seemed to savor that closing phrase, "Positively, Mister Gallagher? Absolutely, Mister Shean!" (In order to emphasize the "mistering" that the song used, in print the word *Mister* customarily was not abbreviated.) In 1965 Landon Laird, for the Kansas City *Times*, recalled how Joe and Coonie sang the number: "Both had good voices and they used to go to town on the song 'Mr. Gallagher and Mr. Shean' and play it to exhaustion. We can hear Joe yell 'Mr. Gallagher! Oh, Mr. Gallagher' and Cooney reply, 'What is it, Mr. Shean?' The boys had many choruses of the piece and as many endings."[9]

In addition to the above ending, Gallagher and Shean occasionally used another, one that Laird recalled hearing Joe and Coonie use. During one of their typical exchanges, Shean asks for a loan of a "couple of bucks," to which Gallagher sings, "Upon my word, as I'm alive, I intended touching you for five." This elicits Shean's indignant "Merry Christmas, Mister Gallagher!" and Gallagher's relieved "Happy New Year, Mister Shean!"[10]

Since Joe and Coonie never recorded the number, we don't know how they sounded when they sang it, but Gallagher and Shean did make recordings of some of their routines. In extant transcriptions one can hear not only Shean's Jewish accent but also two oddities in Gallagher's speech: he pronounced Shean's name as almost a disyllable (i.e., as She-un) and he pronounced *radiator* with a short *a*, recalling Al Smith, in his 1928 bid for the presidency, when he addressed his "friends of the *raddio* audience."[11] A typical verse, as sung by Gallagher and Shean, was the following (with spoken asides in italics):

> SHEAN: O Mister Gallagher!
> GALLAGHER: *Yes? I'm here!*
> SHEAN: Mister Gallagher!
> GALLAGHER: *Well, what is it?*
> SHEAN: Every morning in the bathroom I reduce.
> GALLAGHER: *You reduce?*
> SHEAN: I bend over, up and down; every day I lose a pound. The only suit of clothes I own is getting loose.
> GALLAGHER: *You be careful!* Mister Shean! Mister Shean! Exercising in the bathroom's quite a scene. When you bend over, have a care, if there's a radiator there.
> SHEAN: Oh, there **is** one, Mister Gallagher!
> GALLAGHER: Be sure and face it, Mister Shean![12]

In 1922, Joe and Coonie used "Mister Gallagher and Mister Shean" to help entertain a trainload of Paramount film executives and staff who passed through Kansas City on their way to the studio's annual convention in Los Angeles. With Adolph Zukor, company president, were Vice President Jesse Lasky and a staff of directors and managers. The stopover in Kansas City was mainly to meet and pick up Frank Newman and some Paramount employees. The city's welcoming party included the mayor—he invited the Paramount group to make Kansas City their place for the 1923 convention—and at least a hundred of the city's cinema personnel. And following all this, the

Coon-Sanders orchestra entertained the visitors with a parody on "Mister Gallagher and Mister Shean," with the names changed to "Mister Zukor and Mister Lasky."[13]

Perhaps this is a good time to say something about the popular music of the decade, in particular the type of song that was fetching nonsense. To readers of the last years of the twentieth century, especially those who are accustomed to, and perhaps even aficionados of, popular songs that have "messages" and that strive earnestly for "relevance," much of the music of the Twenties may seem trivial and silly. Obviously, some of it was, just as is true with some music of any other time. One might say, for instance, that many of the songs of the last two decades of the twentieth century seem unmelodic, pretentious, self-important and *deafening*. Many of them seem also to be leading successful crusades to do away with both lyrics and melodies. Eventually, as with the Cheshire Cat's grin, there will be nothing left but the beat.

I have often said that I cannot see how anyone could have played much of the music of the Twenties in a bad mood, or at any rate to have played it and remained in a bad mood. Sometimes the music was inferior and sometimes the lyrics were, and sometimes a song seems today to have miscarried on both counts. But it can't be denied that for sheer good nature, amusing lyrics, and catchy tunes, it would be difficult to find a sprightlier era of songwriting and orchestration than the years 1920 to 1929, especially the second half of that decade. And some of the songs have achieved a certain classic status. Let's examine several of the best-known specimens.

The song that perhaps recalls the Twenties best, "Yes, We Have No Bananas," by Frank Silver and Irving Cohn, is a product of the year 1923 and is pure balderdash. (Though Coon-Sanders never recorded it, they undoubtedly played it.) Sigmund Spaeth, in his writings on American popular music, calls it a "durable freak" and suggests that the ditty's music has some pretty impressive ancestors, the "Hallelujah" from Handel's *Messiah*, for example. And there are several theories of just how the lyrics originated, one being an overheard expostulation by a Greek-American grocer, or some other recent immigrant. After the song, and its inane title, became familiar, all kinds of witticisms were built on it. Mark Sullivan tells of one in which an Army mess officer wished to emphasize to a private that the honorific *sir* was required from a lowly soldier:

> CAPTAIN (sternly): Do I understand there is no dessert today?
> PRIVATE: Yes.
> CAPTAIN: Yes, what?
> PRIVATE: Yes, we have no bananas.[14]

And several years before Joe Sanders tried his hand at songs about comic strips, 1923 saw Billy Rose and Con Conrad produce another song, also catchy nonsense, that was based on a popular cartoon character of the day, Barney Google. (The comic strip survives today as *Snuffy Smith* with Google seldom making an appearance.) Barney Google was drawn as a diminutive fellow with big, bulging eyes, and owner of a nag named Spark Plug. The lyrics were filled with irony about the exploits of Spark Plug and his owner. Google, in the song's wry lyrics, made such romantic idols as Douglas Fairbanks and Rudolph Valentino look like amateurs, and such politicians as Charles Evans Hughes and William Jennings Bryan as perpetual jokes. The ditty was very successfully recorded by Billy Jones and T. E. "Ernie" Hare. Jones (1889–1940) and Hare (1881–1939), known as the "Happiness Boys," were among the very earliest radio personalities; and when they made this recording, they had been in radio broadcasting for two years.[15]

And there were other such songs, some equally popular in their day, others less so, but all of which helped to give the Twenties their special character. Could a graver decade have come up with "Who Takes Care of the Caretaker's Daughter, While the Caretaker's Busy Taking Care"? Or with the rollicking

"Collegiate" as it extolled all the nutty fashions that Sullivan describes as "competition in uncouthness"? In singing, the title was usually pronounced quickly as "c'legiate," and the music accompanying these preposterous dithyrambs was equally animated and delightfully saucy. Or how about Byron Gay and Richard Whiting's 1926 song "Horses," an inane set of lyrics that, if they say anything, seem to be about a fellow who can get nowhere with his inamorata because of her enthusiasm for equines?[16]

Incidentally, "Horses" was one of a number of songs of the era that used the phrase "horse's neck," a popular euphemism and "in-joke" among the era's savvy musicians. Every so often an orchestra, in an impish mood, expressed it musically. First, a band might suddenly insert, somewhere in the middle of a number, the music to "Oh, the monkey wrapped its tail around the flagpole" (which also had naughty connotations). Then, at the very end the musicians might add a little coda, dum-de-dum-dum-dum (sol, me, re, do, do), which initiates understood as "You're a horse's ass."[17] (A good example can be heard, following an instrumental neighing, on a recording of "Yes! We Have No Bananas," by the Great White Way Orchestra, on 26 April 1923.)[18] But unlike a later era when that last word seems unremarkable, the then-unmentionable southern end of a northbound horse was altered in public usage to a euphemistic "neck." And sometimes a song's words employed that term — with a wink. For example, the lyrics of "Horses," as delivered by Fran Frey, popular vocalist with George Olsen's orchestra, has the singer modestly refer to himself as "the horse's neck."[19] (Sigmund Spaeth and Mark Sullivan suggest a relation between "Horses" and Peter Ilyitch Tchaikovsky's *Troika*, though without the "horse's neck" business.[20])

Even the popular, rustic humorist Will Rogers* somehow managed to get into this equine allusion. The story — I think we may regard it as largely apocryphal — told in the Twenties was that while at the Kemper Military Academy, Rogers had irritated teachers with his tendency to hesitate and scratch his head before answering a question. A captain, trying to show Rogers and the other students how to ride a horse, once exclaimed in exasperation, "Rogers, you look like part of a horse!"

Rogers dismounted, drew his sword, and asked, "Which part?"

"The other part," replied the captain.

"Oh," said Rogers, who returned the sword to its scabbard and re-mounted his horse. Fifteen minutes later he scratched his head, frowned, and returned to the captain. "I've been thinkin' about what you told me. Which part is the other part?"

"You're certainly no horse's neck, are you?"

"Of course not," replied Rogers.

"Well?"

Fifteen years later Rogers scratched his head again and frowned, but couldn't find the captain.[21]

But all of this, as well as a lot of other charming musical frivolity, should not make one forget that the decade produced a large number of deeper and more substantial songs, many of them justly considered classics today. Among the many are such as "Look for the Silver Lining," "April Showers," "Swingin' Down the Lane," "Blue Room," "Old Man River," "Lady, Be Good," "The Best Things in Life Are Free," "Can't Help Lovin' That Man," "Who (Stole My Heart Away)?," "What'll I Do?" "Play Gypsies, Dance Gypsies," "Sunny Disposish," and "Remember." The list could be greatly extended.

---

*Will Rogers (1879–1935), vaudeville and film star, humorist, and after-dinner speaker, starred with the Ziegfeld Follies and once said: "Had there been no Ziegfeld and no Follies, I would today have been twelve miles north of Claremore, Oklahoma, plowing for corn, slopping the hogs, running my own still, and knocking the Republican Party — as that is considered one of the chores in my country." See I Can Hear It Now, 1919–1949, Vol. 3, 1919–1932, side 1, band 2.

As already suggested, Coon-Sanders acquired the radio name "Nighthawks" almost immediately, for the term was used in telegrams that arrived no more than three or four days after the very first broadcast. On December 8 or 9, for instance, a message arrived from the Los Angeles Research Laboratories, in California: "Count us in as 'Nighthawks.' Your program's the best ever. Coming in here loud enough to dance by." And H. W. Purcell, Buffalo, N. Y., said: "Give us our initiation ring [of the cowbell] into the Star's 'Nighthawks.' Can we be charter members? Coon-Sanders music great. Long live our organization." In Winnipeg, Canada, E. E. Levine was listening to the third broadcast and said: "We were with you ... with everything except our eyes and feet. It simply was wonderful, and the best broadcasting it has been our privilege to hear." And in the same group of messages was one from Mr. and Mrs. Benjamin W. Fouts, in Tampico, Mexico, who wanted WDAF to know that they were receiving the broadcasts regularly.[22]

The *Kansas City Star's* agent in Washington, D.C., sent back word about a young Nighthawk there, Edward H. Preston, son of James H. Preston, who for many years was superintendent of the Senate press galleries. Edward's parents had for several days become concerned that their son seemed to be getting insufficient sleep. "Go to bed tonight, Son. Your mother is worried over your losing so much sleep." The elder Preston was a little disturbed with how readily his son nodded compliance, and he was further concerned to hear an alarm clock sound in his son's room during the night. The next morning at breakfast, the young boy brightly volunteered: "Well, I put one over on you. I'm an eligible for the Night Hawk Club. I cut in at 1:30 and I got The Star as clear as could be; heard them ring a bell announcing a new member from Oregon and listened in nearly an hour, as other new members were announced, and the program put on." Were the parents upset? Apparently not unduly. In fact, the father decided to get an alarm clock for his own use.[23]

On Christmas Eve the *Star* assessed the success of the innovative broadcasts:

> There is no other similar enterprise in the United States.... In a way it was more of a test for a while to determine how interested the public would be to hear radio. It was certain that if a night program, extending beyond the midnight hour, attracted considerable attention[,] the public was then vitally interested in the science. Success has been attained. With a world audience to its program, the Nighthawk Club was made into a permanent body.... Every night while the musical program is taking place, calls from out-of-town parties praise the novel entertainment which The Star founded. From Atlanta, Detroit, San Francisco and New York reports have come telling of little house dances with Coon-Sanders providing the music, although many miles apart. After-theater parties have found diversion in listening in to the midnight program. Many homes are kept alive until the early morning hours while its occupants tune in as members.... It is also a fraternal organization with a spirit attached to it of good fellowship and benevolence, as evidenced by the many letters received. Its members have their hearts and souls in its development and are ever informing the chief nighthawk of how enjoyable the programs really are ... and now that the Christmas holidays are here, an increase of letters have [sic] been received asking for additional programs.[24]

By December 12 more than 1,100 members had been added to the organization. By the seventeenth the *Star* reported that the new club had "spread their wings over every state in the Union, Mexico, Canada and [Cuba]. Thousands of new members were added to 'the enemies of sleep' and enrolled in their campaign against the manufacturers of bedsprings and mattresses." By Christmas Eve there were more than 5,000 members, with about 300 letters, telegrams, and telephone calls coming in daily. There were over 8,000 members by January 7, and on the previous day the largest delegation to date visited the Plantation Grill in order to hear the band, as they put it, "without headphones." No longer could the Merry Old Chief read all the messages over the radio, and those that he did read were often at least a week old.[25]

Leo Fitzpatrick, the Chief, was himself becoming quite as much an object of interest as was the Coon-Sanders Orchestra. He seems to have been amusing, affable, and glib, someone whose talents were being far better used now than when he had been a police reporter for the *Star*. Of course, the highlight of any Nighthawk broadcast was the music by the band; but when there was talking to be done, it was usually Fitzpatrick's voice the public heard. And it must have been an engaging voice, one that captured attention and whose witty banter evoked laughter and happy reflection. Fitzpatrick's prattle reached all the way to a listener in Martha's Vineyard, Mass., who suggested to the Old Chief that anyone who had difficulty recalling the station's call letters, WDAF, might just remember the phrase "Whole Darn American Family." One issue of the *Star* had a photo of Fitzpatrick dressed in Plains Indian headdress—is this where Calvin Coolidge got the idea?—and described as the "gabbiest fellow" when he was holding forth for the Nighthawks. The *Star* further observed that the photograph "was taken when he wasn't looking, so the feathers are rather in repose. At the sight of a mattress or a bed spring the feathers spread out fan shape, in much the same manner as a lemon pie when struck with a flat surfaced paddle." The Birmingham, Ala., *Age Herald* spoke approvingly of his friendly voice calling out, "All right, Ben, bear on the bell," or "All right, Professor, give this one a charter." (Either Joe or Coonie might be the "Professor," but it was perhaps more often Coonie.) And in Oil City, Penn., Paul Jones, Ed Phillips, Ralph Sigworth, and Guy Fellers heard themselves initiated into the Nighthawk Club with the following injunction from Chief Fitzpatrick: "Ha, ha. Here's a communication from the home of Coal Oil Johnny, Oil City, Pa.... Professor, will you give them a heavy one on the charter[?]"[26]

At first the messages received were such a novelty to both WDAF and the *Star* that almost every issue of the newspaper made references to them, often fully quoting great quantities of them. Among correspondents farthest away were H. M. Stovin and S. W. Wilkinson, in Unity, Saskatchewan, who wrote, "Cowbell us into the 'Nighthawks.'" W. H. Durracott, Winnipeg, Manitoba, said: "You kept me out of bed last night listening to the Coon-Sanders music. I don't suppose nationality makes any difference with you fellows and that a bally* Englishman will make a good 'Nighthawk.'" From Regina, Saskatchewan, came a telegram from J. H. Arnett: "Your 'Nighthawk carrier' wave swoops down here every night and is causing considerable stir among the chickens, to say nothing of the old roosters."[27]

On December 9, A. F. Costa, United States postmaster at Wailuku, Maui, Hawaii, wrote to say he marveled that he could hear the applause at the Plantation Grill despite the distance of some four thousand miles, including 1500 miles of ocean. He told Coon-Sanders that "there is a nighthawk who is not registered with your organisation ... but ... has been attending your meetings regularly every night for the last four nights, unseen, hidden behind his radio receiver in his home in Wailuku.... I was first attracted to you on Tuesday night, December 5 [i.e., the second broadcast], by that jazzy music ... so tempting to the feet...."[28] Perhaps the clear reception in the Hawaiian Islands was connected in some way with increased activity, on the Island of Hawaii, of Kilauea Volcano, which in early January was pouring lava from three breaks in the mountain.[29]

This was one of several letters that Costa wrote over many months to WDAF about the Nighthawk Frolics. The following March he told them he had engaged in a little experiment. He had been listening to WDAF and getting their signal very well, when he had the idea of changing to the station owned by

---

*Which means something along the line of another Briticism, "bloody."

Leo Fitzpatrick ("Merry Old Chief" or "Chief Hawk"), announcer for WDAF's "Nighthawk Frolics." (Courtesy Special Collections, Kansas City [Mo.] Public Library.)

From the Isle of Pines (now called the Isle of Youth), ninety miles south of Havana, Cuba, came a clipping from the Island's paper: "Waldo E. Harris, with the apparatus installed by him in his home, 'Brazo Fuerte,' is enjoying musical programs broadcast in America by The Kansas City Star.... He picked up the 'Nighthawk' concert broadcast by that paper.... The music was exceptionally clear."[31]

On the evening of Monday, December 14, the Nighthawk program was called on to help unite two members of their organization who hadn't seen each other for years. On the preceding Wednesday evening, Harry J. Leake had been enrolled as a member. A short time later Dr. A. F. Barrows, in St. Francisville, Louisiana, wrote:

the Fort Worth, Texas, Star-Telegram, that was picking up the Nighthawks and rebroadcasting their program. WDAF had come in much stronger. Just the evening before, Costa had tuned into the Coon-Sanders Orchestra so that his guests could listen. It was a great treat, because they had never heard radio before. "They never imagined," he wrote, "that your voice could be heard so loud and distinct over here, a distance of about four thousand miles away. Their surprise at the loudness and distinctness of your voice was beyond expression."[30]

In enrolling members into our Nighthawks organization Wednesday I heard you mention the name of Harry J. Leake. Some years ago, under most unusual and mysterious circumstances, a young nephew of mine with that name disappeared. No reason could be assigned for his leaving home. He was married happily, stood well in this community, was editor of the leading newspaper, and had a brilliant future. All effort at locating him has been futile. The announcement of yours the other night may help solve the mystery. If you can help us locate him, it will be another plume in the wonderful record of The Star's radio achievements.[32]

Whether or not the Nighthawks were able to

help Dr. Barrows find his nephew does not seem to be in the records.

A similar, but definitely successful, episode occurred in February of 1923. Two brothers, Roy R. Hosford and J. W. Hosford had been living together but went separate ways in 1912. J. W. went to California, while Roy remained in Kansas City, Kans. A few letters followed, but after about two years correspondence ceased, and after 1914 neither knew the whereabouts of the other. But during a Nighthawk program in early February, the Merry Old Chief was reading out the names of new members: "Better get out the fur-lined charters, professor. Here's a brother from Portland, Ore., seeking admission. He is J. W. Hosford." Roy Hosford had recently been granted a membership charter, and he happened to be listening over a home-made crystal set. Next morning, Roy sent a telegram to his brother in Portland, and the next day he got an answering telegram that ended with "Letter follows."[33]

It is interesting that from the beginning, Coon-Sanders developed its reputation as a great boon for those confined to sickbeds, or otherwise incapacitated. Coonie, especially, became known for his concern for "shut-ins."[34] After only one week of broadcasts, for instance, six-year-old Virginia Parker, in Kansas City, wrote to say that she had chicken pox and couldn't sleep, "so I listen to your music," adding, "I want to be your first little 'Nighthawk.'" Also in Kansas City, 39-year-old Frank Williams found the Nighthawks a pleasant way to help forget his injuries received during a robbery. On March 1, he had encountered several bandits, one of whom shot him and shattered his left femur just above the knee. Not wishing to miss any of his favorite radio program, Williams had a radio set placed at his bedside in the city's General Hospital. Using his bed as a ground and placing the aerial outside the hospital window, he was then able, as the *Star* put it, "to 'listen in' on everything from the early morning market reports to the final jest of 'the merry old chief.'"[35]

Matilda and L. E. Houchin, and F. H. Meredith, in Louisville, Kentucky, requested, "More 'Nighthawk Blues.' Longer programs. We never sleep. Give us [a] ring [of the cow bell] for new members." From Greenville, Mississippi, Mr. and Mrs. L. C. Murrell and J. W. Collins observed, "the 'Nighthawk Blues' had the world shuffling its feet last night."[36]

In the middle of December there arrived a message from O. F. Hawley and H. W. Higgins, of Sioux City, Iowa, that not only expressed their approval but did it in rhyme:

> While listening to the Nighthawks' Club
> We got the grand idea
> That we'd like to have a membership
> And do our best to be a
>
> Reg'lar Nighthawk by attending
> All the meetings of the order.
> It's got the movies cheated
> And it doesn't cost a quarter.
>
> We listen, mindless of the time,
> Till early in the morning,
> Almost in time to see the sun
> The eastern sky adorning.
>
> Of the Nighthawks' growing membership
> We oft receive an inkling,
> The grand initiation
> And the cowbell's merry tinkling.
>
> We've listened to your programs now
> For four nights in succession,
> We only get our forty winks
> But haven't missed a session.
>
> We'd like to join the order
> And give the club a boost,
> So get over all you Nighthawks
> And let us on the roost.[37]

Let's look at a sampling of other December messages: Robert M. Duckett, Raleigh, N.C., "clear and strong ... one of the best stations that we pick up"; H. A. Orr and wife, Beardstown, Ill., "Just sold mattress, springs and bed"; O. E. Frazier, Watts, Calif., alluded to Prohibition with, "First time I knew there were any Nighthawks left after John Barleycorn died"; George P. Curry, Hiawatha, Utah, "none of the gang here will go to bed until you sign off ... it is unanimous with us that your Nighthawk jamborees are just about the best stuff in the air";

F. E. Jaeger, Chicago, Ill., "Your Nighthawk program is the cat's meow"; Harry Copping, Reynoldsville, Pa., "I got the family out of bed to listen to the music"; William M. Garvin, Navy radioman on U.S.S. *Oklahoma*, at anchor at San Pedro, Calif., "Your Nighthawks make the 'gobs' want to hurry to Kansas City. It certainly is the hot stuff"; Tom Orr, Charles Artz, and Roy Hall, Chama, N.M., "We are snowbound in the mountains.... Whoop 'er up tonight"; Mr. and Mrs. W. A. Clark, Nowata, Okla., "We get your Nighthawks stronger than horseradish"; Joe Nauet, Jordan, Mont., "We are one hundred miles from a railroad, north of Miles City, the old cow town, and it sure brought a laugh when you rang the [cow] bell"; Bert Reddish, Mr. and Mrs. F. M. Christmas, Vera Parker, Kelly Miller, Ben C. Bell, and Silpha Bell, Kemmerer, Wyo., "We are buried in snow, but getting the best concert in the United States"; J. P. Funk, Steubenville, Ohio, "Please consider me a member of the 'Nighthawks' Loyal Order of the Knob Twisters"; Beta Chi Fraternity, U. of Ariz., Tucson, "Would like to hear the 'Nighthawk Blues' again tonight"; W. E. Byerly, Velva, N.D., perhaps were referring to Coonie's expertise with hard liquor when they said, "great.... Better stay in Kansas City instead of going to International Falls, Minn. Canadian nightcaps might have a bad effect on Mr. Coon. Why not designate lady members as chicken hawks?"; "Hell Roaring" Jones, Miles City, Mont., "Will you admit a cowboy to the 'Nighthawks'? If so, saddle the goat, I'm raring to go"; W. L. Hitchcock, Portsmouth, Ohio, "Give us more of 'Gallagher and Shean.' Do not wait until 1 o'clock to play 'Three o'Clock in the Morning'"; F. R. Spiegel, Post Commander, American Legion, Vicksburg, Miss., "Please accept applications of 280 members.... We think your program *tres tres bon*"; Charles E. Williams, Barstow, Calif., "wonderful ... for people such as we, living away out from nowhere.... I might mention that my occupation is a miner and I work in the Coffin Mine, in the Funeral Range, Death Valley, which is located in Inyo County on the rim of Death Valley"; and, from Oshawa, Ontario, Robert D. Preston, recalling the old song from 1909, "I Love My Wife but Oh, You Kid!," wrote, "I have a password ... 'I love my bed, but oh you radio!'"[38]

The next month, January, brought even a greater deluge of letters and telegrams. Carl S. Salter, of Brownwood, Texas, wrote of spending the Christmas holidays with friends on a canoe trip down the Colorado River. Said he: "We were entertained every night at a different point by your excellent broadcasting station. We stayed with the 'Nighthawks' every night until they flew off." S. A. Grogan and J. W. Bradbury, with the Mexican Gulf Oil Company, near Tampico, Mexico, wrote, "You just simply smeared your music all over the place last night, and I believe that if it was not of such high class[,] the neighbors would be complaining about having their slumbers disturbed." From Mayaguez, Puerto Rico, Hal Jackson reported that he had picked up the Nighthawk program "and, believe me, they take the crystal detector." Rex McReynolds, in Mexico City, pronounced the Nighthawk Frolics "of the first caliber." John Shepard, Boston, regarded the WDAF midnight rounders as "the best program that reaches Boston."[39]

In late January the *Argus* in Minneapolis had this advice for its readers:

> If you are troubled with an ingrowing disposition or being pesticated with a pet peeve, here's a simple and effective remedy—get a radio set and listen to the Nighthawks Club of the Kansas City Star. This organization is nightly delighting thousands of radio fans all over the United States, and it's a treat to hear the 'initiations' over the radio.
>
> The Chief Nighthawk, who acts as announcer and High Potentate of the order, is the possessor of a ready wit and keen sense of humor, and it's hard to say, which is more entertaining—the chief or the really excellent Nighthawk orchestra.
>
> The writer recently had the pleasure of listening to one of the club's programs over the loud speaker on the set at Bonner's,

2406 Central avenue, and there wasn't a dull minute from the time these Kansas City gloom chasers opened up to the 'sign off.' Hats off to the Nighthawks.[40]

Among the most distant places to receive the Nighthawks' signal would certainly be London, England, where R. H. Ridley, a well-known British amateur radio operator, picked up the program on December 20. To make this reception even more interesting, another fan was listening to the same program in Hawaii. Also in Hawaii, R. Kekoa reported that he got the Nighthawks "regularly." Rex McReynolds, in Mexico City, said that he listened almost every night and that the signal came in "loud and clear." (*Loud and clear!* One sees that phrase used frequently in the days of early radio.) W. C. Boyd, in Nicaragua, scarcely ever missed a night, listening to the program "under a typical tropical moon." Not nearly so far away, but under conditions that made it remarkable, Thomas Skinner, of Passaic, N. J., reported that passengers on a New York subway listened to the Nighthawks while the train was in motion fifty feet underground, and later he witnessed reception in the tube under the Hudson River. Said he: "A successful demonstration of the practicability of receiving radio messages through steel and underground with a simple 20-inch loop was achieved early yesterday morning in the Interborough subway. At one stage at Eighty-sixth street, fifty feet underground, station WDAF ... was picked up."[41]

Two of the most remarkable instances of distant reception involved ships. In January 1923 R. E. Roesch, radio operator on the steamer *Easterner*, reported that when his ship was southwest of Panama and about halfway between South America and New Zealand, not far from Pitcairn Island, by using "one step of amplification" he clearly heard Leo Fitzpatrick initiating members. In August of that year radio operator Verne Munhollon (Mulholland?) was on the merchant ship *Arctic*, anchored in the Arctic Ocean at Baillie Island, 700 miles east of Point Barrow, Alaska, when he picked up the Nighthawk broadcast and thus "entertained the Eskimos." Said the letter writer: This may not be a record for distance, but I can say you will never be heard farther north as this is where you run into the Arctic ice pack...." The seaman quoted his records: "The log: August 23, 1923—Your music starts coming in loud and clear at 7 o'clock, ship's time, or 12 o'clock, Kansas City time. It continues to get louder until it could be heard one deck above the radio room." The ship's radio continued to pick up the program as it moved westward, until by September 7 at Point Barrow the signal was weaker; but then on the eighth, anchored at Wainwright, everything was much louder and clearer. Finally, the listener wrote: "You must have a wonderful station as there is no place in the world that I know of that is harder to get over than the Alaskan mountains, as all radio waves seem to be absorbed by them.... The inspector of the Royal Northwest Mounted Police and the Eskimos enjoyed your frolics immensely. Radio is new to them."[42] These broadcasts heard in the Arctic would not, of course, have been by Coon-Sanders; for the band was on vacation after having finished its engagement in Oklahoma City. The broadcasts from the Plantation Grill were by a band substituting during the original Nighthawks' absence.

But the Nighthawk program, with Coon-Sanders playing, did reach the Arctic on another occasion. Speaking with Charles J. Gilchrest a decade later in Chicago, Coonie recalled how he, Joe, and Leo Fitzpatrick had assisted with an Arctic expedition by the explorer D. B. MacMillan. The latter had reached a point at which it was impossible for him to communicate with his home base, so radio signals were relayed down to Portland, Ore., then to Denver, Colo., next to Kansas City, and from there to the explorer's home base.[43]

In March of 1923, two other messages arrived from ships at sea. About the middle of February, aboard the steamer *Dix*, radio operator George B. McElwain tuned into the Nighthawks when his ship was about 965 miles south of San Francisco. He found the Coon-Sanders band "sure rolling in on the li'l ole two-step." And on February 26, Seaman L. C. Collins, aboard the destroyer U.S.S. *Yarborough* about 600 miles southwest of Balboa, Canal Zone, picked up WDAF. "I have heard your concert," commented Collins, "and will say that it sure helped to drive away the blues." His ship had been at sea for thirteen days, and the young man was responsible for the dreary midnight-to-four shift. He turned on his short wave receiver and brought in Kansas City "easy as pie." It wasn't his first time to hear the Nighthawks on the radio; that was while his ship was at Neah Bay, Washington. But this time he was thrilled when he heard the Merry Old Chief read a letter from Dubuque, Iowa. "I am from Dubuque," wrote Collins, "and know that bird Staufenbaul. His dad owns a jewelry store...."[44]

Though not exactly at sea, J. H. McKinney was on board a barge on the Mississippi River, at Memphis; and he could have sympathized with Seaman Collins' lonely midnight vigil. "I am an operator on this barge line, and believe me your midnight concerts make the lonesome ghost watch a pleasure. I listen in every night to the wonderful orchestra music and the quips of the 'Merry Old Chief.' Keep up the good work."[45]

After the Nighthawk Frolic developed a routine, the highlight of each program was, of course, the band's playing, as well as Joe and Coonie's singing, which they often did through small megaphones. It is of some interest to see, to the extent that records exist, just what songs the band played and how often they played them. In the early days of the programs the *Kansas City Star*, on the preceding Saturday or Sunday, published lists of songs that were to be played each week. These lists show that the Nighthawk program was generally divided into three parts, with each part usually offering three musical numbers. The first part started at 11:45 p.m. and ended at midnight. The second went from 12:15 a.m. to 12:30, and the third from 12:45 to 1:00. Between sections, the Nighthawks Club transacted its business, some of which was to acknowledge as many of the correspondents as possible. The following is a very comprehensive list of the songs played over the air in early 1923 from January 28 through March 18.[46] After each song is the number of times it was played. An asterisk (*) indicates one of Joe Sanders' songs:

"After Every Party"—8, "Aggravatin' Papa"—14, "Am I to Blame?"—13, "Apple Sauce"—3, "Are You Playing Fair?"—3, "Baby Blue Eyes"—11, "Bees Knees"—8, "Billie"—25* (introduced by Nighthawks Friday, 12 January 1923), "Blue"—9, "By the Shalimar"—8, "Carolina Home"—2, "Carolina in the Morning"—2, "China Boy"—2, "Choo-Choo Blues"—8, "Clover Blossom Blues"—6, "Crinoline Days"—7, "Cry"—2, "Crying for You"—1, "Dancin' Fool"—1, "Dearest"—3, "Don't Say Goodbye"—1, "Don't Think You'll Be Missed"—1, "Eleanor"—6, "Fate"—6, "Greenwich Witch"—10, "Gypsy Sweetheart"—1, "Halfpast Kissing Time"—2, "He Loves It"—2, "Homesick"—2, "I Wish I Could Shimmy like My Sister Kate"—9, "I'm Through Shedding Tears"—15, "Ivy"—8, "Jimbo Jumbo"—2, "Journey's End"—2, "Lady of the Evening"—14, "Linger Longer"—6, "Little Rover"—6, "Longing for You"—3, "Lost"—15, "Lovin' Sam"—3, "Maggie Blues"—7, "Martha"—10*, "My Buddy"—8, "Nighthawk Blues"—20*, "No One Just Like You"—5*, "Nola"—6, "One Night in June"—4, "Pack Up Your Sins"—5, "Pale Moon"—9, "Parade of the Wooden Soldiers"—4, "Peggy Dear"—1, "Peruvian Nights"—6*, "Porcelain Maid"—9, "Romany Love"—3, "Rose of the Rio Grande"—2, "Runnin' Wild"—23, "Saint Louis Blues"—11, "Saw Mill River Road"—9, "Seven Eleven"—1, "Somehow"—2*, "Sonja"—2, "Stories"—2, "Sweet Lovin' Mama"—15, "The Sheik of Avenue B"—19, "Think of Me"—6, "Three o'Clock in the Morning"—16, "Toot-toot, Tootsie"—3, "Where the Bamboo Babies Grow"—1, "Where the Blue Begins"—1, "Who

Cares?"—1, "Who Did You Fool after All?"—3, "Whoa, Lillie, Take Your Time"—1, "Without You"—5, "The World Is Waiting for the Sunrise"—10, "You Tell Her, I Stutter"—14, "You've Got to See Mama Every Night"—6

Celebrations of New Year's Eve, 31 December 1923—a Sunday—filled those of the city's hotels and restaurants that offered good dancing facilities, and dance reservations for the city's more popular gathering places had already indicated that there would be an unusually big turnout. Those groups planning their big parties for Saturday night included the Kansas City Club, the Country Club in Mission Hills, the Automobile Club, the Milburn, the Meadow Lake, the Blue Hills, and the Hillcrest. The Muehlebach's big shindig was on Sunday evening. And though the Nighthawks did not regularly play on Sunday evenings, they made an exception on this occasion. In honor of the special season, the broadcast's business session was kept brief. The *Star* promised that "Coon-Sanders will 'out-do' themselves in playing 'Sister Kate,' 'Nighthawk Blues,' and all the numbers made familiar to the members by this popular musical organization." The paper predicted that many would be dancing to the Nighthawks' music in many small towns "where orchestra music is not obtainable," as well as "many homes in the far off northland of Canada and on the plains of New Mexico and Arizona." The Nighthawks held a special meeting to greet the new year shortly before midnight, after which they played until everyone began to grow weary.[47]

On the regular evening broadcast for New Year's Day, a Monday, the Nighthawks helped WDAF and the Kansas City Telephone Company demonstrate a new loudspeaker that had been installed at Convention Hall. The purpose was to show the possibilities of sound amplification, and the estimate was that it would amplify the human voice about eighteen billion times. The new amplified speaker was similar to the one used recently by President Harding at the burial ceremonies for the Unknown Soldier at Arlington Cemetery.[48]

The Nighthawks began their second month of broadcasting while Kansas City was beginning to enjoy the new electric street lights that were replacing the gas lamps. The new illumination wouldn't be so romantic as the gas lamps had been, but romance would have to defer to economy and efficiency. Perhaps that illustrated one of the points made in an article at this time in the *Star*, and written by Frenchwoman Georgette Leblanc Maeterlinc, that Americans were too rushed and too busy with material things to appreciate love and sentiment. "The devil 'Quickly' is the enemy of the god Cupid," she wrote. But, then, so was light, whatever the source, especially for a sheik and his flapper when they were parked on Lover's Lane. But, romantic or not, by the seventh of January all installations of the new lighting had been completed except three small circuits near the bridge in Swope Park, around the zoo, and in a section of Swope Parkway east of the Paseo. Also, a few scattered lights were still to be placed on Pershing Road opposite the Union Station, as well as on the new Boston Boulevard Bridge. Most residential and small-business areas had the new lights, but there were still more than two thousand gas lamps in use.[49] The city's "old lamplighters" doubtless had reason to rejoice when, in early February, on at least two nights the temperature went down to zero.

Over the next several months WDAF and its Nighthawks increased in fame and favor with the public, and perhaps even with one competing radio station. For, when the Sweeney School's station WHB broadcast a twelve-hour program on 1 February 1923 to celebrate the fifteenth year of the school's existence, WDAF cooperated by not broadcasting the Nighthawk Frolic. Instead, The Merry Old Chief was invited to WHB where he granted a few memberships and made a short address to the nation's Nighthawks. It was an impressive act of courtesy, as well as a public-relations coup.[50]

At about the same time, Ted Lewis was entertaining at the Shubert Theater in his "Greenwich Village Follies." He appeared on the Nighthawk program on January 29 and was ceremoniously received into the club and was given his membership card. In the spirit of reciprocity Lewis sang "Fate" and "Three o'Clock in the Morning." He told what was described as a "bedtime" story and later added his clarinet in several numbers with the Coon-Sanders band. Just after he had finished singing — or perhaps talking — the words to "Fate," calls thanking him and the Nighthawks came in from Yankton, S.D., Minneapolis, Minn., and Enid, Okla. Lewis, known as the "Jazz King," had recently introduced "Me and My Shadow," a song with which he was ever after associated.[51]

Occasionally other stars and lesser lights joined the Nighthawk broadcasts. In the first week of March 1923, for instance, Sam Worley, Steve Cady, and Harry Kessel joined Coon-Sanders as vocalists. Coonie and Joe probably welcomed the respite and the opportunity to concentrate on their drums and piano.[52]

WDAF and Leo Fitzpatrick very early developed an especially close association with the *Atlanta Journal's* station WSB, and in early February of 1923 The Merry Old Chief was an honored visitor in Atlanta where he appeared on "The Voice of the South" and was welcomed by Lambdin Kay, a well-known announcer for WSB. Fitzpatrick actually proclaimed some new Nighthawk memberships over WSB and had himself photographed shaking hands with his Atlanta counterpart. Kay's voice was familiar to many in Kansas City, where WSB's powerful signal was easily received. Said the *Kansas City Star*, Kay's "Southern accent is typically 'the voice of the South.'" Apparently the *Star* wasn't aware that Kay was actually from Brooklyn, N.Y.[53] But that was a minor point in what was something that Fitzpatrick was a master in, cultivating good public relations; and it would pay off when the Nighthawks' 1926 road tour took them to Atlanta.

How WDAF and WSB handled this little bit of pioneering radio was given special treatment by the *Kansas City Star*, which described it this way:

> Shortly after midnight last night [February 5-6] the Merry Old Chief of the Kansas City Star "Nighthawks" initiated applicants into his organization from the radio station of the Atlanta Journal, WSB. Preceding the initiations, music from the Hotel Muehlebach was broadcast by WDAF on its regular "Nighthawk" schedule. A switch was turned in the grill room at the Hotel Muehlebach — music by the Coon-Sanders orchestra was sent into the ether — an announcement was made at exactly three minutes after midnight that the Merry Old Chief would open the "Nighthawk" business session from the Atlanta Journal's studio — another switch was turned at The Star's broadcasting station and the transmitting set of WDAF was shut down to enable the "Nighthawk" flock to tune in on WSB for the nocturnal session. The Merry Old Chief conducted the "meeting" until 12:30 o'clock, when The Star resumed its broadcasting from the Hotel Muehlebach until 1 o'clock, the hour when "Nighthawks" doff their ear pieces and return to their roost for the night.[54]

In January 1923, WDAF added another feature to the Nighthawk program. By the early 1920s the theater organ was moving into its position as a regular attraction in motion picture theaters, both as accompanist for the silent films and even as a "feature" in itself. It was later in the decade that it reached its peak of popularity, but even by the early Twenties many larger theaters had already installed them. Kansas City's Globe Theater, for instance, announced that on January 18 it would dedicate its new Robert Morton organ that cost $20,000. But the Newman Theatre, an even more prestigious movie palace, already was known for its theater organ, played at this time by Thomas F. Bruce. On January 20 WDAF added it to the Nighthawk program, and twice a week, during breaks on the Nighthawk programs, Bruce's aeolian tones filled the air. Occasionally he played "The Nighthawk March," a piece he had composed especially for the band.[55] The *Star* described one such concert:

It is midnight. The strains of jazz that have been coming from the orchestra in the Hotel Muehlebach have died away and there follows the soft melodious sound of a pipe organ. An operator in the Plantation Grill has switched the key from the orchestra's microphone to an instrument in the Newman Theater a block away.... At the farther extremity of the deserted theater a musician bends over the keyboard of an organ, dimly outlined behind the glow of a single light.... The empty auditorium has the appearance of a huge tomb. There is utter stillness except for the music, which echoes in the dark corners.... He plays alone. The world listens. The musician opens up with a strain that fairly roars and then dies to a soft melody, and all this is going into the air where thousands [are] listening in wonder at it all.

The operator at The Star peers constantly at the shimmering tubes and dials of the transmitting set. A twist of a knob to tone down the incoming music. The switching of a wire from one microphone to another. He dons a headset to listen. Pulsating meter hands tell him there is too much power. He sets it down and sighs.

The Chief Nighthawk at the hotel is on the line. A word over the telephone and the operator switches another key. The music of the organ dies away.

The strains of jazz are heard. The microphones have been changed. The merry laughter of dancers. A hearty chuckle from the chief. The rattle of a drum, the drone of a saxophone and the blare of the cornet blend into the "pep" that contrasts with the music of the organ.

There had been utter stillness among the thousands of Nighthawks as they listened to the organ. It was different and somewhat solemn compared to the jazz of the Coon-Sanders orchestra. Fifteen minutes of the dance music and the process is repeated.[56]

Such publicity was good for Fitzpatrick, too. He was invited to serve on a committee of twenty radio experts, who in late March of 1923 met with the Department of Commerce, in Washington, to advise the agency on broadcasting and regulations governing the new field. Fitzpatrick represented radio stations owned by newspapers.[57] No doubt the witty Fitzpatrick was especially useful when the committee's work tended to became dull, but he was probably thankful to get back to Kansas City and the clowning of the Nighthawk Frolics.

And in mid-April it was this spirit of hilarity that led the *Star* to tell of geese that allegedly were interfering with the Nighthawks' broadcasts. It had to do with a man in O'Neill, Nebraska, who had a theory about radio static:

> How the Kansas City Star's Nighthawk concerts have been interfered with by flying migratory birds creating static when the atmosphere is dry is shown in the experiments here of Prof. M. H. Horiskey, who is engaged in radio research.
>
> When a recent cold wave hit North Nebraska it brought countless numbers of ducks and geese into this section....
>
> These vast flocks of migratory birds are now winging their way through Nebraska to the colder region of the north lands and creating unusual static interference, according to Professor Horiskey. He says the atmosphere in the upper altitudes is extremely dry at this time of the year and the friction of the air against the feathers of the flying fowl creates static electricity ... [and] the discharge of the static is extremely irritating to the birds, causing them to utter fretful calls and quacks as they fly. These calls, uttered simultaneously with the electric discharge[,] are broadcasted [sic] in various parts of the country....
>
> This theory was recently substantiated during a radio demonstration given in one of the local halls by Prof. John Hiber. In the demonstration the ... Nighthawks were tuned in and the voice of the announcer was heard clear as a bell. The music was interrupted suddenly by a series of quacks and honks. Listeners[-]in suggested that the Professor at Kansas City was evidently giving out some new kinds of charters.
>
> "Charters nothing," said an old time rancher who was listening in, "Them is real ducks and geese."
>
> Investigation disclosed several large flocks of ducks and geese passing over the hall. After they had passed on[,] the Kansas City program again came in with no disturbance noticeable.[58]

It was at the same time that "real ducks" were endangering transmission of the Nighthawk programs that a listener — he signed himself "Dick Wick Hall" and lived in

Salome, Arizona — wrote a fan letter that seemed to identify him as a genial Southwestern codger. Having heard on each Nighthawk broadcast that the programs were coming from the Muehlebach Hotel, he pretended to mistake the hotel's name for Missouri's famed quadruped:

> Dear Chief: Chiquita Bill says one night while I was gone he heard you say you was broadcasting from a mule's back and he wants me to write and tell you be careful, especially when the Professor and his bunch get to hot-fingerin' that music.
> Chiquita rode Tonto Bill Springer's sorrel mule into Phoenix once and come around a corner into a circus parade just as the calliope started and Chiquita says the mule broadcasted him half way across the state of Arizona, so he says you be careful if you're going to do any more mule-back broadcasting. Get yourself a good cinch and a long pair of spurs and when the Professor starts the music just hook 'em in and ride her, cowboy.
> Chiquita was listening to you last night and he says: "I'll bet you ten gallons of Laughing Gas [liquor] that guy never sleeps. Let's close up and go back to Kansas City." We might just as well, I guess, because we're only running the gas station afternoons now, since we joined the Night Hawks. If we go broke listening to you we're going to join the Hoot Owls too and crawl in a prairie dog hole and live on jack rabbits. Good luck to you, Old Timer.[59]

Hall and Chiquita Bill got their memberships, after which they considered themselves "the official Nighthawks of No. 1 Main Street, Salome, Ariz." Then, Hall launched into a hawk-and-bull story about how, when their new radio had began to squawk, Bill suggested it needed "squawk oil," or perhaps even some "hawk oil." Since Salome had none, said Hall in an account reeking strongly of fish, they went to Los Angeles, where, after much searching, they found one store with a supply. Introducing themselves as Nighthawks got them the commodity at a reduced price. Back in Salome, however, their troubles continued, for in the absence of anything taller than sagebrush, their aerial was attached to "Old Squint Eye Kellogg's barbed wire fence." A "dang coyote run a bunch of steers through" it, and Bill had to walk four miles before he found the break. The two men planned to send a team sixty-five miles down to the Colorado River to cut some cottonwood poles for a proper aerial. That, plus the new "loud talker" they had ordered, should give them improved reception. Meanwhile, they made do with what they had. Wrote Hall: "You'd ought to seen my frog sit up and grin when he heard the professor [Sanders] croakin' the other night. The professor was off key a little and missed a note on that last croak — or maybe he's a different kind of a frog. How about it, professor?"[60]

"Hey, Nighthawks," shouted an advertisement to Kansas Citians from Highland Radio Supply, "wear your head set to bed with comfort." What? Wouldn't that be a little uncomfortable? No, not if one wore a pair of the seller's "soft, comfortable pneumatic ear cushions." They cost only two dollars a pair and fitted any earphones; and they would, the ad assured, shut out extraneous noise and keep fixed on radio waves.[61] It was just another indication of the Nighthawks' popularity of which many of the city's merchants were trying to avail themselves.

In fact, the public were becoming so interested in the new radio phenomenon that the Newman Theatre decided to make a film about it. The entertainment weekly *Variety* suggested that one reason for making such a film was to try to attract back to cinema many patrons who had deserted to radio.[62] Thus, in early 1923, with the cooperation of *Scientific American* magazine, the Newman assigned cameramen William Andlauer and Howard Curtiss to take moving pictures of all the personnel and equipment used to produce a Nighthawk program. Titled *Via Radio*— one source gives *Via Wireless*— the film showed the Coon-Sanders Orchestra broadcasting at the Plantation Grill, Leo Fitzpatrick announcing as the Merry Old Chief, radio technicians operating the various stages of broadcasting, other entertainers who had performed over WDAF, Thomas

Bruce at the Newman theater organ, the Newman Theatre Orchestra, and others. After it had been completed, the film was shown at the Royal Theater, in Kansas City, and then at theaters throughout the Southwest.[63] The film was, of course, silent, but it is unfortunate that it apparently is no longer extant.

Another indication of the almost insatiable public appetite for radio in general and the Nighthawks in particular was the popularity of the new medium's exhibit held in the Hotel Muehlebach's ballroom from 17 to 20 January 1923. Called a "peep behind the scenes of a radio studio," it offered a miniature broadcasting station, and opened with the music of Fritz Hanlein's Trianon Ensemble composed of violinists Erling Knutsen and N. Van Vendeloo, cellist Hanlein, contrabass S. V. Gilkison, pianist H. W. Steele, and harpist M. A. Russo. As a special treat, a mock version of the famous Nighthawk Frolic showed the spectators just how the programs were actually broadcast; and the Coon-Sanders Orchestra delighted everyone with such pieces as "Lovin' Sam," "Baby Blue Eyes," "Nighthawk Blues," and "Mister Gallagher and Mister Shean." Besides Joe and Coonie, the orchestra consisted of Elmer "Crab" Kohlman, Hal McLean, Frank M. "Pop" Estep, Harry "Happy" Williams, Carl "Swede" Nordberg, and Harold Thiell. In addition, fourteen jobbers of radio equipment displayed their goods and demonstrated various types of "receivers" suitable for home, auto, or pocket. Almost 700 visitors attended on the first day of the exhibit.[64]

And at the Newman the band kept manufacturing their famous skits that featured songs, especially comedy songs, by Coonie and Joe. Frequently, these "acts" had the band's members out of their seats and cavorting about the stage, often in hilariously absurd costumes. On Christmas Eve, on the program with Gloria Swanson's *The Impossible Mrs. Bellew*, Coon-Sanders put on a novelty called "The Night before Christmas." Beginning Sunday, January 21, the Newman offered the film version of Willard Mack's play *Kick In*, a story that dealt with both the social elite and the underworld. Coon-Sanders prepared a novelty act with the band dressed in convict attire in a setting that purported to be Sing Sing Prison in 1973. On another occasion, when the film was *The Pilgrim*, with Charlie Chaplin, Edna Purviance, Sydney Chaplin, and Mack Swain, Coon-Sanders was ready with another of its droll acts. In the film Chaplin, an escaped prisoner, disguises himself in clerical attire, so each of the band's members sported a Chaplin-type mustache and wore a clerical frock coat and hat. Said a newspaper ad: "This week at the Newman seven Charlie Chaplins [actually there were eight band members] in seven Charlie Chaplin mustaches and 'Pilgrim' frocks hold services as a prologue to the feature picture. The stunt is the most original the boys have yet conceived." Another critic agreed, adding, "And you should have heard the applause...." On another occasion a movie critic had little good to say about most of the Newman's program — it was "terribly sad" — but "Coon-Sanders ... are far from sad and ... they're the one lively spot on the program outside of the overture." Joe and Coonie appeared in blackface and were "riots." With perhaps a pun on *upright*, though Sanders played a grand, the critic added, "Sanders at the piano and with what he's got to make the piano speak right up, and with his voice, grown more accustomed to public presentation, compares favorably with Al Jolson as an entertainer." Elmer Kohlman got a good applause with a cornet novelty. When the Newman showed Constance Talmadge as a Chinese woman in *East Is East*, the Nighthawks dolled themselves up in Chinese attire for a skit they called "A Chinese Laundry." When the Newman showed a film of the popular Arab genre, a critic wrote: "'Sheikish' music is heard from the band in sheikish attire. Beards and swarthy skins and desert attire are the makeup and the boys loll around on pillows and how they play!" The Coon-Sanders skits were, said an ad for the

About spring, 1923, Kansas City, Missouri. Standing: Coon (left) and Sanders; seated (from left): Kohlman, Nordberg, Estep, Williams, McLean, and J. Thiell. (Courtesy Kansas City [Mo.] Museum.)

Newman, "easily the most popular of the Newman presentation features."[65]

In their twenty-fifth week at the Newman, in February of 1923, a newspaper critic had special praise for the orchestra's long engagement at the theater, a feat, said the critic, that had "never been equaled or approached in any sort of vaudeville." "During this time," continued the journalist, "they have just about run the gamut of sense and nonsense, filling in for good measure with divers character acts." The critic called Joe "the truck horse [who] writes every line and note of every act at the Newman. Practically everything they play at the Muehlebach are [sic] his own special arrangements, done by dint of consuming quantities of midnight oil and energy." The article reported that Joe was singing his song "Billie" at the Newman, and that on February 17 he had sold his "No One Just Like You" to the Triangle Music Company, of New York. On another occasion the band, capitalizing on the recent archaeological discovery in Egypt, put on a skit titled "A Little Music from King Tut's Tomb." And one critic, referring to the band's lengthening engagement, said, "The Coon-Sanders orchestra again goes over just as they have for the past umpty-umpty weeks."[66]

The simulated Nighthawk Frolic, that had been so successful at the recent exhibit in the Muehlebach's ballroom, was repeated in the middle of April at the Newman Theatre. A mock-up of the Plantation Grill's bandstand was prepared for the theater's stage, and the presentation was complete with Leo Fitzpatrick as announcer. In its advertisement, the Newman for the first time called the band Coon-Sanders "Nighthawks" instead of the usual "Novelty Orchestra." After this special program, however, the Newman reverted to the original name.[67]

It did not take stations in other cities

Newman Theater, Kansas City, Missouri, April 1923. Band's skit to accompany Charlie Chaplin's film *The Pilgrim*. The garb and Chaplinesque mustaches make identification problematic. (Courtesy Kansas City [Mo.] Museum.)

long to pay the ultimate compliment to the Nighthawk program. In Chicago, for example, the Sun Dodgers began broadcasting a similar, but less popular, program. The Minneapolis station had one, too, and read telegrams from listeners.[68] But all of them were simply less remarkable imitations of "Radio's Aces" from Kansas City.

By late April the Nighthawks had achieved a membership of 35,000 fans, even as WDAF changed to a wavelength of 411 instead of 400 to help avoid interference from such stations as those in Atlanta, Chicago, Fort Worth, Davenport, Detroit, and St. Louis. The "meetings" had settled into a popular routine that consisted of the reading of telegrams by Fitzpatrick, with "Professor" Sanders' or Coon's cowbell ringing the new name into membership. The *Cincinnati Post* admiringly commented that Fitzpatrick had "a better line of patter than in any of the old-time minstrel show interlocutors." And as

the paper also observed, there was something "almost uncanny" about sitting up late at night, when concerts came in clearest and there were fewer stations sending. As for such programs as that of the Nighthawks', said the *Cincinnati Post*, "It's like pulling teeth for a radio bug to shut off the juice and go to bed."[69]

> For radio [continued the *Post*] has a peculiar lure, unlike anything else. This lure is in fact that radio eliminates distance and carries the listener hundreds or thousands of miles in a twinkling. Radio beats the Magic Carpet in the "Arabian Nights."
>
> The time devoted to listening in is not wasted. The music that rushes in from far off is of secondary importance to the listener. His real interest is in the marvel of transmission. In this sense the radio is awakening a scientific sense that will be indispensable to people who want to keep up with the times from now on.
>
> Outfits like the Kansas City Nighthawks ... are embryonic scientific organizations

that incidentally are keeping a lot of people out of mischief.*⁷⁰

In the spring of 1923 the Nighthawks received an offer to take their music in person to their public in another state. Oklahoma City beckoned, so on Saturday, May 26, the band gave its last program at the Newman until the next fall. They also played a concert on Monday, May 28, at a place called the Jack o'Lantern, and apparently played their last Nighthawk program for the season on the evening of that day. On May 29 an aggregation called the Plantation Orchestra took their place at the Plantation Grill, though the programs would still be often called the "Nighthawk Frolic."⁷¹ Before leaving for Oklahoma City, the band's members apparently took a short vacation.

Ever afterward Joe would brag that the Nighthawks were the first dance orchestra to play for radio on a regular schedule. This, however, is one of those claims that are rather difficult to prove. By 1922 there were enough radio stations for at least one other somewhere in the nation to have scheduled an orchestra before the beginning of the Nighthawk programs. And as we have already seen, even on WDAF Eddie Kuhn's Harmony Boys, earlier in 1922, had begun a series called "Forty Minutes of Music." Also, WDAF often featured other bands in such a way that one might call their programs, at least in some degree, scheduled. One difference, however, is that the Nighthawks played every night except Sunday. It may be a little closer to the facts to say that the Nighthawks' programs, even if not the first, were perhaps the first to endure as long as they did and to demonstrate, to a remarkable degree, that there was a vast, late-night audience for their music.

It was at about this time that a journalist attempted to assess the status of the Coon-Sanders aggregation:

> New York has its Paul Whiteman. Kansas City has its Coon-Sanders, Carlton [sic] Coon and Joe Sanders have their jazz band.
> And jazz lovers have their hearts' content of some of the prettiest syncopated music ever run ragged up and down the scale.
> 'Cause when Sanders clips off a staccato measure or two and then the piano laughs tinklingly as he fingers his way up to the high C's and back again to the creepy low accompaniment and when Coon dum-dum's away at his drums in wild rhythmic beat, and the rest of the band lending their stuff—you just can't refuse....
> Both Coon and Sanders have two of the most pleasing parlor voices that blend in jazzy harmony and they intersperse their playing with snappy duets.⁷²

The next day, as the band began a week's vacation and started preparing for Oklahoma City, the newspapers reported that Jess W. Smith, a somewhat mysterious hanger-on and close associate of the Harding administration, had committed suicide at his home in Washington. A historic series of political and private scandals had begun to surface in the nation's capital. They would soon become collectively known as the Teapot Dome Scandals.

It is interesting that many years later, when Joe Sanders put together a scrapbook narrative of the Nighthawks, he did not begin with his famous meeting with Carleton A. Coon in the music store, nor even with their great success at the Newman Theatre and the broadcasts on the Nighthawk Frolics. He began with their first road trip that took them to Oklahoma City.

It is often difficult to be certain when some members joined Coon-Sanders or how long they remained. The Thiell brothers are a typical case, partly because it is easy to confuse their names, but also because Harold left the band briefly before the Oklahoma trip. Some who have written about the band quote Harold Thiell as saying that he was with the orchestra from its formation, which perhaps is correct except for a relatively brief absence in 1923. Certainly he was with the

---

*Which recalls the Nighthawks' song "Keeping out of Mischief Now."

band at least as early as when they made their first recording in March 1921. But when the group went to Oklahoma City in the summer of 1923, Harold, for some reason I have never discovered, was playing with D. Ambert Haley's Fairyland Park Orchestra, as were also the former Coon-Sanders banjoist Robert Norfleet and future band members Robert Pope and Nick Musolino. Also playing with Haley's band at that time was the once and future Coon-Sanders member Floyd Estep.[73] (Estep, as we have already seen, was playing with Coonie when Joe joined the group in 1919.) Harold Thiell's brother John, who joined Coon-Sanders sometime about the first of January 1923, was the one who accompanied the band to Oklahoma.

Expensive Pullman reservations and luxurious Auburn and Cord automobiles were several years into the future. This time Coonie, Joe, John Thiell, Hal McLean, Harry Williams, Elmer Kohlman, Carl Nordberg, and Frank Estep — "The Nomads of the Air," as Joe phrased it — set out in their own automobiles and headed south-southwestward toward Oklahoma City, with Hank Linder as tour manager. They could hardly have chosen a worse time to make such a trip. What was being proclaimed by the *Daily Oklahoman* as the "Worst Floods Since 1904" began to afflict the Coon-Sanders caravan almost immediately but especially after they entered Oklahoma. Sanders drove his Buick — "My old Buick, yclept [named] 'Abner'" — and later proudly said that it was the only one of their cars that traveled under its own power through miles of solid water, and kept going. The others had to be towed and still wouldn't run even after reaching high ground.[74] That automobiles in those days were very high off the ground probably was of little avail in the flooded areas where they traveled.

As he would on the band's many future trips, Joe had his box camera and got the first of a great quantity of snapshots that he later arranged in a scrapbook and provided with catchy titles. One of his first photos from this Oklahoma trip shows their caravan fording the Verdigris River and is titled "another Ford — at a ford." Many bridges were out, especially in the Verdigris River Valley in Oklahoma. According to Joe, several bridges were washed away within an hour after their passage. It was perhaps a bit of dramatic adornment of reality, but there is no doubt that they faced real obstacles and that their successful passage was almost wondrous. According to Joe, on one segment of the trek they traveled through mud and water for three days and covered only seven miles. One of Joe's photos shows John Thiell kissing dry ground after leaving a badly flooded stretch of country. They managed to drag into Tulsa, where they "abandoned" their cars and caught the last train permitted to challenge the high water into Oklahoma City, much of which was under water when they arrived about June 7.[75]

The band's members, awed by the flooded city, moved warily about, some of them taking snapshots of the soggy scene. On June 14 they got some especially awesome photographs of what was regarded as the worst flood in the state's brief history. Paul Braniff was helping the band with their finances, and it was his father-in-law who had built the dam that was the only thing protecting Oklahoma City from even worse flooding. Had that dam broken, there very likely would have been perhaps as much as ten feet of water in the downtown area. Even as it was, Western Avenue, perhaps the hardest hit area in the city, was flooded to such an extent that Sanders was able to get a photo of youngsters swimming in front of a grocery store. The streetcar tracks were considerably below the water's suface.[76]

Their arrival coincided with an announcement from the U. S. Post Office Department that the name of the city would henceforth be not just "Oklahoma" but "Oklahoma City," which everyone could have told them it had been all along. Whatever the name of the city, Coon-Sanders, glad to have arrived, barely made it to their engagement at Spring Lake Pavilion, opposite Lincoln

Heavy rains brought flooding as the band set out on their first road trip as the Nighthawks, June 1923, to Oklahoma City. Here they ford a river. (Courtesy Special Collections, Kansas City [Mo.] Public Library.)

Park. It was, said Joe later, a "plain, barnlike structure that our music converted into a rendezvous for dance lovers from as far away as Tulsa and Guthrie." L. E. Buttrick managed the Pavilion, and Paul Braniff, in Joe's words, "was the guardian of our weekly check." On their first evening, the governor and several other high officials were present.[77] A journalist, a few days later, described how the place looked during the Coon-Sanders engagement:

> Who are the devotees of jazz in Oklahoma City?
> We can't see how, from now on, any distinction among us can be made.
> The Referee was eased out, with a group traveling de luxe in a Ford touring car equipped with shock absorbers, to the scene of light-hearted frolic Tuesday night. Our group sat outside to listen and watch.
> An orchestra made popular over the country thru its radio concerts, was performing and a crowd of dancers swung around the floor gracefully.
> While there could be counted many faces of young swains, now called jelly beans, and many bobbed-hair young women called flappers, we also saw the following stepping to the rhythmic strains:
> A gray-haired former chief justice of the supreme court ... a prominent surgeon.
> And there was no head that appeared more often to have circled the hall than the gray-haired, ex-chief justice, nor no applauder ... more enthusiastic than the prominent surgeon.
> Now what argument could be more conclusive than this for the statement that you never can tell?[78]

On Sunday, June 24, Coon-Sanders augmented their income, but lessened their leisure time, by beginning an eight-week engagement at the Criterion Theater each day at 3:30 and at 8 p.m. On Monday evening, June 25, the same day on which news arrived that Paul Whiteman and his wife had been injured in an automobile accident in England, WKY started broadcasting the Nighthawks' evening programs at 9:30 to 11:30 from Spring Lake.[79] It was as busy a schedule as the band had followed in Kansas City; the the band obviously thrived on such punishment.

Coonie, Pop Estep, and John Thiell lived in a unit at the Monticello Apartments, at Twenty-first Street and North Robinson,

Joe and (behind him) Nordberg beside Joe's Buick ("Abner") on way to Oklahoma City, June 1923. Joe's was the only car that made it through flooded areas under its own power. (Courtesy Special Collections, Kansas City [Mo.] Public Library.)

as did possibly other members of the band. At first, Joe's wife Madeline made a brief visit, during which she and Joe stayed at the Drexel Apartments, at Sixteenth and North Robinson. After Madeline left, Joe moved in with Coonie and the other two men, thus making up what he called the "Four Horsemen." In Sanders' words, there they spent "many happy hours together." Occasionally several of the band went over to the Oklahoma City Country Club, which Joe declared a "dandy golf course" and where his best score was 41.[80]

Just before Coon-Sanders began their second week at the Criterion, a local music store observed that the band used Conn instruments exclusively, reminding the public that the store just happened to sell that brand. The Nighthawks, advertised as having "scored a decided hit the opening week at the Criterion," gave the second week's customers "The Bugle Call Blues," "You've Got

On flooded way to Oklahoma City, June 1923, John Thiell gratefully kisses dry ground. (Courtesy Special Collections, Kansas City [Mo.] Public Library.)

to See Mama Every Night," and "Louisville Lou." In keeping with the Criterion's new policy, Coon-Sanders had to change its program in the middle of each week.[81]

The Criterion Theater lavished great praise on the Nighthawks, even mistakenly saying that they had been broadcasting from the "roof garden" at the Muehlebach — the Plantation Grill was actually in the hotel's basement — and that they had played "for more than ten weeks in succession" at the Newman. Well, they had played much longer than ten weeks, though not quite for the forty weeks that Spring Lake announced. A second Criterion ad gave the figure as "forty weeks." The error may have originated with Joe, who always seemed to have difficulty recalling just how many weeks the band had played at the Newman. (I had to recount several times, too, before I could recall the number — 38 weeks.) Each week the Criterion promised a "rare treat to all pleasure-seekers." In their first week the Nighthawks played such numbers as "The World Is Waiting for the Sunrise," "The Nighthawk Blues," "I Love Me," "Yes, We Have No Bananas," "Weary Blues," "Desires," "Rose of the Rio Grande," and "Farewell Blues."[82]

During the first week of July, while President Warren Harding was starting his fateful trip to Alaska, and the Nighthawks were planning a special program to complement the feature film *The Woman with Four Faces*, the *Daily Oklahoman* carried the news that Dr. A. W. LaForge, a Chicago diagnostician, had gravely informed the American Institute of Homeopathy that "flapperitis" was a disease. "Of course," he said, "it is an expression of modern social conditions, but essentially it is an organic disease of the nervous system due to the strain of living in a jazz age."[83] The article failed to say whether this had generated any laughter, either politely subdued or of a more robust type. And as though this weren't sufficient, a month later the *Daily Oklahoman* reprinted another item from Chicago that might have been seen as coming closer to such a group as Coon-Sanders. Ida B. Allen, a New York dietician, opined: "The jazz age, the flapper, the slicker, the lack of corsets, rolled stockings, bobbed hair and cowbell orchestras are

Headed to Oklahoma City, June 1923, Coon (on left) Nordberg, Estep, and Williams are happy to reach dry land. (Courtesy Special Collections, Kansas City [Mo.] Public Library.)

not due to inherent wickedness but have been traced directly to the improved diet of women—carrots, oranges, lettuce, milk and other foods rich in vitamines [as the word was then often spelled]."[84] Apparently, almost everyone had a theory about jazz, though some observations were more imaginative than others.

Residents of the state's capital and in the general area began sweltering under a terrific July heat wave that set new records. On the eleventh the thermometer reached 100 in Oklahoma City and 102 the next day, the highest since 1889 when statistics began to be kept. On the twenty-fifth the temperature went to 105. But at least the city's population could take some satisfaction in a report by the local press that the Fourth of July had been a much more sober holiday than in times past, when it was more often a "drunken orgy."[85]

Joe and Madeline did a lot of sightseeing in, as Joe put it, "the slow-moving city, wherein we had so many happy hours." Joe, seldom without his camera, took many snapshots as they went about admiring both public and private buildings. Madeline was so taken by one large two-story house, with shade trees on the front lawn, that Joe named it "Madeline's dream home." Both also were fascinated by the thatched roofs on a few buildings, one of them on McKinley Road. Several homes on Classen Boulevard caught their attention, too. All in all, Joe concluded, "Oklahoma City may rightly boast of its many beautiful homes."[86]

On Thursday night, July 12, Coon-Sanders had to take second place to the boxing match between Luis Firpo and Jess Willard, the winner of which would take on Jack Dempsey.* A crowd at Daily Oklahoman Park, at Fourth and Broadway, listened to an announcer, who got reports of the fight by radio and shouted them into a megaphone as he stood at a window of the newspaper's building. Joe and Cooney perhaps made up for it the next evening with a program that included "Electric Girl," "Two Time Dan," "Swinging Down the Lane," "Aggravatin' Papa," "After Every Party," "Nighthawk Blues," and "Ostrich Walk."[87]

It might be interesting to the reader to

---

*Firpo defeated Willard but was defeated by Dempsey on September 14.

see a list of songs that Coon-Sanders played over a three-day period in mid–July at the Spring Lake Pavilion. Obviously over a period of several weeks there were other songs played, but this gives some idea of the band's selection within a typical three-day period:

"Aggravatin' Papa," "Bambalina," "Barcarolla," "Beale Street Mama," "Bees Knees," "Billie," "Bugle Call Rag," "Dreamy Melody," "Electric Girl,"* "I Cried for You," "Ivy," "Kiss Me Again," "Lady of the Evening," "Longing for You Blues,"* "Martha," "My Pillow and Me," "My Sweetie Went Away," "Nighthawk Blues,"* "Parade of the Wooden Soldiers," "Saint Louis Blues," "Sheik of Avenue B," "Some of These Days," "South Sea Eyes," "That's My Baby," "Think of Me," "Two Time Dan," "When Will the Sun Shine for Me?," "Wild Flower," "Wonderful One," "The World Is Waiting for the Sunrise," "Yes, We Have No Bananas," "You Tell 'Em, Ivories," "You Tell Her, I Stutter," and "You've Got to See Mama Every Night."[88]

In the middle of July the Nighthawks tried a novelty at the Criterion that had received a pretty good reception in Kansas City at the Newman Theatre. Something has already been said about the popularity of "Mister Gallagher and Mister Shean" and that Joe and Coonie's rendition always got much enthusiastic applause. The version resurrected for the Criterion was called "Mrs. Gallagher and Mrs. Shean."[89] Unfortunately, there seems to be no record of the lyrics they used, and equally unfortunate is it that they never recorded it.

While Coon-Sanders prepared for their last week at the Criterion and the end of their engagement at Spring Lake, they probably paid some attention to the news about President Warren G. Harding's trip to Alaska and the concern for his health. On his return, looking "gray and worn" according to reporters, he reached San Francisco on July 29. The news that he was suffering from acute indigestion or perhaps even ptomaine poisoning did not seem unduly disturbing, so the huge headline in the *Daily Oklahoman* on Friday, August 3, was startling — "Harding Is Dead."[90] The cause was given as apoplexy, but many conflicting accounts of his last illness were to give rise in the years ahead to a story that is still murky.

So now the nation had a president who, rather ironically, has become as much a part of the legend of the Roaring Twenties as are Prohibition, jazz, Al Capone, flagpole sitting, hip flasks, mah-jongg, and crossword puzzles. Coolidge, however, did not contribute to any of these features of the decade. As Edward R. Murrow puts it on his excellent phonograph recording of the Twenties: "He [Coolidge] was calm, cool, and silent; the people were hot, hyperthyroid, and roaring."[91]

The band's last performance at the Criterion was to have been Saturday, August 12, but the theater asked them to remain one more day and urged the public to "hear them one more time offering a medley of all popular selections rendered by them during their stay in Oklahoma City." After they left, their place at the Spring Lake Pavilion was taken by the Sooner Serenaders Orchestra.[92] Joe, Coonie, and the others left Oklahoma City just as the Governor's dispute with the Klan-dominated legislature became heated. No doubt the band members were happy to let others enjoy such ennobling activities.

"We remained in Oklahoma City all summer," Joe later wrote with some exaggeration, "establishing a popularity that has never been approached. All were loathe [sic] to leave, even tho' the heat was terrific." In addition to the heat, Joe was having problems with two of his players, Carl "Swede" Nordberg† and Elmer "Crab" Kohlman, whom he fired for what he regarded as insubordination. On that sour note the band departed about August 13, the others driving back to Kansas

---

*Played on two occasions.
†By November 1923 Nordberg was playing with Eddie Kuhn's Kansas City Athletic Club Orchestra.

City, and Joe going alone to Joplin, Mo., where Madeline met him. The two of them spent a week's vacation at Lake Taneycomo, on the White River in Taney County, Mo.[93]

This was probably Joe's first visit to Lake Taneycomo and the Branson area, and in the following years he often went there — "God's country," he called it. On this occasion his camera saw much use as they moved about the lake in a boat, especially admiring such sights as the dock at the foot of Cliff House, near Branson. A hotel high up on the rocks was a "stiff climb," admitted Joe, so he and Madeline rented a cottage on more accessible land behind the hotel at Rockaway Beach. At the end of their visit, Joe promised himself to return.[94]

But Joe and Madeline had to cut short their visit to the lake, for word reached them that the band was having additional personnel problems. "We were forced," said Joe later, "to hurry back to Kansas City to recruit a new band." Kohlman and Nordberg, seething over their differences with Joe in Oklahoma City, "set about to wreck our band," as Joe put it. According to Sanders, they took advantage of Joe's and Coonie's absence from Kansas City and persuaded Happy Williams and Hal McLean to quit. "At this stage," said Joe, "Pop Estep and John Thiell proved their loyalty by making frantic efforts to locate Coon and me." They were successful and Joe, starting at 7 p.m., drove into Kansas City the following noon. Coonie had been only a short distance from Kansas City, so he got back first and took immediate steps to save the situation. He hired Ferdy Jacobs and Tom Beckham, and replaced McLean with Orville Knapp. But when Joe arrived on a Thursday, he found that the commitment for the following Saturday was going to be difficult. "It was sad music," he recalled later, "*but we opened* in spite of traitorism." A few months later Joe and Coonie re-hired Harold Thiell and let Jacobs go. All of this apparently worked out well, and according to Joe the band was "soon more popular than ever."[95]

In Kansas City the Royal Plantation Grill Syncopators, under the direction of Louis Forbstein, were playing at the Hotel Muehlebach for what was still being called the Nighthawk Frolic. In the latter part of August the Newman Theatre, not yet in its new fall season, was offering a program that included Fred Waring's Pennsylvanians, billed as a "novelty singing orchestra, 12 men, 40 instruments." (In the following years Coon-Sanders would form a close bond with Waring's group.) After Waring left, his place was taken by Art Landry's Orchestra.[96]

Coon-Sanders returned to the air at the Plantation Grill on Saturday, 1 September 1923, even as news was coming in about the terrible earthquake in Japan—"Tokio [*sic*] an Inferno," said a headline. The band's increasing national fame made them attractive to visiting celebrities, some of whom appeared with them on the Nighthawk Frolic. In early October, for example, comedians Willie and Eugene Howard were appearing in "The Passing Show" at the Shubert, and on October 9 they joined the Nighthawks to offer "songs, jokes and patter."[97] At the same time Emil Chaquette's band was playing at the Baltimore's Pompeiian Terrace, and one ad bid for public patronage for both orchestras during the new season:

> Learn the new dancing steps tonight at dinner. You'll find new dance tunes played in a tantalizing way, awaiting you tonight in both the Pompeiian Terrace and the Plantation Grill. The famous Coon-Sanders Orchestra is back at the Grill after a 3-months' tour, and is playing for both the dinner and late supper period. The popular Pompeiian Players, headed by Emil Chaquette, is playing for both the luncheon and dinner period in the Pompeiian Terrace.[98]

Somehow the Nighthawks managed to find time for yet more appearances, such as that at Convention Hall on September 25 and 26. Sponsored by the Merchants Association of Kansas City, it was the Second Annual Fall Fashion Pageant, an event that positively demanded music in this musical city.

"Street attire" was illustrated by, among others, the Newman Theatre. Joe Sanders wrote the music for the number "Autumn 1923," and Milton M. Feld, of the Newman, the lyrics.[99] Charitable events also often found the band receptive.

September of 1923 was a tolerably rollicking month, with enough violence to stir the hearts of all real he-men. Oklahoma Gov. J. C. Walton declared martial law in his fight with the state's Klan, and the latter, through its minions in the legislature, responded with a threat of impeachment. These were heady times for the treble-K, when it managed to spread itself over much of the nation, though not always without competition. In Williamson County, Ill., where Coon-Sanders would find themselves playing within one year, the Klan, facing competition, was taking on another equally patriotic and public-spirited organization called the Knights of the Flaming Circle.[100] And across the Atlantic, in Munich, Germany, a similarly inclined group called National Socialists were planning big things for November. By comparison, Jack Dempsey's boxing victory over Luis Firpo, on the fourteenth at New York's Polo Grounds, was not even an *hors d'oeuvre*.

According to Johnny Coon, while the Nighthawks were re-acclimating themselves to Kansas City that fall, one of the new members, Orville Knapp, was dating a young local woman named Lucille Fay LeSeur. Occasionally the two of them would drop by the Coon residence, where Eula Coon studied the young woman and decided she wasn't impressed. But apparently many others were, for Miss LeSeur shortly afterward made her way to Hollywood, where as Joan Crawford she became an important figure of what many have called the Golden Age of Hollywood. At about that same time, Orville's sister Evalyn also became a movie actress of some fame, possibly, said Johnny Coon, with Crawford's help.[101]

The Nighthawks returned to the Newman Theatre in mid-fall and continued to be billed as a "novelty singing orchestra." But reading through the files of the *Kansas City Star*, which still sponsored Nighthawk broadcasts, one rarely sees anything about the band, other than the perfunctory notes about the programs in the radio schedules. A year before, almost every issue of the paper had something about the late-night sessions, especially reprints of fan mail. One wonders whether the *Star* no longer considered the Nighthawk program newsworthy, or whether the Nighthawks' earlier close relationship with the paper and its radio station had become stale, if not frayed. Certainly, the broadcasts were as well received by the radio audience as ever.

Coon-Sanders continued to be seen and enjoyed at various places other than the Newman and the Plantation Grill. For example, in the Forum Cafeteria, at Twelfth Street and Grand Avenue, the band furnished the music for the city's newsboys at their annual Thanksgiving Day dinner. Along with the usual holiday food, there was entertainment by juvenile singers John and Edna Fitzpatrick, and even addresses by Sen. James A. Reed and Rep. Henry L. Jost, guests of honor. The Nighthawks agreed to play also for the newsboys' Christmas dinner. An article telling of these events identified the members of the orchestra, in addition to Coonie and Joe, as Ferdy Jacobs and Joe Richolson, trumpets; Pop Estep, bass; Nick Musolino, trombone; Tom Beckham, banjo; and Orville Knapp and John Thiell, saxophones.[102] (Harold Thiell still hadn't returned to the fold.)

Nicholas L. Musolino, the new trombonist, was a native of Quincy, Ill., where he was born 14 October 1898, the son of Louis and Mary Malambri Musolino. He got a standard education in the Quincy public school system and attended also Gem Business College. From Buck O'Farrell, Nick learned to play the trombone, and he decided early that he had no desire to enter his family's fruit and produce business. But before he could follow either of these paths, the nation entered the First World War. Recognizing his skills as a trombonist, the U.S.

Army enlisted him and put him into the 304th Cavalry Band. As he later explained, his first task was to teach a horse how to carry a man whose lips were trying to get meaningful sounds from a horn. That was no longer a problem after the unit had become mechanized and was moved from Leon Springs, Texas, to a motorized contingent at Camp Travis, near San Antonio. There, Sergeant Musolino was part of the Fifth Illinois Infantry Band, 33rd Division. It was considerably south of where Sergeant Joe Sanders, at Camp Bowie, was starting to try his hand at arranging, and it would be about five years before the two started working together. Nick spent two years and four months in the Army. Upon his release from the military, he went back to Quincy and its Gem City Business College. But business couldn't take the place of music for Nick, so he faced facts and went to Chicago to join the entertainment circuit. Eventually he arrived in Kansas City, and it was while he was playing with Haley's Fairyland Orchestra that Joe Sanders contacted him and invited him to join the Nighthawks.[103]

It was at about this time—the end of 1923—that banjoist Tom Beckham left the orchestra and was replaced by Dewey Birge. According to his granddaughter, Cathy Birge Williams, Dewey did not read music, but his interest in several different musical instruments developed into an ability to perform well on the banjo, guitar, violin, piano, and reeds. When he showed up to investigate the possibility of playing with Coon-Sanders, Coonie asked for a demonstration on the banjo and apparently was quite satisfied with what he heard. Later, says his granddaughter, Dewey often tried to give the impression that he was reading the scores right along with everyone else. When he thought he needed to add verisimilitude by turning a page, he did so.[104] But either he kept his secret from the rest of the band, or else he was so good that it was not important.

The Nighthawk Frolics celebrated its first anniversary on Monday, 3 December 1923, with a five-hour program—the actual anniversary was on the fourth. It began at eight o'clock with Ray Stinson's Serenaders playing a special dance program, followed by selections by the Orpheus Quartet. At ten o'clock there was an old-time "fiddlin'" contest that featured "Uncle Dan" Corbin, of Merwin, Mo., and several others. In addition, there were square dances, with a caller, done to the accompaniment of what someone termed "the never-to-be-forgotten tunes of yesteryear," and played by banjo and "three-string" guitar.[105]

At 11:30 p.m. the Nighthawks took over and played a large number of songs they had broadcast to great acclaim the previous season, such pieces as "The Nighthawk Blues," "Mister Gallagher and Mister Shean," and "You Tell Her, I Stutter." After signing off at 1 a.m., the band remained at the Muehlebach another hour and then retired to the WDAF studios where they played requests from the studio. The *Star* did give good coverage of this celebration, and noted that the Nighthawks had worn out four cow bells and taken in more than 80,000 members. The paper observed also that the Nighthawks "is one of the most widely known radio organizations in the country," and that it had never failed to broadcast a midnight program in its entire twelve months.* During this broadcast the Nighthawks' Merry Old Chief, Leo Fitzpatrick, received one of their more unusual telephone calls. From Richmond, Mo., a fan exclaimed that he could no longer talk, because his house was on fire.[106] It must have given new meaning to the popular term "hot music."

In Lincoln, Nebr., there was another variation on the wacky Nighthawk story. According to one listener:

> We had a very modern fright the other night. Returning late from some enter-

---

By the term "Nighthawks," the Star *included the band that had filled in for Coon-Sanders during the previous summer. That is why Coon-Sanders often termed itself the* Original Nighthawk Orchestra.

Henry Dewey Birge and his wife Sara. Birge, Nighthawk banjoist in 1924–25, appears here in band attire. Sara's photograph taken at age 18. (Courtesy Cathy Birge Williams.)

tainment, we braved the imaginary dangers of a dark garage and side porch, which reports of recent robberies seemed to people with crouching bandits, and slid silently through the side door into a dimly lighted house.

Imagine our consternation to hear a husky voice, entirely unfamiliar and unmistakably belonging to a man, in a nearby room, which said, "How do you like that?"

Mental pictures of yeggs gloating over the wife's jewel box or dividing the family silver flashed across our mind. We were undecided whether to make a run for the telephone or to slip back out of the side door when the voice was followed by a crash of dance music and the "Nighthawks" of Kansas City were tempting the universe to dance.

The radio had been unintentionally left on while tuned in for Kansas City and the greeting from the husky voice was the "Jolly Old Chief" asking his listeners how they liked the program.[107]

Three days later the great news event seemed to be that radio, including WDAF, for the first time carried a presidential address. Calvin Coolidge, breaking what had been a considerable silence since his assumption of imperial purple, presented to Congress a speech whose length seemed to belie his reputation for brevity. Coolidge showed on many occasions that regardless of his prosaic reputation, he possessed a flair for engagingly dry humor. Some of it pertained to this very reputation for economy in speech. He once justified his habit of verbal economy with, "I think the American public wants a solemn ass as President and I think I'll go along with them."[108] But what is perhaps a much better-known aphorism comes from a speech Coolidge made in Washington on 17 January 1925, before the American Society of Newspaper Editors: "The business of America is business." It let the editors, and the nation, know just where the government's chief interest would be for at least the next four years. And for the benefit of those nations, America's Allies in the late war, who were hoping that the United States might relent on repayment of war debts, Coolidge came out with another terse pronouncement which showed that when he said *business*, he meant business abroad as well as at home: "They hired the money didn't they? Let them pay it." Of this presidential opinion, the quintessential Englishman, Winston Leonard Spencer Churchill, from whom the world would soon hear plenty more, observed with equal terseness: "This laconic statement was true, but not exhaustive."[109]

But whatever else Mr. Coolidge may have been, he was *not* an orator; and if there is somewhere in space where spent sounds are idling about, my guess is that the Nighthawks would make far better listening for anyone able to tap that sonic limbo.

CHAPTER FIVE

Chicago's Congress Hotel

In 1924 the Nighthawks and the Victor Talking Machine Company had their first contract, which ran for one year, beginning April 5. It provided that "for the purpose of making complete, perfect and approved master records" the Nighthawks would assemble at a Victor recording laboratory and make four recordings, to be selected by Victor, and perhaps more if the Company chose. "No master record shall be considered satisfactory or complete and perfect," said the contract, "until it has been approved by an authorized representative of the Victor Company." The contract further provided that Victor would, within ten days after each recording session, "pay to Mr. Coon and Mr. Sanders or to one of them, the sum of two hundred dollars ... and shall thereupon be without further obligation ... to either of them or to the orchestra or to any member thereof...." In other words, there would be no royalties, which at the time was about standard, especially for a band just beginning its recording career.[1] The band went to Chicago for the recording sessions that lasted from April 5 through April 7. At the first session "Nighthawk Blues" was cut. The next day came "Red-hot Mama," "Oriental Love Dreams," and "There's No One Just Like You." On the final day "Why Don't My Dreams Come True?" and "My Daddy's Dream Time Lullaby" were cut. All recordings were accepted and issued. After the Nighthawks returned to Kansas City, the Victor Company wired Joe and Coonie on May 8 to congratulate them on their first recordings, and to ask them to send, by special delivery, materials that would help create window displays for at least fifty Chicago Victor dealers. "If you wish to cooperate," said the wire, "please send ... two photographs [of the] orchestra for enlargement and fifty photographs within [the] week...."[2]

As New York's *Variety* observed, bands were finding good recordings useful in the place of salesmen. Heretofore, it had been necessary, in arranging distant engagements, for a cafe or hotel owner, or his representative, to visit and hear the band. Now, an orchestra could wrap up some of its best recordings and send them, perhaps with a few photos, for examination.[3]

Most Kansas City bands in the early Twenties seemed to change personnel frequently, and this included even the Night-

5. Chicago's Congress Hotel

On the muddy way to Chicago, near Odessa, Missouri, mid–May 1923. The old taunt "Get on a horse!" was still apt. (Courtesy Special Collections, Kansas City [Mo.] Public Library.)

hawks, at least in their early years. By the time the band was finishing its obligations in Kansas City, in May 1924, however, the band's membership was much more stable. The members now, in addition to Joe and Coonie, were probably as follows: Dewey Birge, banjo; Pop Estep, bass; Orville Knapp, Harold Thiell and John Thiell, reeds; Joe Richolson, trumpet; and Nick Musolino, trombone.

About the time that their contract with the Newman came to an end in the spring of 1924, the band received a letter from Jack Huff, manager of the Lincoln Tavern, in Morton Grove, Ill., on Chicago's north side. Huff expressed an interest in hiring the band. At first, Joe regarded the offer as some sort of joke from a small town, and he answered it in that spirit. About a week later, however, Huff visited the Nighthawks at the Muehlebach, listened to their music, and made a definite offer. As Joe later wrote, "On a cold day in March [1924], I made a flying trip to Chicago, had luncheon at the La Salle, and then drove out 21 miles to see the Lincoln Tavern." He was so impressed by what he saw, and the offer of $1,250 a week, that he turned down an identical offer from Chicago's Rainbo Gardens. This was good pay compared with what the Nighthawks had been getting, though it was less than half of what an even better-known band might make for that much work and in the choicest places. At about the same time, for instance, Vincent Lopez was getting $2,800 for one week at New York's Hippodrome. But it was good enough for Joe, who went before the musicians union and then signed with Huff for the summer.[4]

Eagerly the Nighthawks set out for Morton Grove, via St. Louis. At Odessa, just east of Kansas City, they again confronted the realities of highway travel in the 1920s. The preceding year the Nighthawks had been flooded on their way to Oklahoma City. Now it was just mud, enough of it to supply both parties for that year's presidential campaigns.* Joe got several appalling snapshots

---

*Except that the political weapon of choice in that year's election was not so much mud as oil.

of their line of cars mired down, as a team of horses tugged at Joe's "Thud" Cadillac leading the caravan. Behind him came Coonie's "Scatterbolt" Cadillac, Richolson's "Kiddiecar" Maxwell, Harold and John Thiell in their "Covered Wagon" Buick, Pop Estep in his Buick "Airedale," Musolino's "Cheese Box" Essex, and Knapp's "Paint Job" Studebaker. One of Joe's shots shows the Thiells' car mired to its axles, and Joe's apostrophic exclamation, "Oh! Mud, here is thy victory! What a life! And what a road!" The Thiells' stranded vehicle elicited Joe's comment, "The Thiell Boys sans locomotion!"[5] But the band's excitement over their new engagement apparently compensated for Mother Nature's covering their road to adventure with mud rather than red carpet.

There is an interesting footnote to the Nighthawks' muddy progress to Chicago. Joe said that seven automobiles made the trip—the Thiell brothers rode together. For some reason, Dewey Birge, banjoist, seems not to have driven an automobile with them. But he had not left the band at that time, for Joe pretty clearly says in his records that Birge left them about April 1925, just before the start of their road tour that month.[6] But did Birge travel alone for some reason and join them for their week in St. Louis and their two quick engagements in Illinois? Perhaps he was riding with one of the others. Joe is silent on the point.

Starting on May 4, the band appeared for a week at the Missouri Theater in St. Louis. Their radio fame, now enhanced by some really good phonograph recordings, brought them great acclaim from theater patrons at the Missouri, as well as flattering reviews by the *Globe-Democrat*, whose critic declared Coon-Sanders "deserving of their popularity." The band, said the paper, was "[A] performance in itself." The audience applauded lustily and kept applauding even after the band had ended its program and the feature film was starting. Especially successful were their renditions of "Hula Lou" and "It Ain't Gonna Rain No Mo'."[7]

The latter song was at this time seeing some special use during the congressional and presidential campaigns in 1924. The Republicans were trying to overcome the effects of the Harding scandals, as revealed by Democratic Senator Thomas J. Walsh, of Montana, and his investigators. Newspaper cartoonists, especially Democratic ones, were delighted with all the ramifications of the mess and pilloried such inviting targets as Edward B. McLean, oilmen Harry F. Sinclair and Edward L. Doheny, and cabinet member Edwin N. Denby. McLean was theoretically a newspaper tycoon but was better described as simply a wealthy playboy married to Evelyn Walsh McLean, famous for her Washington parties and for owning the Hope Diamond. Sinclair and Doheny were three hundred-percent American go-getters, and Denby was a rather naïve, but apparently honest, secretary of the Navy. One cartoonist showed a distraught GOP elephant and a happy Democratic donkey doing a vaudeville duet, a take-off on that year's popular song "It Ain't Gonna Rain No Mo'":

> ELEPHANT: O, we ain't gwine steal no mo',
> We ain' gwine steal no mo';
> DONKEY: But how'n the 'ell kin the country tell—You ain' gwine steal no mo'?[8]

Despite much public ridicule and indignation, the Grand Old Party managed to weather the Harding legacy. It was, in fact, not a good time for the Democrats. Their nominating convention, held in terrible heat at New York's Madison Square Garden, dragged on for *ten days* and *103 ballots*. It was a dismal record for length and misery. The party was so divided between Alfred E. Smith's forces for repeal of Prohibition and those backing William Gibbs McAdoo (whose supporters favored Prohibition and soft-pedaled anti–Klan rhetoric) that the convention compromised on an unlikely choice, John W. Davis, a New York lawyer. Calvin Coolidge clobbered them in November.

But the Nighthawks were heading toward Chicago and a much more agreeable and interesting summer than political conventions afforded. The band members most likely were not especially interested in either Republicans or Democrats. Probably the nearest they came to current practical politics was with the aforementioned mud, and with ascertaining the best places in the Chicago area for convenient and potable spirits. They would find the city a hospitable oasis and a population contemptuous of the Volstead Act. In fact, when in December of 1925 Clarence Darrow and the Rev. John Haynes Holmes, a Unitarian from New York, debated Prohibition, the wet Darrow won handily.[9]

Chicago's city officials would give the band little to fear so far as a plentiful supply of social beverages was concerned. William E. Dever, mayor when the Nighthawks arrived, had campaigned on a reform platform, but at the end of his term in 1927 the city had changed little with regard to crime and corruption. He was followed by William Hale Thompson's second term, during which the city's officials were even less effective. Those who disagreed with Prohibition had little to fear from Thompson, or as *Variety* put it, the new mayor was "strong for personal liberty." Mayor Thompson was well aware of the opinions of a majority of Chicagoans about alcoholic beverages, and he endorsed those views absolutely. When his chief of police held his first captains' meeting, the chief ordered his men "to stop kicking in people's doors in the search of home brew." Said the chief, "If a man wants to have a good time, that's his business, as long as he doesn't violate the law or interfere with the rights of others." His object, he said, was to prosecute crooks and thugs, not to engage in wholesale arrests and raids.[10] As it turned out, crooks and thugs, as well, had nothing to fear.

As a matter of fact, Americans were now in their fifth year of Prohibition, quite long enough to find ways around its severities. And if the Nighthawks were ever seriously incommoded by the legislation, there is no evidence of it in any records I've seen. It was at this time that *Variety* concluded that there were, by late 1924, more cabarets, night clubs, and restaurants in the larger cities than there had been in those same cities in 1919. And yet, concluded the same report, prohibition was a success. What! How could that be? Why, because the people had their liquor, and the politicians had their glorious issue. To be "strong for law enforcement" always seemed to resonate well in most American states. *Variety* suggested that "there isn't a politician in any city of consequence in this Union that wants to see prohibition abolished!" This same report added: "When you can send trucks loaded with whiskey in cases from New York to Chicago, over state lines, through cities and counties, and deliver it in Chicago ... Kid, there's something doing somewhere." As one proceeded inland, one found prices rising, even on the Canadian border. But better avoid the booze on the Mexican border, warned *Variety*, "It's poison down there." What the United States government was losing on liquor taxes, the distillers and bootleggers were raking in almost obscenely. Even in Britain the distilleries were working overtime to slake Americans' thirst. What cost $40 a case in New York would cost more in such places as Syracuse, Buffalo, or Cleveland; and by the time the imbiber reached Chicago, he'd better have about $80 or go on the wagon. Some of the cost was a result of having to pay protection. Said *Variety*, the payment ranged from two to five dollars a case, "depending [on] where and when, whom and how." The payment might go through two or three stages with a five dollar payment covering all. In other words, one man might be in charge of a large district, "protecting" everybody. *Variety* asked sarcastically, "Are you listening, Mr. Volstead?"[11] It would appear that the only party not benefiting from this arrangement was the United States Treasury.

Following the week in St. Louis and brief appearances at La Salle and Marseilles, Ill., the Nighthawks pulled into Chicago, all seven cars, traveling duck-fashion with Joe in the lead. They must have attracted quite a lot of attention as they progressed along Chicago's streets, especially at one intersection where

Joe, unfamiliar with local traffic laws, took an illegal left turn and was obediently followed by each of the other cars. A nearby traffic policeman was too surprised to do anything but gape at what Joe termed "our innocent disregard of all signals."[12] Or, perhaps the policeman was concerned with such other, more serious matters as the city's growing problem with so-called *organized* crime — imagine how many corpses might have turned up if it had been *disorganized*! And in a few days the police would be investigating the murder, on May 21, of a young boy named Bobby Franks, by two wealthy, brilliant, socially prominent young men named Richard Loeb and Nathan Leopold, Jr. It would be termed the "crime of the century."

All the evidence suggests that Jack Huff had reason to congratulate himself, not only for his shrewd guessing, but for his good fortune, as well — for Coon-Sanders had turned down some other offers.[13] The Nighthawks apparently were at their best at the Lincoln Tavern, and the public responded handsomely. *Variety*, which earlier had perhaps been prejudiced by the band's connection with radio, was only now beginning to pay some attention to these Kansas City boys. The paper had to admit that though the Lincoln Tavern "had been an elephant," matters were now different; and "with a recognized organization the place has been doing capacity business, though located 20 miles from the city." In a brief sketch of the band, *Variety* spoke of their performance for Huff: "They have a keen conception of rhythm and their arranger is deserving of special mention. The boys work well together, inserting several original novelties." The same writer predicted their success, should they take to the vaudeville circuits.[14] Another of the newspaper's correspondents questioned several of the bands in and around Chicago as to the songs they were asked most often to play. Coon-Sanders said their listeners seemed most to enjoy "June Night," "Spain," "S-h-i-n-e," "Lazy," "Remembering," "Mandalay," and "When Lights Are Low," all of them from 1923 and 1924.[15]

The Nighthawks played for Huff's Lincoln Tavern until the middle of August and pretty clearly enjoyed being in the Chicago area. Joe later boasted that they transformed the "dear old Lincoln Tavern," previously a "white elephant," into a "bonanza." (As we saw just above, *Variety* called the Lincoln Tavern merely "an elephant.") Joe and Madeline, and probably some of the other band members, lived in Evanston at the Evanston Hotel, which Sanders sarcastically referred to as the "Ritzy Evanston." In his opinion, it housed "more old fossils and retired physical wrecks than can be found in any county home." Neither Joe nor Madeline liked the place, but Joe did say that the "inmates" gave him a lot of ideas for future comedy skits.[16]

Sometime during the summer's engagement at the Tavern, Joe swapped his Cadillac for a sportier Moon sedan, which he described as "a good little buggy." It boasted such accessories as sleek, slanting, metal ornaments just behind the rear side windows, and jaunty spare wheels at the front of the running boards.[17]

After the band finished its summer engagement at the Lincoln Tavern, Joe and Madeline checked into Chicago's Sherman Hotel.[18] Eventually, as we shall soon see, they put up at the Surf Hotel. Though Madeline often traveled with Joe, Eula Coon's small children kept her in Kansas City except for occasional short visits with her husband. In the coming years one or more of the Coon family visited from time to time, and sometime about 1930 Coonie's entire family lived in Chicago for about a year.

Jules Caesar Stein was born in South Bend, Ind., on 26 April 1896, about seven months before little Joe Sanders started using his powerful vocal chords. Stein's father, a storekeeper, sent his son to the University of Chicago. There, having paid part of his expenses by playing violin and saxophone in various dance bands, Jules, according to an obituary in *Variety*, was graduated at the early age of eighteen. In 1921 he received his M.D. degree from Rush Medical

Coonie (left) and Joe at Evanston Hotel, Evanston, Illinois, where at least some of the band lived, summer 1924, while playing at Lincoln Tavern. (Courtesy Special Collections, Kansas City [Mo.] Public Library.)

College and the following year began studying ophthalmology at the University of Vienna, in Austria. Having earlier started his residency at Cook County Hospital, he returned there in 1923 to become chief resident in ophthalmology. Meanwhile, he still occasionally played with dance bands, sometimes leading his own. He entered private practice as assistant to Dr. Harry Gradle, and even wrote a treatise, "Telescopic Spectacles and Magnifiers as Aids to Poor Vision."[19]

Dr. Stein was finding himself a very busy fellow, what with his medical practice and his musical commitments. At times his schedule was so complicated that he was unable to play at engagements and had to ask other ensembles to fill in for him. In other words, he had added another activity, that of a part-time agent. It gave him an idea, however, and by 1924 Stein had decided that ophthalmology was less interesting and remunerative than running a booking agency for bands. He and his brother Billy had already been placing a few bands, and Jules was also trying to get Ernie Young, a booking agent with whom he was sharing office space, to work with them to form an agency that would challenge Edgar Benson's well-entrenched organization. For a short period Young and the Steins did work together

About spring of 1924, probably in the Chicago area. Coon in rear; others (from left): J. Thiell, Sanders, Knapp, Birge (?) H. Thiell, Estep, Richolson, and Musolino. (Courtesy Kansas City [Mo.] Museum.)

modestly, but Young wasn't interested in going in the direction that Stein was contemplating. This brought them to a parting, but Stein proposed purchasing one of several business names that Young was using — Music Corporation of America. The price was $10,000, which Stein would soon earn from his first major client, the Nighthawks. Meanwhile, the grand sound of the new company's name was just that, grand in name only. To give it substance, the Steins would need clients, *good* clients, and plenty of them.[20]

In the Chicago area at that time there were plenty of potential clients, some good, but most only so-so. One observer said bands and orchestras outnumbered any other type of vaudeville entertainment at that time in Chicago. A previous demand for such groups had resulted in a plethora by the summer of 1924, when there were about seventy bands under contract with agents. There were even seven female groups and two more exotic ones, one Indian and one Chinese. The problem, however, was that the uneven quality of these groups meant that only a few had been successful in getting bookings. There were cafes and dance halls looking for bands, but the demand was for those with reputation and skill. The Lincoln Tavern had been very lucky in attracting Coon-Sanders. By doing so, Jack Huff had completely turned his luck around, but that was exceptional. More typical was Chicago's College Inn, which in past summers had tried to economize with lesser-known groups and had suffered. In 1924 it bombed royally.[21]

According to Carl Kramer, the Nighthawks were not especially well known in the Chicago area in 1924, except to those who were avid radio fans. But it was at the Lincoln Tavern, in the summer of 1924, that the band met Jules Stein, destined to prove very important to their future fame. Johnny Coon said that the band began to notice a bright-looking young man who kept coming back day after day. After about a week, the stranger sent a note to Coonie and Joe asking for an opportunity to speak with them. He liked what he had been hearing and strongly urged the band to let him send them on a short tour of one-night stands. After some initial reluctance on the part of the band's members, especially Coonie, Joe and Coonie finally agreed, provided Stein would pay the band $10,000. That gave Stein pause, for he knew he didn't have anywhere near that much money. After pondering the matter, however, Stein returned and said he'd give them $2,000 when they signed a contract and the rest when they went on tour. But knowing that he didn't have even the $2,000, Stein cleverly gambled on the band's great popularity throughout the Midwest and the dance halls' willingness to pay fifty percent in advance. He was correct. In this way, says Dennis McDougal, Stein was able to pay off Coon-Sanders before they ever played a note.[22]

Thus, what Stein was proposing would be beneficial almost immediately both to him and to Coon-Sanders. Stein himself had insufficient money to start such an enterprise properly, and the few bands he already had signed up were not likely to bring in enough. As for what Coon-Sanders would get from such an association, years later Johnny Coon observed that back in the early and middle Twenties, bands often had a difficult time getting engagements. Agents, especially good ones, were few; and when bands tried to get gigs on their own, they often met suspicion and even hostility. Moreover, many theaters and auditoriums had poor facilities and were distant from acceptable lodging. A good booking agent could allow an orchestra to concentrate on its music and not waste time and effort on such matters as scheduling of events, travel accommodations, and meals and lodging.[23]

According to Joe Sanders, Stein was not then popular with musicians in the Chicago area, mainly because of their fear of the Benson Agency, which was, in Sanders' phrasing, "king of the ten per centers."[24] Kramer corroborates this and says that the Benson Agency "had a firm hammerlock on the Chicago hotel and cafe business." Stein was looking for more bands to represent, especially good ones; and when he heard the Nighthawks at the Lincoln, says Kramer, he "was immediately captivated by the brilliant performance." Kramer continued:

> Both Joe and Coonie were in their prime and their wonderful singing both in solo and duet, plus the strong beat and contagious rhythms, told him that this was the band he must have for his new company. Again it must be emphasized that the dance beat in the early Twenties was much faster than in later years and this speed seemed to give the dancers a pleasure and exuberance which started to diminish when the slower tempos came into popularity. It is also possible that the average dancer was younger then and more physically able to handle the breaknecking [sic] pace of the speedy one-steps which were so prevalent from about 1914 to 1928. Certainly no orchestra of that time could dish out a faster or more enthusiastic beat than the Coon-Sanders Nighthawks.[25]

Johnny Coon, Carleton's son, said many years later that his father, had he lived, might have been interested in getting out of the band and working in a booking agency. "That's where the money was, anyway," observed Johnny. The younger Coon, who had his own booking agency in later years, said that Jules Stein had approached his father about the latter's joining MCA.[26] Stein seemed to like Coonie, and the two would probably have found each other very compatible.

The contract with Coon-Sanders was only a temporary one, but Stein hoped for something more substantial later. He soon got it, and according to John Coon, Stein ever afterward credited the Nighthawks with, in effect, having been the genesis of the Music Corporation of America, destined to be the giant among booking agencies in

America. In fact, according to Johnny Coon, the Nighthawks, between 1924 and 1932, made more money for Stein and MCA than any other orchestra except Guy Lombardo's, and Lombardo was an exception because he dealt with MCA over a much longer period. Kramer later said that by the late Twenties the Nighthawks were "unquestionably the number one dance orchestra in the Middle West and possibly the entire U.S."[27]

Thus, with hope, shrewd guessing, and not much else, Stein founded the Music Corporation of America — he fancied the name because it reminded him of the prestigious-sounding Radio Corporation of America. By the next year Stein was so involved in this new enterprise, and so encouraged by its success, that he gave up entirely his medical practice. At first he experimented with such groups as the Memphis Five and the Dixieland Jazz Band. With these, and especially with the Coon-Sanders Nighthawks, he pioneered in the one night stand and the exclusive contract. By the summer of 1924 the MCA had advanced sufficiently to advertise jointly with the Ernie Young Music Corporation, in New York's *Variety*. Among the bands in the advertisement were, in first place, the Nighthawks, followed by Paul Biese, Paul Specht, Seattle Harmony Kings, Glenn Welty, Frank Karcher's Egyptian Serenaders, King Oliver's Jazz Band, Bob White and His Hollywood Gang, Billy Goodheart* and the Illinois Collegians, Coonie Conrad, Louis Culp and the Continental Concert Orchestra, Virginia Ramblers, Art Payne, Jack Wright and the Nomads of Syncopation, and J. C. Turner and the Southern Serenaders. And, in a positioning and phraseology reflective of the times, the last named band was that of "Edgar and His Champion Colored Orchestra."[28]

With success came not only prosperity but also envy from competitors. Stein attracted the interest also of a very much more dangerous party. The bootlegging gangsters in the Chicago area, particularly Roger Touhy, began demanding that MCA cut them in on its profits. Stein, explaining later that he had "the guts of a fool," took out a hefty insurance policy on himself and rashly ignored these demands. With even greater bravado, he began selling not only music stands and automobiles to the expected customers, but even liquor to nightclubs.[29] He appeared to be confusing business with suicide.

From the very start of his new enterprise, Stein was aware of the importance of radio and hotels in putting over a band. The Nighthawks were proving it and so would other bands. Hotels were prominent among the engagements that MCA got for Coon-Sanders throughout the Midwest, South, and Atlantic Seaboard; but after he became the agent for the Guy Lombardo Orchestra in 1927, that was the ensemble that Stein promoted on the East Coast. In fact, there are those who believe that the reason Coon-Sanders did not play in New York City until quite late was that by 1928 Stein had switched his main interest to the Lombardo Orchestra and wished it to have no competition in New York from MCA bands. Whatever the truth of that may be, Stein was always careful to see that both of these popular bands, as well as others that he represented, had plenty of exposure on radio and in the best hotels. One of Billy Goodheart's chief duties, in fact, was to sell the MCA's bands to hotels.[30]

Stein's conviction that radio would be important to his bands was quite contrary to what many others in the entertainment industry believed in these early years of the new medium. By the mid–Twenties there was great hostility in the world of the stage — legitimate, operatic, and vaudeville — to what was regarded as radio's parasitism, that is, its use *gratis* of copyrighted songs.[31] Moreover, some critics alleged that radio brought overexposure to stars and thus hurt their attractiveness at the box-office and their reputations as artists. The Musical

---

*Later to work as an MCA administrator.

Managers Association, in fact, forbade its performers to broadcast.[32] This was a debatable assertion and ignored the eagerness that many fans felt in wishing to see popular figures whom they had previously only heard. Perhaps at the base of all this animosity toward radio was the obvious fact that it was keeping many potential ticket buyers at home. It was the same problem that television would create in later years for cinema. And both of them eventually killed old-time radio. (Vaudeville, radio, and film star Fred Allen, who disliked television, explained on one occasion to Tallulah Bankhead that he knew why television was called a *medium*—"Because nothing is well done.")[33]

Some of the editorial board at *Variety* engaged in a vendetta against radio and alternated between scathing articles charging it almost with vampirism, and others in which it gleefully predicted radio's decline. Said the newspaper with relish in one typical article: "Radio is fast losing its grip. That is the combined belief of the owner of a broadcasting station and from a theatre manager on Broadway of a big picture theatre, verified in turn by the manager of another Broadway picture house who states that there has been a tremendous falling off in fan letters."[34] The New York weekly reported in May of 1924 that big-time vaudeville, convinced that melodies "exploited through air" became too familiar, was banning their use. The Keith Vaudeville Circuit forced Vincent Lopez, the previous month, to keep his band off the radio while under contract with them. The allegation was that the public tended to become saturated with radio bands and thus less willing to hear them in theaters.[35] The decision, in the summer of 1924, by the National Music Managers' Association's New York office not to play or book concert artists who appeared on radio was a result of its belief that no artist giving free time on radio improved theater attendance.[36]

Though *Variety* continued its anti-radio crusade, there were some on that paper's staff who, while probably outnumbered, had different opinions. In September 1924 *Variety*, quoting anti-radio elements in both Chicago and New York, again averred that radio's popularity had passed its peak. "Music men generally noted with satisfaction," said one article, "the Washington report in last week's *Variety* that 16 radio stations had reported suspension during August, as against four new stations starting."[37] On the other hand, one finds occasionally in *Variety* references to radio that were fairly free of bias. The paper's own Abel Green observed that though radio had been blamed for damaging the sale of phonograph recordings, one recording artist had told him that the problem lay with the record companies. Radio, said the artist, had developed remarkably, while the making of recordings hadn't changed greatly in ten years.[38] A year, however, would bring in the electrical recording process.

Ironically, it was "variety" itself—that is, vaudeville—that by the mid–Twenties was showing signs of senescence. Many articles in *Variety* spoke of one or another of the symptoms. Poor attendance, for example, though partly a result of competition from radio and Hollywood, had other causes, as well. One factor that became increasingly obvious as the Twenties began to wane was that many vaudeville stars were flirting with radio and cinema, a situation caused partly by the dictatorial attitudes of some of those who controlled the vaudeville circuits.[39] It appears that vaudeville's decline was the result of several causes, and that it probably was "just one of those things" that Cole Porter later celebrated in song. As a matter of fact, vaudeville, as a significant institution, would barely survive the decade.

Nevertheless, many bands, in addition to Coon-Sanders, continued to do well over the radio and to take a commanding position in the development of American jazz and popular music. One of those was Meyer Davis, who in July of 1924 engaged in a little of the hokum that, in retrospect at least, lends so much charm to the decade. Pretending to think the word *jazz* a bit *infra dignitatem* and, as the British might say, *non-U*, he increased his popularity with the public by conducting, via radio, a contest to invent a new, and supposedly better, name for America's new music. At that time Davis's orchestra was playing mainly in Washington, D.C., in his own restaurant called Le Paradis, on Thomas Circle. By the middle of the summer at least 700,000 suggestions had come in. Among them were the following somewhat improbable ones: fron fron, melody rhythmic, rhythmic-reverie, rhapsodoom, rigsody, peppo, ufon, exilera, Hades harmonies, syncodavis, joghop, dancial, merryhop, paradisa, syncosway, glideola, swazee, en cadence, syncomelo, mah song, gee miss, melojings, and besto music.[40] Doubtless the word *jazz* was never in any real danger.

At this point it would be useful to say something about Chicago's night life as it was when the Nighthawks went there. Writing in the fall of 1925 when Coon-Sanders was in its second season at the Congress Hotel, Chicagoan Jack Lait found the city's cabaret life depressing by comparison with what he recalled from earlier years. To describe it, he said, was like writing the obituary of a good friend. "Time was," he added, "and not so long ago, that Chicago had perhaps the most picturesque and colorful night life on the globe, which seems paradoxical for a mid-western, young, rushing commercial center; but it is true." He went on to observe that Chicago had "flashed" the first cabaret in America, and had started the "metropolitan dancing craze" that the world subsequently took up. What was more, he said, "Chicago, with the most sinister and yet the most atmospheric 'line' on the continent when vice was legal, still had the knack of maintaining night life which was buoyant and merry and giddy apart from the scarlet and black of its segregated sins." He ran through a list of the city's hot spots, and concluded that of them all, but few such as Ike Bloom's and Mike Fritzel's had survived. Bloom was still there but had moved downtown above the Garrick Inn. Fritzel now had the Friar's. Lait cited a few other spots and paid a compliment to the Balloon Room at the Hotel Congress, whose Coon-Sanders Orchestra was "excellent." But what of the rest of it? "Well," said Lait, "Chicago is still a city of more than 3,000,000, and in such a population there will always be a demand and an outlet for a few animated spirits. But the zip and rebound have seeped out of my beloved old home burg."[41]

In his unpublished story of the Music Corporation of America, Karl Kramer has given a fairly detailed picture of the musical and dancing scene in Chicago during the late Teens and early Twenties. In an account somewhat less lugubrious than that by Lait, Kramer says that sometime about 1920, the city's dance halls were geographically divided into northern, western, and southern areas. Each had its own dancers who rarely ventured into the other sections. Even the bands and favorite dance steps often tended to differ among areas, though this diversity had pretty much broken down by 1930. "During the pre-radio days, from 1920-25," writes Kramer, "the growth of the name dance orchestra was slow and sporadic. Starting in 1926, the band snowball really started rolling; and, by 1930 ... exploded into orchestras of all sizes and styles...."[42]

According to Kramer, the very early ballrooms included the White City Ballroom, on the Southside, that catered to dancers who attended the park's rides and exhibits nearby. It became so popular that it remained open during the winter when other parts of the park were closed. On the West Side the largest ballroom was Guyon's Paradise. But Kramer says that the "real hot spots" were the two Merry Gardens, one of which was on the North Side and the other on the South Side, both under the same management. They were low-priced and were popular with dancers too young for the cafes or nightclubs.[43]

"The entire ballroom picture of Chicago changed about 1923," says Kramer, "when Andrew Karzas decided that the dancers of Chicago deserved something better than a warehouse, [or] square brick building to do their stuff." On the South Side Karzas built the Trianon, which Kramer calls "the first of the really great and beautiful ballrooms." Its name implied a similarity to the two small palaces built at Versailles by Louis XIV, especially the Petit Trianon that was so popular with Marie Antoinette. The new ballroom drew dancers away from other places, and within two years other dance spots suffered a decline. Some of them even closed. "From that time on," says Kramer, "the Trianon remained as the only big ballroom on the Chicago South Side." It was spectacular with its fine carpets, beautiful drapes, elegant lighting, elaborate decorations, and attractive balconies and restrooms.[44]

Among the other popular dancing spots in 1925 mentioned by Kramer are the following: Alamo Cafe, Crillon Cafe, Citro's Cafe, Deauville, Erie Cafe, Friar's Inn, Frolic's Cafe, Gingham Inn (later the Granada Cafe), Kelly Stables, La Boheme, Liberty Inn, Moulin Rouge, Montmartre, Merry Go Round, Palais de la Rue, Pershing Palace, Rendezvous, Silver Slipper, and Valentino Inn. Though all of them had dance orchestras, rarely did their ads mention them by name. Among the exceptions were Charlie Straight at the Rendezvous, Verne Buck at the Montmartre, Al Handler at the Alamo, and Bernie Cummins at the Pershing Palace. At first the Chez Paree, one of the most popular Chicago nightclubs, did not advertise its orchestras; but by 1925, when Earl Hoffman's band was playing there, it did. Two other popular dance places that year also had distinctive orchestras, the Hotel Sherman's College Inn, which offered Isham Jones, and the Edgewater Beach, which had Ted Fiorito and Danny Russo's Oriole Orchestra.[45] About another dance spot, where Coon-Sanders would later entertain, Kramer had this to say:

> The to-be-famous Dells, most popular north side roadhouse, run by that very nice guy Sam Hare, had an orchestra known as the Genevans, formerly the Inspirators. Neither name survived. Sam in the few short years [he operated] became completely sold on the name dance orchestra and later featured Coon-Sanders and other prominent orchestras. The Dells continued to be the top summer spot until that unfortunate night when Jake Factor was kidnapped coming from the Dells and the authorities never let Sam operate in Cook County again. He was a very generous and likeable fellow, pleasant to do business with, and probably the most generous and open-hearted customer we [i.e., the Music Corporation of America] ever had.[46]

In mid–August, after their remunerative stint at the Lincoln Tavern, the Nighthawks anticipated an exciting and, as it would prove, profitable short tour. Jules Stein was sending them into completely new territory and requiring them to master new tactics—for about five weeks. But what then? Would they return to Kansas City in the fall? Before they began their tour, Jack Huff arranged for Joe and Coonie to talk with H.L. Kaufman, head of Chicago's Hotel Congress. Kaufman promised to give serious consideration, and a quick decision, to hiring the band for the fall and winter.[47]

And so it was that Coon-Sanders began fulfilling their commitment to Jules Stein for a thirty-two-day series of engagements throughout the Midwest. Harold Thiell years later recalled that the tour began on Labor Day of 1924, but Joe Sanders, probably correctly, remembered the date as August 29.[48]

With Hank Linder accompanying them as tour manager and Cory Adams as assistant, they made their first stop at Elkhart, Ind. As soon as the band members stepped off the train, Joe and his camera quickly proceeded to snap everyone's photo. Their baggage of fourteen huge trunks and a number of smaller items must have attracted quite a bit of attention atop the large station trucks. It certainly attracted Joe's attention for he got several shots of them, as well as of Linder carting two rather heavy suitcases. In another picture several redcaps eye the rest of the baggage professionally, and the band members stand idly and watch others handle the heavy stuff. In one photo Harold Thiell

Knapp (left) and Sanders clown for the camera, on tour September 1924. (Courtesy Special Collections, Kansas City [Mo.] Public Library.)

smiles at the camera and shades his eyes from the sun. Later, Joe wrote beneath the photo, "Harold, wearing a smile that was to come off the next day in a wild Yellow Cab cross-country trip." Joe labeled a shot of Orville Knapp as "being his silly, lovable self"; and another snapshot showed, as Joe put it, "'Jawn' Thiell, idol of the sport world." In a style that falls heavily on today's more sensitive ears, Joe described the photo of Nick Musolino as showing "his famous wop smile." The inscription on Pop Estep's photo was phrased in the somewhat heavy-handed humor that Joe sometimes used: "Pop, trying to appear human. What a task!" He took a photo of J. F. Boyer, representative of the Conn Company, makers of musical instruments, for the Nighthawks had a contract for the exclusive use of that company's instruments. Joe wrote on Coonie's snapshot, "Coony, typifying Adonis in the original." But Joe was suffering something of a hangover from what he termed "my big liquid farewell at Lincoln Tavern." And on a snapshot that one of the others took of him, unsmiling and looking like leftover oatmeal, Joe later wrote, "Weak, sick, but not licked. What a head!"[49]

On each future trip, Joe, Coonie, and the others would assiduously do their photography, sometimes even with movie cameras; but this trip, while less stately than future ones would be, was obviously something new, something more professional than the Oklahoma trip of the preceding summer, and far more comfortable. Now they could wear neat business attire while traveling. Thus it was that, unaccustomed to such relative pomp and uncertain as to its permanence, they alternated between clicking their own shutters and posing self-consciously for others'.

Preparing next day to leave Elkhart, they learned that a wreck on the railroad would make them miss their intended connection, so they had to hire taxicabs to make their commitments in Illinois at Kankakee, Decatur, and Centralia. Racing across the countryside in Yellow Cabs, four men to a vehicle, was, in Joe's words, "Not a bit funny!" Apparently, Harold Thiell would have expressed it even more forcefully. Then it was back into Indiana for an engagement at Terre Haute. On the third and fourth of September the band played at Herrin, Ill. Later Joe was to write, "When we were informed that Herrin, in bloody Williamson County, was on our itinerary, we regarded it with mingled emotions."[50] As we have already seen in chapter four, Herrin was at the center of a struggle between the Ku Klux Klan and the Knights of the Flaming Circle, as well as who-knows-what other such groups.

Discreetly reporting *ex post facto* about Herrin, Sanders observed: "This little city ... in the heart of Little Egypt's coal-belt has long been the scene of uprisings, factional warfare and much bloodshed." A number of persons had advised against the Nighthawks' going there. According to Joe, just two days before the band's arrival six men had been killed in a gun battle on a downtown street. But undaunted, or at least trying to appear so, the band put up at the Lymar Hotel. "The kleagle of the Klan occupied the room next to us," said Joe, "and Coonie and I each had a case of Scotch in our trunks. When we checked in, the clerk told us that the war was [a] liquor war and any man caught with a drop on his hip was a dead man." Joe reported that he and Coonie "broke out with prickly heat." (In those days the Klan usually represented themselves as all hot for Prohibition and morality.) But that evening the band had a party with the kleagle and left him stewed or, in the jargon of the era, *blotto*. "At the dance," said Joe, "the badge of admittance was a flaming circle and all the men checked their guns at the door, just as in the old lawless Western days...."[51]

The Nighthawks played at White City Park. Though the Herrin City Library reports that it no longer exists, it was, in Sanders's words, an amusement area that "would do credit to a city of 100,000." There was also a large, well-constructed swimming pool that attracted visitors from all over southern Illinois.[52]

But clearly the Nighthawks felt like civilians in a minefield. "Guns were liable to start popping any minute," Joe decided, "and too much curiosity could easily be decidedly unhealthy." "Herrin," he said, "was definitely the hotbed of unrest and ill will." Nor did Joe care for the local cuisine: "Of all the cities I've visited from coast to coast, Canada to the Gulf, Herrin, beyond a doubt, is America's worst dining place."[53] What Joe didn't understand was that the citizens of Herrin probably regarded culinary deficiency as one of their lesser problems.

An unidentified newspaper clipping in Joe Sanders' papers suggests that the Nighthawks did indeed demonstrate that "music hath charms to soothe the savage breast." The band's first night in Herrin was the second day of the riot, and that evening the crowd danced till twelve. The savage breasts were obviously not only soothed but charmed, and probably well anesthetized on local moonshine. At any rate, they declared a truce until the next day when everyone would probably be more in the mood for trouble. The band's members were taken on a tour of the city's points of interest, starting with the "death car" that had caused the riot, and they were introduced to prominent leaders on both sides of the dispute.[54]

Apparently always keeping in mind the motto *Safety First*, the Nighthawks took their usual quota of snapshots, but Joe pronounced it "dangerous business" and was careful to avoid attracting undue attention. Among the scenic spots he photographed was Smith's Garage, which he described as the "Battle Ground ... one of the gathering places for the rabble," and a place where "any gathering is apt to blaze into a gun-fight." Another photo showed a hotel, about a block from Smith's Garage, about which Joe said, "From the roof of this hotel, a machine gun played over the streets during the riots." And in illustration of the perversity of human

Awaiting transportation in Iowa City, Iowa, September 1924. From left: Richolson, Hank Linder (tour manager), Estep, J. Thiell, and (on right looking at camera) Musolino; others unidentified. (Courtesy Special Collections, Kansas City [Mo.] Public Library.)

nature, Joe's curiosity kept drawing him to other scenes of the bloody fracas. He took careful photos of a car in which bullet holes in the seats gaped eloquently. Under a picture of the hospital where the injured and dead had been taken after the violence, Joe wrote that it "does a thriving business — thanks to the gangsters." At the local cemetery Joe got a photo of Ira Thomas' grave, whose occupant, according to Sanders, "didn't know what fear was." (Had he been available, the Nighthawks could perhaps have told him.) And perhaps to avoid offending even the dead, Joe got a photo also of Glenn Young's grave, "the other leader — killed by Thomas, who in turn, was shot in the back by one of Young's followers."[55] Fortunately for jazz in America, as well as Stein's Music Corporation of America, Joe waited until the band had left town before expressing his opinion of Herrin and Williamson County, and how some of the inhabitants amused themselves.

Sanders was apparently not being melodramatic. Herrin was indeed developing a reputation for violence, and not just that caused by the Klan. On November 20 of the previous year, W. F. "Whitey" Doering, described by an article in the Kansas City *Star* as the chief of "St. Louis Mobsters," was mortally wounded in a shootout with Charles Birger, owner of a resort between Marion and Johnston City, just east of Herrin. Doering lived in St. Louis, where the police regarded him as the "'bad man' of the notorious 'Egan's Rats.'" He was said to have all the secrets of murders, robberies, and other edifying acts committed by the gang, including a mail robbery of $2,283,650. Later in St. Louis, Doering's neighbors, who had always liked him and thought him a good citizen and charming fellow, were surprised when a police raid found a large amount of the stolen money in Doering's bungalow. It was then discovered that he had spent time in the state penitentiary, and that he was even then out on an appeal bond of $90,000. Earlier he had written to the parole board that he realized he was a failure as a bandit and that he now wanted to lead an honest life. But when he was arrested and found to be carrying $8,600 on his person, he was indignant, and explained, "I made that money honestly by bootlegging." On being asked, just before he died, about his last shootout, his only reply was an outburst of profanity. He was thirty-two years of age.[56]

While Sanders' report makes it clear that the band's members were relieved to leave Herrin for the somewhat safer territory of Springfield, his reporting of the two days in Williamson County makes it equally obvious that he was rather proud of having been there. They would visit again during the next several years.

It was perhaps between Herrin and Springfield that they had to change trains in Mattoon, though this may have occurred several days earlier between engagements in Decatur and Centralia. But whenever it was that they found themselves waiting in Mattoon, Sanders discovered that, having inadvertently packed all of his shoes, he had to spend the entire day in slippers. It was bad enough to be without shoes, but without his spats he probably feared arrest for indecent exposure. And as always, the layover at Mattoon gave the shutterbugs more opportunities. Joe, in a lapse of his customary dapper manner, allowed himself to be pho-

A dapper Joe Richolson awaits the train, Mattoon, Illinois, September 1924. Hank Linder, tour manager, in background. (Courtesy Special Collections, Kansas City [Mo.] Public Library.)

tographed displaying one of his slippers, quite a contrast with another photo of a debonair and neatly dressed Joe Richolson leaning complacently against a sign. Harold Thiell, wearing what appeared to be either a monstrous yarmulke or a misshapen fez, was

Waiting for train in Mattoon, Illinois, September 1924. From left: Knapp, J. Thiell, Sanders, Musolino, Cory Adams (assistant tour manager), Birge, Richolson, Estep, and Linder (tour manager). (Courtesy Special Collections, Kansas City [Mo.] Public Library.)

ceremoniously referred to as "Rabbi Thiell." In another photo one sees Joe's portable phonograph on the floor of the depot's public concourse, while the boys crouch or stoop around it and a station employee peers cautiously at them from around a corner. Joe neglects to say what record was playing, but one hopes it was their new recording of "Nighthawk Blues." And Knapp, Coon, Sanders, and Richolson, for whiling away some of their time at the station with a game of tossing coins, got themselves not only photographed but briefly arrested. It almost caused the band to miss their train.[57]

In Springfield's Elks' Club the band played to a thousand dancers and a balcony filled with observers, many of whom had traveled considerable distances to be present. The spacious club had the finest dance facilities in the city and a beautiful floor that was itself an attraction. Above the dance hall, on the roof garden, there were fountain beverages and refreshments. Among the numbers the band played were "Nighthawk Blues," "Red Hot Mama," "There's No One Just Like You," "Oriental Love Dreams," "Why Don't My Dreams Come True?" and "My Daddy's Dreamtime." The dance called the Charleston was not yet very familiar, so the Nighthawks' tempo was probably still very brisk, especially for fast fox trots and one steps. (Despite its reputation, the Charleston necessitated such vigorous, exaggerated movements that accompanying music had to be taken somewhat more slowly than that for fast fox trots.) Coon-Sanders apparently brought everything off with their usual finesse, for the local *Illinois State Journal* pronounced them "a decided success."[58]

After leaving Springfield they spent a week at Milwaukee's Alhambra Theater, where, said Joe, the band was a "sensation." Then on to Joliet, Ill., and next to Dubuque and Sioux City, Iowa. In Grand Island, Nebr., in mid–September, they received confirmation of their opening the next month at the Balloon Room, in Chicago's Congress Hotel.[59] That would occupy them into the following year.

From Grand Island they traveled to Lincoln, Nebr., and then to Fort Dodge to play at the Twin Lakes Pavilion. At the latter city

Joe unintentionally packed all his shoes and was obliged to travel in slippers. Harold Thiell prepares to record the event, while Richolson looks on amused. Depot in Mattoon, Illinois, September 1924. (Courtesy Special Collections, Kansas City [Mo.] Public Library.)

they talked with a reporter from the local *Messenger*. There was the usual chitchat about their road tour, and the band amused the local reporter with stories about their recent visit to Herrin, Ill., with some emphasis on their examination of "the death car that caused the riot." Then they got around to speaking of what they hoped to achieve musically. "Rhythm has come to stay, but the age of discordant jazz is past," was the way the reporter quoted them at the beginning of his piece. (When quoting the two leaders, he seems usually to have synthesized their views.) "Dance music has come a long way," they held, "since the day that a fiddler and an accordian [sic] player wheezed out 'Turkey in the Straw' and 'Old Zip Coon' for the steppers in the barn. Men with fine musical educations and undoubted talent are devoting their careers to the evolution of rhythm to which people can dance." Alluding to the importance of arranging, they said, "[T]he reason ... that rhythm has come to stay is ... that people have always danced, and that they will dance quicker to music which has been written especially to make them desire to dance." Coonie observed that dance orchestras had become "complicated affairs," which necessitated careful instrumentation and, in their case, the carrying about of thirteen large trunks of instruments and music. He further pointed out that modern dance orchestras had "popularized many formerly unknown and little used instruments, which in rhythm today are necessary and desirable in obtaining certain effects." "Every man in the band," said Coonie, "plays from one to a dozen instruments and he is an artist in each." As to the question of how to achieve success, it was a matter of adapting the music to the audience and the locality. "A crowd in Oklahoma," they explained, "will boo our best efforts when we are playing the speedy syncopation that brought a crowd to [their] feet in Illinois."[60]

The *Messenger's* reporter concluded that *versatility* was the key word with Coon and Sanders. "Brought up as legitimate

At depot in Mattoon, Illinois, September 1924, several toss coins and get arrested briefly for it. From left in foreground: Knapp, Sanders, Coon, and Richolson. Others unidentified. (Courtesy Special Collections, Kansas City [Mo.] Public Library.)

musicians," he observed, "they dabbled in newspaper* work, baseball and light opera on the side, and after struggling against the inroads of jazz for four years finally capitulated and started a symphonic syncopation band, which is what jazz bands become these days, when they acquire an expert arranger and composer and real musicians." He noted that Joe was the group's arranger—"Every band has its own arranger now...."—and it was this practice that lent "novelty" and "distinctive characterer" to an orchestra such as the Nighthawks.[61] The entire tour was becoming a triumph, a gratifying and heady experience for so relatively-new an ensemble of young musicians.

With the delightful taste of Ft. Dodge still tingling on their musical tongues, they went on to one more appearance in Iowa, Cedar Rapids, probably on the nineteenth. Then they crossed Old Man River into Illinois for engagements at La Salle, Peoria, and Cairo. The two giant rivers at Cairo fascinated all the amateur photographers, as did the many donkeys to be seen. Someone took a shot of Coonie looking intently at one of the town's equines, and Joe wrote under the photo, "Coonie imploring 'Jack' not to be an 'ass.'" Another shot, later used for publicity purposes, shows Coonie in a two-wheel cart and holding the reins of a donkey, into whose ears Joe apparently whispers sweet nothings. And while in Cairo the Nighthawks chummed with a group of musicians called the Egyptian Serenaders, another MCA band and one very appropriate for Cairo. At the next stop, Marion, Ill., the band had a party in the county jail with "the famous Sheriff Galligan." They met and were impressed by the sheriff's nephew, a beardless fellow of eighteen, who already had six notches on his belt.† After Marion came

---

*How journalism came to be identified with Coon-Sanders is unknown. Perhaps it was another one of the two men's embellishments of truth.
†Chicago obviously had nothing on Southern Illinois.

Waiting for a train in Iowa City, Iowa, September 1924. (Courtesy Special Collections, Kansas City [Mo.] Public Library.)

Terre Haute, Ind.; Aurora and Champaign, Ill.; and Anderson and South Bend, Ind. At South Bend they played two engagements at the Hotel Oliver, one a public dance, the other, Joe emphasized, the Notre Dame Senior Ball for the class that boasted the famous football stars, Notre Dame's Four Horsemen, halfbacks Jim Crowley and Don Miller, quarterback Harry Stuhldreher, and fullback Elmer Layden.[62]

This appearance at Notre Dame was one of the earliest of many such engagements, for Coon-Sanders quickly became a favorite among the college crowd. The excellent and vigorous quality of the band's playing was probably the most important reason for this partiality, but there doubtless was also the attraction of their clowning. With the exception of Pop Estep, the players were not a great deal older than the students, so there was understandably a special sense of empathy and shared outlooks. The entertainment weekly Variety observed that many dance orchestras simply found playing for college groups too debilitating. "The collegiate steppers at a dance forget there is such a thing as intermission," said the New York paper, with the result that there was a great strain on the "average musician." College boys tended to turn any dance into a marathon, to demand encores, and to be impatient during intermissions. It was often a grind that proved a "physical tax on the average musician."[63]

Perhaps the key phrase in Variety's article is "average musicians"; for if the Nighthawks ever found playing on campuses an onerous task, they apparently never showed it. On the contrary, the band enjoyed such gigs and sought them. They cultivated the students at dances. Moreover, on their radio broadcasts they ostentatiously flirted with the college crowd.

The band closed at Columbus, Ohio, where they received an impressive reception but confronted a baggage problem. When they were leaving, their musical instruments and their personal baggage exceeded the weight limit and were held up. This put in doubt their opening at the Balloon Room at Chicago's Congress Hotel, but all the items arrived in Chicago just in time.[64]

As we have already seen, Chicago in the

Depot in Mattoon, Illinois, September 1924. From left: Knapp, J. Thiell, Musolino, Birge (partly hidden), Richolson, H. Thiell, Coon, and Estep. (Courtesy Special Collections, Kansas City [Mo.] Public Library.)

fall of 1924 was well stocked with bands. But in the opinion of *Variety*, there really was none suitable for several current vacancies. Three cafes were scheduled to open during October, and all were hard pressed to find good bands. Said the entertainment weekly, "All of the bands have either played every cafe in town or else have not sufficient drawing power to warrant first class positions."[65] If this assessment was correct, it helps to explain the electric effect that the Nighthawks had on Chicago. Jules Stein, whose Music Corporation of America needed good clients, must have anticipated that effect.

Thus did Coon-Sanders, on October 1, start what Kramer calls "this plush engagement, their first in the city of Chicago proper." They were a hit, even though the Congress Hotel's Balloon Room might not have seemed exactly the right place to attract crowds. Despite Sanders's description of it as "the world's most beautiful supper club," the somewhat staid, dignified atmosphere of the place, as well as its location, was not what Kramer thought was attractive to younger dancers, especially those of limited means.

But though many younger dancers may have stayed away, Sanders proved the better judge of success, and even at fifteen dollars per person, the place was often sold out. According to Joe, "The band proved to be the sensation of Chicago and succeeded in putting over the only financially successful supper club the Congress Hotel ever had." Two previous efforts had flopped.[66]

"During the opera season," said Joe, "the room was a blaze of color and dazzling jewels. Most any night found millions of dollars dancing to our music on the black walnut floor." Westinghouse Station KYW allowed the band, in Joe's words, "free rein" to broadcast. The two leaders dreamed up some gimmicks, one of which was the Insomnia Club, a continuation of the "enemies of sleep" theme they had used in Kansas City. It was an experiment that proved as popular with the growing number of radio listeners as the Kansas City show had been. The club was broadcast from 1 to 2 a.m., and on Sundays until 3 a.m. KYW, the Westinghouse station directed by Scoop Wetherbee and Shorty Fall, was so powerful that a fan from

Coonie braces for the worst, while Joe implores Jack not to be an ass. Cairo, Illinois, 22 September 1924. (Courtesy Special Collections, Kansas City [Mo.] Public Library.)

Apia, Samoa, wrote to say that the program, which reached Samoa about 7 p.m., afforded delightful dinner music. This meant an astounding seven thousand miles at least that the station's signal was carrying. Said the *Chicago Tribune*: "Apparently there is little interference developing in the South Seas, although thousands of ships on the Pacific are transmitting on 600 meters and KYW's wave-length is 535.5 meters, for Mr. Dunwoodie [the fan in Samoa] does not report any trouble in picking up KYW's carrier wave and holding it as long as he likes."[67]

On Wednesday, 26 November 1924, Frank Haben Clark, the Chicago *Evening American*'s program director, announced that the newspaper's station KYW would, that evening, have "Our Own Gang" broadcast "for the crowned heads of Europe." The several programs would air from 10 p.m. until 2 a.m., which meant that Europe would, by their time, receive the airings some six or more hours later. That would still be fairly early, whether for crowned heads or simply plebeian heads wearing mere earphones. But in 1924 there doubtless were a lot of listeners in Europe willing to sacrifice a little sleep to hear American jazz. The artists that KYW's broadcast would feature included "Polly" Willis, Sallie Menkes, Bobby Brown "and his overseas uke," Art Linick, Uncle Bob (Walter Wilson), Charlie Schultz, and Herby Mintz. What were described as "two powerful Hawaiian guitars" would be managed by "Jacobson and Ray." At midnight J. Remington Welsh would play the theater organ at the McVicker's Theater. And there would be stars of vaudeville and the legitimate theater, those such as Ruth Donnally, appearing in *Cheaper to Marry*, at the Playhouse Theater, and Joe Laurie, Jr., star of *Plain Jane*, at the Illinois Theater. "At frequent intervals during the evening," said Clark, "the Coon-Sanders Original Night Hawks will be heard from the Balloon Room of the Congress Hotel."[68]

There is an interesting aspect of the Nighthawks' broadcasting over KYW. At about this time, the American Society of Composers, Authors and Publishers set a precedent by allowing the Congress Hotel and its radio station, for an annual license

Joe's "Nighthawk Pyramid," depot in Iowa City, Iowa, about 20 September 1924. On baggage across top: Birge, Knapp (with pipe), J. Thiell, Musolino, Adams (assistant tour manager) Richolson; in center; Linder (tour manager, on left), and Sanders; across bottom: H. Thiell (with camera), Coon, and Estep (standing far right). (Courtesy Special Collections Kansas City [Mo.] Public Library.)

fee of a thousand dollars, broadcast the society's songs seven hours a week. Many radio stations were already using these songs *gratis* but only with much legal protesting by ASCAP. An agreement such as this between the society and KYW would perhaps help lead to a harmonious solution to the problem, so often complained of by many in the entertainment field, of copyright infringement. Why ASCAP chose KYW was a mystery to many at the time. It was an unlicensed station and was the only one in Chicago that was then, under protest by ASCAP, using "tax-free" songs. Furthermore, ASCAP had turned down similar requests for licenses from such applicants in New York as the Rendezvous Cafe, Roseland Ballroom, the Mark Strand Theatre, and the Cinderella Ballroom, all of which broadcast over New York's WJZ, also an unlicensed station. *Variety*, in reporting on the matter, said:

> The American Society could increase its income considerably from these special dispensations to applicants who desired the use of an unlicensed station for a limited number of hours weekly, but is desirous rather of licensing the stations direct.
>
> In the case of WJZ, the total of the number of applicants in New York would probably more than equal the license fee which would permit the station an unlimited use of the A. S.'s catalog, so it is not a question therefore of revenue from that source.[69]

The Nighthawks' reputation was such that during this first winter in Chicago, an offer came from New York's Palace Theater, the acme of American vaudeville. Most actors and bands would have done almost anything to appear there, but for some reason the Nighthawks didn't go. Joe suggests in his memoirs that he simply turned the offer down.[70] On the other hand, some seem to suggest that it wasn't Coon-Sanders' refusal to go to New York that delayed their doing so, but rather that the Music Corporation of America had other bands they wanted to present there instead, and without competition.[71] Whatever the reason, Coon-Sanders would not play in New York City until 1931. It is clear, though, that Joe and probably the rest of the band were quite satisfied with the reception Chicago was giving them, especially when it was sufficient to eat into the business that Isham Jones's popular band was getting at the Sherman. Jones left and took *his* band to New York.[72]

For over twenty-five years the Congress had been a popular place to celebrate the new year, and the hotel announced for 31 December 1924 the "most elaborate program in the history of the Congress." The ads proclaimed, "Coon-Sanders Original Night Hawks will play all night in the Balloon Room. Theirs is the music that sets feet to dancing." In other parts of the hotel there would be other bands, for instance, Husk O'Hare's Casino Club Ensemble in the Pompeiian Room and George Mellin and His Royal Syncopators in the Gold Room. The Congress would put on its usual elaborate affair. Some of the Nighthawks perhaps thought the restaurant's menu for the evening a little chichi, what with such items as "Souper de Luxe," "canape of Astrakan caviar," "French peas etuvee," and "petits fours."[73] From now on, however, all the Nighthawks, even those who still preferred a good hash house, would see plenty of such menus.

During that first winter in Chicago, the Nighthawks continued to expand the horizons of radio. And they did it as they had in Kansas City, by opening a new phase of the war on sleep. Whether it was simply the Insomnia Club going by an alias or perhaps an entirely new arrangement is not clear. But early in 1925 KYW announced a Nighthawks club, broadcasting at the same time slot, called the Wakeful Order of the Midnight Sons. From the Congress Hotel's Balloon Room, the band broadcast from 1 until 2 every morning except Monday and Tuesday. The first broadcast was on Sunday, 1 February 1925. To become a charter member, one tuned into KYW during the hour following 1 a.m. and, as one newspaper article put it, "hear the Coon-Sanders Nighthawk Orchestra trounce out their zippiest melodies for the benefit of insomnia disciples all over the United States." The band would take requests as in Kansas City days, and with "special mystic incantations," souvenirs would go out to all those who sent in telegrams containing their addresses. The band's area in the Balloon Room was arranged somewhat as their broadcasting platform had been at the Muehlebach. The room's guests would be the visible audience, and Fred Hill of KYW's engineering staff was announcer. There was a microphone for Hill's use but close enough for Joe and Coonie to be heard "with their novelties." And all of it would be managed from the "Little Red studio atop the Congress Hotel."[74]

In the spring of 1925 from his station in New Orleans, O. M. Samuel was helping *Variety* develop a new method to report radio's status. It targeted the entire nation and even some foreign areas. Samuel would observe the new medium and, in the words of the New York weekly, condense what he found "lightly and briefly." One evening in early March, Samuel remarked about the "peppy jazzful strains" he heard coming from the East and West Coasts, often rather drowning out more prosaic lecturers. Station PWX in Havana, Cuba, came through with "delectable Spanish strains." Then he heard a pianist in Atlanta, Ga., some balladists in the Windy City, an instrumental quintet in Cincinnati, and sounds from Washington indicating that that city's "dry" cabarets were successfully helping to inaugurate President

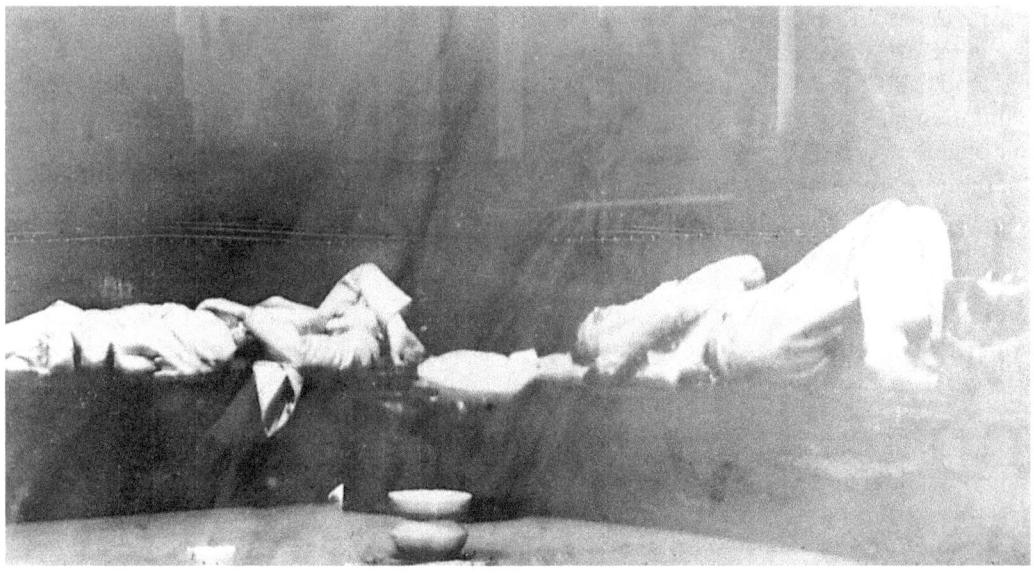

Band members on tour sometimes slept when and where they could. About 1925 in an unidentified railroad station. (Courtesy Special Collections, Kansas City [Mo.] Public Library.)

Coolidge. Shortly after midnight, Samuel heard Meyer Davis' Lido Venice Orchestra play its last number in New York City, after which the announcer looked at his watch, declared it 12:13, and signed off. But, hinted Samuel, don't be misled into thinking radio was turning in. "About that time," said the New Orleans correspondent, "those Kansas City 'Night Hawks' were just beginning their evening." "They rule the air in the early hours of the morning," said Samuel, "and keep a million farmers from sleeping. With his radio in good trim, a jug of cider on the table and jazz artists like the Kansas City gang for company, the American farmer should worry over lost sleep."[75]

The Nighthawks might have been making a strong case for listening to radio, but there was growing animosity in some entertainment circles toward the medium, especially in New York City, the Vatican of vaudeville. *Variety* continued to be one of the most outspoken and persistent detractors. "Radio now is the biggest thing the amusement business ever has had to encounter as opposition," opined the New York publication, and the only recourse the theater had was to "keep quiet and wait."

Whether radio's listeners would continue to patronize it avidly would depend upon whether the new medium could continue to come up with material that would "hold the public at home at the receiving sets." *Variety*, whose primary interest lay with the stage, grumbled that the only ones being helped by radio were the bands. The magazine's greatest complaint, of course, was that theater attendance was dropping, but aggravating this situation was radio's continued free use of copyrighted songs. And when the possibility arose of radio's using plays to attract even more listeners, *Variety* sneered, "Radio has grown so bold it appears to think it can employ anything without pay." It didn't help when a Federal court in Cincinnati, Ohio, on 6 January 1925, decided against music publisher Jerome H. Remick & Company. The Crosley Radio Corporation, said the court, was not to be considered in violation of the copyright law when its stations broadcast songs. The court found such use not a performance for profit. Congress was no help, said the paper, for "[t]here is not a Congressman or Senator in Washington who will not feel the pressure of radio."[76]

One of those congressmen was New

Band about 1925, apparently trying to demonstrate versatility. From left: Musolino, Pop Estep, Richolson, Sanders, Coon, Haid, J. Thiell, Knapp, and H. Thiell. (Courtesy Harvey C. Rettberg.)

York's own Sol Bloom, who in September of 1924 predicted that within five years radio would "kill off" the theater in towns of 75,000 or fewer inhabitants, unless something occurred to prevent it. In fact, he went even further and said that it would ruin theater in cities of 100,000 or or even of larger ones if they were not near one of the nation's main metropolitan areas.[77]

The anti-radio critics also charged discrimination by publishers of dance music in favor of bands. A customer, who identified himself as "A Musician," said that he had recently gone to T. B. Harms, "the first publisher of dance music to adhere to the policy of charging 25 cents for dance orchestrations." The angry customer said he had gone there quite willing to pay for his arrangements, and that while there he overheard Jim Derkin, an employee, tell another person that Harms did not charge hotels "because it's considered a favor ... when a hotel plays a Harms number." Abel Green, of *Variety*, admitted that it was indeed a practice by publishers "when the stand of the orchestra merits it." "But free orchestrations," observed Green, "must be curbed by an arbitrary method, if there is any question and publishers most likely do discriminate according to the circumstances."[78]

Now that the Nighthawks were ensconced in Chicago, Victor had them make more recordings. According to Brian Rust, on Sunday, November 9, the band recorded three numbers, "Lazy Waters," "Moonlight and You," and "Bright Eyes," the last of which was rejected for distribution. On the following Thursday they recorded "Some of These Days," which was accepted, and "My Best Gal," which was not. On the following Sunday the band recorded "Brown Eyes," "Show Me the Way," and "Jing-a-Ling-a-Ling," with only the second number regarded as acceptable.[79] The band now had ten Victor recordings circulating, though as usual, they were paid only for the recording sessions. But the publicity generated by phonograph records was worth plenty.

Meanwhile, Jules Stein, even though he did not yet have an exclusive contract to manage the band, was trying to put together a tentative tour schedule for the Nighthawks after the termination in the following spring of their engagement with the Congress. Indeed, Stein hired Karl Kramer for the purpose of planning such a tour. Kramer had been working for vaudeville's Orpheum Circuit, a block away from MCA, where he had been doing publicity and promotions for headline attractions. Stein assigned him to do what Kramer later called a "complete publicity kit" for the band's tour. "As I remember it," says Kramer in his memoirs, "I wrote about a dozen newspaper stories complete with catch lines, ad layouts and various other ideas which had been used with great success in vaudeville." It involved also cutting stencils and making mimeographic copies that Kramer delivered to MCA. He says he received sixty-five dollars for the work, not especially great payment but, as he put it, "my efforts were more than rewarded in later years."[80]

Apparently quoting Johnny Coon, Joe Popper says it was very soon after MCA began managing bookings for Coon-Sanders that Stein urged both Joe and Coonie, each of whom was earning about two thousand dollars a week, to let him invest some of their earnings for them. They refused. "Prodigals both," says Popper, "money seemed to vanish from their hands. Coon made no excuses. Money was for spending, he insisted. Once, when his wife suggested they should begin planning an estate, he responded, 'Hell, no! I'm not going to leave my kids anything. Let 'em make their own.'" In conversation with Johnny Coon, I heard him corroborate this.[81]

Helped substantially by the publicity and the profits that Coon-Sanders was bringing in, Stein's efforts to develop a booking agency were very successful. "It is immaterial as to in just what order MCA started taking over band bookings in Chicago," says Kramer, "but it was not too long before we had the big spots, the College Inn, the Edgewater Beach, the Bismarck, the Dells and Lincoln Tavern in summer, and a great number of smaller cafes like the Vanity Fair, Pershing Palace, and even a Chinese restaurant, the Golden Pumpkin, which had the largest capacity in the entire town." MCA was delighted to increase the number of its clients, but it meant hard work. When Stein began dealing with Coon-Sanders in 1924, the number of orchestras he represented, according to Kramer, "could have been counted on two hands, maybe even one." Some of the first were Paul Biese, Ted Weems, Charles Dornberger, Eddie Neibauer, and the Egyptian Serenaders. In a relatively short while they added such others as Ben Bernie, Ray Miller, Don Bestor, and Jack Crawford. All of these were top features, and the list kept growing. By 1930 the number had increased to more than a hundred.[82] Kramer believed that if Paul Biese had not died early, his band, not the Nighthawks, might have been the first dance orchestra of any significance to be booked by MCA in its early years.[83]

But it *was* the Nighthawks that first starred for MCA, and that band maintained its contact with Stein's agency right up to the spring of 1932, when the band, for all practical purposes, died with Coonie. Though the association continued to be profitable for both parties, it did not, according to Kramer, remain quite so warm a relationship as it had been earlier, or as those with other bands were. Over thirty years later Kramer mused about the altered relationship:

> Again, it was not any one big thing, but in the little matters that Sanders seemed to antagonize people. One small incident that seems to stick in my memory happened in 1928 when MCA essayed a brief and unsuccessful venture into the music publishing business. We bought two songs in New York and had dance arrangements made for orchestras. We went to the various bands that we booked in Chicago and asked them to play the tunes to their audiences to see if they had any value. Every orchestra in Chicago played the tunes for us except Coon-Sanders, and though Joe had charge of the repertoire[,] he did not include these numbers in his program even once. Coonie, on the other hand, was a very well-liked individual and it is probably true that while they were together he made up a lot for his partner's aloofness.[84]

Part of Joe's reason for refusing to play

the songs may have been his competitive spirit that, in this instance, perhaps manifested itself in sensitiveness toward another composer's work. Johnny Coon remembered Joe as often jealous of other bands, but if the charge is justified at all, the reason may have been partly that Joe was such a musical perfectionist that he was reluctant to trust any part of his program to any other arranger. There certainly is no question that Joe was among the very best arrangers.

On the other hand, some band leaders and publishers believed that popular music had reached a place where there were simply too many tunes being published, and, thus, too many to play — or "plug"— them all. One anonymous publisher told *Variety*, "No matter how friendly the musician may be with the publishing houses, it is an impossibility to play even the hits consistently or enough to warrant a genuine 'plug' like in the days gone by." There was also, the publisher said, the tendency to flood the market with imitations of successful songs, and the result was that all of them, the original and the imitations, lost some of their appeal. Nor did he like the more elaborate arrangements that were becoming fashionable:

> On the matter of arrangements I've been preaching special orchestrations and 18-bar modulations for the last three or four years. But the trouble is that every band tries to outdo [Paul] Whiteman. When Paul first came to the East with his unique style he started a fad which has caused many band leaders to attempt to outdo him on the "special" arrangement gag. The result is that the original melody is so camouflaged by a wealth of fancy musical trimmings it requires a musical detective to locate the theme melody which really sells the song and should have its greatest appeal. This practice of "over-dressing" a simple strain with all this musical hokum is not only a fault on the records (where it might be considered pardonable), but even more so when rendered for the dance public.[85]

According to this critic, the problem of over-arrangement had become so severe that many cafe managers were getting complaints from guests. "Generally they use the melody for a trombone solo and the real melody is thus covered up by all sorts of counterpoint," he said. As a result, the bands were told to play ninety percent of the numbers as "straight" music from printed arrangements. To do otherwise was to forget "the foundation of dance rhythm." "It may be pretty to listen to," he added, "but it doesn't belong for dance purposes. The continuity is lost, as is the rhythm, because no band can go from the rhythm and modulate into a different character in melody and still maintain that rhythm." He believed that the worst was past, however, and that the situation was improving. Moreover: "The better musicians and arrangers ... are making their arrangements so interesting that an intelligent leader can find enough harmony in the printed arrangements of the individual tunes to make them sound effective, yet danceable with all the rhythmic appeal intact."[86]

The Nighthawks' completion on 6 April 1925 of their engagement at the Congress Hotel accompanied preparation for their road trip. Despite Stein's having hired Karl Kramer to plan the Nighthawks' 1925 tour, Coon-Sanders was not yet fully committed to MCA. Stein and the band had signed a three-year contract on 1 December 1924, but it would not go fully into effect until the following April 11. And even then, any engagements that Coon-Sanders had already made would not be affected by the contract with MCA.[87]

Technically, the 1925 road trip was not handled by MCA but rather by the Ernie Young Music Corporation, with which Stein still had a joint operation. As a matter of fact, Jules Stein signed the contract for the Young agency. It billed the Nighthawks as "The Orchestra [or Band] That Made Radio Famous," a phrase that resonated and was one of several that Coon-Sanders used for the rest of its existence. The Young agency had already printed tickets with the agent's and the band's names, below which was space for filling in with pen the name of the place and the date. The stub had the band's logo and the ticket number.[88]

Coonie giving Knapp a lift and deciding they'd better stick to the railroad. Niles, Michigan, where they apparently only changed trains, spring 1925. (Courtesy Special Collections, Kansas City [Mo.] Public Library.)

Booking agencies seem to have offered their bands any of several contractual arrangements, depending upon preference or peculiar circumstances. The Ernie Young Music Corporation, for instance, offered a choice of two contracts. One guaranteed $700 of the gross receipts over $1,000, less taxes. The other was a guarantee of $500 plus 65 percent of the gross receipts over $700, minus taxes. The Young agency's opinion of the Nighthawk Orchestra was expressed in it promotional statement: "Coon-Sanders orchestra tour of 1924 demonstrated its unquestioned superiority as an attraction, establishing records of attendance unequalled by an organization."[89]

The three-year contract with the Music Corporation of America, signed on 1 December 1924 by Joe, Coonie, and Jules Stein, included the following stipulations:

- The Coon-Sanders Original Kansas City Nighthawks would not allow their band, "or any other orchestra or orchestras of theirs," to be advertised by any other party without MCA's consent.
- MCA would spend at least $1,000 per year for publicity.
- MCA agreed to pay the Nighthawks at least $1,500 per week for the nine-member band.
- If the band added musicians, MCA agreed to pay $70 per week for each additional member, and Coon-Sanders agreed to accept a $70 deduction per week for each person less than nine.
- Where the contract price was $1,550 or less per week, MCA would receive $50 per week. If the agreed price was between $1,550 and $1,599 per week, MCA would be entitled to $50 per week and an additional amount each week equal to one-half the amount over $1,550 per week. If the agreed price was between $1,600 and $1,699 per week, MCA would receive five percent of the amount. If the amount was

between $1,700 and $1,799 per week, MCA would receive six percent of the amount. If between $1,800 and $1,899, MCA would receive seven percent. If between $1,900 and $1,999, MCA would receive eight percent. If between $2,000 and $2,250, MCA would get nine percent. And if over $2,250 per week, MCA would get ten percent.
- The terms of this contract would not include Coon-Sanders' work at either the Congress Hotel or that done for the Victor Talking Machine Company, both of which engagements antedated this contract.
- If, during the three-year period of this contract, the gross receipts for Coon-Sanders were at least $100,000 each year, the contract could be renewed automatically for another three years.[90]

The agency provided free advertising materials such as large posters, window cards, circulars, photographs of the orchestra and the leaders, newspaper stories and photos, admission tickets "serially numbered for advance sale," Nighthawk tags for identification of paid admissions, and Nighthawk souvenir programs.[91]

After the band closed at the Congress, everyone took a five-day break. Then they launched what Joe called "our first extensive tour." Thus, as Joe later put it, after he "dropped" Dewey Birge, banjoist — actually Birge quit to help his wife care for their two young children — and engaged Bill Haid, they opened at Davenport, Iowa, on Easter Sunday, April 12. Here the band appeared at the Eagles Auditorium and had to share the town with Frank Westphal and His Columbians, who appeared at the Coliseum. But as the Davenport *Daily Times* put it, "Both are great bands. So take your pick now. Maybe you can get to both places." The paper published large photos of the bands and their leaders, with Westphal's sandwiched between pictures of Coonie and Joe. Describing the Nighthawks as "one of the greatest dance orchestras in the country," the *Times* added, "These are the same boys who have broadcast to millions of fans all over the country and they will play a program of old favorites and new numbers." In an interview with the paper, Sanders spoke in terms that he tended to use from place to place: "We realize that thousands of dancers want us to play the big hits we have done over the radio. We have been asked this in so many places that we are literally forced to do so. However, we will do enough new stuff to keep the crowd interested."[92]

It was at this time that the entertainment weekly *Variety* began to pay slightly more attention to the Nighthawks. *Variety* was among the severest critics of radio and frequently expressed its contempt for the new, brassy entertainment medium. Coon-Sanders' close connection with radio was perhaps an important reason that the New York paper had been somewhat slow to take notice of the band and why it was restrained even after it did. Of course, that the Nighthawks did not play in New York until the end of their career was doubtless another important reason. It is difficult to find an issue of *Variety* in the Twenties that does not contain at least one mention of such bands as those led by Paul Whiteman, Ben Bernie, Vincent Lopez, and George Olsen, all of which spent much of their time in New York City. That Coon-Sanders managed to get even belated attention in *Variety* was probably due to the work of Jules Stein and his energetic Music Corporation of America, especially after the office in New York had begun to function fully. Even still, Coon-Sanders never received as much attention as did such other MCA bands as Ben Bernie's and Guy Lombardo's.

MCA's full-page ad in *Variety's* issue for 22 April 1925 paired Coon-Sanders with Paul Biese's band and described the Nighthawks as "The Band That Made Radio Famous." The ad also announced that Coon-Sanders would play that summer at Young's Million-Dollar Pier, in Atlantic City.[93] That in itself was perhaps enough to make the New York weekly take at least a little more notice than

Tip-toeing behind the tulips at Niles, Michigan, spring 1925. They did not play here but apparently changed trains. From left: Haid, J. Thiell, Richolson, Sanders, Coon, Knapp, H. Thiell, Musolino, and Estep. (Courtesy Special Collections, Kansas City [Mo.] Public Library.)

usual, for Atlantic City in those days was almost a sixth New York borough.

Meanwhile, *Variety* continued its campaign against radio and everyone associated with it. A typical attack, in June of 1925, contained the statement that the new medium was becoming increasingly boring. "Thursday night on the radio," said one article, "was a dull evening. That's running true to form and therefore not particularly startling in import."[94] Another item reported absurdly on a so-called "radio rash" from Van Nuys, Calif. This "new disease," allegedly diagnosed by a local physician, was said to be brought on by the rubbing of radio earphones against the skin: "The discoverer of the new malady is Joe Lithicum, who lives on a ranch near here. Joe came to town with his ear phones and said, 'Danged if I ain't off these yere ear phones for good. The blamed things had my ears and sides of my face all messed up with a pimply rash. Where's this fellow what sells them loud speakers?'"[95]

Variety was even dubious about the honesty of the handling of huge numbers of telegrams received by such radio programs as those featuring the Nighthawks—the magazine did not name any particular bands. The New York weekly suggested that the "frequent request to 'wire' regarding radio entertainment or requests, with Western Union usually designated, was not altogether altruistic on the part of the announcers or some of them who send this 'suggestion' so frequently over the ether." "It is unknown," said *Variety*, "whether announcers who do this keep tab of wires received for a commission to be collected on the gross paid the telegraph company, but the suspicion is about."[96]

And without comment, the magazine observed that the Department of Commerce was expected to use a large portion of $125,000, allocated to investigate conditions in the radio industry, to ascertain whether the airwaves were involved in the illegal alcohol traffic. It seems that there were charges that some broadcasting stations had been sending messages in code, either by choice of popular songs or in coded statements in lectures, as advance notification on the best times and ways to transport booze.[97]

Even if it is improbable that radio was helping in rumrunning, the complaint that the pesky medium was drawing customers away from theaters had more substance and was more justified, especially in light of the copyright dispute. There was a movement early in 1925 to urge the world's composers and authors to make a concerted demand that radio broadcasters pay for the use of copyrighted materials.[98] An article in late 1924 called radio "the Sponger" and "a paradox in its relation to show business." "The thorough showman," said *Variety's* Abel Green, "at first and last thought condemns radio as a bane of show business. He cannot see any good in the gratis ether entertainment and in many instances sees harm." Contradicting this position, the broadcasters insisted that radio, for the most part, "appealed to a certain large class of always 'stay-at-home' folks who from inclination or circumstances contented themselves with an evening by the lamplight with a newspaper or periodical." A radio was simply an enhancement of such an evening. And besides, broadcasting an artist or a band over the radio was excellent advertisement. Despite this response from broadcasters, Green insisted that radio was a leech on the entertainment world. Moreover, he flatly charged that it was harmful to musical hits. As an example, he cited the song "I Love You," that he called "a sensational production hit which ... was so widely done by the bands that it 'killed' the song's chances on sheet music sales." Green concluded: "Radio has 'sponged' now for many, many months on the artistic efforts of its talent. It must wake to the fact—and soon!—that the salvation of broadcasting lies in choicer talent, a selectivity that can only be obtained through a system of remuneration for its radio artists."[99]

But with little or no anxiety about *Variety's* radio war, the Nighthawks swept through the Midwest on their first major tour. From Davenport their itinerary took them to Waterloo, Mason City, and Sioux City, all in Iowa. Then came Lincoln, Nebr., and after that, back into Iowa to Des Moines and Cedar Rapids. After what Joe called "a terrific jump" back into Illinois for an engagement at La Salle, they backtracked westward to Omaha in what Joe said was "another awful jump." In Omaha they played at *the* social event of the season and, according to Sanders, gave their competition, Art Landry's Orchestra, "a sound beating two straight nights." Another one of those Coon-Sanders jumps, as the Nighthawk flies, took them eastward again into Illinois for engagements at Rockford, Peoria, and Monmouth. Yet another big shifting of gears took them back westward to Burlington, Iowa. Situated on the Mississippi, a river that seemed to have some special fascination for members of the band, Burlington gave the gang an opportunity to hire a launch for what Joe called "a spin up the Mississippi ... and a nice time was had by all!" Joe's camera, always handy, got several shots of the river and of the band members leaning against the boat's railing, for viewing. Joe tried to get a picture of an old fellow in another boat, but the churlish old "'salt' ... positively refused to pose for his picture." Next it was north to Milwaukee, where they played at the city's Wisconsin Roof. Minneapolis proved to be a rare flop, mainly, said Joe, because they had been improperly promoted. Strangely, the competition was Paul Biese, another client of MCA. When the Nighthawks left, he was in jail for defaulting on alimony. (Biese would not live much longer.) While they were in Minneapolis, the Nighthawks were guests of Harry Wilcox, maker of Wilcox trucks. He had his own island, Gin Isle, in the Mississippi River, and

Nighthawk baggage dominates the depot's concourse at Niles, Michigan, spring 1925. (Courtesy Special Collections, Kansas City [Mo.] Public Library.)

here the band had what Joe termed "loads of fun." That probably meant that Wilcox's island was appropriately named and had a bountiful supply of high-class wet goods. Several of the band members had their wives with them, and Jean Richolson, Doll Haid, and Madeline Sanders are much in evidence in some of the photos that Joe and others took. Joe clowns in one picture, pretending to be about to go over the bank. Under the photo he later wrote: "Ali—oop! If Joe misses—Bam! Right into the Mississippi River." One of Joe's snapshots caught the Richolsons in what he described as "a peaceful, one might say amorously inclined mood." Madeline and Joe took advantage of a little extra time to visit such scenic and historic places nearby as Minnehaha Falls, associated with the Hiawatha story.[100]

After all this relatively free time, the band dashed back into Illinois for a dance at Anderson, where, in Joe's words, "we broke all attendance records, with 4,250 paid admissions." By this time, one would suppose, the Nighthawks' wings would be too tired to keep them going, but one would suppose wrong. That record-breaking appearance in Anderson perhaps helped them catch their second wind. Besides, the Nighthawks seemed to thrive on a fast-paced schedule. Well might they have used Al Jolson's phrase, "You ain't seen nothing, yet!" Next came Indianapolis, where they played for the Hoosier Athletic Club. Then, they left the Mississippi River in peace and crossed the Ohio.[101]

The next set of engagements would take them from the upper South to the Canadian border. First came Lexington, Ky., where Mary Boswell, one of their radio fans, feted them at a grand dinner. Cincinnati came next and a packed house received them wildly. From there they went to Kokomo, and then on to Terre Haute to play for St. Mary's of the Woods, a Catholic girls' school. After appearing at Silver Lake, Ind., and Kalamazoo, Mich., they arrived in Detroit, where they played at the University of Detroit's Junior Prom. Port Huron, Mich., their next stop, gave the band what in the Twenties must have been regarded as a valuable fringe benefit, namely, an opportunity to get over to wet territory in Sarnia, Ontario. There, said Joe, "We filled our pockets with liquor." They "brought back plenty — inside and out." On the band's return to Prohibition, the American inspectors either were bored and careless or else were civilized gentlemen, for they made no fuss.[102]

Doubtless the band's members always breathed a bit more easily when enjoying liquor whose origin they knew. There were always disturbing reports about the potentially lethal witches' brews that were being offered for thirsty gullets. Many of the reports were probably exaggerated, but one could scarcely help wondering which ones and how much. In September of that very year, for instance, J. W. Quillen, a federal chemist, was quoted in news accounts as warning of "two new and deadly poisons in the bootleg liquor." One of the poisons was brucine sulfate that was described as having about the same effect on the heart as that of strychnine. Nicotine alcohol, a byproduct of the tobacco industry, and made even more harmful "through a chemical process," was showing up in liquors of dubious origin. Quillen flatly predicted an increase in deaths. He said that even such materials as kerosene, pine tar, camphor, and benzol (i.e., benzene), camouflaged with clever flavorings, were showing up here and there.[103] It was almost enough to make the water wagon look inviting — *almost*.

After hitting Battle Creek, Mich., the Nighthawks played on May 15 in South Bend, Ind., at Notre Dame. The campus was still glorying in the excitement generated by their victorious football team. Having won all its games the preceding fall, it went on to defeat Stanford 17–10 in the Rose Bowl. And it had been in the game with Army at New York's Polo Grounds, on 18 October 1924, that Knute Rockne's team won 13–7. On that day the great sports journalist and broadcaster Grantland Rice coined a term to describe the famous quartet of Harry Stuhldreher, Elmer Layden, Don Miller, and Jim Crowley. Reported Rice, "Outlined against a blue-gray October sky, the Four Horsemen rode again.... They formed the crest of the South Bend cyclone."[104] Both the team and their coach were becoming legends, and so was Grantland Rice.

Two bands had been engaged to furnish the music for Notre Dame's annual Senior Ball, Coon-Sanders and Harry Denny's Collegians. (Denny's, apparently a campus group, sometimes used the name Harry Denny and His Notre Dame Orchestra.) Preliminaries for the Senior Ball began at the Oliver Hotel, from four to six in the afternoon. Denny's group played for that, as well as early in the evening for those arriving before the main event, and the Nighthawks would play for the main ball that started at ten o'clock in the Palais Royale. George Laughlin headed the program committee, whose sponsors were Professor and Mrs. W.L. Benitz, Dean and Mrs. T. J. Konop, Coach and Mrs. Knute Rockne, and professors Charles Phillips and Paul Fenlon.[105]

Notre Dame's colors of blue and gold, as well as ornamental shields bearing the senior class pin, dominated the decorations in the dance hall at the Palais Royale. The Nighthawks played from an area partly enclosed by an arrangement of ferns. One source says there were 275 couples present, while another says 235. Whatever the number, there undoubtedly was considerable suspense as everyone waited for ten o'clock. And at the appointed time class president Donald C. Miller and his date Isabell Joyce prepared to lead off the grand march. The *South Bend News-Times* described in some detail Joyce's attire — a tight bodice and a flesh-colored chiffon dress heavily beaded in crystal and with an uneven hemline — but gave no hint as to the height of that uneven hemline. The Nighthawks, all of whom were more or less connoisseurs of feminine beauty, could keep but one eye on Joyce and the other charming women present. The other eye was on Joe Sanders. He gave the beat and the band began to play for a long program that would not end until 3 a.m. It was, according to *The Notre Dame Scholastic*, "[s]plendidly picturesque and colorful, with all dignity attaching to the most important social event of the scholastic year...."[106]

The *Scholastic*, observing that the Nighthawks were scheduled soon to play at Atlantic City's Million Dollar Pier, remarked that this was the second consecutive year in which the band playing for their Senior Ball had gone on to that New Jersey location. The previous year it had been Don Bestor's orchestra.[107]

Back in Illinois, the Nighthawks played in Champaign and next at Pontiac (Illinois, not Michigan). At the latter city they added to their schedule a *gratis* appearance at the state's reformatory, even though many of the citizens in the area probably thought that jazz was one of the reasons the state needed a reformatory. After that came Vincennes, Ind., and then Nashville, Tenn., where the band gave two sensational programs at the Orpheum Theater. In Tennessee they played also at Knoxville and at Johnson City. Joe was much taken with Knoxville, pronouncing it "one of the loveliest cities I have ever visited." He and Madeline had their photos taken in various parts of the city, sometimes identifying themselves below the snapshots as the "girl- and boyfriend" or as "Mr. and Mrs. N. Hawk." Joe took several bird's-eye views from the roof of the Hermitage Hotel. From East Tennessee they swung back northward for a return appearance at Lexington, Ky., and all along the train's route Joe got photos of the beautiful Cumberland Mountains. "What a country!" Joe wrote on one photo, but adding, "Rich in beauty with poverty on all sides!"[108] So much for Appalachia!

They next played a return program in Cincinnati, Ohio, then entertained audiences at Bucyrus and Coshocton in the same state, and followed these appearances with yet another visit to Columbus, Ohio. After that, they hit Indianapolis a second time, where the band were much taken by the excitement and masculine panache of the motor speedway during its 1925 Memorial Day endurance contest. The Nighthawks arrived just in time to catch some of the race, which a baby-faced Peter DePaulo, in his little cream-colored racer, won at an average speed of 101.13 miles per hour. His uncle, Ralph De Palma, finished seventh. The winner's prize was $20,000, as well as about $7,800 in "lap" prizes and $10,000 from makers of automobile accessories. One of Joe's snapshots shows DePaulo's auto just approaching the finish line, with two other vehicles right on his tail. Another photo shows DePalma's racer, in Joe's phrasing, "going at a dizzy rate of speed."[109]

It was not just racing that occupied the band's free time in Indianapolis. The city was attractive and interesting, and Joe's camera has left evidence that he and Madeline found much to admire. They were taken by such street scenes as a downtown view, "just off the Circle," facing the Capitol. Madeline snapped a nattily clad Joe, who stands on a sidewalk and studies a picture in a cardboard frame, as he later put it, "assiduously digesting High Art." Another photo, taken by some third party from behind them, shows Joe and Madeline head-to-head and studying something closely, perhaps another piece of "high art."[110]

Their schedule next took the band back into Illinois for gigs at Marseilles, Oregon, Quincy, Benid, Herrin, and Cairo. The band's engagement at Quincy was on Tuesday, June 2, and both the *Daily Herald* and the *Whig-Journal* gave it publicity, the latter making a point of reminding the public that the band's Nick Musolino was a hometown boy. The *Herald* described the band's engagement at the Highland Rose Garden as the "biggest event of the season." From 9 p.m. until 1 a.m. more than a thousand dancers, including over three hundred out-of-town fans, gave the Neighthawks an enthusiastic welcome and filled the large dance floor to capacity.[111]

Another turn south took them to Jackson, Tenn., and then back northward to Carmel, Ill., Owensboro, Ky., New Albany, Ind., Cincinnati, Ohio, Kentland, Ind., Akron, Ohio, and so on and on, until they ended at Philipsburg, Pa., on July 4. It had been truly a grinding schedule, but the members of the band were young and seemed to enjoy and even thrive on such punishment. Nevertheless, the band took a three-day rest. Said Sanders, "Three days to most bands is no rest at all, but being inured to constant steady going, to our weary band it was a godsend." They had a major engagement before them, but at least it would all be in the same place, Atlantic City, N.J.[112]

While Noel Coward prepared to come to America to act in his own work, *Vortex*, and Gallagher and Shean were ending their professional association, the Nighthawks arrived in Atlantic City for a six-week engagement at Young's Million Dollar Pier. Joe and Madeline, and probably at least some of the other members of the band, put up at the Shelburne Hotel, which, said Joe, "became my Atlantic City home during our successful ... engagement."[113]

Meanwhile, John T. Scopes, Clarence Darrow, William Jennings Bryan, Henry L. Mencken, and all the rest of the "monkey trial" cast were assembling at Dayton, Tenn. Thus, while the Nighthawks prepared for their first gig on the Eastern Seaboard, the Dayton notables and lesser lights would try to decide, in effect, whether humans and apes might be practically kissing cousins. More to the point, the trial would be the first step in deciding whether Tennessee might forbid its public school teachers to discuss the claims of the Evolutionists. Galileo would have understood the issue quite well. As a headline in *Variety* put it, "Ballyhooed Hullabaloo; Dayton, Tenn., Full of Scribes and Riff Raff."[114]

The band had a comfortable schedule at Atlantic City — Joe called it "ridiculously easy"— from 8 p.m. to midnight, alternating with Charlie Fry's Orchestra, a band that *Variety* called a "fixture" at Young's Million Dollar Pier. Joe declared afterward, however, that they had had some concern about adapting to the new dance called the Charleston, which required a slower tempo than they usually played. It had a lively, if brief, rage that peaked about 1925 and then, with a similar dance called the black bottom, ended with the decade. But while it lasted, it was enthusiastically and vigorously executed on dance floors, and predictably denounced elsewhere.[115]

The Charleston is a symbol of the Twenties as are bathtub gin, flivvers, Florida real estate, and the Coué System. It came on the scene rather suddenly and seemed to have caught everyone by surprise, delighted or appalled as the case might have been. Its bizarre gymnastics were exactly right for irritating those who seemed to enjoy being irritated, and for its aficionados, it was one more unequivocal way to proclaim oneself up-to-the-minute. The Charleston was definitely "mean" and "hotter than hot."

In early 1926 another new dance, the *raunch*, was being discussed in white circles. As was the Charleston, the raunch was an African-American invention. It was apparently taking the place of the Charleston, which by that date was said to be *passé* in black communities. Unlike white dancers, black couples performing the Charleston on dance floors had generally separated to allow each person to strut solo. This was also the practice for the raunch, which was being described in Harlem as making one seem to be moving backwards while one actually went forward.[116] Apparently the raunch never had much effect on the white community.

More often than not it is risky business to proclaim the absolute origin of something that was as sudden, popular, and widespread as the Charleston. Nevertheless, for what it's worth, here's what Elida Webb, of New York, had to say. He had been on the road with the famous black show *Shuffle Along*. Upon returning to New York in May of 1922, he saw some black children on the streets doing a simple dance they called "the Charleston," because they had learned the steps from neighborhood children whose family had just moved up from Charleston, S.C. Said Webb, "There was something about the rhythm that was fascinating, and it caught me." He took the rather simple, one-routine movement that the youngsters were doing and added some complementary steps. Later, when in July of 1922 he was engaged to stage the chorus numbers in the black revue *Runnin' Wild*, he used the dance in a number with sixteen women and three men. They opened in Washington on 20 August 1922, the first opportunity the public had to see the Charleston as a finished product. In the fall of 1922, the mother of Bee Jackson, a white dancer, asked Webb to instruct her daughter in the dance, and in February of 1923 Jackson opened at the Silver Slipper. She was, said Webb, "the best of all the 'Charleston' dancers, white or colored, and surely if anyone should know, I should." Webb went on to teach the dance to others such as William Reardon and Dorothy Clark, both of them white, as well as Josephine Baker, black, who was at the time rehearsing with Eubie Blake and Noble Sissle for *Chocolate Dandies*. Baker later carried the dance to Paris.[117]

As one would expect, there were those who disputed Webb's claim and urged their own priority. One such was Ned Wayburn, who insisted that he originated the Charleston in October, 1923, "long before its present popularity." He was, he said, producing a series of six one-reel moving pictures "demonstrating the intricacies of the various Charleston steps which will be ready for release within a few weeks."[118] Perhaps so, but his claim seemed less convincing than Webb's.

Hardly any dance since the shimmy had brought such a storm of protest and such melodramatics as did the Charleston. On 4 July 1925, the dance floor of Boston's Pickwick Club completely collapsed and killed many persons. It had been a dilapidated, weakened structure, but many critics, blaming the new dance's vigorous movements for the disaster, referred to the Charleston as a "death dance." A Boston censor girded up his loins and banned it from the city's ballrooms.[119] Out in Antelope, California, near Sacramento, the Grange Hall was in so dangerous a condition that it would need to be rebuilt. It had, said some, been weakened by "continuous dancing of the 'Charleston.'" Even Mori's Cabaret, in New York's Greenwich Village, found the Charleston intolerable. Many other towns and cities probably reacted as did Des Moines, Iowa, where the supervisor of public dance halls declared, "No matter how popular the step is, the commission regulating dance halls won't allow it — it's indecent." It apparently could also be hazardous for one's health, for in that same city, a few months later, Melvin Eusiere cracked a bone in his knee while doing the Charleston at a house party. He would spend several weeks wearing a splint.[120]

Several months went by and Des Moines took a slightly more tolerant and practical approach to the problem. While keeping in mind the need to protect the less adventurous dancers from the dervishes, the forces of law and order helped devise some rules to keep the Charleston dancer on a leash. Such persons as Madame La Cuta, "sponsor of the down-south antics as a dancing instructor," as well as someone else identified only as "Cesar," whose cabaret had banned the new dance, came up with the following rules:

- Absolutely forbidden was the "stage" Charleston, "with its swinging feet and limbs."
- To make falling less likely, Charleston dancers would not be allowed to swing their feet more than two feet off the floor.
- In order to avoid kicking other dancers in their shins, dancers attempting the new steps must not kick more than twelve inches to either side.
- In order to avoid the possibility of bringing down buildings, Charleston aficionados must not move their bodies above the waist.
- Dancers were to lift their feet quickly and

set them down lightly in order to eliminate undue noise and heavy jarring.[121]

Chicago, not wishing to follow slavishly in New York's footsteps, at first affected a condescending detachment and pretended to see the new dance as less a shocker than a dud:

> Exit the "Charleston," Chicago's prize flop of the season. The dance step that struck New York like a bolt and is sticking like glue has been voted "out" in the Windy City.
> Chicago usually takes to jazz dances more quickly than any other city and more often invents them. That city's steps always held [the] limelight in New York. Some were good and some not so good, but all gained many New York followers, while the "Charleston," probably the snappiest of them all, has been rejected by Chicago's best and worst alike.[122]

Rejected? Well, not entirely, for the following October there was a Charleston contest, sponsored by the Hearst paper *Herald-Examiner*. Dancers in several ballrooms all around Chicago went through the new dance's vigorous exercises. At the Coliseum, alone, there were five thousand who attended. That doesn't sound exactly like rejection.

But whatever the Windy City's true feelings may have been regarding the Charleston, Atlantic City was neither an ambivalent Chicago nor an uncritical New York, and certainly not a sniffish Boston, so the Nighthawks persevered and must have adjusted to the new dance without difficulty. At any rate, the hall was filled each evening. Crowds of visiting celebrities came to hear them, stars such as Al Jolson, soon to make the first movie with dialogue. In fact, he showed up repeatedly. Sanders met and became friends with Benny Davis, composer of such songs as "Margie," "Baby Face," and "Goodbye, Broadway, Hello, France." The two of them even collaborated on several unsuccessful songs. Sanders spent an afternoon with Irving Berlin and listened to him play and sing his latest song, "(You Forgot to) Remember." Other stars who came to listen included George Jessel, De Wolf Hopper, Chic Sale, Bee Palmer,* and many others who took advantage of New York's proximity to Atlantic City. Popular orchestra leaders such as Irving Aaronson and Tom and Fred Waring came by. And perhaps most important to Joe was the acquaintance he formed with composers Gus Kahn and Walter Donaldson.[123] Sanders and Kahn became close friends and collaborated on several songs, some of which had some popularity. Kahn himself was a lyricist of some of America's favorite songs, such classics as "Memories," "I'll See You in My Dreams," "It Had to Be You," "Carolina in the Morning," "Toot, Toot, Tootsie," and "I'm Bringing a Red Red Rose," the last of which three years later Paul Whiteman recorded to good effect. "Little Orphan Annie" and "Beloved" are two songs which Kahn and Sanders later produced and that had some popularity.

There was much competition for the Nighthawks in Atlantic City that summer. Irving Aaronson's Commanders, a very popular dance orchestra, and soon to be a prolific recording band, was at the Ritz-Carlton. Dorothy Braun was at the Follies Bergere, as was also Evelyn Nesbit. (The latter was still deriving some benefit from the notoriety she had received in 1906 from her peripheral involvement when Harry K. Thaw, on the roof of New York's old Madison Square Garden, publically murdered the famous

---

George Jessel (1898–1981), actor and comedian, admired for his singing of "My Mother's Eyes" and for his starring in the stage production of The Jazz Singer, *and later for his after-dinner speeches that earned him the nickname of "Toastmaster-General." De Wolf Hopper (1858–1935), actor and comedian famous for his recitation of "Casey at the Bat," later married to actress and columnist Hedda Hopper (1890–1966), both of them parents of William Hopper (1915–1970), who played Paul Drake on Raymond Burr's* Perry Mason *television series. Charles "Chic" Sale (1885–1936), actor, was then appearing at the Steeplechase in* So This Is Paris. *Bee Palmer was renowned for her shimmy dancing.*

architect Stanford White.)* Jon Lucas's band was at the Traymore Hotel, Ed Hutchison's Revue was at the Breakers Roof, and Martin's Cafe offered the Music Weavers Band, Francis Renault, and Beth Chalis. Bee Palmer was appearing at the New Embassy Club, on the Boardwalk. At the Silver Slipper there was a group with the curious name of the California Nighthawks.[124] (Indeed, there was also a band, elsewhere in the nation and perhaps a few months later, called the "Original Kentucky Nighthawks," led by Al Shayne.)[125]

Within a week of their arrival, *Variety* praised the Nighthawks as "a sensation," and thought it might be profitable for some New York cafe to engage them. Elsewhere, in a special review of the band the New York weekly said: "This crack combination ... speaks forcibly for itself when facts and figures are mentioned in connection with the pier engagement." The Nighthawks, said the reviewer, were getting $2,500 a week, a record for Young's Million Dollar Pier and made all the sweeter by the relaxed nature of the commitment. Except for Sundays, the band did not play on afternoons, and in the evenings the orchestra alternated with Charlie Fry's band. "It's a corking band," said *Variety's* critic, "and the various reports that this combination would wow 'em in vaudeville or at a New York cafe are not exaggerated." The reporter misspelled the Thiell brothers' last name, identified the bass player as "Frank E. Stept," and seemed to confuse Nick Musolino with the upstart dictator in Italy. Nevertheless, there were plenty of compliments to Joe, Coonie, and the other members of the band: "That sax section, comprising Harold and John Thiel [sic] and Orville Knapp, is great. Joe Richolson, at the trumpet, and Nick Mussolini [sic], trombone, are first-class brass men." The band members, said the critique, were eager to test the New York waters, but Joe and Coonie thought they weren't quite ready.[126]

In fact, Coon-Sanders were being so well received in Atlantic City that they got offers in New York City for engagements, but Jules Stein turned them down on the grounds of his having already committed the band during the remainder of the summer. Moreover, the Congress Hotel was expecting them back for the fall. Stein apparently believed that when the Congress's fall commitment had been satisfied, he might even send the Nighthawks abroad during the winter, and if that happened, he might let them "stop over" in New York briefly.[127] Of course, the Nighthawks were not destined to go abroad.

Just as radio had added a revolutionary new dimension to entertainment in the new decade, the art of recording sound was on the verge of an innovation hardly less important. In this year 1925 the reproduction of sound on discs was basically what it had been when Thomas Alva Edison made his first recording in 1877. Though a few improvements had been made, huge megaphones were still needed to pick up the sound waves that, once created, were on their own. But now electricity was about to become a part of the process, and a number of individuals and companies were working on the matter. On August 14, in New York, the Brunswick Recording Laboratories demonstrated for the press a new method of reproducing sound. Trade-named "Panatrope," it claimed to reproduce all musical ranges and octaves electrically. Instead of the usual method that made recordings with eighty grooves to an inch, Panatrope created 500, an improvement that accommodated a forty-minute recording on a twelve-inch disc. Brunswick believed its experimental product would be a great boon to radio. Charles A. Hoxie, of General Electric, was announced as the inventor of the system that was described as differing from Lee DeForest's "Phonofilm."[128]

A few miles from Atlantic City, in

---

*Among the many well-known buildings that White designed was the old Madison Square Garden, in whose tower he lived and on whose roof garden he was murdered. Evelyn Nesbit was the hypotenuse of a triangle involving rivals Thaw and White.

Camden, the Victor Company had been experimenting with an improved method of recording, one that used electricity and a microphone instead of a horn and unaided sound waves. The new tests aimed both at greater clarity and a more thorough capturing of the sound. Though there had been some success, several artists who had experimented with it complained that it produced what they described as a "back in the horn" effect, that is, "as if the band or vocalist were in another room and their music amplified by the 'mike' and thus registered on the wax." But Victor seemed to be making progress with the new idea, and Paul Whiteman, in early May, had gone to Victor's Camden facilities and used the new method to record several test sides. A little later *Variety*, in reporting further on these experimental exercises, observed somewhat facetiously: "The new electric recording process on the Victor [records] is so fine and faithful in reproducing the human voice that it oversteps itself. For instance, in the case of John McCormack, some laboratory tests transformed his tenor into a baritone on the wax."[129] A practical method of recording electrically was still several months away.

Victor was also working on a new type of phonograph—or "Victrola," to use the trade name that eventually became almost a generic term for a phonograph. Before a number of government officials in Washington, the company demonstrated what it called its "greatest discovery" since Edison's original phonograph in 1877. The machine ran without batteries or tubes and could record or reproduce as low as 113 vibrations up to an almost unlimited extent.[130]

By this time Victor had issued ten sides by Coon-Sanders, all of them recorded in Chicago. Now it was convenient for the band to record at the company's headquarters, a mere fifty-five or sixty miles away. Thus it was that on July 13 the band went to Camden and recorded "I'm Gonna Charleston Back to Charleston," "Alone at Last," and "I Can't Realize," the last of which was rejected for issuing.[131] Johnny Coon recalled visiting his father while the Nighthawks were in Atlantic City and accompanying them to Camden for a recording session. It may have been this first one, though he wasn't sure. At any rate, many years later Johnny reminisced about it:

> I remember distinctly that it was in the afternoon and they recorded the first side, and it printed right away. In other words, the recording master said 'It's a go' and they printed it in about five or six minutes. They just played the tune one time and he said it was just fine. But the second one they did—and I don't remember the name of it—they had a time with that, and they spent about forty-five minutes or an hour on that particular song. I don't know what the problem was, or whether balance between sections wasn't good or whether there was something wrong with something else in the way they played the particular song. And I was sitting there listening; but being about thirteen years old, I wouldn't know from sickum [?] about what the problems were, really. But I do know that I observed that they worked on it about—oh, between thirty and forty-five minutes before they got official word from the recording master to print it.[132]

Of course, all of these were acoustical records, for the electrical process would not arrive until the end of this year, 1925. Recording sessions still were clumsy affairs that required special huddling and spacing around the megaphone-like horn or horns—sometimes more than one horn was used. And, as before, the band received no royalties on these recordings, only what Victor paid for the session.

Four days before this first recording session, Henry Busse's Buzzards had recorded "Deep Elm," which Victor paired with "I'm Gonna Charleston Back to Charleston." The Busse number still sounds excellent and the disc today is an especially desirable collector's item.[133]

The band went to Camden twice more to record. On July 27, Coon-Sanders recorded "I Can't Realize," or rather re-recorded it since it had been rejected at the first session. The second number was "Yes,

Sir, That's My Baby." Then came "Everything is Hotsy-Totsy Now," which was rejected, and finally "Dreaming of Tomorrow." The last session, on August 7, consisted of "Hong Kong Dream Girl," "Who Wouldn't Love You?" "That's All There Is," and another, and this time successful, recording of "Everything Is Hotsy-Totsy Now."[134]

But not *everything* was hotsy-totsy. The next day, in Washington, D.C., the Ku Klux Klan staged a huge, three-hour parade down Pennsylvania Avenue. Apparently no one interfered, except the elements, which disrupted the proceedings with a thunderstorm. And barely two weeks before that, a court in Dayton, Tenn., had found John T. Scopes guilty of teaching evolution in a Tennessee public school, and also (by implication) that the world was indeed created in 4004 B.C. Appropriately, Will Rogers, in his newspaper column "The Bull's Eye," observed: "Some people certainly are making a fight against the ape. It seems the truth kinder hurts. Now, if a man didn't act like a monkey, he wouldn't have to be proving that he didn't come from one." Even a popular comic strip got into the issue. One daily "Mutt and Jeff" strip shows them walking in a zoo when they see a strange-looking monkey. Jeff walks over to the animal and whispers something, and the next picture shows both men tumbling head over heels, with a brick trailing them for good measure. "For the love of Mike," exclaims Mutt, "what did you say to the monk?" Replied Jeff, "I asked him if he was Bryan's cousin."[135] The humor in the comic strip may have proved inappropriate when prosecutor William Jennings Bryan died five days later.

Joe complained that he had been kept so busy arranging and recording that he and Madeline had been unable to do much sightseeing or even to spend much time together. He was unable even to do any bathing in the ocean, "scarcely a hundred feet from the Shelburne," as he said plaintively. He did manage to get in a bit of recreation, though. Something he called the "Deep Sea Net Haul and the accompanying lecture by Capt. Young, owner of the Pier" proved entertaining. Young gave these lectures twice daily.[136] This was a typical situation for Joe, hard at work on music and spending his few spare moments on intellectual pursuits.

The Nighthawks closed on August 9. There were many warm goodbyes by everyone, and Joe spent his last hours at the Embassy Club and at Benny Davis's apartment writing songs. Said Sanders, "Thus ended a busy and successful engagement at Atlantic City — America's great county fair. Selah!"[137]

Having finished their commitment at Atlantic City, the Nighthawks set out on the second part of their road tour for the year and on August 10 played at Philipsburg, Penn. Remaining in the state for several days, they subsequently played at Uniontown, Oakmont (immediately northeast of Pittsburgh), and Franklin. The band did their usual sightseeing while in the Keystone State, including a tour of Philadelphia. Here Joe confused Betsy Ross's house with that in Frederick, Md., where Whittier's heroine Barbara Frietchie poked her head through a window and scolded the Boys in Gray. (Though they would have liked to, the Confederates never made it to Philadelphia.) In Tyrone, Fred Waring's home, the band "killed time," as Joe put it, changing trains. Waring's mother made them a "lovely cake" and had Fred's brother Tom take it down to the station for them. At another town — "somewhere in Pennsylvania," as Joe vaguely remembered — Sanders got a good shot of Yalmar "Axle Flooey" Lovendahl, whom Joe identified as "assistant tour manager and official drunkard." (To be declared "official drunkard" of *this* outfit was no trifling distinction.) Joe got another good snapshot of Nick Musolino, a pipe in his mouth, standing next to a train and looking very suave in a white suit. In Franklin, Penn., they found a long wooden stairway at the train station and got someone to take a photo of the entire band standing one to a step. Joe called it the "Night Hawk Pyramid." Starting with Pop Estep on the bottom, there were Nick

Madeline and Joe enjoy a gondola outside their accommodations at the Shelburne Hotel, Atlantic City, New Jersey, mid-summer 1925. (Courtesy Special Collections, Kansas City [Mo.] Public Library.)

Musolino, John Thiell, "Flooey" Lovendahl, Harold Thiell, Joe Richolson, Coonie, Hank Linder, Bill Haid, Orville Knapp, and Joe at the top.[138] Then the band headed west to play at Dayton, Ohio, and Anderson, Ind. In Illinois they played at Lincoln, Decatur, Spring Valley, Sterling, Bloomington, and, finally, Lewistown, which Joe was interested to learn was the state's first capital. Orville Knapp and Nick Musolino were about to take their leave of the Nighthawks, and under a photo of Musolino Joe wrote, "Good old Nick — his last trip — hence his last appearance on these pages."[139]

While still in Atlantic City, Joe had purchased, by wire, a new Auburn brougham, and it was waiting for him in Lewistown, Ill. This was apparently the first contact any of the Nighthawks had with the Auburn Automobile Company, an association that in six years would become a famous, important part of the Nighthawk story. It was the first of six vehicles made by the Auburn Company that Sanders would own. In no time at all Joe was hooked on them and, as he later put it, "began to sing their praises." He even invested in the company's stock and became close friends with company executive Roy Faulkner.[140]

Now that they had finished the second part of their road trip, everyone took a break. Undoubtedly proud, elated, and still awed by the car's newness and elegance, Joe got into his Auburn and headed for Kansas City—"HOME!" as he emphasized it. He left Lewistown at 2 a.m. and arrived in St. Louis at 7:30 a.m. Joe Richolson and his wife Jean had started out in their Maxwell in order to drive with him, but on the dark road the two vehicles became separated and Joe lost time searching vainly for them. After driving for twenty-one hours without sleep—in one place he says forty-eight hours—and 538 miles, he reached Kansas City at 10 p.m. He failed to say when the Richolsons arrived.[141]

Joe spent part of his break in Kansas City involved with personnel changes in the

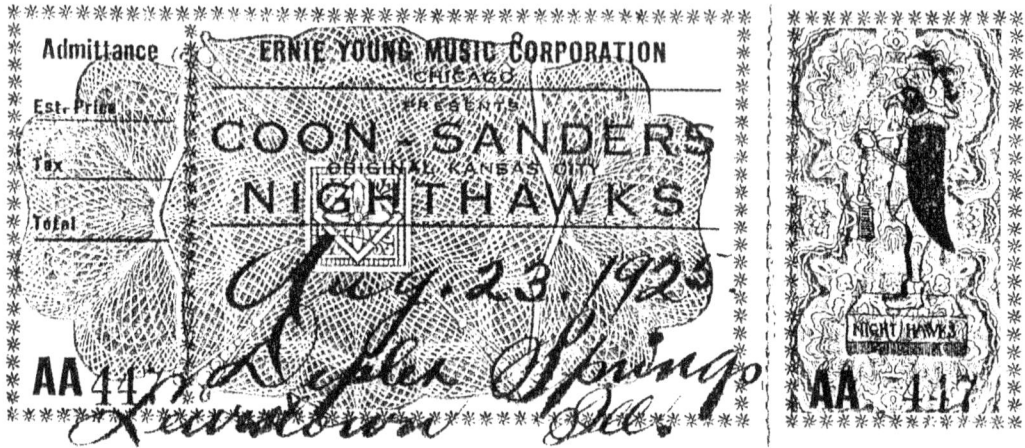

Ticket used for the band's dances. This was for the engagement at Lewistown, Illinois, 23 August 1925. (Courtesy Special Collections, Kansas City [Mo.] Public Library.)

band. Though the story is still a bit murky, it appears that both Musolino and Knapp had decided sometime during the Atlantic City engagement that they wanted to leave the band. Joe later seemed to suggest that the changes were his idea. (In an interview in 1961 with Harvey Rettberg, Joe said that Musolino had "lost his lip.") Thus, suddenly in need of two replacements, Joe remembered Floyd Estep, a fine young musician back in Kansas City and son of the Nighthawks' bass player. As we have already seen, Floyd had played with the early band and, in fact, was playing with Coonie's group at the time Joe returned from the Army. But it wasn't long before Estep realized that his and Joe's personalities tended to clash. "We were a couple of hardheads; we didn't get along at all," recalled Floyd. "We'd go over and play three-cushion billiards; and if I whipped him, he wouldn't speak to me all night." So, Floyd left the band but remained in Kansas City.[142]

According to Floyd Estep, as stated to Harvey Rettberg in 1961, in the summer of 1925 Estep got what he called "the most wonderful wire" from Sanders in Atlantic City. Referring to their past differences, Joe's telegram said, "Now that we've both grown up, would you like to rejoin the band? And get me a trombone player." That was about all the wire said, and Estep must have ac-

cepted fairly promptly. At any rate, as soon as Joe got back to Kansas City, he went out to Fairyland Park where Floyd and Rex Downing were playing. Thus, whether the changes in the band's personnel were a result of Musolino's and Knapp's own decisions, or whether, as Joe later seemed to suggest, the changes were his own idea, it didn't take Joe long to recognize that Estep and Downing "would do." The two men joined the Nighthawks for researsals during the last three days of the band's vacation, and reported to play with it at Joplin, Mo., on September 14. All of this accords pretty well with Rex Downing's recollections many years later.[143]

The Nighthawks then opened the third and final lap of their 1925 road tour. From Joplin, Mo., they went on to Independence, Kans.; Tulsa, Okla.; Dallas, Houston, and Galveston, Tex.; Shreveport, La.; and El Dorado, Texarkana, and Little Rock, Ark. Then they made a tremendous jump of 630 miles to Indianapolis and Lafayette, Ind.; Streator and Sterling, Ill.; and, finally, to Garrett, Ind. The tour had been, said Joe, "highly successful, very interesting, and opened new territory for MCA."[144]

Maybe the tour was "very interesting" for Joe, but for Rex Downing it was a somewhat tense period. The band rather let him fend for himself. Except for Downing and Floyd Estep, the members knew the routine and the arrangements but for some reason did not properly introduce Rex to them. If Floyd Estep was having similar problems, Downing apparently didn't know about it. But every time the band prepared to play a number, poor Rex had to struggle to find his place. And when the band played in Little Rock, Ark., Joe, after reminding the audience that Downing was a local boy, insisted upon his singing four or five of the pieces played. Said Downing later, "Now, I haven't been able to carry a tune before or since then, but to them that was a big joke, and the people seemed to enjoy it."[145]

The trombone is sufficiently loud so that Rex was never concerned about volume, but he apparently did experiment with achieving a variety of tones. One of his methods was to set up a megaphone on a stand, stuff a towel into its mouth, and play his trombone into the large opening. Johnny Coon, who recalled this, said Rex often used it for four to eight bars in special arrangements. Whether Rex had invented the tactic Johnny could not recall.[146]

It was a somewhat different band that made its way back to Chicago. This made the term *original*, as in "The *Original* Nighthawks," problematic.* As a matter of fact,

Nick Musolino just before leaving the band, late summer 1925. (Courtesy Special Collections, Kansas City [Mo.] Public Library.)

aside from Joe and Coonie, there were now only two of the band from the summer of 1923 that were still playing, John Thiell and Pop Estep. Everyone else had come in after that tour, with the exception of Harold Thiell who had been away most of 1923, and Floyd Estep who had only recently returned

---

*Of course, Coon-Sanders meant the term "original" to mean primarily that they were the band, or at least the latest version of the band, that had started the Nighthawk programs in Kansas City.

Joe Sanders' first Auburn, 1925. (Courtesy Special Collections, Kansas City [Mo.] Public Library.)

after a long break. After 1925, changes in personnel were fewer and less frequent.

Whatever the circumstances of Estep and Downing's joining the flock, the Chicago Musicians Union, according to Johnny Coon, seemed likely to raise objections to hiring two players from outside the Chicago area. The local union was headed by James Caesar Petrillo, a man with strong opinions and a gargantuan ego. Controversy was his bosom companion. He felt comfortable with discord and perhaps judged his success by its intensity. Even when in 1924 union men got into a dispute with some nonunion ones, and a bomb badly damaged Petrillo's residence, he managed to appear not especially frightened.[147] Negotiating with him, while not necessarily unpleasant, was usually not easy, as a congressional committee would discover in January of 1948, by which time Petrillo was national head of the American Federation of Musicians.[148] Obviously, getting him to approve the hiring of Downing and Estep was going to require careful dealing by someone of great tact and delicate instincts. Since that excluded Joe, who might instead have gotten the entire band blacklisted, the job fell to Coonie. Thus, armed with a gift for charming gab and a bottle of the best booze (probably Scotch), he paid Petrillo a visit. Of course it worked, for who, especially in those arid days, could resist the eighty-proof charms of Carleton A. Coon? Petrillo's decision: Downing and Estep would do just fine, and drop by anytime there's a problem.[149]

Petrillo was re-elected many times to the local's presidency, and he seems to have taken his work seriously. He presided over a large union that, in 1925, had at least 7,000 paid-up members, a thousand of whom had joined that year. Petrillo believed that the great surge in membership had been due primarily to radio.[150]

In Petrillo the city of Chicago certainly had a municipal institution, but he was hardly the only metropolitan oddity. In a city where life was made more dramatic by such curiosities as the splashiest gangsters, weak city government (and even that adjective puts the best face on it), and cold winds off the lake, there were many others that autumn that must have furnished Chicagoans with diversion, and certainly with fewer concerns than the first three named. At Balaban & Katz's new Uptown Theatre, for instance, Jay McGee lost his voice and had to miss several scenes. He was certain that the cause was that his dressing room was numbered 13. The theater changed the room's number to 12-B, and McGee had no further trouble.[151] And in the city's divorce court, the vaudevillian H. M. Burgess discovered that jokes which might seem merely stale to audiences could quickly become mental cruelty to a wife. Mrs. Burgess had heard them long enough and told a court she thought she had earned a divorce.

Floyd Eugene Estep, son of the band's bass player, joined on reeds in late summer 1925. Occasionally he made the arrangements. (Courtesy Claude and Ruth Anderson.)

MRS. BURGESS: I used to grit my teeth when he told those jokes.
JUDGE: What were the jokes?
MRS. BURGESS: One of them began like this: Once there were two Irishmen, Pat and Mike…
JUDGE: That's enough! Decree granted.[152]

As a matter of fact, Chicago seemed to be where many in the entertainment world went to be freed of marital restraints. Though local courts were concerned and vowed not to become another Reno, Nevada, disgruntled couples kept pouring in. By 1928 there was a backlog of ten thousand suits. But Reno, Nevada, still had something of a mystique, and in the spring of 1931, Taft Schreiber at MCA said that twelve of their band leaders in the East were pleading to get six-week engagements in Reno. They were willing to take cuts in pay just for the opportunity to take "the cure" in that Western clinic.[153]

As Joe and Madeline set up house again at the Surf Hotel, the Nighthawks opened their second season at the Congress Hotel's Balloon Room. By this time, the band had

The strain of the heavy schedule seems to have gotten to Coonie and Joe. Uniontown, Pennsylvania, August 1925. (Courtesy Special Collections, Kansas City [Mo.] Public Library.)

become so popular that *Radio Digest* picked them for its first-place award. As Joe put it, the band beat out "every famous announcer, all radio bands and every radio entertainer." Their announcer was Harold Isbell, from Los Angeles. The Nighthawks, in fact, were so popular at the Congress that often the hotel had to display an announcement: "Sold out tonight in the Balloon Room. We regret that we cannot accept any more reservations for tonight."[154]

Another group that would develop a great radio popularity was at this time preparing to send some "mean" sounds into the ether. Harry Reser, a native of Piqua, Ohio, was born the same year as Joe Sanders. (They would die the same year, as well.) He found his way to New York, where on 3 December 1925 his Eskimos began broadcasting over sixteen radio stations. Under the sponsorship and name of a beverage producer, the Cliquot Club Eskimos became radio favorites for the snappy style they employed, the interesting, if nasal, singing of Tom Stacks, and the masterful banjo playing by Reser.[155] The Eskimos' recordings of such numbers as "My Sunday Girl" and "Collegiate Sam" are still available on more recent releases.

In Chicago on December 20 and 21, the Nighthawks had two more recording sessions for Victor. By this time, the electrical process had arrived, so recordings were losing their "telephone" tone quality. In late 1925 and early 1926 record companies were doing exceedingly well in sales, and Victor was at the top.[156] On the twentieth Coon-Sanders recorded "Too Bad" and "Don't Be a Fool, You Fool," the first of which Brian Rust says was rejected. The four numbers recorded the next day were "Louise, You Tease," "Flamin' Mamie," "Sittin' Around," and "Moon Dear." "Sittin' Around" was rejected for distribution but was successfully re-recorded at a later session.[157] "Flamin' Mamie" remains one of the favorites for Coon-Sanders fanatics, among whom I count myself.

Flaming Mamie was probably the kind of flapper who would have gravitated to every new fad as readily as metal filings do to a magnet, and one such fad at present involved wearing garters with an initial on them. Such garters had to be fancy, the kind that came into view when the lass sat down. The monogram could be of any form or color. Said one commentator, "If the girl declines to give a plausible reason for it being there, that is looked upon as an admission the initial goes into the anklet class, with the single letter signifying there is someone in the background she is always thinking of." An earlier, but similar, fad was the "dog collar" or "necklet," which was available at five-and-ten-cent stores for about a half dollar. That affectation was said to have originated with Gertrude Lawrence when she appeared in *Charlot's Revue*.[158]

It was at about this time that Joe Sanders, who was not always eager to help plug someone else's song, joined Art Kahn and Charley Straight in praising a recent publication by Leo Feist, in New York. A Feist ad boasted, "Chicago's leading orchestra leaders all pick 'Sleepy Time Gal,' the new sensational song and dance hit!" In a telegram to Phil Kornheiser, at Feist's offices, Joe had wired: "No one should know better than you that I seldom enthuse over a tune. Hence you will doubtless be speechless that I take this method of offering sincere congratulations on your sensational song 'Sleepy Time Gal.' Both from the dance floor and over the air it is tremendous."[159]

There was another and very common method of plugging songs against which Joe took a strong and much-publicized stand. It had been the habit for many in the songwriting industry to persuade or perhaps even pressure band leaders to hold so-called "celebrity nights," often just an excuse to get an orchestra to puff pet songs. Joe wrote a letter to most music firms in the Chicago area to inform them that his orchestra would play such tunes provided the promoters paid a standard fee of $25 for the special arrangements. In commenting on this interesting development, *Variety* suggested that perhaps it would bring on the "long-awaited explosion in the song pluggers vs. band leaders," especially since the Nighthawks were "recognized in the midwest as strictly on the square in its dealings with the music men."

The letter was interpreted by the music industry as "an out-and-out slam by direct allusion at hooey celebrity nights, running riot around this town."[160]

According to Brian Rust's discography, Bob Pope played with the Nighthawks on those December recordings. The same source shows that Pope had recently left Jack Ford's Arcadia Peacock Orchestra of St. Louis, with which he made recordings in St. Louis from November of 1923 until March 1925.[161]

Less than three months later, in Chicago on March 9, the band had a rather busy recording session during which they cut five numbers, one of which was an acceptable re-recording of "Sittin' Around." The others were "Everything's Gonna Be All Right," "Deep Henderson," and two that were rejected, "Here Comes the Hot Tamale Man" and "I'd Rather Be Alone." On all five Russ Stout replaced Bill Haid on banjo.[162]

But what could the Nighthawks anticipate for the fall of 1926? Would they continue at the Congress? Sanders insisted that having given the Congress two successful seasons, they certainly could not consider returning for the same amount of money. According to Joe, however, H. L. Kaufman thought himself alone responsible for the Nighthawks' successful appearances at the Balloon Room. "It was his contention," said Sanders, "that [he] having made the band, we should, from a sense of appreciation, return to him at the same figure." Rex Downing said that one night Joe called the band together and explained their situation. He told them of a possible engagement at the Blackhawk Restaurant in Chicago's Loop and that Otto Roth, the proprietor, had offered a good contract for the following year. Nevertheless, all of the band's members should take a good look at the proposition and pass judgment. After the other members had considered the Blackhawk's offer, Joe seemed to be the only one who thought it a good idea. He eventually won over the other members, however, and the band prepared for its 1926 road tour, now fully under the auspices of the Music Corporation of America.[163]

About 1925, probably Chicago. Standing: Coon (left) and Sanders; seated (from left): Musolino, Estep, Richolson, Haid, J. Thiell, Knapp, and H. Thiell. Insets: Coon (left) and Sanders. (Courtesy Harvey C. Rettberg.)

The MCA, too, had an important role in the move to the Blackhawk. Karl Kramer later wrote: "With the Nighthawks now firmly in the MCA stable, the next step was to place them in a permanent Chicago location which could be their home base between tours." The problem was that the Benson Agency still had a stronghold on Chicago's best places. So MCA decided, as Kramer put it, "to create a new job especially for this orchestra." He continues:

> About a block and a half from the MCA office was located the Blackhawk Restaurant on Wabash Avenue near Randolph Street. The MCA boys* used to have lunch there frequently and became very friendly with the proprietor, Otto Roth. Roth was always complaining about poor business, a habit which he continued even through the following years which saw his place thronged from opening to closing, but in early 1925 his restaurant business must have been slipping because he was very receptive to the radical idea Stein proposed to him. That was to convert the Blackhawk from a straight restaurant to a dine and dance establishment and to open this policy with the Coon-Sanders Nighthawks Orchestra. The deal was made and the place renovated to provide for a dance floor. In the fall of 1925 [actually 1926] the Blackhawk Restaurant began its band policy which was to become so successful that this establishment became nationally famous as the "House of Bands."[164]

With the end of March 1926, it was time for what was becoming Coon-Sanders' annual road tour. Their engagement with the Congress Hotel at an end, Charles Dornberger's band took over and the Nighthawks set out.[165] In addition to playing gigs, this meant checking rail schedules, getting Pullman accommodations, and trying to find decent and affordable hotel reservations—

---

*Including both Jules C. Stein and William R. "Billy" Goodheart, the "supersalesmen" whom Kramer gave credit for finally persuading Roth to open the Blackhawk to dancing.

5. Chicago's Congress Hotel

Framed Nighthawk display for an egagement about late 1925. Clockwise from top-right: Sanders, H. Thiell, F. Estep, J. Thiell, Haid, Downing, Pope, Richolson, Pop Estep, and Coon. (Courtesy Claude and Ruth Anderson.)

all the things that a good road manager would do. Hank Linder acted in that capacity until May 7 in Richmond, Ind., at which point Dudley Wilkinson replaced him. Wilkinson had once been an accompanist for Nora Bayes* and business manager for one of Florenz Ziegfeld's† shows. Sanders regarded him as a "wizard" at reading railroad timetables, in those days a useful and rare talent.[166] Sanders enjoyed travel by rail and probably considered it one of the most agreeable aspects of his work. Much of his photography involved railroads, and in his notebook he often indicated details of the lines they took to get to their appointments.

Though the band's great popularity was the main reason, it was perhaps partly due to the imaginative efforts of Jules Stein and the MCA that the Nighthawks had, among other perquisites, a free supply of clothing for their engagements. The makers of Society suits and Kingly shirts provided these items if the band's members would wear them as endorsements. Moreover, when the band had engagements in towns where stores sold those products, the national companies arranged with local dealers to have attractive window displays showing all the Nighthawks handsomely clothed. Placards reminded the viewer that the band, thus magnificently attired, would appear at such and such a theater or ballroom on a certain date. Apparently no other of Stein's clients, at least at this time, received this benefit.[167] It paid off immediately.

Thus, after boning up on timetables, these jolly Nighthawks-errant hit the rails for their first engagement, Anderson, Ind., where on April 4 they checked into the Grand Hotel and played that evening at the Green Lantern. A local dealer in men's clothing, E. A. Smith, announced to the public that Coon-Sanders was "America's most famous band," and seemed to imply that one reason for that fame was that its members "unanimously choose Society brand Clothes to be worn at all appearances—in famous hotels and every place where well dressed people gather." Not to be outdone, Hoyt Wright, of "The Store That Does Things," reminded the public: "Look at their shirts; they're all Kingly's," for which Wright just happened to have the "exclusive agency." Anderson's citizens, probably more interested in the Nighthawks' music than in the clothes they wore, allowed them to earn the considerable sum of $832.50.[168] (The most they received for a single appearance on this trip was $1500, which they got in each of Columbus, Ohio, Evansville, Ind., and Champaign, Ill.)

From Anderson they went on to one-nighters in Vincennes, Evansville, and Terre Haute, Ind. At Vincennes, on the fifth, the band played in a vaudeville type program at the junior high school from 7:45 until 9 p.m. After an hour's break they played until 2 a.m. at the Union Depot Hotel, where the band members also stayed. They earned, for both appearances, $721.50. Following Vincennes, they moved on to Evansville, stayed at the McCurdy Hotel, and picked up $636.[169]

The next day, April 7, the band played in Terre Haute at the Trianon and made $750. They stayed at the Deming Hotel. David N. Lewis, of the Vigo County Public Library, tells me that the Trianon, located in a brick building at 2831 Wabash Avenue, was probably the city's best-known ballroom. Ordinarily, says Mr. Lewis, admission to the Trianon was fifteen cents, with an additional charge of ten cents to dance.[170] For a special appearance such as that by the Coon-Sanders band, the charge probably was higher.

Then it was to Dayton, Ohio, and $900

---

*Bayes (1880–1928) star singer of such songs as "Shine On Harvest Moon" and "Down Where the Wurzburger Flows," the latter earning her the nickname of the "Wurzburger Girl." She married Jack Norworth (1879–1959), pianist and composer of such songs as "Take Me Out to the Ball Game" and "Shine On Harvest Moon."
†Florenz Ziegfeld (1869–1932), theatrical producer famous for his Follies.

Late 1925 or early 1926. Back row (from left): Coon, Sanders, and Pop Estep; front row (from left): J. Thiell, F. Estep, H. Thiell, Haid, Richolson, and Downing. (Courtesy Claude and Ruth Anderson.)

for each of two nights of playing for the Delco-Frigidaire National Convention, whose special guest was Will Rogers. This was followed by two evenings at Castle Farm in Cincinnati, Ohio. Then they crossed the Ohio River into West Virginia to play on the twelfth at Huntington, where they put up at the Pritchard Hotel and made $900.[171] The local *Herald-Dispatch* gave them good coverage, flatly declaring them the greatest dance band in the country. The dance was at the Vanity Fair Ballroom, where admission was $1.65 per person. The paper paid tribute to Joe and Coonie's singing, calling it a "pleasant feature of the program," and adding, "At swinging swaying syncopation they are supreme, and no dancer can resist the rhythms played by this peppy, youthful and versatile aggregation." The paper continued:

This is Station KYW, Chicago — How many radio fans throughout the country have listened for these call letters, knowing that they would hear one of the most famous dance bands in the country[?]… It is one of the few really distinctive band organizations of the day and will always be remembered by radio fans as the first orchestra to become famous on the air. Curiously enough, most of the broadcasting done by the Nighthawks has been after 1 a.m., and this is how their name originated.[172]

From Huntington Coon-Sanders went to Williamson for a dance on the thirteenth, after which the band left West Virginia for Chillicothe, Ohio. After checking into the Warner Hotel, they played for a "post Lenten dance" at the Winter Garden on the evening of April 14. An ad called them "famous and original" and praised their "peppy rhythms." (*Pep* and its corresponding adjective were popular words in the Twenties.) The local

Scioto Gazette called them "an orchestra with a hundred personalities." "An orchestra has a personality, you know," said the anonymous writer, suggesting as an example the "dignified symphony atmosphere" that Paul Whiteman offered, or Ted Lewis's "jazzy struttings." "But the trouble with most modern musical organizations," continued the writer, "is that they have but one personality apiece." Sounding almost like a psychiatrist, the journalist explained, "There are individuals with more than one personality — and appearing at the Winter Garden is an orchestra with a hundred personalities, moods, surprises, talents or what you will." The city's fans of good music were reminded that the Nighthawks had founded the Insomnia Club, "the members of which sat up all night, preferring the mellifluous strains of the Night Hawks, to the pleasures of slumber." The engagement was so well attended that the band received $610.30, as well as an invitation to return soon.[173] They did, about a month later.

One more appearance in Ohio, at Toledo on the fifteenth, and Coon-Sanders headed feverishly onward — to Detroit and Battle Creek, Michigan, and then to Streator and Galena, Ill., appearing in the latter place at the Royal Dance Palais, on Monday, April 19. The band stayed at the De Soto Hotel and made $400. (The Galena Public Library tells me that the dance hall was demolished in the summer of 1998.)[174] Then came La Crosse, Wis., where they made $646 playing for a dance at the Winter Gardens on the twentieth. "Gents" paid $1.50 and ladies fifty cents. Three different ads in the *La Crosse Tribune* managed to use three different versions of the Nighthawk logo, one of which showed a vaguely avian creature whose eyes were quite crossed, perhaps from travel fatigue, or possibly even from liquid lunches at the Standard Hotel, where the band stayed.[175]

In the first two weeks of their tour they had made $11,000, and somehow the information got to New York, where *Variety* duly reported it.[176] Perhaps MCA was trying to suggest to other bands that the new Chicago agency was the way to wealth. MCA's new office in New York would have been pleased to receive any new clients.

There followed a dash over to Davenport, Iowa, for an engagement on April 21. The band checked into a hotel with the interesting name of Blackhawk and made $500 playing at Danceland.[177] The local press described them as "far above the general run of dance orchestras" with "talent, cleverness and originality" and a "super-syncopating ensemble." And yet more:

> People who pick their phonograph jazz records with subtle discrimination, rating rhythm and melody above mere noise, have encountered time and again the name and art of the Coon-Sanders Original Night Hawks.... This orchestra — the first to attain nation[al] fame in radio — guides jazz music into the realms of stage entertainment, and yet it has the smoothest dance rhythms of any band known. It does tricks with popular tunes, achieves novelties that are original and amusing. And through it all is that subdued commotion, that fine art of time and melody which gently excites and stirs, pleasing dancer and listener alike. The charm, urge and emotion of modern music are nowhere more deftly displayed than by the Coon-Sanders Night Hawks.[178]

Following an engagement at Cedar Rapids on the twenty-second, the Nighthawks headed to a one-night gig in Chicago. Reaching Dubuque on the twenty-third, they received some special treatment by the Chicago, Burlington & Quincy Railroad that Sanders must have regarded as an unexpected treat. There was a trifling two-mile stretch of track that linked Dubuque with East Dubuque, Ill., across the Mississippi River. Running on that short line was a small locomotive and single coach, half baggage and half passenger. Though the little train was apparently not in service when the Nighthawks reached the Dubuque station, the railroad ran the train just for the band and someone even attached to the side of the coach a Coon-Sanders placard. Before leaving Dubuque, the band's members lined up

Joe labeled this "A very busy body of young men — working very hard at doing nothing." Waiting for a train, Dubuque, Iowa, late summer 1925. (Courtesy Special Collections, Kansas City [Mo.] Public Library.)

beside the coach and posed for several photos. Joe drolly called the train the *Toonerville*, a reference to a rickety trolley in a comic strip of that day, but he was clearly delighted by the experience.[179]

The band played in Milwaukee's Wisconsin Theater from April 24 through the 30 and stayed at the Wisconsin Hotel. The *Milwaukee Journal*, managing to spell Coonie's first name correctly, lavishly praised the band as "The most popular radio orchestra in the world today," and stated that their performance at the Wisconsin would be broadcast over WHAD. Actually, they broadcast twice in the evening, first for a few minutes following 8:30 from the radio studio, then after 9:30 from the theater's stage. This extended visit to Milwaukee netted them $2,750.[180] In Portsmouth, Ohio, where the band appeared on May 6, the *Daily Times* announced that at the Athletic Club, the "Coon-Sanders Original Kansas City Nighthawks…will give you the thrill that comes once in a lifetime." The *Portsmouth Morning Sun* described the band in much the same manner and even sentences — obviously at least some of the information had been supplied by MCA — as had appeared in the press in previous places, though adding: "It has the smoothest dance rhythms of any band known. It does tricks with popular tunes, achieves novelties that are original and amusing. And through it all is that subdued commotion, that fine art of time and melody which gently excites and stirs, pleasing dancer and listener alike." For some reason, prices in Portsmouth seem to have been a little higher than those in some other places. Admission for a couple or an unaccompanied man was $3.30, and for an unaccompanied woman $1.10, with the number of tickets limited to 400. The band stayed at the Washington Hotel.[181]

On May 7, while Mae West's play *Sex* was starting to fascinate some and shock others in New York City, the band made the first of two appearances during this tour at Richmond, Ind. A local merchant advertised that "Coon-Sander's [sic] Original Night Hawks use Conn instruments, sold exclusively

Danny Danford's orchestra played at the same place. The band's compensation was $501.85.[182] On May 8 in Terre Haute, Ind., the Nighthawks put up at the Deming Hotel, their same stopping place on their visit April 7. As on that previous occasion, they gave an evening program at the Trianon. In the little appointment book he usually carried with him, Joe jotted down, "Tell Miss Doyle I saw Miss Schmitz," one of many such notations whose significance is now lost. They made the very gratifying sum of $900, $150 more than on the previous appearance. Some of the guests were probably students from nearby colleges, for Coon-Sanders was already becoming popular with the college crowd. At Manitowoc, Wis., on May 10, they made $385, by their standards only a fair gate.[183]

An issue of *Variety* brought attention to an arrangement between Jules Stein's MCA and the Nighthawks, and suggested that the band was perhaps unique in that it maintained a scale of prices for single engagements. There was a request of a flat price of $1,000 per night, "with a preference for as low as $375 guarantee against an 80 per cent. take on the gate." Coonie and Joe had worked up a schedule of percentages ranging downward from $700 to $375, with the percentage increasing accordingly. If a flat price of $1,000 was not accepted, the band would take fifty-five percent of the gross with a guarantee of $700, or sixty percent against a $600 guarantee, or sixty-five percent with a guarantee of $500.[184]

Carleton and Eula Coon, about 1925. (Courtesy Special Collections, Kansas City [Mo.] Public Library.)

On 11 May 1926, at Manitowoc, Wis., the band chartered a boat, the *Pere Marquette 21*, and crossed Lake Michigan to Ludington, Mich. It afforded everyone a novel break in routine, and some unusual subjects for the amateur photographers. In fact, Joe declared the trip "the one bright spot in a chill, drab month."

in Richmond by Runge's Music Store." The Nighthawks put up at the Westcott Hotel and played at Athletic Park Pavilion, 9 p.m. to 1 a.m. Admission was forty cents, four times what was charged the next night when

Joe's camera caught Coonie leaning against the ship's rail and in what seemed an uncharacteristically introspective mood, or as Joe later put it, "romancing over the blue waters of Lake Michigan." "Isn't this a dandy little old tub to be the private transport of Coon-Sanders?" wrote Joe beneath a snapshot of a very considerable deck and superstructure. In fact, the ship must have been at least two hundred feet long. It was a wonderful outing, and they were back in time for their next engagement, that evening at Wausau, Wis. The train that took them from Manitowoc to Wausau, as train-enthusiast Sanders carefully recorded, was part freight and part passenger. Someone got Joe's picture as he was about to board the caboose.[185]

And on they went. On the twelfth and thirteenth they played in Marshfield and Norrie, Wis. Then on the fourteenth it was again into Michigan for an engagement at Iron Mountain, where they made $509.28. Then back into Wisconsin for Milwaukee on the fifteenth and Appleton the next day. At the Cinderella Ball Room, in Appleton, the band apparently shared the Sunday evening with a "semi final Charleston contest," and apparently even provided the music for the dancers. Nine couples from the general area participated in the contest that began at 11 p.m.[186]

Then it was into Michigan again, from the seventeenth through the twenty-second,

Coonie and his Hudson, 30 April 1926, en route to Chicago. (Courtesy Special Collections, Kansas City [Mo.] Public Library.)

for gigs at Ludington, Traverse City, Cadillac, Grand Rapids, a university prom at Ann Arbor, and then Battle Creek. Laurence Fuller, conductor of Fuller's Orchestra, had already announced to the *bons vivants* of Traverse City, Mich., that a dance scheduled at the Opera House for Saturday, the fifteenth, had been cancelled. But, he added, anyone feeling disappointment would be "fully recompensed" by the Nighthawks on

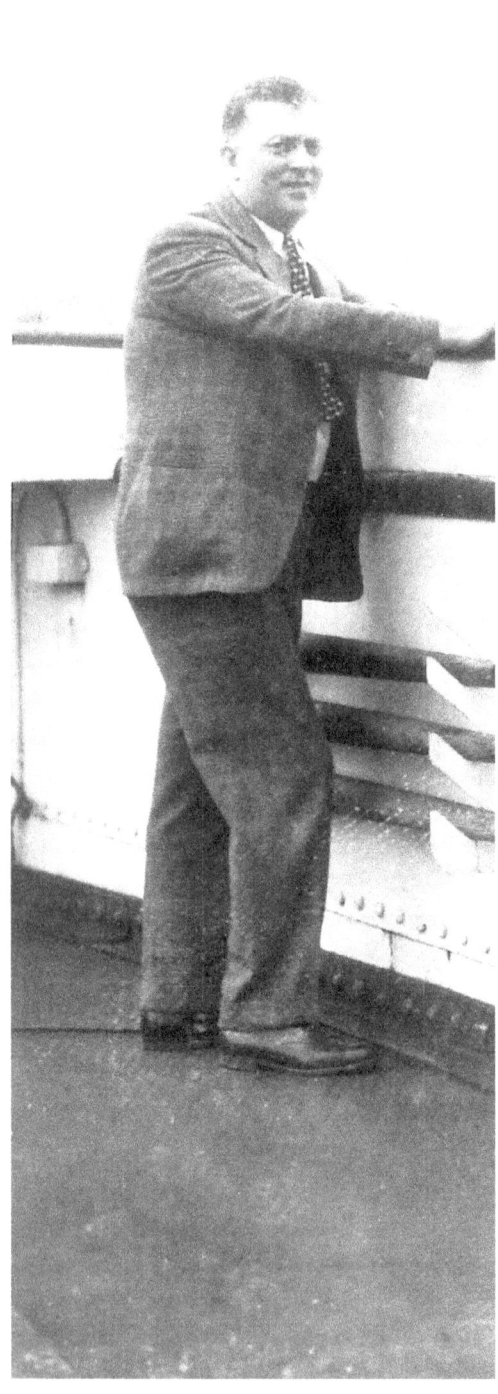

Coonie caught off-guard in a meditative moment, 11 May 1926, aboard *Pere Marquette 21*, Lake Michigan between Manitowoc, Wisconsin, and Ludington, Michigan. (Courtesy Special Collections, Kansas City [Mo.] Public Library.)

the following Tuesday. "Those planning to attend," said the *Record-Eagle*, "have been counting the days, and as there remain only three more, it is expected that tickets will be disposed of in great number within that time." In fact, as a precaution against too little space, the gallery had been enlarged for Coon-Sanders' first invasion of Traverse City. It would be, said the best estimates, the biggest crowd of dancers for the season. However, in the words of a headline in the local paper, "Best Dance Orchestra Ever Heard Here Entertains Few." What happened? "The Night Hawks presented excellent instrument[al] music, good vocal music and plenty of comedy," said the press, but only about two hundred dancers showed up, and few occupied the balcony. But those present responded enthusiastically. In his notes, Joe Sanders says nothing about the occasion, other than that they played there, even though he was often inclined to comment frankly about engagements, whether successful or not.[187]

How they kept that grueling a pace is a marvel, but they did, and their sense of humor as well. At Cadillac someone in the band found a huge straw sailor hat, big enough to fit even the head of a movie mogul. Both Joe and Coonie were photographed wearing it, with plenty of room to spare, while they stood in the middle of the street. In the background there looms the sinister sign of a dentist's office. Said Joe, "Two heads are better than one — and even two couldn't fill this hat."[188]

An unseasonable blast of cold weather on the nineteenth in Cadillac kept the crowd smaller than it might have been. By 11 p.m., the thermometer had dropped to twenty-eight degrees, and even inside the Oak Ridge Park Pavilion, with its shutters in place, the amount of warmth was somewhat less than ideal for playing musical instruments. Nevertheless, said the Cadillac *Evening News*, "the Nighthawks proved the best dance orchestra to be heard in Cadillac in several years." The paper described the repertoire as varied and full of "steppy" music. The dance, along with that in Traverse City the day before, had been promoted by Laurence Fuller, conductor of Fuller's Orchestra.[189]

The engagement at Battle Creek was their second appearance there on this tour — their first had been on April 17. Staying again at the Post Tavern, the Nighthawks played for several hundred dancers, including many from such outlying places as Albion and Marshall. The occasion, billed as a "William Ryan party," was held at the local Masonic Temple. Potted ferns and floor lamps with brilliant shades decorated the stage on which the colors orchid and white predominated.[190]

Joe liked to jot down lyrics, personal observations, individuals' names, odd bits of information, etc., in his 5½ × 3-inch Voss Diary notebook. Most of the lyrics were probably his own, but perhaps sometimes they were words he had seen elsewhere and was trying to remember. During this tour, for example, he put down the following two verses:

> There's a saying True love comes but once
> To everyone beneath the sun, Dear.
> I could not believe that it was so,
> Until the day you came my way, dear.
> Never knew real happiness before,
> Just went along, but I was wrong, Dear.
> Never dreamed that love could mean so much;
> I know it's true, since I met you, Dear.

And perhaps the makings of another:

> Always blue — constantly reaching for you, Dear;
> Lonely, friendless, each passing day seems endless —
> No one who cares what I do.

One finds the following, better-developed lyrics of what he titled "Forbidden":

> I may not put into your hands
> My own, or go your way with you.
> I may not look into your eyes
> So deeply tender and so true.
> I may not even speak your name
> Across the void of years to be.
> But, ah, my dear,
> Not God Himself can change

What you have meant to me.

Or the following song without a title:

> Honest Injun, I can't begin to tell you
> How I love you.
> Honest Injun, ever since I fell,
> You've made me forget
> The others I've met;
> Don't make me guess — say yes,
> And sign on the dot;
> What it takes to make
> Me dizzy (jealous) [sic] you've got.
> Honest Injun, can't begin to tell
> How I love you.[191]

Sometimes the jottings explained photos he had taken, such as those in Atlanta and at Niagara Falls. Some are of more practical matters, for example, his listing of the checks that he had sent back to Madeline, for a total of $6,995.90. One check for $1,000 is called a "bonus," perhaps from MCA, though Joe doesn't explain. The largest amount, $2,440, was sent from Detroit. Some notes were apparently put down as song lists for programs, such as that made for their appearance at (apparently) Lakeview Park, in Lakeville, Ohio, and included the following: "Night Hawk Blues," "Chinky Butterfly," "Just a Little Drink," "Military Blues," "Nighty Night," "Here Comes the Hot Tamale Man,"* and "Everybody Stomp." Encores were "Spring Fever," "I Love My Baby," "Tiger Rag," "Somebody Loves Me," and "Sugar Foot Stomp." (What a program that must have been!) And there is a list of personal items, probably for purchasing, including a deck of cards for bridge, Camel cigarettes, and an "ensemble vanity," the latter probably for Madeline.[192]

The band continued its tour without respite, and on Friday, May 28, they were back for a second time in Huntington, W.Va., where they again put up at the Pritchard, and again they played at the Vanity Fair Ballroom. This time admission was $1.10 per person, fifty-five cents less than the previous month, and they netted $600 in-

---

*Recorded by Coon-Sanders on 9 March 1926, but rejected — and do I wish I could have heard this one!

Niagara Falls, about 25 July 1926. From left: F. Estep, Pope, Downing, Stout, Bud Wilkinson (tour manager), Sanders, Johnny Coon (Coonie's son), Pop Estep and Richolson. (Courtesy Special Collections Kansas City [Mo.] Public Library.)

stead of the previous $900. On May 29 they returned to Richmond, Ind., again playing at the Athletic Park Pavilion, and made a relatively modest $400 — admission was only seventy-five cents and dancing was free. As they had before, the band stayed at the Westcott. It was at Richmond that "Good old Dudley Wilkinson," as Joe described him, took over from Hank Linder as tour manager. Joe later described Wilkinson as the best they ever had.[193]

On Friday, June 4, the Nighthawks arrived in Atlanta from Nashville, via the Louisville and Nashville Railroad. They registered at the Henry Grady Hotel and prepared for the Georgia Tech graduation celebrations. The band was scheduled to play Friday, Saturday, and Monday, which meant that there would be what Joe later called "our first open night in three years of touring." What he meant was that Georgia had a strict system of blue laws that forbade bookings on Sunday, and thus by chance everyone had a welcome break.[194]

Atlanta offered not only the usual fans but also a radio station, WSB, and parent newspaper, the *Atlanta Journal*, that were decidedly in the Nighthawks' corner. Lambdin Kay, head of WSB's broadcasting, had become well acquainted with the Nighthawks, Leo Fitzpatrick, and WDAF in Kansas City when the band was broadcasting from the Hotel Muehlebach. Kay apparently served as host for the visiting band, and in an article in the *Journal* he praised the musicians highly and did it with the humor they naturally elicited. And even though he made a number of misstatements in his article — e.g., "For more than four years there has been no change in personnel" — he nevertheless told their story without mangling the truth too badly. While playing for the Georgia Tech dances in the campus gymnasium, Atlanta's WSB broadcast the numbers, and the Nighthawks did a special show for WSB at noon on Monday. Then, on Monday evening, they did a "transcontinental" broadcast over WSB. Kay added that "brother and sister nighthawks who think the fabulous old 'Nighthawk Blues' is the national anthem, will be happy to hear that Joe Sanders and Carlton [sic] Coon are still generating melodies." He specifically mentioned "Hi-Diddle-Diddle" that "is now sweeping the country," a statement that, for reasons we will see, may have irritated Joe.[195]

Atlanta's Lambdin Kay, heard and admired by many radio listeners from his announcing on WSB, reveled in his opportunities to meet entertainers. Sometimes he was even able to help them along their ways to success and fame. Art Gilham, for instance, who recorded many songs with his own piano accompaniment, owed his sobriquet "the Whispering Pianist" to Kay, who noticed Gilham's manner of almost whispering into the microphone. Others in the recording studio could scarcely hear him, but Gilham's voice was quite clear on the recordings.[196]

Dudley Wilkinson, tour manager after Hank Linder's departure. Taken about April 1926, possibly at Richmond, Indiana. (Courtesy Special Collections, Kansas City [Mo.] Public Library.)

The band spent much of its free Sunday sightseeing. Edwin Hess, manager of the Flint Motor Company's Atlanta branch, was host for the band's tour of Stone Mountain and its unfinished Confederate memorial. Sculptor Gutzon Borglum (1867–1941) had begun the work in 1917 but stopped after a short while because of the war. He resumed work in 1923 but in 1925 was dismissed after a dispute with the memorial association. When the Nighthawks saw the mountain, Augustus Lukeman had taken over the project.[197] (This probably made Coonie curious enough to seek out Borglum a few years later, as we shall see, when the Coon family stopped at Mount Rushmore, where Borglum was then sculpturing the four presidents.) It was probably also on Sunday that Joe managed to get some snapshots. He took some at Emory University and at the home of Asa G. Candler, whose name Joe confused with "Chandler." Other photos included some of the Atlanta skyline, the federal penitentiary, and Georgia Tech, where they had played. After finishing their Monday engagement, they got back on an L & N train and headed for Louisville, Ky. Atlanta had left the band better off by $2,750, not bad at all for three nights' work and a Sunday break.[198] College campuses would always be among the Nighthawks' best supporters.

It was at about this time that an amusing incident occurred, one that Johnny Coon heard from Pop Estep. Somewhere in the Middle West — Johnny wasn't sure where — the Nighthawks were on a train heading for their next commitment. Pop walked through two or three cars to get to the dining car, and whom should he meet there but the orchestra leader Abe Lyman.* Lyman, somewhat

---

*Abe Lyman (1897–1957) was a drummer and bandleader, mainly in the Twenties, but later was a restaurateur in association with his brother William. He also composed such songs as "I Cried for You" and "After I Say I'm Sorry."

Frank M. "Pop" Estep, bass player, about 1927. (Courtesy Claude and Ruth Anderson.)

quite successful, mainly because many of the customers took advantage of the opportunity to hear two outstanding orchestras.[199]

Whether this double billing by MCA was rare is not clear. At least one other case that I've discovered involved MCA's actually billing three groups for the same city, though it did not involve the Nighthawks. On 7 February 1926 Stein's agency presented Jack Crawford's Slaves of Music, the Egyptian Serenaders, and Ross Reynolds' band simultaneously in Columbus, Ohio.[200]

It was also at this time that MCA ran an ad in *Variety* and titled it "Throwing Bouquets." It included nine of that agency's bands, and put the Nighthawks in first place. Others included Ted Weems, Don Bestor, Charlie Straight, and Zez Confrey. Each band was represented with a bit of doggerel, with the Nighthawks making a play on Irving Berlin's popular "Always": "We're in the M.C.A., Not for just a day, Not for just a year, But always." With a reference to his most popular piano composition, "Kitten on the Keys," Confrey said: "Through the country I've been flittin', With my pianistic kitten, and I only want to say, That my tour has been a pleasure, And successful without measure, Thanks to the M.C.A."[201]

MCA had just moved to a new office, one in the new Masonic Temple at 32 West Randolph Street in Chicago. Stein's new quarters occupied half of the eighteenth floor, quite a change from his situation of three years before when he had but one small

disconcerted to learn that his was not the only band on the train, asked gingerly where his competitors were headed, only to discover that it was his destination, also. It turned out that MCA had made the Nighthawks share a town with another MCA orchestra. To make matters even worse, their two dance halls, quite near each other, had for some time been battling for the public's patronage. Nevertheless, both engagements were peaceful and

Loading the band's baggage from railroad truck to van at Raub, Indiana, 23 May 1926, for overland trek to Silver Lake. Joe in foreground; Harold Thiell in right background. (Courtesy Special Collections, Kansas City [Mo.] Public Library.)

office. As a musician, Stein had kept a piano in his old office; but Masonic rules, for some odd reason, forbade musical instruments in their building. Stein had no choice but to sell his piano. Well, without the distraction of his piano he could perhaps concentrate more single-mindedly on planning his new office in New York, which he would open shortly.[202]

The band played in Marion, Ohio, on June 17 and made $595. It was the hometown of the late President Warren G. Harding, whose name adorned the hotel where the band stayed. Harding's reputation by now had suffered from the revelation of several corrupt dealings in his administration, none of which involved the president himself, except to the extent that he was being revealed as childishly trustful of untrustworthy persons. It would not be until the following year that the book *The President's Daughter*, written by a young woman named Nan Britton, would make a plausible charge that she and Harding had carried on an affair that had produced a daughter. But the book's story was still generally unknown, and the other scandals did not keep the Nighthawks from visiting Harding's home and tomb and taking both still and motion pictures.[203]

Starting on Sunday, the twenty-seventh, Coon-Sanders spent a week at the Allen Theater in Cleveland, Ohio, for which they received $2,612.50. In contrast to most other places where they appeared, the press of Cleveland (aside from favorable comments probably furnished by MCA) gave only lukewarm reviews at best. Of three newspapers I have examined, the *Cleveland News* came closest to a favorable report with the terse journalistic murmur, "The band offers popular 'jazz' music that is very pleasing to the audience."[204] On the other hand, the *Cleveland Plain Dealer*'s critic said:

> To the Allen Theater, followers of jazz music will also look this week, for here will be Coon-Sanders "Night Hawks," nationally famous radio orchestra, originally at Kansas City and more recently at Station KYW, Chicago. This organization has

many followers especially among radio listeners. Concerning their music ability we must confess we know nothing. They are, however, an organization of the type of Ev Jones and his Merry Makers at WTAM and offer much the same sort of program, although we have heard many say that Ev Jones puts on a better program."[205]

After another of the paper's critic had heard the Nighthawks, he had this to say:

> The Coon-Sanders "Kansas City Nighthawks" orchestra, of radio fame, is the Allen's current attraction. In comparison with Waring's Pennsylvanians [who had just played in Cleveland], Brooke John's "Oklahoma Collegians," [Irving] Aaronson's "Commanders" and the other A-1 orchestras the Allen has been featuring, the "Nighthawks" is just a fairly good dance orchestra. The organization is at its best in "red hot" jazz and offers some novel orchestral effects and singing in "Hot Tamale" and "Flaming Mamie."[206]

George Davis, critic for the *Cleveland Press*, dismissed the Nighthawks curtly with the statement that they turned out to be "just another band, whose music sounds rather rough after hearing Waring's Pennsylvanians." He added, "The Night Hawks are at their best as entertainers, to judge by their program Sunday at the Allen."[207] One wonders what he understood the word "entertainers" to mean, and why whatever he thought it meant was inferior to whatever he thought Waring was. It isn't likely that Waring would have agreed with the reviewer.

Shaking Cleveland's dust from their sandals, the Nighthawks headed next day to Vermilion, Ohio, where they would play on two evenings, July 4 and 5. Unlike the press's reaction in the larger city, the *Vermilion News*, two weeks before their arrival, heralded the Nighthawks as "by far the greatest attraction ever attempted in this section." In an ad on July 1, the same paper announced that Coon-Sanders would appear at Crystal Gardens, and advised the public, "Trot along to the best dancing party of the year — speedy, soothing syncopation by this wonderful orchestra." A week after the Nighthawks' departure, the *News* still maintained that even with all the good weather, careful driving by thousands of automobiles, the great crowds, and the beautiful fireworks, "Coon-Sanders and their Radio famed Night Hawks was [*sic*] the center attraction at Crystal." The Nighthawks had made $996.30.[208]

By an unusual booking, the band played two programs, two weeks apart, at Huntington, Ind. The first engagement, on July 13, was at the Idle Hour Pavilion, whose proprietor, Claude Cline, had been trying for some time to get the Nighthawks. They were so well received that Cline brought them back to the same dance hall on Sunday, August first. Coon-Sanders made $525.85 for the first appearance, $652.54 for the second.[209]

The band played at Buffalo, N.Y., on Sunday, July 25, and stayed at the Statler. Though it doesn't appear in Joe's date book records for this tour, he later wrote in a scrapbook that they "played in Canada — two concerts at Beach." Crystal Beach, perhaps? Wherever they were, the programs must have been quick ones with everyone hurrying about even more than usual. It was at this time that the band visited Niagara Falls. He duly recorded that the Niagara River dumped 13,000,000 cubic feet of water per minute into the gorge.* He took about eight snapshots from the American side, some showing the boat *Maid of the Mist*, and a few looking directly down into the abyss. It may also be reasonably assumed that the band's members took advantage of Canada's refusal to follow in Prohibition's footsteps. As a matter of fact, Joe took a photo of the gang aboard the *Maid of the Mist* and cap-

---

*To Oscar Wilde, in 1882, it has been different — "a vast unnecessary amount of water going the wrong way and then falling over unnecessary rocks." See Hesketh Pearson, Oscar Wilde: His Life and Wit. New York; London: Harper & Brothers, 1946.

tioned it, "Skipper Pope sights land, while First Mate Thiel smells liquor in the offing." Coonie's son Johnny, dressed in light-colored knickers, dark jacket, and bow tie, was with the band; and there is a good photo of Johnny, taken by Coonie, while to Johnny's side stands Joe trying to set his camera to snap Coonie.[210]

The band's members knew the value of forays into Canada during these years, and probably heard from the natives that exactly a year before, the United States Coast Guard had stepped up its policing of the Great Lakes, and of Lake Ontario in particular. At first there had seemed to be a slight diminution of the supply of distilled and malt liquors in the Rochester area, and the prices of Canadian ale, highly esteemed in the Northeast, jumped from $1.25 to $1.65 a quart retail, sometimes even more. Shortly thereafter, however, the Fates relented and the supply apparently picked up. Both Dawes Ale and Keefe's "three percent," for instance, were flowing again quite agreeably. Despite the Coast Guard's speedboat and its machine gun, the liquor supply remained fairly steady, mainly because of the large stocks already on hand. Draft beer was in plentiful supply at ten to twenty cents.[211] Even down in Washington, where some journalists had feared the government's new drive might portend dry times ahead, an investigation showed the warning more alarmist than real. If anything, there were even more social lubricants available than

Harold Thiell (left) and Pop Estep, about 1926, place unidentified. (Courtesy Special Collections, Kansas City [Mo.] Public Library.)

before, some of them fairly reputable. In the Potomac Flats, "synthetic" gin was selling for three or four dollars a bottle, and Scotch, represented as "thought to be imported,"

Niagara Falls, about 25 July 1926. Joe adjusts his camera while Coonie snaps both Joe and Johnny. Person behind Johnny unidentified. (Courtesy Special Collections, Kansas City [Mo.] Public Library.)

brought eight to ten dollars. Though imported gin and any kind of cognac were apparently hard to come by, there was a reassuring quantity of other such staples.[212] It seemed certain that neither journalism, jazz, nor legislating would suffer any perilous droughts in the foreseeable future.

Bootleggers were remarkably pragmatic about the risks and opportunities in their line of work, and in August of 1924 those in the New York area held a convention in Union Hill, N.J. At the top of their list of items for discussion were how to keep prices high, and how to encourage contributions to defend those caught merchandising their wares.[213]

It is good testimony of the ineffectiveness of the Volstead Act that periodicals such as *Variety* discussed the liquor supply quite openly and matter-of-factly. The preceding fall the entertainment weekly had given a very detailed estimate of the supply of liquors and brewery products. In late September of 1925, *Variety* stated that there was so great a difference in the price and quality of these products that one could actually set it down in writing, and it proceeded to do so. "Scotch at $38 [a case] is a mixture of raw alcohol," said the periodical, "while the good Scotch quoted at $48 is cut with malt. This latter Scotch also ranges up to $65 a case, dependent upon the bootlegger and his customers, although prices here quoted are known as dealers' prices." During the past month good Scotch had dropped from fifty-five dollars a case to forty-eight. Brandy was a different matter: "The $75 a case brandy is 'terrible' while the $110 brandy may be relied upon." As for malt beverages, there was one type of alleged beer that sold for $38 a barrel (120 bottles). Known as "needles" or "needle beer," it was much inferior to pre–Prohibition beer but was about the best available in the East. This "etherized" beer was readily available, and if the drinker didn't have too accurate a memory of beer in

Joe and Pop perhaps practicing for encounters with Prohibition agents. (Courtesy Special Collections, Kansas City [Mo.] Public Library.)

the old days, it was passable. Sometimes the only way a person could be certain which kind of beer he was consuming was to drink the stuff and try to decide whether it gave him that old feeling.[214] Small wonder that the Nighthawks, and many others as well, were always happy to drop by and pay their respects to the more sober-minded Canadians.

After Buffalo, the gang went to Franklin, Johnsonburg, and Carrolltown, all in Pennsylvania, and followed with a quick touchdown in West Virginia, at Keyser. There, on the twenty-ninth, they played at the Knights of Pythias Armory for four hours starting at 9 p.m., with one fifteen-minute intermission. Admission was $2.50 for men and fifty cents for women, but the size of the hall entailed a limit of two hundred dance tickets. Balcony seats cost fifty cents, and the public were warned that none would be reserved. Though Coon-Sanders fans always seemed inclined not to let hot weather interfere with a chance to see this famous orchestra, the management provided plenty of electric fans and advertised that there would be chilled beverages and other refreshments in the basement. According to the local paper, the place was filled to capacity. "No one," it reported, "was disappointed in the music; the duets and solos by Coon and Sanders were encored again and again."

The band made $400 and then headed northwest on a short jump to Connellsville, Pa. The local paper in Keyser hoped the Nighthawks would soon return, but apparently they never did.[215]

On August 4 the Nighthawks returned to Vincennes, Ind., where they had played in early April. Again they put up at the Union Depot Hotel. The dance was at Lake Lawrence; and though spectators paid but a quarter, tickets for dancing couples cost $3.50, a considerably higher charge than usual. Said an ad in the *Vincennes Sun*: "This is a case where the Chickens follow the Hawks. The entire city of Vincennes wants to be at Lake Lawrence ... when Coon-Sanders' famous Nighthawks fill their only engagement in this section. Trot along to the best dancing party of the year. Speedy, soothing, syncopation by this wonderful orchestra."[216]

On August 13, at Madisonville, Ky., the band added another legend to their already bulging collection. According to Quin A. Ryan, in an article for *College Humor* in 1930, the Coon-Sanders aggregation was the only nationally known orchestra to play for a dance in their bare feet. The occasion was what Ryan called a "spiffy hop," but the band had been unable to make train connections. Ryan says they therefore chartered automobiles, and Joe's records do indeed show the use of autos for that leg of the tour. They were going uphill along a river, but the road was so muddy that one of the cars began to slide toward the river and finally became deeply mired. Everyone jumped out to save the vehicle and push it along, and they eventually had to remove shoes and socks. Then, somehow a wave from the river washed away much if not all of the footwear. Afterward, they trudged barefoot into the Oakdale Park dance hall; since they were already quite late, the promoters of the dance insisted on their playing unshod until enough old boots and slippers could be collected. They were doubtless relieved, after the dance, to be able to get back to their rooms at the Grand Central to clean up. They had made $581.75 at the dance, whose admission was one dollar each for both spectators and dancers.[217]

And inexorably on they went. By now even the hardiest and most enthusiastic members of the band must have been feeling some strain. They had played in ninety-four places and still had seventeen more. There had been no vacation and scarcely a break, though the week spent in Milwaukee in late April had afforded at least a slight respite from rushing to and from trains. They made some use of Pullman accommodations, but whether they frequently used sleepers is impossible to say. Obviously, Pullman would have been an uneconomical luxury on short hops. In one of his notations in this 1926 tour book, Joe shows reservations for four lower berths and five uppers.[218] Since the band had by now ten players, and there was at least one tour manager along, this would suggest that there was some doubling up, probably on lower berths. But even in the most expensive and spacious rail accommodations, only the most devoted of rail fans, and the most exhausted of other travelers, can sleep well on a train, so the week spent at each of St. Louis, Cleveland, and Omaha doubtless was very welcome. Certainly, by the time the group took a real vacation, from August 16 to the 31, the relief must have been inexpressible. Preparing for the band's vacation, and almost with a child's eager anticipation, Joe scribbled in his small notebook the rail schedules out of Mt. Carmel, Ill., their last engagement: "Lve. Mt. Carmel at 1:57 a.m., arr. St. Louis 7:26. Lve. St. L. 9:03, Alton or Wabash [Railroads]. Both leave U. Depot same time, arr. K. C. same time."[219] He seemed as nutty over trains as he was over sports.

At least most of the band apparently went back to Kansas City during the August break. Joe did and Coonie almost certainly did. As Joe put it in his scrapbook, "After a perfect, much needed vacation spent in dear old Kansas City, we most reluctantly bade 'adieux' until next year and launched upon the last lap of our long tedious summer." That last lap started on Wednesday, Sep-

The World Theater, Omaha, Nebraska, where the band appeared 3–9 September 1926. (Courtesy Special Collections, Kansas City [Mo.] Public Library.)

tember 1, in Mendota, Ill. The band was paid a good $500, and moved on to Cedar Rapids, Iowa.[220]

From Cedar Rapids the band went into Nebraska and checked into Omaha's Fontenelle Hotel. There, from September 3 through 9 they made $2,750 at the World Theater, playing a thirty-minute stretch on a program that included several other acts. Newspaper notices hailed them as the "Orchestra of Radio Fame" and as offering "syncopated surprises such as you have never heard before."[221] The Omaha *Bee* cited the Nighthawks' importance to radio and remarked about the two clubs they had founded, first the Nighthawk Club and later, in Chicago, the Insomnia Club. According to a column in the *World Herald*, this band, whose salaries were "among the largest in vaudeville," were "literally stopping the show so favorably are their selections being received." Their rendition of "Nighty Night" was especially well received.[222]

At Sioux City, Iowa, on Sunday the twelfth, the band appeared at the Roof Garden, starting at 8:30 p.m. Local station WEAU broadcast the entire dance. The *Sioux City Journal* earlier that day had informed its readers that this popular band would play many of "the latest hits from the east and many of the pieces that helped to win them national popularity as radio entertainers and Victor recording artists." Elsewhere in the same issue the *Journal* quoted, "This is station KYW, Chicago!" and observed, "Radio fans throughout the country have listened patiently into the sma' hours for these call letters, knowing that they would have Coon-Saunders [sic] Original Nighthawks, who are coming to the Roof Garden here tonight on their annual transcontinental tour." It mentioned also their popular Insomnia Club broadcasts over the same Chicago station. Along with the article the paper printed good photographs of Joe and Coonie, individual shots that the two men often used and that showed them looking very distinguished in wing collars and black bow ties. The band stayed at the Martin Hotel and made $400 for the dance, not too bad, especially by comparison with the mere $204.08 they would get two days later in Sibley, Iowa.[223]

At Denison, Iowa, on September 17, an

Joe and Madeline Sanders' Nighthawk Club membership card, signed by Leo Fitzpatrick. (Courtesy Special Collections, Kansas City [Mo.] Public Library.)

engagement for the Uwana dance brought the Nighthawks $370.30. Said the *Denison Bulletin*, "Although the Uwana management is paying them a round sum to appear here, there will be no raise in the price of admission." On the nineteenth they played at Dubuque's Union Park, where they made $400. An evening at Green Bay, Wis., brought another $600 and ended the 1926 trek. What Joe described as the "long tedious summer" was over. Now they could look forward to three days of rest, before taking on their new engagement at the Blackhawk Restaurant in Chicago.[224]

The Nighthawks were certainly making a heavy use of the nation's railroads, and Stein and the MCA were doing a beautiful job of providing rail transportation for them and the other clients. It wasn't always easy, as was demonstrated on one occasion by the Ray Miller band at about the time Coon-Sanders opened at the Blackhawk. For some murky reason, MCA had booked Miller for two engagements on the same day, one in Urichsville, Ohio, the other in Battle Creek, Mich. The only way that Stein could figure the matter, the Pennsylvania train out of Urichsville needed to stop at West Manchester, Ohio, to allow Miller's group to catch a train to Jackson, Mich., and go from there via the Michigan Central to Battle Creek. The Pennsylvania's refusal to stop at Manchester elicited Stein's threat to cease doing business with the road. But before carrying out that threat, MCA had a bold idea. Miller, having been made privy to the plan, went ahead and caught his train in Urichsville. Then, a man from MCA's Chicago office hurried to the Manchester junction, and stationing himself about six blocks from the depot, he vigorously waved a red flag as the train approached. Miller and his men were ready. As the train came to a quick stop, the band dashed for the exits, at the same time asking loudly what the trouble was. They stepped off casually, as though to get out to observe the excitement; but once their feet were on the ground, they dashed madly away. Later, the MCA man was arrested, but after giving the matter consideration, the Pennsylvania officials decided to treat it as a joke. Miller's band made its two appointments, though how they managed to retrieve their instruments and baggage during their hasty exit was never made clear.[225] The Nighthawks probably never had to use such tactics for any of their rail connections.

The Nighthawks were opening at the Blackhawk just as Prohibition agents were starting to turn the screws in earnest on Chicago's night life. It centered on Al Tearney's Town Club, whose attorney, Maclay Hoyne, sought to protect his client from a proposed permanent injunction against the cafe's allowing its patrons to consume their own liquor on the premises. Hoyne's argument was that the establishment's serving of ice and ginger ale was not a violation of existing laws, even if those patrons used it for their own liquor. Cafe owners in Chicago feared the case boded ill for the city's night life.[226]

The Nighthawks had survived that relentless tour schedule of 1926. Karl Kramer writes that this successful round of engagements had not only "built up the bankroll" of MCA but also had "proved conclusively that the one-night bandstand could be built into a very successful business." The agency now knew that the customers were there for good attractions, which gave Jules Stein even more incentive to sign up more top-flight bands.[227] For the Nighthawks it had been a tiring but very remunerative summer tour. In all, they had traveled 18,148 miles and netted $76,756.47. Let's remember that these were "Coolidge dollars."[228]

CHAPTER SIX

The Blackhawk Years

As soon as the band returned to Chicago, Sanders called on Otto Roth at the Blackhawk Restaurant to see, as Joe put it, "our winter home." He didn't like what he saw, even though Roth had, at Jules Stein's suggestion, redecorated the restaurant and made some alterations. The proprietor had remodeled the entire dining area and improved the appearance generally — new color effects, lights, furnishings, and the like. Johnny Coon recalled the restaurant as accommodating about two hundred diners, "perhaps a few more." And Roth even ordered cards printed to advertise the opening. Written in flowing cursive script, they proclaimed: "Announcing the Formal Opening of The Black Hawk, with Supper Dancing, Saturday, September twenty-fifth, Eleven o'clock, P. M., Coon-Sanders Night Hawks."[1] (Despite this writing of the restaurant's and the band's names, each was usually spelled as one word.)

In persuading Roth into this adventure, both Jules Stein and Billy Goodheart had gone to a lot of trouble, and Stein, wishing to provide his best band, had proposed the Nighthawks. Nevertheless, Joe was dubious:

To say that I was deeply disappointed would be putting it mildly. It appeared that, for the third time in Chicago, we were fated to put over a "white elephant." The cafe had never before boasted of a band, having always been a family dining place, famous for good food. Friends (?) unanimously predicted a nice solid "flop" for us. Frankly the prospect was none too encouraging. One must "open" and so we did, without attracting too much attention. Before long it became obvious that we could not possibly make of the Blackhawk a night club, hence we cast about for ideas. We finally arrived at the conclusion that, were we to put over this luscious white elephant, we needs must attract the younger element, the collegiates. Chicago being the hub of the Big 10, we concentrated on these schools. A "college night," an innovation, was inaugurated and, in a surprisingly short time, the cafe swarmed with huge throngs of college kids. With the installation of WBBM's wire, we started the "Nutty Club," a popular radio club on Saturday night.[2]

Joe used the phrase "white elephant" so often, however, that one becomes suspicious of its being a device to accentuate the Nighthawks's subsequent successes. But all of the band's members were dubious about their chances for success at the Blackhawk.

Rex Downing, too, later spoke of the doubts that had plagued him and other members of the band during that September of 1926. They were betting they wouldn't last a week. "That's how much I knew about it," said Rex later.[3] The Nighthawks acquired Charlie Garland as radio announcer and proceeded to duplicate to some extent what they had done in Kansas City. At once the band was deluged with telegrams that requested numbers, or paid compliments, or just passed the time of night. Business picked up and the restaurant, already famous for its good food, now added the fame of an orchestra that was developing a reputation for distinction, even uniqueness. According to Sanders, Roth couldn't believe it was happening, and in one of Joe's catty moments, he observed that Roth, "being a Hebrew, promptly decided that he should have 100 percent profit instead of 90 percent." He added, "Thereupon the Blackhawk's famous food became the world's worst."[4] This was almost certainly an exaggeration, for both the restaurant and the band continued to be popular.

As often happened where Coon-Sanders was concerned, the entertainment weekly *Variety* seemed to take a slightly coy attitude toward the band's new situation. Right after the Nighthawks opened at the Blackhawk, the New York weekly remarked about the restaurant's experiment, spoke of the alterations such as a new floor, and mentioned the cover charges—fifty cents on weeknights and a dollar on Saturdays. The paper predicted a good business from the after-theater crowd, and also from the movie crowds, and then added the ambiguous statement, "Just their speed." The article went on to say that there was no question about the band's musical ability, but that thanks to the bad acoustics in the restaurant, the musicians were obliged to play rather loudly. It added, "After feeling the place out they will undoubtedly soften a great deal." But, admitted *Variety*, the band members looked good and played "with gusto and [were] plenty warm."[5]

The Nighthawks quickly developed quite a liking for their new situation. How many of them followed Sanders' example is unknown, but he had personal stationery made with the Blackhawk letterhead. Joe's carried the statement:

The Blackhawk
Featuring Coon-Sanders Nighthawks
Wabash Avenue at Randolph
Telephones Dearborn 6260 — 6262

Just below, at the left margin, Joe's stationery had "Joe L. Sanders."[6] Clearly, and contrary to what he is quoted above as saying, Sanders was pleased by the way everything had turned out. There is every indication that the other members of the band were as well.

There were times, however, when Roth and Sanders found each other less than engaging. Kramer says that one such occasion followed Roth's purchase of a new grand piano for his new orchestra. Anyone familiar with musical instruments knows that pianos, and grands especially, are very considerable investments. And since Joe was a heavy smoker and coffee drinker, Roth was careful to provide pads on which Joe could place his cigarettes and cups. Nevertheless, within about a month the top of the piano was badly burned and stained. Roth never forgot it.[7]

This first season at the Blackhawk was musically productive for Sanders, who again lived at the Surf Hotel. Among the pieces he wrote at about this time were "Brainstorm," "High Fever," "Nighty Night," "Hallucinations," "Blazin'," "Sluefoot," "The Wail," and "Tennessee Lazy." Also, he made an arrangement of several famous college fight songs that became a regular feature of their programs. According to Joe, it was eventually "copied by every band of note in America." The Nutty Club proved very popular and was an important factor in the band's being declared, in a 1931 survey, the "World's Most Popular Band." It was also during this first season that the band did its first commercial broadcast, a local half-hour for Hudson Motors. This was their first work done on the air for which they were paid.[8]

But it is partly to Coonie that another composition, in late 1925 or early 1926, must be credited. Harvey Rettberg, who got his information from Harold Thiell, says that on one occasion when the band was playing an engagement, the composer Hal Keidel dropped in to listen. A little later he proposed to Joe that the two of them collaborate on a song he had in mind, but Joe declined with the excuse that he was already quite involved in composing and arranging. Keidel then made the same suggestion to Coonie, who accepted the offer. The result of this collaboration was "Hi-Diddle-Diddle," which was published in 1926 by Leo Feist and went on to considerable success with other orchestras—but not with Coon-Sanders. Years later Thiell told Rettberg that Joe resented the number and refused to play it. And Rettberg suspects that Coonie, perhaps in retaliation, rather put his foot down on "Beloved," on which Joe and Gus Kahn had collaborated.[9]

Related to this was a curious situation that *Variety* commented about in the summer of 1928, by which time there had developed a rivalry between the Nighthawks and the Royal Canadians. (This was perhaps at least partly a result of Stein's attitude toward his two top orchestras.) The New York weekly observed that both the Nighthawks and the Royal Canadians not only were popular orchestras in Chicago but also that the leaders of both were composers. Joe, however, would not play any Lombardo numbers.[10] *Variety*, which seemed to be suggesting that such rivalry was more noticeable in Chicago than elsewhere, failed to say whether Lombardo was equally reticent about playing Joe's compositions or, if so, to offer any reasons for it. The Royal Canadians did, however, record at least one of Joe's songs, "Beloved," which they did for Columbia in Chicago on 23 March 1928. In October of 1929, in a two-part recording for Columbia, Lombardo paid Joe the ultimate compliment with the imitative "College Medley Foxtrot," featuring the "Big Ten" institutions.[11]

Variety went on to say, however, that this competitive spirit was found in some of Chicago's other bands as well and that one of them stumbled upon a way around it. A band leader in the city discovered that one of his songs, on which he had used an alias, was readily picked up and played by other bands. He therefore informed his publishers to stop using his real name entirely, and his first tune released under a new pseudonym "hit the best seller class."[12]

It was at about this time that the dance called the black bottom barged upon the popular scene as suddenly and obtrusively as the Charleston had a year or so before, and threatened to eclipse the latter. The two were similar and were danced to about the same beat. But the black bottom was newer, and brassy neophilia could be called the decade's chief charm. The black bottom, however, was a more complicated step and required much more instruction. Described by some as a "syncopated cooch," the music cued the dancer who stepped against the beat and, without moving the feet very high from the floor, executed a body-twisting, semi-circular rotation of the feet. Though there was much hip movement, it was perhaps mostly for effect. One observer said, "The against-rhythm 'stomping' produces a highly effective syncopated and broken-rhythm idea," and suggested that dancers commonly affected a facial expression to denote "ultra revelry in the 'mean' dance."[13]

According to *Variety* the black bottom craze had even spread to Europe and was winning adherents in Germany and France. Paris was allegedly "mad" about it, and patrons were swarming into dance halls in Berlin for it. The British liked it too, but as English speakers and perhaps somewhat staid English speakers at that, they found the name embarrassing and were seeking a more seemly one. Having learned that the dance had been invented by African-Americans in the South, the English were experimenting with such terms as *black base*, and *black bed*.

They learned also that the black bottom was very similar to another dance, from some years back, called the *pas ma la*.[14] Probably none of that was of any help for what the French have been known to call *la délicatesse anglaise*. But whatever the truth of that may have been, in both Europe and America the Charleston, by 1926, seemed to be taking second place to newer dance fads.

The British problem in the Twenties with the black bottom's nomenclature recalls a similar awkwardness in the eighteenth century when, on one occasion in a public establishment, Dr. Samuel Johnson was trying to convey to several acquaintances that a certain woman possessed solidity and strength of character. The term he used was the then-common English expression "bottom." It was well known to everyone in London that the great literary arbiter was very sensitive about any suggestion that he was being ridiculed, so he put his listeners into a bind by gravely saying of the woman that she "had a bottom of good sense." Aware of the suppressed amusement around the table, Johnson angrily asked, "Where's the merriment?" and even compounded the awkwardness with an explanation that "the *woman* was *fundamentally* sensible."[15]

The opening of the Blackhawk's restaurant and band combination coincided with an observation by *Variety* that while cabarets and night clubs seemed to be disappearing in Chicago, their places were being taken by "dine and dance" establishments. The entertainment weekly suspected that the reason was that places without floor entertainment, by thus saving money, could offer their customers better prices. In addition, *Variety* suggested that such establishments as the Blackhawk had better public images than did night clubs—"the respectability angle."[16]

As for that "respectability angle," an event in early December of 1926 perhaps had a role in the disappearance of some of the night clubs. Federal agents had continued nosing about the city for some time, checking those places where customers brought their own liquor and the establishments furnished such items as glasses, ice, and mixers. These clubs always pretended ignorance of how their customers might have been using those items, but three of Chicago's most popular night clubs—Moulin Rouge, Friars' Inn, and Town Club—were declared in violation of the Volstead Act. The federal agents ordered the three places padlocked, but a writ of *supersedeas** delayed the matter while the three continued to pretend an unawareness of what customers were doing.[17] It is remarkable that even while other nearby establishments found themselves, from time to time, in trouble with Prohibition authorities, the Blackhawk seemed to avoid the worst of those problems.

At about this same time, another federal agent, a member of the U.S. House of Representatives, had been doing some snooping, not into the nation's drinking habits but rather into what it read. It was, he concluded, a dark picture. Since burning at the stake, except for lynchings, was not an option in the United States, he went before his congressional peers to demand legislation to stop the publication or production of what he deemed naughty magazines and stage productions. Getting considerable applause in the House chamber, he threatened publishers and producers with hearings before the Interstate Commerce Committee. It was not just the so called "art" magazines that upset him but even such more decorous ones as *Scribner's*. Also on the list were *Life* (not the later Luce magazine but an earlier one that featured John Held, Jr's popular cartoons) and *Judge*. *College Humor*, that occasionally had articles on the Nighthawks, was on the honor roll. Bernarr Macfadden's sensationalistic *New York Evening Graphic* came in for special attention, as did H. L. Mencken's highly respected *American Mercury*, whose green cover was almost a badge

---

**A writ commanding a stay in a legal proceeding.*

of honor on many a college campus.* Plays that the congressman found vexing included Anita Loos' *Gentlemen Prefer Blondes* and Michael Arlen's *The Green Hat*. He excoriated especially the spicier magazines such as *Fig Leaf*, published in Monroe, Wis., that displayed "bad text and sketches." Many were variously denounced as "risqué," "obscene," or just "vulgar." Others had "erotic pictures," "nudity," "sex confessions," or "questionable advertising." Some of the magazines had even *names* that must have convinced the honorable House member that Satan was hard by and causing mischief again. What else could one make, for example, of something called *Low Down*, or another named *Flappers' Experiences*, or even *Jim Jam Jems*, or yet again, *Folly-ology*. Others, with such titles as *I Confess*, *Saucy Stories*, and *Whiz Bang*, were just asking for it. It all must have been so disturbing that the congressman might have recalled as almost benign the venerable *Police Gazette*, of an earlier era's all-male hangouts—except that it was on Wilson's list, too.[18] What an onerous task it must have been to plow through all those *belles lettres*!

Shortly before all this avid congressional interest in literary matters, Coon-Sanders again visited the Victor studios in Chicago for two more recording sessions. On 8 December 1826 they recorded "High Fever," "My Baby Knows How," and "Brainstorm," the latter an instrumental subtitled "An Erratic Blues," which Joe arranged and published in Chicago the following year with Forster Music Publishers. The following December 17 the band recorded only "I Need Lovin'." All four takes were issued.[19]

According to Karl Kramer, the Blackhawk-Nighthawk combination "hit Chicago like a Kansas tornado." It seemed to have everything that guaranteed success. "Formerly," said Kramer, "the Nighthawks had played for high prices and more exclusive spots, but the Blackhawk appealed more to the younger dancers, who thronged the place nightly." The radio, said Kramer, was even more important to the fame of the restaurant, orchestra, and MCA than was immediately recognized. There were far more radios in the nation now than there had been during the Muehlebach years, and for those who afterward remembered the Nighthawks at all, the band would be identified most often with Chicago and the restaurant at Wabash and Randolph. Many other orchestras would follow them at the Blackhawk, but the Nighthawks were the first. This primacy clothed both the Nighthawks and the Blackhawk with an aura of legend. Kramer declared the Blackhawk "the biggest band-building spot in Chicago, or maybe in the entire United States."[20]

More than three decades later Kramer attempted to assess the significance of what MCA and Coon-Sanders had accomplished by opening at the Blackhawk. He believed that success had resulted from a combination of good location, popular orchestra, and fortuitous timing that caught the great dance craze following 1920. On top of all this, radio was only then beginning to reach a significant number of Americans. Starting on station WBBM, the Nighthawks later went to WGN, which though not yet part of any great network, was powerful enough to reach throughout the Midwest and into much of the rest of the nation. It guaranteed the Nighthawks a large, invisible audience and created potential customers for those intensive tours that would engage the band in its few remaining years.[21]

The Nighthawks closed their first season at the Blackhawk on 30 March 1927 and were replaced by Ralph Williams' orchestra for the spring and summer. "Once more," said Joe, "we developed itchy feet for the winding road," but those "itchy feet" were going to risk becoming very tired ones. For

---

Mencken and his American Mercury, *in the spring of 1926, had already been indicted and exonerated in the famous "Hatrack" case, an event that made his magazine even more of a symbol of free speech. See Carl Bode,* Mencken *(Carbondale and Edwardsville: Southern Illinois University Press, 1969), pp. 270–275.*

6. The Blackhawk Years

reasons that will soon be discussed, this year's tour would last even longer than had that of the preceding year. The band would play in about ninety cities and towns, and it appears from Joe's entries in his small notebook that their financial rewards proved at least as gratifying as those of the previous summer. For example, their five-day commitment in Omaha, starting on April 3, brought them $2,750. The next day at Columbia, Mo., they received $500, still a good amount for one night. As we have already seen in the terms of the contract, and as Karl Kramer later recalled, MCA guaranteed the band a certain basic amount, and if the "take" was larger, they got a percentage of that. (Someone — according to Johnny Coon it was often Coonie — stood at the entrance to count attenders, in order not to be obliged to take the local management's word.) This next tour would prove to be the band's most lucrative, because it was also by far the most protracted.[22]

After playing on March 31 at Cedar Rapids, Iowa, they went to Omaha for a week's engagement at the World Theatre, where they had played the preceding September. Again they received $2,750, but on this occasion they were saluted as the "Monarchs of Jazz" and "Rulers of the Land of Jazz," and ads showed Joe and Coonie wearing crowns and regal smiles. This time the ads promised "entirely new" numbers.[23]

Carleton Coon, about 1927. (Courtesy Kansas City [Mo.] Museum.)

"Not one number has been retained from the original act," said the Omaha *Bee*, "which broke all attendance records when the organization first appeared at the World [Theater] eight months ago." Ed Patton's Music Company ran an ad that assured the public that the Nighthawks "use and indorse Conn instruments exclusively." An ad for the World Theater represented the band as saying, "Right here in Omaha we've been accorded the greatest receptions in our career. We're grateful and we'll give you the best

Coonie seems to be trying to sell a car to a skeptical Joe. Omaha, Nebraska, first week in April 1927. (Courtesy Special Collections, Kansas City [Mo.] Public Library.)

that's in us."[24] Here's how the *Evening World Herald* described the show in which the Nighthawks were a part:

> Audiences at the World theater Friday were given a surprise. That was when the vanished console of the pipe organ appeared, gradually ascending, with Arthur Hays dispensing music as the banks of keys slowly came into view. While he played the familiar air, "This Is My Lucky Day," amusing lyrics of a topical character were displayed on the screen. As prepared by Arthur Frudenfeld, these timely verses prove a popular hit.
>
> The chief feature of the new bill is contributed by the Coon-Sanders jazz orchestra, the Nighthawks. There are a half score of instrumentalists, who blend vocal work with their other music. One of the most popular numbers is "Somebody Loves Me." An amazing hit is the jazz wedding, with the trombone and trumpet making queer responses in the marriage ritual.[25]

After Omaha came Columbia, Mo., where on April 8 Coon-Sanders played for a dance at the Sigma Nu Fraternity House, and lodged at the Daniel Boone Tavern. From Columbia they went into St. Louis for a week at the Missouri Theatre.[26]

On Easter Sunday, April 17, Coon-Sanders played at the Danceland Ballroom in Davenport, Iowa. As could sometimes happen even this early in the year, the weather was rather warm for an indoor dance. For the Danceland to have had even one of the primitive, rare cooling systems then in existence would have been unusual. But the Nighthawks had been well received the previous season and had generated such great anticipation for this second visit that neither warm weather nor competition from an excursion on the Mississippi River could prevent the band from succeeding and making $500. The next day at La Salle, Ill., a lot of mud, and many cars mired in it, did not keep the band from having what Joe termed a "terrific opening." Guaranteed $350, the Nighthawks received $554.[27] But the Mississippi River and many of its tributaries were

Stout (left), Downing, and Pope, as Joe identified them, mulling over portentous matters. Probably 1927, place unidentified. (Courtesy Special Collections, Kansas City [Mo.] Public Library.)

already entering one of the worst flood seasons in U.S. history.

It is at this point that there occurred one of the most famous events of the Nighthawk legend, namely, the band's direct encounter with a tornado. They had played for a charity ball on April 18 at Spring Valley, Ill., where the extremely heavy rains had made many vehicles bog down on what Joe termed "terrible" roads.[28] Back on the train, they started south for their commitment that evening at Springfield. When at about 1 p.m. their train was just a few miles northeast of Springfield, it almost collided with a tornado that had already damaged Carrollton and Loami and clipped the edge of Springfield. Inexorably the twister then tore through the little towns and villages of Riverton, Buffalo Hart, Cornland, Mt. Pulaski, and Chestnut. The Nighthawks' train apparently encountered the storm's funnel at Cornland, and though the train was not seriously damaged, it stopped there first, partly because the track was badly littered with debris. Some of those on the train, including the Nighthawks, quickly set up an emergency hospital in the baggage car, and, as Joe later put it, "Dr. Coon undoubtedly saved several lives." They probably took some injured on board the train to carry them on into Springfield, as did some other trains. The Nighthawks' train stayed at Cornland at least an hour. Then, moving his coaches slowly ahead, the engineer had to stop four times within just a mile in order to clear the track, but the train next reached Buffalo Hart, where it again stopped. There, among the victims of whom the band members had knowledge, were an adult named Charlie Crabtree and young Harold Lewis Hardy, a five-year-old resident of the little community. Flying debris had killed Crabtree a few feet from his house near the depot. Little Hardy was perhaps killed instantly, too, but accounts suggest the possibility that he died after being taken to Springfield. Joe mentioned later that he had held a dying infant in his arms for an hour, though he did not say whether this was during the ride into Springfield and whether it was young Hardy. The Nighthawks' train

Snapshot taken by Joe near Cornland and Buffalo Hart, Illinois, 19 April 1927, just after the Nighthawks' train nearly collided with a tornado about 1 p.m. (Courtesy Special Collections, Kansas City [Mo.] Public Library.)

took a large number of the injured into Springfield. On the following day, the Springfield *Illinois State Journal* reported nineteen known fatalities and probably one hundred persons injured. Some communities were nearly leveled and hospitals in Springfield were flooded with the injured.[29]

As one would assume, Joe's camera got another workout, and not more than five minutes after the storm hit Cornland, he was recording the devastation. According to Sanders, his photos were the only ones taken immediately after the storm and some of them were used later by the press. One shot was of the Buffalo Hart railway depot and showed overturned boxcars and the demolished station's bare walls. Another showed an expanse of what had been forest but now looked like a much-contested battlefield. Photos of the railroad's right-of-way showed the trees and other debris that littered the track for quite a distance and slowed the train's progress into Springfield.[30]

After Coonie and Joe were interviewed three years later by a representative of *College Humor*, the reporter gave the following account of the Nighthawks' experiences in the tornado:

Cooney [sic] carried with him on all jumps a medical kit for the purpose of setting finger bones or bandaging bruises incurred by his instrumentalists while playing baseball. [The band's members often enjoyed batting and catching baseballs.] Traveling from Chicago [sic] to Springfield, they were lolling about and playing cards in their Pullman car, and suddenly the early evening sky became black as midnight. The boys rushed for their cameras. Then one wise old head shouted "Tornado!" There was a whistle of wind that grew more violent, and the very train was slowed down to a stop by the force of it! The lights went out — a telegraph pole flopped on the roof — windows were sucked out like balloons. Brr! Crash! Wreckage! But, as they later learned, the tornado proper bounced over the vicinity of the train and took its toll a short distance away. It destroyed the villages of Cornland and Buffalo Heart [sic].

Breathless time passed and there was [sic] scurrying and shouting. Then up to the train there stumbled a torn and bleeding villager, crying for a doctor. Towns razed to the ground! Scores maimed and injured! Emergency aid needed! No surgeons on the train nor in the village!

So the train was backed up, and Cooney and his U. of K[ansas] medical school work came to the rescue, Joe Sanders will tell you today. The dining car became an operating room. Bed sheets and tablecloths became bandages. The orchestra boys worked far into the night, perhaps saving many lives and certainly alleviating much suffering among the townspeople.[31]

That's the way the legend has it, and there certainly is some truth in it, but there is assuredly some myth as well. The biggest problem, as has already been stated, is that Coonie never went to medical school nor even to college. That he carried a bag of medical implements on his travels seems fairly well established, and that he had an interest in medicine is equally well established. It isn't difficult to imagine that he could have been of some medical assistance on this occasion, especially in the absence of physicians, and he may even have saved some lives, perhaps by something as elementary as stanching the flow of blood. And if Coonie could face such injuries without losing control of himself, he already had a considerable advantage over many others. But beyond this—well, one is skeptical, especially in light of the well-known proclivity of both Coonie and Joe for exaggeration and even an occasional mauling of facts.

Even such a relatively minor matter as when the storm struck is a problem. The reporter for *College Humor*, almost certainly getting his information—perhaps imperfectly understood—from Joe and Coonie, said that the storm struck in the early evening.* This is obviously an error considering the good snapshots that Joe's simple box camera was able to get on the scene just minutes after the storm hit. In his own account, Joe said the storm appeared at about 3 p.m., a forgivable error considering the circumstances. But the actual time, as stated by contemporary articles in the Springfield press, was at about 1 p.m.[32]

That the orchestra's men did good work trying to alleviate the suffering and to get the injured onto the train for transport to Springfield is certainly plausible and even probable, but that they worked "far into the night" is next to impossible. In fact, the band was scheduled to appear at Springfield's Knights of Columbus auditorium that night, from nine until 1 a.m.; and if they failed to meet that obligation, I've seen no evidence of it. As a matter of fact, Joe's pocket date book indicates that they stayed at the Abraham Lincoln Hotel and, guaranteed at least $350, actually made $554.55.[33]

Oddly, an item four days earlier in the Springfield paper erroneously reported that the band had just spent three days in Camden, N.J., making several phonograph records, whereas they had actually been touring Nebraska, Iowa, Missouri, and Illinois. (More Coon-Sanders *dis*-information?) Not only had they not just recorded in Camden, there is no indication that they had recorded anything since the previous December. And records indicate that the only time the band recorded in Camden was during the summer of 1925.[34]

Apparently the first notification that the band would play in Springfield on Tuesday, the nineteenth, had appeared in Springfield's *Illinois State Journal* on April 3. In that notice, the paper observed: "To spend five years in only two cities without the public tiring of its music is quite a feat for any orchestra. However, this is the record established by Coon-Sanders' Original Nighthawks." The paper went on to say that "if it were possible to fill one-fourth of the engagements offered, the organization would be very busy for the next twenty-five years."[35] That perhaps was *less* exaggeration.

Torrential downpours continued. "Rain! Rain! Rain!" was Joe's plaintive entry

---

Of course, in earlier years many Americans, especially in more rural areas such as the Midwest and South, understood the word evening *to include the afternoon. I recall hearing it often so used in Mississippi in the 1930s and 1940s.*

Joe and Madeline at Rock Island Monument, Joliet, Illinois, where the band played 25–27 July 1927. (Courtesy Special Collections, Kansas City [Mo.] Public Library.)

in his notebook. The twentieth found the band in Joliet, Ill., where they stayed at the Woodruff Inn and played for a dance. Not only did the Nighthawks have to deal with the bad weather, grumbled Joe, but also with the promoters' error of trying to put over a "society" dance in an industrial town. Nevertheless, what Joe termed a mostly "out of town crowd" netted Coon-Sanders an acceptable $400.[36]

Later, at some Midwestern city, the other band members were filing into a dance for a second evening's program, when they spied Joe and Coonie in work clothes, with hammer and saw as they busily constructed an extension to the small bandstand. Joe nonchalantly explained that the night before he had fallen off the bandstand several times, so they were enlarging it. Thus, here again Joe was rashly courting injury to his hands.[37]

At this time, according to a report in the Aurora, Ill., *Daily Beacon*, every member of the band was insured against any bodily injury that would prevent his playing—for example, Joe Richolson's lips and Joe's fingers. Whether the insurance had been taken out by the several members themselves, or whether Stein's MCA had done it, isn't clear. But the ten members of the band were reported to have been insured for more than a half-million dollars.[38]

On April 22 and 23 the Nighthawks were back in Chicago to play at the Sherman Hotel the first night and at the South Shore Country Club on the next. According to Joe's notes, the appearance at the Sherman competed with a ball at the Hotel Stevens' Crystal Room, where Jack Chapman's Orchestra was playing. Of course it brought out Sanders' competitiveness, and referring to both orchestra and the Benson Agency, Joe commented, "Gave Benson's pet, Jack Chapman, a fine beating. Turned away 5000. Went over tremendously." The next night, at the South Shore, Joe described it as a "Riot!" adding, "Went over great—packed house," though he regretted that all his old friends were absent.[39]

At this time music stores were advertising new recordings that would quickly catch the public's approval and endure as collectors' classics. Ted Lewis, for example, had a hit in "When My Baby Smiles at Me," as did the Cliquot Club Eskimos with their snappy version of "My Sunday Girl" (featuring Tom Stacks' distinctive vocalizing). Art Gilham, who often talked to his fingers and was known as the "Whispering Pianist," offered "Let's Make Up," and Ruth Etting's "Hoosier Sweetheart" was hardly the "torch song" that many of her later recordings would be. Comic dialog reached a milestone with the first recording of Moran and Mack's "Two Black Crows" series.[40] Their vaudeville-type blackface humor was popular, much quoted, and often imitated.

At Fort Wayne, where the band remained for four days, they stayed at the Keenan Hotel and played at the Palace Theater. According to that theater's alliterative ad, "Now for the first time Fort Wayne can see and hear these merry, mad-cap monarchs [sic] of mirth and melody who make musicland stop, look and listen with their jingling, jangling, joyous syncopating." In his pocket engagement book Joe wrote, "Broke all house records. Band a sensation." On the last night, April 27, Coon-Sanders teamed up with several other bands from local theaters, as well as with several local persons, for a benefit evening for victims of what was becoming a flood season of record proportions. There were Wilbur Pickett and His Melody Men, from the Palace Theater; Gaston Bailhe and the Strand Orchestra; and Louis A. Pike and the Music Masters, from the Jefferson Theater. If these bands and Coon-Sanders received any remuneration for the benefit performance, I've

Richolson on a train, about 1927, place unidentified. (Courtesy Special Collections, Kansas City [Mo.] Public Library.)

seen no evidence of it. The dance started at 11 p.m. and lasted until 2 a.m., familiar territory for Nighthawks, though the other bands may have been dragging.[41]

Coon-Sanders spent May's first twenty-eight days in Cincinnati, where at Castle Farm's Dream Cafe they played to a total of 25,000 people and, according to Joe, "broke all attendance records, Whiteman included." The band even had several splendid photos of themselves taken standing on the dance floor's dais. All of them looked chic in their

Joe leans against his Hertz rental car in Cincinnati, Ohio, where the band spent nearly all of May 1927. (Courtesy Special Collections, Kansas City [Mo.] Public Library.)

white summer double-breasted suits with polka dot bow ties. The only visible lack of uniformity was John Thiell's slight slouch and Floyd Estep's unbuttoned coat. The band met some General Motors executives, whom Joe rather Pecksniffishly pronounced a "drunken crew." Also, they started another radio club, the "Pitchfork Club — Hey! Hey!" Madeline joined Joe here and did much sight-seeing with him.[42]

The Cincinnati press regaled the Nighthawks with high praise, a typical specimen of which appeared in the Cincinnati *Enquirer*:

> Before one of the largest Sunday night crowds in the history of Castle Farm the Kansas City Nighthawks more than live up to their reputation as America's greatest entertaining orchestra. Coon and Sanders, popular leaders of the Nighthawks, kept the crowd in an uproar with their comedy, harmony singing and funny antics throughout the evening.
>
> After listening to the Nighthawks, it is not a hard matter to tell why they were recently voted the most popular radio band in the United States by radio fans in a contest conducted by "Radio Age." The orchestra offers 12 special entertaining numbers, each one of a different variety. Probably the best feature of the evening is the piano specialty played by Al [*sic*] Sanders.[43]

The long engagement in Cincinnati gave the band not only a rest but also a good opportunity for sightseeing and photography. Apparently some, if not all, of the band stayed at Kemper Lane Apartments, behind which was a huge swimming pool. One of Joe's snapshots was of Rex and his wife enjoying a swim. Joe apparently rented a car, and he and Madeline took in such sights as the zoo—"Mr. Bear" and "lovely little fauns." And there was the Baldwin Company, which, carrying Madeline's maiden name — though there was no connection — produced Joe's favorite brand of piano. The local baseball park naturally attracted Joe, and at Redland Field he got snapshots of such players as Pie Traynor and Glenn Wright. A shot of their dugout revealed Vic

At Castle Farm, Cincinnati, Ohio, where the band played 1–28 May 1927. Back row: Joe and Coonie; second row (from left): Pop Estep, Pope, Downing, and Stout; front row (from left): J. Thiell, F. Estep, H. Thiell, and Richolson. (Courtesy Special Collections, Kansas City [Mo.] Public Library.)

Aldridge, Lee Meadows, Hal Rhyne, Ray Kremer, and others. And Joe probably found Latonia Racetrack irresistible, for horse racing apparently interested him almost as much as golf did. Also, the track afforded him material for still more snapshots.[44]

That was an exciting month and spring in Cincinnati and the nation. Movies, for example, had just taken a big step, and the city was marveling at Warner Brothers Vitaphone, a system to bring sound to films. Projectors were equipped with an attachment for 13- to 17-inch disc-type records that could provide musical sound accompaniment for an entire reel of moving picture film. There was even modest progress with work to record dialog. The new device had been introduced on 6 August 1926, but it had taken a while for cinemas to acquire the necessary equipment. Cincinnati was seeing it for the first time this mid–May. The Capitol Theater offered it for a week, starting on Sunday the fifteenth. This demonstration film offered a talk by Will H. Hays, president of the Motion Picture Producers and Distributors of America. There was a bit of an opera; guitar, banjo, and ukelele solos by Roy Smeck; a comic monolog by George Jessel; and perhaps to try to lend "class," the "Quartet" from *Rigoletto*, sung by Marion Talley, Benjamino Gigli, Jeanne Gordon, and Giuseppe De Luca.[45] As the moving picture industry made further, tentative advances, new terms, some less than complimentary, were invented to describe the clumsy groping for true sound on film. Today we usually call a sound film a *talkie*, but in these early days of experimentation the word was usually *talker*. That often gave way to the more-critical *squawker*, and such films as *squawking pictures*, in jeering reference to the poor quality of the sound.[46]

The city and the nation were following a number of other interesting developments. There was, for instance, the latest news from aviation that on the thirteenth bad weather was delaying a contest by three aviators to be the first to fly non-stop to Europe. But one of them, Charles A. Lindbergh, set out on Friday, the twentieth, to follow the "great circle route" to Paris. On Saturday he was "officially reported over Ireland," and on the twenty-third the *Times-Star* announced that Lindbergh was being honored in Paris. There was more down-to-earth news that the lower Mississippi River was threatening a large area, especially parts of Louisiana and Mississippi, and that, by the thirteenth, there was the first break in the levee system protecting central and southern Louisiana. And, less violently, women were being advised that the most fashionable hats were small, close-fitting, and untrimmed.[47]

From Cincinnati the Nighthawks went northeastward, stopping first for another crack at Marion, Ohio, where they stayed again at the Harding Inn. (This was the year in which the alleged liaison between Nan Britton and President Warren Harding became public knowledge.) Marion gave the band a third consecutive record attendance and sent them merrily to their next stop at Pittsburgh. That was a six-day engagement and a great success, said Joe, "far better than [that by Jan] Garber, who preceded us." Some of the band played golf at the Oakmont Golf Course and attended a baseball game between the Pirates and the Phillies. They stayed at the Saunders Hotel, where the band broadcast yet another club, "The Joy-Casters — Grab a Little Rainbow."[48]

From June 5 through August 9 the band visited thirty-three towns and cities, most of them for one-nighters. Sandusky, Ohio, the first place after Pittsburgh, had some unseasonably cool weather that, oddly, kept attendance down. "Typical Ohio date," grumbled Joe; "Blah!!!" In Altoona, Pa., where they stayed at the Penn Alto, the attendance was "not so good," but the next stop made up for it. In Mahanoy City, Pa., Joe proudly noted, Coon-Sanders outdrew Vincent Lopez. Joe couldn't resist a comment: "We played opposite 'Miss' Lopez and gave 'her' a damned artistic trimming. We had 1800 and Lopez 350. After the dance Sister Lopez' dainty little mustache was drooping disconsolately."[49] Where Lopez was concerned, Joe tended to have trouble distinguishing gender.*

How the band managed to do it is almost painful to imagine, but between Mahanoy City, Pa., on the ninth, and Springfield, Mass., on the tenth, they stopped off long enough in New York City to do some sightseeing and to indulge in the usual photography. At Springfield they put up at the Bridgeway Hotel and entertained a good audience that had ignored the heavy rain. In his pocket date book Joe scribbled afterward, "Made them like it — damned Yanks!" Staying at the Bournehurst in Buzzards Bay, Mass., the Nighthawks discovered that the summer resort had not yet opened. This provided the band with only a small crowd, but the Nighthawks found the area and the Pine Tree Inn interesting and beautiful. In New Bedford, on the twelfth, the band stayed at the New Bedford Hotel and was what Joe termed a "knockout." The thirteenth found them in Waltham to play at Nutting's-on-the-Charles, though they put up at the Statler of Boston. The Waltham program was a great success, but by then both Coonie and Joe were ill with influenza. It is difficult to know from the records whether they were, at least on occasion, too sick to play; but whatever the situation, all seemed to go well when they appeared in Waltham, as well as in Lowell, Lawrence, Salem, Taunton, and — for the last engagement in New England — back to Salem on the eighteenth. In Lowell the band played at the Commodore's ballroom but stayed at the North American. Their other hotels were the Franklin in Lawrence and the Hawthorne in Salem. Joe

---

*Vincent Joseph Lopez began his dance band career in 1921 at New York's Pennsylvania Hotel and pioneered in early radio when by "remote" pickup over station WJZ he played from that hotel. As every crossword puzzle fan knows, his theme song was "Nola." Lopez died, age 80, on 20 September 1975 in a Miami Beach, Fla., nursing home.

failed to mention where they stayed in Taunton.[50]

This New England tour was clearly a success. In his diary Joe wrote after the appearance at New Bedford, "Band a knockout." "Sensation!" was his description for Waltham. In Lowell he said it was "Another K.O.," and then just "Another" for the last five places. The *Lowell Sun* hailed Coon-Sanders as "the first orchestra to become famous on the air," an accolade more easily supported than the one, by the Galena, Ill., *Daily Gazette* the following August, that they were "the first orchestra to ever broadcast over a radio." As often happened when time permitted, the main program in Lowell was preceded by a short concert in which, unfettered by the demands of steady dance music, the band played several novelties and comedy numbers. For Joe and Coonie, however, their flu must have made the whole thing a real test of the old saw that "the show must go on." Joe's comment regarding his and Coonie's illness was, "Each day it was simply a matter of the first man able to stand buying the other a drink," a comment that might make one wonder whether their "flu" was of the viral or of the spirituous variety. "We broke record after record for Cy Schribman, the promoter," said Joe later. And those in the band who were photographers took advantage of this attractive, historical part of the nation. Said Joe, "We obtained many beautiful and interesting pictures of this vicinity, rich in tradition."[51]

The Nighthawks' appearance in New Bedford, Mass., afforded the opportunity for another "seafaring" trip similar to the one across Lake Michigan in May of 1926. This one was across Buzzard's Bay from Onset to New Bedford. Joe got a shot of Pop Estep, sporty in his straw sailor hat and looking inscrutable as he sat next to the skipper. Later, the band was in Boston where Joe got several shots of the restoration of U.S.S. *Constitution*, "Old Ironsides." He took photos also of such other Boston landmarks as Faneuil Hall, Breed's Hill, and the old Granary Cemetery that contains the graves of such notables as Paul Revere, John Hancock, and Benjamin Franklin's parents. As at least a nominal Christian Scientist, Coonie perhaps was interested to see the Mother Church, and Joe got several good views of it. Salem and its environs are, of course, a must for the tourist and offered the Nighthawks plenty of photographic fodder. Joe got several shots of the House of the Seven Gables, boulders along the beach near Salem, what Joe termed the "Old Puritan and 'Witches' burying grounds," and the Plaza showing the statue of Roger Williams. Gloucester offered views of the Henry Frick estate, cod drying in the sun, and the famous statue of the helmsman and its dedicatory caption, "They that go down to the sea in ships."[52]

Perhaps it was about now when, not too far from where the band was playing, a youngster named Bob Harrington, walking along Main Street in Greenfield, Mass., happened to hear music coming from a phonograph in a music store. (He relates it only as "in the summer of 1927.") The music sounded unfamiliar and exciting, so Harrington went up to one of the clerks and asked what record was playing. The clerk went over to the phonograph, stopped the turntable, and examined the record. "It's the Coon-Sanders Nighthawks Orchestra playing 'Flamin' Mamie,'" he replied. Young Harrington didn't have the seventy-five cents to buy it, so he went down to the Victoria Theatre where his mother played the piano for silent movies and vaudeville shows. He asked her for money and said he would explain his reason later. Since she was involved in furnishing music for *Lilac Time*, she told him to take the money from her handbag. Years later, Harrington mused,

> Maybe if my mother had said 'No,' that she didn't have any change handy, my entire life might well have taken a different course. But I bought the record and proceeded to drive my family over the edge by playing it over and over until I knew every nuance, every inflection. It was the beginning of my life in the world of jazz. By the time I was 15, every Saturday night found me close by the big Majestic radio console

to hear the Coon-Sanders Nighthawks, direct from the Blackhawk Restaurant...! Saturday night without fail, and I never missed a broadcast.[53]

Coon-Sanders spent June 19 getting from New England to Butler, Pa., where they put up at the Penn Butler. On the twentieth they played to somewhat more than three hundred couples with tickets at $3.30 each. As usual, Joe sought comparisons with other bands and was pleased to learn that George Olsen's orchestra had recently attracted only seventeen couples in Johnstown, and Vincent Lopez, Joe's special *bête noire*, had played to only five in the same town.[54]

After Butler, they played at Oberlin and East Liverpool, in Ohio, then returned to New York for an appearance at Batavia, and back into Ohio for one at Canton on the twenty-fourth. Afterward, while the rest of the band were sleeping at Canton's McKinley Hotel, Joe apparently spent the night making arrangements. Next day they dashed to Chicago and recorded "I Ain't Got Nobody" and "Roodles." That evening they played in Coloma, Mich., where they stayed at the Woodward Hotel. They had been in six states in five days![55] And though every member of the band had to have been under a strain, Joe's energy and dedication were prodigious and obviously the chief source of the band's momentum.

And speaking of momentum, I suggest that in traveling from Canton, Ohio, where they appeared on June 24, to Coloma, Michigan, for an engagement on the twenty-fifth, they must have been expending a great amount of it to be able to appear also in Chicago on the twenty-fifth to make their two recordings. But according to Brian Rust's discography, that's what they did, though Joe mentions nothing about it, either in his vest-pocket schedule book or his scrapbook memoirs.[56]

The rest of their appearances preceding their vacation in August, though wearing on them, were fairly routine. They were in Cincinnati from June 27 through July 17, a longer commitment and thus one that allowed them more time to relax. On July 22 they played a few miles outside Iowa City, at a tiny community named Lone Tree, where they received $500 for a dance at the Circle Inn Pavilion. Two days later put them in Aurora, Ill. Here they stayed at the Illinois Hotel and played at the Fox Vaudeville Theatre, where ads promised the public "novelties galore" and "irresistible melodies."[57]

The matter of the band's members having been insured was raised again when the Aurora, Ill., *Daily Beacon* marveled that the Nighthawks represented a "half million dollars worth of musical fingers, lips, voices and other expressions of talent." "That is the sum total of insurance recently issued," said the paper, "to members of the Coon-Sanders Nighthawks acclaimed by all critics as one of the three absolutely greatest dance and entertainment orchestras in the country." Moreover,

> Every man in the famous ensemble commands a salary equal to that of the average captain of industry. But unlike an ordinary business man, a musician's earning capacity depends almost entirely upon the physical parts of the body used to play his instrument. If a pianist lost the index finger of his right hand, if a violinist severed a nerve in his left hand, if a horn player had an accident to his lips—he would be useless in a modern orchestra. The musical intellect would remain but the means of presenting his art to the public would be lost. That is why the members of the Coon-Sanders orchestra have insured individual parts of their hands, etc., for a sum in excess of $500,000, one of the most unique policies ever recorded.[58]

In Joliet, Ill., the band's three-day engagement coincided with the Miss Joliet beauty contest, the winner of which would compete for Miss Illinois. No doubt all the members of the band were delighted at this happy coincidence, and they immediately appointed themselves to an unofficial panel of judges. Their decision was for a young woman named Lois Delander, who did manage to become Miss Joliet, then Miss Illinois, and finally Miss America. From the twenty-eighth to the thirtieth the band played at the Palace in Fort Wayne, Ind., and put up at the Keenan Hotel. The Fort Wayne *Journal-Gazette* ran an ad, no doubt made up by MCA, that described the Nighthawks as producing "a new and greater whirl of haunting melody and song."[59]

Often when the Nighthawks were in Indiana, one of their staunchest fans would get into his car in South Bend and drive to wherever they were playing, sometimes even as far as Chicago. Knute Rockne* became a favorite with the band's members, especially with Coonie. In fact, Johnny Coon said that Rockne regularly listened to Coon-Sanders' radio broadcasts, and that Coonie and Rockne had lunch together about once a month.[60]

In Lafayette, Ind., on August 8, the Nighthawks registered at the Fowler Hotel and played at the Lincoln Lodge. For Joe, however, the highlight of this stage of their road trip came at their next engagement, in Vincennes. It was here that his new "factory" Auburn was delivered to him. As we have already seen, Joe bought his first Auburn in the summer of 1925, apparently from some local dealer. But sometime later Maury Olds introduced Joe to Roy Faulkner, vice president of the Auburn Company, and their friendship led Joe to get a second Auburn. Ever afterward, said Joe, he "was to shout Auburn's praises." But, now he had to get the new car back to Kansas City. In Joe's phrasing, "old faithful Pop Estep" came to his rescue and agreed to drive it home. Said Joe later, "It must have been a tiresome journey at 25 miles per hour." This typically accommodating gesture by Pop allowed Madeline and Joe Sanders to set out at once on their vacation in Canada.[61]

Though I've seen no record of it, my suspicion is that the Auburn Company, through Roy Faulkner, began at some point giving Joe one of the company's automobiles, Auburns first and finally Cords. It may be that when Faulkner finally became president of the company, he decided to include the entire band in this generous gesture. After all, it was good publicity for the company, because from the very first car that Joe owned, the company painted on it the band's and the happy leader's names.

From 10 August 1927 to the end of the month, the Nighthawks were on a very welcome respite. Joe went by train to Chicago and, arriving at 10:40 a.m. on the tenth, he immediately called on Stein at MCA. But he must not have remained long in Chicago, for he had made reservations in Indianapolis for his and Madeline's trip to Banff and Lake Louise, Canada. Following what Joe proclaimed as "the most delightful vacation ever," he and Madeline returned to Kansas City, where several other members of the band probably already were.[62]

It may have been during this break in routine that the band did some moonlighting. It would probably be impossible to know the total number of covert recordings made by the Nighthawks, sometimes by only some of them. Their contract with Victor forbade them to record for any other label, but they did so under aliases on occasion, as did many other bands of that day. According to Brian Rust's discography, in Chicago sometime in August of 1927, Vocalian recorded several sides with Joe Richolson, Rex Downing, Harold Thiell, John Thiel, and Floyd Estep, as well as former Nighthawk Bill Haid and several others, though not including Joe and Coonie. The group was identified as the Castle Farms Serenaders, and the numbers were "Ol' Man River," "'Tain't So, Honey, 'Tain't So," "Silver Moon," "Chili Blues," "Tennessee Lazy," and "High Up on a Hilltop."[63]

This is the time to insert a note about two men who had no direct connection with the band but who would play a very important role in later years for Coon-Sanders— Harvey Rettberg and Clyde Hahn, who in 1959 founded the new Coon-Sanders Nighthawks Club. Harvey, in the academic

---

*Knute Kenneth Rockne (1888–1931), famed football coach at Notre Dame University.

year 1927-1928, was a freshman at Pennsylvania State Forestry School. His parents had sent him a wind-up Victrola, and he eventually bought a dozen records, one of which was a Coon-Sanders number. He was charmed by it and particularly by Rex Downing's trombone playing. Meanwhile, he discovered that his school was being taken over by Pennsylvania State. Harvey and about forty others "didn't take to that at all" and transferred to North Carolina State, in Raleigh. They rented two houses, bought furniture, and moved in. Harvey also had brought his beloved Victrola and records, and he bought a Victor radio, a "nice console job" as he later described it, on top of which was an electric phonograph attachment. Harvey and several of his friends often sat around listening to dance bands and, of course, gravitated to Chicago's WGN. They became regulars, and around midnight they listened expectantly for Joe Sanders' "Howja do—howja do—howja do!" Harvey in particular was hooked and continued to listen to the Nighthawks on the air as long as they existed.[64]

Clyde Hahn's interest in the Nighthawks antedated Harvey's a bit, for Clyde was a little older and first listened to them about 1924. At that time he was playing tenor banjo for a campus band at Elon College, in North Carolina. By 1926 he was playing with the King Cotton Serenaders, the first dance band to broadcast over nearby Greensboro's first radio station, WNRC. From then on he played with "territory" bands and with Del Luper's Orchestra from Florida. He quit playing in 1932, the year that also saw the end of the Nighthawks.[65]

It was at about the time, after the Nighthawks had returned from vacation and gone for their next gig at Mineral Point, Wis., that MCA and Jules Stein were hit with an unexpected and very disagreeable development. When the agency again approached Otto Roth for the Nighthawks' next season at the Blackhawk, Stein was annoyed to learn that the restaurant's owner had made other plans. Roth, believing that his good business in the preceding season had been due mainly to the quality of his food, had decided to hire a different band for the next season. While he acknowledged that Coon-Sanders was a fine orchestra, he was certain that he could do just as well with a less expensive one. After considering the orchestras available, Roth decided upon Ben Pollock's Orchestra.[66]

At that time, Pollock's style was regarded by many in the world of popular music as eccentric and experimental. As George Simon would later write, "Ben Pollock led one of the greatest big bands of its day, one that broke up just before one of the many brilliant musicians he had uncovered, Benny Goodman, started the whole big band craze, and several years before another graduate, Glenn Miller, took over as the Number One Leader." Pollock's roster of players was an impressive one, but only to those reading it at a later date. It included, in addition to Goodman and Miller, such musicians as Jack and Charlie Teagarden, Charlie Spivak, and Jimmy McPartland. As Karl Kramer later wrote, Pollock is remembered today as an experimenter, one who was admired very much by other musicians. But they played what would later be recognized as more advanced jazz, not the type of music that dancers preferred, the "sweet" music by such as Coon-Sanders and Guy Lombardo, music in which melody was greatly respected. "At first," writes Kramer, "the young people came to hear the orchestra and enjoy their favorite dance rendezvous, but with each succeeding week business dwindled and the dancers stayed away in droves." Kramer concluded that Pollock's orchestra, though a good one, was several years ahead of its time. Even Benny Goodman considered the band "too far out" for the Chicago dancers. But while there was a falling off of Roth's business, he nevertheless did enjoy the patronage of a good many of Chicago's musicians who were interested in what Pollock was doing. Kramer says that there was a story that one night Guy Lombardo and his band went to the Blackhawk to hear Pollock, and that some of Lombardo's musicians suggested that they try what Pollock was doing. Guy replied, "If you do, you will starve to death."[67]

As a matter of fact, the late Johnny Coon liked to tell a story about how greatly the jazz purists disliked the music that Guy Lombardo's band and many others were playing. That Guy was doing well financially made his popularity all the more galling, for, as Coon pointed out, players of "hard" jazz rarely made any money at it. Two practitioners of "hard" jazz decided to barge into a prestigious club where the Lombardo band was appearing before a very appreciative audience. The two marched down to the bandstand and, while the players were taking a break, said something to the effect, "That's not jazz you're playing. That stuff stinks! We wouldn't be caught dead playing that junk!" Carmen Lombardo, one of Guy's brothers, shot back with, "Oh? And where are *you* playing?"[68]

Nevertheless, since Roth had committed himself to a different band and a different type of music, there was nothing for the Nighthawks to do but to continue what was already quite a protracted tour, at least until something new developed. From Wisconsin they went back into Illinois for appearances at Galena and Elgin, then into Ohio for gigs at Fremont and Toledo. They swung west again into Indiana to Wawasee, and from there back into Michigan for a gig at Putnam, then eastward into Pennsylvania for one at Connellsville. And so they went here, there, and yonder, like bolts of lightning and sometimes striking the same place twice. On September 17 and 18 they again risked an appearance in Herrin, Ill., hoping to catch the several gangs during an armistice. The next day they dashed south into Dixie for appearances at Memphis, Nashville, and Chattanooga. For some reason, John Thiell did not play for the Nashville engagement on the twentieth, and his place was taken by a man, apparently local, named Bill McDowell.[69]

Chattanooga, where the band appeared on September 21, gave them a pretty good buildup. The local press even managed to spell Coonie's first name correctly. (As Babe Ruth often said, don't worry about what they say about you as long as they spell your name right.) The day before the event, the *Chattanooga News* reported that Polk Smartt, manager of the Memorial Auditorium, where the band would play, predicted that "many another staid Chattanoogan is expected to get a severe case of 'hey! hey!' fever … when the original Kansas City Nighthawks cut loose." He was referring to the Nighthawks' current "Pitchfork Club — Hey! Hey!" Smartt further informed the area that the Nighthawks had over a thousand pieces in their repertoire, and that those planning to attend the program should send in their favorites to allow the band to play the ones with the most nominations.[70]

The dance was a great success and must have delighted not only Smartt and the band but the Music Corporation of America, as well. At least 1,500 attended, with anywhere from 800 to 1,000 persons actually getting onto the dance floor. "The program started promptly at nine o'clock," reported the *Chattanooga Times*, "and lasted until 1 this morning, and when the last strains died away many of the dancers were loath to leave the building."[71] But leave they had to, as did Coon-Sanders later that day for their next engagement in Louisville, Ky. But Coonie, Joe, and some of the others in the band managed to get the usual camera shots, both still and motion pictures. Coonie's movie film of Civil War sites about the city ended up, long after his death, on a family videotape.

Chattanoogans who had happened to catch "hey-hey" fever perhaps found some interest in a revival, somewhat to the west of the city, by the Rev. Mr. Wade House. At his appearance in Columbia he promised to reserve a section of seats for "bootleggers and their families." And in case the section was not filled, he announced a special train to import reformed scofflaws and moonshiners from the general area.[72] But Billy Sunday and Gypsy Smith were strong competition, and I've seen nothing to suggest that they had anything to fear from House's efforts. On the other hand, Sunday's vow to make America so dry that one would have to "prime a man before he can spit"[73] must have begun to seem as bogus as the latest hot item in Benarr Mcfadden's *New York Evening Graphic*.

It was at this time that William S. Paley started a new radio network that would give the National Broadcasting Company some good competition, as well as have a special relationship with the Music Corporation of America. During the planning stage, Paley spoke with Joe and Coonie about what strategy they thought he ought to use in lining up stations, for the three men knew that many stations were hard pressed to fill air time with good programs. Though the National Broadcasting Company was already making some progress, Paley believed that if he could offer good scheduling, he probably could get a fair percentage of the market. He respected Joe's and Coonie's opinions and later apparently thought he had profited from them. On 18 September 1927 Arthur Judson's Columbia Phonograph Broadcasting System (the network soon dropped the word *phonograph*) had come on the air rather shakily. A little later Paley took it over and was successful. In Chicago, the railroad station called to tell Coonie and Joe that there was a dog waiting for them. It was a chow that Paley, as a thank-you gift, had sent from New York.[74]

Following their appearances in Tennessee, the band moved about the Middle West. On September 29 at Portsmouth, Ohio, they checked into the Hurth Hotel and appeared at Baesman Hall. An item in the *Portsmouth Daily Times* stated that the announcement of the imminent arrival of this "real Victor recording orchestra" had caused the auditorium to be "besieged with requests to have the band include several of the musical numbers which have made the orchestra popular." This must have included their latest Victor release, recorded on June 25, of "I Ain't Got Nobody" and "Roodles." Summers & Son—what a delightful name!—placed an ad in the local paper to remind the public that "I Ain't Got Nobody," the Nighthawks' "biggest hit," was available at 906 Gallia Street.[75]

And back across the Ohio River into West Virginia went the restless flock to play at Huntington, Hinton, and Williamson. At Hinton, Joe later wrote, "We played for Joe Hinton. Town so-named." It apparently was on a second quick dash into West Virginia, on October 1, that a flying machine gave new meaning to the word *Nighthawk*. The band had just played in Zanesville, Ohio, and needed to be in Charleston the next evening. A young pilot named Ralph Charles, flying his handsome monoplane *Miss Buckeye*, ferried at least some of the Nighthawks to their commitment. Joe, unintimidated by the open cockpit, clutched his camera and got several photos from the airplane, some of them dramatically showing the craft's guy wires and wings. In 1927 this was real adventure and romance. In one photo there is the wide Ohio and not much else; under it Joe wrote, "My first flight—no 'chutes'—wasn't strapped in—no possible place to land—can't swim!" (Fortunately he didn't have to!) On Joe's flight the pilot swooped low over the stadium where, as a publicity stunt, they dropped flowers on the West Virginia and Washington and Lee football teams. The band managed to make it to the game in time to be the guests of the president of the University of West Virginia. When Joe later put the photos into his album, under three showing their approach to the landing field in Charleston, he wrote in undulating lines, "Approaching Charleston without positive knowledge that there was a landing field and the air was full of pockets that made us go up and down like this!" It was Joe's first flight and seemed to leave him eager for more.[76]

On and on they dashed along the entertainment trail until the sixth of October, when they went again on a week's vacation. Then it was to St. Louis for engagements at the Hotel Chase and Loew's State Theater, from October 15, Joe's birthday, through December 3. The Chase had a fine masonry garage that provided suitably elegant cover

Ralph Charles and biplane *Miss Buckeye* that carried Joe on his first airplane ride, from Zanesville, Ohio, to Charleston, West Virginia, where the band played on 1 October 1927. (Courtesy Special Collections, Kansas City [Mo.] Public Library.)

for the Nighthawks' motor cars. The city, however, was still groggy from a lethal tornado that had hit on September 29. In fact, the tornado had done so much damage that the band had feared they might not be able to get the important engagement. Nevertheless, they did open and were well received. They had some trouble with the general managers who, according to Joe, "warred among themselves so constantly that we received no co-operation." But, said Joe, "We ... went over with a bang ... and were granted a police escort nightly from the theatre to the hotel." In his free time Joe as usual got his old box camera out and took many photographs of the areas where the tornado had hit. He also enjoyed the zoo, facetiously suggesting that, the city's "populace proving to be most obtuse," he spent his "idle hours" with the animals.[77]

There followed two weeks in Kansas City, December 9 through 25, for what Joe described as a "local boy makes good" celebration. The band drove into Kansas City, arriving on Thursday, the eighth; and then, in a manner that smelled strongly of ham, they went down to the Union Station the next day for an *official* arrival. Jack Quinlan, manager of the Pantages Theatre, where the band would appear first, had arranged a lavish welcome.[78]

At noon, with outrageous theatricality that must have appealed strongly to both Coonie and Joe, the band went through the motions of stepping from a Chicago & Alton train, after which they confronted mobs of well-wishers and a huge welcome sign. A committee of fifteen members, headed by Councilman George Goldman, shook hands with all the band members, presented them with a key to the city, and then escorted them into the station's lobby where three bands and a mob of fans hailed them. Billy Andlauer's movie camera captured it all on film. As Joe, Coonie, and the other players sat on their baggage inside the station, Phil Baxter's band regaled them with good brassy jazz, and a photographer got a shot of them

One of Madeline Sanders' snapshots at the official welcome for the band's visit to Kansas City, 9 December 1927. Joe (left) and Coonie wait for the parade to start at Union Station. (Courtesy Special Collections, Kansas City [Mo.] Public Library.)

just as Joe, his spats much in evidence, was turning to Coonie to say that it surely was "hot" back in the old home town. Then the real spectacle took place.

With the collaboration of the local Ford auto dealer, Quinlan had organized a parade for the Nighthawks. At Convention Hall there was a display of new Fords that had not yet been seen on the city's streets, and three of these were put into service to transport the band's members from the Station Plaza in fitting style. The Nighthawks were escorted out to the Station Plaza where the new Fords awaited them. Among the many photographers was Madeline Sanders, who caught Joe (in derby and very ample fur coat) and Coonie (wearing a fedora and a more modest cloth coat) standing in front of the new Fords. As Joe put it, "The darling just trotted her dear little legs off 'getting' daddy's big moment." A photographer for the *Kansas City Post* took a photo of Joe behind the wheel of the first Ford, with Coonie as back-seat driver. Looking back at a grinning Coonie, Joe risked his standing with the Auburn Company by suggesting that it might be nice to buy one of the new Fords. The rest of the band climbed into the other two cars, and then, as Joe later described it, "It was a sort of a free-for-all, in which anyone with a car could join in." In the *Post*'s phrasing, "these ambassadors of Jazzland" were then paraded from the station through the downtown district. They went up Grand Avenue to Fourteenth Street, west to Main, north to Eleventh, east to Grand again, south to Twelfth, and finally east to the Pantages Theater, where they would later perform and where that afternoon could be seen the moving pictures taken of the band's arrival and welcoming parade.[79]

At noon the following day the Nighthawks made a personal appearance at Rudolph Wurlitzer's music store, 1015 Grand Avenue, to play several of their best-known numbers. The music store also advised the public that during the Nighthawks's appearance, the store would play some of their recordings "marvelously reproduced on the new Orthophonic Victrola."[80]

It was all a fine buildup, said Joe, for a subsequent flop. Part of the problem almost

Assembling a parade at Kansas City's Union Station, 9 December 1927, to welcome the Nighthawks back home for a visit. (Courtesy Special Collections, Kansas City [Mo.] Public Library.)

certainly was that Joe and Coonie had another bout with the flu, or *grippe* as it was then often called. But whatever one calls it, the victim, even if able to sing, scarcely feels the inclination. Another reason may have been resentment by some Kansas Citians of what they perceived as the Nighthawks' desertion to Chicago. The *Kansas City Star*, once a loyal and important supporter, seems to have been particularly cool to the band's homecoming, though the *Kansas City Post* fully compensated with its coverage. Joe thought another reason was the proverbial prophet unhonored in his own country, and that the city just expected too much of them. Nevertheless, according to Joe, they did break house records at the Pantages Theatre and were splendid at El Torreon Ballroom. They shared billing with Phil Baxter's orchestra at the latter place.[81]

But adding to their problems were contract and labor difficulties. The local De Molay organization wanted the band for a dance, but the Pantages Theatre would not release them. Joe telephoned or wired Los Angeles, Chicago, and New York to try to settle the matter. Eventually, the Nighthawks solved the problem by playing for De Molay *gratis*. It soured the return of the prodigals, though they were happy to be "home," especially for the Christmas holidays. And though he was pleased to spend Christmas with his father, who had less than two years to live, Sanders later described the return to Kansas City as "a real headache." Said Joe, "I heaved a fervent sigh of relief when it was all over."[82]

While the band were in Kansas City, they recorded eight numbers for Victor, the only ones done for Victor in Kansas City. On the thirteenth they cut "Louder and Funnier,"* "Sluefoot," "Wabash Blues," and "Mine, All Mine." The next day they recorded "The Wail," "Hallucinations," "Stay Out of the South," and "Is She My Girl Friend?"[83] These are highly prized by Coon-Sanders aficionados.

The last lap of the unusually long tour

---

*This song, written by Joe Sanders, took its title from the famous derisive shout used by bored vaudeville audiences when inept comedians were on the stage.

A band serenades the Nighthawks inside Kansas City Union Station, 9 December 1927, during the welcome for the band's visit home. (Courtesy Harvey C. Rettberg.)

of 1927 included five more cities. After Elgin, Ill., on the twenty-sixth, the band crossed the Mississippi into Iowa, and played next day at Ft. Dodge, where they had been very successful in September of 1924. From Ft. Dodge, they moved on to Sioux City on the twenty-eighth, then Cedar Rapids on the twenty-ninth, and Des Moines on the thirtieth. Actually, the final engagement was back in Chicago, where the band played for the New Year's Eve party at the Standard Club. Said Joe, in another of his competitive moods, "Played opposite Roy Bargy and administered a thorough spanking." The return to Chicago had involved train travel through a frigid countryside, and as Joe put it, their "wheezing over-worked locomotive limped into Chicago covered with snow." It was the last train able to go eastbound for the next twenty-four hours. A real blizzard was hitting the Middle West, and all along the railroad the Nighthawks could see hundreds of automobiles buried in snowdrifts. As Joe later described their arrival:

> We arrived barely in time to fill our engagement at the Standard Club.... Upon leaving the club just before dawn, we discovered that the blizzard had raged all night and that the temperature had dropped many degrees below zero. No cabs to be had so, after having gone for 48 hours without sleep, I started to walk home. Finally at the bridge a ten dollar bill turned the trick and I "cabbed" it on out to home sweet home.[84]

The next night found Coon-Sanders back at the old bandstand at the Blackhawk and starting a very heavy schedule by playing for a capacity crowd that hoped to hear some familiar dance music. By this time, even Otto Roth was probably delighted — well, perhaps *resigned* is an apter word — to see the Nighthawks again, even though it was with what, according to Kramer, was "a big increase in price." It proved to be an active time, those first few months of 1928, and a profitable one for all parties, especially for MCA, which now was beginning to overtake the Benson Agency. As Kramer put it, "Starting with the Blackhawk, it was not too long before MCA added one after another [of] a great many of the important night dance spots in Chicago." In addition to all the rest of their activities, the Nighthawks also played for their first commercial broadcast, a half-hour spot for Hudson-Essex automobiles.[85]

I have already mentioned that Joe and Coonie's singing was a special feature of Nighthawk music, and there is an interesting fact about that singing that made them different from many other singers of the time. Most distinctive periods of popular music, at least since the early 1900s, have had their faddish pet phrases, affectations, and musical exclamations in the singing of songs. Who knows how they get started? The decade of the Twenties is well remembered as the time of the nonsense expression *vo-do-de-oh-do* and its variations. The song "Crazy Words" includes the expression in its list of the era's silly verbalisms. But however popular all this was with some singers, Joe and Coonie apparently seldom if ever resorted to them. Nor did they take up later similar balderdash when most had grown weary of *vo-do-de-oh*. By 1928 such new affectations were reported as *barup, baroo, poo, poo* and *skedunk, kadoo, doo, doo*. Some said that all that sort of business began with the expression *skinamarink*, from the time of Harrigan and Hart, about 1872–1884, and early burlesque.[86] Perhaps so, but whatever their origins and forms, like all fads, they quickly become tiresome.

The Nighthawks broadcast over WBBM, and on Saturday nights there was the Nutty Club, with Charley Garland again at the microphone. In addition, the band managed to squeeze in a few extra engagements, all but one of which were outside Chicago. In April they played at Battle Creek and Detroit, in Michigan; Green Bay and Lacrosse, in Wisconsin; and Cedar Rapids, Iowa.[87]

At Battle Creek, on April 12, about three hundred couples danced to Coon-Sanders' melodies at another dance given by William Ryan, and held again at the Masonic Temple. Said the local *Moon-Journal*, "Many novel effects were introduced and each number was enthusiastically applauded." Those "softly shaded lights and pretty floor lamps" that the paper mentioned were probably the same items that had furnished Nighthawk decor two years before. In addition, there were the orchestra's black and gold banners bearing the band's name, as well as a drawing of a microphone and a hawk across the front of the stage. In the audience were also many youngsters from the surrounding areas.[88]

At La Crosse, Wis., where Coon-Sanders played on the eighteenth, the *La Crosse Tribune* announced that the occasion was the grand opening of the New Avalon. The management assured the public that "We believed in the beginning that you and all of us want — and will always cling to — wholesome, CLEAN entertainment and dancing." The ad on the day of the dance printed individual photos of all the band's members, with the admonition "Dance — to the best — with the best — at the best." On April 27 they were back in Chicago for a dance at Merry Gardens.[89]

In May they played at Putnam, Mich., South Bend, Ind., and Gambier, Ohio. Joe was not well and had left his sick bed to play these last three engagements, quite against the orders of his physician, Dr. Schenkelberger. Previously, in fact, on Sunday, May 6, he had collapsed while he and Madeline were dining at the Blackhawk. But Sanders had a strong sense of duty and obligation to his patrons, and if there was anything wrong with his performance, it apparently wasn't evident during these three widely separated engagements.[90] The commitment in South Bend, for instance, was for another Notre Dame Senior Ball, a repeat of the Nighthawks' appearance for the same event in 1925. It must have put the Nighthawks and everyone else through the old wringer, for it lasted five hours, starting at 10 p.m. This farewell to the Class of 1928 was also held in the Palais Royale amid the customary decorations. For the delectation of the 300 couples present, there was in the center of the hall a pergola of white posts and latticework with trailing vines. In the center of this was a revolving vase of apple blossoms. The *Notre Dame Scholastic* makes a tantalizing reference to those decorations, saying not only that they completely masked the dance hall but also that they "nearly caused the sudden demise of several particularly dignified seniors."[91] Nothing in the description of the decorations sounds especially hazardous, but it adds force to the story of the Scandinavian god Balder and his lethal enounter with mistletoe. Balder's problem was caused by the evil Loki; but the source of the problem at Notre Dame was more likely centered in the campus swains and what the *South Bend News-Times* referred to as "Hundreds of girls, representing many cities."[92]

By this time the Nighthawks, among the nation's top orchestras, had worked out especially close relations with such orchestra leaders as Ben Bernie and Fred Waring. According to Johnny Coon, in fact, Waring was probably Coonie's best friend in the music business. Johnny said he was traveling somewhere in the 1950s and was listening to Fred Waring on the car radio. At one point, Waring said, "Today is my mother's birthday. Mom, this next song is for you." Then, before the band played the number, Waring added, "You'd think that my orchestra would be my mother's favorite, but it isn't. Coon-Sanders is still my mother's favorite orchestra." Johnny said that when he heard that, he "almost fell out of the car."[93]

Others who were celebrities, or in some cases would later become celebrities, began to cultivate the Nighthawks' acquaintance. There was Kate Smith, not yet well known but already on stage as what Thomas A. DeLong has termed "on-stage knockabout comic relief and the target of dumb fat girl jokes." Her singing of "God, Bless America" and her top-rated radio shows with Ted Collins were well into the future. And one summer in Chicago, Coonie came home and told his oldest son Johnny that the two of them were scheduled the following day to play golf. Johnny learned that it was with Paul Whiteman, whose band was appearing at the Edgewater Beach. Another lifelong fan was Arthur Godfrey,* a Coast Guard enlistee soon to find his place in radio, and in the 1940s and 1950s, to recall the Nighthawks often. Harold Gray, who created the cartoon *Little Orphan Annie*, was a close friend. Joe Sanders' song "Little Orphan Annie" was without doubt a factor in that association.[94]

Another fan was the future comic strip artist Milton Caniff, who would eventually produce two popular comic strips, *Terry and the Pirates* and *Steve Canyon*. Years later, in his Canyon strip for 12 February 1962, Caniff shows several military officials discussing a problem of radio reception and its role in an attempted rescue operation. In the last frame, a major general muses, "I recall when the biggest problem in radio was trying to bring in Coon-Saunders [sic], and the Kansas City Night Hawks on a crystal set." When that installment of the strip appeared, its author received many calls and letters from fans of the former orchestra, some of whom reminded Caniff that he had misspelled Joe Sanders' last name. "I realized too late," wrote Caniff to Harvey Rettberg, "that

---

*Arthur Godfrey (1903–1983), radio and television star whose theme song was "Seems Like Old Times." "The old redhead" was famous for playing the ukelele and for his relaxed manner and ad-libs that sometimes disturbed studio executives.

Sanders' name had been misspelled and I am mighty sorry about this. It reminds me to double-check everything, no matter how late the hour." Most Coon-Sanders addicts probably thought the misspelling was far outweighed by Caniff's remembering the band at all. In fact, Clyde Hahn immediately sent Caniff a membership card in the new Nighthawks club. But Caniff, just to be sure, sent Harvey Rettberg a sheet on which he had redrawn the offending square, but with the general getting it right the second time.[95]

The Nighthawks maintained good relations with most bands, some of whom credited Coon-Sanders with having influenced their own playing. From time to time leaders showed up in their audiences, as on one occasion when Rudy Vallee, who was playing in Chicago for a week, walked down and stood in front of their bandstand. After exchanging pleasantries, Vallee explained that he had taken the week in Chicago just to give him a chance to hear the Nighthawks. The band had a room above the restaurant where they could relax during breaks, and at the next break several of them took Vallee up there and taught him how to play pool.[96]

Johnny Coon said that his father, after finishing his own work, often enjoyed going out to hear other bands and entertainers in Chicago. He liked, for example, to go to the Grand Terrace Cafe to hear Earl "Fatha" Hines* and his band. With the inevitable cigar in his mouth, Hines could always be expected to do some very engaging piano playing. Fortunately for Coonie, the Blackhawk closed at 1 a.m., while the Hines Orchestra usually played much later. Coonie never sat in with the band, but Hines always made a point of recognizing him and introducing him to the audience. Johnny said that on one occasion when he, his father, and his sister Nancy had dropped in to hear Hines, the band leader Ted Lewis came in and, noticing Coonie and his children, went over and sat with them. While Lewis and Coonie were talking, Hines suddenly proclaimed,

"Ladies and gentlemen, we have Mr. Ted Lewis with us tonight. Maybe we can get him to do a number." Lewis in his act often did a special version of "Me and My Shadow," which consisted of working with a young African-American who followed Lewis's movements precisely to simulate a shadow. Coonie turned to his daughter and said, "Honey, you're going to get to see a five-thousand-dollar act for free."[97] Lewis became famous for his battered top hat, a cane or a clarinet in his hand, and half-talking his way through such songs as "When My Baby Smiles at Me," "The Sweetheart of Sigma Chi," and "Is Everybody Happy Now?" Sometimes he would knock his hat off, let it roll down his arm, and then catch it in his hand. And every so often he called out, "Is EV'rybody happy?" Many critics in the big band era panned his orchestra and his own musicianship, but Lewis remained a popular entertainer for many years and was especially friendly with the Nighthawks.[98]

Another person, already becoming a celebrity from his years with Paul Whiteman, was Bing Crosby, who was often with his brother Everett in the audience at the Blackhawk. Bing was an avid golfer, and sometimes he would sit there talking about their "plumbers" tournament, a term he gave to their golf competitions. They were always held at the same country club where Coonie belonged and where, according to Johnny Coon, one had to be a Mason to belong — most, if not all, the Nighthawks were members of the club. Johnny still had until the time of his death a trophy awarded in 1927 at one of these tournaments.[99]

Meeting other well-known orchestra leaders was always exciting for young Johnny Coon when he visited his father. On one occasion when Johnny was with his father in Chicago, Coonie took his son to a theatrical supply house. After renting a gorilla suit, Coonie took his son to a theater that was featuring Jan Garber's Orchestra. They entered the theater and went to the manager's office

---

*Earl Kenneth "Fatha" Hines (1905–1983), composer, author, conductor, pianist, and cigar smoker.

where Coonie explained that he wanted to change into the costume. The manager knew Coonie and said sure, go ahead, though he probably wondered "Now what?" After Coonie got into the garb, he and his son went down to the main auditorium, at the back of one of the aisles. While Garber's band played on the stage, Coonie and Johnny started down the aisle. The perplexed members of the audience, perhaps wondering whether this was somehow a demonstration of Evolution and just how far man had descended, began to titter and laugh. The tittering and laughter increased in amperage as the "ape" proceeded in the most approved simian manner to the front of the auditorium. Garber later said that he could tell that something was happening but had no idea what it was, especially since the theater was somewhat darkened. But by the time Coonie got to the front row of seats, Garber could see some idiot in a gorilla suit, and while the bandleader's face registered a what-the-hell-is-this expression, Coonie walked on up the side steps and then onto the stage. Meanwhile, the band continued to play, that is, as well as they could through their laughter. Garber was flabbergasted about the disruption but had no idea what to do about it. Coonie walked to the center of the stage, next to Garber, and removed the head of the costume. Garber, recognizing him at once, laughed and turned to the audience: "Ladies and gentlemen, this *gorilla* is Carleton Coon of Coon-Sanders Nighthawks." The audience laughed and clapped appreciatively. It had been a typical — shall we say it? — *monkeyshine* by an ardent practitioner.[100]

It was during this second Coon-Sanders season at the Blackhawk that James C. Petrillo, head of the Chicago Federation of Musicians, decreed that as of Sunday, February 19, there would be no more remote control tie-ups in a ballroom or cafe by any of the city's twenty-seven radio stations, unless a station maintained its own band or orchestra. Only five stations met that criterion — WGN, WENR, WCFL, WBBM, and WMAQ. Each of these stations, by having such a band, added about a thousand dollars a week to its payroll. Some had expected stations owned by newspapers to raise a ruckus about this ruling, but they apparently did not.[101]

From time to time — Johnny Coon said about three times a year — the Blackhawk got a call from Al Capone,* who rather liked the place and always made a reservation for himself and a few others at a table where he could keep his back to the wall. The mobster, a large man, often wore his overcoat merely draped over him with his arms free, and always arrived with about a half-dozen of his men. Once he had settled himself into a chair, Capone usually tore a hundred-dollar bill into halves, one half of which he sent up to the bandstand with a note that said, in effect, "Play several of my favorites and I'll send the other half."[102] (Sometimes this anecdote is rendered as having Joe Sanders reply to Capone's request with a curt statement that the band would play some of the gangster's favorites if there was time. I doubt that Joe would have replied in that way to anyone, and certainly not to Capone — armed with a hundred dollars.)

But Capone was unwittingly helping the Nighthawks in their annual philanthropy. Johnny Coon said that Pop Estep was "treasurer" of the Coon-Sanders tip fund. And though male entertainers rarely got very many tips, the band put their annual accumulations into a savings account at a local bank. Then, at Christmastime they donated the money to help some of the neediest families identified by the *Chicago Tribune*. The band divided the money among ten different families. But once, when Estep had taken the money to the bank for a deposit, the teller asked who the devil was splitting all those hundred-dollar bills. "I'd sure like to give him a piece of my mind!" exclaimed the teller. Pop thought it better for the teller's *peace* of mind not to know. Later, when Pop

---

*Alphonse "Al" Capone (1899–1947) was Chicago's best-known mobster in the '20s.

told Johnny about it, he said, "John, if I'd told that pipsqueak bank teller who was tearing those bills, he'd have gone right through the roof."[103]

Several members of the Nighthawks seem to have had at least a nodding acquaintance with Capone and some of his gang. Johnny told of an occasion when he and his father went into the Henry C. Litton clothing store to buy some items. There, standing before one of the counters, was the man called — except to his face — "Scarface." Coonie said to Johnny, "Son, that fellow in the nice-looking overcoat — that's Al Capone." Johnny carefully examined the man, as well as his nice-looking overcoat, which Capone was typically wearing draped across his shoulders. Young Coon also observed the several men accompanying Capone. The gangster had told them to get whatever shirts and ties they wanted, and as each man selected an item, he placed it on the counter in front of Capone. Coonie didn't introduce Johnny to Capone, but Capone waved to them.[104]

The Nighthawks might well have been leery of too close a contact with Capone, for the mobster was known occasionally to take advantage, sometimes violent advantage, of entertainers. For instance, Jay Robert Nash has described how Capone, who had a very strong liking for nightclubs and theaters, was known occasionally to impose on his favorite stars. There was the notorious case of Joe E. Lewis whom "Machine Gun" Jack McGurn (1904–1936), one of Capone's thugs, almost killed when the entertainer refused to leave one nightclub and go to another in which Capone had an interest. McGurn slashed Lewis's throat, almost fatally. (McGurn, whose name was originally James De Mora, was believed to be one of the killers at the St. Valentine's Day Massacre.) In another outrageous act, Capone had the Ritz Brothers briefly kidnapped and carried to the gangster's residence at the Hawthorne Hotel, in Cicero, Ill. There they had to entertain Scarface Al until dawn.[105]

Many years later, in April 1976, Rex Downing regaled Bob Harrington with stories about the old days when the Nighthawks, in their more relaxed moments, enjoyed socializing with other musicians. Full of questions, Harrington began by asking about Coon-Sanders' relations with such Whiteman musicians as Jack Teagarden (1905–1964) and Bix Beiderbecke (1903–1931). Downing stated that the Nighthawks always maintained close relations with Paul Whiteman's players and often heard them and enjoyed their company when they were in the Chicago area. On one occasion Downing and the other Nighthawks had a jam session with several of the Whiteman men, including Bing Crosby and the Rhythm Boys, Jimmy Dorsey, Bix Beiderbecke, and Jack Teagarden. "I especially remember that meeting," said Downing,

> because after our regular show was over some of us, including Bob Pope, Teagarden, Bing, Jimmy Dorsey and Bix went over to the Palmer House [and] after a while, when the ballroom was empty, we started fooling around, playing some of Bing's tunes. I remember this quite well because I accidentally picked up the wrong trombone. And, my God, the response was unbelievable. I just couldn't believe there was such a horn. Afterwards, I asked Teagarden where he got it — that I would have to get one just like it. He gave me a big grin and said, "It's yours," just like that. And I've kept that horn to this day.[106]

During the spring and early summer of 1928, the Nighthawks made three visits to the Victor studios in Chicago for recording sessions. On May 29 they recorded "Indian Cradle Song," "Ready for the River," and "Oh! You Have No Idea." On June 27 they did "Too Busy!" and "Blazin'." Then, two days later they recorded "Down Where the Sun Goes Down." All of these were issued.[107]

At the conclusion of the Blackhawk season, Coon-Sanders went out to Morton Grove, Ill., where on Dempster Road a dinner club named The Dells advertised the Nighthawks and assured the public that there were "only two places for good food: The Dells and home." Sam Hare, manager, got

Contract for the band to play at George Griffiths' private Christmas party, 1930, at Chicago's Palmer House. The band received $6,000. (Courtesy Kansas City [Mo.] Museum.)

out fliers, some three-by-five inches in size, advertising the band's engagement. Photos of Coonie and Joe showed them wearing black tuxedos, black bow ties, and wing collars, and looking as sober as a bank president or a head of the Anti-Saloon League.[108]

Rex Downing recalled The Dells as "a beautiful supper club." According to Rex, who was apparently remembering times after the Nighthawk years, he learned that The Dells was reputed to have connections with some of Chicago's less-shining lights. The revelation came as a result of the kidnapping of John "Jake the Barber" Factor, while he was leaving one night. "The next day," said Downing, "we were all over the front pages." Florence Stout recalled seeing a machine gun on the roof at The Dells and two "hoods" patrolling the grounds.[109]

But Rex and Florence were apparently confusing their occasions. Factor's alleged kidnapping — it was later proved bogus — had taken place on 1 July 1933, about a year after the end of the Nighthawks. Factor, who began as a barber, eventually rose to become a millionaire stockbroker. At the time, the version given to the press was that Jake and several others were returning from a party at The Dells. Riding with Factor was Al Epstein, a Chicago attorney. Factor's son Jerome, a student at Northwestern University, was riding with a chauffeur in a second car. (Jerome himself had been kidnapped several months before but was released unharmed eight days later.) Suddenly Jake Factor's car was stopped, and several men seized the two passengers. After telling the chauffeur and the son to keep moving and to keep their mouths shut, the kidnappers then rode off with the elder Factor and Epstein. A short time later, the kidnappers stopped and kicked Epstein out. It became an item of considerable interest to the nation and was much reported in the press. But it happened *after* the demise of the Nighthawks.[110]

Russ Stout said that the Lincoln Tavern, where the Nighthawks had played back in 1924, and just a mile up the road from The Dells, was owned by Bugs Moran. Outside the building there were armaments similar to those at The Dells. Oddly, Stout and the other band members seemed not unduly disapproving of such magnificos as Moran and Capone. "I know Al Capone was really bad," commented Stout, "but he treated the musicians and entertainers royally. The boys in the band used to play poker with him during intermissions when he was there."[111]

According to Randy Skretvedt, on August 13 the Nighthawks had another "covert" recording session for Vocalion Records. This time the entire orchestra played, but Harry Maxfield did the vocals. The session was held in Chicago, and the name of the band was given as the Louisiana Rhythm Kings. The four sides were "When You're Smiling," "Dusky Stevedore," "Skinner's Sock," and "Hallucinations."[112]

Six days after the Nighthawks made their recording for Vocalion Records, Joe purchased a bungalow in Kansas City, the address of which was 22 East Seventieth Street Terrace, in the Armour Hills area. He paid $9,000 for it and made the purchase through Paul Hamilton, with the J. C. Nichols Investment Company.[113]

On the last night that the band played at The Dells in the summer of 1928, Henry Sellinger, newly appointed director at the *Chicago Tribune's* station WGN, was in the club and made a very attractive offer to the band for programs on the radio station. Joe regarded the offer as especially timely, because he thought he had discovered some skullduggery between WBBM and at least some of those at MCA. "It so happened," he later wrote, "that we had uncovered a little WBBM–Quodback [*sic*]–B. Stein–Lombardo plot which was to give Coon-Sanders a merry licking during the coming winter's broadcasting." And thus it was that, as Sanders put it, "before going home for vacation, it was a sealed bargain that we were to become the ace attraction of the World's Greatest Newspaper, the Chicago Tribune."[114]

As for the "plot" that Sanders was talking about, there is some disagreement as to how

The Dells, a nightclub in Morton Grove, Illinois, where the band played several summers in the late '20s. Joe's Auburn stands under the canopy. (Courtesy Special Collections, Kansas City [Mo.] Public Library.)

Jules Stein and MCA first became aware of Lombardo. According to Johnny Coon, it was Coonie who first heard Lombardo in Cleveland and notified Jules Stein to look into getting them into MCA.[115] Dennis McDougal, however, in his fascinating recent book about the MCA, seems to suggest that MCA found the orchestra through its own personnel. In 1926, says McDougal, Jules Stein's brother Bill, the agency's talent scout, made a trip to Cleveland, Ohio, where he encountered a new band called the Royal Canadians, led by Guy Lombardo. Eventually, Stein and MCA became persuaded that the Canadians were a hotter item than the Nighthawks. As he had done several years before with the Nighthawks, Jules Stein went to Cleveland to meet Lombardo and began the process that would let Lombardo's orchestra take the favored place that the Nighthawks had occupied.[116]

Though his opinion was debatable at that time, just as it is today, Jules Stein was so taken by the Lombardo group that he could say years later (1975), "Starting in 1929, there was no question that the Guy Lombardo Orchestra was the biggest dance band attraction in the entire country."[117] But back when Lombardo was getting started, Coon-Sanders gave the Royal Canadians the "impetus" to move forward. And when Billy Stein made his effort in 1926 to lure Lombardo to Chicago and MCA, Lombardo was not moved by Stein's impressive list of the bands they represented, until he saw the name Coon-Sanders. And even a short time later, when Lombardo, without an agent, had begun to pick up great momentum, he asked himself why they needed MCA. They had done their own booking and, he believed, "broken Coon-Saunders' [sic] records."[118]

Nevertheless, join he did, and the Lombardo orchestra began to supplant Coon-Sanders in MCA's estimation. This shift of preference by the Music Corporation of America is today something of a mystery, for it is difficult to see that MCA could have regarded Lombardo's group as superior musically to the Nighthawks. As good as the Royal Canadians were — and I have always particularly liked them — I can see no real contest concerning the ability of the musicians and, especially, the quality of the arrangements. As much as I

Advertisement for Coon-Sanders at The Dells, Morton Grove, Illinois. (Courtesy Special Collections, Kansas City [Mo.] Public Library.)

enjoy Lombardo, I think his arrangements were very predictable; whereas, unpredictability was one one of the Nighthawks' chief charms. I'm led to think that at least some of the answer to this riddle lies in the personalities of those involved. Joe Sanders was a man of strong opinions and often explosive reactions, and I can easily imagine that Jules Stein, who even then was well on the way to becoming the hard-bitten tycoon, clashed on occasion with Sanders. The only thing that keeps me from being certain of that is that I find nothing in Joe Sanders' recollections about any disagreements with Stein. It would seem that the two men maintained an excellent relationship.

Karl Kramer gingerly refers to MCA's jilting of Coon-Sanders: "However, by this time [1927] another orchestra had loomed on the horizon to challenge the Coon-Sanders status of being the number one dance orchestra in Chicago. This was the Guy Lombardo Royal Canadians who were playing at the Granada Cafe on the South Side." Kramer goes on to describe a "battle" that took place between the two orchestras on one occasion:

There was a tremendous rivalry between the two orchestras. Each had his supporters and many of us liked both bands, but for entirely different reasons. Capitalizing on this rivalry which was a very hot issue in dance circles, the Associated Fraternities of Northwestern University came to MCA and bought both bands for a Battle of Music to be played in the grand ballroom of the Stevens Hotel. As I remember there were over 5,000 dancers attending this affair at a price of $5 per head and it was probably the greatest Battle of Music ever staged. In the early part of the evening the Coon-Sanders Orchestra with its tremendous spirit almost blasted Lombardo out of the ballroom, but strange to say as the evening progressed Lombardo's hold on the dancers kept getting stronger and when the final number was played it was the general concensus [sic] of both the audience and the professional critics that this famous battle of music ended in a draw — that Coon-Sanders had its own style as did Lombardo, and that they must be considered Co-Champions of the Chicago Dance League.[119]

The Al Quodbach that Joe singled out for censure is described by McDougal as "a tall, loud club owner from Chicago's seedy South Side." Quodbach owned three gambling establishments: the Granada Cafe, The Dells, and Venetian Gardens, the latter, says

McDougal, "a Capone enterprise." Apparently, so far as Sanders was concerned, Jules Stein, as well as such others at MCA as Karl Kramer and Billy Goodheart, were not involved in the effort to advance Lombardo over the Nighthawks.[120] But, as we have seen, Jules Stein was heavily instrumental in it.

If Sanders or any of the other members of the band resented the advancement of the Royal Canadians, there is scarcely any evidence of it in any records I've seen. Aside from some expected professional competition, excellent relations seem to have existed between the two orchestras. Nevertheless, it appears that Lombardo's early posting to New York and his close identification with the Roosevelt Hotel in that city were the result of a very studied strategy by MCA. In addition, that agency's *not* sending Coon-Sanders there until quite late was probably a deliberate tactic to avoid detracting from Lombardo. But if such was the case, Sanders apparently never hinted either that he suspected it, or that he resented it if he ever had suspected it. On the contrary, Sanders always said that the Nighthawks stayed in Chicago because they liked it and had no desire to go to New York. When they did finally get to New York, they could hardly wait to return to Chicago. As a matter of fact, it is entirely possible that it was simply a matter of Stein's and Sanders' wishes happening to coincide.

McDougal, however, says flatly that Coon-Sanders remained in Chicago because Stein wanted them there. "MCA no longer just booked bands," he writes, "it owned them and told them when and where to play." As though to dramatize his assertions, McDougal, in his history of MCA, several times uses the word *stable* to suggest how MCA regarded their clients. And speaking of Stein's having finally persuaded the Nighthawks to use his agency, even Karl Kramer later described the band as "firmly in the MCA stable."[121]

In Kramer's description of the famous musical combat between those two orchestras, as quoted above, he makes a point that seems sound and fair to both of these bands, namely that to contest the qualities of Coon-Sanders and the Royal Canadians would be almost like arguing about two excellent desserts. And as one who, like Kramer, admires both bands, I can say that I too like both, but for different reasons. The Nighthawks, thanks to Joe Sanders, had some of the very best arrangements created at that time, and the band had some of the best and most harmonious (in both senses) musicians available to play those arrangements. On the other hand, Lombardo's orchestra had a very pleasant quality about its music, a relaxed, suave character that was evident even in their *con brio* numbers. In addition, the Royal Canadians, by comparison with the Nighthawks, were much more sedate and, perhaps to some audiences, more seemly. Some doubtless saw the Nighthawks as often verging on the bizarre, both in their playing and in their romping behavior. All that I can say, finally, is what a treat it must have been for those Northwestern University fraternities that night at the Stevens Hotel!

It is ironic that until the recent publication of McDougal's book about MCA, few knew, or remembered, that Coon-Sanders was the band that got the Music Corporation of America started. Karl Kramer's history of MCA had an entire chapter on the Nighthawks, but his book was never published. Even George T. Simon, in his generally excellent *The Big Bands*, makes no reference to the Nighthawks in his discussion of Jules Stein's "Star Spangled Octopus," as he calls the MCA.[122]

Incidentally, as would be expected from someone inclined to dismiss many of the more traditional, or "sweet," bands as "mickey mouse" and "ricky-tick,"* Simon has his criticisms of Lombardo's orchestra —

---

*Though the big bands, the ones that Simon praises, were all the rage during my teen years in the 1940s, I always preferred the smaller groups of an earlier time, or such holdouts as Guy Lombardo and Sammy Kaye, the latter almost revolting to Simon.

The band about 1929, probably Chicago. In foreground: announcer Sen Kaney, Coonie (above) and Joe; back (from left): Richolson, Krebs, H. Thiell, Pope, Stout, J. Thiell, Estep, and Downing. (Courtesy Special Collections, Kansas City [Mo.] Public Library.)

"less than knocked out by his music"; "exaggerated sax vibratos"; "clippety brass phrases with their illegitimate tones"; "the little use made of the five rhythm instruments"; "style of singing that lets you hear all consonants and no vowels." And yet, Simon's book quotes something he had written in February 1942 for *Metronome,* and it just misses being a charming bit of praise of "The Sweetest Music This Side of Heaven":

> It [Lombardo's orchestra] hits superb tempos, and though it doesn't produce a rhythmically inspiring beat, it produces a succession of steady, unobtrusive beats that make it a pleasure to take your girl out on the floor and move around to the best of your ability. If you can dance at all, you can dance to Lombardo's music....*
>
> Lombardo's band is also a wonderful band to talk to. It never plays so loudly that you've got to say 'what?' whenever somebody asks you a question. If you catch it at dinner sessions, you can even hear a mashed potato drop....
>
> And Lombardo plays wonderful tunes .... For Lombardo, with his years and years of experience, knows how to select tunes that create a mood, an intimate, cozy mood.[123]

It was during this third season at the Blackhawk that the Nighthawks moved into a special niche at WGN—the call letters were an abbreviation of World's Greatest Newspaper, the paper's slogan. Said Joe many years later, "The tie-up with WGN proved to be a happy one and we became fast friends with [Henry] Sellinger, Quin Ryan and Pat Barnes." Earl Rickard was their master of ceremonies. At midnight on Saturday

---

*Simon must be correct, for though I was never, even charitably speaking, a dancer, I remember going to a church in town on Sunday evenings during one summer, about 1949, and to the accompaniment of a Lombardo recording, learning to dance the schottische—at least that's what they said it was.

About 1930. Top row (from left): Pope and Richolson; middle row (from left): Krebs, Downing, H. Thiell, and Stout; front row (from left): Sanders, Coon, Estep, and J. Thiell. (Courtesy Special Collections, Kansas City [Mo.] Public Library.)

nights there was a new club called "The Knights and Ladies of the Bath," a title that was Pat Barnes's brainchild. According to Dan Schroeder, this schedule was followed into the early Thirties. Schroeder said also that at the Blackhawk during this period, each member of the band was paid $125 per week, and summer engagements at The Dells brought each band member $150 per week. Between the end of the Dells' engagement and the start of the Blackhawk's main season, the band had a three- or four-week vacation.[124]

In August of 1969 Rex Downing, by that time living in Harrisburg, Ark., recalled that Coonie formed the Shut-In Club over WGN. The station allowed the Nighthawks several hours of airtime to use as they wished, so the compassionate Coonie dreamed up another Coon-Sanders club to try to cheer up listeners who were sick or physically incapacitated. "The control box to open the line to the studio," said Downing, "was under my chair. The program was opened 'very formally' with the announcement 'We now take you to the Black Hawk Restaurant.' I would flip the switch, Joe would call a few numbers and we were off and running." Whoever was announcing on a particular evening—Pierre Andre, Quinn Ryan, Bob Zelston, or someone else—would leave the studio for a cup of coffee, "or to the nearest speakeasy," and the band would hear nothing from them for long stretches. "I took it for granted," said Downing, "that they left an engineer at the studio although I am not pos[i]tive about that." Then the band played several numbers and read telegrams. Between "sets" on the air, the band members shot the breeze during each set's fifteen or twenty minutes—"sometimes longer," said Downing, "if we had to go find Bob Pope in the mens room or Russ [Stout] and Harold [Thiell] in the pool room on the third floor."[125]

6. The Blackhawk Years

It was at about this time, early 1928, that Frank M. "Pop" Estep, bass player, decided to leave the band. It has often been assumed that Pop left the band sometime in 1925, but there is clear evidence that he was with it much longer. In fact, when the Nighthawks played their engagement in Kansas City from the ninth through the twenty-third of December, 1927, at least one newspaper ad clearly shows Pop with the band. Shortly afterward he joined Phil Baxter's orchestra as bass player. And since Baxter was playing in Kansas City at the same time the Nighthawks were there, it is a fair assumption that it was at this time that Estep and Baxter reached an agreement.[126]

It is entirely possible—in light of what Johnny Coon and Joe Sanders in later years said, it seems almost certain—that Pop had begun to feel victimized and unwanted. Ever since joining the band, he had increasingly become the butt of many of the pranks the other band members pulled on stage and off, and in his written recollections Joe patronizingly referred to Estep as the band's "official worrier." Though several of the band's members reacted sharply to tickling, none did so more vigorously than Pop. It made him an especially tempting victim. Estep was a good-natured man, but his temper, when put to severe tests, often exploded. One favorite prank by other band members, for instance, was to throw wads of paper into the inviting bell of his sousaphone. Joe, for example, often quickly learned his piano part of an arrangement and then played from memory. The piano score, propelled by Joe's good left pitching arm, occasionally wound up in Pop's bass horn. On one occasion at the Muehlebach's Plantation Grill, someone put empty bottles inside the horn, whence they tumbled during a broadcast. The irate hotel manager fired the entire band but had to bow to an amused public and rehire them immediately. According to Johnny Coon, once while the band was playing at Chicago's Congress Hotel, several members of the band had assembled in the lobby and placed a whoopee cushion in the chair where Pop would sit, to embarrass him before the other guests. Even on Carleton Coon's home movies one can see that Pop was often the victim of some pretty vigorous tickling, or "goosing," as Johnny Coon phrased it.[127]

John Coon, who as a teenager spent a good bit of time with the band, draws an interesting picture of some of the typical insanities committed by the band's members. The Nighthawks, said Johnny,

> were probably the craziest bunch of actors on a stage you ever saw. They were goosing each other all the time. It was the darndest thing I ever ran into in my life, and ... the people were watching them and knew what they were doing. And, of course, some people when they get goosed, they respond kind of wildly, and Pop Estep, the bass player—he was a big man—Pop weighed about 260 and he was ... part [American] Indian. And if they touched him off, boy! he'd start throwing stuff, and he was big enough to pick you up and throw you.[128]

Johnny Coon mentioned several other times when Pop reacted involuntarily to sudden stimuli. On one occasion the Nighthawks were appearing in Minneapolis, Minn., at the same time that the Women's Christian Temperance Union were having their convention. And both the band and the women's group were staying at the Schroeder Hotel. Coonie and Pop had just entered an elevator to go downstairs when they encountered several women whose badges proclaimed their WCTU membership. Coonie and Pop, both of whom perhaps had some pretty strong opinions about these would-be Carrie Nations, probably had already made several guarded, choice comments about them. From what Johnny said, it would seem probable that Pop was merely intending to make a pleasant remark to his female fellow passengers, something to make the passengers' descent on the elevator more sociable and less awkward. At any rate, just as Pop came out with "Three cheers for the WCTU," Coonie struck and turned Pop's soft-spoken pleasantry into a battle cry. What was worse, Pop reacted so violently to

Coonie's tickling that he almost pulled the blouse off the nearest woman. Both men began sputtering apologies, but the incident probably convinced the women that the WCTU had a perilous and even bloody road ahead of it.[129]

When the Nighthawks were playing at The Dells, they often went across Dempster Road to a saloon called Murphy's. On one occasion, Pop and several other band members were standing at the bar. Pop had a mug in his hand, and when someone suddenly tickled him, he threw the mug into the mirror behind the bar. The several Nighthawks had to pay for the damage.[130]

In an interview in 1961 with Harvey Rettberg, Sanders said that he became dissatisfied with Pop's ability to play bass, and suggested that Estep's playing was of a rather ordinary, oompah style, quite inferior to that of Elmer Krebs' who replaced him. "He [Pop] just came and quit one day, and I was very happy to see him go," said Sanders. "I loved him — wonderful person — but he just didn't fit. He wasn't a good musician. We were on the way up then, and he *was* holding us back." Krebs, so Joe thought, played the tuba so deftly that it almost at times sounded like a cello. It allowed Joe to make arrangements in which the bass soloed, though Joe said that Krebs could not improvise and thus had to have his solo parts written out.[131]

Whatever truth there may have been in Joe's estimation of Pop Estep's musical ability, it seems rather ungrateful to have described him as he did, especially since Pop had been with them those five or six years when the band enjoyed what was perhaps its greatest popularity and made some of its best recordings. Also, as Joe himself said occasionally, Pop was an unusually obliging fellow. But his relations with the rest of the Nighthawks were beginning to cause him health problems, and his physician suggested he quit the band.[132] What Floyd Estep thought of his father's situation seems not to have been recorded.

This season of 1928-1929 was a busy and profitable one for the band. Joe was, as usual, very creative and composed and arranged a number of pieces, including "Beloved" (whose lyrics were Gus Kahn's), "What a Girl! What a Night!," and "Got a Great Big Date with a Little Bitty* Girl." In addition, at the *Chicago Tribune*'s suggestion, he wrote some songs based on comic strip characters. There were at least two, "Little Orphan Annie" and "Harold Teen," the second of which was used by WGN for a radio program based on that old comic strip drawn by Carl Ed.[133]

Though Joe could not be blamed for it, the radio program *Harold Teen* got some harsh criticism. *Variety*'s reviewer listened to several episodes of it and pronounced it a "peculiarly puerile and annoying species of punning, self-conscious humor." He marveled that the cast were able to "maintain their unnatural characterizations and to read lines that would outrage any imaginative actor." The show's tempo, he said, was "as slow as molasses," and how could anyone connect the insipid scripts with the sponsor's Colgate "Seventeen" perfume. To emphasize the intellectual level of the program, the reviewer closed with the lines about the show's hero, Harold Teen: "He is romance personified; his credentials are bona fide."[134]

It seems possible that Joe's title "Got a Great Big Date with a Little Bitty Girl" was suggested by another song published the previous year, "Gotta Big Date with a Little Girl." It was written by Harry, Charles, and Henry Tobias, and published by Leo Feist.[135] I haven't heard the Tobias number, and though Joe's song is hardly well known today, my suspicion is that his is more interesting.

According to Brian Rust's discography, starting on 20 November 1928 the band, over

---

*For some reason, the word bitty in this title has usually been rendered as bitta, as on the Victor recording, but anyone familiar with the very common diminutive knows the final vowel is a y. I haven't seen Joe's manuscript of the lyrics, but I doubt that he would have spelled it bitta.

Chicago, probably at the Blackhawk, about 1929. From left: Krebs, Joe, Coonie, Stout, Richolson, H. Thiell, Pope, F. Estep, Downing, J. Thiell. (Courtesy Harvey C. Rettberg.)

a period of thirteen weeks, recorded a dozen numbers. They did "My Suppressed Desire" and "What a Girl! What a Night!" on the first date. Subsequently, they recorded as follows: November 27, "Smilin' Skies," "Here Comes My Ball and Chain," and "Who Wouldn't Be Jealous of You?"; December 3, "That's How I Feel about You" and "Little Orphan Annie"; December 12, "Rhythm King" and "Bless You, Sister"; February 12, "Mississippi, Here I Am" and "Tennessee Lazy"; and February 23, "Kansas City Kitty." Only one, "That's How I Feel about You," was rejected for issuance.[136]

The band continued busily both inside Chicago and on tour. On February 8 they played at the University of Michigan, Ann Arbor; March 15 at the Edgewater Beach, Chicago; April 2 for the De Molays in Peoria, Ill.; April 25 in Gary, Ind.; and April 26 at the University of Indiana, Bloomington. In Chicago the Nighthawks started a second sponsored program over WGN, this one for the Florsheim Shoe Company. For this, says Schroeder, each man received an additional $50 per broadcast, "much to their surprise." This great activity measurably improved each member's finances, and it also helped Joe endure the death of his father in February. Then, at the end of the Blackhawk engagement, the band took a vacation. Joe left immediately after the last program and drove directly to Kansas City, and he did it in record time. As he later put it, "In my incomparable Cord, I left the Blackhawk door at 4:00 A.M., drove 586 miles and parked in my driveway at 2:00 P.M.., ten hours flat." And this was over 1929 roads! No wonder the band was known for its vigorous mobility![137]

Joe, Coonie, and Madeline mug for the camera, about 1929. (Courtesy John A. Coon.)

Joe, Madeline, and several friends went to Joe's favorite vacation spot, Lake Taneycomo in Missouri's Ozarks, where they stayed at Wheatley Cottage. According to Joe's personal journal, it was at this time that he cancelled the band's contract with Victor.[138] (Since the Nighthawks continued to make recordings for Victor, there must have been more contracts, but I have not seen copies.)

In the summer of 1929 the Nighthawks again betook themselves to Morton Grove, Ill., and a second season at The Dells. It was an engagement that proved as successful as the first had been, though, thanks to Chicago business methods of that day, somewhat more rollicking than the previous year's had been. It is interesting that owner Sam Hare had for a while attempted to operate a gambling room in The Dells, but police interference had caused him instead to hire an orchestra and to discover that good music was at least as remunerative as a casino.[139] Whether he actually had abandoned gambling is a moot question. Thus it was, however, that Coon-Sanders happened to have been hired for 1928 and were now returning for the second of what would be three summers at the nightclub.

For a period of several years Hare was engaged in a struggle with rival, envious parties among the Chicago underworld. Even as early as May of 1929, the nightclub was damaged by an explosion of suspicious origin, and threatening events would continue into the early 1930s. During this second Nighthawk season at The Dells, at mid-afternoon of August first, Hare's assistant Lewis Spielman saw smoke coming from a corner of the building and called the nearby fire departments. The Nighthawks were preparing to play that evening, and since they had played late into the previous night, most of the men probably had not been long out of bed. At least one, Joe Richolson, was having breakfast. The fire alarm caught him by surprise, and before he could leave the building, he was overcome by smoke. Firemen rescued him and he was apparently none the worse for the experience. The building, however, was heavily damaged.[140]

In a subsequent comment on The Dells' adventures, Joe Sanders refers to this summer of 1929 — he mistakenly recalled it as 1930. "Due to intense rivalry among roadhouse owners," wrote Joe later, "our summer of 1930 was full of strange happenings." He goes on to mention a bombing, several early morning fires, and the above-mentioned mid-afternoon fire which destroyed one entire side of the building. Such events in and around Chicago during the Twenties were hardly rare; successful businesses, and nightclubs especially, were always under the greedy watch of mobsters. But the likable Sam Hare wasn't easily cowed. The place opened as usual the evening following the fire, with even the members of the band, apparently including Joe Richolson, helping to get the floor ready. As Sanders put it, "We all pitched in, got on our knees and mopped up the water-soaked floor with tablecoths." While the band played to a capacity crowd on the one undamaged side of the house, stars twinkled beyond the wet draperies and through gaping holes.[141]

Of course, Coon-Sanders was only one of many bands that Sam Hare engaged for The Dells, and it was this practice that, in the spring of 1931, led the Rev. Elmer L. Williams, a Methodist clergyman, to start a crusade against Hare and his club. Williams, no longer holding down a pulpit, was by 1931 a full-time reformer, and he suspected that Hare had not discontinued his casino. Part of Williams' efforts went into publishing a paper titled *Lightning*. How, Williams wondered in his June issue, could a mere dining establishment pay $100,000 in a sixteen-week period for name bands? The Dells, alleged the cleric, was not a "chicken and steak dinner dispensary" but rather a gambling den. For the spring and summer Hare had engaged such bands as those led by George Olsen, Ben Bernie, Fred Waring, and Ted Lewis. They would, said the clergyman, be paid about $6,500, and he contemptuously referred to this as simply payment for the bait that would lure gamblers "out into the verdant suburbs of a summer evening." The clergyman had thus far been unable to arouse much indignation in the community against Sam Hare and his road house. The Dells was too popular with Chicagoans, and musicians regarded the nightclub as a very desirable employer. Besides, everyone spoke well of Sam Hare.[142]

While playing at The Dells in the summer of 1929, the band held two recording sessions for Victor in Chicago. On July 24 they recorded "And Especially You!," "True Blue Lou," and "Because You Said 'I Love You,'" the last of which was rejected for issuance. Two days later they recorded "The Flippety Flop" and "Got a Great Big Date with a Little Bitty Girl."[143]

The fourth season at the Blackhawk began in the fall of 1929. The club scene in Chicago was clouded a bit when federal Prohibition authorities closed such popular places as the Frolics, Chez Pierre, and the Rainbo. The Blackhawk itself had what Joe termed "a most attractive injunction sign" in its window, but business continued. The teletype machine was again on the bandstand, and shows began with Joe's famous greeting, "Howja do, howja do, howja do — you great big ol' raddio pooblic!" Then followed a program filled with amusing patter, comic dialog, and incomparable music. Even the churlish conduct of Uncle Sam's agents, as well as the "egg" laid by Wall Street in October, could not keep the season from being successful.[144] (Surely nearly everyone is familiar with *Variety's* famous headline in its issue for 30 October 1929, "Wall Street Lays an Egg.")

November of 1929 brought two more

Victor recording sessions, one on the eighteenth that produced "Harlem Madness" and "Moanin' for You," and the second on the twenty-ninth, when the band recorded "Music in the Moonlight," which was rejected, "Ain't You, Baby?," and "We Love Us." The next month, December, offered two more sessions. On the sixth the Nighthawks recorded "Sweepin' the Clouds Away," "Alone in the Rain," and "After You've Gone." On the twelfth they recorded "The Darktown Strutters' Ball," "Take Me" which was rejected, and "Music in the Moonlight, the last which was a re-recording."[145] Just how they managed, in December of 1929, to record "Sweepin' the Cluds Away" isn't clear, for the song bears a copyright date of 1930.[146]

In addition to a shaky national economy and pesky federal agents, there was another cloud on the Nighthawk horizon, one that for Coonie was an unpleasant and, in light of future events, almost ominous episode. In the early part of 1930 Coonie dropped out of the public scene for several weeks, and Joe had to carry on alone during that time as a vocalist. (I've seen nothing to indicate whom Joe found to play drums, but it could have been young William Paley, relative of the William Paley of the new Columbia Broadcasting System.) The official, and probably correct, explanation for Coonie's absence was that he had undergone an operation, which according to the *Kansas City Star*, as well as his son Johnny, was an appendectomy.[147] At that time appendicitis could be a very serious matter, as Rudolph Valentino had proved four years before. But in Coonie's case there was more to the story than an inflamed appendix.

Coonie and his family now found themselves facing rumors that his absence for the past several weeks had been caused by his having been kidnapped and held for ransom by Chicago thugs. His previous brushes with mobsters probably lent plausibility to the story.[148]

Shortly after the band moved to Chicago in 1924, Coonie bought himself a five-carat diamond ring, set in a Masonic pattern. It was a very extraordinary item. If the lighting was favorable when he played drums, his ring sparkled in a spectacular way, but it apparently sparkled too spectacularly for the wrong person while the band was playing at The Dells. Coonie was driving home one night, and another car came up alongside his own and forced him off the road. The other man walked over to Coonie, who, suspecting robbery, had put the ring into his mouth before the other driver got in beside him. With the ring in his mouth, Coonie betrayed himself when he tried to speak. "Spit it out!" demanded the stranger. Coonie did so, and away went the robber with not only the expensive ring but also about $450 in cash. When the other band members heard about it next day, one of them sent word to Al Capone. Theoretically, Scarface Al's goodwill was an asset in such a situation in Chicago, but for Coonie on this occasion, *theoretically* was the key word. Though Capone was reported to have put out word that he wasn't happy about the theft and that the culprit had better return the goods "yesterday," the only solace that Coonie got came in the form of an anonymous phone call offering to sell the ring back to him. Coonie refused.[149]

Obviously, either Capone's influence was waning or else the outlaw couldn't be unduly bothered by what happened to non-mobsters. Another possibility is that since both the Blackhawk and The Dells were on the north side of Chicago, which was more in George "Bugs" Moran's* bailiwick, Capone really didn't have much power in the matter. Besides, at this time Capone had more serious things to worry about, for he was engaged in a mortal struggle with Moran for control of bootlegging in the entire city. For several of Moran's henchmen (but not Moran), it would culminate fatally in what

---

*Moran (1893–1957) by 1927 was the chief survivor of the Dion O'Banion gang, and Capone's main competition for the area's criminal pickings.

is called the St. Valentine's Day Massacre in February 1929. Capone's turn came a little later in a losing struggle with the United States Internal Revenue Service and tertiary syphilis.

The foregoing account of Coonie's loss of his ring is the version I heard from Johnny Coon, but Rex Downing told a different version. Coonie's loss did get around among his fellow musicians, and Rex must have heard Coonie talk about it. "Coonie used to wear a big diamond ring on his pinky finger," said Rex.

> It was [Downing continued] something a lot of show folk used to do. It was quite an attractive ring and it's quite a story. One night when Coonie was driving home ... some car forced him off the highway. A couple of gangsters came over to him and told him to get out of the car. One of them threw Coonie face down onto the road. Coonie figured they wanted the cash he was carrying on him. Still facing the ground, Coonie said, "Listen, fellers, I don't know who you are, I can't see you ..., so take my car and my diamond ring. Don't shoot me, I don't know who you are. Just take everything and let me live. That way you won't have a murder rap hanging over your head. I promise you I won't say a word if you spare my life." His plea must have fallen on attentive ears. They thought it over, took his diamond and his wallet and as they drove off, one of them said, "If you talk, I'll get you and blow your head off." They then drove away in their car.[150]

According to Downing, nothing happened for about two weeks. Then Joe, noticing that Coonie was not wearing the ring, asked about it. Coonie, at first reluctant to discuss it, after about two days told Joe the whole story. Joe then made two phone calls that resulted in a visit from an unknown man dressed as a chauffeur and bearing a package that contained Coonie's ring and wallet. There was a note with the package: "This will never happen again. The boys who did this have been taken care of. Hope to visit you soon." It was signed "Your friend, Al Capone."[151]

On the basis of what Dennis McDougal says about Jules Stein and the MCA's connections with the Chicago Mob, it is possible that — assuming that Rex Downing's version is correct — Joe called Stein, who perhaps directly or indirectly contacted Capone. McDougal makes an interesting and persuasive charge that Stein and his organization had, from the beginning, some ties to the Mob.[152]

On another occasion four gangsters tried to extort $20,000 from Coonie, but he reported them to the police, and they were arrested.[153]

As a result of these incidents, and perhaps others that were never reported, Coonie hired a bodyguard to accompany him around the Chicago area. Lonely drives through rural areas and even some suburban areas of northeastern Illinois, especially in those days when gangs often seemed to wield greater power than municipal authorities, made Coonie's precaution a prudent one. On one occasion, or at least one that Coonie's son John knew about, the bodyguard was of very effective assistance. Coonie and his companion were driving out to the Grand Terrace and quickly overtook another automobile that was being driven in the middle of the road in such a way that made passing it impossible. Blowing the horn had no effect. The bodyguard said, "Coonie, move over to this side a little." Coonie did so, and the bodyguard took out his 38-caliber pistol and shot the other car's right rear tire. The mystery vehicle went off to the side at once.[154]

Thus it was that this new rumor obliged Coonie and his family to deny or confirm it. They chose the former course. By 27 March 1930 Coonie was back at his apartment at the Lake Shore Athletic Club, where he was kept busy insisting that he had neither been kidnapped nor received threatening letters.[155]

In Kansas City, at her home at 820 West Seventy-first Street Terrace, Eula Coon first heard about the alleged crime on the radio. She immediately called Chicago and heard her husband deny the story. Then she had to face querelous reporters from the *Kansas*

City Star. According to the *Star*, she replied to the reporter as follows:

> There positively cannot be any truth in it. I was with him in Chicago until a week ago and he is just out of the hospital. But I was with him and know exactly where he was. Possibly his presence in a hospital might be attributed to a beating he received in a kidnaping [sic]; I have heard that story, too. But I know he went to [the] hospital because of appendicitis; that he was operated upon, and his surgeon will vouch for that.[156]

The reporter observed that Eula was said to have reported prowlers around the Coon home in Kansas City. Coonie's wife confirmed this but said, in effect, so what? What neighborhood doesn't have prowlers occasionally? As far as she was concerned, there was no connection between the prowlers and the alleged kidnapping. The *Star's* reporter, perhaps a little disappointed, suggested later that the report may have been generated by the knowledge that the Coon-Sanders band was very famous and financially successful. And where the money was, there, often, were the mobsters.[157]

As for Capone by this time—1929 and 1930—he was probably enjoying his greatest power and influence, and he carried himself with ostentatious cockiness. Even by 1927 it was estimated that his gang was bringing in about $175,000,000 a year, mainly with its bootlegging enterprise. So his response to criticism was feigned self-pity, and perhaps even some remark about how his was a thankless task. Here he was, supplying the area with its liquor, and all the thanks he got was to be the butt of all those unkind remarks. He was going to leave for Florida and let the city get its booze the best way it could. Probably barely suppressing a laugh, he added, "I've been spending the best years of my life as a public benefactor."[158]

Mel Tormé (1925–1999), in his autobiography *It Wasn't All Velvet*, tells how his personal acquaintance with the Nighthawks, as well as his singing career, began. "The Velvet Fog" was born in 1925, but as early as 1929 he became a devoted radio fan. "With so much music going on around me," he writes, "it should come as no surprise that my favorite household item was a Stromberg-Carlson Cathedral model table radio." And Coon-Sanders was one of his favorite programs. While he pushed his Lionel train around the floor, he listened to the band, and was especially struck by their rendition of "You're Driving Me Crazy." He delighted in hearing not only the music but also the background noises—"the murmur of the Blackhawk patrons and the tinkle of silverware and glasses." One Monday night, probably in November or December, his parents dressed him in a sailor suit and took him to dinner at his favorite restaurant. "I sat at a front table," writes Tormé, "my eyes glowing at the sight of the burnished horns, the ebony piano, the shiny massive bell of the tuba, the drums and cymbals." He knew every selection by heart and sang along with each. All this interest in a four-year-old boy caught the attention of several dancers, one of whom told Joe Sanders. At intermission Joe went over to the Tormés' table and spoke with them about their enthusiastic son. Then Joe went back to the bandstand, spoke to Coonie, and asked him to play a drum roll. After the house had quieted expectantly, Joe said to the audience, "Folks, we have with us tonight our youngest and most devoted fan, little Melvin Howard Tormé." As Tormé later wrote, "He pronounced it 'Tormee,' as did most people at that time." Continuing, Joe said, "Little Melvin's parents tell me he listens to our broadcasts and knows every number we play. Well, whadaya say we give him a chance to prove it, eh?" And while Joe led the applause, little Melvin strode confidently up to the bandstand. Joe shook his hand, sat down at his piano, and asked what song Melvin would like to sing.[159]

When he wrote his autobiography, Tormé remembered that the song was "You're Driving Me Crazy." However, either the occasion was later than 1929 or else it was some song other than "You're Driving Me Crazy," which was not published until 1930.

But whatever the song, Joe gave the downbeat, and, as Tormé later wrote, "My career began at that moment." There was great applause. "My memories of that evening are absolutely indelible," writes Tormé. "I remember Carlton [sic] Coon lifting me up onto his lap behind the drums and my bouncing up and down each time he worked the bass drum pedal. I fell in love with drums that night." Later, Joe spoke with Mel's parents and asked whether their son might be there every Monday night as a special feature. They were willing — Mel emphasized that they did not press him to do it — and the young boy readily agreed. He appeared with the Nighthawks for nearly six months and was paid fifteen dollars each evening. It was his first time to sing publicly.[160]

Both Joe and Coonie were always alert to special and interesting patrons, as in the case just cited of Tormé. Another one had to do with a young invalid named George — Joe was unable in later years to recall his last name. The young man, confined to a wheel chair, came to the band's attention while they were playing at the Blackhawk, and Joe arranged for George to be carried into the Blackhawk where the young guest got his first look at a nightclub and spent his visit near the band as it played.[161]

It was also in 1929 that the Nighthawks made a deal with Maytag Corporation to broadcast under the latter's sponsorship. The program was the *Maytag Frolics* and featured the Nighthawks in a half-hour spot. At the time the Nighthawks aired the program, Maytag was experimenting with a new process, apparently called "Sonotone," for making recorded transcriptions of programs for later radio broadcast. According to Orville Butler, in more recent times an archivist of the Maytag Corporation, the new type of transcription was intended to improve the quality of the sound; but some broadcasters feared that the new method might play havoc with live broadcasting.[162] How many broadcasts the Nighthawks made for Maytag is perhaps impossible to discover, but a recording still exists of their program on 17 January 1929.* There were such numbers as "What a Girl! What a Night!," "Bless You, Sister," "Kansas City Kitty," "Mississippi, Here I Am," and Joe's compositions "Sittin' and Whittlin'" and "Harold Teen." One of Coonie's compositions was on the program, too, a slow number called "Way Down in the Deep, Low South." When he sang "Bless You, Sister," Coonie, not pressed by a phonograph recording's limitations, took the lyrics much more leisurely, and with more improvising, than we hear on their Victor recording of that number. In addition, the band played their famous medley of football fight songs that had received so much praise and had become one of their most popular features. There was chitchat between numbers by the announcer, and occasionally one hears Joe, Coonie, or some of the band members with their comments. The "football medley," played and sung amid much cheering by the band and audience, contained all or parts of the fight songs of such colleges as Yale, Annapolis, West Point, Georgia Tech, California, and Washington and Lee. The last item in the medley was what Joe announced in his stentorian voice as "everybody's alma mater," "Hail, Hail, the Gang's All Here." The band had already, in the Georgia Tech song's phrase "and a hell of an engineer," risked shocking the 1929 radio audience, when Joe boomed out the word *hell* clearly over much of America. And for good measure, at the very end, Elmer Krebs gave a few derisive hoots on his sousaphone. Then, in case there were perhaps a few listeners who had somehow not quite heard everything, the singing of "Hail, Hail, the Gang's All Here" assured everyone "What the hell do we care." Such toying with what

---

*For this information about the *Maytag Frolic* I am indebted in part to Orville Butler, formerly an archivist with Maytag, and Nate Stoller, of the Collectors Club, in California. Inexplicably, the Maytag Corporation seems not to have preserved its archival records.

was then often humorously termed "the naughty word" must have been treading on risky terrain. The band were obviously showing themselves as not overly concerned about the issue, and even emphasized the irony, when in a repetition, they demurely sang,

> Hail, hail, the gang's all here;
> Mustn't say the naughty word!
> Mustn't say the naughty word![163]

On November 7 Joe became a Mason, got his second degree a week later, and his third degree a week after that. Joe declared the process as "one of the greatest moments" of his life. Coonie had already become a member and may have had something to do with not only Joe's membership but that of several of the other band members. Johnny Coon assured me that Coonie and Joe also were instrumental in introducing Masonry to both Freeman Gosden and Charles Correll, the stars of radio's *Amos 'n' Andy*.[164]

The telegraphic flood that had begun back in Kansas City, in 1922, continued in Chicago. Let's examine some of the messages that the band received on their broadcasts in 1929 and early 1930. The Nighthawks' medley of football fight songs, though extensive, could mention but a few of the hundreds of colleges in the nation. Patti Winans, of Chicago, wired on 27 April 1929 to complain: "Don't Texas colleges sing songs?" The following November 24, N. Barry, of Chicago, cabled, "What's the matter with Ohio's fight song?" Some telegrams complained of what their senders regarded as failure to recognize some player's great feat, as did F. W. Bellman, also of Chicago, in late November of 1929. He wired, "Why not give Tom Lieb some credit playing Notre Dame[?]" On the "Knights and Ladies of the Bath," messages came in making puns on the name of the program. A Sigma Phi Epsilon chapter bade, "Make us members; we need a bath. Play anything." J. W. Roe, Houston, Texas, in March 1929 said, "Can we join Knights of the Bath? Not so pure but [you can] clean up till daylight." Jean Singer, of Chicago, wired on 22 December 1929: "Merry Christmas. Please send a knight over to give a lady a bath and play Lover Come Back." There were messages from old friends and former professional associates, such as Harry Nordberg, who from Kansas City, on 30 December 1928, must have sent all the band's members into uproarious laughter. Nordberg wired: "Your programs always good. Hooray for Haroldtine [*i.e.*, "Harold Teen"] and Darby Hicks."* Celebrities listened and sent wires. Edward E. "Zez" Confrey on 1 January 1928, from Albany, N.Y., said, "Wish you loads of success and happy new year." Charley Straight, bandleader and composer, wired on 2 January 1928, from Chicago: "Welcome home. May your salary always increase and your tempo never decrease." On 24 December 1929, from South Bend, Ind., Knute Rockne wired: "Many thanks for some very pleasant evenings during my illness. Merry Christmas to you all." One wonders what bandleader Jean Goldkette thought, if he heard the telegram from P. M. Bentzell, of York, Pa., who wired on 31 December 1929: "Please play Oh, Look What You Done to Me, for Jean Goldkette." (By that time Goldkette had given up his orchestra.) Joe probably got a good laugh from King Stanley, of Wichita, Kans., who on 8 January 1928 wired: "Dear Joe, play music and leave out the bull. We have plenty to take care of the cows here." A message from T. A. Gannon, of Chicago, said: "Play Mary Della for three doctors before high blood pressure sets in." Brooks Y. Stroupe, of Memphis, on 13 January 1929 wired: "Music hotter than depot stove. Play it tight like that." Sometimes telegrams brought a lump to the throat, as did that from H. W. Chadwick, Chicago, who on 31 December 1929 wrote: "Listening in tonight. Children quarantined with scarlet fever and diphtheria and

---

*As we have already seen, "Darby Hicks" was a fictitious character and a running joke for the Nighthawks.

wife with an abcess. Please play Singin in the Rain, and Believe me, I love you."[165]

It was probably from the colleges in these years of the late '20s that Coon-Sanders received the most attention, for the band continued to cultivate them. On 12 April 1929 "The Committee" in Bloomington, Ind., wired: "Please play collegiate melody [*sic*, probably meant *medley*]. We are anxiously waiting for you to play the 1929 junior prom." (Well, that's probably why Coon-Sanders was in Bloomington on April 26.) The Sigma Nu chapter at State College, Pa., on 1 December 1929 wired: "It's plenty cold in these mountains. Turn on the heat." Also asking for the band to stoke the fire was the Lambda Chi Alpha house, University of Arkansas, probably in 1929, that wired, "We want those St. Louis Blues, and we want 'em hot." Lambda Chi Alpha, of Alabama Polytechnic Institute (now Auburn University), on 11 January 1930, wired, "Please play Some of These Days on midnite program." Many of the collegiate messages came from Southern schools, evidence that Coon-Sanders was clearly received and enjoyed there. Another message came from Auburn's rival, the University of Alabama, where on 24 November 1929 the Sigma Alpha Nu chapter asked, "Please play Yea, Alabama, or St. Louis Blues." And on 18 January 1930, on the same campus, the Alpha Phi Gamma wired: "We are all having a big house party and wish you and your bunch were here to make it a hundred percent better. Please play Hello, Baby for the bunch at one o'clock."[166] The following are yet more collegiate messages:

- Sigma Chi, Indiana University, 11 January 1930: "Would like [to] be Knights of Bath. Request Sweetheart of Sigma Chi."
- R. Blackwell, Chicago, 17 March 1929: "Please play Illinois — one of the old grads nineteen eleven."
- Bob Johnston, Cincinnati, 24 November 1929: "How's tricks, Joe? Play Hail to Old Purdue. Bet you don't know it."
- John Connor, Vanderbilt University, 24 November 1929: "Please play Girl of My Dreams, dedicated to Miss Mildred Hutton."
- Bob Griffith and Alex McKee, Birmingham, Ala., 17 March 1929: "Please play Alabama Swing and have Joe Sanders sing it."
- Lewis Suydam Wilder, University of Massachusetts, 19 January 1930: "Please play I Ain't Got Nobody for Chi Phi Fraternity at Amherst."
- Tau Epsilon Phi, University of Illinois, 11 January 1930: "If you have anything like final exam blues, play it."
- Phi Delta Epsilon, University of Illinois, 12 January 1930: "Play Take Away Darkness. Exams soon."
- Alpha Sigma Phi, Pennsylvania State, 24 November 1929: "Please play Diana and Tiger Rag. Shake it up."
- Alpha Chi Rho "Regulars," Lehigh University, 10 January 1930: "Would like to hear After You've Gone. Would it be possible for you to play a Lehigh number if we send you the orchestration[?]"
- Sigma Phi Epsilon, Cornell University, 24 February 1929: "Please play [Here Comes My] Ball and Chain or some other Cornell song." (Was this suggesting that Cornell was like a ball and chain?)
- Chuck Greenlee, Syracuse, N.Y., 24 November 1929: "Four University of Illinois Phi Psis marooned in Syracuse, New York, waiting to hear Here Comes My Ball and Chain."
- L. L. Voigt, Jr., Cornell University, 18 January 1930: "Not particular at Cornell. Tiger Rag or Some of These Days."
- Sigma Nu, Purdue University, 11 January 1930: "Waiting feverishly to hear What a Girl! What a Night!"
- Upsilon House, Hamilton College, 11 January 1930: "Listen every night ten thirty to eleven. Please play tonight Collegiate Sam and Tiger Rag. Hope Joe is better." [Doubtless one of his periodic bouts with flu.]
- "The Blue Flames," Phi Kappa Tau, Purdue University, 16 March 1929: "How for Diana? We're holding a hot session."[167]

It was in the early part of 1930 that the band did the first of two seasons of the *Florsheim Shoe Frolic* for the National Broadcasting Company. The program originated in NBC's Michigan Avenue studios, with Sen Kaney as announcer — "good old Sen of 20th floor Congress days," as Joe put it. Ted Pearson was program director. One of the best-known photographs of the Nighthawks is a posed one for this program. It shows Kaney smiling broadly before a microphone, while Joe, Coonie, and the rest of the band cluster about, gazing intently at him, and mirroring his happy countenance.[168]

After finishing the Blackhawk commitment, the band fulfilled fourteen engagements on a brief tour before going to The Dells. Beginning with the University of Illinois on March 28, the Nighthawks set out on a somewhat irregular schedule. On April third they fulfilled an engagement at Waukegan, Ill. The next day they played in Madison, at the University of Wisconsin's Military Ball. And as Steve Masar with the University Archives tells me, his research shows that this was at a time when the Reserve Officers' Training Corps was very strong. At least 850 couples attended.[169]

On April 10, in Davenport, Iowa, the Nighthawks played at the Danceland Ball Room, where men's admission was a dollar each and women's half that.[170] Thereafter, they appeared at the University of Iowa on the eleventh; Northwestern University on the sixteenth; Milwaukee, Wis., on the twenty-third; and St. Louis, Mo., on the twenty-fourth.

The annual prom at Saint Louis University had for years been a big event, perhaps *the* event of the year. On Wednesday, March 26, the campus *Varsity Breeze* announced that thanks to Robert Denvir, prom chairman, and his co-workers, the 1930 version would be graced by the Nighthawks. The committee regarded having snared this band as a real coup, and the campus paper described the committee as "brimming over with smiles" about it. But Coon-Sanders would have to be paid; and though tickets cost five dollars per student couple and ten for each patron couple, quite a number would have to be sold. And all this as the nation had begun to fear that "Old Man Depression" just might be more than a brief visitor. Said the *Breeze*, "Popular with university men and women all over the nation, Coon-Sanders have a 'rep' that enables them to ask for a big price for special trips." And they had, said the paper, "asked [for] plenty — and they got it."[171] Now, hinted the campus journalist, the students were going to have to respond and plan to "prom-trot" on April 24. Moreover:

> Realizing the immense crowds that the orchestra itself will attract, [continued the paper] the prom committeemen have been scratching their worn brows in anxiety. But they have increased the facilities at the West Pine barn and promise that it will accomodate [sic] everyone comfortably. A big crowd make a big time, but too many hoofers in a small hall results too often in scuffed shines, shoes and such. Denvir and his cohorts promise that there'll be plenty of room to wax poetic with whirligig terpsichore.[172]

The *Varsity Breeze's* announcement reminded its readers of the Nighthawks' history — their start in Kansas City, their move to Chicago, and especially their connection with radio. And since Chairman Denvir realized the popularity of the band on the air, he had decided to "give radio addicts their innings by having KMOX, 'The Voice of St. Louis,' broadcast the music and gaiety direct from the gym." But the Nighthawks worked even more effectively with live audiences:

> One big thing in favor of the Nighthawks as a collegiate ballroom band is their ability to mix with the crowd. Every one of the boys saw something or other of a college and knows what kind of syncopation Joe College and his girl friend like to hop to. If milady wants to blow the alto clarinet, well, it's she to be pleased; the clarinet player is getting paid and doesn't mind taking a furlough while she bravely tries to eke squeks [sic] out of the maltreated swinette.[173]

Of course, the campus journalist had to

recount some of the standard Coon-Sanders myths. Coonie was described as "an overgrown medic who decided that it's more fun thumping tom toms than carving appendixes." Going even further into the realm of imagination, the *Breeze* stated that in Kansas City, "the whoopie outpost for the oil and cattle get-rich-quicks, he [i.e., Coonie] was allowed to hide his knee-breeches behind his bass drum even while in grade school. He stuck to the books until he got half way through Kansas U. medicine school, when he fled the laboratory and the cadaver...." Some of the story, such as how Coonie and Joe happened to meet, was a little closer to reality. And the account of how the name *Nighthawk* was born was reasonably accurate, as was the writer's observation that Coonie's inadvertent comment over the live microphone "almost lifted the postoffice out of its deficit."[174]

The event apparently lived up to expectations, though the *Varsity Breeze* eschewed superlatives as "too ordinary to use" in describing the affair. The elite of St. Louis were well represented, as were the campus belles. The Court of Love and Beauty consisted of the following: Alice Shores, Julia Maloney, Wilhelmina Muntsch, Margaret Vollet, Rosemary Edom, Dorothy Mudd, Rosaline Madden, Josephine Jones, Helen Bonner, Margaret Clopton, and Florence Shaughnessy. As for the males: "Even at college affairs there are Jimmie Walkers [apparently referring to New York's dapper mayor], but the greater part of the assemblage started hoofing on schedule." The Nighthawks played ten numbers in all. After the first four, there was the coronation. Everything thus far had been fairly standard, despite what the campus reporter said were the usual undependable suspender buttons, or faulty hook-and-eyes on the ladies' gowns. Then — well, let's let the reporter tell it:

> The sides of the big canopy were looped up deftly, a la Arabe, so that the more bashful, or footsore, couples could hold hands ... and [then with] the Coronation March from something-or-other, played by the Windy City tunesters, the promenade started. The gaily-garbed ladies with their gaily-disposed gentlemen marched round and round until it was decided that it would be just as well to place the crown on the queen's classic brow and let everybody go back to enjoying themselves.
>
> No sooner said than done and the queen, Julia Maloney, duly coronated, sat in regal splendor to endure the antics of several small-time vaudeville actors, who disported themselves ... in the best manner possible for her doubtful enjoyment. She bore it all bravely though, and is hereby invited to drop in at the office any day to receive a broken chair rung, or some other highly journalistic souvenir from the paper's staff. The Varsity Breeze isn't run on a business-like enough basis for the writers to be able to afford orchids. She does deserve them.[175]

It was all suitably pert and cynical for a world and a society that, by this year of 1930, appeared increasingly shaky. But for a few rollicking hours it was old times. The Nighthawks got unvarnished praise. Said the campus journalist: "Maybe the color of the queen's slippers didn't suit everyone, but Joe and Cooney soothed the displeased with their dulcet strains. The [N]ighthawks made the party what it was." Rex Downing, his trombone laid aside during intermissions as he calmly smoked his battered briar pipe, was declared the "most optimistic member of the orchestra." Someone got Joe Sanders' ear and asked what he wanted to be when he grew up. A songwriter, Joe averred. Was it true that Joe had actually had twenty-seven strikeouts in nine innings? Yes, indeed. Later, the questioner wished he had asked Joe whether he was pitching or batting. At some point a fellow in horn-rimmed glasses persuaded every one of the Nighthawks to autograph one of their phonograph records in white ink.[176]

Vignettes of the dance: The young ladies present had managed remarkably to appear in dissimilar but very colorful attire, which lent credence to the suspicion that there had been collusion.... One rumor had it that a number of susceptible females allegedly mistook Woody Kose, the "grinning"

KMOX announcer, for Rudy Vallee, the popular band leader and crooner. Kose's tendency to whisper into the microphone was the basis of that canard.... Sound effects from either Bob Pope or Joe Richolson embarrassed a page whose trumpet began to blow before he got it to his lips, and there was general embarrassment far and wide when the radio announcer named the wrong girl as the new queen.... From the balcony, one looked down on the dancers who, said the campus paper, "just moved with the crowd, and the crowd didn't move".... Clustered about the band were non-dancers who simply enjoyed the Nighthawks' music.... At the end, there were the remains of battered formal trains and about ten yards of "motley-hued silks and satins."[177]

There is every indication that the 1930 Prom was entirely successful. As for the Nighthawks' role in it, the *Varsity Breeze* had nothing but praise. It summed up as follows:

> As might have been expected, the Coon-Sanders bunch did its bit to make the evening enjoyable and when, early the next morn, the danced-out couples departed, they chatted heureusement about the excellent performance of the tone artists. This journal didn't distribute any radio applause cards, but it may be taken for granted that the ether audience fully concurred with the sentiments of the trotters.[178]

From St. Louis the band went on to the remaining five engagements: Purdue University on April 25; Midland Club, Chicago, on May 1; Mt. Carmel Prom, Drake Hotel, Chicago, on the second; Grand Rapids, Mich., on the eighth; the University of Notre Dame on the ninth; and Mendota, Ill., on the fourteenth. Following these appearances, the band took a vacation and, on June 9, opened their third season at The Dells, Dempster Road, Morton Grove, Ill.

In the fall it was back to the Blackhawk. Restaurants were beginning to feel the effects of the Wall Street collapse and the incipient depression — the word would very soon become a proper noun. The Blackhawk, while doing better than most, was obviously not enjoying the business that it previously had.[179]

It occurred to Stein and MCA that if Roth would release the band, it might be profitable to take it on a road tour for the month of December. Joe, however, always expecting and believing the best of Stein and the worst of Roth, blamed "faint hearted Roth," who according to Joe thought "December a bad month and eager to save salaries, released the band." They therefore spent the month of December, 1930, on the road doing one-nighters at twenty-six locations.[180] Since there is evidence that business at the Blackhawk was suffering somewhat, Stein may have thought that the Nighthawks could bring in some better earnings on the road.

According to Joe, the December engagements amounted to their most "sensational tour." They even managed their commitments so that they could get back to Chicago for their Florsheim radio programs, which meant returning to the city on Sundays and Tuesdays. They missed only one of those broadcasts, and it was because of illness. Ted Weems substituted for them and, according to Joe, "did a nice job of it." Though, as always, the band tended to thrive on such a punishing schedule, Joe had to admit that "At the end of the trip we were wrecks, but we had cleaned up." Their most profitable engagement was on Christmas night, 1930. In fact Stein's MCA received the largest payment for a single engagement in the years before the Second World War — a check for six thousand dollars. The occasion was Coon-Sanders' playing at George W. Griffiths' party at Chicago's Palmer House. The band's commitment was from 8 p.m. to 1 a.m. The contract had been signed the previous June 9, and the payment was made on December 30.[181]

Following the Griffiths party, the band had to jump on a train and head for the old home town, and the only vacation they got was that of the three-day appearance in Kansas City from the 26th through the 28th of December. Then, after three more appearances—Springfield and Chicago, Ill., and Milwaukee, Wis.—they found themselves back at the Blackhawk for New Year's Night.

Despite some evidence to the contrary, Joe later recalled that business at this time was excellent at the Blackhawk. "Everyone in the cafe wanted to kiss us," he said, "for Ted Fiorito, 'subbing' for us in December had been a horrible 'bust.'" Joe said waiters told him that often Fiorito played to only four or five parties. But Sanders and Roth were apparently now finding each other almost insufferable. Joe remarked, "During the latter part of this, our last season at the Blackhawk, Snatch-Penny Roth, the world's worst loser for whom we had made a fortune, became very nasty." Joe alleged that Roth, "accustomed to 90% profit ... could not stand a small loss when others were losing their 'shirts.'"[182] (Unfortunately, we don't have Roth's side of this matter.)

It was in January 1931 that the Music Corporation of America put the National Broadcasting Company into a bind in Chicago; for MCA, an independent, unaffiliated agency, controlled twenty-one of the area's radio outlets. (Unofficially, MCA and the Columbia Broadcasting System were allies.) There was an awkward situation, for instance, when Paul Whiteman returned to the Granada Cafe to do a commercial over KYW for NBC and the Sherwin-Williams Friday night program, and then went to Columbia-owned WBBM for regular nightly broadcasts. NBC could not even force one of its own bands upon one of its own stations, if the owner of the outlet or the commercial account preferred another, non–NBC outfit. This left many NBC stations open to competition. Among the major MCA bands that NBC had to accept as regular NBC features were Johnny Hamp, at the Congress Hotel's Balloon Room, and Coon-Sanders at the Blackhawk. It seemed odd that NBC, with all of its great resources, would find itself in such a position. One observer explained it by saying that Columbia, notably WBBM, had "made hay in Chicago while NBC was concentrating until last September in New York." But, said the same source, it went beyond that: "NBC's policy is not favorable to the large-salaried name band and the effort of the NBC Artist Bureau at all times is to sell a studio band." NBC proposed to solve the problem by taking to Chicago some thirty-five sustaining programs and to try to organize so that a series of programs might be handled by about two studio orchestras, with perhaps a variety of featured leaders. This, the company hoped, would lead to the sharing of commercials by one or two permanent studio bands. But, as was stated by the same independent observer, "This is diametrically opposed to the interests and financial profit of the individual name bandsman who sells his musical wares to the highest bidder and with a stated agreement to share in any radio melons that happen along." Such bands feared NBC's very bigness and "institutional aloofness" and regarded the network as a menace to their independence. To compound the problem for NBC, CBS had, in effect, "dibs" on such top-notch MCA bands (in addition to Coon-Sanders, Johnny Hamp, and Paul Whiteman) as Ben Bernie, Jan Garber, Wayne King, Ted Weems, and Husk O'Hare.[183]

NBC, however, was not content to let its competition thus operate in Chicago without a fight, and by mid–1931 the National Broadcasting Company was quickly working toward sewing up the Chicago broadcasting business. After having taken over the Northwestern Broadcasting System, NBC acquired controlling interest in the *Chicago Daily News*' station WMAQ. Col. Frank Knox, a Republican who would serve as secretary of the Navy in Franklin D. Roosevelt's wartime cabinet, had recently bought controlling interest in the daily but had no interest in the radio station. Since WMAQ had program alignments with CBS, Knox contacted William Paley but was unable to reach an agreement with him. Knox then contacted NBC, which closed a deal. This left the Columbia Broadcasting System without a full-time outlet in the city. To those in the industry, it appeared that NBC was determined upon a wholesale-buying binge of radio stations. On September first, *Variety* reported, "Rumbles of this impending switch in policy from one of station grabbing through affiliation to the more secure method of self-intrenchment by cutting in on ownership have been emanating in recent weeks from the office of NBC's top executives." It was, said *Variety*, a reversal of the relative positions that NBC and CBS had occupied a short while before. However, the New York weekly still thought the odds favored Columbia, which at least still owned WBBM and WJJD, even though neither was a full-time outlet, and WJJD had old equipment and, thus, a low rating.[184]

But Coon-Sanders, Hamp, Bernie, Garber, and a few others, though the agency's best, were hardly all that MCA boasted. At this time Jules Stein had exclusive management of about a hundred orchestras. The agency announced in early February its financial statement for the year 1930, and it was impressive. The company had done a gross business of $2,994,000, just with its orchestras, while it brought in another $1,000,000 from what it called its convention, club, and novelty departments. The net profit to MCA was $250,000. Stein announced in April that MCA would spend $100,000 for advertising in the *Saturday Evening Post*. *Variety* declared this unprecedented, the first time such an agency had advertised nationally to inform the public about its operations.[185]

These figures are all the more remarkable when one considers that the nation was already well into economic depression, with the number of unemployed growing. In Chicago there was an increasing problem with petty hoodlums. But where these pests had once simply threatened their victims with bodily harm if not accommodated, they now often added a spiel about the "hard times." Entertainers, perhaps easier to identify and to find, were especially feeling the brunt of this new crime wave, and the criminals were becoming so bold as to haunt hotels as well as side doors to theaters. The band leader Ben Bernie was accosted in his hotel, and Paul Ash was waylaid in the alley behind the Uptown Theatre. These two incidents were enough to convince entertainers to avoid alleys in preference for entrances and exits through front lobbies.[186]

Chicago was having to cope also with robberies of theatres' box offices and safes. During the winter of 1931, the Grand began paying off its players each night. That left less money in the building and smaller amounts to be taken to banks. The Grand hired two armed policemen to guard both the box office and, afterward, the office. These measures were a result of two robberies during a run of the play *Lysistrata*.[187]

Among the increasing army of unemployed were some musicians. At this time, of course, the more popular bands such as the Nighthawks were still doing well, but smaller groups were becoming apprehensive. Even when they could find engagements, they usually had to accept smaller payments than in the past. The prospects for the summer of 1931 were very gloomy. *Variety* reported that the small bands in the New York area, as well as other places in the East, were facing a "workless summer," especially if those bands were in a salary range under $1,000. Even so well known a band as Art Kassel's found itself, in May, in a Chicago department store, playing and sweating amid the notions, toilet goods, and underwear. Those groups without "names" might even have to lay off some of their players. Most of the exceptions to this retrenchment were those establishments under long contracts to booking agencies, mainly hotels but also a few dance halls. Adding to this problem was that many resorts had installed equipment to take music directly off phonograph recordings or radio.[188]

Well, thank goodness for radio! And broadcasting certainly had come a long way. With a decade of experience, the new medium was developing some polish and even sophistication as compared with those early, cruder efforts when almost anything one could hear was deemed worth hearing. But much of broadcasting was still live and, hence, unpredictable. Already, many stations about the nation were building up a collection of gaffes, and the industry would continue to be plagued by the problem. Chicago, especially, had, in Jimmy Durante's words, "a million of 'em," some of which, by the standards of that day, were shocking and unprintable. On one occasion an announcer was merely performing the seemingly ordinary act of giving the correct time — "At the gong signal the time will be exactly nine o'clock." Nothing to it. Only, it wasn't nine o'clock. It was seven o'clock, and someone else in the studio frantically signaled that fact. The announcer looked at his watch, and perhaps thinking himself with the boys in the nearest speakeasy, he murmured, "Damn if it ain't." Since most listeners to a local ball game were males, there was little said about a sports announcer's observation that one of the teams had been "caught with their pants down." After all, who hasn't been on occasion. Live, untended microphones have accounted for a large share of such contretemps. The reader will perhaps recall that such a situation gave the Nighthawks their name. Since most such blunders aren't that harmless, however, studios began to install red lights that warned of live mikes. But even this innovation took some time to become fully appreciated, and one announcer blurted out over the air, "What the hell is this red light for?" Nor would a light of any color be of much help when, as on one occasion, a visitor strode into a broadcasting area and said to a young fellow standing next to a live microphone, "Where the hell is the john around this joint, buddy?" What is probably the most famous gaffe in radio history occurred not in Chicago but in New York City, and it involved a microphone that had been left on too long. It concerned Don Carney, who, as "Uncle Don," conducted a program of children's chitchat and music on early radio. The story is that he once signed off and, not realizing the microphone was still live, blurted out, "There! I think that'll hold the little bastards!" He spent the rest of his life denying it ever happened, and charging jealous rivals with having concocted the story.[189] Live radio was indeed a hazardous undertaking.

For the second season the Nighthawks broadcast the *Florsheim Shoe Frolic*. The show started at 7:30 p.m., Central Standard Time, on Tuesday, March 10, and was aired thereafter every Tuesday through May 26. The programs were broadcast over the National Broadcasting Corporation and were heard on forty-three stations, including WDAF in Kansas City and WGN in Chicago. NBC's ad praised the Nighthawks' "nationally famous compositions and original arrangements of the latest 'hits.'" Again, Sen Kaney was the announcer, assisted by his smiling face and full mustache.[190]

Sanders' scrapbook indicates that Harold Florsheim was so eager for the Nighthawks to start playing under his aegis that he had the band do several programs for him while they were still at The Dells the previous summer. Coon-Sanders featured some black spirituals, which Joe said "became the rage and Whiteman and others started to feature like numbers." Later in the broadcast season, the *Frolic* directly followed Whiteman, and Joe averred, "I think I may safely say, and in all due modesty, that we outshone him every week."[191]

Just how independent and plainspoken Joe Sanders could be was illustrated by a little disagreement in April 1931 between Joe and Coonie on one side and NBC on the other. *Variety* gleefully reported that the difference of opinion became pretty heated. The Nighthawks were rehearsing for that evening's *Florsheim Frolic* when an NBC announcer strode in flourishing a copy of the evening's script. He pointed to a song on one page and said that the band would have to substitute something else.

"Says who?" demanded Sanders.

The announcer suavely explained that since Paul Whiteman was going to use that same number, the Nighthawks would have to omit it.

"Nothing doing," said Joe.

"Ditto here," said Coonie.

Both men followed that with, "And that goes for both of us."

The announcer was adamant: "But Mr. Whiteman has that number on his program."

"The number stands as is," said Joe.

"Ditto here," said Coonie.

"And that ends that," added both Joe and Coonie.

Except that it didn't end the matter, for the announcer stood his ground. Voices increased in volume and vehemence, until Harold Florsheim, who had been observing all this from the ringside, stepped up to the contestants. If NBC kept tinkering with his band's program, he warned, he'd take his show off the air.

"I'll tell you what it's all about!" Joe shouted. "These people are fighting for jobs with the Music Corporation of America, and we're being discriminated against because we're an MCA band." Then, someone came to the Nighthawks' rescue by observing that it was really too near broadcast time to make any switches, anyway. That bit of logic was enough to calm matters; the boys went back to work, and the number stayed in the program.[192]

According to Sanders, it was at this point that he was approached by "certain persons" to attempt a one-man show of the type done by Phil Cook, who had become famous at this time by singing his own songs on the Columbia Broadcasting System. Joe's account of what followed was that he gave an audition for Quaker Oats and "walked off with it, because I 'sold' a thought, whereas Little Jack Little* and others merely sold songs." Joe was to receive $1,400 a week and would broadcast each morning at 6:30, 7:30 on the West Coast. There was even a promise to run a wire to Joe's hotel so that he could do the show from his apartment. "The whole affair ... fell thru," said Sanders, "for the simple reason that I was presented by a company rival to NBC." Actually, it was Phil Cook (1893–1958) who became the "Quaker Oats Man."[193]

But Joe said that his audition had drawn attention, and a number of other possible sponsors approached him, chief among whom were Swift, the meatpacking company; Pepsodent, maker of toothpaste and sponsor of *Amos 'n' Andy*; and the Fuller Brush Company. Yet instead of these companies, it was Florsheim Shoes that asked Joe to try to put something together. Florsheim had been looking for a program to fill a brief period on Sundays. Joe asked Coonie to work with him, and the two did thirteen weekly programs for Florsheim over NBC. It was called the *Florsheim Sunday Radio "Feeture,"* and presented Coonie — the ad naturally omitted the *e* in Carleton — and Joe as "The Harmony Duo of Coon-Sanders Original Nighthawks." There is still extant a dated but (for me) strangely appealing recording, perhaps part of one of these programs, in which Joe and Coonie harmonize on Joe's composition "Lonesome (I Wonder If You're Lonesome Too)." An advertisement for the program used a photo of the two men that showed them looking at an old NBC microphone, with Joe leaning over his keyboard and Coonie standing and leaning against the grand piano. Joe later said that a number of persons told him they liked the "*Feeture*" more than the entire band's *Frolic*. Joe, "to make the program distinctive," as he put it, wrote and presented each Sunday what he termed "an original piano mood." These "moods" caught some attention, so publishers began asking for them. Robbins took them for publication, and Joe was "very proud" when he received the first sample copy of "Improvisations," which included his "Embers," "Intangibility," "Southology," and "Inhibition." "It was an achievement for me," said Sanders, "aside from the lucrative phase, for it had always been Madeline's

---

*Little (1902–1956) was a radio singer and pianist whose theme song was "Little by Little."

dream that one day I'd do something a bit tastier than mere danceable tunes."[194]

Over thirty years later Joe, in a taped conversation with Harvey Rettberg, discussed another of the piano "moods" that he wrote for use on the programs for Harold Florsheim. It was titled "Sparks," which, said Joe,

> defies Leonard Bernstein, Josef Hofmann — the greatest living pianists — Oscar Levant — I defy anybody to play it. It can't *be* played. It gives the impression of a fire just starting. It might be an outdoor fire; it might be a fire in a fireplace. It's just smoldering.... Just starting to flame. Starts out very, very quietly, very softly, and very melodiously. And all of a sudden the fire crackles and so did the notes. I couldn't play it! I was never so embarrassed in my life, I took it up there on a Sunday afternoon — has to go fast — no man living — I don't care *who* he is, how great a pianist — *concert* pianist — it's *impossible* to play at the speed for which it was intended. I could slow it down and play it, *yes*, but "Sparks" means something after the fire starts burning. Couldn't *do* it. I stumbled all over myself that Sunday afternoon. [Then, in reply to someone who said he couldn't hear anything wrong with it:] That's because you didn't write it.[195]

"A letter from Robbins made me very happy," wrote Sanders later. He stated that the London Victor representative, upon hearing "Southology," pronounced it "quite the loveliest thing he had heard for ages." In addition, Robbins acclaimed the Nighthawks as the band of the highest value to them in "making" songs. Moreover, a poll voted Coon-Sanders the most popular band in America. Joe was proud of the acclaim: "All this, mind you, without recording assistance. Again during this season we turned down as high as $8,500.00 from theatres. My folio, incidentally, boosted me to class 'C' in the Authors and Composers Society."[196]

Carleton A. Coon, Jr., says that it was at about this time, 1930 or 1931, that Coonie brought his family to live with him for a year in Chicago. The younger son recalls that he went to school there and that the family lived at 5510 Sheridan Road, on the tenth floor of a tall apartment building. It was across from the Edgewater Beach and near where Paul Whiteman used to give concerts. Carleton, Jr., liked to swim in a pool there and on one occasion ran into some of the Whiteman orchestra. To young Carleton all this was magical stuff. He remembers also that the orchestra leader Ted Fiorito once had some tickets to a Northwestern football game, but, unable to use them, he gave them to Coonie's family. It was also at this time that young Carleton started collecting foreign postmarks that his father received from some of the orchestra's fans in other countries.[197]

During their years in Chicago the band's members became fans of the Chicago Cubs and even of players on visiting teams. Coonie, especially, got to know and be close friends with many members of the various teams, as well as with sports announcers; sometimes Coonie and his son Johnny sat in the broadcasting booth during games. Johnny Coon remembered an incident that happened when he was about seventeen and when he and his mother and siblings were spending a year with Coonie in Chicago. Johnny's father called him from the Blackhawk and said: "Son, get one of the cars and come down to the Blackhawk. I've got something I want you to do for me." When Johnny arrived, the band was playing, so he took a seat. At a break in the program, Coonie walked over to him and explained confidentially: "I've got a couple of ball players here that are getting awful drunk." He cautiously indicated where they were, and Johnny saw that his father wasn't exaggerating. Then Coonie whispered, "I want you to be sure and get them over to their hotel." Johnny went over to their table and discovered that they were New York players, one of whom was William Harold "Bill" Terry, a six-foot-one giant of about two hundred pounds. Coonie explained to the semi-conscious duo what Johnny was going to do. He then wished the men luck in avoiding trouble with their manager, especially since there was a game next day with the Cubs at

Wrigley Field. Following his father's instructions, Johnny took them into their hotel through the back way and managed to get them into the freight elevator. Then, hoping they'd remember their floor and room numbers, young Johnny left them there.[198]

It was perhaps also at this time that Coonie's own consumption of alcohol started to increase to an extent that threatened to interfere with his work and even his family life. Johnny Coon told Joe Popper, and in more recent years he told me, that his father during his last two or three years seemed to be a very unhappy man. Coonie had reached the point where he often consumed a glass of Scotch early in the morning. In fact, Coonie seemed able to imbibe a considerable quantity of Scotch or other liquor without very obvious signs of intoxication. Nevertheless, it eventually showed in such other ways as occasional antic behavior, weight gain, and deteriorating relations within his family. And, eventually, it affected his professional obligations.[199]

Johnny Coon recalled an incident that caused his mother much upset. The family at the time had three automobiles, but Coonie often liked to take a cab to and from engagements. He liked to carry a bottle of liquor with him, as he was doing on this occasion, and didn't wish to worry about trying to drive. At some point on Sheridan Road he asked the cabbie to put him out at a diner to get a snack. Gregarious Coonie immediately struck up a conversation with a milk delivery man, who found Coonie as agreeable as he did Coonie's bottle of liquor. The two men talked and talked, and drank and drank, until both were in a state that would have given Billy Sunday enough material for several sermons. But eventually the bottle's contents were exhausted, as were perhaps also the bottle-scarred veterans. Now Coonie had to face the problem of getting home. Always resourceful, especially where money was concerned, he offered to buy his new friend's milk wagon, its contents, and the horse. Johnny Coon didn't say how much his father offered, but it was acceptable, and Coonie drove the wagon home to an incredulous and furious Eula.[200]

The commitment at the Blackhawk, their last at that famous restaurant, ended on 15 May 1931. But even during the previous February, April, and May, the Nighthawks appeared in at least twenty-eight places other than the Blackhawk, and most of them outside Chicago. The majority of the engagements were one-nighters. This entailed having to return quickly to Chicago on those Sundays and Tuesdays when they were obligated to broadcast the Florsheim shows.

In Youngstown, Pa., on April 16, the Nighthawks played at Idora Park for that city's Stadler Spring Festival. The band had a popular following in Youngstown, for four thousand had listened to them with great acclaim two years earlier at Yankee Lake. As the *Youngstown Vindicator* put it: "With Carlton [sic] Coon headlining the vocal portion of the musical entertainment together with the marvelous band directed by Joe Sanders, the affair should be a huge success."[201]

As soon as the last trumpet had sounded at the Blackhawk, the band, as Joe put it, "bade the Blackhawk a none too tearful farewell."[202] It had been a profitable association for all parties, but it apparently had taken its toll on personalities and temperaments. Roth was perhaps as glad to see Joe go as Joe was to leave. How the rest of the band felt is difficult to know, nor do we know what Stein and MCA thought about it. Apparently, Roth subsequently let it be said that he believed the Nighthawks had begun to slip in popularity. When in the following autumn he engaged Earl Burtnett's orchestra, he perhaps was the source of *Variety*'s report that said, "A new orchestra, a new policy, and a new silver ceiling are counted upon by the auspices to improve business at the Blackhawk this year." Roth was described as hopeful that the new arrangement would "attract … some of the abundant patronage that last year went to Clark and Randolph for Ben Bernie and the

College Inn."[203] He and Joe had clearly had enough of each other, at least for a while.

In these early days of 1931 there was much speculation about an alleged drop in popularity of radio bands. *Variety* raised the issue and blamed it on a practice called "cut-ins." Some bands, apparently including some of the more famous ones, had ties with music publishers who bribed the leaders to play and promote certain songs. There were cases in which bands had so many cut-in agreements that there was little room left for playing pieces that might be newer or more interesting. The result, according to *Variety*, was that the bands had little opportunity for improving their programs, and radio listeners were becoming aware of it. Some broadcasting companies had begun searching for "leader-substitutes," that is, lesser-known bands with good potential. It was, said *Variety*, a move perhaps more effective than anything the American Society of Musicians might have been planning.[204] There was no suggestion that this problem involved Coon-Sanders, nor was it Joe's policy to get himself into such agreements that would have interfered with his fiercely protected independence.

Among the automobiles of the Twenties, few had as much glamor as did the Auburn, the Cord, and the Duesenberg. Those who know classic automobiles still salivate over these three. And the Duesenberg was so carefully made and was so expensive that relatively few of them were made and sold. In fact, so esteemed was the Duesenberg's name that a shortening of it went into the English language as synonymous with the ultimate, as in the expression "It's a Duesy." (Many Americans would pronounce that *doozy* rather than the preferable, if somewhat prissier, *dewsey*.) Auburns and their swankier siblings were among the most prized vehicles of the day. A cartoon published by the Auburn Company showed a puzzled man trying to find his automobile among many others in a parking lot. Says the cartoon's message, "Owner of new auto, which looks like half a dozen other makes, tries to pick it out of a row of parked cars." (Most drivers today would not find that situation nearly so unusual as they would a sign in the cartoon that says "Parking 10c.")[205] The Auburn Company prided itself on the distinctiveness of its products.

A great deal has been said by Coon-Sanders fans about the Nighthawks' relations with the Auburn company, and as we have already seen, Joe Sanders began buying Auburn products as early as 1925. In the course of his dealings with the company, Sanders became a close friend of Roy H. Faulkner, a vice president. The two men would meet for a meal together, perhaps, or Faulkner would hear the band whenever he was near enough to attend their engagements.

In mid–1928, for instance, after Joe had just purchased his third Auburn, Faulkner was in Chicago and had dinner with Joe. Coon and Sanders, said Faulkner in one of his subsequent columns in the company publication, were famous and "the idols of the Mid-west college students." The automaker expatiated for his readers:

> With all of this "Joe" is still boyish, lovable and unspoiled. I was complimenting him on the way he had accepted his success and he gave me this answer, "Why shouldn't I be humble[?] Suppose I lost my talent in music tomorrow, could Auburn employ me at anything like my present income? Could I take up anything else in the world and enjoy a like success? I couldn't, so I am continually thankful for the talent that has been given me and appreciative of the fact that I have been able to retain my popularity and my friends."[206]

Faulkner went on to say, "I always thought 'Joe' was a great guy but after that I knew he was great because I have seen so many people swell up and burst with popularity and success."[207]

One of the favorite parts of the Nighthawk legend has been that the band were taken to the company's factory in Auburn, Ind., where each member received a free automobile. This happens to be true, though it occurred much later in the band's story than most Coon-Sanders fans realize. Also, the transactions were tehnically sales. Each member was invited to *buy*, for the token price of a dollar, any Auburn on the floor. The only stipulation was that all had to have the same model, though each new owner might choose his color. The band settled on the 1931 Custom Phaeton Sedan. Rex Downing, many years later, remembered the elation that he and the others felt at being "turned loose" in that incomparable showroom. Joe and Coonie each were "sold" a Cord, a somewhat more prestigious vehicle.[208]

The company made a spectacular production of the occasion. After each man had chosen his color, his automobile was given a special final touch. Across the rear luggage trunk was written "Coon-Sanders Orchestra," and below that the owner's name. (Photographs show that earlier, when Joe was buying his own Auburn products, the company put his name on his cars.) Then the new cars were lined up in front of the main building, each car backed diagonally into the curb and with the proud owner standing outside the driver's door. Then a photographer captured the moment for advertising purposes. The cars were rearranged slightly for other photographs, one of which shows the band's members, shoulder to shoulder and dressed nattily in uniform topcoats and fedoras— well, except Krebs who wore a golfer's cap— standing in front of one car parked horizonally to the building. Three of the photographs taken appeared in the June issue of the company's publication.[209]

On 2 May 1931 the band's members wrote the following letter, which sported an elegant subjunctive form of the verb *to be*, to Roy Faulkner:

> Dear Mr. Faulkner:
> We are but newcomers in the Auburn family, yet we can readily understand why Auburn-Cord has forged ahead so rapidly during this period of utter depression among other automobile manufacturers.
> It is quite impossible for us to express our gratitude for your personal supervision of the equipment which goes to make up the finest cars we have ever owned. If, in lauding AUBURN to the skies be a method of reciprocation, please know that your efforts to make us HAPPY AUBURN DRIVERS shall not be in vain.[210]

Then the band's members signed the letter. That is to say, the following seven did: Harold Thiell, Floyd Estep, Bob Pope, Rex Downing, Elmer Krebs, John P. Thiell, and Russ Stout. But no Joe Richolson. There is a general assumption that Richolson got his Auburn at a later date. Perhaps Joe Sanders' reason for not being present was that he had already received his free Cord. In fact, my suspicion is that he had already received one or two cars *gratis*, and Faulkner, when he became president shortly before this time, perhaps had the inspiration to extend this courtesy to the entire band. The article in *The Accelerator* mentions that in addition to the seven Auburns, one Cord was "purchased" by a band member; and in the photograph of the eight cars parked in front of the Auburn Company's main showroom, the man standing at the left end in the picture, next to the lone Cord, is pretty clearly *not* Joe Sanders. Joe added a postscript to the letter that the seven new Auburn owners wrote:

> After glancing at the above glowing endorsement of your cars, it behooves me to say a brief word. After having driven FOUR AUBURNS and TWO CORDS, I regret to state that it becomes impossible for me to concur in the foregoing rhapsody. So thoroughly am I set against your products that I give you my word that I shall never drive an AUBURN product — beyond the age of 100.[211]

Many years later Rex Downing recalled that magical day at the Auburn factory and showroom in Auburn, Indiana:

> Once there, we were told that we could select any auto we wanted as long as it was the same model and we chose a gorgeous convertible sedan. Believe me, it was the most sought after car at that time. We were

told we could have any color we wanted and could then go about the showroom and pick out accessories—that is to say, running board spotlights, fog lights, special tires and so on. And to make the deal legal and binding, we each paid one dollar for each car.

Can you imagine turning a bunch of knucklehead musicians loose in an automobile showroom and telling them to take whatever they wanted? Well, this gift of autos proved to be a most profitable deal for the Auburn people. Due to the great popularity of the band, a great number of people got to see those beautiful cars as we drove about the country. They—the cars and the musicians—got to be a show all by themselves, and it turned out to be that the sales of the Auburn went up that year, while every other car went down in sales. This might have been the first time in history that a band made an auto famous.[212]

Well, it would be nearer the truth to say that the band made the already-famous automobile yet more famous, or at least identified it with the Nighthawks. Joe had already become interested in the company and had already invested heavily in Auburn stock.

The new automobiles became almost as much a feature of the band as were the distinctive duets that Joe and Coonie often sang. Downing said that frequently the band drove the autos from engagement to engagement, usually with all cars traveling in a row. As the Nighthawks pulled into a city, the residents

Clarence Russell "Russ" Stout, perhaps about spring 1926, place unidentified. (Courtesy Special Collections, Kansas City [Mo.] Public Library.)

habitually gawked and admired the gorgeous, sporty sight. One assumes that onlookers uttered plenty of such then-current jargon as "Hot dog!" and thought the beautiful vehicles the "bees' knees," "mean," and

Eight of the band pose with their new cars, Auburn, Indiana, about 2 May 1931. Coonie and his Cord L29 on left. Richolson and Sanders not in picture. (Courtesy Auburn Cord Duesenberg Museum, Auburn, Indiana.)

"hot." In each large city the Auburn Company sent a crew who took the cars back to the local agency's shop to clean and polish them while the boys were playing their gig. Then, the Auburn crew returned them and parked them ostentatiously in a row near the dance hall. It was highly successful publicity for both the band and the Auburn Company. Too bad Faulkner hadn't tried it earlier, in years when the Nighthawks were doing their heaviest one-nighting. The reason may be that Errett Lobban Cord, the company's president, did not wish to do any such type of publicity. In February of 1931, however, Cord retired and Roy Faulkner, Joe Sanders' good friend, took over.[213]

Downing's car was a Fauntleroy blue, while Florence Stout, Russ's widow, recalled that theirs was a "light beige with genuine brown leather upholstery." Coonie's Cord, according to Johnny Coon, was a mother-of-pearl color outside and a sort of eggshell color inside. Afterward, two of the cars were stolen, Downing's in New York City and Stout's in Chicago. When the Chicago police found Stout's car, it was up on blocks and had been completely stripped and gutted. Said Florence Stout, "We kept our golf clubs in the car, and, of course, they were gone, too." In later years Downing recalled that occasionally one of the band borrowed another member's car to go someplace where he didn't wish to be recognized, and caused the actual owner to get blamed. Rex particularly remembered catching it from his wife on such an occasion. On the other hand, that may have been the way some of the members tried to explain how their cars happened to

Joe and his 1931 Cord, showing his and the band's names on the trunk. (Courtesy Special Collections, Kansas City [Mo.] Public Library.)

be seen in embarassing situations. Florence "Sis" Stout remembered that often, after her husband had played at an engagement, she drove their Auburn while he slept on the back seat. "I was the youngest member in the group," recalled Florence, "and to me it was all one big good time. And driving those cars — they were so wonderful — never a speck of trouble."[214]

Coon-Sanders' fans, having heard much about the band's connection with these fine cars, will perhaps be disappointed to learn that, except for Joe Sanders, who had already acquired several Auburn products on his own, the rest of the band flaunted their Auburn products for little more than a year. Downing and Stout, as we have just seen, enjoyed them even more briefly.

This identification of the Nighthawks with those flashy Auburn products perhaps helped fuel the formation of a new, but apparently short-lived, Nighthawk fan club, which *Variety* said was being touted by "hot-feet gals" on both coasts, as well as in Canada and Missouri. It was described as the first fan club boosting a radio band (a questionable statement in light of the Nighthawks' own earlier club back in Kansas City). "Coon and Sanders are sitting by quietly," said *Variety*, "while a group of local gals stir up the country. So far, the band boys think it's an oke idea." But, added the periodical, there could be painful afterthoughts if they suddenly discover that the "pash femmes" might get delusions of grandeur and "start demanding special favors over the air in the way of tunes, mention, etc., besides giving 'em advice on how to eat spaghetti."[215]

The first place on the 1931 tour was right there in Chicago, a two-week engagement at

Harold Thiell's Auburn, showing his and the band's names on the trunk, Auburn, Indiana, about 2 May 1931. (Courtesy Auburn Cord Duesenberg Museum, Auburn, Indiana.)

Auburn Automobile company's donation of cars to the band, Auburn, Indiana, about 2 May 1931. From left: Stout, Krebs, Downing, Pope, Estep, H. Thiell, and J. Thiell. (Courtesy Auburn Cord Duesenberg Museum, Auburn, Indiana.)

the Trianon, as well as some appearances at the Aragon. The main purpose of these two commitments was to occupy the band in Chicago while they did the last two Florsheim broadcasts. Joe missed the last program as well as the last week at the Trianon, and in his written recollections he is coy as to the reasons—"a story not for these pages," as he puts it.[216]

Another view of Joe and his 1931 Cord, a gift from the Auburn Company. (Courtesy Special Collections, Kansas City [Mo.] Public Library.)

After closing at the Aragon on May 31, the band prepared to leave for Pittsburgh, the first stop on a brief road trip. Roy Sanders and his wife Mary came to Chicago to drive Joe's Cord back home. That it was very heavily loaded with baggage is probably why Madeline returned to Kansas City by train. After hailing a cab and piloting Roy to his route out of the city, Joe dashed to the depot and joined the band on their private Pullman. There seemed to be a general feeling of relief at leaving Chicago and a desire to stay away for at least a year. Nevertheless, Joe closed this part of his recollections with, "Adieu, Chicago, my beloved Chicago! Au revoir, dear old Surf Hotel!"[217]

CHAPTER SEVEN

The Final Year

The band pulled out of Chicago on June first for a brief but remunerative tour. I have no idea what persuaded them to hire their own Pullman car, nor do I know whether MCA provided it for them. They used it for the entire trip, and Joe later pronounced it "the only way to travel." While at Pittsburgh, the first stop, Joe indulged his love of baseball and went to Forbes Field, where he ran into orchestra leader Don Bestor and his young daughter. After Pittsburgh they appeared in York and Mahanoy City, both in Pennsylvania; then at Lexington, Va.; Wilkes-Barre, Pa.; Johnson City, N.Y.; Hershey, Pa.; Olean, N.Y.; and finally at Union City, Pa. At Olean, where they played for the Nighthawks' friend Bob Fisher, they made $1,700. At Hershey they grossed $2,300, an almost unprecedented amount for one night. Every commitment was a one-nighter except that at Lexington, Va., where they tarried from the fifth through the tenth of June.[1]

The six-day engagement at Lexington, Va., seems to have been the highlight of the tour. They played three nights for the Washington and Lee "Finals" and three at Virginia Military Institute. According to Joe, they "had a barrel of fun and made a host of new friends," which probably means that both barrel and friends were full of the beverages of choice. The band apparently stayed at the Mayflower Inn, at which Joe said their "liquor cache [was] only ten gallons of corn."[2] The Nighthawks played for a series of dances on Friday and Saturday, June 5–6, and on Friday evening they opened the week-long "Inter-Fraternity Dance" season. On Saturday morning at ten o'clock, they played for the Pan-White Friar Dansant in the gymnasium, and that afternoon from two until six for the Delta Upsilon Fraternity Dance, held at the Robert E. Lee Hotel. Then, after the University's second and third regatta crews had raced at 5:30 p.m. on the North River, everyone got ready for the Nighthawks' final dance, starting at nine, for the Sigma German. Fletcher Henderson's Orchestra played for the rest of the events.[3]

The band's apparance at VMI called for them to play for several occasions, one of which was on Tuesday, June 9, at 10 p.m. The campus *Cadet* described the dance:

> With Coon-Sanders' boys again furnishing the syncopation, dancing began at 10 o'clock Tuesday night, and about 11:30 the

6. The Final Year

floor was cleared for the Final German Figure. This dance was the last bow of the First [i.e., graduating] Class which was so soon to go out from the shelter of these grey walls. For many it was an event slightly tinged with sadness, as they watched the immaculately white figures of the First Classmen accompanied by their fair and blushing damsels sweep by in long rows. The figure which wound itself about the spacious floor in gracefully intricate curves and finally formed the letters V M I and then broke again to form the figure 31 [for the year], was led by Woods Talman, president of the class, and Miss Elizabeth Watkins, of Richmond. They were ably assisted by George Shell and Miss Medora Ford of Lexington. The dance following the figure was one of the best ever held at the Institute, thanks to the capable management of the Hop Committee and the sparkling music put out by Coon-Sanders' Orchestra. Two o'clock came too soon, and as the orchestra finished playing a college medley the staccato beats of the O. D.'s drum ended the festivities for the night.[4]

On the next evening, Wednesday, the Class of 1932, or "Second Class," honored the graduating class with the last dance of the year. "For the first time," reported the *Cadet*, "the Second Classmen appeared in their new paletots and showed them off to the utmost in the beautiful figure with which the Ball, 'The Social Military Highlight of the South,' was commenced." This was led by Rand Turner, president of the Class of 1932, and Sally Sackett, assisted by Johnny Monks and Rhoda Monks. "The girls," said the campus paper, "dressed in white to match the brilliancy of the white uniforms, carried beautiful corsages. The red of the flowers furnished a contrast in color." Those present thought it one of the most impressive such occasions ever seen at VMI. "No small factor in the phenomenal success of the 1931 Finals," concluded the *Cadet*, "was the inspiring—and inspired—music of Coon-Sanders' Orchestra. They played with unexampled pep throughout the last three dances, and did a great deal towards setting so high a standard of scintillating enthusiasm." Joe and Coonie, said the paper, "were show enough for the price of admission."[5]

Those days in the Lexington area gave Joe an opportunity to slake his thirst not only for "corn" but also for snapshots. Joe and Coonie, both of whom always seemed to have a soft spot in their hearts for Confederate history, were much impressed by such places as Stonewall Jackson's and Robert E. Lee's burial places. Carleton, his camera hanging from his right hand, had his picture taken as he leaned against the sign to Jackson's tomb. Joe declared Washington and Lee "one of the loveliest campuses in the world," and the gymnasium where the band played as "splendid." VMI, with its stronger atmosphere of the military, perhaps reminded Joe of his frustrating weeks at Camp Bowie in the Great War. If so, it was perhaps less appealing. Nevertheless, he took pictures on that campus, too, and thought the gymnasium, with its fortress-like façade, interesting enough to photograph.[6]

The proximity of Lexington to Virginia's Natural Bridge lured at least Joe and Coonie there. Joe took numerous photos of the bridge and the area, and was delighted to see a place on the rocks where George Washington had carved his "G. W." (Well, at least the letters are there. Opinions differ as to who carved them.) Not to be outdone, even by George Washington, Joe and a friend, "Doggy" Stone, climbed several feet up on one of the rocky areas and carved *their* initials, and got themselves photographed doing it. One of his snapshots shows Joe standing under the arch and looking up in awe, much as Thomas Jefferson had done about 160 years before when he bought the bridge and over seven hundred surrounding acres.[7]

On June 15, at the behest of Bob and Eleanor Fisher, the band played at Olean, N.Y., and made $1,700, a splendid take for one night. Darling Shops' shoe department informed the city, "While Coon-Sanders syncopates there's dance rhythm in your toes in these shoes." "Dancette pumps" were available for $5.90 a pair. How many of the area's flappers and matrons availed themselves of Darling's offer was not reported, but

Joe beneath Natural Bridge, in Virginia, early June 1931. The band played in Lexington at Washington and Lee and Virginia Military Institute. (Courtesy Special Collections, Kansas City [Mo.] Public Library.)

over sixteen hundred fans paid $1.50 each to enter the Olean State Armory to hear the Nighthawks play some of their favorite pieces, as well as the newly released "Losing You," which tenor Ted Torrey sang. According to the press, "Every number ... was done with good taste, showmanship and true sense of comedy and entertainment values." According to this same account, the band catered to both old and young, playing such brisk items as "Tiger Rag" as well as softer, crooning waltzes. The good turnout, the splendid clothes displayed, and the beautiful flowers and other "necessaries" in abundance moved a local commentator to say, "Does it SOUND like honest-to-goodness depression? Aren't we all 'kidding' ourselves just a little bit?"[8] President Hoover would have appreciated that wisp of support.

Near Olean was Rock City, another place of overwhelming natural beauty, so Joe's camera got another workout. Later, he described the area:

> One walks carefully and, suddenly comes to a dead stop on the brink of nothingness. Fissures, some of them only inches wide, and bottomless chasms. One scrambles, squirms and crawls down, ever downward, and, having reached the bottom of a pit, looks upward, and far, far above, can just discern daylight. Some of the holes are so narrow as to be inaccessible, as afore said [sic], apparently bottomless.[9]

And in downtown Olean, Joe snapped a photo of Coonie occupying the rear seat of a convertible and with a woman on each side of him, one of whom was Eleanor Fisher. Coonie's appearance reminds one of an Oriental potentate — a *portly* Oriental potentate — a very *complacent*, portly Oriental potentate. Joe later labeled the photo "Coonie has his moments." Bob and Eleanor Fisher entertained the entire band at their home.[10]

From Olean the band made a modest jump to their last stop, Union City, Pa., near Erie. There they went through the usual sightseeing, and Joe got photos of Commodore Oliver Hazard Perry's flagship, the brigantine U.S.S. *Niagara*. From Erie the Nighthawks went back to Chicago for a break—"We disbanded in Chicago," said Joe in something of a pun.[11]

Among his preparations to leave Chicago, Joe probably made a call upon Jules Stein in his office at the city's Loop. With his life reported to be insured for a million dollars, Stein decided to swear off flying, permanently. Though he had previously made great use of the airplane, Knute Rockne's recent death in a flying accident had shaken him. Well, sometimes changes were necessary, even for Stein; at about the same time that he quit the air, he installed a little red light on his telephone. He hated the harshness of the bell.[12]

The men went their several ways, but Joe was ailing and had to spend a week at the Congress to be close to Dr. Smith. Despite his illness, he had what he termed "many happy moments" with Smith and such other friends as Harold Van Ohrman and Claire Shanley. He then spent a week with Madeline at the "Old Riding Academy." Following that, they went to Kansas City for two or three days, after which he, his brother Roy, and Harry Johnston spent "two perfect weeks" at the Wheatley Camp in Joe's beloved Ozarks at Lake Taneycomo.[13]

Upon his return to Kansas City, Joe learned that their summer plans had changed. In fact, there seems to have been several changes in the band's plans that spring and early summer. For example, *Variety* reported in mid–May that they were scheduled to play again at Atlantic City's Million Dollar Pier, though they did not. They had been scheduled also to go to a place in New York named Hollywood Gardens, on Pelham Parkway, but MCA thought it so badly deteriorated physically that the agency cancelled all its bands' engagements there. Probably because of previous agreements, however, MCA's cancellations at Hollywood Gardens did not prevent Abe Lyman's Orchestra's playing there in mid–July and Ben Bernie's following him. When Bernie left, his place was taken by amateur wrestling bouts.[14]

Instead, Coon-Sanders was signed up for a two-week appearance at Lakeside Park, in Denver, Colorado. "Having never played that far west," said Joe later, "the outcome was, to us, a matter of conjecture. As is, and has been ever, our lot, we found that Lakeside was another of those 'white elephants' that had passed in review before our flying notes."[15]

The Nighthawks discovered that their old competitor Isham Jones (1894–1956) was playing in the area. Naturally this brought out Joe's competitive spirit, and with sardonic relish he referred to Jones as "the toast of Denver." "He was," said Joe, "intrenched in the 'smart' spot, Elitch Gardens. At the end of the first week, the 'toast' had become a 'moldy crust.'" According to Sanders, the Nighthawks "were a smashing sensation, much to our surprise, Selah!"[16]

Lakeside Park was rather the typical sort of amusement park with a sort of roller coaster that skirted the shore of the lake. The building in which the band played, a dance hall called El Patio, was a fairly large, substantial, but unremarkable-looking structure with a wide porch that ran across much of the front of the building. To reach the porch, one ascended a flight of stairs of at least a dozen steps. As Joe put it, this was the place "where we smashed all records, giving Isham Jones the beating of his young life."[17] (Jones was two years older than Joe.)

Since the band had never been so far west before, they took good advantage of the nearby scenic areas. Madeline was with Joe, and the two enjoyed Pikes Peak, Estes Park, Echo Lake, Troutdale-in-the-Pines, Evergreen Lake, Red Rock Park, and Bear Creek Canyon. There was even a trip to Cheyenne where Joe saw his first rodeo. On some of the outings, such as to the rodeo, Coonie accompanied Joe and Madeline. The local

El Patio, Lakeside Park, Denver, Colorado, where the band played 18–31 July 1931. (Courtesy Special Collections, Kansas City [Mo.] Public Library.)

Auburn-Cord distributor, E. J. Johnston, continued the courtesy extended by dealers to the east of lending the band members vehicles for use in the area. And Joe's automobile was often to be seen at Denver's Lakeside Country Club—"What a 19th hole I played."[18]

Some of the scenery Joe found overwhelming, but when his snapshots were returned later, he thought the photo developer of his exposures along Lookout Mountain Drive, as well as those looking at Golden, Colo., from Twin Mesas, must have been an amateur. Whoever had developed the film had almost ruined several scenes. With another couple, they ascended to Pikes Peak and made the customary stop at Glen Cove Rest House, halfway up, to let their car's motor cool. Here, said Joe, one took a deep breath, or at least as deep a breath as the altitude permitted. The "bottomless pit" near the summit impressed him deeply and moved him to conclude, "A facile way of going into permanent coma is to simply slip over the side—if you like." He also had to recognize that the area taught one "how infinitesimal one really is." Another view moved him to slip into a philosophical mood: "Limitless—Vast—What is this thing called 'Man'?" The entire trip to the summit took them two and a half hours, "not bad," he concluded, "for a plainsman," and adding, "Thrills! Shivers! Chills!" At Big Thompson Canyon Joe thought he saw an answer to the divorce problem: "An endless succession of breath-taking panoramas, each more lovely than the last! If you *could* think you no longer love your wife, drive it *with her!!!!!!*" Two more views elicited, "Was it here—or here—that I said, 'Joe, *your* wife is the loveliest of women'?"[19]

After the engagement in Denver ended, most of the band returned to Kansas City, but Joe was there only a night and a day, just long enough to see his family and get out to his country place to examine the progress of work on a bass lake. The "Advisory Board" seemed satisfied with how the work was going, including the mules—"Missouri Canaries," Joe called them—hauling away the earth.[20] Joe was familiar with Missouri's fame as a mule producing state, and he almost certainly had heard the old vaudeville quip:

> STRAIGHT MAN: Missouri stands at the head in raising mules.
> COMIC: That's the safest place to stand when fooling around with mules.[21]

It was probably at about this time that Coonie's family persuaded him to take them to Yellowstone National Park. Both Johnny Coon and his brother Carleton, Jr., still remember the trip as a delightful adventure. Before leaving Chicago, Coonie went to Abercrombie and Fitch, where he bought a rifle and a shotgun. The trip to Yellowstone took them through Rapid City, S.D., where Gutzon Borglum, who several years earlier had begun the work on the Confederate Memorial at Stone Mountain, Ga., was now working at Mount Rushmore on the memorial to four presidents. He had not been working long and Washington's face was all that the Coon family could see. They were nevertheless quite impressed. Borglum was a fan of the radio Nighthawks, and when he learned that Coonie and his family were at the visitors station, he was impressed, too, and quickly descended to meet them. The Coons spent about two hours talking with the sculptor. Coonie was surprised to learn that Borglum was working without salary and that he got only whatever contributions visitors left. The ever-generous Coonie donated a hundred dollars.[22]

After leaving Rapid City, the Coons proceeded to Yellowstone Park, where an official asked whether they had firearms. Coonie produced his two pieces, and the official put wire through the mechanisms of both weapons and sealed them. So far as John Coon ever knew, his father never fired either piece, during the trip or afterward.[23]

There are in the records hints that Joe Sanders was becoming increasingly concerned by his partner's behavior, especially what Joe regarded as Coonie's growing dependence upon alcohol. (As a drinker, Joe himself was no amateur.) It is also a matter of record that Madeline Sanders was finding Coonie annoying and at times embarrassing, though Madeline was entering a period when she herself was finding life's problems increasingly onerous. As for Coonie, it would seem that he was experiencing great spiritual and physical stress. What caused this, if indeed it was a fact, is anyone's guess. My own opinion is that part of Coonie's problem was the frequent, protracted absences from his family, especially his children. In the early years of the band, Coonie seems to have enjoyed being free of the responsibilities of family life, but perhaps in these later times he was developing an accusing conscience. If so, this could easily have caused him problems, including a greater dependence upon alcohol.

There is a touching letter that in February of 1929 Coonie typed to his oldest child, and that was among Johnny's most-prized possessions:

> My darling Sunny Boy:
> Today is your BIRTHDAY.
> Another mile-stone added to the Great Book of Life, as you travel it.
> My wish to you today—as your DAD—is that it will ever hold all the glorious and wonderful things that I am wishing in my heart of hearts for you—and that you will find the roadway a little easier, because of those who love you.
> I am mighty proud of you John—I get to thinking about you sometimes, and I feel the surge of PRIDE and ADORATION come sweeping over me—because you are such a realization of MANY DREAMS that your PRECIOUS MOTHER and I have dreamed—
> Wondered what you would be like—wondered if you would be the manly fellow that you are—wondered if you would be half the joy to us that we prayed that you might be—
> AND YOU HAVE "DELIVERED."
> So—your old Dad is pretty darned glad to shout CONGRATULATIONS to you from the house tops and wish you the loveliest returns of the day.
> I am enclosing a little check that you can use for anything that your heart desires.

> Mother tells me that you need a few little things — so here it is boy — and may you find joy and happiness in what you choose —
>
> Bye PRECIOUS SON OF MINE — and were you here I would love to crush you against my heart and look into your sweet clean boyish face and tell you that I love you better than life itself.
>
> And don't forget to always and ever live so that I can eternally be proud that you are MY VERY OWN ORIGINAL "SONNY [he had first typed SUNNY and then typed over it] BOY."
>
> EVER AND EVER—
> "Dad"[24]

I have trouble with this letter. Of course, I have seen very little that Coonie wrote and suspect, in fact, that he did not write much. (By contrast, Joe did a great deal of writing — letters, memoirs, etc. — through which one gets some definite impressions of his personality.) Therefore, it is probably risky to try to deduce much from one letter. And yet — there seems to me a sad quality about it. Was the emotion in it genuine, or was much of it just rhetoric? My inclination is to accept it as an actual expression of Coonie's feelings, and as an admission of a fear of having somehow failed his son. At any rate, and lacking anything to the contrary, I shall consider this letter to his eldest child a pathetic, heartfelt cry.

At 12:30 Sunday morning, August second, Joe left Kansas City for Illinois in his brown Cord touring car, Illinois license plate 496-552.[25] In his written recollections he says that he went *via* Louisiana, Mo. But he must have run into poor driving conditions around that little town, for he pronounced the choice of routes "an error." In these early years of his career, Sanders was often inclined to push himself and his vehicle with hard driving. Usually he got away with it, but this time perhaps his fatigue caught up with him and his luck ran out. He records that he reached Springfield at seven in the morning, quite a feat, even by his standards, for he had driven from Kansas City to Springfield in only six and a half hours. But then, as he left Springfield, he "collided heavily with another car," as he put it, adding that it was "a long story." He continued:

> Briefly, due to the long (and, in this instance, erroneous) arm of the law, I was forcibly detained until late in the day — sans sleep — sans good disposition and — finally — sans money and car. A slight error just here, for the car was hastily repaired just sufficiently to allow me to crawl along to my destination, Bloomington. En route a tire blew with violent finality and a few new cuss words were born right there in the wide open spaces.[26]

After the Bloomington engagement, Joe and a member of the band whom Sanders did not identify drove into Chicago for a meeting with Florsheim, who was not in town. Nothing seemed to be going right! Joe observed later that it ought to have made him wary about the future. He put up at the Congress, arose early the next morning, and made arrangements with the Auburn factory to pick up the car for repairs. At noon he had lunch with Jules Stein but lingered too long over it, and for the second time in his road trip history he missed the train — the "damned train," as he put it. Well, he'd be thoroughly modern and check the flight schedules. He could just make the last plane for Toledo, where the next program was scheduled, and his second time on an airplane got him to his destination on time.[27]

But the schedule for the remainder of the summer was already so flawed that the band found itself with too much "vacation," or when working, with too little to show for it. The Nighthawks played in Toledo on August 6, the next day in Columbus, and the day after in Dayton. On August 9 Joe rose early and caught the train to Auburn, Ind., where he picked up his car, and from there he made a dash for Hudson Lake, Ind., where the band was to play that evening. The next day brought a break that allowed a visit with the Auburn Company's Roy Faulkner at the latter's cottage in Lake Klinger, Mich. It was, said, Joe, a "wonderful time." On August 11 the band were in Saginaw, Mich., a place with unpleasant memories for Joe. During the months just after America's entry in the World War, when Joe was singing at the Bancroft Roof with the U.S. Four Quartette, he had been involved in what he termed "a nice bout of fisticuffs." This time Saginaw treated him better, but the visit was followed by a hard drive across Michigan to Coloma, a little town on Paw Paw Lake, where the band appeared on the twelfth. Then it was back to Chicago for an appearance on the thirteenth at the Trianon. The next day they dashed into Wisconsin for a program at Sun Prairie.[28]

Paul Karberg was there and remembered the night as warm and starry. Droves of youngsters from Madison and other nearby places, said Karberg, "made the Sun Prairie road a mighty dangerous place for frogs to be crossing." Each Nighthawk arrived at Angell Park in a brightly colored Auburn, and though each of the two leaders was expected to be driving his Cord, they arrived instead in a small, dark roadster. As Karberg puts it, "Nattily attired in blue suit coats and light, pin-striped trousers, Coon and Sanders were handsome, athletic chaps—by no means disillusioning to any admirers whose hearts they had palpitated via the loudspeaker." He goes on to describe the concert:

> A crowded pavilion, plus the Nighthawks' torrid-tunes—each begun by stomping of Joe's heel—made the temperature soar! Soon Joe and "Coonie," happy but perspiring, were coatless, tieless, and with sleeves rolled, as they alternated on vocals or blended voices in the delightful manner that had won them critical acclaim as "greatest singers in jazz."
>
> With no microphones at hand, the pianist and drummer used small megaphones through which to croon tender love ballads and to "raise the roof" with more vociferous offers as "Here Comes My Ball and Chain," "What a Girl!," "Slewfoot [sic]," "Darktown Strutters' Ball," "Georgia on My Mind," and "Cryin' for the Carolines."[29]

The fifteenth and sixteenth found them at Hartford, Wis., but next day they had another hard drive for an appearance in the evening at Maquoketa, Iowa. There followed engagements in Decatur and Mounds, Ill., on the eighteenth and nineteenth. From Mounds they headed south and on the twentieth played at Memphis, where Joe said they "broke all records," a phrase he often used and that in some cases is of uncertain accuracy.[30] There is no doubt that the Nighthawks were popular with Memphians, and it is reasonable to suppose that they did get a good reception. The South always seemed to like them, and they apparently reciprocated the affection.

MCA next scheduled them for Little Rock, Ark., where on August 21 they played for a dance and for three shows at the Arkansas Theatre, though Madeline's journal says they played for four. Madeline arrived in Little Rock on the Missouri Pacific Railroad, but her train was twenty minutes late. Mack Howard, the band's tour manager, met her and took her to her hotel. Alone in her eighth-floor room, Madeline sat down to write in her journal. She was still obviously awed by her husband's fame and often seemed unsure of her ability to perform properly as a celebrity's wife. "He is playing now—the act is on," she wrote. "My first reaction after an absence of three weeks [is] to serve him in any way possible. He is using himself up on trifles. Ordering dinner and answering phone etc." Gazing from her hotel window, she could see the theater and was thrilled by "the huge crowd trying to get in" and sensitive of the disappointment of those who had to be turned away. Well, so much for all that! She needed to get ready to receive Louise Bren, a friend who lived in Little Rock and was due to arrive soon. Furthermore, Joe was expecting her to attend the evening dance. With perhaps a shrug of resignation, she wrote, "Tho tired, I shall go."[31]

When the band arrived next day in Monroe, La., Madeline was already finding her trip tedious. And though she later concluded that Monroe seemed to appreciate the

Nighthawks more than Little Rock had, she made clear her own mood in her bald characterization of the Deep South as "Negroes and indolence and liquor."[32] The boys played at the Edgewater Nite Club from 11 to 3 a.m., for what was billed as the First Annual Harvest Time Dance. Red Guy's Orchestra preceded them for an hour and a half. The local *News-Star* gave the Nighthawks a friendly notice and promised those planning to attend that "Melodies sweet and melodies hot will predominate ... when the Coon-Sanders aggregation of internationally renowned jazzists bow to entertainment seekers and dance lovers of Edgewater Nite club." Furthermore,

> Joe Sanders and Carleton Coon are active members of their own band. Joe is the ever-smiling, blue singing fellow at the piano, while Carleton Coon, better known as "Coonie," banks [sic] away at the drums and also bursts forth in occasional vocal offerings. Therefore, the pianist and drummer are the men whose names have become a password wherever good music and satisfying entertainment values are discussed.[33]

Right after the dance, the band broke up and began heading individually for New Orleans, the city for their next engagement. If everyone took the same route, it was to drive east from Monroe, across the Mississippi River to Jackson, Miss., and then straight south. Apparently every member was driving his Auburn product—Coonie's ecru Cord, Joe and Madeline in their tan Cord, Downing in his Fauntleroy blue Auburn, Bob Pope in his black Auburn, etc. It probably was on this trip that Downing had a mishap, for he described it in later years as happening in Mississippi. (I know of no other time that the band members were in Mississippi.) That evening, apparently as he was driving in south Mississippi, Downing put too much of a strain on his battery. As he later put it, "I had everything on, spotlights, heater, radio and so on, and the car came to a stop." It was too much for the battery, but somehow he got the thing recharged and probably beat the Sanderses to New Orleans.* How the other band members made out is apparently unrecorded.[34]

Joe and Madeline, however, made their departure somewhat more leisurely. They spent the night in Monroe, sleeping until about noon, and left a short time later. Madeline was obviously uncomfortable and was suffering not only from having slept badly but also from indigestion. "Too much food or driving," she surmised. Joe, always interested in the sights along his route, decided that they needed to take a quick look at Vicksburg's national military park and cemetery, so after crossing the Mississippi River, he pulled off the road. (According to Madeline, they left Monroe about 1:45 p.m. and arrived in Vicksburg at 2 p.m., clearly impossible even today and certainly so in 1931.) As usual Joe got his snapshots—"Old Man River" seen from the heights below the city, another of Madeline standing just below the barrel of a cannon atop the bluff overlooking the river, yet another shot of the entrance to the park and cemetery, and other sights. The observation tower caught Joe's attention, so up he climbed to take more pictures, one of which shows Madeline driving the car up just below to pick him up. "Entranced by the beauty and historic glamor of this lovely park and 'city of dead heroes,'" said Joe later, "we lingered until the afternoon shadows reminded us that we had barely started." But before they could get out of Vicksburg, the car's left front tire went flat. Joe had no tools, but though it was a Sunday, they found a garage that repaired the tire, and they were off for Jackson, where they arrived, as Joe put it, "right side up." They then headed south toward the Crescent City, with its romance, lusty history, summer heat, and mosquitoes.[35]

"*Then it started!*" Joe later wrote with

---

*Downing was probably telling this in an off-hand, careless manner, for it isn't likely that he would have been running his heater in south Mississippi — in August!

Club Forest, New Orleans, Louisiana, where the band played for three weeks in August–September 1931. (Courtesy Special Collections, Kansas City [Mo.] Public Library.)

emphasis. "Oh, what roads! Loose gravel! Narrow roads! Dust clouds so thick we travelled with full driving lights on. Night came on and we were millions of miles from New Orleans." Surprisingly, however, Madeline seemed to be feeling considerably better than she had earlier. At 7:30 they stopped for what Madeline thought a good dinner. In fact, she thought it a beautiful night. Moreover, she seemed to be really enjoying their ninth wedding anniversary.* "Nothing marred our peace & happiness," she told her journal, "until at ten we met with an accident."[36]

Just over the state line in Louisiana, a little north of Roseland, Joe was steering the car through a deserted area of woods and swamps, so typical of that area and much more gothic than he cared for. It was "the most God-forsaken stretch of road" he had ever seen. Suddenly in the car's headlights Joe and Madeline saw two men walking along the roadside, on their left. One seemed to be staggering.

> Naturally thinking him very drunk, [Joe later wrote] I slowed down to avoid striking him. As we drew abreast, I saw him draw back his hand. Subconsciously I straightened in my seat to protect Madeline, from whatever was to come, and I *knew* something was coming! Then came a smashing impact and Madeline screamed! Of course I instinctively knew something heavy had been thrown! My first thought was of Madeline's eyes (she was wearing goggles). We both thanked God that her eyes had been spared! Upon checking up — still going at top speed (when I divined that something was about to happen, I *floored* the accel[er]ator), we discovered that, barring a bruise on my left shoulder and minor scratches, we were unharmed. A miracle! On the windshield appeared another miracle!

---

*See the previous discussion of the disagreement over the actual date of their marriage (page 79).

It just happened that it was our ninth anniversary! On the windshield (where a rock had hit it) appeared a perfect heart upside down. It was truly uncanny, for the windshield undoubtedly saved our faces.[37]

After racing for about a mile, they stopped, brushed off bits of broken glass, and steadied their nerves. Then, about ten miles beyond where this happened, they came upon the outskirts of Roseland, where Joe stopped for gasoline and oil. The station attendant noticed the cracked windshield and Joe told him what had happened. "You don't know how lucky you are!" exclaimed the attendant. "That section of Dismal Swamp land up there is inhabited by wild, half civilized people called the Red Necks." It was a new term to Joe and Madeline, and probably sounded to both of them like something out of a tale by Edgar Allan Poe, though Poe's characters had the grace to be fictitious. According to the station's attendant, such welcoming parties "employ a ruse to get a motorist to stop. They then rob him and, if he offers resistance, kill him. If there is a woman, she is outraged. After these indignities, the Red Necks vanish into the swamps and the law can't find them." It had been a terrifying experience, and thereafter Madeline tended to duck every time they passed anyone. Another reason for her to dislike the Deep South![38]

But New Orleans was hardly typical of the Deep South or anything else. Joe and Madeline arrived there at 1:30 Monday morning, the twenty-fourth, checked into the Jung Hotel, and, as Madeline put it, "slept furiously" until early afternoon. After taking a good look at their accommodations, they decided they didn't like them, and so moved to the Roosevelt Hotel, whose manager, Franklyn Moore, was from Kansas City. They liked their new surroundings and discovered that the hotel's famous restaurant offered a Creole gumbo that quickly became one of their favorite foods.[39]

Nor was that all the Roosevelt was famous for. There was, for instance, its Ramos gin fizz that contained gin, milk, powdered sugar, and both lemon and lime juice, as well as drops of orange-flower water over ice to provide the fizz. One of its chief advocates was none other than Louisiana's "Kingfish," Huey Pierce Long (1893–1935), formerly governor and now, in 1931, the new U.S. senator. Though now working in Washington, D.C., Long continued to control the state's politics in such a way as to suggest an American brand of fascism, but one made more bizarre by the "Kingfish's" antic personality. Though none of the band reports it, they might well have crossed paths with Long, who, according to Garry Boulard, regarded the Roosevelt Hotel as his "home away from home." (Long would have loved the Nighthawks. Too bad they never met.) And across the street from the Roosevelt was the 1-2-3 Club, one of the city's gambling establishments. Its owner, and owner as well of the Roosevelt, was Long's friend Seymour Weiss, not related to Karl Weiss who ended Long's career four years later.[40]

By coincidence, the Sanderses occupied the suite at the Roosevelt that had recently been vacated by Abe Lyman, whose orchestra had just closed. Madeline liked it and felt settled, but this recent presence of another band leader was certain to raise Joe's blood pressure and his competitive instinct. (Joe couldn't resist stating later that "our opening was bigger than Abe Lyman's.") Later in the afternoon he contacted the other band members and held rehearsals for the evening's program, the first of a three-week engagement at Club Forest, and the Nighthawks' sole commitment in the Crescent City. Madeline sent Joe flowers to celebrate his opening.[41]

According to *Variety*, the nightclubs and roadhouses in New Orleans that summer were engaged in "hot rivalry." Club Forest had started it by engaging name bands. First there was Abe Lyman and then Coon-Sanders. Suburban Gardens countered with Vincent Lopez. The two clubs went to considerable trouble to advertise in local newspapers, buying ads larger than those of any of the city's cinemas. Each establishment offered a gambling casino as well as a floor show, and neither had a cover charge. Club Forest had a slight advantage in that Suburban Gardens was situated a mile farther out, but the latter was doing quite well. The Gardens seemed to be more attractive to the younger crowd, to whom it catered by giving the youngsters, as *Variety* put it, "more leeway ... that is always evident in their long, loud, noisome whopee-making [sic]."42

Joe liked Club Forest and thought it a beautiful building and location, not the "white elephant" he so often complained about. The show's advertisement in the *New Orleans States* reminded the public that Club Forest was twenty degrees cooler, because it was "cooled by iced air," an important amenity in New Orleans during any August. But Joe had been warned that he might find it difficult to follow Abe Lyman — "We were expected to 'lay a huge egg,'" he reported. In addition, appearing at the same time in New Orleans as the Nighthawks were Louis Armstrong and Vincent Lopez. As for Lopez, Joe's comment was the relatively mild "our second meeting and his second licking." Joe and the band were hardly inclined to doubt their musical prowess, and in Joe's words, "We stepped right out and 'busted hell' out of all existing records." On the same show were Grace Hayes, Broadway musical comedy star; the McCue sisters, singers and dancers; and George McQueen, a popular Southern master-of-ceremonies. The band started playing at 9 and finished at 3 a.m., four on Saturdays and Sundays. It was a fearsome schedule, but the boys were used to it and apparently enjoyed such exquisite torture. Nothing that one really enjoys doing is work. The club was always packed, and no one got in without reservations.43

Paying special compliments to Joe's singing and Coonie's "clowning," the *New Orleans Item* cited the Nighthawks' sparkling twelve-year history — their success on radio and at Chicago's dancing and dining places, and the orchestra's stable membership. The paper told its readers also that Coon-Sanders was scheduled in the fall to begin a long engagement with the Hotel New Yorker, that city's newest fine hotel.44

The *New Orleans States*, while saying that Grace Hayes was the "greatest sensation of the new show," nevertheless had good things to say about the band:

> Monday night was marked with the opening of the Coon-Sanders organization at Club Forest before a capacity crowd and the most enthusiastic reception ever offered at the resort greeted them and the other talent offered. The first-nighters found an excellent dance band that lived up to the expectations developed as they had been heard in radio broadcasts since the days of the Kansas City Nighthawks at WDAF during the pioneering days of radio development.
>
> Carleton Coon and Joe Saunders [sic] offered their distinctive personalities at the drums and piano respectively and the nimble fingers of Sanders on the keys brought much comment. The leading pair offered the comedy and novelty[,] and sang, in addition to their instrumental efforts. The band numbers consisted mostly of straight dance music.45

By contrast, the New Orleans *Times-Picayune* seemed to pay less attention to the Nighthawks. It gave rather perfunctory notice of their appearance in the city, and the city's entire press seemed to regard Vincent Lopez's engagement as more important. If this observation is correct, it must have galled Sanders. Moreover, it would have been one of several indications that the Nighthawks were experiencing a change of fortune in their final year.

A three-week engagement gave the band's members an unusual amount of free time, and they took advantage of it in one of the world's most interesting cities. Unfortunately, we don't have much information about where the other members spent their leisure time in New Orleans, and not much about Coonie's activities there, but both Joe and Madeline have left a number of accounts. Joe, for instance, was much impressed by the gambling facilities — "the finest I've seen"— and of course was busy with his camera. He liked the views from their hotel suite and got several on film.[46]

Most of the Sanderses' sightseeing consisted of moving about the French Quarter, going into shops, snapping pictures, dining — the usual things tourists do there. But Joe did it with intelligent curiosity, for Joe was a better-informed and more systematic observer than the average tourist. And since his interest in New Orleans was largely confined to the Vieux Carré — i.e., the "Old Square" or French Quarter — he could, on foot and without any great exertion or travel, cram quite a lot of investigation and photography into a relatively short time.

The Sanderses seem to have begun in the Quarter at Canal and Royal streets, at the Merchants' Exchange at 126 Royal. Then they moved on to buildings connected with such historical figures as filibusterer and adventurer William Walker (1824–1860), pirate Jean Lafitte (1780–1825?), and chess genius Paul Morphy (1837–1884). All the while he kept his camera busy and took many notes. The courtyard of Morphy's house, with its "lovely old lantern," particularly interested him; and he got two good pictures of it, one of which shows Madeline ("my Mama") standing in the center. At the Spanish Arms patio, 616 Royal, he was forbidden to take pictures, but he surreptitiously managed one, from the street, of the archway and the patio beyond. He admired and photographed the famous fence at 915 Royal, erected in 1834, whose wrought iron represents corn and wheat. And he observed the visitation sites of such literary figures as William Thackeray, Mark Twain, O. Henry, and Lafcadio Hearn. The Old Orleans Theatre, once the site of "famous quadroon balls," reminded Joe of a song from his childhood, one called "My Pretty Quadroon" that he remembered hearing his parents sing. "How well I recall those idyllic kid days, after dinner, Mother's lovely soprano blending with Dad's rich tenor to the accompaniment of Dad's old Gibson guitar (*best* to this day), I lying on the grass, head against Mother's knee, lazily wondering, '*What is* a quadroon?'"[47]

Joe seems to have taken many more photos in New Orleans than he did anywhere else. At any rate, there are far more photos of New Orleans in his scrapbook than from any other single city. "I can truthfully say," he explained, "that New Orleans is the most interesting city I have ever visited, surpassing even Boston in color, tradition and historical interest." And when, on the way to Barataria,* he discovered an old black man singing and strumming a guitar, Joe snapped his picture and quipped, "Now I know where [Rudy] Vallee, [Bing] Crosby, and [Russ] Columbo started their bleating careers."[48] As far as his description of his sightseeing is concerned, this was probably as close as Joe came to an examination of New Orleans' black music. If he visited any of the city's places where jazz was played, there is nothing about it in his written account of those three weeks. And his only reference to Louis Armstrong, who was appearing in New Orleans' Suburban Gardens at that time, was that this famous jazz artist was some of the Nighthawks' competition.[49] Unfortunately, except for a few brief comments about Coonie, I have never seen any records about where the other Coon-Sanders members went while in New Orleans; but it is difficult, even in light of racial attitudes of that day, to believe that all of them failed to take advantage of this magnificent opportunity to hear jazz played in its birthplace.

A new friend, Pardue Geren, whom Joe described as a "scion of a fine aristocratic old Southern family," helped them see New Orleans to better advantage. Their car had been repaired and was returned to them Tuesday, the twenty-fifth, which allowed them to get about the city and to nearby places. At one

---

*The Baratarian coast south of New Orleans had been the realm of the pirate Jean Lafitte, who from 1810 to 1814 used it to prey on shipping, mostly Spanish. He aided Andrew Jackson at the Battle of New Orleans, 9 January 1815.

Joe (left) and brother Roy, whom Joe idolized. Time and place unidentified. (Courtesy Special Collections, Kansas City [Mo.] Public Library.)

point they lost their way, exited the French Quarter unawares, and thus went on to see more distant places such as the old Spanish fort — "Rather dumb but one of the sights," wrote Madeline in her journal. (Clearly Madeline was not so enthusiastic a tourist as Joe was.) That evening Coonie — Madeline called him simply "Coon" — entertained Joe and Madeline at Arnaud's Restaurant. After Coonie and Joe left for Club Forest, Madeline saw a movie starring Charles "Chic" Sale.[50]

The next day, Wednesday the twenty-sixth, was very rainy. Madeline breakfasted alone downstairs, and later a piano was brought in for Joe. On Thursday the two of them got an early start to see the Quarter and took "loads of pictures." They stopped for refreshments at a tearoom, where Madeline thought the tea-reader "pretty clever." "To see everything here, one must walk," she observed, though on Friday, with a man from the garage helping them with directions, they used the Cord to see some sights farther away, among them parks and the beautiful homes. Dinner took them again to Arnaud's. Madeline later recorded in her journal that since it was "fish day," they tried the pompano. Joe didn't much care for it, and Madeline concluded that they both preferred fried catfish.[51]

On Saturday the two went through the old St. Louis Street Cemetery, where in addition to taking many snapshots, they provided sustenance for the mosquitoes. The remarkable feature of the cemetery is that tombs are above the ground to protect bodies from the area's high water level. Having heard that some tombs were broken and that remains were visible, Madeline and Joe searched in vain for one such tomb and had to get the caretaker to take them to one.

"Sure enough," Madeline recorded, "there was a skull & bones of a body." She declared it "rather gruesome to see," and Joe observed poetically, "Tho utter moldy silence prevails, these tombs seem alive."[52]

Later, Coonie bought Madeline a huge bouquet, which perhaps made them feel it necessary to invite him to dinner. While they dined, Coonie persuaded Madeline to go out to see the show at Club Forest; so at 11 p.m. she took a cab out to the club and barely managed to get in. She had to share a table with Grace Hayes, the musical comedy star who was also mistress-of-ceremonies. After the show ended at 4 a.m., Madeline met several other persons, but complained that she couldn't remember them very well. "The bourbon is plenty strong down here," she explained. (One almost wonders why anyone bothered to repeal the Eighteenth Amendment.) She and Joe got back to their hotel by 6 a.m.[53] Though Joe still seemed to thrive on such a schedule, Madeline makes it clear in her personal records that she did not.

Sunday, August 30, was rather slow and gave them a chance to get some rest. And though next day the Nighthawks crossed swords with the local music union for not filing their contracts with them, it proved not to be a serious problem.[54] There were, however, union problems between both Suburban Gardens and Club Forest and the musicians' union. By the end of August, the American Federation of Musicians notified musicians playing at both places not to render services after giving the customary two weeks' notice.[55]

Madeline remained in New Orleans for the three weeks the band was there. It was probably on September 12 that Joe took her to the railroad station for her return to Kansas City, where she arrived on the thirteenth and had dinner with her parents.[56] Joe had already said goodbye to such friends as Pardue "Duca" Geren and his wife. Then, after their last performance and their goodbyes to everyone at Club Forest, the band left the city. With Mack Howard as a passenger, Joe set out northward in his Cord.

But the primitive road conditions of the day, as well as the dearth of good directional aids, made Joe miss an important turn. Instead of heading for Jackson, Miss., Joe discovered soon that he was on the road to Baton Rouge. He got back on the right road, but then, trying to make up lost time, he drove too fast and landed in a ditch. Though neither he nor Howard was hurt, the car had some minor damage. Finally, as Joe put it, they pulled into Memphis "after dinner [and] sans scars." They got a good night's sleep, but since the ditch accident necessitated some repairs to the car, they did not get away from Memphis until just before noon. Then they set out for Milwaukee, the place of the Nighthawks' next engagement, and had to drive the last three hundred miles in heavy fog, which, said Joe, "forced standing-on-running board driving." Nevertheless, they reached Milwaukee at 1:30 a.m. and put up at the Hotel Schroeder. The day of their arrival was very likely Tuesday, the fifteenth. Their two-week engagement at the Schroeder Hotel would start the next day.[57]

And with another of those coy statements that Joe sometimes teasingly throws into his memoirs, he said, "A shock or two awaited me there which must necessarily be deleted from these pages." It seems likely that the problem was simply that Joe did not like to play in the middle of the day, and the hotel expected them to do so. And they did, and at the dinner hour and late into the evening, as well. But whoever heard of Nighthawks playing in midday? Joe probably wondered. He didn't like it and growled that it "did not serve to soothe our nerves." (He would again be annoyed by noon commitments when they got to the Hotel New Yorker in October.) They were very happy when their engagement ended, though the band apparently had been well received. Their success, grumbled Sanders, had come in spite of "the hotel's von Hindenburg methods." Whatever the cause of Joe's annoyance at the Hotel Schroeder, he summed it up with, "The least said about the Schroeder, the best."[58]

They broadcast at noon while at the Schroeder, over local station WTMJ, and on Saturdays from about midnight to as late as 2:30 Sunday morning. It was a typical dine-and-dance situation that came ironically while the local press ran an article about the dangers of such dining. It quoted T. Swann Harding as saying "that harsh, fast music of the jazz type" was not good for digestion. Furthermore, said Harding, "The highly emotional stimulus of dancing between the courses of a meal, as now is popular in many restaurants, must be even more dangerous." Perhaps the slower tempos that the *Milwaukee Journal* heralded would help that situation: "We're in for a season of slower dance music and sentimental songs," said the *Journal's* writer, "with still less dissonant jazz, more rhythmic melodies and many lyrics of the semi-ballad type."[59]

Now it was on to four brief appearances, a short vacation, and then their New York commitment, the latter of which was to prove unhappy for several of the band. Joe thought it unwise to take his estimable Cord to New York—"Allah be praised!" he later said. Instead, he "sold" it back to the Auburn Company, and they picked it up in Chicago. At Lake Klinger, Mich., Sanders managed to spend a brief time with his friend Roy Faulkner, and while there drove a speed boat for the first time. At Starved Rock, Ill., Coonie, Eula Coon, Joe, Mack Howard, and Mickey Rockford cavorted, enjoyed the beautiful scenery, and got more photographs. Calling them David and Goliath, Joe got two shots of Coonie and Mickey as if in combat, and so posed as to emphasize Coonie's much greater size.[60]

En route to their commitment at the Hotel New Yorker, they played at four towns: Waukegan, Ill., on September 30; Springfield, Ohio, on October 1; Franklin, Pa., on the second; and Olean, N.Y., on the third. The 1930–1931 road tour that had begun in December, must have been an exhausting experience, but it had been, on the whole, a successful one. It was also their last. The entire band were probably happy to see the summer end, and they doubtless relished the prospect of a long run in New York City. Though they didn't know it, their engagement in Olean, N.Y., on October 3 was the last of their famous "one-nighters." And the long engagement at the New Yorker would be Coon-Sanders' antepenultimate gig.

Stein's Music Corporation of America had arranged a booking for the Nighthawks to start in October at Manhattan's new Hotel New Yorker, Thirty-fourth Street and Eighth Avenue. Over a year before, Joe had told Anne Steward, of *Radio Digest*, that the reason the band had never gone to New York was that they liked Chicago and that the city had been very good to them. "We don't want to go away," he had told her. Well, going to New York need not have involved leaving Chicago for very long, but this engagement would last about six months and may even have been originally intended for longer. According to *Variety*, Coon-Sanders had deliberately avoided New York and "not long ago" had turned down an offer from the Pennsylvania Hotel.[61]

The several members of the band began arriving in New York at least as early as October fourth, the day that Joe himself arrived. Madeline would arrive a bit later. He went at once to the New Yorker, checked in, and dined in his room with Rocco Vocco and Mack Howard. He spent a good bit of the evening—he called it a "wild evening"—teaching Rocco how to play three-cushion billiards. At some point in the afternoon or evening Sanders wandered down to have a look at the Terrace Room to get some idea of what their working conditions would be. He spied Eddie Cantor sitting alone. Cantor, one of many popular entertainers in Kansas City in the early Twenties, had starred for the past several years in several Ziegfeld shows, and recently had repeated his stage role in the film version of *Whoopee*. Now he had his own radio show on CBS. Joe walked over and spoke to Cantor, who graciously predicted that the Nighthawks ought to go over well. On Monday, the fifth, Joe and

Rocco took in a World's Series baseball game, Joe's first.[62]

The band opened in the Terrace Restaurant on Wednesday night, October 7, and the crowds showed that New York had been waiting a long time for this opportunity. According to surviving records, the band was a sellout, with everyone who amounted to anything in the music business in attendance. On the following day, the New Yorker's ad proclaimed, "Coon-Sanders Win!" "Yes, sir!" gushed the hotel's advertisement, "Coon-Sanders and their gay Nighthawks orchestra have New Yorkers going around in circles! Literally going around in cirlces ... utterly delighted at the brand new way these boys have of making them dance. Wild, thrilling rhythms, like nothing you ever heard before...."[63] Of course, it was to the Hotel New Yorker's advantage to be enthusiastic about their new band, but this accords quite well with other sources. As Karl Kramer observed, this good turnout and the equally good ones in the following months were an indication of the drawing power that this band still had, especially now that there were far more good bands than there had been only three or four years earlier. And while he thought they were still one of the best bands, it is significant that he now said "top ten" rather than one of the top four or five. His slight reticence was an indication that the Nighthawks were on the verge of having to change their style or be regarded by many in the music business as old fashioned.[64]

But not yet. It really was a spectacular turnout for the band's New York debut, despite Joe's suggestion that some of the audience had doubts about their success. He later recorded his impressions of the celebrities who had attended:

> Every big name was present.... Rudy Vallee and his exotic (if somewhat artificial) new wife, Russ Columbo, Morton Downey, Bing Crosby, Bing Crosby's brother [probably Everett], Mr. [and] Mrs. Jess Crawford, Irene Bordoni, good old Dudley Wilkinson, the Lombardos, Abe Lyman, Kate Smith, Dorothy Fields, Benny Davis, Harry Richman, Belle Baker, Freddie Rich, Ed Schueing (N.B.C. president), Eddie Cantor, [Dave] Rubinoff, Bert Lown (the first New York leader to cross the floor and wish us well), Vincent Lopez,* Lillian Roth, Al Katz, Marty Hackett (Lord, Thomas & Logan), Ralph Wonders (artist bureau of C.B.S.) and many other nationally famous artists. Despite the apparent success of the opening, I am convinced that we were not acceeded [sic] a chance. As a matter of fact, many predicted that we could not last over three weeks. The gentlemen of the press (present at the opening) were very fair, if not enthusiastic. Nick Kenny, Walter Winchell, Mark Hellinger, Louis Sobol, Jerry Wald, et al., were most complimentary, if a bit vague.[65]

Nevertheless, despite all this public display of support, and the bonhommie and praise from many in the audience, Joe was dubious and uneasy. Some of his disquiet centered on his growing anxiety about his partner. "Coonie," grumbled Joe, "celebrated the opening by becoming most unmistakeably [sic] drunk." "It was evident that my partner was going to be a decided liability. The 'bottle' was finally claiming him for its own and I could see a definite and final break hovering in the offing." Later, "in the most welcome sanctuary of my own room," as Joe put it, he fretted over the evening's performance and was uncertain about the band's "ultimate success" in the city. Moreover, he said he had discovered "to my amazement, that I was already lonesome for my beloved Chicago."[66] He apparently did not communicate these dark musings to the other members of the band, but Joe's misgivings clearly boded no good for the few remaining months left to the Nighthawks. Joe's state of mind was also going to create headaches for Jules Stein and the Music Corporation of America.

Joe's negative impressions, his sometimes abrasive manner toward others, and

---

*Joe must have been thrilled to see Lopez there.

his moody periods soon started to sour the band's relations with the hotel's management. In the first place, Sanders seemed to regard the present engagement as just one more of the band's dealings with a string of what he always called "white elephants." He said that "many fine bands had, in the parlance of the profession, 'laid' a remarkable assorted sequence of 'omelettes' in the Terrace Room." "So often," he continued, "had we been called in, as musical specialists, to cure the ills of sick cafes, that this phase failed to strike terror within our hearts." He saw the Nighthawks in this instance, as in previous ones, rather as "a good honest doctor" undertaking to "revive a stricken patient." It was just another assignment "to do the impossible." But, Joe gloomily concluded, "Only a handful of old friends believed in us, among them Joe Stool, Rocco Vocco, Walter Donovan and Willie Horowitz."[67]

Despite Joe's serious misgivings, it would appear that the other band members, as well as the hotel's management, were pleased with the way things were going. Except for Saturdays and holidays, there was no cover charge at dinner, though after 10 p.m. there was a charge of one dollar. It is somewhat remarkable that the Nighthawks, or any other band, managed to maintain their drawing power in a society that was about to enter the third year of a severe financial recession that was quickly becoming a depression with a capital D. Young Johnny Coon, a freshman back at the University of Kansas, had asked his father to let him know at once how the opening had gone. Very quickly a telegram arrived at Johnny's Sigma Nu House with the words, "We picked the kiss out of them." Johnny thought that his father's witticism would make an excellent title for a book about the Nighthawks.[68] I decided not to use it.

And yet, Harvey Rettberg, who recalls listening by radio to the Nighthawks at the New Yorker, says that the band found their situation somewhat inhibiting and that they were unable to do many of the things they had done on previous engagements. For one thing, they weren't allowed to take requests, and Joe had to be more restrained in his announcing. Rettberg says that their style changed, partly because Joe almost ceased arranging. Instead, he bought arrangements or let a young fellow named Joe Keet do his arranging.[69] This alone would have created a different sound, for Joe's arrangements gave the band distinction.

In addition to all this, Joe had personnel problems. Elmer Krebs, either for personal reasons or perhaps because he had begun to sense imminent problems of morale, decided to go back to his home in Milwaukee, Wisconsin. There is just a hint of resentment about this in Joe's comment made after Coonie's death: "I corrected the one glaring weakness of the band — the tuba. Pat Pattison, who had been a member only because of Krebs' sudden decision to devote his time to the selling of potato salad and pretzels, was released. Two men 'tried out' for the position and my selection, Wilbur (Eddie) Edwards, has, to date, proved a most happy one." Edwards' increasing use of string bass, instead of tuba or sousaphone, was another indication of changing styles in music. The other problem with band membership was the one between Joe and Coonie. Rettberg believes all of these problems affected their music, and that it was inferior to that of just a short while before.[70]

The band had two recording sessions in New York for Victor, one on March 9 and the other on the twenty-fourth. In the first session, for which Joe did the vocals, they recorded "Lo and Behold," "Let That Be a Lesson to You," "What a Life!" and "Sing a New Song." In his 1961 interview with Harvey Rettberg, Joe charges Coonie with inexcusable absences from these recording sessions. In fact, he said that he had to do all the vocals, an assertion not completely correct. Coonie sang the lyrics for the very last record the band made, "On Revival Day." The other recordings in that last session for Victor were "'Round My Heart," "Keepin' out of Mischief, Now," "I Know You're Lying," and "I

Want to Go Home." Another number, "Give Her a Kiss for Me," was rejected for issuance. Rettberg insists that the recordings made in these two sessions just "didn't sound like the old band."[71] To some extent I think he's right, but only a purist such as Harvey would quibble about those delightful final recordings. I must confess, however, to hearing as much of the Thirties as the Twenties in some of them. But, after all, it now *was* the Thirties.

Variety's reviewer spoke well of these last discs by Coon-Sanders, observing that, like George Olsen's orchestra, the Nighthawks had been "prolifically recording." They were, said the reviewer, "all in the same brisk Coon-Sanders manner. The boys sock out their stepology in decisive tempos, with Joe Sanders per usual vocalizing."[72]

It was at about this time that Coon-Sanders was reported by *Variety* as being under suspicion, by the American Society of Composers, Authors & Publishers, of having violated the "tie-in" ruling by the society seven months before. The allegation was that the band, at the Hotel New Yorker, would not play any song requested by a composer or publisher unless paid for it. The article said nothing more about that matter, nor have I seen any subsequent information on the subject. That may perhaps be taken as evidence that the charge was not substantiated.[73]

Variety at this same time suggested that perhaps the most common example of musical "plugs" was that of theme songs, most of which were old, non-selling numbers. Night after night, consistently, orchestras repeated the songs, a practice that, said *Variety*, "so far as its commercial value is concerned, is more or less wasted." If all that effort had been expended on new songs, said the weekly, it would almost assure their popularity. To illustrate the point, *Variety* printed a long list of many bands' current themes, including Paul Whiteman's "Rhapsody in Blue," Coon-Sanders' "My Paradise," and Ben Bernie's three alternating ones, "Lonesome Old Town," "One of Us Was Wrong," and "Pleasant Dreams." Guy Lombardo's Orchestra had not yet become associated with "Auld Lang Syne," but used rather another equally old Scottish strathspey to another Robert Burns poem "Comin' Thro' the Rye."[74]

At the same time that *Variety* took notice of the "tie-in" charge against Coon-Sanders, it reported the first actual charge by ASCAP of such a violation. It was against class-A ASCAP members Robbins Music Publishers and songwriters Fred E. Ahlert and Roy Turk. The charge was that Robbins was publishing more than six songs (not identified in the news item) that cut in radio artists as co-writers. Ahlert and Turk were accused of having cut in Bing Crosby, the popular singer with the Columbia Broadcasting Company, as a co-author of "Where the Blue of the Night Meets the Gold of the Day." (Sigmund Spaeth, a pretty careful authority on popular American Songs, credits Crosby's co-authorship.) Bing Crosby was using the number as his "signature," but ASCAP denied that Crosby had had any part in writing it. ASCAP said that Robbins admitted to having made such attributions in the past, but excused itself by saying that other companies were doing it, as well. A class-A publisher such as Robbins, if convicted, would have lost about $25,000, a figure based on the previous year's income by a publisher in that category. "Songwriters, under the non-participating clause," said *Variety*, "would lose about $3,000 on last year's basis."[75]

On a more positive note, this same *Variety* that had for years been damning radio as a bane to the music industry now had to admit that radio was providing at least one benefit. Whereas a new song once took months before its success could be established *via* phonograph recording or the vaudeville stage, it was now possible, with radio's "quick public reactions," to do so quickly and economically. The entertainment weekly estimated that in earlier times between $5,000 and $20,000 might easily have been invested in testing a new song, and the money was a gamble. The song publishers, in an effort to recoup some of their losses, often used "artificial stimulation" to unload turkeys. By 1930, songs often weren't actually published until they were already on their way to popularity. Another saving that radio had brought was that instead of maintaining publishers' offices in many cities throughout the nation, there now were but two, New York and Chicago. In smaller places the business was handled by traveling representatives. And vaudeville actors, once so important to publishers and so welcomed by them, were by the end of the Twenties hard-pressed to get attention.[76]

Of course, the great complaint in the music industry, and one that had long been made very vocal by *Variety*, was the free use by radio of copyrighted music. There had been over the past decade much discussion, grumbling, and theorizing on the matter; but by the spring of 1932 there seemed to be some real progress toward a solution. On April 19, *Variety* announced that, as ASCAP had already notified all radio stations in the nation, effective June first, the new license fees would be activated. The charge would be five percent of a station's annual income. And since ASCAP reckoned that during the previous year, radio had grossed about $60,000,000, that would mean a payment of $3,000,000 from radio, plus nearly $1,000,000 from the sustaining music licenses, or a total of about $4,000,000. This would be more than four times what ASCAP had received the previous year, namely $900,000. It was assumed that the major share of payment would be on the networks. As for the sustaining rate for each station, in addition to the five percent surcharge for commercials, it would be based on the station's power, wavelength, location, and number of listeners within a certain radius.[77]

According to Rettberg, Victor's recording director, Eddie King, was "dictatorial." It was he who decided what recordings Coon-Sanders would make, just as he had done with Jean Goldkette's and other orchestras. (Rettberg is indignant that King "took a dim view of Bix [Beiderbecke].") The Nighthawks found King's lack of humor and imagination extremely irritating, and they decided to get even with him at the first opportunity. It was entirely by accident that one of the band dropped a mute during a recording session, but King was annoyed. So — the "accidents" continued, and the harried director's smoldering ire burst into flame. At some point King, realizing that he was being deliberately baited, rushed out of the studio, quickly returned with a pillow, laid it at the feet of the offender, and snarled, "Let the mute fall on the pillow — *or else!*"[78]

The hotel kept praising the Nighthawks in glowing advertisements. And perhaps advertisements weren't entirely unnecessary; for this was, after all, New York and there was a lot of competition. *The Band Wagon*, for example, starred Fred and Adele Astaire, and Al Jolson was appearing in *The Wonder Bar*. Those so inclined could enjoy an array of good vaudeville, drama, and musical comedy, and jazz aficionados were still making their way uptown to Harlem. For those who wished to do more than listen passively, the city always offered a good choice of dance orchestras. Rudy Vallee and his Connecticut Yankees, for instance, were appearing at the Hotel Pennsylvania. Hardly anyone ever suggested that Vallee had a great orchestra, certainly not one of the caliber of the Nighthawks, though it was popular and did draw good crowds.

But the Nighthawks continued to be well received and untroubled by their competition. "The band gained steadily in popularity," said Joe, "and we were soon doing the business of the town — we had 'arrived' on Broadway, or, to speak correctly, west of Broadway." Joe rather gloated that "we went serenely on our way, mystifying those who had predicted for us a quick exodus, breaking all records giving Lombardo (at the Roosevelt) a sound licking and utterly annihilating Vallee (our closest competition) at the Pennsylvania."[79] Jules Stein and the MCA might have pursed their lips at that comment about Lombardo.

Sometimes the Nighthawks managed to get out to hear some of their competition and to enjoy much of the city's superabundance of entertainment. Dan Schroeder speaks of how the band often went out on the town, especially to those places with good orchestras. Cab Calloway, for instance, was playing up in Harlem. He had long been a Nighthawks fan and said that Joe's singing had influenced his own. And the Nighthawks were equally admirers of Calloway's orchestra and peculiar style of singing.[80]

Johnny Coon remembered hearing his father speak about Jean Harlow (1911–1937), a sultry platinum blonde actress who arrived in New York to publicize a new film while Coon-Sanders was at the New Yorker. Since the hotel was new and popular, that's where the slinky blonde decided to put up. Upon entering the lobby to register, Harlow noticed a nearby poster that announced the Coon-Sanders Orchestra. *Carleton Coon!* Why, that was the guy who had married her mother's friend Eula Jenkins! This required investigation. Harlow sashayed into the Terrace Restaurant, picked a table where she could be fairly safe from distractions, and proceeded to write a note to Coonie telling him she'd like to meet him. The other members of the band were fully aware of all this activity and noticed especially the dress that Harlow was wearing. What was more to the point, they concluded, after studying the matter carefully, that the dress and shoes were apparently *all* she was wearing. They noticed also that at every intermission, Coonie went over to speak with her.[81] But Eula Coon apparently never learned about Coonie's momentary distraction, nor need she have worried if she had. It was apparently harmless.

But Coonie had already received his comeuppance sometime before in Chicago. On most days when she was in town, Eula simply joined Coonie for meals wherever he was playing; for he rarely ate dinner at home, except on Sundays. At the Blackhawk she usually took her seat at a table fairly near the bandstand. Eula was an attractive woman, and on one occasion at the Blackhawk a man, somewhat older than she, arrived and began to make overtures to her. He tried to make chitchat and even asked her to dance. Coonie immediately noticed it and went down to suggest to the fellow that he find, not better, but *other* objects for his attention. Everything turned out happily, however, when Eula and Coonie found the fellow to be well-intentioned and amiable. Indeed, it was Dr. William Scholl,* the physician and podiatrist. The three of them became close friends, and Scholl in later years became famous and wealthy from his business of selling podiatric supplies. He often sent them expensive gifts from his travels, and died a bachelor at the age of eighty-eight.[82]

On Wednesday, October 21, Joe's spirits got a boost, for at noon Madeline arrived at Grand Central Station on the *Commodore Vanderbilt*. He and Mack Howard were about a minute late in meeting her, which gave her a brief moment of anxiety. In the taxi to the New Yorker, Madeline was awed by the crowded streets, the fast-moving vehicles, and all the various sights that Joe was trying to point out to her. She thought it all looked jumbled and very much like Chicago. Joe escorted her up to his room, 2109; but construction on that floor made everything look unattractive. They therefore moved to suite 3909–10, much more pleasing accommodations, where they lived until they moved to an apartment — "I do miss my good cooking," Madeline said.[83]

The rest of the day they did little but rest. The management sent flowers up to Madeline, and the assistant manager, a Mr. Schneider, called to ask whether everything was satisfactory. Joe and Madeline dined alone, probably in the hotel's dining room,

---

*William Mathias Scholl (1882–1968), famous for his Foot-Eazer arch supports and his campaigning for standardization of shoe sizes. Many often express surprise that "Dr. Scholl" was not just a trade name but an actual person.

A very ample Coonie, with female chaperones, Olean, New York, 3 October 1931. On Coonie's left is Eleanor Fisher, who with husband Bob, was instrumental in bringing the band to Olean. Others unidentified. (Courtesy Special Collections, Kansas City [Mo.] Public Library.)

since Madeline mentioned enjoying the music. They received several phone calls from friends, including Dorothy Lingham, though one from Donald Blair failed to reach them. On Saturday, Mack Howard took Madeline to the *Ziegfeld Follies* where, seated on the front row, she could closely observe Harry Richman, the master of ceremonies. Afterward, Howard took her to Richman's club, where George Olsen's* orchestra was playing. She was awed by the presence of so many celebrities. Though they stayed until 3 a.m., Joe never arrived. Many women would have been delightfully dazzled by all this exposure to New York's nightlife, but Madeline was not. To her it was, at best, like an ordinary night in Chicago.[84] A quiet evening with her husband, with perhaps one or two close friends, was Madeline's conception of a charming way to pass the time. Obviously, dashing madly about mad Manhattan was not.

Joe and Madeline woke up late the next day, Sunday, October 25. Apparently Billy Goodheart, from M.C.A., had breakfast with them, and he and Joe talked about what Madeline called simply "the audition that was to have been today." She doesn't explain what it was for, but her phrasing implies that it was cancelled. Afterward, she and Joe walked about town. Joe bought some hats, probably at Madeline's urging, since she insisted he needed them. Later, while Joe prepared for a broadcast from 6:15 to 6:45, Madeline dressed and had dinner, apparently alone. While dining she saw, and spoke with, a number of persons, some of whom she recognized, such as the Nighthawks' former

---

*George Olsen (1893–1971) had one of the most popular and successful orchestras in the 1920s. I had the pleasure of dining with him in 1969 at his restaurant in Paramus, N.J., and observed at one point, "Mr. Olsen, you had a very good orchestra." He corrected me: "We had a hell of a good orchestra!"

tour manager Dudley Wilkinson. There was present also the wife of the composer Benny Davis. Though she doesn't say, Madeline might have met her when the Nighthawks were in Atlantic City in 1925 and Joe and Benny Davis collaborated on songs. Another person she met, apparently for the first time, was Joe's new arranger, Joe Keet, dining with his wife. Madeline thought Keet a "nice kid." Mack Howard then took her to see *Singin' the Blues*, which she pronounced "fair." Afterward, she returned home, did some reading, and then turned in — to be awakened by Joe who "popped in" at midnight. "I never know when he'll be in," she tartly told her journal. Joe ordered sandwiches and milk, which caused Madeline to fear that so much late eating was going to make her "get fat as a butterball."[85]

Though there was much in New York that Madeline found interesting, it is quite clear that she became increasingly unhappy there. A few days later, probably on Saturday the thirty-first, she and Joe had "breakfast" with Dudley Wilkinson, who later took her to the Palace Theater and left her on her own. She walked over two miles after leaving the theater and shopped at Saks Fifth Avenue, Altman's, and some other stores, rather pleased that she was at last getting some familiarity with at least a little of Manhattan. But she spent so much time shopping that she had to rush back to the hotel to dress for dinner. And that wasn't all. "Joe was a little cross," she said, "because he told me something three times and I wasn't listening." It gave her her "first spell of the blues." She spent the evening upstairs, apparently alone, even though Marquette and Mack Howard had invited her to go with them to the Hollywood Club. She just wasn't in the mood for it and promised to do it some other time. Besides, she had found it unsettling to hear that chorus girls at the Hollywood Club danced in the nude. When Joe arrived at midnight, he found her trying to get control of his newspaper clippings, though they seemed to be engulfing her. Joe apparently went back out but later returned with Mack Howard and some sandwiches. "What a life!" confided a distraught Madeline to her journal.[86] But she was no longer making her journal entries, or dating them, quite so precisely as she had earlier.

Apparently on November 1, a Sunday, Joe and Madeline slept late, then read the papers until dinner time. Eula Coon arrived about 7:30, though whether she had dinner with the Sanderses isn't clear, nor is whether Coonie was present. He probably wasn't, for Madeline would most likely have said so. But while they were eating, the hotel's manager and several others dropped by. Since the Nighthawks didn't play later than 9 p.m. on Sundays, after dinner Joe took Madeline to catch Dudley Wilkinson's act at the Palace. Following that, they joined Wilkinson and his date for a jaunt to Connie's, where there was a black orchestra and revue. "My, such dancing," observed Madeline, who thought it "downright suggestive." From Connie's the four went to Ruben's for a late snack — it was now after 3 a.m.— and sat next to a party of four men who were talking rather loudly. One of them used the word "stupacious," and Madeline was so amused that she laughed and wrote it down. She then pushed the note over for Wilkinson to read. He handed it back with his own note telling her that the man who had said that was Walter Winchell. "My God," she thought, "and here I made fun of him." Whether she knew that the Nighthawks were soon to appear on Winchell's show isn't recorded, but she probably did. It upset her so much that she lost her appetite. By the time she and Joe got back to the hotel, she was in a real funk and later cried herself to sleep. Even the next morning her depression had not left her — she "felt low for several reasons," as she recorded in her journal. Fortunately, Dudley Wilkinson dropped by, and they took a cab over to Pier 57 to see French Premier Pierre Laval leave on the *Ile de France*. (Laval later collaborated with the Nazis and was executed after World War II.) She thought it a fine opportunity to see a large ocean liner.[87]

On another Sunday evening, probably November eighth, at about ten-thirty, acclaimed theater organist Jesse Crawford (1895–1962) and his wife Helen — the two of them were famous for their duets on twin organ consoles at Manhattan's Paramount Theater — called on Joe and Madeline. The Crawfords had also brought Helen's grandmother, which for some reason annoyed Madeline. Coonie and Eula joined them, and they all went to the Cotton Club where Cab Calloway was playing. Unfortunately for Joe's wife, she was in another of her depressed moods and thus found it "a long evening." Coonie perhaps had something to do with it, for she later recorded, "Carleton acted too silly for words with the grandmother — embarrassed everyone." Since she failed to give any particulars, my assumption is that Coonie had been drinking, though it could simply have been that Madeline, whose temperament was now almost always volatile, was unable to appreciate Coonie's type of humor. The group then had a late dinner at Lindy's and got home at five in the morning — "dead tired," added Madeline.[88]

Madeline's fragile state of mind was evident also later in the week when Jack Diamond dropped by Wednesday evening to take her to the opening of *Here Goes the Bride*. She had gone to a lot of trouble to dress formally, only to discover that the rest of the party had not. It was not something that should have troubled her, but of course it did. "Imagine my confusion," she later confided to her diary, for "it well-nigh ruined my evening." She did like the show, however, mainly because of the antics of Bobby Clark and Paul McCullough.* After the show she and Diamond had sandwiches and ice cream with Joe.[89]

Next day Madeline had lunch with Tillie (Mrs. Max) Winslow at the Waldorf-Astoria — "lamb hash!" Madeline was careful to note exclamatorily. She thought the hotel was beautiful but allowed that she would "never feel at home in such spaciousness." She did seem to enjoy the shopping afterward, however, and bought two hats "for fun." Winslow's chauffeur took her home afterward.[90]

Rex and Maybelle Downing and several of the other band members lived at the New Yorker, but Russ and Florence Stout did not. They rented an apartment out in Forest Hills, on Long Island; for, as Florence later said, "We were thoroughly tired of eating on the road."[91]

Madeline Sanders, too, had no intention of spending her entire time in New York in a hotel room. One Sunday afternoon, perhaps November 8, Joe and Madeline were guests of the de Cordovas in their apartment at the Franconia Hotel, 20 W. Seventy-second Street. After a delicious early afternoon meal of roast beef and mashed potatoes, their hosts informed them about a temporarily vacant, furnished apartment in the hotel. The following Tuesday, both Madeline and Joe examined it, considered the monthly rent of $250 acceptable, and were generally pleased with the prospect. Joe described it as "sumptuously furnished" and was interested to learn that Jack Robbins and Ben Bornzstein were neighbors. Signing a lease involved a slight delay.[92]

But Madeline still struggled with her social obligations. On Thursday, the twelfth, Rose Perfect and Mack Howard, both of whom Madeline liked, had dinner with her; and the Robert Fishers, friends of Joe's from Olean, N.Y., came by later in the evening. Madeline became suddenly ill and had to excuse herself. Perfect called her on Friday to say that she too had become ill upon arriving at home, and even Howard had found himself ailing. Madeline blamed it on the "ptomaine" sausages they had eaten, and she remained very quiet for a day or two after-

---

Bobby Clark (1888–1960) and Paul McCullough (1883–1936) were two zany comedians in vaudeville and motion pictures. Clark was famous for appearing with "glasses" painted on his face. McCullough's life ended in suicide.

ward. This gave her a chance to get back to sorting Joe's clippings. Even when her mind wandered to the many persons downstairs whom she knew and others she probably would have liked to know, she still opted to be alone. "One must sometimes," she concluded. Nevertheless, her solitude was soon interrupted by the Winslows and by Mel Washburn from New Orleans. On Saturday, Joe went to a football game while she spent some time shopping for a hat and having her hair done. Upon returning to the New Yorker, she got a call from Leo Kaffir and was pleased, as she put it, "that he was natural for the first few minutes." She neglected to say what he was after that. Later, having survived Kaffir's visit, she called Eula Coon, and the two had dinner in Madeline's suite. "From then on," said Madeline rather ambiguously to her journal, "the evening was hers." Perhaps Eula was speaking of personal problems, some of which may well have concerned her husband. Whatever Eula's situation was, Madeline added, "I certainly have pity for her and anything we can do to make life easier [for her] we want to do. So much for that."[93]

It was at this time that Jules Stein's MCA was negotiating with its occasional adversary, the National Broadcasting Company. MCA's New York office had, for several weeks, been making exploratory negotiations with NBC's offices on Manhattan. As explained to the public, the purpose of these talks was to try to work out a co-operative booking deal regarding a list of bands available for the Lucky Strike programs. At Stein's invitation, executives of NBC's Artists Service traveled to Chicago to continue dickering on MCA's own turf, and remained there until November ninth. NBC agreed to allow MCA exclusive right to all hotel engagements under contract with the network. Also, there would be an assurance of a chain hookup for all MCA bands when possible. In return, Stein yielded all rights to cuts on commercial programs and theater engagements that NBC's Artists Service obtained for MCA bands. These arrangements rather surprised another booking agency, Kennaway, Inc., that had earlier entered into an agreement with NBC for a split-commission booking arrangement. That arrangement, however, was apparently only verbal. To complicate the matter further, Gerald Barry, Kennaway's booker assigned to execute Kennaway's part of the agreement, suffered a nervous breakdown. Kennaway had assumed that NBC was completely satisfied with the agreement, though MCA and NBC, still not at a definite point of agreement, continued discussions. Representatives from both sides, including Jules Stein, were back in New York by mid–November and still little if any closer to an understanding. MCA simply was loath to commit itself exclusively to NBC, thinking it better to be free to conduct business independently with both NBC and CBS. Meanwhile, NBC still had not begun to share in MCA's bookings for the Lucky Strike programs.[94]

The Nighthawks' broadcasts at the New Yorker were carried locally over WMCA by the National Broadcasting Company. According to *Variety*, the network was exploiting Coon-Sanders "as though it were its own band and for which the Artists' Bureau was collecting a 15% commis[sion]." But, said the weekly, the band was "strictly MCA." The only connection that Coon-Sanders had with NBC was that it was the network's wire over which the band was being heard from the hotel. Ralph Hitz, the New Yorker's manager, had established the terms for the broadcasts. CBS had been ready to step in if the New Yorker had been unable to work out a deal with NBC.[95]

Sanders regarded their first few programs as "decidedly 'sad'" and blamed the network's operators, who he said, "were palpably accustomed to 'sugary' bands and wheezy crooners." But eventually Joe and Coonie beguiled such operators and announcers as Kelvin Keach, Ford Bond, and David Ross, and then the fan mail increased dramatically. On Saturday nights the band broadcast their new club, the Night Riders, and provided an appropriate theme song for the half-hour program that began at midnight. They used a Western Union ticker-tape machine, but the station was not a powerful one and relatively few wires came in, most of them from the New York area. Later, popular demand forced NBC to give the Nighthawks a full hour and a powerful coast-to-coast hookup. That was the beginning of a great increase in public response. The band got special acclaim from the West Coast.[96]

Though the contract with the New Yorker did not allow the band to recognize individuals over the air, as they had elsewhere in the past, Coon-Sanders did still recognize, and often support, certain non-commercial groups and causes. On November 11, what then was called Armistice Day, Vincent J. Kane, president of the Uniformed Firemen's Association of Greater New York, Local 94, wrote to Coonie and Joe to thank them for giving publicity, the previous evening, to the union in its campaign for better working conditions. Said Kane:

> May we ask that you send us the words of the song you composed for the occasion? Too bad, indeed that you could not have heard the applause of the men in the engine house where I got the broadcast. Another request: may we have the autographed pictures of yourselves and your band so that we may place them on the walls of our headquarters with the other artists who have given their talent in our behalf. We have a gallery of celebrities framed and hung on our walls and these are for posterity. We wish those coming afterwards and benefitting from the eight hour day to know who helped.[97]

Another acknowledgment of help from Coon-Sanders came in March of 1932 when Robert A. LeRoux, adjutant of the American Legion Post No. 16, Hoquiam, Wash., wrote to express gratitude for a recent recognition of the Post's work with ailing youngsters. The letter was written on spruce from the same trees that produced the wood used in Lindbergh's *Spirit of St. Louis*. "We certainly were knocked over hard," wrote LeRoux, "when we received the information this was your farewell broadcast — you were leaving the Little Old Hotel New Yorker in New York City." The members of the post put together "a little testimonial" for the band and asked for an address where to send it. "Give us your address — send us a picture of your good fellows — give us some news of the band run by two of our buddies," said LeRoux, and adding, "These sick boys have adopted you and you're to be prepared to hear from them regularly."[98]

On Thanksgiving, November 26, the Nighthawks played the first of several engagements for the Walter Winchell program, *The Lucky Strike Dance Hour*, sponsored by Lucky Strike Cigarettes. The first two programs originated from the NBC studios on Fifth Avenue and were under the direction of Jack Nelson, a Chicagoan. Winchell (1897–1972), in earlier years had been an entertainer in vaudeville, at first as a part of Gus Edwards' kiddie revue. But by 1931 he had given all that up and was well known, in newspapers and on radio, as a controversial dispenser of inconsequential chitchat, social gossip, and offbeat news, with all of it reported in his rapid, staccato, nasal delivery.

According to *Variety*, Winchell was the first person to appear on air under a double sponsorship. He had already been under a contract with the Geraldine Company since about the first of October 1931, and that company consented to his also undertaking a Lucky Strike contract. His first doubleheader evening was on Tuesday, November third, when at 8:45 he was on for the Geraldine weekly program, and at ten for the first tri-weekly program for Lucky Strike. He broadcast for Luckies also on Thursdays and Saturdays. During each Tuesday's Lucky Strike hour, Winchell did two two-and-a-half-minute periods of gossip. For these programs Winchell would have music by Andy Sanella, Wayne King, and Gus Arnheim, as well as such others as Coon-Sanders. As a result of this double sponsorship, as well as the thrice-weekly programs for Luckies, Winchell decided to stop reviewing drama premieres for the New York *Daily News*, but he would continue his daily column in that paper, as well as provide another for a new Sunday edition, planned to start the following January, of the New York *Daily Mirror*.[99]

Jules Stein's Music Corporation of America was the exclusive supplier of the bands for *The Lucky Strike Dance Hour*, and now had at least sixty-five top-notch bands to choose from. As we've already seen, the Nighthawks had become associated with Stein at the start of his agency and brought in the first profits sufficient to put the agency on a sound basis. Gus Arnheim came in somewhat later. Arnheim had already become closely associated with the Cocoanut Grove, Los Angeles, where he was often called "The star of entertainers and the entertainer of stars."[100]

Years later Joe Sanders said that the band were all uncharacteristically edgy just before that first Winchell show. After all, Winchell was *big*, almost the personification of Broadway. While preliminaries were taking place, Joe, who was a heavy smoker, reached for one of his Camels. "You want the sponsors to throw us out of here?" asked Winchell confidentially. Joe looked puzzled. Winchell asked whether he knew who the sponsor was. Well, yes, said Joe, Lucky Strikes. "And what are you smoking?" asked Winchell, with a slight gesture toward the little booth where a representative from the sponsor usually sat. For the rest of that evening Joe was careful about how he reached for a cigarette, and on later broadcasts he always put his Camels inside a Lucky Strike box. But that wasn't the only problem. According to Sanders, Winchell could sense the nervousness in the Nighthawks. Even Coonie missed a beat at one point. So to help them relax, Winchell delved back into his old vaudeville experience and did a deft little toe-tapping routine during one of their practice numbers. Perhaps it helped, for there were no more problems. Joe appreciated Winchell's relaxed manner and wit and ever afterward spoke of him in admiring terms.[101]

Rex Downing, many years later, recalled a minor mishap that Coonie experienced on one of the Walter Winchell shows, though whether it was the one that Joe mentions above is unclear. Said Rex:

> Joe had prepared a patriotic program, and Coonie had two or three things to play on the timpani. Well, now, Coonie didn't have any timpani. But the resident drummer, that is, the studio NBC drummer there—Smitty—had a fine set of timps, and he had all of the autographs of all of the people who had passed through the studios. I can remember, for instance, Jack Dempsey and [Gene] Tunney ... that I read on one of the heads of the timps. So, we rehearsed the program, and Coonie reached back and hit the timp. We got on the program that night and when it came time ... for him to play the timpani, Joe nodded at him, and Coonie reached back with his drumstick and stabbed the timpani and tore it all part ... It was hard to keep from breaking up.[102]

The show, broadcast from 10 to 11 p.m., began with one chorus and vocal refrain of the theme song, "Happy Days Are Here Again." The announcer, Howard Claney, one of the best in radio, was described by the NBC Artists Service as "clear-voiced [and] an expert in selling psychology, and blessed with an air personality which strikes a note of genuine sincerity into his excellent delivery." On this occasion he bade the radio listeners to sit back and enjoy "two great dance orchestras, from Los Angeles, and from New York." "Sixty Modern Minutes," he exclaimed, "with the world's finest dance orchestras—and the one and only Walter Winchell of the New York *Daily Mirror*, whose gossip of today, becomes the news of tomorrow."[103]

Claney's "Mr. Walter Winchell!" was the cue for the host to deliver his opening which, despite the times or the sponsor, changed little over the years: "Good evening, Mr. and Mrs. Everybody from Broadway, New York, to Broadway, Los Angeles, California!" In sharp contrast with his usual fast talking, he sometimes did a little sentimental patter, usually delivered more slowly and often with sentences broken up to dramatize each phrase. "I trust you all were thankful for something today — and that if you weren't — that the sweeter breaks will come real soon — to give you reason enough to be happier."* And with a typical Winchell effort at humor and punning, he continued, "I didn't have much of a chance to celebrate the holiday with the usual trimmin's — but frankly — I would rather talk Turkey, than eat it!" Winchell then introduced his guests: "Our stars tonight are Gus Arnheim, and his swelegant† orchestra playing all the way from Los Angeles, who will share honors with the Coon-Sanders crew of blazing bandsmen right here in New York. We're on that magic carpet, Gus! Catch us now! And please push some of those Rockies out of our way for California, here we come!"[104]

In reply, Arnheim tut-tutted that the Rockies were "only molehills." His orchestra played "I Love Louisa," "Love Everlasting," "Who's Your Little Whoozis?" and a medley titled "Flying High." At the conclusion of these, Arnheim showed he could deal in neologisms, too. "And now," he said, "for some of Walter's Winchellizing, the lightning express is leaving Los Angeles for New York City, and the Lucky Strike Dance Hour — Let 'er go!" Then Winchell went into the following typical patter:

> That was plenty good, Gus, but you probably think I'm being paid to say so.... I'll bet you all are having yourselves some jolly moments out there, Gus. Broadway has lost its glamour for me, now that the "Follies" dollies have gone to Philadelphia. I don't know, Gus, the Follies dolls, somehow, make the Street more exciting — ask the florists, who will tell you that they sold more orchids and posies during the recent run of the Follies than during any other.... I know, too, Gus, that right now, several of the Follies kids are sitting in their undressing rooms, listening to our program between their changes of costume. Pull up that left stocking, Mary Carroll, I can see you! And you, Joan Burgess, your shoulder strap is slipping![105]

This was Winchell's cue to go into some of his gossiping about such current luminaries as Earl Sande and Marion Kummer, as well as James Dunn and Molly O'Day. And with a reference to the actress Peggy Hopkins Joyce, of matrimonial and gold-digging fame, he reported, "The other day, Sande decorated the dainty engagement ring finger of widow Kummer with a blinding sparkler that would make Peggy Joyce blink."[106]

At a likely spot in the program, Howard Claney came in with a commercial that referred to a popular cowboy actor of the time. Today the sponsor's commercial makes one a little uncomfortable. "You know, Walter," said Claney, "that Bill Boyd [1898–1972] takes the best possible care of that voice of his? Even in the cigarette he smokes he is careful to get the utmost throat protection." Boyd had provided a testimonial letter that avowed he had been smoking Luckies since 1917, and added, "In my profession, I must consider my throat, and LUCKIES do not cause throat irritation." After a bit more chatter, with Walter getting off another of his neologisms — *ridiculummox* — he brought in the Nighthawks. "And now," he said, "to introduce our newest horn-tooters, THE COON-SANDERS Orchestra who recently came from Chicago, and whose triumphs in New York have placed them high on the list of favorites, already. There are lots of good orchestras in town, but the Coon-Sanders lads lost little time in crashing the Broadway heavens. They have a way about them, which you will soon discover, a contagious way, that makes you want to dance with the other feller's girl. Get ready Mr. Coon and Mr. Sanders. They're tuning in from Vancouver to Key West, to hear you play, 'March of Time,' 'Sweet and Lovely,' and 'Jig Time.' Ladies and Gentlemen, the Coon-Sanders Orchestra!"[107]

---

*In later years, Winchell's introduction was something more on the order of "Good evening, Mr. and Mrs. North and South America, and all the ships at sea; let's go to press! Flash!...." Then, each new "bulletin" would be prefaced by the clicking sound of an apparent news receiver.

†He was famous for coining words, usually combinations of two or more truncated words.

There was some irony in Coon-Sanders' playing "Sweet and Lovely." Not only was it a work by Gus Arnheim*— with Harry Tobias and Jules Lemare—it also was Arnheim's theme song. Very likely that's why the Nighthawks decided to use it. Too bad Arnheim didn't play "Nighthawk Blues" or at least "My Paradise"! (In Arnheim's past were the Syncopated Five and his work as accompanist for Sophie Tucker. In 1930 his orchestra worked with the Rhythm Boys— Bing Crosby, Harry Barris, and Al Rinker.)[108]

Later in the program, right after a station break, Winchell said: "Get ready Coon-Sanders and your grand orchestra. I didn't get enough of you last time. Not only are your old Chicago admirers listening, I'll bet, but think of the new friends you've made all over these good old United States. Keep them happy, fellas—the big idea is to make the LUCKY STRIKE Dance Hour seem too short." The Nighthawks led off with "Singing the Blues," then played "Cuban Love Song," and ended with "Pray, Children, Pray," a piece that had originally been scheduled for the first part of the program. Winchell exclaimed that the Coon-Sanders Orchestra was "Chicago's loss and New York's gain!" After the final number, he said, "Thanks again, Mr. Coon and Mr. Sanders, and all your simply swelegant syncopaters!" At the end of the show, Winchell gave one of his typical closings: "Until Saturday night at the same time, then—I am—as ever—Mrs. Winchell's rambling rascal, Walter—who found out a long time ago, that relatives are people, who wonder, how you contrive to keep on, fooling the world!"[109]

Rex Downing, speaking near the end of his life, thought that the band played "several" times for the Winchell show from the network's Fifth Avenue studios. On the other hand, it was Joe's recollection that the first two, under the direction of Jack Nelson, were done on Fifth Avenue, and the others from the New Yorker. Joe's memory is probably correct, for he was recalling events nearer the time and had been more intimately concerned with arrangements. The first two shows had been so successful that Joe averred they had drawn more mail "than any two bands that had been presented." This popularity meant that they had several more engagements for Winchell's show, but all of them made from the New Yorker's Terrace Room. And since the programs used a public address system, all the guests could get the entire program. It was during these broadcasts that Joe presented many celebrities to the hotel and radio audience. Among them were Jean Harlow, Maurice Chevalier, Fannie Brice, Gloria Swanson, Fifi D'Orsay, and William S. Hart. Joe personally arranged for Hart's presentation. When the famous cowboy actor learned that he was going to be called upon to speak, he wired the "boys" at his ranch to install a radio in the stables so that his horse Pinto could hear his voice. Winchell was so charmed by all this that he used the story on a later program. Joe came to like and admire Hart, calling him "one of the most lovable characters it has ever been my pleasure to know." And Hart was sufficiently taken by Joe to invite him to visit him at his ranch in Vallejo, Calif.[110]

It was quite a coup for Coon-Sanders to be invited to play for the Winchell show. For many years, regardless of whether the sponsor was Lucky Strikes or Jurgens, Walter Winchell's was a name that drew a large audience, sharply divided between those who swore by him and others who swore at him. Joe's opinion of Winchell was glowing: "Walter Winchell proved to be a real person and was distinctly a friend and booster."[111]

Winchell was a plain-spoken, often abrasive, man. In later years the admiration he had felt for Franklin D. Roosevelt turned to contemptuous disdain for the latter's successor. At the end of one of his Sunday eve-

---

*Gus Arnheim, in addition to his eight years at Los Angeles' famous Cocoanut Grove, played at Chicago's Chez Paree, New York's Palace, and in George White's Scandals. He died at age 56 on 12 January 1955.

ning broadcasts, about 1950, Winchell commented on President Truman's recent remark that there were several newsmen he'd like to punch in the nose. Winchell said he didn't know whether he was one of those the president had in mind, but if so, "I regret that I have but one nose to give for my country." Truman had perhaps heard of such Winchelisms, including the newsman's assertion that he now knew "the difference between FDR and HST: from a chicken in every pot to a skeleton in every closet." This referred to the controversy over some of Truman's cronies and associates, which elicited Winchell's additional observation that the president had a reputation for standing up for his friends, but that some of the president's friends were "low, dirty people."[112] Harry Truman was peppery and plain-spoken, too. and it's a wonder that only Winchell's nose was in danger.

I have seen very little information about what the other members of the band were doing during these six months at the New Yorker. Rex Downing, however, had good reason to remember this sojourn in the Big Apple, and he often spoke of it in later years. He had been parking his beautiful Auburn on a street near the New Yorker, where he and Maybelle were living. One night it was stolen. A few days later Downing found his car parked on a different street, and he drove it back to his hotel. A bit later he received a phone call from an anonymous caller who said, "That car you just took. Bring it back or we'll blow your ___ing head off." Rex notified the police and was advised to consider his car gone and to be thankful he hadn't lost anything more.[113] Perhaps Mayor Jimmie Walker was too busy defending himself against charges of corruption to put a little starch into his police force. At least Rex wasn't out any money, though the Auburn Company was missing its advertisement.

Downing also recalled the pleasure of going out on the town with Fanny Brice and Gloria Swanson, and especially of meeting such New York musicians as Red Nichols, Irving M. "Miff" Mole, Phil Napoleon, Emanuel K. "Manny" Klein, Joseph L. "Fud" Livingston, Jimmy Lytell, and Arthur Shutt. They enjoyed some wonderful jam sessions in various parts of Manhattan and the Bronx.[114]

On December 14, the Forster Music Publishers asked Joe's help with arranging. They intended to revive the 1918 song "Hindustan," in the belief that it had an excellent chance right then, "there being nothing on the market on that order." Frank Skinner was making an arrangement of it but wouldn't have it completed for several weeks. If Joe would make an arrangement, not only would it be a good one but also it would provide Coon-Sanders with something they could use immediately. In addition, the company asked him to consider making arrangements for "I May Be Dreaming" and "I'll See You Later in Slumberland."[115] Whether Joe did help Forster Music with these arrangements does not appear in any of Joe's records that I've seen. My guess is that he did not, or he would most likely have recorded the fact. After all, he was decidedly not in a good frame of mind, and did little arranging even for his own broadcasts, during these months in New York.

Meanwhile, Madeline still struggled with her situation. Sundays seemed especially difficult for her, and on one of them in late November, she and Joe awoke groggily after an unusually late night. "Sunday again and both of us have heads. Dear me, this can't go on," was her weary entry in her journal. Jesse and Helen Crawford, again with Helen's mother, had dropped by the previous evening—"late as usual," complained Madeline—and all of them went out clubbing, and wound up at Lindy's. The Sanderses got back at 6 a.m. Sunday. "I don't even remember getting to bed—so tired! Oh, my!" was Madeline's reaction to it all.[116] Clearly the Volstead Act was a farce.

Madeline's troubles with visitors, late hours, and midnight snacks continued. "Keeping very late hours and gaining weight," she wailed to her journal. On one occasion

Clare and Harold Van Ohrman dropped by and asked her to join a party, but she declined. Then, a short time later the wife of the New Yorker's manager arrived and persuaded her to go out. She "dressed hurriedly" and shortly found herself seated next to "Crane," whom she remembered as formerly head waiter at a restaurant she had patronized, apparently in the Chicago area, and who "also was the friend of Earl Wiggs." As did many other things, this disturbed her. The party lasted in the Hitz's hotel suite until after 3 a.m. Then several of them went to the Sanderses' suite. The following Sunday had been intended as a day to move into the new apartment, but neither Joe nor Madeline could work it. That evening a friend from Cincinnati dropped by and stayed until Joe arrived at nine.[117]

The next day, however, Madeline and Joe managed to move into their new apartment, 1201 of the Hotel Franconia. Mack Howard helped them move and made himself generally useful. Joe and Madeline would spend many evenings there, or rather, considering the band's schedule, mornings. And since on Sundays the band played only for dinner, a typical Sunday schedule for the Sanderses allowed them to go out, perhaps, for a hockey match at Madison Square Garden, and then go "home for a bottle," as Joe put it. He said they afterward often went to "either the Cotton Club to see Cab Calloway or Connie's to watch Snake Hips."[118]

The evening of "moving day" Madeline had dinner with the de Cordovas at their apartment in the Franconia, but Joe ate downtown. The next day, Tuesday, was given over to unpacking, which left Madeline very weary by dinnertime. Joe nevertheless asked her to dress and join him, but after they got underway, Madeline's nerves gave way and she started weeping. "Cried so that I didn't dare go in with him, a celebrity," Madeline later confided to her diary. Managing to get control of herself, she and Joe went on to Lindy's where she "ate too much chicken livers." Later they went to see *Band Wagon*, which Madeline pronounced "fair." But after returning home, she spent a miserable night—"Sick, oh so sick."[119]

All day Wednesday Madeline was ill and unable to eat anything, so Joe went out alone to shop for a number of household items they needed. "This woman's kitchen," wrote Madeline, "contains no niceties of a good housewife at all." But at least Joe seemed in an understanding mood, and Madeline made a point of recording that "Joe is very kind to me—seems to understand that I am all in." Thursday found her still unwell but able to get to Martini's Beauty Shop. Joe went out alone for a walk but had returned by the time Madeline got back, and she found him irritable and nervous. It was already 6 p.m., and he needed his clothes, but she was carrying the keys to the closets. A letter from her mother helped, but having Joe upset with her was always an especially severe trial.[120]

And yet, Joe could show Madeline great affection and attention. On January 6, when most Americans were already finding it difficult to buy life's necessities, he bought her a mink coat for $850. "Value is much greater," she wrote in her diary, "but at this time I could get a good buy. Joe & I feel proud of this. Just another of his promises fulfilled."[121]

But while the Nighthawks might be enjoying such things as fine dining and mink coats, most citizens in New York and throughout the nation were having to concern themselves with more substantial and necessary products. By early 1932, the Nighthawks, as they walked about New York, doubtless had already been seeing increasing numbers of unemployed, as well as early versions of soup kitchens and breadlines. And as for those who could still pay for their food, even these were searching for bargains. In fact, *Variety* spoke of a "food fight" that was going on along Broadway. Restaurants were more numerous than any other type of business in the Times Square area, so competition was keen. There was still a great variety of such establishments, from what *Variety* called "the throw it at yourself joints to the class spots," and they were having to lower prices to attract customers. It was impossible to find a block where there wasn't at least one restaurant of some kind, and every one displayed new low prices. A meal for which one might once have paid a half-dollar now cost a quarter. Many businesses were almost using trickery to lure customers. There might be free second or third cups of coffee, or inexpensive combinations for all three daily meals, or even extra servings of a customer's favorite course. One thing that annoyed the restaurateurs was that candy stores, too, were offering discounts and special deals. And before one laughs at that, consider that some individuals were perhaps eating candy as a cheaper way to satisfy the appetite, possibly even the only available way.[122]

At this time the Depression was manifesting itself in an increasing number of ways. There were, for instance, many vacant stores in Manhattan's best business areas. As early as January 1931, on Broadway between Times Square and Columbus Circle, there were fifty-four vacant stores, or an average of more than three to a block. After reaching a high point in 1921, show business on Broadway plummeted in 1930 to an all-time low. The next year was even worse. There were, however, a few positive effects of the worsening economy. Curiously, hard times had put the bootlegging industry on a sounder basis, and as a result, the consumer was finding a better quality of liquor at a lower price. Scotch and uncut rye, for instance, were available at much lower prices, and good beer at a quarter a glass was becoming the favorite beverage in New York and elsewhere in the nation. Also, that many of New York's unemployed white-collar workers were driving taxis, suggested one observer, might explain why the city's cabbies seemed more amiable of late.[123]

On the same day in November on which the Sanderses signed the sub-lease for the Franconia apartment, Eula Coon left New York to return to Kansas City. It was perhaps an unfortunate time for her to do so, but she had her small children to care for. It would appear that she knew her husband was drifting into a perilous condition, and the choice between him and her children must have been a painful one.[124]

The constant pressure on Coonie had apparently brought him to a critical point that was becoming obvious to the other members of the band. That he was still a warm, lovable person made their concern all the more poignant. At times he was clearly not himself. Joe had already concluded that Coonie's drinking was interfering with his work, and according to Harold Thiell, on one occasion Coonie showed up intoxicated and with a blonde whom Coonie introduced as the "most beautiful woman in the world." Harvey Rettberg, who got the information from Harold Thiell, says that Coonie was often absent when the band was scheduled to play. As Dan Schroeder puts it, "Coonie's gusto for life was catching up with him." And though, as Johnny Coon wrote in a letter to Clyde Hahn, all the band had begun to hate New York "with a 'purple Passion,'" Coonie seemed to be even unhappier than the others. One night Coonie, after a night on the town, went into Joe's room and said he was going home, and pulled out a travel ticket to prove it. "God knows," wrote Joe afterward, "what he would have lived on, had I not, by appealing to his manhood, shamed him into seeing it thro." I have seen only Joe's account of this, and he adds that he did manage to talk Coonie out of it. Whatever happened, both Joe and Coonie were going through a very difficult time, and, as Schroeder says, it was under these circumstances that Joe composed "I Want to Go Home." Sanders wrote it for a new theme song, though "My Paradise" was serving that purpose at the end of 1931.[125] But "I Want to Go Home" was a disturbing contrast to such jolly pieces as "Nighthawk Blues." The words are stark, pathetic, and ominous, and, coupled with a melody that slowly descends the scale, formed an appropriate theme for the band, as well as a descant on the worsening national economy:

> I'm tired of the grind for fortune and fame,
> I'm weary of mind and sick of the game,
> I long for the folks who call me by name,
> I want to go home....[126]

If Joe can be believed—and I have no reason to doubt him—Coonie's situation deteriorated quite rapidly until there was more than alcohol to be concerned about. After the band had achieved great popularity about 1928 or 1929, Coonie sometimes became lax in holding up his part of the work. "All this [success]," said Joe, perhaps with some exaggeration, "was accomplished without help from Coonie, who was going to pieces at an alarming rate." Liquor, said Joe, was no longer strong enough for the troubled co-leader. "From being merely a drunkard," Sanders states in his recollections, "the combination of liquor and opiates—and the woman whom he was keeping—began to undermine his mentality. I was finally *forced* to keep him off the air to protect the band *and* the man." Then, with what seems cruel phrasing, Joe adds, "His mind was so puerile that he could not read lyrics right before his eyes."[127]

Johnny Coon acknowledged that his father was an extremely unhappy man at this period, and that Coonie and Joe were having disagreements that were becoming very personal. There are extant letters in which the younger Coon expresses extremely bitter comments about Sanders. As a matter of fact, Coonie's oldest child never forgave what he regarded as Joe's bad treatment of his father at this time. In later years, John Coon made a point of avoiding Joe, even though the two lived fairly near each other.[128] Harvey Rettberg suspects that part of the trouble arose from Joe's tendency to look down on Coonie as a musician, and it is a matter of record that by late 1931 Joe was looking for a way to end their association.[129] In 1960 Johnny Coon put his opinions into unequivocal terms:

> My dad really had a time with Joe in NY as Joe got impossible to live with! The big-shot complex took him over.... This is what I think actually killed dad. He drank pretty good about this time, and with good reason.... They could have broken up back in 1924 or '25 — who knows! He decided he would stick it out — who knows which was the correct route?[130]

In addition to "I Want to Go Home," Joe wrote two other songs which also were, as he put it, "born of homesickness." One was "In the Hills of Old Missouri." The other, "There's a Light in the Window," was written with Gus Kahn and finished after the band returned to Chicago. It was sold to George Marlo, while the other two were sold to George Piantadosi for Remick and Witmark, publishers.[131]

At some other time that I haven't been able to identify, Joe perhaps—they are among his papers without attribution—wrote lyrics similar to the above but without the apparent dejection of those words quoted above from "I Want to Go Home." The following song was titled "Somebody from Home":

> Have you ever been a long long way from home,
> Alone, without a friendly hand,
> A stranger in a stranger land?
> Have you ever wished you'd never left to roam,
> Marooned upon a foreign strand?
> Then you'll understand:
>
> *Chorus*
>
> When you're a long long way
>   from the ones who care
> And ev'ry face you see wears a vacant stare,
> Gee, but it's sweet to meet somebody from home.
> When you'd give all you own for a friendly pat
> And have to call your home
>   where you hang your hat,
> Gee, but it's sweet to meet somebody from home.
> When a pal says, "Gee, I'm glad to see
>   ya — how be ya?" It's grand.
> Then you feel you'll never get too
>   much of the touch of his hand.
> And then you realize that the world is small
> And you are glad you're part of it, after all.
> Gee, but it's sweet to
>   meet somebody from home.[132]

And yet another with a similar theme, though this one was written after the Nighthawk era:

"The House Isn't Home without You"

Four bare walls—and a rug or two.
Four bare walls—and a bug or two
Took advantage just because you're gone.
One bare heart — sorely needing you.
One bare heart — that is pleading you
Please come back and start the day
With dawn—from now on:

Chorus

Since you are gone, the days are long.
The nites are endless, too.
I'm lonely — so lonely —
The house isn't home without you.
With my spirits low, there's the radio!
It will make me forget what I had.
Turn it on — and then — turn it off again,
For the music is gloomy and sad.
Why should I lie? I'm high and dry
Like a ship without a crew.
I'm lonely — so lonely —
The house isn't home without you.[133]

Joe's notes for "The House Isn't Home without You" indicate that he intended to include the following "dramatic recitation," a popular device by singers at that time, during a playing of the chorus:

> My chair where you placed it —
> And your chair that faced it —
> In that little room with a view.
> The clock just behind me
> To hourly remind me
> The house isn't home without you.[134]

It is pretty clear that Sanders was having his own serious problems with morale in New York City. He later said that both he and Madeline thought New York "a hideous nightmare, a cesspool of insincerity, a hotbed of double-crossers, a maze of 'angles.'"[135] These moods may explain why Joe practically stopped arranging and bought arrangements from others. A little earlier he had found some relief in putting the finishing touches on the series of piano pieces, previously discussed and that Joe termed "mood" pieces, or *solo improvisations*— "Embers," "Intangibility," "Inhibition," and "Southology," all four copyrighted in 1931. And yet, there were a few bright spots that he later spoke of:

In our connection with WMCA occurred a most unusual coincidence. Way back in 1927 we established radio contact with Central America. Every Saturday night, on our Knights and Ladies of the Bath program, we received regularly a radiogram from O. W. Penny, listening in at Santa Marta, Colombia. On our third Nite Riders program at the New Yorker a new control man came in. After we had signed off, he walked over to me and said, "Did you ever hear of a chap by the name of O. W. Penny?" At once I said, "Of course. He was our steady Central America correspondent." To which he replied that he was that man. The next Saturday he brought along photos to prove his statements. What a small world after all.[136]

And like other non–New Yorkers, he could find the view from the Empire State Building a "never-to-be-forgotten thrill." There was also the Georgia-NYU football game — Georgia 6, NYU nothing — at which Joe sat with the Georgia fans. He appreciated Bill Melia's friendliness, and he later made an appreciative but cryptic mention of "the Whistler and his 'dog' at the New Yorker." The only clue he provided was "ask the boys."[137]

But much of what New York offered had quickly become flat to him. He thought Greenwich Village "most disappointing." "Winter walks in over-rated Central Park," he complained, "[are] not to be compared with Lincoln Park in Chicago." The much-touted Christmas shopping on Fifth Avenue, he concluded, was a bust. Celebration of the holiday was "a lost art in mad Manhattan," for he sensed an "utter lack of Christmas spirit." And he deplored the "endless parade of push-carts, filled with cheap dresses and fur coats (many cats were sacrificed upon the altar of cheap merchandise)."[138]

Joe got a brief lift in spirits when in February he learned that Gov. Flem D. Sampson, of Kentucky, had made him a colonel on his staff. The honor followed Sampson's visit to New York where he apparently had heard the Nighthawks at the New Yorker. It was said at the time that Sanders was the first musician so honored by Kentucky. The

Governor had long been a fan of Coon-Sanders but conferred the honor in particular for Joe's composition "My Paradise," then being used as the band's theme song in its nationwide broadcasts.[139]

There were other memories, both pleasant and otherwise, that Joe was sure he would take with him: his accommodating black cab driver, Harold Peace, "whose devotion gave me a private car at my disposal constantly"; "Abe Lyman's obvious disgust over our success"; "46th and Broadway, mink coats and the bread line"; attending the Cotton Club with the Jesse Crawfords; "the sincere delight which was ours when we encountered someone from old Chicago"; "Madeline struggling with her toy electric cooking plate"; "the 'Anvil Chorus' sung by rival bandsmen, a few publishers and asinine Jerry Wald"; the "Bedlamville" of Central Park West; "insincerity, flop-houses, Harlem madness, four-flushers, pan-handlers, 'angles'"; and, finally, the "sanctuary at 20 W. 72nd," from whose windows Joe and Madeline could see both the East and Hudson Rivers, the Statue of Liberty, and the Battery. It would be a very mixed Memory Lane.[140]

Joe's distress was palpable. It is quite likely that some of Madeline's unhappiness was getting through to him, or maybe his was getting through to her, or, yet again, perhaps it was a joint project. But Joe had been, from the very start, disgusted with the band's commitment at the New Yorker. In addition to evening programs, the contract had called for the band to play for about fifteen minutes at noon. Joe did so the first day, but never afterward. Coonie had to find someone to fill in for his partner. Since Joe often discarded his piano part after the first one or two playings and thereafter played from memory, getting the piano's part of the arrangements was a problem. When the (nearly) six-month engagement closed, the hotel deducted from Joe's payment what they thought would compensate for his noon absences. Joe was furious.[141] This set-to caused the band's agency much concern, but MCA's New York office contacted the New Yorker and helped calm the hotel's management. Billy Goodheart, on behalf of the agency, wrote to Joe on 25 March 1932 with some advice that Joe would have done well to remember. Goodheart told him that everything had been "straightened out" at the New Yorker. He hoped that upon their departure, as well as at their next engagement in Detroit and even beyond, they would not have burned their bridges. It was vital, wrote Goodheart, "to have the good will of all these people for Joe Sanders, looking ahead to … the coming Fall."[142] As MCA's Karl Kramer put it years later, "All of this, of course, made bad feeling and when the band started on the way down, no one extended a helping hand."[143] Kramer clearly was speaking of the band's brief existence after Coonie's death.

In his memoirs Joe wrote, "The entire personnel of the New Yorker bade us farewell reluctantly and not a few actually cried good honest manly tears." (Joe must have forgotten Ralph Hitz, manager of the New Yorker, whose tears would have been of the crocodile variety.) His German busboy even went to Grand Central Station to see him off. All of this made Joe feel, as he put it, "that I had waged a good fight against almost insurmountable odds. He dubbed Ralph Hitz, manager of the New Yorker, the "Little Napoleon of the hotel industry, [who] exhibited very little appreciation for our efforts in giving to him his *first* successful season in the Terrace Room." The band had originally been engaged for a longer period, but probably all parties were relieved to terminate what had become a general ordeal. MCA probably had little difficulty in getting the New Yorker's management to release the band. "Somehow we finally terminated the engagement," said Joe, adding, "There is much that I needs must leave unwritten, many unhappy situations better to delete." His conclusion: "All things material must end, hence we closed an eminently successful, tho seemingly endless, season on April 26th." (Joe meant *March* 26, a Saturday.)[144]

The Nighthawks, after leaving New York, spent about a week at the Book-Cadillac Hotel, in Detroit. This Detroit engagement was a welcome delight, quite aside from the fact that almost anything would have been a relief after the past six months. In addition to their playing for the hotel, starting on April 3 the band played each afternoon and evening at the city's Convention Hall for a General Motors exhibit. To sweeten matters yet further, Leo Fitzpatrick, the Nighthawks' "Merry Old Chief" from Kansas City days, was now director of his own local radio station in Detroit and brought a party of friends. There was, according to Joe, "an old Night Hawk session." All of them "staged a merry party at the station" as they awaited the arrival of the band's train that would take them to Chicago. They bade farewell to Ed T. Lawless, managing director of the hotel and, as Joe put it, "a splendid fellow."[145]

It was at this same hotel, almost two years before, that Joseph T. Schenck, of the very popular vaudeville and recording team of Van and Schenck, died of a heart attack at the early age of thirty-nine.[146] Coincidentally, Coonie too had just had his thirty-ninth, and final, birthday.

While the band was in Detroit, the *Detroit Free Press* came out with some more of the pleasant prattle and poppycock that had always followed both Joe and Coonie. After disposing of the matter as to who was the band's leader—"Neither is in the usual sense since no one wields a baton or bow in front of the musicians"—the speculation then played around the two men's athletic abilities. And while the newspaper correctly repeated the bit about Joe's having struck out twenty-seven men in nine innings, the writer repeated the old myth about Coonie's having gone to the University of Kansas, and embellished it by saying that he also had been an end on its football team.[147]

On April 7, Lawless wrote Joe to express the hotel's appreciation for "the spirit with which you and your boys have worked during your engagement here at the Book-Cadillac." He assured Joe that he had made many friends for the hotel, and that he wished them the greatest success on their return to Chicago.[148] Stein and the MCA were doubtless relieved, but Joe was likely so happy to leave New York that he probably would have been gracious even to Vincent Lopez.

Their return to Chicago! No doubt it seemed a godsend to every member of the band; as he had promised himself to do, Joe stepped from the train and bent down to kiss the first plot of Chicago he stepped onto. As Dan Schroeder puts it, "there was a tremendous greeting from their Chicago fans ... who considered the Nighthawks their home town band, and certainly, along with Kansas City, the band considered Chicago their home town." Madeline and Joe returned to the Surf. "We've maligned it, wearied of it, sworn we'd never go back," said Joe, "but somehow the dear old Surf is *always* 'home, sweet home.'" Gratz, the Surf's manager, had met their train and he personally escorted them to their old apartment in 906. "Our old home," said Joe, "was just as we had left it, even to Madeline's little china closet drapes." He figuratively drank-in Lake Michigan and said he wouldn't trade it for the seven seas. "[I] could have cried when I saw the familiar shore line—*after Manhattan!*"[149]

Just as the Nighthawks were preparing to return to Chicago, Joe and Coonie, perhaps elated by their leaving New York, drolly announced their candidacies in that year's political rites—on both the Republican and Democratic tickets. There is every indication that neither President Hoover nor such possible Democratic candidates as Franklin D. Roosevelt and Alfred E. Smith showed any concern. Joe would "run" for the presidency and Coonie the second office. Said the two "candidates":

> Not to be outdone by other presidential aspirants and confident that we will carry the north, south, east and west, not forgetting the good old middle west, we hereby throw our hats and musical instruments into the ring for nomination on both the Republican and Democratic tickets for the president and vice-president.
>
> Coon-Sanders campaign headquarters

will be established soon at the Hotel Sherman in Chicago. The speaking rostrum will be the bandstand of the College Inn. Our supporters will gather there nightly to devise new ways and means of furthering our candidacy.

Suggestions for campaign slogans are now in order. Make them short and snappy. Our campaign platform is also open to suggestions. Be liberal in your platform planks as we are out to build a boardwalk to the White House.[150]

Bobby Mellin, in his column "Slices of Mellin, published on March 26 in the *Motion Picture Herald*, picked up the story and explained, among other things, that the Knights and Ladies of the Bath would handle the campaign in Chicago. For those with short memories, Mellin reminded his readers that the KLB was "the radio order started by Joe and Coonie during their broadcasting days in Chicago and has as its membership radio fans from coast to coast." According to Mellin, the joke — though he was careful not to use that word — had occurred to the two men during one of their orchestra's rehearsals.[151]

A joke it was, but no greater than that of some other, serious candidacies for the presidency, both before that time and since. And after we've had our chuckles about it, there remains, somewhat tugging at our imaginations, the mischievous question Why Not? And isn't it unfortunate that the two men couldn't have continued their adventure into politics? It would certainly have been uproarious. But though old times seemed to have returned at the Hotel Sherman's College Inn, it very soon became obvious that they never would again.

Even though the College Inn was regarded as, in Joe's phrasing, "Ben Bernie's personal bailiwick," the Nighthawks were well received when they opened, possibly on April 8, though a WBBM "release" of March 7 said the Nighthawks would open at the College Inn on April 15. "The opening was sensational," recorded Joe later, "and it was indeed gratifying to observe all the old boosters of the band." There were many floral pieces on the stage. One of them, presented by Augie Kieckhoffer and Willie Hoppe, represented a billiard table with two crossed cue sticks. The master-of-ceremonies was Julius Tannen with what Joe termed his "rather mouldy 'gags.'" On the second night the band did a program for Lucky Strikes and then, in Joe's words, settled down "to the serious business of doing business after the season was officially closed." "The Thursday theatrical nights," he added, "were continued and were, to the amazement of all, highly successful. Hundreds of famous stars of the stage, screen and radio made personal appearances and contributed to the success of these nights."[152]

It is interesting at this point to quote from Joe's recollections of events that followed:

> W.B.B.M. was our station, outlet for our coast to coast Columbia hookups. The ensuing fan mail was the conclusive evidence that Coon-Sanders still ruled the air. However, it was Coon-Sanders in name only, for poor Coonie had listened too long to the song of the bottle and it was too apparent that he was irrevocably through. It would be unwise to set down on these pages what transpired latterly. One night a substitute appeared, and the next night, and the next. Dr. Hibbe, his dentist, called me on the fourth day and said that Coonie was confined in Henrotin Hospital. (Coonie had complained of an inflamed gum condition — while yet at work the swelling was noticeable.) Two operations on his throat followed and ... Coonie died from general septosemia [sic]. The details are not pleasant, nor for me to divulge.[153]

The substitute drummer Joe mentions was William A. Paley, an accomplished musician and a cousin of the Columbia Broadcasting System's William Paley. The younger Paley was associated with CBS's Chicago office for many years, much of the time as assistant music director at station WBBM.[154] All evidence is that he was a very competent drummer, so it probably was an easy matter for him to take over for Coonie. In fact, he very likely had filled in on such other occasions as during Coonie's appendectomy.

Exactly when Coonie's problem with his tooth and jaw started has been variously reported. The obituary that appeared in *Variety* says that Coonie became ill on April 18, while he was playing with the orchestra. This was probably accurate, though the same obituary misspelled his first name, said his birthplace was Kansas City, and gave his date of death as May 3.[155] Everyone else in the band knew that Coonie was having trouble with a tooth, but at first it seemed nothing out of the ordinary. Who doesn't sooner or later have dental problems, perhaps even abscesses? There was some swelling in the jaw, but that didn't seem ominous, either. From Joe's notes, quoted above, it would seem that Coonie's jaw infection had already made him miss some performances before he entered Henrotin Memorial Hospital, though Joe seems to be saying that Coonie's problem was alcoholic, not dental. The date of his admission to the hospital has been a matter of some speculation and guessing; but his death certificate, whose medical section was completed by attending physician John J. Eichstaedt, states that Coonie's ulcerated tooth and lower-jaw infection were first noticed on April 18. He probably entered the hospital on April 23, the day when Eichstaedt first started treating him, and two days later there was the first of two operations. On the thirtieth the physician discovered "general septicemia," or blood poisoning. Antibiotics were then unknown, of course, and Coonie's carefree lifestyle had probably weakened his immune system. Moreoever, he had perhaps lost the will to live. There was a second operation on May 3, but Coonie's time had run out. He died at 1:10 a.m. on May 4, one day short of three months past his thirty-ninth birthday.[156]

As soon as word went out about his perilous condition, Coonie's family rushed to Chicago. Eula arrived first and stayed in a room just down the hall from where her husband lay. Then the two oldest children, John and Nancy arrived. Eula's mother Mrs. Henrietta Johnson, got there as soon as she received word.[157] According to the late Clyde Hahn, Joe was directing the band in one of their favorite numbers, "Jig Time," when word came that Coonie was at the point of death. "Joe Sanders," says Hahn, "stunned by the news, dropped his baton and rushed to Coonie's bedside. But the end had already come."[158] Many friends, family members, and others concerned had visited Coon at the hospital; and while he was still able to talk, he did so with various ones. Johnny Coon said that his father, on the afternoon before he died, said to him, "I've made too many people love me and then hurt them." And several of the band members later told Harvey Rettberg that Eula Coon, sadly anticipating her husband's death, said to them, "That's not the Coonie I used to know."[159]

Even on this occasion some of the press continued to repeat legends about Coonie. The *Chicago American*, for instance, brought up the old business of his alleged connection with medicine. "Coon was intended for the profession of medicine," it stated, adding that he had studied it for three and a half years, an embellishment on the usually-reported three years. (If Coonie had lived a little longer, he might eventually have been reported as having received his medical degree!) Coon, so the paper said, "first took up the drumsticks as a cadet member of the Wentworth Military Academy band — and never really laid them down until death stilled his hand."[160] But, as we have already seen, if he went to WMA, it was for so brief a time that the school has no record of him. The *Chicago Daily News* said Coonie had been born "38 years ago," and the Kansas City *Star* said he was born in 1894. The *Star* also repeated the myth that Coonie had attended the University of Kansas, even adding that he had met his future wife there.[161] These papers probably got their information partly from the family, and family members are generally notorious for not knowing one another's exact birth dates and for being hazy about certain other biographical details. This perhaps is another illustration of it. The mistake in the obituaries concerning his year of birth is probably the reason for its almost invariable misstatement in later times. But his oldest son's recollection, in conversations with the author of this book, was always that in February 1932 Coonie had his thirty-ninth birthday. And on his tomb his year of birth is given as 1893. That *should* clear the matter up. Perhaps the error was Coonie's last prank.

Logically, it is difficult to see how Coonie could have found three years in which to study medicine or anything else in college. He married in his late teens and was only twenty when his first child, John, was born. Johnny estimated that his father had begun playing in jazz groups about 1911, at age eighteen.[162]

While plans were being made for a funeral in Kansas City, there were matters to be addressed in Chicago. The evening after Coonie died, Joe and the orchestra had to go ahead and fulfill their obligation at College Inn, but Ben Bernie immediately agreed to take over thereafter for the Nighthawks, and, in tribute to Coonie, without compensation. Coonie's body lay in state in Chicago on the fourth, from 2:30 to 6 p.m., at a funeral chapel at 3409 West Madison Street, after which it was taken by train to Kansas City for the funeral on Friday.[163] Madeline sent a telegram to her mother to tell her about Coonie's death and the band's obligation to play that evening — "The show must go on." She also asked her mother to help Coonie's widow in any way possible, and to order flowers for all of them, "something unusual as a lyre. Do not spare expense. Put your names and ours on card." She and Joe made train reservations, and the other members of the band would travel in their automobiles.[164] It must have been a stunned and anxious group of Nighthawks that made their way to Kansas City.

Joe and Madeline had at first intended to fly to Kansas City. Instead, with Jules and Doris Stein, they took the California Limited and arrived at 9 a.m. Friday. Traveling together doubtless gave Joe and Jules an opportunity to discuss possible future plans for the band. Coonie's body, accompanied by his wife and her mother, had already arrived in Kansas City at 8:10 a.m. Thursday, the fifth, and had been taken to Freeman's Funeral Home, Forty-second Street and Baltimore Avenue. John and Nancy Coon arrived later that day by automobile; the two youngest children, Virginia and Carleton, Jr., had remained in Kansas City. Eula Coon was met at the station by her three brothers, Wayne, Allan, and Jack Jenkins, and the latter's wife.[165]

The funeral took place at 2 p.m. on Friday, the sixth. Instead of the more customary six, there were ten pallbearers — Harold and John Thiell, Floyd Estep, Joe Richolson, Robert Pope, Rex Downing, Russell Stout, Pat Pattison,* William Paley, and John Jarman. The *Star* spoke of the "quiet simplicity" that marked the funeral and observed that there was no eulogy in the Christian Science service conducted by Thomas B. Lee, of the Third Church. The pallbearers carried the casket from the chapel between rows of flowers that Joe reckoned as having cost thousands of dollars. They had come from hundreds of friends, relatives, and fellow musicians. These floral gifts, recorded Joe later, "and hundreds of telegrams bore mute testimony that the actual good he had done — his indisputable charm and comaraderie, his dynamic personality, his devotion to his 'shut-ins'— had won for Coonie the undying love of millions." Among the impressive gifts of flowers were those from Fred Waring's orchestra. It was a blanket of roses that covered the top of the casket. Special music consisted of Helen Smith's solo and Mrs. Frederic C. Shaw's organ accompaniment. Joe and Madeline sat with the family in an adjoining private area. At the conclusion of the service, the casket was taken to Mt. Moriah Cemetery. In his written recollections, Joe states that there was a temporary burial to await "final disposition

---

Joe spelled the name with two Ts, while a newspaper item used only one.

6. The Final Year

The Temple, a huge mausoleum near the entrance of Mt. Moriah Cemetery, Kansas City, Missouri. Coonie's body and Eula Coon Stookey's ashes are here. (Author's photograph.)

by mutual agreement by the family." Carleton, Jr., recalls no such temporary burial and doubts that there would have been any difficulty in opening a place in the huge mausoleum at Mt. Moriah. It is possible, however, that there might have been a slight waiting period until the crypt could be prepared, or a decision about whether, indeed, to use the mausoleum. Joe and the band returned that evening to Chicago to resume their obligations at the Sherman Hotel's College Inn.[166]

As Joe puts it in his written recollections:

> So endeth a brilliant and all too short career. So goeth Coonie (I do believe) blithely on his way — carefree, happy-go-lucky, ever smiling — a guy who somehow never reached Man's est [sic]. He lived for today — worked hard — played harder — lived more vastly than any ten men I know. If he chose to go out as he had lived, who are we to censor?
>
> A man learns to love a partner who has shared the pranks of fickle Dame Fortune. When men have worked together, slept together, fought shoulder to shoulder, smiled as one when the going was rugged, rejoiced, as one heart, when a victory was won — those men *know* each the other. I buried the *real* Coonie two years before he became lifeless clay. My tears were not for the stranger who now sleeps in Kansas City. No — my heart communes with the *old-time buddy!*
>
> Vale, Coonie! May you find what you are seeking!
>
> Your partner and brother,
> Joe L. Sanders[162]

Today both Coonie and Joe occupy graves at Mt. Moriah Cemetery, in Kansas City. Joe lies in space fourteen, lot twenty, in a section numbered twenty-three and named "Angels." His stone marker, flush with the earth, states:

> "Joe"
> Joseph L. Sanders
> Oct. 15, 1896
> May 14, 1965

Joe's grave in Mt. Moriah Cemetery, space 14, lot 20, section 23 ("Angels"), Kansas City, Missouri. Trudy Sanders' grave is to viewer's left. (Author's photograph.)

In the center of the inscription is a lyre. On Joe's right is buried Gertrude "Trudy" Sanders, his second wife. (Madeline Sanders is buried in her parents' lot, elsewhere in the cemetery.)

Coonie's burial site is somewhat more dramatic. As one enters the cemetery from Holmes Road, there looms up directly in front a huge mausoleum named the Temple, which in good Masonic style looks like something at ancient Karnak. Two Egyptian sphinxes guard the Temple's main entrance, an impressive metal double-door. Passing through this door, I descended thirteen steps into a multi-chambered crypt, turned right into the first corridor, and saw on my right a utility room and, next to it, a private family crypt. The next section was designated as "Z." Facing the twelve burial compartments, I discovered that the occupant of the top right was "Carleton A. Coon, 1893–1932." It was an impressive, if somber, setting, and I seemed to be the only person in the mausoleum. Though the experience was not depressing, I could not help sensing the incongruity of the surroundings with what I knew of the occupant's jolly, mischievous nature. In fact, as I gazed at Coonie's resting place and its vicinity, I was reminded of an exchange between two wits, Reginald Turner and Oscar Wilde, when the latter was on his deathbed and, thus, in an uncharacteristically gloomy mood:

> WILDE: I have had a dreadful dream. I dreamt that I was dining with the dead.
> TURNER: My dear Oscar, I am sure you were the life and soul of the party.[167]

Fine

Epilogue

At about the time that Coonie died, *Radio Digest* received a letter, published in its summer issue, from Phil Clarke, Jr., Charles S. Arms, and Barton Cameron, of Asheville, N.C. The three had nominations for what they called an ideal "All Star Dance Orchestra." "We think that this would be the finest possible combination in the country if it were organized into one dance orchestra. There would be no conductor, as all its members would play some instrument—for co-directors, however, we nominate Carleton Coon and Joe Sanders." The nominees were the following: Joe Sanders, piano and vocals; Carleton Coon, drums; Harry Reser, banjo; Louis Panico, 1st trumpet; Victor Lombardo, 2nd trumpet; Carmen Lombardo, 1st saxophone; Wayne King, 2nd saxophone; Art Kassel, 3rd saxophone; Rex Downing, trombone; and Elmer Krebs, bass.[1] In more modern terms, this might have been the "dream team," though it's difficult to see how one could have considered by-passing the other members of the Nighthawk Orchestra.

After Coonie's death, the assumption was that Joe would keep the band together. Johnny Coon told Clyde Hahn that Jules Stein recommended keeping the name Coon-Sanders, and that Sanders might even hire Johnny Coon himself to help justify doing so. Joe refused to become associated with Johnny, and even the younger Coon thought that, for once, Joe was right. "I would never work with Joe," said Johnny, "because I am a redhead and I know that he and I would have been at each other all the time!"[2]

Johnny Coon said that sometime after his father's death, Joe Richolson visited him somewhere in Iowa and asked him to invite all the old Nighthawks to join him in reorganizing the Nighthawks. Johnny refused that, too.[3]

Nevertheless, the Blackhawk was still hoping to recapture the glamor of those past years when the Nighthawks started the restaurant on its career of featuring bands. In March of 1934 Hal Kemp's orchestra was playing there, but the restaurant hoped a revived Coon-Sanders group would take over after Kemp had left for a summer at the Lincoln Tavern. Stein's MCA thought it had persuaded Joe to take on Johnny Coon, but as *Variety* put it, "With details all completed, Joe backed out of the proposed Blackhawk restaurant engagment at the last minute."

He had decided to take a vacation in Kansas City, instead.[4] This would suggest that Johnny Coon had agreed to become associated with Joe, but in later years the younger Coon insisted he had *never* considered it.

As a matter of fact, Joe did try for a short while to continue with the band, not under the name of Coon-Sanders but as the Nighthawks. It didn't work. As some of the band's members later said, Coonie's ghost haunted both the band and the audiences. At various times during performances, many in the dance hall or theater came up to express condolences and to say how much Coonie was missed. It just became too much for the band to endure; Joe, perhaps for several complex reasons, began to find it uncomfortable, perhaps even intolerable.[5] The band had obviously lost both its spirit and its heart.

What Joe's relations were subsequently with Coonie's family is difficult to determine. In later years Joe maintained that he was concerned with making sure that Eula Coon and her children did not suffer financially. Meryl Friedel, in an article about Joe's life after Coonie's death, and perhaps written with Sanders' help, reports that Joe "took upon his shoulders the care of Mrs. Coon and her [children], seeing that she received her husband's insurance, and arranging that she got a share of the orchestra's earnings so long as it existed." The article goes on to say that Joe went to considerable trouble to pay his late partner's debts—"Debts cropped [up] everywhere," he averred. On the other hand, I made a point of asking Johnny Coon what he remembered of all this, and his memory was very much at odds with the version in the Friedel article. Johnny could recall his mother's getting not more than about five hundred dollars.[6] Perhaps, as so often happens, the truth lies somewhere between these very different recollections.

The band members scattered. Joe and Madeline went to Hollywood and spent some months working with the film industry. Meryl Friedel records that Joe and Madeline were sitting in the bleachers at the Rose Bowl game, New Year's of 1935, when Joe decided to form another band. On the following May 18, he opened at the Blackhawk, representing himself as the Old Left-Hander, a reference to his early days in amateur baseball. This band had some success and made several recordings, but its popularity was never even close to what Joe's band had achieved, as George T. Simon puts it, when it "sported a hyphen."[7] Joe's new band played mostly in the Midwest, but he sometimes played over the radio and did programs to entertain military personnel during the Second World War. For instance, the Sanders band was featured on 13 August 1943, over the Blue Network, in its series, sponsored by Coca-Cola, "The Victory Parade of Spotlight Bands." On 16 April 1947 Texas City, Texas, suffered a terrible explosion caused by nitrates on ships at the dock. Joe's orchestra participated in a disaster benefit program that included also Mickey Rooney, Victor Borge, Jane Russell, Ann Blyth, Celeste Holm, Kay Keyser's orchestra, Jerry Wald's orchestra, Sonny Tufts, Harry Babbitt, and Marion Morgan.[8] Earlier that same year, on February 16, Madeline Sanders died at the age of forty-nine. According to Priscilla Sanders, one of Joe's relatives, her death was at least partly the result of alcoholism. Joe ended his career as an orchestra leader in 1953.[9]

Upon retirement Sanders returned to Kansas City, Mo. His financial situation became straitened and made his last years increasingly difficult, though his second wife Trudy provided him with steadfast love and support. In the summer of 1961 he was forced to leave his home and to rent a smaller one. He even lost his piano, and though neighbors started a fund to buy him another, it came when he was no longer able to play. As he often told visitors at this period, he was "learning the true meaning of humility."[10]

Various individuals and groups were of some help to Joe and Trudy Sanders, but Joe's desperate situation led him to ask so many for assistance that he developed a reputation as a mendicant. On the basis of some extant records, it seems that in previous years he had alienated some who now refused assistance, and others who, while not alienated, refused *further* assistance. Even Jules Stein and the Music Corporation of America, who for old times' sake had tried to help Joe, reached a point at which they felt they had done enough. "We, as a company and I, as an individual," wrote Stein to Clyde Hahn, "have given him substantial monies over the recent years. We do not feel we wish to support him any longer."[11]

But there were others, new friends, who continued to take an interest and tried to make his last years easier. Joe was particularly helped by such generous friends as Cliff W. Halliburton and good neighbors such as Pauline McMeachin and her two sons Jim and Bob, all of whom were instrumental in getting Joe a grand piano. They also contacted local disc jockeys, journalists, and others who could call the public's attention to Joe's difficult circumstances, as well as to remind a new generation of Joe's celebrated past.[11] And in early 1965, Victor Records, acting through the urging of such fans and friends as the new Nighthawks Club's Harvey Rettberg, Clyde Hahn, and Paul F. Karberg, issued a volume in its Vintage Series, on which there were good quality copies of sixteen Coon-Sanders recordings. But all of this was so near the end of Joe's life, and he was by then so infirm, that these friendly gestures proved mostly symbolic for the Old Left-Hander. Apparently, the only time Joe heard any of the newly issued long-playing record was when he was practically on his deathbed. In fact, when a friend called Joe to tell him about the new record and placed the phone near the phonograph for him to hear, the Old Left-hander suffered a slight heart attack.[12] Perhaps the excitement was too much.

At last Joe's irritating months at Camp Bowie, back in 1918 and 1919, were paying off. As a veteran, he was eligible for admission to the Kansas City Veterans Hospital. There, after suffering several strokes, he went into a coma and died on 14 May 1965. He was sixty-eight years old.[13]

Joe Sanders' life had been an unusually interesting and productive one. About two years after his retirement in 1953, he told an interviewer that he estimated that he had composed about 500 songs, of which about a fifth had been published.[14] It seems inescapable that if his practical business ability had been equal to his musical talents, his later life and certainly his last days would have been much easier.

Clyde Hahn, of Pleasant Garden, N.C., and Harvey Rettberg, of Sunset, S.C., had earlier discovered that they had a mutual interest in the old Nighthawks of Kansas City and Chicago, so on 26 September 1959 they started the new Coon-Sanders Nighthawks Club. It quickly attracted the attention of others, not only many who remembered hearing the band in person or over the radio but also many who were too young to have heard them except on old phonograph records. In the years since its founding, the organization has held its annual meetings in Huntington, W. Va. As of this writing, Dale Jones is president of the club. He has been of great help in my work on this history. (His email address is Coonsander@aol.com.)

In 1961, while Joe and a number of other veterans of the Coon-Sanders band were still living, Harvey Rettberg decided to visit them and record the interviews on tape. Leaving their home in South Carolina, Harvey and his wife Hilda drove all the way to the West Coast. In Los Angeles they visited Floyd Estep, as well as Nancy Searles, Coonie's daughter, and in Bakersfield, Calif., they saw Joe Richolson. On 16 July 1961 they were in Kansas City where they visited with Joe and Trudy Sanders, even as the latter were moving into a different, smaller home. Harvey taped at least an hour of their conversation. As the Rettbergs were leaving and were walking to their car, Harvey asked Joe to pose for a snapshot. Joe did so, and as a parting gesture, raised his hand — his *left* hand, of course. Leaving Kansas City, Harvey headed down to Arkansas, where he saw Rex Downing, who had exchanged his trombone for a gavel as county judge. In St.

Floyd Eugene Estep, at age 87, Los Angeles, California. (Courtesy Claude and Ruth Anderson.)

Augustine, Fla., the Rettbergs visited Harold Thiell and recorded some of his talk. One other old veteran, Russ Stout, visited the Rettbergs in Sunset, S.C. And some of the sounds of these meetings are still preserved on tape.

Thanks to such enthusiasts as Harvey Rettberg, Clyde Hahn, and other members of the new Nighthawks fan club, in more recent years there have been several other reissuings of original Nighthawk recordings, both on vinyl long-playing discs and on compact discs. For years such collectors as Rettberg and Hahn have swapped recordings and tapes of recordings until there must be many hundreds of them scattered about the nation. The author of this book was one of those fortunate recipients, for Rettberg went to considerable trouble to see that he got every Coon-Sanders recording he had. In addition, I was fortunate to meet another Nighthawk aficionado, Willis Morrisette, at his home in Wilson, N.C., and to receive a considerable quantity of his tapes and old phonograph recordings.

What's left to say? The Coon-Sanders Nighthawks were certainly not only one of the very best of the dance orchestras of the Twenties, but also perhaps the most unaccountable. In these later times when few seem to understand the meaning of the word *unique*, I think it could be well, and correctly, applied to this remarkable band of musicians. Other orchestras of their day played good music — often outstanding music — such orchestras as those led by Paul Whiteman, George Olsen, Duke Ellington, Fred Waring, Bennie Moten, Ben Bernie, and Ted Weems. I've talked with quite a number of persons skilled in music and familiar with the Nighthawks. All of them have agreed that the Nighthawks were excellent musicians and that they were certainly among the very best in the nation of that day. Arrangements by Joe Sanders, and such of his players as Floyd Estep, were of the highest quality. They were designed to allow every member of the orchestra to do solo work and to demonstrate virtuosity. Joe's musical skills brought innovations in such matters as arranging, voicing of instruments, and employment of breaks. It has been said, in fact, that Joe Sanders could get more breaks into one number than other arrangers would employ in many. All of these characteristics helped keep Coon-Sanders' music from falling into a routine.

Joe's home at 7626 Pennsylvania Avenue, Kansas City, Missouri, 16 July 1961. Waving goodbye to Harvey and Hilda Rettberg. Joe of course uses his left hand. (Courtesy Harvey C. Rettberg.)

Milton Caniff's *Steve Canyon* comic strip for 12 February 1962. The general refers to listening to Coon-Sanders over Kansas City's WDAF. Caniff misspelled Sanders' last name, later apologized and redrew that block for private distribution. (Permission granted by the estate of Milton Caniff.)

But it was not merely in the quality of their music that the Nighthawks stood out. From the days of their earliest appearances in Kansas City they had the reputation of offering not only good music but a good show as well. Many reviews of their appearances in Kansas City, Chicago, and other cities and towns about the nation spoke of their delightful antics. And the chief practitioner of such shenanigans was, of course, Carleton Coon. He was famous for his mugging for the dancers and spectators, for his funny comments, and for his pranks upon his fellow bandsmen. But Coonie was only the *chief* zany, for all of the players entered into the spirit of charming madness and thus gave their audiences both an aural and a visual treat. They could, on special occasions, regale listeners with engaging renderings of musical novelty, instrumentation, and farce. But as Johnny Coon often said, the band never forgot that their primary function was to ensure a clear, accurate, steady beat for their dancers.

Though tremendously popular on radio, they achieved far greater fame when their fans could both see and hear them. Contrary to the theory by some in the mid–Twenties that exposure on radio tended to dull popular interest in performers, Coon-Sanders showed that it sometimes actually increased it. Under the very able agency of the Music Corporation of America, they pioneered in road tours and the one night stand.

I have often pondered how prodigal the Nighthawks were of their resources and talents. While other, often inferior bands, through good business planning, went on to achieve greater permanence and financial success, the Nighthawks seemed content to do what they enjoyed most, namely, to play their hearts out and please their fans. They apparently disdained to cater to well-placed promoters, or make publicized trips abroad, or, as with such orchestras as those led by Vincent Lopez and Jean Goldkette, to maintain several bands to increase the number of engagements. That method probably struck them as too like a musical factory.

They played hard, devilishly hard schedules, but seemed to draw strength from them. How these men stood up under such exacting, if self-imposed, discipline is still something of a mystery. But it was the Twenties! It was the era of boundless energy, of a live-for-the-moment philosophy, and of "flaming youth." Sadly, the flame was a brief one, and all we have now to evoke those wonderful Nighthawks are a relatively few recordings. But at least we have those few, those *fetching* few.

Notes

1. Joe and Coonie

1. Author's conversation with John Coon, Auburn, Ala., 19 January 1995.
2. Author's memory, from childhood, of conversations with those who lived during the Twenties.
3. Author's conversation with John Coon, Auburn, Ala., 19 January 1995.
4. Joe Sanders' *Voss Diary, 1926*; box 11, JLSC; *Date Book for Season 1927–1928*, *ibid*; author's conversation with John Coon, 19 January 1995, Auburn, Ala.
5. Joe Sanders' *Voss Diary, 1926* and *Date Book for Season 1927–1928*, JLSC; Joe Sanders, "Join Coon-Sanders and See America," Sanders' scrapbook history of the Nighthawks, *ibid*, *passim*.
6. Author's conversation with John Coon, 19 January 1995, Auburn, Ala.; tape 5 (i.e., tape 3, side 1) of six tapes, now in author's possession, made by Coon just before his death and left with Sherry and Steve Drummond.
7. Author's conversation with John Coon, Auburn, Ala., 19 January 1995.
8. *Ibid*.; Joe Popper, "America's Band," *Kansas City Star's* Sunday supplement, 9 July 1989, p. 9.
9. Author's conversation with John Coon, Auburn, Ala., 19 January 1995.
10. *Ibid*.
11. *Ibid*.
12. *Ibid*.
13. *Ibid*.; author's telephone conversation, 9 May 2001, with Wentworth Military Academy.
14. Author's conversation with John Coon, Auburn, Ala., 19 January 1995.
15. *Ibid*.; Eula Coon Stookey to Harvey Rettberg, 15 May 1961, in HRC.
16. See, for example, Duncan Schiedt, *The Jazz State of Indiana* (Pittsboro, Ind.: Duncan P. Schiedt, 1977), p. 159.
17. Author's conversation with John Coon, Auburn, Ala., 19 January 1995. For statement about Jack Riley, see item in SC1, box 15, folder 2, JLSC.
18. Author's conversation with John Coon, Auburn, Ala., 19 January 1995.
19. *Ibid*.; Joe Sanders, "The Coon-Sanders Story (Part II)," *Jazz Notes*, vol. VI, no. 1 ns (1961?), p. 3.
20. Author's conversation with John Coon, Auburn, Ala., 19 January 1995; author's telephone conversation with the University of Kansas Alumni Association, 9 May 2001.
21. Author's conversation with John Coon, Auburn, Ala., 19 January 1995.
22. *Ibid*.
23. *Ibid*.
24. *Ibid*.
25. Janet K. Miller, Joe Sanders' great-niece, in electronic-mail message to author, 16 February 2001.
26. Jerry Wald, "Not on the Air," *Jazz Notes*, pub. by the Indianapolis (Ind.) Jazz Club, vol. VI, nos. 2/3 (February, March 1961), p. 9; Janet K. Miller's electronic mail to author, 19 June 2001.
27. Joe Sanders, "The Coon-Sanders Story [Part 1]," *Jazz Notes*, February/March 1961, p. 2.
28. *Ibid*.
29. *Ibid*., pp. 2, 4.

30. *Ibid.*, p. 2; programs for recitals, concerts, etc., miscellaneous musical programs, JLSC.
31. *Ibid.*, p. 4.
32. Programs for recitals, concerts, etc., miscellaneous materials, *passim*, JLSC.
33. Olmstead to Joe Sanders, 11 September 1911, in miscellaneous materials, *ibid.*
34. Program's bulletin among miscellaneous materials, *ibid.*
35. Various program bulletins, newspaper clippings, etc., among miscellaneous materials, *ibid.*
36. Sanders, "The Coon-Sanders Story [Part I]," p. 4.
37. Various program bulletins, newspaper clippings, etc., among miscellaneous materials, JLSC.
38. J. A. Lewis to Georgia Murphy, 13 August 1914, *ibid.*
39. Newspaper clipping, *ibid.*
40. Program bulletins, newspaper clippings, etc., *ibid.*
41. Newspaper clipping, unidentified source and date, *Ibid.*
42. Various unidentified newspaper clippings, etc., *ibid.*; Sanders, "The Coon-Sanders Story [Part I]," p. 5; Anthony Slide, *The Vaudevillians: A Dictionary of Vaudeville Performers* (Westport, Conn.: Arlington House, 1981), pp. xiii–xiv, hereinafter cited as *The Vaudevillians*.
43. Unidentified newspaper clipping (probably from a Ft. Worth, Texas, paper of early February, 1919), among miscellaneous materials, JLSC.
44. Mark Sullivan, *Our Times, 1900–1925*, vol. 5: *Over Here, 1914–1918* (New York: Charles Scribner's, 1933), pp. 304, 424–440.
45. Victor recording 18455-A (Camden, N.J.: Victor Talking Machine Co., 1917).
46. Sigmund Spaeth, *A History of Popular Music in America* (New York: Random House, 1948), p. 629; "I Don't Want to Get Well," Victor recording 18413-B (Camden, N.J.: Victor Talking Machine Co., [1917?]).
47. Spaeth, *A History of Popular Music in America*, p. 407; "They Were All out of Step but Jim," Columbia recording A2630 (N.p.: Columbia Graphophone Co., [1918?]).
48. Miscellaneous materials, JLSC; used with permission of the Kansas City Public Library.
49. See *Presenting That Celebrated Maestro Max Morath in a Scintillating Program of Waltzes, Shouts, Novelties, Rags, Blues, Ballads and Stomps*, Epic recording BN 26066 (N.p.: Epic Records/A Product of CBS, 1963).
50. "Former Belton Boy a Song Writer of Unusual Ability," this and other unidentified newspaper clippings, in miscellaneous materials, JLSC.
51. Janet K. Miller, electronic message to author, 16 February 2001; see also miscellaneous unidentified newspaper clippings, JLSC.
52. Sanders, "The Coon-Sanders Story (Part II)," p. 1; see newspaper clipping "Belton's Star Hurler Doing Good Work," 21 August 1918, from unidentified newspaper, in miscellaneous items, JLSC.
53. *Ibid.*, pp. 1–2.
54. *Ibid.*, p. 2.
55. *Ibid.*, pp. 2–3.
56. Unidentified newspaper clipping, among miscellaneous materials, JLSC.
57. Sanders, "The Coon-Sanders Story (Part II)," p. 3.
58. *Ibid.*
59. Author's conversation with John Coon, Auburn, Ala., 19 January 1995.
60. Sanders, "The Coon-Sanders Story (Part II)," pp. 3–4.
61. *Ibid.*, p. 4.

2. Postwar Kansas City

1. "Over 100,000 in 79 Cities; U. S. Census to July 1, 1924," *Variety*, 23 July 1924, p. 2.
2. "Starbeams," *Kansas City Star*, 25 August 1922.
3. Lois Gordon and Alan Gordon, *American Chronicle: Six Decades in American Life, 1920–1980* (New York: Atheneum, 1987), p. 14, hereinafter cited as *American Chronicle*.
4. Arthur Mizener, *The Far Side of Paradise: A Biography of F. Scott Fitzgerald* (Boston: Houghton Mifflin, 1965), p. 88.
5. "Starbeams," *Kansas City Star*, 12 April 1922.
6. *Kansas City Times*, 1 February 1919.
7. *Ibid.*, 13, 14, and 27 November, and 9 December 1921.
8. *Ibid.*, 12 March 1920.
9. *I Can Hear It Now, 1919–1949*, Columbia Masterworks recording album D3L 366, vol. 3: 1919–1932, side 1, band 2 (New York: Columbia Records, n.d.); Elizabeth Stevenson, *Babbits and Bohemians: The American 1920s* (New York: Macmillan Company, 1967), pp. 74, 127.
10. Stevenson, *Babbits and Bohemians: The American 1920s*, p. 130.
11. Henry L. Mencken, *On Politics: A Carnival of Buncombe* (Baltimore: Johns Hopkins University Press, 1956), p. 18.
12. *I Can Hear It Now, 1919–1949*, vol. 1, 1919–1932, side 1, band 2; Gordon and Gordon, *American Chronicle*, p. 7.
13. Henry L. Mencken, *H.L. Mencken: The American Scene, a Reader* (New York: Knopf, 1965), pp. 8–9.
14. James J. Montague, "The Flapper to the Bar," *Kansas City Star*, 13 April 1922, p. 15.
15. Article about Ed Howe, *Kansas City Star*, 11 July 1922; "Kansas Notes," *ibid.*, 17 April 1922; cartoon "A Rag, a Bone — and Less Than a Hank of Hair," *ibid.*, 6 August 1922.

16. "The Flapper and the Flopper," *Kansas City Star*, 16 April 1922, p. 1D.
17. Sullivan, *Our Times, 1900–1925*, vol. 6: *The Twenties*, p. 562.
18. "Signals by Girls Wearing Goloshes [*sic*]," *Variety*, 10 February 1926, p. 13.
19. "Roll 'Em, Girls," Victor record 19838-B (Camden, N.J.: Victor Talking Machine Co., [1926?]).
20. Letters to the editor, *Kansas City Star*, 14 September 1921.
21. Alice Cole, "Speaking the Public Mind," *ibid.*, 11 August 1921.
22. "1920 Clothes Not for the Buxom Maid," *ibid.*, 8 March 1920.
23. *Ibid.*
24. "Dance and Grow Thin," Victor record 18258-B (Camden, N.J.: Victor Talking Machine Co., n.d.).
25. *Kansas City Star*, 29 August 1921.
26. "The Cake," *Kansas City Star*, 17 April 1922.
27. H. W. Davis, "As the King's English Changes," *Kansas City Star*, 13 April 1922, p. 15.
28. "As 12th Street Says It," *ibid.*, 16 April 1922, p. 19-A.
29. *Ibid.*
30. *Ibid.*, 17 April 1922.
31. "A Cake Eater," *ibid.*, 29 January 1922; "Start War on Sissyism," *ibid.*, 16 February 1922; "Cheer a Cake Eater Critic," *ibid.*, 31 May 1922.
32. "A Cake Eater?" *ibid.*, 29 January 1922.
33. *Ibid.*, 13 January 1922.
34. "Best Dressed 'Caker' and Flapper Picked at Door," *Variety*, 16 December 1925, p. 4.
35. "Why Censure the Flapper?" *Kansas City Star*, 11 April 1922.
36. *Ibid.*, 24 February 1920.
37. *Ibid.*, 1 February 1920.
38. *Ibid.*, 23 February 1919 and 31 March 1922.
39. *Ibid.*, 4 February 1923.
40. *Ibid.*, 27 April 1922.
41. Robert Kimball, ed., *Cole* (New York: Holt, Rinehart & Winston, 1971), p. 124.
42. *Kansas City Star*, 1920–1922, *passim*.
43. *Ibid.*, 27 April 1922.
44. *Wonderful Nonsense: Fun Songs of the Roaring Twenties*, compact disc TT503 CD (Los Angeles: Take Two Records, 1999), disc 2, band 2.
45. Henry Louis Mencken, *A Mencken Chrestomathy* (New York: Alfred A. Knopf, 1949), p. 282.
46. *Kansas City Star*, 27 October 1921, 4 April and 28 May 1922; *I Can Hear It Now* vol. III, 1919–1932, Columbia Masterworks recording ML 4261, side 1, band 4.
47. Told to the author in the late 1940s by R.E. Miles, a merchant in Meridian, Miss., and recalled from his life during the Twenties.
48. *Kansas City Star*, 24 February 1920, and 7, 29, and 30 April 1922.
49. "Inside Stuff on Music," *Variety*, 4 November 1925, p. 44.
50. "English Gags," *ibid.*, 7 July 1926, p. 27; ad for *The Private Life of Helen of Troy*, *ibid.*, 8 February 1928, p. 17.
51. "An Old Acquaintance," *ibid.*, 17 January 1923, p. 13.
52. *Ibid.*, 22 January 1923.
53. *Ibid.*, 13 October 1922.
54. *Ibid.*, 10 December 1921.
55. *Ibid.*, 29 October 1922.
56. Ethan Mordden, *That Jazz!: An Ideosyncratic Social History of the American Twenties* (New York: Putnam's, 1978), p. 64 — hereinafter cited as *That Jazz!*
57. "K. K. K.'s Klantauquas in '25," *Variety*, 16 July 1924, pp. 1, 25.
58. "Klan Leader Travels in Arsenal," *ibid.*, 23 July 1924, pp. 1, 5.
59. "Inside Stuff of Vaudeville," *ibid.*, 10 February 1926, p. 9.
60. Sullivan, *Our Times, 1900–1925*, vol. 6: *The Twenties*, pp. 545–47; Mordden, *That Jazz!*, pp. 64–66; Stevenson, *Babbits and Bohemians: The American 1920s*, pp. 155–156.
61. "K. K. K.'s Internal Strife May Close All Klantauquas," *Variety*, 25 February 1925, p. 36.
62. *Kansas City Times*, 1 February 1919.
63. *Hark! The Years! A Scrapbook of Sound*, phonograph recording S-282 (N. p.: Capitol Records, Inc., n.d. [1954?]), side 2.
64. "Alcoholic Blues," Silvertone phonograph record 5025-A, and (side 2) "You Don't Need the Wine to Have a Wonderful Time," Silvertone phonograph record 5025-B (Chicago, Ill.: Sears, Roebuck & Co., n.d. [1919?]).
65. Spaeth, *A History of Popular Music in America*, pp. 632, 426, 429; "I Married the Bootlegger's Daughter," Victor recording 19738-A (Camden, N.J.: Victor Talking Machine Co., n.d.).
66. Among song lyrics, JLSC; used with Kansas City Public Library's permission.
67. "The Streets Ran Booze," *Kansas City Star*, 23 February 1922.
68. "Whisky Now $155 a Case," *ibid.*, 25 January 1922, p. 4.
69. *Ibid.*
70. *Ibid.*, 9 May 1923.
71. Conversation with John Coon, Auburn, Ala., 19 January 1995.
72. "Starbeams," *Kansas City Star*, 19 December 1921.
73. "Oh, Man," *ibid.*, 16 November 1921, p. 20.
74. "Thirsty Eighty [remainder of title missing]," *ibid.*, 1 January 1923, p. 1.
75. *Ibid.*
76. *Ibid.*
77. *Ibid.*
78. *Ibid.*; "Locks for Chicken Farms," *ibid.*, 2 June 1922.

79. "As We Go Dancing Around," *ibid.*, 26 November 1922, p. 1-E.
80. *Ibid.*
81. *Kansas City Star*, 1919–1924, *passim*; Slide, *The Vaudevillians*, pp. 146–147. For reaction to Eddie Cantor, see "The Stage and Stage People," *Kansas City Star*, 7 April 1923.
82. *Kansas City Star*, theater ads, 3 September 1921.
83. *Kansas City Times*, theater ads, 1 March 1920.
84. *Kansas City Star*, 31 January 1919 and theater ads and reviews 1920–1923, *passim*.
85. *Ibid.*, Globe's ad, 17 January 1923.
86. *Ibid.*, 29 September 1922, p. 19.
87. *Kansas City Times*, 8 February 1920.
88. See, for example, "Your Thanksgiving Dinner," *Kansas City Star*, 29 November 1922, p. 7.
89. *Kansas City Star*, 15 June 1922.
90. *Ibid.*, 28 May 1922; *ibid.*, 5 August 1921.
91. Sullivan, *Our Times*, vol. 4, *The War Begins, 1909–1914*, pp. 252–255.
92. "Starbeams," *Kansas City Star*, 21 June 1922.
93. See *The American Heritage Dictionary of the English Language* (Boston, etc.: Houghton Mifflin, 1980), p. 1195.
94. "Ban on 'Shimmy Shiver,'" *Kansas City Star*, 2 February 1919.
95. "Shimme [sic] Caused Her Fall," *ibid.*, 5 September 1921.
96. Classified ads, *ibid.*, 9 October 1921.
97. *Kansas City Star*, 24 February, 4 March 1920.
98. "Starbeams," *ibid.*, 14 June 1922.
99. *Kansas City Star*, 1919–1924, *passim*.
100. Brian Rust, *Jazz Records A–Z, 1897–1931*, 2nd ed. (Hatch End, Middlesex, England: 1962), pp. 431–434; George T. Simon, *The Big Bands* (New York: Macmillan, 1967), pp. 498–499.
101. "Enter the Jazz Waltz," *Kansas City Star*, 9 October 1921.
102. "Some of the Methods of Dancing the Welfare Board Frowns On," *ibid.*, 4 October 1923, p. 3.
103. "Guilty Verdict on Dance," *ibid.*, 24 January 1922, p. 5.
104. *Ibid.*
105. *Ibid.*
106. "Jazz Like Booze Problem," *ibid.*, 11 February 1922, p. 2.
107. "Some of the Methods of Dancing the Welfare Board Frowns On," *ibid.*, 4 October 1923, p. 3.
108. "A Jazz Ban in Schools," *ibid.*, 10 September 1922.
109. "Enter the 'Jazz' Waltz; Dancers Find a Way around a Ban," *ibid.*, 9 October 1921. This is edited for clarity of reading.
110. "Methodists Recommend," *Variety*, 14 May 1924, p. 1.
111. *Kansas City Star*, 1 October 1922.
112. "City's Dress Suit Ready," *ibid.*, 28 October 1921; *ibid.*, Doric Theater ad, 30 October 1921; Truman Committee, *ibid.*, 17 October 1921; "Police Ready for Crooks," *ibid.*, 29 October 1921.
113. "A Legion Song Contest," *Kansas City Star*, 31 August 1921; see also miscellaneous materials, JLSC.
114. *Kansas City Star*, 13 October 1922.
115. "Big Race Sunday," *ibid.*, 16 September 1922; "One Racer Killed," *Kansas City Times*, 18 September 1922; see also letters to the editor, *Kansas City Star*, 21 September 1922.
116. See, for example, *Kansas City Star*, 10 April and 1 July 1922.
117. *Ibid.*, 16 May 1923, 30 September 1921.
118. "A New Car to Kansas City," *ibid.*, 1 February 1920.
119. *Ibid.*, 1 February 1920.
120. *Ibid.*, 5 December 1921.
121. *Ibid.*, 5 March 1922.
122. *Ibid.*, 1 February 1920.
123. "A New Signal in Penn Valley," *ibid.*, 16 October 1922, p. 4.
124. James W. Farlow, "A Fool and His Car Are Soon Busted," *ibid.*, 1 February 1920.
125. *Kansas City Star*, 31 August 1921, 10 May 1923.
126. Company's ad, *ibid.*, 19 February 1922.
127. *Ibid.*, 19 November 1921.
128. See, for example, *ibid.*, 10 September 1921, *et seq.*, *passim*.
129. "Starbeams," *ibid.*, 25 January 1922.
130. "Spy Hunting in Kansas City," *ibid.*, 2 February 1919.
131. "Have We Lost Control of Civilization Forces?" *ibid.*, 5 July 1922, p. 18; also, lead editorial, *ibid.*, 11 November 1922.
132. Eric F. Goldman, *Rendezvous with Destiny: A History of Modern American Reform* (New York: Vintage Books, 1956), pp. 196–197.
133. "Actors Fear Theater Reform," *Kansas City Star*, 30 January 1920.
134. "They're All Radio 'Fans,'" *ibid.*, 17 January 1922, p. 1; "Starbeams," *ibid.*, 17 March 1922.
135. "Sending Stations in 21 Cities," *ibid.*, 26 February 1922; "Radio Stations Listed," *ibid.*, 16 April 1922, p. 14-A; *ibid.*, 3 May 1922, p. 12; "Radio Sweeps Nation," *ibid.*, 15 October 1922; *ibid.*, 7 January 1923; "A Million Radio Sets in Use," *ibid.*, p. 6.
136. "Mr. Radio Man," Paul Whiteman's orchestra, Victor recording 19330-B (Camden, N.J.: Victor Talking Machine Co., n.d.); Billy Jones and Ernie Hare (The Happiness Boys), "Twisting the Dials," 2 sides, Victor recording 35953-A and B (Camden, N.J.: Victor Talking Machine Co., n.d.).
137. Joe Hayman, "Cohen Buys a Wireless Set," Columbia record A-3832 (New York, N.Y.:

Columbia Graphophone Co., n.d., but about early 1923).

138. "Tune in at 375 Meters," *Kansas City Star*, 16 February 1922, p. 1; "Next Concert Wednesday," *ibid.*, 17 February 1922, p. 1.

139. "Two of Best Orchestras in West Will Play for the Post's Radio Concert," *Kansas City Post*, 19 May 1922; "WDAF Will Talk Tonight," *Kansas City Star*, 5 June 1922, p. 1; Sweeney Auto School's ad, *ibid.*, 15 August 1922, p. 24.

140. "The Ravings of a Radio-Maniac," *Kansas City Star*, 5 March 1922, p. 1D.

141. "A Great Boon to Parents," *ibid.*, 18 April 1922, p. 15.

142. "Radio Stations Listed," "Paste This Near Your Set," "Radio Questions and Answers," and "The Bootlegger into Radio," *ibid.*, 16 April 1922, p. 14A.

143. "Listen in with the Shaves," *ibid.*, 22 February 1922, p. 1; *ibid*, 28 June 1922.

144. "A 'Radio Shop' Raided," *ibid.*, 8 December 1922, p. 20.

145. "There Is Jazz — and Jazz," *ibid.*, 15 March 1922, p. 1.

146. Reproduced in Sullivan's *Our Times, 1900–1925*, vol. VI: *The Twenties*, p. 479.

147. *Ibid.*, pp. 478–479.

148. *Ibid.*, p. 481.

149. "A Restful Evening," *Kansas City Star*, 9 July 1922, p. 7-C.

150. "A War on Jazz Music," *ibid.*, 8 January 1922, p. 8A; "Enemies of Jazz Speak," *ibid.*, 10 February 1922, p. 7; "Starbeams," *ibid.*, 25 April 1922.

151. "A Real Jazz Disease," *ibid.*, 27 May 1922, p. 16.

152. See, for example, "They Stopped the Show," Audio Rarities recording LPA 2290 (N.p.: Audio Rarities, n.d. [c. 1957]).

153. "No Jazz for Mary," *Kansas City Star*, 6 March 1922.

154. Ad for *Ladies' Home Journal*, in *ibid.*, 4 November 1921.

155. "Blames Jazz for Crime," *Kansas City Star*, 21 January 1922.

156. "Sees Menace in Jazz," *ibid.*, 29 December 1921, p. 13.

157. "Not Exactly," cartoon in *Kansas City Star*, 21 April 1922, p. 30; "Proof," cartoon in *Kansas City Star*, 3 March 1922.

158. "Starbeams," *ibid.*, 27 February 1922; "Starbeams," *ibid.*, 8 December 1922.

159. "Starbeams," *ibid.*, 13 February 1922; "Starbeams," *ibid.*, 12 March 1922.

160. "Jazz Pioneer Is at Pantages," *Kansas City Star*, 3 January 1923, p. 3; Rust, *Jazz Records A–Z, 1897–1931*, p. 474; Brian Rust, *The American Dance Band Discography, 1917–1942*, 2 vols., I: p. 543.

161. "Fox Trot on Ganz's Program; Miss Millar Finds the Conductor Is a Brave Man," *Kansas City Star*, 7 November 1921.

162. "The Stage and Stage People," *Kansas City Star*, 2 July 1922, p. 6D.

163. *Kansas City Star*, 24 February 1920.

164. "Starbeams," *Kansas City Star*, 29 January 1922.

165. Helen Hullitt Lowry, "New York Is Taking the Gymnastics Out of Jazz," *Kansas City Star*, 28 February 1922, p. 11; "Paul Whiteman Denies Jazz; Plays 'Syncopated Rhythm," *Variety*, 3 January 1924, p. 4.

166. "The Man Who Tamed Jazz," *Kansas City Star*, 7 October 1923.

167. Thomas A. DeLong, *Pops: Paul Whiteman, King of Jazz* (Piscataway, N.J.: New Century Publishers, 1983), pp. 3–10.

3. Coon-Sanders Novelty Orchestra

1. Joe Sanders, "The Coon-Sanders Story (Part II)," p. 4; unidentified newspaper clipping affixed to a sheet of paper, miscellaneous materials, JLSC.

2. Joe Sanders, "The Coon-Sanders Story (Part II), p. 4; scrapbooks of miscellany, JLSC.

3. *Ibid.*

4. John Coon on tape #1 of two made solo in Prairie Village, Kans., about January 1995, for author's use, in author's possession.

5. Joe Sanders, "The Coon-Sanders Story (Part II)," pp. 4-5.

6. *Ibid.*

7. *Ibid.*

8. *Ibid.*

9. Sullivan, *Our Times, 1900-1925*, vol. 6, *The Twenties*, pp. 343-344; Frederick Lewis Allen, *Only Yesterday: An Informal History of the Nineteen-Twenties* (New York: Harper & Brothers, 1931), p. 138, hereinafter cited as *Only Yesterday*.

10. Quin A. Ryan, "Coon-Sanders," *College Humor*, April 1930, p. 108; Sanders, "The Coon-Sanders Story (Part II)," p. 5.

11. Slide, *The Vaudevillians*, p. 65.

12. James Fisher, "Guinan, Texas," *American National Biography*, 24 vols. (New York: Oxford University Press, 1999), 9: 713; "Texas Guinan Is Getting $1,000 and Worth It," *Variety*, 13 August 1924, p. 37.

13. Fisher, "Guinan, Texas," p. 713; "Hello Sucker," *Variety*, 13 August 1924, p. 30.

14. Joe Sanders, "The Coon-Sanders Story [Part I]," p. 4.

15. Unidentified clipping, miscellaneous materials, JLSC.

16. Landon Laird, "About Town," *Kansas City Times*, 20 May 1965, p. 15D; "Roy G. Sanders Dies," *Kansas City Star*, 17 January 1950, clip-

ping among miscellaneous items, JLSC; "Sanders to Coach at K. U.," *Kansas City Star*, 3 February 1920.

17. Anne Steward, "Cooney and Joe Hard Workers," *Radio Digest*, April 1930, p. 106.

18. Clipping from *Kansas City Star*, of 26 December 1926, in miscellaneous materials, JLSC; Robert Ripley, "Believe It or Not," *Kansas City Star*, 3 June 1923.

19. Newspaper clippings pasted on a sheet, miscellaneous materials, JLSC.

20. *Kansas City Star*, 1919-1921, *passim*.

21. Author's conversation with Johnny Coon, 20 January 1995, Auburn, Ala.

22. Jimmie Selby, "News and Gossip of the Hotel Muehlebach," clipping among miscellaneous materials, JLSC.

23. Jimmie Selby, "News and Gossip of the Hotel Muehlebach," clipping among miscellaneous materials, JLSC.

24. *Ibid*; also, unidentified newspaper clipping affixed to sheet of paper, miscellaneous materials, JLSC.

25. Jimmie Selby, "News and Gossip of the Hotel Muehlebach," clipping affixed to sheet of paper, miscellaneous materials, JLSC.

26. "'Twas a Cheerful Party," unidentified newspaper clipping fixed to sheet, among miscellaneous materials, JLSC.

27. Rust, *The American Dance Band Discography, 1917–1942*, vol. 1, p. 348.

28. Several ads clipped from newspapers and affixed to a sheet, in miscellaneous materials, JLSC.

29. Various clippings affixed to sheets, miscellaneous materials, JLSC.

30. Newspaper clipping affixed to sheet, in miscellaneous materials, JLSC.

31. "The Coon-Sanders Orchestra Grabs Off Big Honors," newspaper clipping affixed to sheet, in miscellaneous materials, JLSC.

32. Newspaper clipping affixed to sheet, in miscellaneous materials, JLSC; Slide, *The Vaudevillians*, p. 133.

33. "Is Al Jolson Right on This?" "They Made the Columbia Records," and several other unidentified newspaper and periodical clippings affixed to a sheet, among miscellaneous materials, JLSC.

34. *Kansas City Star*, 28 October 1921.

35. "Comes a Jazz Bandwagon," *Kansas City Star*, 24 January 1922.

36. Newspaper clipping affixed to sheet, in miscellaneous materials, JLSC.

37. Joe Popper, "America's Band," *Kansas City Star Magazine*, 9 July 1989, p. 9.

38. Schubert Theater ad, *Kansas City Star*, 25 November 1921; Mainstreet Theater ad, *ibid*., 11 December 1921; Newman Theater ad, *ibid*., 11 December 1921; Mainstreet Theater ad, *ibid*., 18 December 1921.

39. "Starbeams," *Kansas City Star*, 20 January 1922, copied from "Society Personals" in the *Wichita Beacon*.

40. "Is Traffic Cop Doomed?" *Kansas City Star*, 21 January 1922.

41. Tape made solo by John Coon for author's use, Prairie Village, Kans., about January 1995, now in author's possession; also, author's conversation with John Coon, 20 January 1995, Auburn, Ala.

42. *Ibid*.

43. Sanders, "Join Coon-Sanders and See America," p. 9A (back); "Pennsylvania Town Listens In and Receives Charter," *Kansas City Star*, 14 January 1923, p. 8A.

44. "Hollywood Heeds It Not," *Kansas City Star*, 8 February 1922; "Into Mystic Love Cult," *ibid*., 9 February 1922.

45. "A 'Lease' on the Air Asked; Radio Company Needs a 'Clear Track' for Program," *Kansas City Star*, 6 February 1922.

46. "Tune In at 375 Meters," *Kansas City Star*, 16 February 1922, p. 1; "Next Concert Wednesday," *ibid*., 17 February 1922, p. 1; "Starbeams," *ibid*., 20 February 1922.

47. "Radio Music Replaced Orchestra," *Kansas City Star*, 17 February 1922, p. 2.

48. "Countless Hundreds Heard," *Kansas City Star*, 5 March 1922.

49. Satterlee ad, *Kansas City Star*, 3 March 1922; Radio Supply ad, *ibid*., 16 March 1922; Robinson Shoe ad, *ibid*., 27 March 1922; J. W. Jenkins ad, *ibid*., 7 April 1922.

50. "Tune in at 360 Tonight," *Kansas City Star*, 4 March 1922; "Starbeams," *ibid*.; "A Concert Every Night," *ibid*., 5 March 1922.

51. A. G. Clark, "The Tuning Troubles of Messrs. Gallagher and Shean," *Radio Broadcast*, May 1923, p. 28.

52. Bryan's speech before Philadelphia Academy of Music, *Kansas City Star*, 6 March 1922; "Forty Minutes of Music," *ibid*.; Kuhn's eliminating jazz, radio section, *ibid*., 10 March 1922.

53. "The Star's New Radio Set," *Kansas City Star*, 7 May 1922.

54. "The Star's New Radio Set," *Kansas City Star*, 7 May 1922. For Joe Sanders' misstatement of the number of radio stations, see Harvey Rettberg's taped interview with Sanders, 16 July 1961, Kansas City, Mo.

55. "Stage Set for Par Excellent Radio Program Friday Night" and several lesser newspaper clippings, apparently from the *Kansas City Post*, all affixed to a sheet, in miscellaneous materials, JLSC.

56. Harvey Rettberg's taped interview with Joe Sanders, 16 July 1961, Kansas City, Mo.

57. "Two of Best Orchestras in West Will Play for the Post's Radio Concert," *Kansas City Post* newspaper clipping affixed to a sheet, in miscellaneous materials, JLSC.

58. "Radio Concert, Perfect in All Appointments, Pleased Folks," newspaper clipping, apparently from the *Kansas City Post*, affixed to sheet, in miscellaneous materials, JLSC.

59. "Stage Set for Par Excellent Radio program Friday Night," newspaper clipping, apparently from *Kansas City Post*, affixed to sheet, in miscellaneous materials, JLSC.

60. "A Great Treat" and Jenkins ad affixed to sheets, in miscellaneous materials, JLSC.

61. "WDAF Will Talk Tonight," *Kansas City Star*, 5 June 1922, p. 1; "Radio 'Dead Spot' Is Gone," *ibid.*, 6 June 1922, p. 2.

62. "Ready for Midnight Frolic," *Kansas City Star*, 21 June 1922; *ibid.*, 15 July 1922; "'Bits' from the Midnight Radio Frolic," *ibid.*, 30 July 1922, p. 15A.

63. "The Kansas City Star Radio Radio Station, WDAF," *Kansas City Star*, 5 June 1922, p. 1.

64. "WDAF," *Kansas City Star*, 22 September 1922, p. 4.

65. "Musical Comedy by Radio," *Kansas City Star*, 9 July 1922, p. 2B.

66. *Ibid.*
67. *Ibid.*
68. *Ibid.*
69. *Ibid.*

70. Rust, *The American Dance Band Discography, 1917-1942*, vol. 2, pp. 1975-1978; "Inside Stuff on Music," *Variety*, 31 March 1926, p. 45.

71. *Kansas City Star*, 17 June 1922; "Dial Trouble Will Pass," *ibid.*, 19 June 1922; "Starbeams," *ibid.*

72. "Starbeams," *Kansas City Star*, 10 October 1922.

73. "Starbeams," *Kansas City Star*, 24 May 1922.

74. *Kansas City Star*, 15 August 1922; Sweeney School's ad, *ibid.*, p. 24.

75. "Coon-Sanders Orchestra to Broadcast Program," unidentified newspaper clipping affixed to sheet, among miscellaneous materials, JLSC.

76. For term "uglies," see *Kansas City Star*'s article about a lean-to beside the Federal Building, 10 September 1922; Alderman John J. Manning's remarks in *Kansas City Star*, 23 August 1922; temperature given in *ibid.*, 24 August 1922.

77. Article about phone building in *Kansas City Star*, 19 June 1922; article on Truman, *ibid.*, 2 August 1922; Coon-Sanders at Newman, *ibid.*, 3 September 1922.

78. Janet K. Miller's electronic mail to the author, 19 June 2001; Madeline Sanders' journal for 23 August 1923; Joe Sanders, "Join Coon-Sanders and See America," p. 73 (back); "Forty Years Ago in the Star," *Kansas City Star-Times*, 19 January 1962, newspaper clipping with letter from Mary Higbee to Harvey Rettberg, undated but sometime in 1962, HRC.

79. 12th Street Theater ad, *Kansas City Star*, 4 September 1921.

80. Newman Theater ad, *Kansas City Star*, 3 September 1922; Sanders' song at Newman, see unidentified newspaper clipping "Newman— 'Fascination,'" affixed to sheet, miscellaneous materials, JLSC.

81. Newman ad, *Kansas City Star*, 3 September 1922.

82. Newman ad, *Kansas City Star*, 22 September 1922.

83. Newman ad, *ibid.*, 1 October 1922.

84. Slide, *The Vaudevillians*, p. 158.

85. "Longer Wave to WDAF," *Kansas City Star*, 18 October 1922.

86. "A Street Tests Drivers," *Kansas CityStar*, 20 October 1922; cartoons against "spederinos," *ibid.*, 27 October 1922; see related articles also in *ibid.*, 18 and 19 October 1922.

87. Article about Leo Davis orchestra, *Kansas City Star*, 5 November 1922; Coon-Sanders and desert jazz theme, *ibid.*, 29 October 1922; Coon-Sanders and blues program, *ibid.*, 5 November 1922; Coon-Sanders Christmas program, *ibid.*, 24 November 1922.

88. Tape no. 1, of two made solo by Johnny Coon for author's use, Prairie Village, Kans., January 1995.

89. Special program on WDAF, *Kansas City Star*, 26 November 1922

4. The Nighthawks

1. Lambdin Kay, "Famed Coon-Sanders Nighthawk Band Will Play for Noon Concert Monday," *Atlanta Journal*, 6 June 1926, WSB section, p. 1.

2. Newman ad, *Kansas City Star*, 3 December 1922; "Concerts at Midnight," *ibid.*, p. 14A.

3. Kay, "Famed Coon-Sanders Nighthawks Will Play for Noon Concert Monday."

4. "Its Audience a Continent," *Kansas City Star*, 10 December 1922, p. 6B; "Nighthawks Defy Sleep," *ibid.*

5. See, for example, "Nighthawk Brood Grows," *Kansas City Star*, 17 December 1922, p. 2B.

6. "A 'Nighthawk' Emblem Suggested," *ibid.*, 12 December 1922, p. 4.

7. Sheet music, JLSC.

8. "Song Sold for a 'Song,'" *Kansas City Star*, 23 September 1922, p. 18; Slide, *The Vaudevillians*, pp. 61–63.

9. Laird, "About Town."

10. *Ziegfeld Follies*, phonograph recording VM 107 (New York: Veritas Records, 1967), side 2, band 3.

11. *Ibid.*
12. *Ibid.*

13. "Paramount Film Representatives Stop in

City," unidentified newspaper clipping, miscellaneous materials, JLSC.

14. Spaeth, *A History of Popular Music in America*, 437; Sullivan, *Our Times: 1900–1925*, vol. 6, *The Twenties*, pp. 456–457.

15. Thomas A. DeLong, *Radio Stars: An Illustrated Biographical Dictionary of 953 Performers, 1920 through 1960* (Jefferson, N.C.: McFarland, 1996), no. 459, hereinafter cited as *Radio Stars*; John Dunning, *On the Air: The Encyclopedia of Old-Time Radio* (New York: Oxford University Press, 1998), p. 309, hereinafter cited as *On the Air*.

16. Sullivan, *Our Times: 1900–1925*, vol. 6, *The Twenties*, p. 454.

17. From author's conversations with Douglas E. Mitchell, Mobile, Ala., in the 1940s and 1950s.

18. Rust, *The American Dance Band Discography, 1917–1942*, vol. 1, p. 654; "Yes! We Have No Bananas," Victor recording 19068-A (Camden, N.J.: Victor Talking machine Co., [1923]).

19. "*George Olsen and His Music*," RCA Victor recording LPV-549 (New York: RCA, 1968), side 1, band 5.

20. Sullivan, *Our Times: 1900–1925*, vol. 6, *The Twenties*, p. 459; Spaeth, *A History of Popular Music in America*, p. 454.

21. Claude Binyon, "Inaccurate Biographies: Will Rogers," *Variety*, 21 January 1931, p. 49.

22. "Other Nations Hear WDAF," *Kansas City Star*, 9 December 1922, p. 1.

23. "The Late Bird Got This Worm," *ibid.*, 13 December 1922, p. 1.

24. "Radio Club Covers Globe," *ibid.*, 24 December 1922, p. 2B.

25. "A 'Nighthawk' Emblem Suggested," *ibid.*, 12 December 1922, p. 4; "Nighthawk Brood Grows," *ibid.*, 17 December 1922, p. 2B; "Radio Club Covers Globe," *ibid.*, 24 December 1922, p. 2B; "Nighthawks Visit Here," *ibid.*, 7 January 1923, p. 15A.

26. "WDAF in the Odd Places," *ibid.*, 2 February 1923, p. 1; "The Merry Old Chief Nighthawk," *ibid.*, 21 January 1923, p. 15A; "Nighthawks in Birmingham," *ibid.*, 28 December 1922, p. 1; "Nighthawks in Oil City," *ibid.*, 14 January 1923, p. 8A.

27. "Nighthawks Defy Sleep," *ibid.*, 10 December 1922, p. 6B; "Nighthawks in Air Again," *ibid.*, 12 December 1922, p. 8.

28. "Now Hawaii Listens In," *ibid.*, 20 December 1922, p. 1.

29. "Kilauea Volcano More Active," *ibid.*, 9 January 1923, p. 22.

30. "Nighthawks into Hawaii," *ibid.*, 18 March 1923, p. 19A.

31. "'Nighthawks' in Isle of Pines," *ibid.*, 14 December 1922, p. 1.

32. "A Nighthawk Is 'Lost,'" *ibid.*, 18 December 1922, p. 1.

33. "Radio Unites Lost Brothers," *ibid.*, 12 February 1923, p. 1.

34. See, for example, Joe Sanders, "Join Coon-Sanders and See America," p. 86 (back).

35. "'Nighthawks' in Air Again," *Kansas City Star*, 12 December 1922, p. 8; "Bandit Fighter Still a 'Nighthawk,'" *ibid.*, 7 March 1923, p. 1.

36. "'Nighthawks' Defy Sleep," *ibid.*, 10 December 1922, p. 6B.

37. "Nighthawk Brood Grows," *ibid.*, 17 December 1922, p. 2B.

38. See *Kansas City Star* for following dates in December 1922 and pages: 9th, p.1; 10th, p. 6B; 12th, p. 8; 17th, p. 2B; 24th, p. 2B; 31st, p. 9A.

39. See *Kansas City Star* for following pages and dates in January 1923: 9th, p. 22; 31st, p. 2; 28th, p. 2B; 3rd, p. 1.

40. "An Ethereal Enemy of Gloom," quoted in *Kansas City Star*, 28 January 1923, p. 2B.

41. "WDAF's Radio Waves Penetrate the Antipodes," *Kansas City Star*, 15 February 1923, p. 1; "'Hawks' on Land and Sea," *ibid.*, 28 January 1923, p. 2B; "Hear WDAF in Subway," *ibid.*, 24 January 1923, p. 1.

42. "WDAF Radio Waves Penetrate the Antipodes," *Kansas City Star*, 15 February 1923, p. 1; "WDAF to the Eskimos," unidentified newspaper clipping but probably *ibid.*, among similar items affixed to sheet, in miscellaneous materials, JLSC.

43. Charles J. Gilchrest, "Popular Radio Favorites Recall Old Times as Interviewer Tours Studio," *Chicago Daily News*, 20 April 1932, clipping in JLSC, SC1, box 15, folder 1.

44. "Gets WDAF Far at Sea," *Kansas City Star*, 1 March 1923, p. 1; "WDAF Entertains Canal Zone," *ibid.*, 8 March 1923, p. 1.

45. "WDAF in the Odd Places," *Kansas City Star*, 2 February 1923, p. 1.

46. For lists of songs played by Coon-Sanders, see *Kansas City Star* 28 January through 18 March 1923.

47. "Holiday Parties Two Nights," *Kansas City Star*, 26 December 1922, p. 1; "A Midnight Radio Frolic," *ibid.*, 31 December 1922, p. 9A.

48. "Tests for Loud Speaker," *Kansas City Star*, 31 December 1922, p. 9A.

49. "Gas Lamps Flicker Out," *Kansas City Star*, 7 January 1923; Georgette Leblanc Maeterlinc's article, *ibid.*, 6 January 1923.

50. "WHB in 12-Hour Program," *Kansas City Star*, 31 January 1923, p. 2.

51. "Ted Lewis into Nighthawks," 30 January 19123, p. 11; Slide, *The Vaudevillians*, p. 92.

52. See radio section, *Kansas City Star*, 2 March 1923.

53. "'The Voice of the South' and the 'Chief' Meet," *Kansas City Star*, 11 February 1923, p. 17A; "Radio Chatter," *Variety*, 19 April 1932, p. 56.

54. "Nighthawk Rites by WSB," *Kansas City Star*, 6 February 1923, p. 4.

55. Globe Theater's ad, *Kansas City Star*, 17

January 1923; "Plays Alone for Nation," *ibid.*, 21 January 1923, p. 15A; "'Hawks' on Land and Sea," *ibid.*, 28 January 1923, p. 2B.

56. "Plays Alone for Nation," *Kansas City Star*, 21 January 1923, p. 15A.

57. "The Radio Conference Opens," *Kansas City Star*, 20 March 1923, p. 8.

58. "Them Were Real Ducks," *Kansas City Star*, 15 April 1923, p. 13A.

59. "A Pitfall of Broadcasting," *Kansas City Star*, 15 April 1923, p. 13A.

60. "Salome Hawks Have Trouble," *Kansas City Star*, 25 March 1923, p. 13A.

61. Highland Radio Supply ad, *Kansas City Star*, 18 February 1923, p. 15A.

62. "Giant Radio Idea Launched," *Variety*, 1 March 1922, p. 2.

63. "The 'Nighthawks' into Movies," *Kansas City Star*, 11 February 1923, p. 16A; "Nighthawk Movies Next Week," *ibid.*, 18 February 1923, p. 14A; "Movies to Explain Radio," *ibid.*, 22 February 1923, p. 1; "The Nighthawk Movies Today," *ibid.*, 25 February 1923, p. 12A.

64. "Radio Exhibit This Week," *Kansas City Star*, 14 January 1923, p. 8A; ad for the exhibit, *ibid.*, 16 January 1923, p. 5; "Radio Secrets on View," unidentified newspaper clipping fixed on sheet, among miscellaneous materials, JLSC.

65. Various newspaper clippings affixed to several sheets of miscellaneous scrapbook materials, JLSC.

66. Unidentified newspaper clipping affixed to sheet, among miscellaneous materials, JLSC.

67. Newman Theatre's ad, *Kansas City Star*, 18 April 1923.

68. "Radio Nighthawks," reprinted from *Cincinnati Post*, in *Kansas City Star*, 8 April 1923, p. 12A.

69. "Radio Nighthawks," quoted in *ibid.*, 8 April 1923, p. 12A; for discussion of new wavelength, see *ibid.*, 18 April 1923.

70. "Radio Nighthawks," quoted in *ibid.*, 8 April 1923, p. 12A.

71. "Farewell Week," *Kansas City Star*, 20 May 1923; "Coon-Sanders to Leave," *ibid.*, 27 May 1923, p. 2B; article about Plantation Orchestra, *ibid.*, 29 May 1923, radio section.

72. "Coon-Sanders, Jazz Banders," *Joslin's Jazz Journal* (Parsons, Kans.), February 1983, p. 4.

73. For the personnel in the Haley orchestra in June 1923, see "Haley's Fairyland Park Orchestra," *Kansas City Star*, 10 June 1923, p. 2B.

74. Joe Sanders, "Join Coon-Sanders and See America," p. 1 (front); "Worst Floods since 1904 Raging," *Daily Oklahoman*, 10 June 1923.

75. Joe Sanders, "Join Coon-Sanders and See America," pp. 1 (front) and 2 (back).

76. *Ibid.*, p. 2 (back).

77. *Ibid.*, pp. 1 (back) and 2 (back); item about post office, *Daily Oklahoman*, 10 June 1923.

78. Unidentified newspaper clipping (probably from *Daily Oklahoman*), affixed to sheet among miscellaneous materials, JLSC.

79. Ad for Criterion Theater, *Daily Oklahoman*, 24 June 1923; "WKY Is To Present Coon Saunder's [*sic*] Fun," *ibid.*, 22 June 1923.

80. Joe Sanders, "Join Coon-Sanders and See America," pp. 1 (back) and 2 (front).

81. Ad for Frederickson-Kroh Music Store, *Daily Oklahoman*, 29 June 1923; Criterion Theater's ad, *ibid.*, 1 July 1923.

82. Criterion ad, *Daily Oklahoman*, 24 June 1923; "Criterion," *ibid.*; item about Spring Lake Pavilion, *ibid.*, 11 June 1923.

83. *Daily Oklahoman*, 5 July 1923.

84. *Daily Oklahoman*, 1 August 1923.

85. *Daily Oklahoman*, 5, 12 and 25 July 1923;

86. Joe Sanders, "Join Coon Sanders and See America," pp. 1 (back) and 2 (front).

87. *Daily Oklahoman*, 13 July 1923.

88. *Ibid.*, 11- 14 July 1923.

89. "Criterion," *ibid.*, 15 July 1923.

90. "Harding Is Dead," *ibid.*, 3 August 1923; Sullivan, *Our Times, 1900–1925* vol. 6: *The Twenties*, pp. 247–250.

91. "*I Can Hear It Now, 1919–1949,*" vol. 3, 1919–1932, side 1, band 4.

92. *Daily Oklahoman*, 7, 12, and 13 August 1923.

93. Joe Sanders, "Join Coon-Sanders and See America," pp. 1 (back), 3 (front and back).

94. *Ibid.*, p. 3 (front).

95. *Ibid.*, p. 3 (back).

96. *Kansas City Star*, 15 and 26 August 1923, 9 September 1923.

97. "They're Back!" ad for Hotel Muehlebach, newspaper clipping affixed to sheet, among miscellaneous materials, JLSC; earthquake article, *Kansas City Star*, 2 September 1923; Willie and Eugene Howard item, *Kansas City Star*'s radio section, 9 October 1923.

98. Hotel Muehlebach ad, *Kansas City Star*, 10 September 1923.

99. Pageant program, miscellaneous materials, JLSC.

100. *Kansas City Star*, 20 September 1923.

101. Tape no. 1, of two made for author by John Coon, Prairie Village, Kans., about January 1995.

102. "Entertain Kansas City Newsboys," newspaper clipping dated 29 November 1923, probably from the Kansas City *Journal-Post*, though not so identified; "Orchestra Volunteers for Newsboys' Christmas Fete," newspaper clipping, probably also from the *Journal-Post*, and probably of 30 November 1923; both clippings are glued to a sheet found in the miscellaneous materials, JLSC.

103. Carl Landrum, "Nick Musolino Played with Big Band Greats," Quincy, Ill., *Herald-Whig*, 5 May 1996; Bill Bradshaw, "'Nick' Musolino Found Niche Tooting His Horn," *ibid.*, 26 July

1976; Karl Karberg, "Coon-Sanders Vet Plays Trombone in Post Bands," unidentified newspaper clipping affixed to sheet of paper, miscellaneous materials, JLSC.
  104. Cathy Birge Williams to author, via electronic mail, 16 February 2001.
  105. "Fun for the Nighthawks," *Kansas City Star*, 2 December 1923, p. 3B.
  106. *Ibid.*; "It Was Nighthawk Night," unidentified newspaper clipping, but probably from the *Kansas City Star*, in SC1, box 15, folder 2, JLSC; "Starbeams," *Kansas City Star*, 5 December 1923.
  107. "What Others Think of WDAF," *Kansas City Star*, 10 December 1922, p. 2B.
  108. *Kansas City Star*, 6 December 1923; Bill Adler, *Presidential Wit from Washington to Johnson* (New York: Trident Press, 1966), p. 119.
  109. Bruce Bohle, *The Home Book of American Quotations* (New York: Dodd, Mead & Co., 1967), p. 70; "*I Can Hear It Now*," *1919–1949*," vol. 3, 1919–1932, side 1, band 4; Kay Halle, *The Irrepressible Churchill: A Treasury of Winston Churchill's Wit* (Cleveland & New York: World Publishing Co., 1966), p. 94.

5. *Chicago's Congress Hotel*

  1. Contract with Victor Talking Machine Co., miscallaneous materials, JLSC.
  2. Joe Sanders, "Join Coon-Sanders and See America," sheet 3 (back); Rust, *The American Dance Band Discography, 1917–1942*, vol. 1, p 348; telegram Victor Company to Carleton Coon and Joe Sanders, 8 May 1924, scrap books, JLSC.
  3. "Cabaret," *Variety*, 9 August 1923, p. 18.
  4. Joe Sanders, "Join Coon-Sanders and See America," sheet 3 (back); "Lopez Band at $2800," *Variety*, 10 January 1924, p. 5.
  5. Joe Sanders, "Join Coon-Sanders and See America," sheet 3 (back).
  6. *Ibid.*, p. 9A (back).
  7. "Missouri Features Coon-Sanders Orchestra; Why Men Leave Home at Skouras Houses," St. Louis, Mo., *Daily Globe-Democrat*, 5 May 1924.
  8. Sullivan, *Our Times, 1900–1925*, vol. 6: *The Twenties*, p. 362.
  9. "News from the Dailies: Chicago," *Variety*, 9 December 1925, p. 20.
  10. *Encyclopaedia Britannica*, 1965 ed., s.v. "Chicago," by Bessie Louise Pierce; "Chicago Chief Strong for Personal Liberty," *Variety*, 4 May 1927, p. 52.
  11. "Booze — More or Less," *Variety*, 31 December 1924, p. 8.
  12. Joe Sanders, "Join Coon-Sanders and See America," p. 3 (back); Dan Schroeder, "Coon-Sanders Kansas City Nighthawks," typescript, HRC. But a number of those writing about this episode in Nighthawk history have assumed that it occurred late in the band's existence, rather than in May of 1924, as Sanders makes clear in his memoirs.
  13. Joe Sanders, "Join Coon-Sanders and See America," p. 3 (back).
  14. "Many Bands, but They Must Be Good," *Variety*, 6 August 1924, p. 37; "Coon-Sanders Orchestra," *ibid.*, 13 August 1924, p. 36.
  15. "Popular Songs Now in Demand in Chicago," *Variety*, p. 26.
  16. Joe Sanders, "Join Coon-Sanders and See America," p. 3 (back).
  17. *Ibid.*
  18. *Ibid.*
  19. "Jules Stein Rites a 'Joyous' Affair; Warm Tributes, Big Band Sendoff," *Variety Obituaries, 1905–1992*. 14 vols. (New York; London: Garland Publishing, Inc., 1988–1994), for 6 May 1981.
  20. *Ibid.*; Dennis McDougal, *The Last Mogul: Lew Wasserman, MCA, and the Hidden History of Hollywood* (N.p.: Da Capo Press, 2001), pp. 13–14, hereinafter cited as *The Last Mogul*; Karl Kramer, unpublished history of the Music Corporation of America, chapter 8, p. 4, HRC.
  21. "Many Bands, but They Must Be Good," *Variety*, 6 August 1924, p.37.
  22. McDougal, *The Last Mogul*, pp. 13–14; Joe Sanders, "Join Coon-Sanders and See America," p. 4 (front); Kramer, unpublished history of the MCA, chapter 8, pp. 4–5; tape no. 1, of two, made solo by John Coon for author, Prairie Village, Kans., January 1995.
  23. John Coon, tape no. 1, of two made solo for author, Prairie Village, Kans., January 1995.
  24. Joe Sanders, "Join Coon-Sanders and See America," p. 4 (front).
  25. Kramer, unpublished history of the Music Corporation of America, chap. 8, p. 4.
  26. Author's interview of John Coon, Auburn, Ala., 18 January 1995.
  27. Author's interview with John Coon, 19 January 1995, Auburn, Ala.; Kramer, unpublished history of MCA, chapter 8, p. 4.
  28. Kramer, unpublished history of MCA, chapter 8, p. 4; also, M.C.A. advertisement, *Variety*, 6 August 1924, p. 56.
  29. "Jules Stein Rites a 'Joyous' Affair; Warm Tributes, Big Band Sendoff," *Variety Obituaries, 1905–1992*, 6 May 1981.
  30. See, for example, McDougal, *The Last Mogul*, p. 16. In this reference the author says "Muehlbach [sic] Hotel" though *Congress Hotel* is probably meant.
  31. See, for instance, almost any issue of *Variety* in the mid-Twenties.
  32. "'Radio Voices' Injure Reps of Singers," *Variety*, 6 August 1924, p. 35.
  33. *Fred Allen Looks at Life: Comedy Highlights from His Greatest Radio Shows*. Bagdad phonograph recording album S-6969. (N.p.: Bagdad Records, n.d. [c1971]), side 4.

34. "Radio Interest Wanes 90%; Fan Letters Few; Wires, Too," *Variety*, 21 October 1925, p. 39.

35. "'Radio Songs' Barred Out of Big Time Vaudeville," *ibid*, 14 May 1924, pp. 1, 45; "Forced to Quit Radio," *ibid*., 16 April 1924, pp. 1, 46; "Keith's New Season Contracts Contain Strong Radio Clause," *ibid*., p. 4.

36. "Radio Formally Barred and Banned in Any Way for Concert Artists," *Variety*, 2 July 1924, p. 5.

37. "Peak of Radio Craze Has Been Passed," *Variety*, 24 September 1924, p. 26-A.

38. Abel Green, "Abel's Comment," *Variety*, 1 October 1924, p. 32.

39. See, for example, "Can Vaudeville Be Revived?" *Variety*, 5 May 1926, p. 41.

40. "Synonyms for Jazz," *ibid*., 30 July 1924, p. 38.

41. Jack Lait, "Night Life of the World: Chicago," *ibid*., 7 October 1925, pp. 5, 60.

42. Kramer, Unpublished history of the Music Corporation of America, chapter 4, p. 1, in HRC.

43. *Ibid.*, p. 4.

44. *Ibid.*

45. *Ibid.*, pp. 1–2.

46. *Ibid.*, p. 2.

47. Joe Sanders, "Join Coon-Sanders and See America," p. 4 (front).

48. Schroeder, "Coon-Sanders Kansas City Nighthawks,"; Joe Sanders, "Join Coon-Sanders and See America," p. 4 (front).

49. Joe Sanders, "Join Coon-Sanders and See America," pp. 4 (front) and 5 (front).

50. *Ibid.*, pp. 4 (front), 5 (front), and 6 (front).

51. *Ibid.*, p. 6 (front).

52. *Ibid.*

53. *Ibid.*

54. Unidentified newspaper clipping, among miscellaneous items, JLSC; Joe Sanders, "Join Coon-Sanders and See America," pp. 6 (front and back).

55. Joe Sanders, "Join Coon-Sanders and See America," pp. 6 (front and back).

56. Article about W. F. "Whitey" Doering, *Kansas City Star*, 20 November 1923.

57. Joe Sanders, "Join Coon-Sanders and See America," pp. 5 (front and back).

58. "Crowds Enjoy Dance at Elks," *Illinois State Journal*, 6 September 1924, p. 2.

59. Joe Sanders, "Join Coon-Sanders and See America," p. 4 (front).

60. The source of this is an unidentified newspaper clipping titled "Discordant Jazz Age Is Past, Say Nighthawk Men," in miscellaneous materials, JLSC; but internal evidence suggests that it appeared in the Ft. Dodge, Ia., *Messenger* of 18 September 1924.

61. *Ibid.*

62. Joe Sanders, "Join Coon-Sanders and See America," pp. 6 (front), 7 (back), 8 (front and back), and 9A (front);

63. "Collegian Dance Hounds Can Out-Dance Any Band," *Variety*, 9 September 1925, p. 1

64. Joe Sanders, "Join Coon-Sanders and See America," p. 9A (front).

65. "Need Bands," *Variety*, 1 October 1924, p. 28.

66. Kramer, unpublished history of the MCA, chapter 8, p. 4; Joe Sanders, "Join Coon-Sanders and See America," p. 9A (front).

67. Joe Sanders, "Join Coon-Sanders and See America," p. 22 (front); "Dine in Samoa to KYW Jazz," *Chicago Tribune*, 22 March 1925.

68. Frank Haben Clark, "Europe Tunes in on KYW Tonight," newspaper clipping from Chicago *Evening American*, of 26 November 1924, in SC1, box 15, folder 2, JLSC.

69. "Special Radio License Sets Precedent for Hotel Band," *Variety*, 19 November 1924, p. 32.

70. Joe Sanders, "Join Coon-Sanders and See America," p. 9A (front).

71. See, for example, McDougal, *The Last Mogul*, pp. 21–25.

72. Joe Sanders, "Join Coon-Sanders and See America," p. 9A (front).

73. Congress Hotel's menu for 31 December 1924, miscellaneous materials, JLSC.

74. "Midnight Sons from Congress New Feature," unidentified newspaper article of 31 January 1925, probably from the Chicago *Evening American*, SC1, box 15, folder 2, JLSC.

75. O. M. Samuel, "Nighthawks and Farmers," *Variety*, 11 March 1925, p. 45.

76. "Radio," *Variety*, 10 December 1924, p. 16; "Remick's Radio Decision Appealed," *ibid*, 7 January 1925, p. 39.

77. "Radio Will Kill Off Theatres in Towns of 75,000 within 5 Years," *ibid*., 10 September 1924, pp. 12, 50.

78. Abel Green, "Abel's Comment," *ibid*., 17 December 1924, p. 41.

79. Rust, *The American Dance Band Discography, 1917–1942*, vol. 1, p. 348.

80. Kramer, unpublished history of MCA, chapter 8, p. 5.

81. Joe Popper, "America's Band," *Kansas City Star Magazine*, 9 July 1989, p. 26; author's conversation with John Coon, Auburn, Ala., 19 January 1995.

82. Kramer, unpublished history of MCA, chapter 4, pp. 8, 12.

83. *Ibid.*, chapter 8, p. 1.

84. *Ibid.*, pp. 11–12.

85. "Mimicry and Tunes Galore," *Variety*, 1 October 1924, p. 29.

86. *Ibid.*

87. Joe Sanders, "Join Coon-Sanders and See America," p. 9A (back); Kramer, unpublished history of MCA, chapter 8, p. 5; Nighthawks' contract with MCA, miscellaneous materials, JLSC.

88. Nighthawks' contract with MCA and Ernie

Young agencies, miscellaneous materials, JLSC; "Schedule of Prices" advertisement by Ernie Young Music Corporation for Coon-Sanders, *ibid.*; program ticket for Coon-Sanders on 23 August 1925 at Lewistown, Ill., *ibid.*

89. "Schedule of Prices" advertisement by Ernie Young Music Corporation, *ibid.*

90. Nighthawks' contract with MCA and Ernie Young agencies, *ibid.*

91. *Ibid.*

92. Joe Sanders, "Join Coon-Sanders and See America," p. 9A (back); Cathy Birge Williams' electronic mail message to author, 16 February 2001; Davenport, Iowa, *Daily Times*, 4 April 1925, p. 8, and 11 April 1925, p. 8.

93. MCA ad, *Variety*, 22 April 1925, p. 56.

94. "Any 'Air' Night Dull as Usual," *Variety*, 17 June 1925, p. 39.

95. "'The Radio Rash' Is Not a Song," *Variety*, 29 April 1925, p. 38.

96. "Radio's 'Thank-o-Grams,'" *Variety*, 8 April 1925, p. 1.

97. "Radio and Rum," *Variety*, 4 March 1925, p. 40.

98. "International Combine of Authors Will Demand Radio Pay for Material," *Variety*, 18 February 1925, p. 35.

99. Abel Green, "Radio—The 'Sponger,'" *Variety*, 31 December 1924, pp. 1, 136.

100. Joe Sanders, "Join Coon-Sanders and See America," pp. 9A (back), 10 (front and back).

101. *Ibid.*, p. 9A (back).

102. *Ibid.*, pp. 9A (back), 14 (front).

103. "New Poisons in Bootleg Booze," *Variety*, 9 September 1925, p. 39.

104. David L. Porter (ed), *Biographical Dictionary of American Sports: Football* (New York: Greenwood Press, 1987), pp. 187, 505–506; "*I Can Hear It Now*," *1919–1949*, vol. 3, 1919–1932, side 1, band 4.

105. *Notre Dame Scholastic*, 24 April, 1 May, and 15 May 1925; for name of Denny's orchestra, see Rust, *The American Dance Band Discography, 1917–1942*, vol. 1, p. 399.

106. *Notre Dame Scholastic*, 15 May 1925; South Bend (Ind.) *News Times*, 16 May 1925.

107. *Notre Dame Scholastic*, 24 April 1925.

108. Joe Sanders, "Join Coon-Sanders and See America," pp. 9A (back), 14 (back), and 15 (front and back).

109. Joe Sanders, "Join Coon-Sanders and See America," pp. 9A (back), 11 (front and back), 12 (front); "D'Paolo Wins in Automobile Race," *Meridian* (Miss.) *Star*, 31 May 1925, p. 1.

110. Joe Sanders, "Join Coon-Sanders and See America," pp. 11 (front and back).

111. "Famous Night Hawks to Play Here Tuesday," Quincy, Ill., *Whig-Journal*, 1 June 1925; "Coon-Sanders Night Hawks Attract Many," *ibid.*, 3 June 1925; "Night Hawks Will Play at Highland," Quincy, Ill., *Daily Herald*, 2 June 1925.

112. Joe Sanders, "Join Coon-Sanders and See America," pp. 9A (back) and 16 (front).

113. *Variety*, 8 July 1925, pp. 2, 5; Joe Sanders, "Join Coon-Sanders and See America," p. 16 (front).

114. Jack Lait, *Variety*, 15 July 1925, p. 1.

115. Joe Sanders, "Join Coon-Sanders and See America," p. 16 (front); "Atlantic City Full of Bands in Cabaret," *Variety*, 8 July 1925, p. 47.

116. "'The Raunch' Dance," *Variety*, 31 March 1926, p. 4.

117. Elida Webb, "'Charleston' Accidental Discovery," *ibid.*, 9 December 1925, p. 4.

118. "Wayburn Claims His 'Charleston' First," *ibid.*, 9 December 1925, p. 5.

119. "Charleston—Death Dance," *Variety*, 8 July 1925, p. 1; "'Charleston' Out in Dance Halls," *ibid.*, 15 July 1925, pp. 1, 40.

120. "'Charleston' Weakened," *ibid.*, 13 January 1926, p. 47; "'Charleston' Barred," *ibid.*, 9 December 1925, p. 6; "'Charleston' Taboo in Iowa," *ibid.*, 12 August 1925, p. 37; "'Charleston' Dancer Hurt," *ibid.*, 2 December 1925, p. 3.

121. "'Charleston' Rules," *ibid.*, 3 February 1926, p. 47.

122. "Chi. Off Charleston," *Variety*, 13 May 1925, p. 15.

123. Joe Sanders, "Join Coon-Sanders and See America," p. 16 (front).

124. "Atlantic City Full of Bands in Cabaret," *Variety*, 8 July 1925, p. 47.

125. "Here and There," *ibid.*, 23 March 1927, p. 47.

126. *Ibid.*; "Band Reviews," *ibid.*, 12 August 1925, p. 35.

127. "Stein Turns Offers," *ibid.*, 15 July 1925, p. 37.

128. "New Sound Panatrope," *ibid.*, 19 August 1925, p. 42.

129. "Victor's New Process," *ibid.*, 13 May 1925, p. 4; "Inside Stuff on Music," *ibid.*, 19 August 1925, p. 42.

130. "Improved Victrola Given Demonstration," *ibid.*, 21 October 1925, p. 39.

131. Rust, *The American Dance Band Discography, 1917–1942*, vol. 1, p. 348.

132. Author's conversation with John Coon, 19 January 1995, Auburn, Ala.

133. Rust, *The American Dance Band Discography, 1917–1942*, vol. 1, p. 348; Rust, *Jazz Records, A-Z, 1897–1931*, p. 83.

134. Rust, *The American Dance Band Discography, 1917–1942*, vol. 1, p. 348.

135. "Thousands in Klan Parade," *Meridian* (Miss.) *Star*, 9 August 1925, p. 1; Will Rogers, "The Bull's Eye," *ibid.*, 26 July 1925, p. 6; "Mutt and Jeff," *ibid.*, 21 July 1925, p. 7.

136. Joe Sanders, "Join Coon-Sanders and See America," p. 16 (front).

137. *Ibid.*

138. *Ibid.*, pp. 11 (back), 16 (back), 17 (front

and back), 18 (front and back), 19 (front and back).

139. *Ibid.*, p. 20 (front).

140. *Ibid.*, pp. 20 (front), 50 (front); author's conversation with Harvey Rettberg, 19 November 1993, Pickens, S.C.

141. Joe Sanders, "Join Coon-Sanders and See America," pp. 17 (back), 20 (front).

142. *Ibid.*, p. 20 (front); Harvey Rettberg's taped interview with Joe Sanders, 16 July 1961, Kansas City, Mo.; Harvey Rettberg's taped interview with Floyd Estep, early July 1996, Los Angeles, Calif., in author's possession.

143. Harvey Rettberg's taped interview with Floyd Estep, early July 1961, Los Angeles, Calif.; Joe Sanders, "Join Coon-Sanders and See America," p. 20 (front); Bob Harrington, "Tales of Coon-Sanders," *The Mississippi Rag*, April 1991, p. 10.

144. Joe Sanders, "Join Coon-Sanders and See America," p. 20 (front).

145. Rex Downing at Coon-Sanders Nighthawks Fan Club's 1977 annual convention, Huntington, W.Va., recorded by Willis Morrisette; tape in author's possession.

146. Author's conversation with John Coon, Auburn, Ala., 19 January 1995.

147. "Bomb Wrecks Petrillo's Home," *Variety*, 20 August 1924, p. 7; McDougal, *The Last Mogul*, p. 38.

148. *"I Can Hear It Now," 1919–1949*, [vol. 2] 1945–1949, side 2, band 1.

149. Author's conversation with John Coon, 18 January 1995, Auburn, Ala.

150. "News from the Dailies: Chicago," *Variety*, 2 December 1925, p. 10.

151. "Hoodoo No. 13 Room," *ibid.*, 7 October 1925, p. 5.

152. "4 Pet Jokes Cost 1 Wife," *ibid.*, p. 5.

153. "Chicago Remains Main Center for Divorce Actions Despite 10,000 Suits Awaiting Trial," *ibid.*, 26 September 1928, p. 29; "Bands Will Even Cut for That Reno Cure," *ibid.*, 20 May 1931, p. 1.

154. Joe Sanders, "Join Coon-Sanders and See America," p. 22 (front); "sold out" flier, among miscellaneous materials, JLSC.

155. William McKenna, album notes on *Harry Reser's Novelty Groups* phonograph recording TT-202 (Los Angeles: Take Two Records, 1978).

156. "Inside Stuff on Music," *Variety*, 24 February 1926, p. 48.

157. Rust, *The American Dance Band Discography, 1917–1942*, vol. 1, p. 349.

158. "Initial on Garter Latest Nutty Fad," *Variety*, 24 March 1926, p. 13.

159. Feist ad, *ibid.*, 2 December 1925, p. 61.

160. "Chiseling and Hooey Theme of Coon-Sanders' Hot Letter," *ibid.*, 4 February 1931, p. 80.

161. Rust, *The American Dance Band Discography, 1917–1942*, vol. 1, pp. 39, 349.

162. *Ibid.*, p. 349.

163. Joe Sanders, "Join Coon-Sanders and See America," p. 33 (front); Harrington, "Tales of Coon-Sanders," p. 11.

164. Kramer, unpublished history of the MCA, chapter 8, p. 5.

165. "Here and There," *Variety*, 31 March 1926, p. 45.

166. Joe Sanders, "Join Coon-Sanders and See America," p. 22 (back).

167. "Inside Stuff on Music," *Variety*, 26 May 1926, p. 48.

168. E. A. Smith and Hoyt Wright ads, *Anderson* (Ind.) *Herald*, 4 April 1926; Joe Sanders' *Voss Diary 1926*, 4 April, in miscellaneous materials, JLSC.

169. "Famous Radio Orchestra coming to Junior High," *Vincennes* (Ind.) *Morning Commercial*, 2 April 1926; program ad, *ibid.*, 4 April 1926; Joe Sanders' *Voss Diary 1926*, 5 and 6 April.

170. Joe Sanders' *Voss Diary 1926*, April 7; David N. Lewis to author, Terre Haute, Ind., 5 July 2000.

171. Joe Sanders' *Voss Diary 1926*, April 12; Sanders, "Join Coon-Sanders and See America," p. 22 (back).

172. "Greatest Dance Band in Country Here One Night," Huntington, W. Va., *Herald-Dispatch*, 11 April 1926.

173. Joe Sanders' *Voss Diary 1926*, April 14; "Coon-Sanders Nighthawks," Chillicothe, Ohio, *Scioto Gazette*, 13 April 1926; Winter Garden ad, *ibid.*, 8 April 1926.

174. Joe Sanders' *Voss Diary 1926*, April 19; Royal Dance Palais ad, Galena, Ill., *Daily Gazette*, 17 April 1926.

175. Joe Sanders' *Voss Diary 1926*, April 20; Winter Garden ad, *La Crosse* (Wisc.) *Tribune*, 19 April 1926.

176. "Coon-Sanders on Tour Did $11,000 in 14 Days," *Variety*, 28 April 1926, p. 81.

177. Joe Sanders' *Voss Diary 1926*, April 21.

178. "Coming to Danceland Wednesday," *Davenport* (Iowa) *Democrat*, 18 April 1926, p. 19; "Coon-Sanders Night Hawks at Danceland," *Davenport* (Iowa) *Times*, 17 April 1926, p. 8.

179. Joe Sanders, "Join Coon-Sanders and See America," p. 23 (back).

180. "Nighthawks in Theater Revue," *Milwaukee Journal*, 25 April 1926; Joe Sanders' *Voss Diary 1926*, April 24–30.

181. Athletic Club ad, *Portsmouth* (Ohio) *Daily Times*, 5 May 1926; "Coon-Sanders Night Hawks to Play for Dancers at Athletic Club," *Portsmouth Morning Sun*, 4 May 1926, p. 16; Joe Sanders' *Voss Diary 1926*, May 6.

182. Athletic Park Pavilion and Runge's Music Store ads, *Richmond* (Ind.) *Item*, 7 May 1926; *Richmond Palladium and Sun-Telegram*, 7 May 1926, p. 12; Joe Sanders' *Voss Diary 1926*, May 7.

183. David N. Lewis, Vigo County Public Library, to author, Terre Haute, Ind., 5 July 2000; Joe Sanders' *Voss Diary 1926*, May 8 and 10.
184. "Band's Scale of Prices for 1-Nighters," *Variety*, 5 May 1926, p. 25.
185. Joe Sanders, "Join Coon-Sanders and See America," pp. 25 (back and front), 26 (back and front).
186. Sanders' *Voss Diary 1926*, May 12–15; ads for Irving Zuelke and for Cinderella Ball Room, *Appleton* (Wisc.) *Post-Crescent*, 15 May 1926.
187. "Prepare for Hawks," Traverse City, Mich., *Record-Eagle*, 15 May 1926, p. 6; "Night Hawks Tonight," *ibid.*, 18 May 1926, p. 3; "Coon-Sanders Music's Great," *ibid.*, 19 May 1926, p. 3; Sanders' *Voss Diary 1926*, 18 May.
188. Joe Sanders, "Join Coon-Sanders and See America," p. 27 (front).
189. "Famous Orchestra Coming Wednesday," *Cadillac* (Mich.) *Evening News*, 18 May 1926, p. 8; "Nighthawks Great Despite the Cold," *ibid.*, 20 May 1926, p. 2.
190. "Many Enjoyed Nighthawks," *Battle Creek* (Mich.) *Enquirer*, 23 May 1926, p. 6; Sanders' *Voss Diary 1926*, May 22.
191. Sanders' *Voss Diary 1926*, dates for February and March; quoted with permission of Kansas City Public Library.
192. Sanders' *Voss Diary 1926*, *passim*.
193. Vanity Fair Ball Room ad, Huntington, W. Va., *Herald-Dispatch*, 26 May 1926; Athletic Park Pavilion ad, Richmond (Ind.) *Palladium*, 29 May 1926, p. 13; Joe Sanders' *Voss Diary 1926*, 28 and 29 May; Joe Sanders, "Join Coon-Sanders and See America," p. 22 (back).
194. Joe Sanders' *Voss Diary 1926*, train listings page [7]; *ibid.*, June 4–7; Lambdin Kay, "Famed Coon-Sanders Nighthawk Band Will Play for Noon Concert Monday," *Atlanta* (Ga.) *Journal*, 6 June 1926, WSB section, p. 1; Joe Sanders, "Join Coon-Sanders and See America," p. 22 (back).
195. Kay, "Famed Coon-Sanders Nighthawk Band Will Play for Noon Concert Monday"; "Coon-Sanders Band to Play for WSB Monday at 10:45," *Atlanta Journal*, 7 June 1926, p. 10.
196. "Art Gilham Is Shot," *Variety*, 18 November 1925, p. 45.
197. "Nighthawks See Stone Mountain as Flint Co.'s Guests," *Atlanta* (Ga.) *Journal*, 6 June 1926, sec. A, p. 4; *Encyclopaedia Britannica*, 1965 ed., s.v. "Stone Mountain Memorial," by A. K. McComb.
198. Joe Sanders, "Join Coon-Sanders and See America," pp. 27 (back), 28 (front and back); Joe Sanders' *Voss Diary 1926*, train listings p. [7], engagement for June 8.
199. Tape one of two made solo by John Coon for the author, Prairie Village, Kans., January 1995.
200. "Here and There," *Variety*, 17 February 1926, p. 46.
201. MCA ad, *ibid.*, 16 June 1926, p. 56.
202. "Orchestra Booking Co. in Non-Musical Bldg.," *ibid.*, 12 May 1926, p. 48.
203. Joe Sanders' *Voss Diary 1926*, June 17; Allen, *Only Yesterday*, pp. 128–129; Joe Sanders, "Join Coon-Sanders and See America," p. 32 (back); Carleton Coon's moving pictures on videotape, copy in author's possession.
204. Joe Sanders' *Voss Diary 1926*, June 27–July 3; "'What Price Glory' Still Tops Theatrical Bills," *Cleveland* (Ohio) *News*, 28 June 1926, p. 18.
205. John T. Vorpe, "In the Land of Jazz with the Orchestras and Entertainers," *Cleveland* (Ohio) *Plain Dealer*, 27 June 1926, p. 2.
206. "Allen," *Cleveland* (Ohio) *Plain Dealer*, 29 June 1926, p. 16.
207. George Davis, "Night Hawks at Allen," *Cleveland* (Ohio) *Press*, 28 June 1926, p. 20.
208. "Independence Day," *Vermilion* (Ohio) *News*, 17 June 1926; Crystal Gardens ad, *ibid.*, 1 July 1926; "Fourth of July in Vermilion," *ibid.*, 8 July 1926; Joe Sanders' *Voss Diary 1926*, July 4–5.
209. "Original Nighthawks to Play at Idle Hour," *Huntington* (Ind.) *Herald*, 13 July 1926, p. 3; "Large Crowd Hears Famous Nighthawks," *ibid.*, 2 August 1926, p. 6; Joe Sanders' *Voss Diary 1926*, July 13 and August 1.
210. Joe Sanders' *Voss Diary 1926*, July 25, and pp. [13–14]; Joe Sanders, "Join Coon-Sanders and See America," pp. 30 (back), 31 (front and back), 32 (front).
211. "Ale Price Jumps Up," *Variety*, 11 July 1925, p. 36.
212. "Booze in Washington," *ibid.*, 22 July 1925, p. 1.
213. "Bootlegger's Convention," *ibid.*, 20 August 1924, pp. 1, 54.
214. "Phoney and Good Liquor," *ibid.*, 30 September 1925, p. 1.
215. "Coon-Sanders Nighthawks in Keyser Tonight," Keyser, W. Va. *Mineral Daily News Tribune*, 29 July 1926; "Coon-Sanders Orchestra Pleases," *ibid.*, 30 July 1926; Joe Sanders' *Voss Diary 1926*, July 29.
216. Coon-Sanders ad, *Vincennes* (Ind.) *Sun*, 3 August 1926, p. 5; Joe Sanders' *Voss Diary 1926*, August 4.
217. Ryan, "Coon Sanders," pp. 46–47; Joe Sanders' *Voss Diary 1926*, August 13.
218. Joe Sanders' *Voss Diary 1926*, p. [3].
219. *Ibid.*, August 16–17.
220. Joe Sanders, "Join Coon-Sanders and See America," p. 33 (front); Joe Sanders' *Voss Diary 1926*, September 1–2.
221. Joe Sanders' *Voss Diary 1926*, September 3–9; World Theater ad, Omaha, Neb., *World-Herald*, 3 September 1926; "New Bills at the Theaters: World," *ibid.*, 5 September 1926.
222. "At the Theaters: World," Omaha *World-Herald*, 1 September 1926; World Theater ad,

ibid., 4 September 1926; "Advance Notices from Theater Managers: World," *Omaha Bee*, 5 September 1926.

223. *Sioux City* (Iowa) *Journal*, 12 September 1926, pp. 31, 34; Joe Sanders' *Voss Diary 1926*, September 12 and 14.

224. "Kansas City Night Hawks Coming," *Denison* (Iowa) *Bulletin*, 15 September 1926; Joe Sanders, "Join Coon-Sanders and See America," p. 33 (front); Sanders' *Voss Diary 1926*, September 17 and 19; see also *Voss Diary, 1926*, also, p. [12], for mileage of entire tour.

225. "M.C.A. Man Waved Flag to Stop Train," *Variety*, 20 October 1926, p. 101.

226. "'Hip Booze' Makes Chi's Night Life Look Dismal," *ibid.*, 14 July 1926, p. 1.

227. Kramer, typescript of unpublished history of MCA, chapter 8, p. 5

228. See Joe Sanders' *Voss Diary 1926*, introductory pages, for distance traveled, and, on September 22, for money earned.

6. The Blackhawk Years

1. Joe Sanders, "Join Coon-Sanders and See America," p. 33 (front and back); author's conversation with John Coon, 19 January 1995, Auburn, Ala.; miscellaneous materials, JLSC.

2. Joe Sanders, "Join Coon-Sanders and See America," p. 33 (front and back); "Blackhawk Cafe," *Variety*, 6 October 1926, p. 87.

3. Joe Sanders, "Join Coon-Sanders and See America," p. 33 (front and back); Rex Downing, on tape made by Willis Morrisette at Coon-Sanders Nighthawk Club's annual convention, April 1977, Huntington, W. Va., in author's collection.

4. Joe Sanders, "Join Coon-Sanders and See America," p. 33 (back).

5. "Blackhawk Cafe," *Variety*, 6 October 1926, p. 87.

6. Miscellaneous materials, JLSC.

7. Kramer, unpublished history of MCA., chapter 8, p. 11.

8. Joe Sanders, "Join Coon-Sanders and See America," p. 33 (back).

9. Author's conversation with Harvey Rettberg, 19 November 1993, Pickens, S.C.; Feist ad, *Variety*, 19 May 1926, p. 53.

10. "Chatter in the Loop: Rival Musicians," *Variety*, 8 August 1928, p. 41.

11. Rust, *The American Dance Band Discography, 1917-1942*, vol. 2, pp. 1109-1110; "Inside Stuff — Music," *Variety*, 22 August 1928, p. 59.

12. "Inside Stuff — Music," *Variety*, 22 August 1928, p. 59.

13. "'Black Bottom' Dance Described," *ibid.*, 15 September 1926, p. 28.

14. "Black Bottom Hits Europe," *ibid.*, 8 December 1926, p. 1; "Black Bottom Name Is Worrying English," *ibid.*, 24 November 1926, p. 57.

15. T. H. White, *The Age of Scandal: An Excursion through a Minor Period* (New York: G. P. Putnam's Sons, 1950), pp. 80-81.

16. "Chi Night Clubs Passing; 'Dine and Dance' Cafes," *Variety*, 15 December 1926, p. 1.

17. "'Observation' Evidence of Booze on Person Held Sufficient — 3 Loop Clubs," *ibid.*, 15 December 1926, pp. 2, 26.

18. "69 Mags and 67 Plays Labeled Fit for Censoring by Wilson," *ibid.*, 23 February 1927, p. 37.

19. Rust, *The American Dance Band Discography, 1917-1942*, vol. 1, p. 349; "Brainstorm," "An erratic blues." (Chicago: Forster Music Publisher, 1927), "Arranged and recorded by the composer."

20. Kramer, unpublished history of M.C.A., chapter 4, p. 6.

21. *Ibid.*, chapter 8, pp. 6-7.

22. Joe Sanders, "Join Coon-Sanders and See America,"p. 34 (front).; "Here and There," *Variety*, 6 April 1927, p. 53; typed sheets of road tour engagements, miscellaneous items, JLSC; Sanders' pocket *Voss Diary, 1926* and *Date Book for Season 1927-1928*; author's conversation with John Coon, 18 January 1995, Auburn, Ala.

23. Ads, Omaha, Neb., *Evening World Herald*, March 30 and 31 and 1 April 1927.

24. "Coon and Sanders to Headline at World," *Omaha* (Neb.) *Bee*, 31 March 1927; Ed Patton's ad, Omaha *Evening World Herald*, 1 April 1927; World Theatre ad, *ibid.*, 4 April 1927.

25. "World — 'Nighthawks,'" Omaha *Evening World Herald*, 2 April 1927.

26. Joe Sanders, "Join Coon-Sanders and See America," p. 34 (front); cited date in Joe Sanders' *Date Book for Season 1927-1928*, miscellaneous materials, JLSC.

27. Cited date in Joe Sanders' pocket *Date Book for Season 1927-1928*.

28. Cited date in *ibid*.

29. "Nineteen Killed, 100 Hurt As Tornado Hits Central Illinois," Springfield *Illinois State Journal*, 20 April 1927, pp. 1, 3; Joe Sanders, "Join Coon-Sanders and See America," pp. 37 (back), 38 (front).

30. Joe Sanders, "Join Coon-Sanders and See America," pp. 37 (back) and 38 (front); Joe Sanders' *Datebook for Season 1927-1928*, "memoranda" opposite April 10 and 11, and entry for April 19.

31. Ryan, "Coon-Sanders," p. 108.

32. Compare Sanders' account in his scrapbook (cited just above) and several accounts in Springfield *Illinois State Journal*, 20 April 1927, p. 1.

33. Joe Sanders' *Date Book for Season 1927-1928*, entry for April 19.

34. "Nighthawks Make Discs; Start West," Springfield, *Illinois State Journal*, 15 April 1927, p. 9; Rust, *The American Dance Band Discography 1917–1942*, vol. 1, pp. 348-351.

35. "Coon-Sanders' Nighthawks to Play in City," Springfield *Illinois State Journal*, sec. 3, p. 10.
36. Sanders' *Date Book for Season 1927–1928*, entry for April 20.
37. Dan Schroeder, "Coon-Sanders Kansas City Nighthawks," p. 16.
38. Aurora, Ill., *Daily Beacon*, 23 July 1927, p. 12.
39. *Ibid.*, April 22 and 23.
40. Ad for Chubb and Steinberg's Music Shop, Cincinnati, Ohio, *Times-Star*, 5 May 1927.
41. Palace Theater's ad, *Fort Wayne* (Ind.) *Journal Gazette*, 24 April 1927; ad for "Big Benefit Dance!" *ibid.*, 27 April 1927; Sanders' *Datebook for Season 1927–1928*, 24–27 April 1927.
42. Sanders' *Date Book for Season 1927-28*, 1–28 May 1927; Joe Sanders, "Join Coon-Sanders and See America," pp. 39 (front and back), 40 (front and back).
43. "Castle Farm," Cincinnati *Enquirer*, 2 May 1927.
44. Joe Sanders, "Join Coon-Sanders and See America," pp. 39–40 (front and back), 41 (front).
45. "Initial Vitaphone Program at Capitol Escites Wonder and Admiration," Cincinnati *Times-Star*, 16 May 1927; *Encyclopaedia Britannica*, 1965 ed., s.v. "Motion Pictures," by Arthur Knight.
46. "Squawking Pictures," *Variety*, 11 July 1928, p. 5; "Sound Devices Hit Snag," *ibid.*, p. 7.
47. Cincinnati *Times-Star*, 3, 14, 20, 21, 23 May 1927; Cincinnati *Enquirer*, 1, 13 May 1927.
48. Joe Sanders' *Date Book for Season 1927–1928*, 29 May–4 June 1927; Joe Sanders, "Join Coon-Sanders and See America," p. 34 (front).
49. Joe Sanders, "Join Coon-Sanders and See America," p. 34 (front); Sanders' *Date Book for Season 1927–1928*, 5, 8–9 June 1927.
50. Joe Sanders, "Join Coon-Sanders and See America," pp. 34 (front and back); Joe Sanders' *Date Book for Season 1927-1928*, 10-18 June 1927.
51. Joe Sanders' *Date Book for Season 1927–1928*, 10–18 June 1927; "Radio Orchestra at the Comodore [sic]," *Lowell* (Mass.) *Sun*, 14 June 1927; "Famous Radio Band at the Commodore," *ibid.*; "Coon-Sanders Original Kansas City Nighthawks Coming September 2," *Galena* (Ill.) *Daily Gazette*, 31 August 1927; Joe Sanders, "Join Coon-Sanders and See America," pp. 34 (front and back).
52. Joe Sanders, "Join Coon-Sanders and See America," pp. 44 (back), 45–49 (all front and back).
53. Harrington, "Tales of Coon-Sanders," p. 10.
54. Sanders' *Date Book for Season 1927–1928*, 19–20 June 1927.
55. *Ibid.*, 20–25 June 1927; Joe Sanders, "Join Coon-Sanders and See America," p. 50 (front); Rust, *The American Dance Band Discography, 1917–1942*," vol. 1, p. 349.
56. Rust, *The American Dance Band Discography, 1917–1942*, vol. 1, p. 349; Joe Sanders' *Date Book for Season 1927–1928*, 24–25 June 1927; Sanders, "Join Coon-Sanders and See America," p. 34 (back).
57. Joe Sanders' *Date Book for Season 1927–1928*, 27 June–24 July 1927; Iowa City *Press-Citizen*, p. 5; Fox Theater ad, *Aurora* (Ill.) *Daily Beacon*, 23 July 1927.
58. *Aurora* (Ill.) *Daily Beacon*, 23 July 1927.
59. "The Stage: Rialto," Joliet, Ill., *Evening Herald-News*, 27 July 1927, p. 17; for reference to Miss Illinois, see Joe Sanders, "Join Coon-Sanders and See America," p. 33 (back); Sanders' *Date Book for Season 1927–1928*, 25–30 July 1927; Palace Theater ad, Ft. Wayne, Ind., *Journal-Gazette*, 29 July 1927.
60. Tape one of two made solo for the author by John Coon, Prairie Village, Kans. January 1995.
61. Joe Sanders' *Date Book for Season 1927–1928*, 8–9 August 1927; Lafayette, Ind., *Journal and Courier*, 6 August 1927; Joe Sanders, "Join Coon-Sanders and See America," pp. 50 (front), 52 (front).
62. Joe Sanders' *Date Book for Season 1927–1928*, 10–31 August 1927; Joe Sanders, "Join Coon-Sanders and See America," p. 52 (front).
63. Rust, *The American Dance Band Discography, 1917–1942*, vol. 1, p. 291.
64. Author's interview with Harvey Rettberg, Pickens, S. C., 19 November 1993.
65. Johnson, "The Happy-Go-Lucky Sounds of Coon-Sanders Nighthawks," p. 9; Clyde Hahn, "The Story of the Coon-Sanders Original Nighthawks Club (...and How It Grew — or, It Went This-away!)," *Jazz Notes*, vol. VI, no. 1 ns, pp. 9–10.
66. Joe Sanders, "Join Coon-Sanders and See America," p. 52 (front); Kramer, unpublished history of MCA, chap. 8, p. 9.
67. Kramer, unpublished history of MCA, chap. 8, p. 9; Simon, *The Big Bands*, p. 499.
68. Tape 11 (i.e., tape 6, side 1) of six microcassettes made solo by John Coon, about 1998, Prairie Village, Kans., in author's possession.
69. Joe Sanders, "Join Coon-Sanders and See America," p. 53 (back).
70. "1,000 Pieces on Nighthawks' List," *Chattanooga* (Tenn.) *News*, 20 September 1927, p. 9; for Babe Ruth statement, see *Hark! The Years!: A Scrapbook of Sound*, phonograph recording S282 (N.P.: Capitol Records, n.d. [1954?]), side 2.
71. "Great Crowd Greets Nighthawk Orchestra," *Chattanooga* (Tenn.) *Times*, 22 September 1927, p. 13.
72. "Revivalist Reserves Seats for 'Legger,'" *ibid.*

73. For Sunday's statement, see *The Voices of the 20th Century*, phonograph recording CRL 57308 (New York: Coral Records, n.d.[196_]), side 1.
74. John Coon's tape no. 1, of two made solo for author, Prairie Village, Kans., January 1995; Dunning, *On the Air*, p. 174.
75. "Kansas City Night Hawks Here Thursday," *Portsmouth* (Ohio) *Daily Times*, 28 September 1927, p. 10.
76. Joe Sanders, "Join Coon-Sanders and See America," pp. 53 (back), 54 (front).
77. *Ibid.*, pp. 54 (back), 55 (front).
78. *Ibid.*, p. 56 (front).
79. *Ibid.*, p. 56 (front); "Ford Car Tie-Up," *Variety*, 14 December 1927, p. 1; "City Hangs Out Welcome Sign for Orchestra," *Kansas City Post*, 9 December 1927, p. 10B.
80. "City Hangs Out Welcome Sign for Orchestra," *Kansas City Post*, 9 December 1927, p. 10B; ad for Wurlitzer's, *ibid.*, p. 14A.
81. Joe Sanders, "Join Coon-Sanders and See America," p. 56 (front).
82. *Ibid.*
83. Rust, *The American Dance Band Discography, 1917–1942*, vol. 1, p. 349.
84. Joe Sanders, "Join Coon-Sanders and See America," p. 58 (front).
85. *Ibid.*; Kramer, unpublished history of MCA, chap. 4, p. 7.
86. "Inside Stuff—Music," *Variety*, 12 September 1928, p. 56.
87. Joe Sanders, "Join Coon-Sanders and See America," p. 58 (front).
88. "Many Enjoy Party," Battle Creek, Mich., *Moon-Journal*, 13 April 1928.
89. Joe Sanders, "Join Coon-Sanders and See America," p. 58 (front); New Avalon ads, *La Crosse* (Wisc.) *Tribune*, 17 April 1928, p. 12, and 18 April 1928, p. 10.
90. Joe Sanders, "Join Coon-Sanders and See America," p. 58 (front).
91. "Society," *South Bend* (Ind.) *News-Times*, 12 May 1928; "Senior Ball Marks Social Exit of Class of 1928," *Notre Dame Scholastic*, 18 May 1928.
92. "Society," *South Bend* (Ind.) *News-Times*, 12 May 1928.
93. Author's conversation with John Coon, 19 January 1995, Auburn, Ala.; John Coon's tape no. 1, of two made solo for the author, Prairie Village, Kans., January 1995.
94. Thomas A. DeLong, *Radio Stars*, entry 796; author's conversation with John Coon, 20 January 1995, Auburn, Ala.
95. Author's conversation with Harvey Rettberg, Pickens, S.C., 19 November 1993; *Steve Canyon* comic strip, *Meridian* (Miss.) *Star*, 12 February 1962; Milton Caniff's letter to Harvey Rettberg, 22 February 1962, and Caniff's corrected drawing, in HRC.

96. Author's conversation with John Coon, 19 January 1995, Auburn, Ala.
97. John Coon's tape no. 2, of two made solo for the author, Prairie Village, Kans., January 1995.
98. See, for example, Simon, *The Big Bands*, pp. 497–498.
99. John Coon's tape no. 2, of two made solo for author, Prairie Village, Kans., January 1995.
100. *Ibid.*
101. "Stoppage of Remote Control Goes into Effect in Chicago," *Variety*, 22 February 1928, p. 53; "Chicago Stations Stop All Dance Music," *ibid.*, 7 March 1928, p. 56.
102. John Coon's tape no. 2, of two two made solo for author, Paririe Village, Kans., January 1995.
103. *Ibid.*
104. *Ibid*; tape 3 (i.e., tape 2, side 1) of six tapes John Coon made solo shortly before his death in 1999, now in author's possession.
105. Jay Robert Nash, *Almanac of World Crime* (New York: Bonanza Books, 1981), p. 138; Carl Sifakis, *The Encyclopedia of American Crime* (New York: Smithmark, 1992), pp. 456-457.
106. Harrington, "Tales of Coon-Sanders," p. 10.
107. Rust, *The American Dance Band Discography, 1917–1942*, vol. 1, p. 349.
108. "The New Dells" flier, among miscellaneous materials, JLSC.
109. Harrington, "Tales of Coon-Sanders," p. 11.
110. "John Factor Is Kidnapped by Autoists," *Meridian* (Miss.) *Star*, 1 July 1933, p. 1.
111. Harrington, "Tales of Coon-Sanders."
112. Randy Skretvedt, liner notes for compact disc MB 113, *Coon-Sanders' Original Nighthawk Orchestra*, vol. 3 (N.p.: The Old Masters, n.d.), p. 1.
113. Newspaper clipping from *Kansas City Star* of 19 August 1928, SC1, box 15, folder 2, JLSC.
114. Joe Sanders, "Join Coon-Sanders and See America," p. 58 (front).
115. John Coon on tape 5 (i.e., side 1, tape 3) of five cassette tapes he made solo just before his death, in author's possession.
116. McDougal, *The Last Mogul*, pp. 21–22.
117. Guy Lombardo, *Auld Acquaintance* (Garden City, N.Y.: Doubleday, 1975), p.x.
118. *Ibid.*, pp. 49, 54, 56.
119. Kramer, unpublished history of MCA, chap. 8, pp. 9–10.
120. McDougal, *The Last Mogul*, pp. 22–23.
121. *Ibid.*, p. 19; regarding use of word *stable*, see *ibid.*, pp. 198–199, 218, 369; Kramer, unpublished history of MCA, chapter 8, p. 5.
122. Simon, *The Big Bands*, pp. 48–49.
123. *Ibid.*, p. 321.
124. Joe Sanders, "Join Coon-Sanders and See America," pp. 58 (front and back), 59 (front);

Schroeder, "Coon-Sanders Kansas City Nighthawks," p. 15.

125. Rex Downing to Harvey Rettberg, Harrisburg, Ark., 29 August 1969, HRC.

126. Rust, *The American Dance Band Discography, 1917–1942*, vol. 1, pp. 348–349; Wurlitzer's ad, *Kansas City Post*, 9 December 1927, p. 14A.

127. John Coon's tape no. 2, of two made solo for the author, Prairie Village, Kans., January 1995; author's conversation with John Coon, 19 January 1995, Auburn, Ala.; John Coon's videocassette containing home movies made in the mid-Twenties by his father, copy in author's possession.

128. John Coon's tape no. 2, of two made solo for the author, Prairie Village, Kans., January 1995.

129. *Ibid.*

130. John Coon's tape no. 1, of two made solo for the author, Prairie Village, Kans., January 1995.

131. Harvey Rettberg's recorded interview with Joe Sanders, 16 July 1961, Kansas City, Mo., copy in author's possession.

132. Author's conversation with John Coon, 19 January 1995, Auburn, Ala.; Rust, *The American Dance Band Discography, 1917–1942*, vol. 1, p. 132.

133. Joe Sanders, "Join Coon-Sanders and See America," pp. 58 (front and back).

134. "Radio Reports: 'Harold Teen,'" *Variety*, 11 March 1931, p. 66.

135. Leo Feist ad, *Variety*, 27 June 1928, pp. 32–33.

136. Rust, *The American Dance Band Discography, 1917–1942*, vol. 1, p. 350.

137. Joe Sanders, "Join Coon-Sanders and See America," pp. 58 (front and back), 59 (front); Schroeder, "Coon-Sanders Kansas City Nighthawks," p. 15.

138. Joe Sanders, "Join Coon-Sanders and See America," p. 58 (back).

139. "Fire Destroys The Dells; Arson Is Suspected," *Chicago Tribune*, 1 August 1929 (the author is indebted for this item to Charles Sengstock); Joe Sanders, "Join Coon-Sanders and See America," p. 59 (front).

140. "Fire Destroys The Dells; Arson Is Suspected," *Chicago Tribune*, 1 August 1929.

141. Joe Sanders, "Join Coon-Sanders and See America," p. 59 (front).

142. "Olsen, Bernie and Waring as Lure for Gamblers, Sez Chi Reformer," *Variety*, 27 May 1931, p. 100.

143. Rust, *The American Dance Band Discography, 1917–1942*, vol. 1, p. 350.

144. Sanders, "Join Coon-Sanders and See America," pp. 58 (back), 59 (front).

145. Rust, *The American Dance Band Discography, 1917–1942*, vol. 1, p. 350.

146. See, for example, Gottlieb and Kimball, *Reading Lyrics*, p. 358; also, Nat Shapiro (ed.), *Popular Music: An Annotated Index of American Popular Songs*, vol. 4, *1930–1939* (New York: Adrian Press, 1968), p. 33.

147. "Carlton [*sic*] Coon at Work," *Kansas City* (Mo.) *Star*, 27 March 1930; author's telephone conversation with John Coon, 2 August 1998.

148. "Carlton [*sic*] Coon at Work," *Kansas City* (Mo.) *Star*, 27 March 1930.

149. Tape no. 2, of two, made solo by John Coon, Prairie Village, Kans., January 1995, for author's use.

150. Harrington, "Tales of Coon-Sanders," pp. 11–12.

151. *Ibid.*, p. 12.

152. McDougal, *The Last Mogul*, pp. 22–25 and *passim*.

153. Author's telephone conversation with John Coon, 19 May 1998.

154. John Coon's tape no. 2, of two made solo for the author, Prairie Village, Kas., January 1995.

155. "Carlton [*sic*] Coon at Work," *Kansas City Star*, 27 March 1930.

156. *Ibid.*

157. *Ibid.*

158. Gordon and Gordon, *American Chronicle*, pp. 70, 77.

159. Mel Tormé, *It Wasn't All Velvet* (New York: Viking Penguin, 1988), pp. 3–4.

160. Spaeth, *A History of Popular Music in America*, p. 482; Tormé, *It Wasn't All Velvet*, p. 4.

161. Harvey Rettberg's taped interview with Joe Sanders, Kansas City, Mo., 16 July 1961.

162. Skretvedt, liner notes for compact disc MB 113, *Coon-Sanders' Original Nighthawk Orchestra*, vol. 3, pp. 9–10; author's telephone conversation with Orville Butler, sometime in early 1998.

163. *Coon-Sanders Original Nighthawk Orchestra*, compact disc MB 113 (N.p.: The Old Masters, n.d.), bands 13–17.

164. Joe Sanders, "Join Coon-Sanders and See America," p. 58 (back); author's conversation with John Coon, 19 January 1995, Auburn, Ala.

165. Box 17, scrapbook 8, JLSC.

166. *Ibid.*

167. *Ibid.*

168. Joe Sanders, "Join Coon-Sanders and See America," p. 59 (front); NBC ad for *Florsheim Shoe Frolic*, miscellaneous materials, JLSC.

169. Steve Masar's electronic mail to author, 22 September 2000.

170. Ad for Danceland, *Davenport* (Iowa) *Times*, 10 April 1930, p. 5.

171. "Radio Stars for Prom," St. Louis University *Varsity Breeze*, 26 March 1930, p. 1.

172. *Ibid.*

173. *Ibid.*

174. *Ibid.*

175. "Prom Presented a Scene of Glorious Pageantry," *ibid.*, 30 April 1930, p. 1.
176. "Prom Notes by L. J. K.," *ibid.*, p. 1.
177. *Ibid.*; "Prom Presented a Scene of Glorious Pageantry," *ibid.*, 30 April 1930, p. 1.
178. "Prom Presented a Scene of Glorious Pageantry," *ibid.*, 30 April 1930, p. 1.
179. Joe Sanders, "Join Coon-Sanders and See America," p. 59 (back).
180. *Ibid.*, pp. 59 (back), 60 (front).
181. *Ibid.*; original check and contract for Griffith party, Kansas City Museum, Kansas City, Mo.
182. Joe Sanders, "Join Coon-Sanders and See America," p. 60 (front).
183. "'Name' Bandsmen Favor Columbia in Chi as NBC Pushes Studio Bands over Midwest for Commercial Jobs," *Variety*, 21 January 1931, p. 67.
184. "Chi Network Status Reversed Overnite as WMAQ Goes NBC; CBS Minus 100% Outlet in Chi," *ibid.*, 1 September 1931, pp. 59–60.
185. "MCA Nat'l Advertiser after $2,994,000 Year," *ibid.*, 11 February 1931, p. 73.
186. "News from the Dailies: Chicago," *ibid.*, 11 February 1931, p. 49.
187. "Chicago Precaution," *ibid.*, 18 February 1931, p. 58.
188. "Small Bands in East Face Summer Panic," *ibid.*, 18 February 1931, p. 69; "Pepping Biz with Band's Pop Music in Chi Dept. Stores," *ibid.*, 20 May 1931, p. 1.
189. "Bad Radio Tongue Slips," *ibid.*, 11 February 1931, pp. 1, 12; John Dunning, *On the Air: The Encyclopedia of Old-Time Radio* (New York: Oxford University Press, 1998), p. 689.
190. Program schedule's ad, miscellaneous materials, JLSC.
191. Joe Sanders, "Join Coon-Sanders and See America," p. 59 (front).
192. "Coon-Sanders Sasses NBC," *Variety*, 15 April 1931, p. 75.
193. Joe Sanders, "Join Coon-Sanders and See America," pp. 59 (front and back); DeLong, *Radio Stars*, p. 62.
194. Joe Sanders, "Join Coon-Sanders and See America," p. 59 (back); ad for Florsheim's "Feeture" broadcast, miscellaneous materials, JLSC.
195. Taped conversation between Joe Sanders and Harvey Rettberg, Kansas City, Mo., 16 July 1961.
196. Joe Sanders, "Join Coon-Sanders and See America," p. 59 (back).
197. Author's telephone conversation with Carleton A. Coon, Jr., 27 October 2000.
198. John Coon's tape no. 2, of two made solo for the author, Prairie Village, Kans., January 1995.
199. Author's conversation with John Coon, 19 January 1995, Auburn, Ala.; Popper, "America's Band," p. 26.
200. John Coon's tape no. 2, of two made solo for author, Prairie Village, Kans., January 1995.

201. "Coon-Sanders Band is Feature of Stadler Party at Idora Park," *Youngstown* (Ohio) *Vindicator*, 16 April 1931, p. 18.
202. Joe Sanders, "Join Coon-Sanders and See America," p. 60 (front).
203. "Blackhawk," *Variety*, 6 October 1931, p. 96.
204. "Radio Bands Fading Fast," *Variety*, 8 April 1931, p. 1.
205. Cartoon "Forlorn Figures," *The Accelerator*, the Auburn Automobile Co., August 1928, p. 5.
206. "Faulkner Speaking, Straight from the Shoulder," *ibid.*
207. *Ibid.*
208. "Coon-Sanders, Nationally Popular Radio Orchestra, Has Gone Auburn," *ibid.*, June 1931, p. 3; Harrington, "Tales of Coon-Sanders," p. 12; tape one of two made solo for author by John Coon, Prairie Village, Kas., January 1995.
209. "Coon-Sanders, Nationally Popular Radio Orchestra, Has Gone Auburn," *The Accelerator*, June 1931, p. 3.
210. *Ibid.*
211. *Ibid.*
212. Harrington, "Tales of Coon-Sanders," p. 12.
213. *Ibid.*; author's conversation with Gregg Buttermore at the Auburn Cord Duesenberg Museum, Auburn, Ind., 13 October 2000.
214. Harrington, "Tales of Coon-Sanders," pp. 12–13; tape no. 2 of two made solo by John Coon for author, Prairie Village, Kans., January 1995.
215. "Coon-Sanders May Find Out About Pash Femmes," *Variety*, 20 May 1931, p. 139.
216. Joe Sanders, "Join Coon-Sanders and See America," p. 60 (front).
217. *Ibid.*, pp. 60 (front), 62 (front)

7. The Final Year

1. Joe Sanders, "Join Coon-Sanders and See America," p. 62 (front).
2. *Ibid.*, pp. 62 (front), 63 (front).
3. "Program Complete for 1931 Final Set of Dances Here," Washington and Lee University *Ring-tum Phi*, 22 May 1931, p. 1.
4. "First Classmen Give Their Last Dance of Year," Virginia Military Institute *Cadet*, 10 June 1931, pp. 1–4.
5. "Final Ball Climaxes Series of Gala Dances," *ibid.*, pp. 1–4.
6. Joe Sanders, "Join Coon-Sanders and See America," pp. 62 (back), 63 (front and back).
7. *Ibid.*, pp. 64 (front and back).
8. *Ibid.*, p. 62 (front); newspaper clippings, box 15, folder 1, SC1, JLSC.

9. Joe Sanders, "Join Coon-Sanders and See America," p. 66 (front).
10. *Ibid.*, pp. 65 (back), 66 (back).
11. *Ibid.*, pp. 66 (back), 67 (front).
12. "Chatter: Loop," *Variety*, 15 April 1931, p. 58; "Chatter: Loop," *ibid.*, 2 June 1931, p. 47.
13. *Ibid.*, p. 67 (front).
14. *Ibid.*; "Bands Shuffled," *Variety*, 13 May 1931, p. 92; full-page ad for Lyman's orchestra, *ibid.*, 14 July 1931, p. 56; "Hollywood Garden [*sic*] Show Out, Wrestling In," *ibid.*, 21 July 1931, p. 48.
15. Joe Sanders, "Join Coon-Sanders and See America," p. 67 (front).
16. *Ibid.*
17. *Ibid.*
18. *Ibid.*, pp. 67–69 (fronts and backs), 70 (front).
19. *Ibid.*, pp. 69–70 (fronts and backs).
20. *Ibid.*, p. 72 (front).
21. From the author's memory of having read this, as a child, in some old joke book, probably one of the Thomas W. Jackson joke books once sold especially in railroad stations. It could have been *Through Missouri on a Mule*, published in the early 1900s. Most of the material in these books consisted of old vaudeville routines and one-liners. The first book of the series, I believe, was *On a Slow Train through Arkansas*.
22. John Coon's second of two tapes made solo for author, Prairie Village, Kas., January 1995; author's phone conversation with Carleton A. Coon, Jr., 27 October 2000.
23. John Coon's second of two tapes made solo for author, Prairie Village, Kas., January 1995.
24. From a copy, in the author's possession, made from John Coon's original. I have no idea what disposition was made of the original after John's death.
25. For Sanders' driver's license, see miscellaneous materials SC1, JLSC.
26. Joe Sanders, "Join Coon-Sanders and See America," p. 72 (front).
27. *Ibid.*
28. *Ibid.*, p. 72 (back).
29. Paul Karberg, "Coon-Sanders Band 'Sent' the Young Folks in '20s," Madison, Wisc., *Capitol Times Green*, 15 April 1961, p. 1.
30. Joe Sanders, "Join Coon-Sanders and See America," p. 72 (back).
31. *Ibid.*; Madeline Sanders' journal, entry for 21 August 1931, in scrapbook of miscellaneous correspondence, JLSC.
32. Madeline Sanders' journal, entry for 22 August 1931, in scrapbook of miscellaneous correspondence, JLSC.
33. "Orchestra Leader," *Monroe* (La.) *News-Star*, 21 August 1931, p. 5.
34. Harrington, "Tales of Coon-Sanders," pp. 12–13.
35. Joe Sanders, "Join Coon-Sanders and See America," pp. 72 (back) and 73 (front and back); Madeline Sanders' journal, entry for 23 August 1931.
36. Joe Sanders, "Join Coon-Sanders and See America," p. 73 (back); Madeline Sanders' journal, entry for 23 August 1931.
37. Joe Sanders, "Join Coon-Sanders and See America," pp. 73 (back), 74 (front); Madeline Sanders' journal, entry for 23 August 1931.
38. Joe Sanders, "Join Coon-Sanders and See America," p. 74 (front); Madeline Sanders' journal, entry for 23 August 1931.
39. Joe Sanders, "Join Coon-Sanders and See America," p. 74 (front); Madeline Sanders' journal, entry for 23 August 1931.
40. Garry Boulard, *Huey Long Invades New Orleans: The Siege of a City, 1934–36* (Gretna, La.: Pelican Publishing Company, 1998), pp. 21–25, 128.
41. Joe Sanders, "Join Coon-Sanders and See America," p. 74 (front); Madeline Sanders' journal, entries for 23 and 24 August 1931.
42. "Hot Rivalry," *Variety*, 1 September 1931, p. 60; "Suburban Gardens," *ibid.*, 22 September 1931, p. 61.
43. "Club Forest," *New Orleans* (La.) *States*, 26 August 1931, p. 4; "Coon-Sanders Nighthawks Open at Club Forest," *New Orleans* (La.) *Item*, 24 August 1931, p. 3; Joe Sanders, "Join Coon-Sanders and See America," p. 74 (front); Madeline Sanders' journal, entry for 24 August 1931.
44. "Coon-Sanders Nighthawks Open at Club Forest," *New Orleans* (La.) *Item*, 24 August 1931, p. 3.
45. "Club Forest," *New Orleans* (La.) *States*, 26 August 1931, p. 4.
46. See, for example, his "Join Coon-Sanders and See America," pp. 74–81 (back and front).
47. *Ibid.*, pp. 75 (front and back), 77 (front and back).
48. *Ibid.*, p. 81 (front).
49. *Ibid.*, p. 74 (front).
50. *Ibid.*; Madeline Sanders' journal, entry for August 25.
51. Madeline Sanders' journal, entries for 26–28 August 1931.
52. Madeline Sanders' journal, entry for 29 August 1931; Joe Sanders, "Join Coon-Sanders and See America," pp. 79 (back), 80 (front).
53. Madeline Sanders' journal, entry for 29 August 1931.
54. Madeline Sanders' journal, entries for 30 and 31 August 1931.
55. "N.O. Clubs and Unions," *Variety*, 1 September 1931, p. 60.
56. Madeline Sanders' journal, entry for 13 September 1931.
57. Joe Sanders, "Join Coon-Sanders and See America," p. 81 (front); ad for Hotel Schroeder, *Milwaukee* (Wisc.) *Journal*, 15 September 1931, p. 8 [sec. 1]; ad for Hotel Schroeder, *ibid.*, 29 September 1931, p. 14 [sec. 1].

58. Joe Sanders, "Join Coon-Sanders and See America," p. 81 (front).
59. "Jazz Tunes with Meals Called Bad for Digestion," *Milwaukee Journal*, 24 September 1931, p. 2 ["Green Sheet"]; "Slower Tempos Mark New Era in Dance Music," *ibid.*, 27 September 1931, p. 9 [sports sec.].
60. Joe Sanders, "Join Coon-Sanders and See America," pp. 81 (front), 82)front).
61. Steward, "Cooney and Joe Hard Workers," p. 24; "Coon-Sanders Break Rule to Play New York," *Variety*, 14 July 1931, p. 49.
62. Joe Sanders, "Join Coon-Sanders and See America," p. 82 (back).
63. New Yorker's ad in the *New York Times*, 8 October 1931, p. 19; Joe Sanders, "Join Coon-Sanders and See America," p. 82 (back).
64. Kramer, unpublished history of MCA, chap. 8, p. 10.
65. Joe Sanders, "Join Coon-Sanders and See America," p. 82 (back).
66. *Ibid.*
67. Joe Sanders, "Join Coon Sanders and See America," pp. 82 (back), 83 (front).
68. Hotel New Yorker's ad, *New York Times*, 15 October 1931, p. 15; author's interview with John Coon, 19 January 1995, Auburn, Ala.
69. Author's interview with Harvey Rettberg, Pickens, S.C., 19 November 1993.
70. Joe Sanders, "Join Coon-Sanders and See America," p. 87 (front); author's interview with Harvey Rettberg, 19 November 1993, Pickens, S.C.
71. Rust, *The American Dance Band Discography, 1917–1942*, vol. 1, p. 351; Harvey Rettberg's interview with Joe Sanders, 16 July 1961, Kansas City, Mo.; author's interview with Harvey Rettberg, 19 November 1993, Pickens, S.C.
72. "Disc Reviews: Coon-Sanders," *Variety*, 26 April 1932, p. 53.
73. "Society's 1st Cut-In Violation Charges Are against Robbins, Turk, Ahlert," *Variety*, 3 November 1931, p. 59.
74. "Radio's Biggest Music Plug, Theme Songs, Devoted Mostly to Non-Selling Old Numbers," *ibid.*, 17 November 1931, p. 61; Spaeth, *A History of Popular Music in America*, pp. 53–54, 66.
75. "Society's 1st Cut-In Violation Charges Are Against Robbins, Turk, Ahlert," *Variety*, 3 November 1931, p. 59; Spaeth, *A History of Popular Music in America*, p. 487.
76. "Radio's Lone Advantage for Music is Quick Decision over New Songs," *Variety*, 17 November 1931, p. 60.
77. "$4,000,000 from Radio," *ibid.*, 19 April 1932, p. 61.
78. Author's interview with Harvey Rettberg, 19 November 1993, Pickens, S. C.
79. Joe Sanders, "Join Coon-Sanders and See America," p. 83 (back).
80. Schroeder, "Coon-Sanders Kansas City Nighthawks," p. 21.
81. Tape no. 1 of two made *solo* by John Coon, Prairie Village, Kans., January 1995, for the author.
82. *Ibid.*
83. Madeline Sanders' journal, entry for "New York City," 21 October 1931.
84. *Ibid.*, probably entry for 24 October 1931, though Madeline at this time had ceased dating entries carefully.
85. *Ibid.*, entry apparently for 25 October 1931.
86. *Ibid.*, entry for Saturday (probably 31 October 1931).
87. *Ibid.*, entries for Sunday and Monday (probably 1–2 November 1931).
88. *Ibid.*, entry for Sunday, either 1 or 8 November 1931.
89. *Ibid.*, entry for Wednesday, either 4 or 11 November 1931.
90. *Ibid.*, entry for Thursday, either 5 or 12 November 1931.
91. Harrington, "Tales of Coon-Sanders," p. 13.
92. Joe Sanders, "Join Coon-Sanders and See America," p. 83 (back); Madeline Sanders' journal, entry for Tuesday, 10 (possibly 17) November 1931.
93. Madeline Sanders' journal, entries for Thursday, 12 or 19 November 1931, through Saturday, 14 or 21 November 1931.
94. "NBC-MCA Conferences in Chi Move to N.Y.," *Variety*, 10 November 1931, p. 60; "NBC-MCA Band Get-Together Hot and Cold," *ibid.*, 17 November 1931, p. 61.
95. "Inside Stuff—Radio," *ibid.*, 29 September 1931, p. 50.
96. Joe Sanders, "Join Coon-Sanders and See America," p. 83 (front).
97. Vincent J. Kane, President, Uniformed Firemen's Association, to Carleton Coon and Joe Sanders, 11 November 1931, New York, N.Y., miscellaneous correspondence, JLSC.
98. Robert A. LeRoux, post adjutant, to Joe Sanders, March (no day) 1932, Hoquiam, Wash., typed copy of original, miscellaneous correspondence, JLSC.
99. "Winchell with Lucky Strike Hour and Only Ad Double on Radio," *Variety*, 3 November 1931, p. 57.
100. MCA's ad for the Lucky Strike Dance Hour, miscellaneous materials, JLSC; *Gus Arnheim live from the World Famous Cocoanut Grove, 1933*," Mark56 long-play recording no. 705 (Anaheim, Cal.: Mark56 Records, 1975), side 1, band 1.
101. Sanders, "Join Coon-Sanders and See America," p. 83 (front); Harvey Rettberg's taped conversation with Joe Sanders, Kansas City, Mo., 17 July 1961.
102. Tape recording of Rex Downing at an-

nual meeting of the New Nighthawk Club, Huntington, W. Va., in 1977; tape in Willis Morrisette collection, now owned by author.

103. Program script for "The Lucky Strike Dance Hour," of 26 November 1931, in miscellaneous items, JLSC; DeLong, *Radio Stars*, p. 55.

104. Program script for "The Lucky Strike Dance Hour," of 26 November 1931.

105. *Ibid.*

106. *Ibid.*

107. *Ibid.*

108. *The ASCAP Biographical Dictionary of Composers, Authors and Publishers* 1966 ed. (New York: The American Society of Composers, Authors and Publishers, 1966), pp. 35, 604.

109. Program script for "The Lucky Strike Dance Hour," of 26 November 1931.

110. Harrington, "Tales of Coon-Sanders," p. 14; Joe Sanders, "Join Coon-Sanders and See America," pp. 83 (front and back).

111. Joe Sanders, "Join Coon-Sanders and See America," p. 83 (front).

112. From the author's memory of hearing those broadcasts about 1950.

113. Harrington, "Tales of Coon-Sanders," p. 13.

114. *Ibid.*

115. Foster Music Publishing to Joe Sanders, 14 December 1931, miscellaneous correspondence, JLSC.

116. Madeline Sanders' journal, entry for Sunday, November 15 or 22.

117. Entries for 17 or 24 November and 22 or 29 November 1931, *ibid.*

118. Joe Sanders, "Join Coon-Sanders and See America," p. 83 (back); Madeline Sanders' journal, entry for Tuesday, 10 or 17 November 1931.

119. Madeline Sanders' journal, entry for 23 or 30 November 1931.

120. Entries for 25 November or 2 December and 26 November or 3 December 1931, *ibid.*

121. Entry for 6 January 1932, *ibid.*

122. "Times Sq. Food Fight with All Kinds of Prices," *Variety*, 1 March 1932, p. 43.

123. "Those Broadway Empty Stores," *Variety*, 28 January 1931, p. 57; "Bad Times Bring Reorganization to the Business of Booze-Selling," *ibid.*, 23 June 1931, pp. 1, 10; "Beer Is Licking Liquor," *ibid.*, 11 August 1931, pp, 1, 43; "White Collar Idle Turning to Taxis, Bring New Type Drivers to B'way," *ibid.*, 26 January 1932, p. 1.

124. Madeline Sanders' journal, entry for 17 or 24 November 1931).

125. Joe Sanders, "Join Coon-Sanders and See America," pp. 82 (back) and 83 (back); author's interview with Harvey Rettberg, 19 November 1993, Pickens, S.C.; Schroeder, "Coon-Sanders Kansas City Nighthawks," p. 21; John Coon to Clyde Hahn, Kansas City, Mo., 21 July 1960, typed copy in HRC; "Radio's Biggest Music Plug, Theme Songs, Devoted Mostly to Non-Selling Old Numbers," *Variety*, 17 November 1931, p. 61.

126. Phonograph recording, Victor 22972 (Camden, N.J.: Victor Talking Machine Co., 1932).

127. Joe Sanders, "Join Coon-Sanders and See America," p. 83 (back).

128. Tape no. 1, of two, made solo for author by John Coon, January 1995, Prairie Village, Kans.; also, several informal conversations with John Coon since that date, in person and by telephone.

129. Author's interview with Harvey Rettberg, 19 November 1993, Pickens, S.C.; Joe Sanders, "Join Coon-Sanders and See America," p. 86 (front).

130. John Coon to Clyde Hahn, Kansas City, Mo., 21 July 1960, typed copy in HRC.

131. Joe Sanders, "Join Coon-Sanders and See America," p. 83-A (front).

132. Miscellaneous lyrics, JLSC; used with permission from Kansas City Public Library.

133. *Ibid.*

134. *Ibid.*

135. Joe Sanders, "Join Coon-Sanders and See America," p. 83 (back).

136. *Ibid.*, p. 83 (front).

137. *Ibid.*, pp. 83-A (front) and 84 (back).

138. *Ibid.*, p. 83-A (front).

139. Unidentified newspaper clipping, dated 19 February 1932, in SC1, box 15, folder 1, JLSC.

140. Sanders, "Join Coon-Sanders and See America," pp. 83-A (front and back).

141. Author's interview with Harvey Rettberg, 19 November 1993, Pickens, S.C.; also, Kramer, unpublished history of MCA., chapter 8, p. 11.

142. W. R. Goodheart to Joe Sanders, 25 March 1932, New York, N. Y., miscellaneous correspondence, JLSC.

143. Kramer, unpublished history of M. C. A., chapter 8, p. 11.

144. Joe Sanders, "Join Coon-Sanders and See America," pp. 83 (back) and 83-A (front).

145. *Ibid.*, p. 85 (back); clipping from the *Detroit Times*, 3 April 1932, in SC1, box 15, folder 1, JLSC.

146. Slide, *The Vaudevillians*, p. 158.

147. "It's Gridder Coon, and Pitcher Sanders," *Detroit* (Mich.) *Free Press*, 2 April 1932, clipping in miscellaneous materials, JLSC.

148. Ed T. Lawless to Joe Sanders, 7 April 1932, miscellaneous correspondence, JLSC.

149. Joe Sanders, "Join Coon-Sanders and See America," p. 85 (back).

150. WBBM "Air Theatre" news release for 7 March 1932, in SC1, scrapbook no. 1, JLSC.

151. Bobby Mellin, "Slices of Mellin," *Motion Picture Herald* of 26 March 1932, filed in *ibid.*

152. *Ibid.*, p. 86 (front); for WBBM air "release," see SC1, scrapbook no. 1, JLSC.

153. *Ibid.*

154. *Variety Obituaries, 1905–1992*, p. for 26

December 1979; author's conversation with John Coon, Auburn, Ala., 18 January 1995.

155. *Variety Obituaries, 1905–1992*, p. for 10 May 1932.

156. Xerographic copy of Coon's death certificate in author's possession. Also, "Coon Dead but Famed Band Plays On," *Chicago American*, 4 May 1932, p. 18, and "Carlton [sic] Coon Dies; Leader of Radio Band," *Chicago Daily News*, 4 May 1932, p. 8, clippings in miscellaneous materials, JLSC; author's conversation with John Coon, Auburn, Alabama, 19 January 1995.

157. "Coon Dead but Famed Band Plays On," *Chicago American*, 4 May 1932, p. 18, and "Carlton [sic] Coon Dies; Leader of Radio Band," *Chicago Daily News*, 4 May 1932, p. 8, clippings in miscellaneous matierals, JLSC; author's conversation with John Coon, Auburn, Alabama, 19 January 1995.

158. Clyde Hahn, "The Story of the Original Coon-Sanders Nighthawks," p. 8.

159. Author's conversation with Harvey Rettberg, Pickens, S.C., 19 November 1993; author's conversation with John Coon, Auburn, Alabama, 19 January 1995.

160. "Coon Dead but Famed Band Plays On," *Chicago American*, 4 May 1932, p. 8, news clipping among miscellaneous materials, JLSC.

161. "Carlton [sic] Coon Dies; Leader of Radio Band," *Chicago Daily News*, 4 May 1932, p. 8, clipping in miscellaneous materials, JLSC; "Friend of Years Gone," *Kansas City Star*, 4 May 1932, news clipping in *ibid*.

162. Author's conversation with John Coon, Auburn, Ala., 19 January 1995.

163. Joe Sanders, "Join Coon-Sanders and See America," p. 86 (front); "Carleton Coon Dies; Leader of Radio Band," *Chicago Daily News*, 4 May 1932.

164. Madeline Sanders' telegram to her mother Libbie Baldwin, 4 May 1932, SC1, box 15, folder 2, JLSC; Joe Sanders, "Join Coon-Sanders and See America," p. 86 (front).

165. "Rites for Carlton [sic] Coon," *Kansas City Star*, 6 May 1932; "Carlton [sic] Coon Rites Friday," *ibid.*, 5 May 1932.

166. "Rites for Carlton [sic] Coon," *Kansas City Star*, 6 May 1932; Joe Sanders, "Join Coon-Sanders and See America," pp. 86 (front and back); author's telephone conversation with Carleton A. Coon, Jr., 27 October 2000.

167. Joe Sanders, "Join Coon-Sanders and See America," p. 86 (back).

168. Hesketh Pearson, *OscarWilde: His Life and Wit* (New York and London: Harper & Brothers, 1946), p. 331.

Epilogue

1. "All Star Orchestra," clipping from "summer *Radio Digest*, 1932, in SC1, box 15, folder 2, JLSC.

2. Typed copy of letter from John Coon to Clyde Hahn, 11 July 1960, HRC.

3. Author's telephone conversation with John Coon, 19 May 1998.

4. "Sanders Backs Out," *Variety*, 13 March 1934, p. 48.

5. Meryl Friedel, "Too Many Friends for Joe," article from unidentified source and with unnumbered pages, box 15, folder 2, JLSC.

6. *Ibid.* ; author's telephone conversation with John Coon, 2 August 1998.

7. Friedel, "Too Many Friends for Joe"; George T. Simon, *The Big Bands*, p. 496.

8. "The Coca-Cola Company Presents 'The Victory Parade of Spotlight Bands,'" program script for 13 August 1943 over Blue Network, in JLSC; R. B. Blanton, of the Port Arthur Chamber of Commerce, to Joe Sanders, 6 May 1947, Port Arthur, Texas, *ibid.*; also, various photographs, *ibid*.

9. Madeline Sanders' obituary, *Variety Obituaries, 1905–1992*, p. for 26 February 1947; Priscilla Sanders to Clyde Hahn, 4 February [1965], HRC; "Old Nighthawk Music Recalled," *Kansas City Times*, 16 March 1963, pp. 1, 5, miscellaneous clippings, JLSC.

10. Harvey Rettberg's taped interview with Joe Sanders, Kansas City, Mo., 16 July 1961.

11. Jules C. Stein to Clyde Hahn, 19 September 1960, New York, N.Y., HRC.

12. "No Piano for Music Man's Tunes," *Kansas City Star*, 18 January 1965, p. 22; Cliff W. Halliburton's letters to Harvey Rettberg, Kansas City, Mo., 19, 21, and 22 January 1965, HRC.

13. Bruce Beard, "No Piano for Music Man's Tunes," *Kansas City Star*, 18 January 1965.

14. "Joe Sanders Is Dead," *Kansas City Times*, 15 May 1965.

15. Hugh Wylie, "Sanders, 'Ole Lefthander,' Is Leading Simple Life Now," Louisville, Ky., *Courier-Journal*, 20 August 1955, clipping in miscellaneous materials, JLSC.

APPENDIX A

The Band's Personnel

A note of clarification: I have of course striven to be accurate with the following information, but I fear that some of the various sources I've consulted often are vague and, occasionally, of doubtful accuracy. I have listed Joe Sanders and Carleton Coon as co-leaders, though occasionally one sees Coon spoken of as business manager, and Sanders as leader. In at least one place in his reminiscences, however, Sanders refers to his partner as "co-leader." In another place Sanders facetiously refers to Coon as "Da Sakratary."

Earliest period: Other than Joe Sanders, Carleton Coon, and Floyd Estep, the earliest players are perhaps impossible to discover. There very likely were many of them, most of whom probably were with the band for only short periods. Even Joe, in his articles for *Jazz Notes*, failed to identify almost all of his earliest co-players. Floyd Estep, in a recorded interview in 1961 with Harvey Rettberg, said that he had already been playing with Coonie's group when Sanders returned from the Army. Even if Harold Thiell was correct in stating that he was with the band from the beginning, there was at least one break, for he did not play with Coon-Sanders during most of 1923. At that time his brother John took his place, while Harold was playing with D. Ambert Haley's Fairyland Park Orchestra, in Kansas City.

1920: A well-publicized photograph dated "circa 1920" of the Coon-Sanders Novelty Orchestra identifies the personnel of that period. They were: Clyde Hendrix (trumpet), Carl "Swede" Nordberg (trombone), Bob Norfleet (banjo), Harry Silverstone (violin), Harold Thiell (alto saxophone), Hal McLean (alto saxophone), Joe Sanders (piano, vocals, co-leader), and Carleton Coon (drums, vocals, co-leader).

March 1921: According to Brian Rust, when Coon-Sanders made their first recording on 24 March 1921, the band's personnel were: Joe Sanders (piano, vocals, co-leader), Carleton Coon (drums, vocals, co-leader), Clyde Hendrix (trumpet), Carl Nordberg (trombone), Hal McLean and Harold Thiell (saxophones), Harry Silverstone (violin), and Bob Norfleet (banjo).

May 1922: Sometime earlier, Harry Williams had replaced Bob Norfleet on banjo, and on 19 May 1922, when the *Kansas City Post* made its first broadcast, the band's personnel

About to board a coach for a two-mile trip from Dubuque, Iowa, to East Dubuque, Illinois, probably 23 April 1926. From left: Downing, F. Estep, Stout, Pope, Sanders, Pop Estep, Linder (tour manager), J. Thiell, H. Thiell and Richolson. Note the Nighthawk placard. (Courtesy Special Collections, Kansas City [Mo.] Public Library.)

were as follows: Carleton Coon (drums, vocals, co-leader), Joe Sanders (piano, vocals, co-leader), Harold Thiell and Hal McLean (saxophones), Clyde Hendrix (cornet), Carl Nordberg (trombone), Harry Silverstone (violin), Harry "Happy" Williams (banjo).

January 1923: The band's personnel were Joe Sanders (piano, vocals, co-leader), Carleton Coon (drums, vocals, co-leader), Elmer "Crab" Kohlman (trumpet), Hal McLean and Harold Thiell (saxophones), Frank M. "Pop" Estep (bass), Harry Williams (banjo), and Carl Nordberg (trombone).

Summer 1923: At the time of the trip to Oklahoma City, the members were Carleton Coon (drums, vocals, co-leader), Joe Sanders (piano, vocals, co-leader), John Thiell and Hal McLean (saxophones), Harry Williams (banjo), Elmer Kohlman (trumpet), Carl Nordberg (trombone), and Pop Estep (bass).

Note: At the time that Coon-Sanders went to Oklahoma City in the summer of 1923, not only was Harold Thiell playing with D. Ambert Haley's Fairyland Orchestra, in Kansas City, but so were the future Nighthawks Robert Pope, Nicholas Musolino, and Floyd Estep.

Late summer 1923: Band's personnel were Sanders (piano, vocals, co-leader) Coon (drums, vocals, co-leader), John Thiell and Orville Knapp (saxophones), Ferdy Jacobs (trumpet), Pop Estep (bass), Nicholas L. Musolino (trombone), and Tom Beckham (banjo).

December 1923: Exactly when Ferdy Jacobs left and Joe Richolson arrived are uncertain, but both are shown as trumpeters in the orchestra at Thanksgiving of 1923. By the end of 1923, the band probably consisted of Sanders (piano, vocals, co-leader), Coon (drums, vocals, co-leader), Joe Richolson (trumpet), Pop Estep (bass), Nick Musolino (trombone), Tom Beckham (banjo), and Orville Knapp and John Thiell (saxophones). Note: Dewey Birge perhaps had already replaced Beckham on banjo at this time.

Summer 1924: When the band went to Chicago, the personnel were Sanders (piano, vocals, co-leader); Coon (drums, vocals, co-leader); Pop Estep (bass); Dewey Birge

Sanders (left), Pop Estep, Pope, and Harold Thiell, about 1926, place unidentified. (Courtesy Special Collections, Kansas City [Mo.] Public Library.)

(banjo); Orville Knapp, Harold Thiell, and John Thiell (saxophones); Joe Richolson (trumpet); and Nick Musolino (trombone).

Spring 1925: At this time the band consisted of Coon (drums, vocals, co-leader); Sanders (piano, vocals, co-leader); Nick Musolino (trombone); Pop Estep (bass); John Thiell, Harold Thiell, and Orville Knapp (saxophones); Joe Richolson (trumpet); and Bill Haid (banjo). According to Sanders' records, Dewey Birge, banjoist, left the band shortly before the start of Coon-Sanders 1925 road tour in April.

December 1925: Sanders (piano, vocals, co-leader); Coon (drums, vocals, co-leader); Bob Pope and Joe Richolson (trumpets); Rex Downing (trombone); Harold Thiell, John Thiell, and Floyd Estep (saxophones); Bill Haid (banjo); and Pop Estep (bass). Note: Brian Rust shows Elmer Krebs as having joined the band by this time on bass, but several sources show Pop Estep with the band in 1927, definitely to the end of December and probably over into early 1928.

March 1926: Sanders (piano, vocals, co-leader); Coon (drums, vocals, co-leader); Bob Pope and Joe Richolson (trumpets); Rex Downing (trombone); Harold Thiell, John Thiell, and Floyd Estep (saxophones); Russ Stout (banjo); and Pop Estep (bass).

1927 and 1928: Same as above, except that Elmer Krebs took Pop Estep's place on bass sometime perhaps about January 1928.

Early 1929: Sanders (piano, vocals, co-leader); Coon (drums, vocals, co-leader); Bob Pope and Joe Richolson (trumpets); Rex Downing (trombone); Harold Thiell, John Thiell, and Floyd Estep (saxophones); Russ Stout (banjo); Elmer Krebs (bass).

About March 1932: Sanders (piano, vocals, co-leader); Coon (drums, vocals, co-leader); Bob Pope and Joe Richolson (trumpets); Rex Downing (trombone); Harold Thiell, John Thiell, and Floyd Estep (saxophones); Russ Stout (banjo); Wilbur "Eddie" Edwards (bass). Note: Pat Pattison took over on bass briefly after Krebs' departure (late 1931 or early 1932) and was soon replaced by Edwards. Brian Rust's discography mentions that John "Lop" Jarman joined the band at about this time on mellophone, and Joe Sanders' records show Jarman with the band after its return to Chicago. But Jarman perhaps was playing more than just the mellophone.

APPENDIX B

Nighthawks and Their Associates

Unfortunately, I have been unable to trace the subsequent lives of a good number of those who, in one way or another, were closely associated with the Nighthawks. It is frustrating to reflect that, had I known years ago that I should later be writing the band's history, I might have talked with many of the principals. However, the following information will perhaps be of some interest to readers.

Tom Beckham succeeded Harry Williams on banjo in the late summer of 1923 and was followed, late that year or early the next, by Dewey Birge. Beckham is apparently the same person who, with his wife Kate, on 5 March 1960 was found shot to death in their home in suburban Kansas City. The police concluded that Beckham, distraught over his wife's poor health, had shot her and then killed himself. In earlier years the two had been a musical team, and at one time he had led an orchestra.

Henry Dewey Birge (whose name is pronounced with a soft *g*, to rhyme with *urge*) took over from Tom Beckham as banjoist in late 1923 or early 1924. Dewey's son David tells me that his father had great natural musical talent but no formal training. Dewey's family had lived on a farm where his father did not encourage his young son's musical interests. Nevertheless, Dewey's older brother, an evangelist, sometimes took Dewey with him and thus provided him access to an organ that was used in religious services. Later, Dewey learned to play the violin and at one time worked as a roving violinist in a restaurant. However, fearing that the violin was less likely to offer him many opportunities in the jazz bands that were then becoming popular, he taught himself to get some good chords out of the banjo. His strong interest in music was not limited to the organ, violin, and banjo, but led him to other instruments. He even composed a song titled "Lonely Night." Since he did not understand musical notation, he had a friend write the song down and make an arrangement of it. Birge was with the Nighthawks when they made their first Victor recordings in the spring of 1924 and for a year after they went to Chicago, and he was with the band in September 1924 when they made their first tour of one-nighters. But by this time he and his wife Sara Ortbals Birge had two sons, Hank (born 1921) and David (born 1922). It was to avoid obliging his wife to care for them alone that Dewey left the Nighthawks just before they began their road tour in April of 1925. Bill Haid replaced him.

Dewey later moved his family to St. Louis, where he was employed by Wenzlick Real Estate Company. In 1929, at about the same time that his two sons joined the Marine Corps, he was diagnosed as tubercular, but the infected lung was successfully removed. While crossing a street in St. Louis on 15 October 1958, Dewey was struck by a bus. The blow broke a rib that pierced his remaining lung and caused his death. His wife Sara died in October 1999 at the age of 101. Dewey's granddaughter Cathy Williams, who has kindly furnished much of this information, tells me that she still owns his banjo, a gift from the Nighthawks when he left the band. His fellow musicians had affixed a brass plate on it with a suitable inscription.

John Allyn Coon, Eula and Carleton's oldest child, was born 7 February 1913 and was graduated in 1931 from Southwest High School, Kansas City, Mo. He attended the University of Kansas for the academic year 1931–1932, where one of his roommates was the future playwright William Inge. He started his own band in December 1932 and led it not under his own name but as Carleton A. Coon, Jr. For about a year Johnny employed former Nighthawk Frank M. "Pop" Estep as the orchestra's manager. Coon's group played over much of the nation from Denver, Colo., to the East Coast, though mainly in the Midwest, for Coon said he had had no desire to travel extensively. The band lasted until 1974. Coon was married 1 June 1937 and settled in Kansas City, Mo. For thirty-five years, starting in 1945, he and his wife Maxine operated the Johnny Coon Theatrical Agency, whose clients included such stars as Morey Amsterdam, Roy Acuff, and Red Foley. Coon was a member of the American Federation of Musicians, Local 34, in Kansas City, and a founding member of Red Bridge Sertoma. He was active also in the Lions, Elks, and Moose Clubs, as well as the Kansas City Chamber of Commerce. In his later years, when he was a widower, he met an old high-school chum named Dorothy Drummond, herself a widow. They became very close friends, and the author was fortunate to become acquainted with them and to see how each enriched and gladdened the other's last years. Johnny spent his last years mainly in Lenexa and Prairie Village, Kans. As of this writing, Mrs. Drummond still lives, but Johnny died on 5 May 1999. His body was cremated. Curiously, Johnny's birthday was two days after his father's, and the day of his death was one day after his father's.

Rex Downing, trombonist for the Nighthawks after Nick Musolino left in 1925, was from Little Rock, Arkansas, and in later years lived at various times in both Harrisburg and Weiner. According to Bob Harrington, Downing attended the Wentworth Military Academy, Lexington, Missouri. Downing recalled in the 1970s that he started his musical career in Kansas City at the Hotel Baltimore, while Coon-Sanders was playing at the Newman Theater and the Muehlebach's Plantation Grill. After the breakup of the Nighthawks, he played briefly with the Joe Sanders Orchestra and later went to the National Broadcasting Company, under director Roy Shields. Rex joined the Navy in 1942 and played in an orchestra during the war years. He eventually entered his state's politics by becoming county judge in Harrisburg, Ark. He was an honored guest during the new Nighthawk Club's 1977 annual reunion in Huntington, W. Va. According to a letter in the Harvey Rettberg Collection written 13 April 1962 to Clyde Hahn, Downing's grandfather, A. R. Downing, fought with the Union during the Civil War and was stationed in Memphis, Tenn. He served also in Arkansas. Leaving his home in Hastings, Neb., after the war, Rex's grandfather returned to the Memphis and Arkansas area. While living in Weiner, Ark.,

"Somewhere in Indiana," said Joe, probably about July 1926. From left: H. Thiell, Coonie, Stout, Pop Estep, Pope, J. Thiell, Joe, Downing, Richolson, F. Estep, and Johnny Coon. (Courtesy Special Collections, Kansas City [Mo.] Public Library.)

he purchased cattle and, about 1900, acquired some cattle land in Orlando, Okla. This property later was of some value to Rex as oil land. According to Paul F. Karberg, Downing died on 11 June 1980.

Floyd Eugene Estep was Pop Estep's son and a valued reed player for the Nighthawks. His early work included a period with Carleton A. Coon, before the latter's partnership with Sanders. Later Estep played with D. Ambert Haley's orchestra. After the Nighthawks ended, he eventually worked his way to Los Angeles, Calif., where his outstanding musical abilities, both as instrumentalist and as arranger, were in great demand, including work with the motion picture industry. One of his early jobs in California came in the 1940s with Ken Murray's *Blackouts*, a long-running revue, at Hollywood's El Capitan Theatre. Gene Autry was among those for whom he did arranging. Estep was born 17 January 1900 and died, at age 98, on 21 January 1998, very likely the last survivor of all who had ever played with Coon-Sanders. His body was cremated, and on February 1, at 2:15 p.m., pilot William Fuller Gilchrist scattered Estep's ashes in the Pacific Ocean off the California coast, latitude 32 degrees, 40 minutes north, longitude 117 degrees, 20 minutes west. His wife, Mildred Alline Heinze Estep, was born 4 August 1902 in Texas and died in Los Angeles, Calif., 24 March 1982. They had two sons, one of whom died in the Army during World War II, the other in an automobile accident shortly after the war. The sons apparently had no children.

Frank M. "Pop" Estep, in his youth, played guitar for dances and country music groups. A little later he took up bass saxophone, as well as tuba and string bass. Claude F. Anderson, his son-in-law, doubts that he ever had any formal musical instruction. He was born in Adrian, Mo., in 1878, and had some American Indian ancestry.

Anderson is unsure exactly what his middle name was but said it was an Indian name such as *Monoque*, and pronounced by Anderson in such a way that I at first thought he had said *Montague*. Before going with the Nighthawks, Pop played bass for the orchestra employed by Sweeney Radio Station WHB, in Kansas City. He played bass with the Nighthawks from about late 1922 or early 1923 until December 1927 or early 1928. Many have thought that he left the band sometime about 1925, but Joe Sanders' personal papers, as well as newspaper accounts of their appearance in Kansas City in December of 1927, make it clear that he was still playing with the Nighthawks at least until just after Christmas of 1927. Since Phil Baxter's band was playing in Kansas City while the Nighthawks were there in December 1927, it is quite possible that at that time he and Baxter made an agreement for Pop to join that group. At any rate, by 1929, he was playing bass with Phil Baxter's orchestra. For one year, about 1933, Pop managed the young Johnny Coon's orchestra, right after the latter had started his musical career under the name "Carleton A. Coon, Jr." Pop eventually moved to California, where he died in 1949. He and his wife Lulu M. Estep (1877–1967) are buried at the cemetery on Foothill Boulevard in La Verne, Calif., a suburb of Los Angeles. Frank Estep was about 6'3" tall and weighed about 275 pounds. Since he was older than any of the other players in Coon-Sanders, and since his son Floyd called him Pop, the other band members also used that nickname. Pop, a thirty-second-degree Mason, at one time played with the Kansas City Masonic Band.

Leo J. Fitzpatrick was a veteran of the First World War and commander of Kansas City's William R. Nelson Post of the American Legion. Originally a police reporter for the *Kansas City Star*, he apparently began his radio work when he announced for the original Nighthawk broadcasts at the Hotel Muehlebach, Kansas City, Mo., in December of 1922. Later, President Herbert Hoover appointed him to the Federal Radio Conference, a forerunner of the Federal Communications Commission. *Variety*, of 30 September 1925 (page 45), reported that he had accepted the position of announcer with Detroit's station WJR. According to his obituary in *Variety*, he became general manager and part-owner of that station, and later part-owner of Cleveland's WGAR. It was at WJR, in 1926, that Fitzpatrick introduced the Rev. Charles E. Coughlin as a radio minister, but when that priest's speeches became bitter and anti–Semitic, Fitzpatrick ended the association. In 1946 he disposed of both stations and bought WGR, in Buffalo, N.Y. During World War II he was a consultant for the Office of War Information and later was on the occupational staff in Japan, where he directed radio facilities in both Japan and Korea. *Variety* reported that he died, at age 77, on 15 September 1971 in a hospital in Detroit.

William R. "Billy" Goodheart, Jr., an original partner in the Music Corporation of America, was mainly responsible for the corporation's interests in the New York area. Retiring to farm life in 1943, he operated a ranch at Eaton, Ohio, and remained there until his eight-year-old son was killed by a tractor. He later was executive vice president of the Russ Lyon Realty Corporation, in Phoenix, Ariz., where he died, at age 58, on 26 June 1960.

Bill Haid, banjoist with Coon-Sanders, left in late 1925 or early 1926 and was replaced by Clarence Russell "Russ" Stout. According to Brian Rust, in 1928 Haid had his own groups, Bill Haid and His Thieves of Sleep and Bill Haid and His Cubs. The first-named perhaps owed something to the Nighthawks' slogan "Enemies of Sleep." Though it may not be the same person, Rust's compilation shows a Bill Haid, in New York in 1924, playing piano with Harl Smith and His Orchestra.

Ferdy Jacobs played trumpet briefly with the Nighthawks in the latter part of 1923, following Elmer Kohlman. He seems to have continued with the band after a second trumpeter, Joe Richolson, arrived; for both

Pop Estep's and his wife's graves, Vista, California. (Courtesy Claude and Ruth Anderson.)

are shown as playing with the band at a Thanksgiving dinner for newsboys of the Kansas City *Journal-Post*.

John "Lop" Jarman played the mellophone with Coon-Sanders and was with them during at least part of their 1931–32 engagement at the Hotel New Yorker, as well as up to the time of Coon's death. According to Brian Rust, Jarman played mellophone in the mid–Twenties with Willard Robison's Deep River Orchestra. In later years, Floyd Estep urged Jarman to join him for Ken Muray's *Blackouts*, a long-running revue in Hollywood, but reminded him to be sure to develop his "lip." Jarman perhaps failed to take the second piece of advice, for he was not accepted for the revue.

Orville Knapp played reeds. Before playing with the Nighthawks, Knapp was a member of Leo R. Davis's Orchestra, as well as with Charles Gray's Society Orchestra and Edward Werner's Orchestra. After he left Coon-Sanders in the summer of 1925, he eventually clicked with his own band that he started in 1934. According to Brian Rust, Knapp's orchestra recorded at least thirty-two sides, mostly for Decca. George T. Simon, in his *The Big Bands*, says that Knapp's short engagement at the Beverly-Wilshire, in 1934, started him on a successful career, cut short when on 16 July 1936 the plane he was piloting crashed near Boston, Mass. Perhaps his prior association with Coon-Sanders led to his association, as a band leader, with the Music Corporation of America.

Karl Kramer, hired in 1926 by the Music Corporation of America, quickly became an important part of its senior management. His obituary in *Variety* notes that in the early days of television he was head of Revue television, later MCA-TV. He retired in the early 1960s at about the same time that he wrote a history, apparently never published, of MCA. Kramer died, at age 81, on 14 October 1980 in Los Angeles.

Elmer Krebs, who took over from Pop Estep on bass in late 1927 or early 1928, was from Milwaukee, Wisc., and returned there after leaving the Nighthawks (suddenly, according to Joe Sanders) in late 1931 or early 1932. Joe, who always regarded Krebs as one of the band's best musicians, said nevertheless that Krebs could not improvise and had to have his solos written out. In addition to bass, he also could play piano and trombone. After leaving Coon-Sanders, he played with bands under Abe Lyman and Charley Straight; and he was featured in "Down by Herman's," a show that aired on CBS from Milwaukee. He was director of station WISN's studio orchestra for twenty years until 1951. He died in early September 1953 at the age of 53.

Hal McLean, an early saxophonist with Coon-Sanders, later played with Paul Whiteman's orchestra and, after that, with Walt Roesner's stage band at the Capitol Theater, New York City. He died of pneumonia on 15 May 1928, at age 33, and was buried in Kansas City. (An unidentified clipping, printed just after Coon-Sanders' first recording, 1921, in the miscellaneous items of Joe Sanders Collection, Kansas City Public Library, gives his first name as Harley.)

George McQueen was associated with the Nighthawks during their 1931 appearance in New Orleans. Before 1932 he was a star in vaudeville and a popular singer-emcee at the Club Forest, where the Nighthawks played. "A Fool in Love" was one of his compositions. He died 14 August 1963 at age 65.

Irving Milfred "Miff" Mole was a virtuoso jazz and classical trombonist. While the Nighthawks were playing in New York, 1931-1932, some of the band chummed and held jam sessions with him. After playing under Fritz Reiner and Bruno Walter, he was with Paul Whiteman. He toured with the Orpheum Circuit, later joined Phil Napoleon and the Memphis Five, and yet later formed a partnership with Red Nichols. For a while he played with Benny Goodman. Later he played for eleven years with the NBC Symphony Orchestra. He died in New York City on 29 April 1961, age 63.

Nicholas L. Musolino was a native of Quincy, Ill. Before going to the Nighthawks, Musolino played with D. Ambert Haley's Orchestra, as well as with the orchestra of the Sweeney Radio Station WHB, in Kansas City. He was married on 29 November 1921, in Kansas City, Mo., to Gladys Leu, and they had one son, Rudy. After leaving the Nighthawks in the summer of 1925, he played with other groups, including Howard Steed and His Seven Syncopating Soldiers and with a band led by Carl Landrum. He worked with the Pantages vaudeville circuit out of Chicago and shared stages with such performers as a very young Bob Hope. Eventually, Musolino quit the big bands and returned to commercial business by joining Pittsburgh Glass, in Wichita, Kans., and, later, the Wohl Shoe Company. During the Second World War Nick found himself back in uniform and on a bandstand. Working under the command of Major Wayne King, a nationally famous band leader known as the "Waltz King," Nick led the 1620th Service Company's band. Back in Quincy he worked in the Block and Kuhl Shoe Store and retired in 1963. Musolino settled in Las Vegas, Nev., which he said he liked because he didn't gamble. Outliving both his wife and his son, Nick died in Las Vegas on 5 March 1996, at the age of 97. Probably the next-to-last surviving member of the Nighthawks (Floyd Estep died in 1998), he had been living in Las Vegas with the Larry Fisher family.

Carl Nordberg was an early trombone player for Coon-Sanders and was with the band when they made their first recording in 1921 and until just after the band returned from its engagement in Oklahoma City in the late summer of 1923. By the following November he was playing with Eddie Kuhn's Kansas City Athletic Club Orchestra. Arthur Nordberg, perhaps a brother, in March of 1922 was conductor and violinist of Loew's Garden Orchestra, in Kansas City, and broadcast over the *Kansas City Star's* early radio stations.

William A. Paley, a cousin to William Paley, founder of the Columbia Broadcasting System, was drummer with the Nighthawks briefly after Coon became unable to play in the latter part of April, 1932. Paley later was a much-employed drummer with a number of big bands in the Midwest, in addition to his duties for thirty-one years with the CBS interests in Chicago. In later life, as an amputee, he was an inspiration to others similarly disabled. He died, age 75, in Tulsa, Okla., on 19 December 1979.

Pat Pattison (as Joe Sanders spelled the last name, though I've seen it also as *Patterson* and *Patison*) played bass briefly after Elmer Krebs left suddenly in late 1931 or early 1932. Pattison's place was quickly taken by John J. "Lop" Jarman. Brian Rust records that one Pat Patterson played in the early 1940s with Tiny Hill's orchestra.

Bob Pope, before playing trumpet with Coon-Sanders, was, according to Brian Rust, a member of the Arcadia Peacock Orchestra, St. Louis. He also played with the Kansas City bands under D. Ambert Haley and Ray Stinson. In later years he lived in Charlotte, N.C., and had his own band, Bob Pope and His Hotel Charlotte Orchestra, that made a number of recordings in 1936 and 1937, in both Charlotte and in Birmingham, Ala. According to Joe Sanders in 1961, Pope died on a bandstand while performing in Indianapolis, Ind., apparently sometime in the 1950s.

Joe Richolson was playing trumpet with Coon-Sanders as early as Thanksgiving of 1923, right after being graduated from military school. He later lived in Bakersfield, Calif., and was interviewed by Harvey Rettberg during the latter's "Coon-Sanders Revisited" trip in the summer of 1961.

Madeline Esther Baldwin Sanders, Joe's first wife, died in Chicago, Ill., 13 February 1947, age 49. She is buried in her father's lot, Mt. Moriah Cemetery, Kansas City, Mo.

Roy Garvin Sanders, Joe's older brother, was born in Stafford, Kan. It was first in Belton, Mo., where he distinguished himself in high school athletics. Following that, he excelled in baseball and football during his three years at William Jewell College. Interested for a time in medical school, he decided instead to join the Muskogee, Okla., baseball team in the Western Association, but the team suddenly disbanded and Sanders returned to Belton. He next worked for a paint company in Omaha, Neb., and pitched for that city's team in home games. His success in Omaha won him an offer from the Kansas City Blues, for whom he pitched from 1915 to 1917, after which he went to the Pittsburgh Pirates. At the end of the season, a disagreement over salary caused him to quit and return to Kansas City, where he played semi-professional baseball and coached Ban Johnson teams. In the spring of 1920 he was hired to help with the baseball team at the University of Kansas. In the following years he was active as a player in the area's semi-professional clubs.

During the Second World War, Sanders was recreational director of the North American Aircraft Corporation's bomber plant, Fairfax District. In 1946 he coached a Burnett Meat company team which captured the semi-professional state championship. Later, he was employed by automobile dealers and by the Chamber of Commerce. He worked on Tuesday, 17 January 1950 without apparent problems, but his wife Mary found him the next morning dead in bed, where he had suffered a heart attack. He was fifty-seven.

Jules Caesar Stein remained sole owner of the Music Corporation of America until 1954, when he distributed fifty-four percent of it in shares to a number of associates and employees, some of whom subsequently became quite wealthy. During World War II, Stein, Bette Davis, and others established the Hollywood Canteen to entertain members of the military. In 1946 a California amusement park owner sued the MCA for antitrust activities and won. At about the same time, however, MCA played a role in breaking up the notorious studio contract system in Hollywood. Also, despite its reputation as an "octopus," in 1949 MCA formed Revue Productions and went into television production. In his later years Stein and his wife Doris dealt in real estate and antiques. Revue Productions purchased television re-runs

Sanders bats to Richolson, behind whom is "Axel Flooey" Lovendahl (assistant tour guide), while waiting for train in Marion, Ohio, about 18 June 1926. (Courtesy Special Collections, Kansas City [Mo.] Public Library.)

and such vintage films as the pre–1948 Paramount collection. In 1959 MCA bought University City Studios, but by 1961 the U. S. Justice Department began to attack MCA's growing activities.

In 1960 Stein returned to his first interest, the field of eye research. In that year he founded Research to Prevent Blindness, based in New York. In 1963 the American Foundation for the Blind awarded Stein its Migel Medal, and in 1964 he became an honorary member of the Association for Research in Ophthalmology. In 1966 the Jules Stein Eye Institute, with a donation of more than $1,500,000 of Stein's money, opened with a five-floor, sixty-bed hospital. In 1973 he retired as board chairman of MCA, and for the rest of his life he had a continuing series of awards and honors. He died in Los Angeles, Calif., on 29 April 1981, at the age of 85. His funeral brought out almost every well-known person in Hollywood and the entertainment industry. Among the honorary pallbearers was President Ronald Reagan.

Eula Coon Stookey, Coonie's widow, later remarried but survived her second husband. In July of 1969 she was visiting a daughter in Denver, Colo., and died there on the 15th in a hospital. Her body was cremated, and her ashes are in a niche on the same floor of the mausoleum where Carleton lies, but around the corner and down another corridor.

Clarence Russell "Russ" Stout, was born in Fremont, Ohio, and later lived in Fond du Lac, Wisc. He was the last, and best known, banjoist-guitarist with Coon-Sanders. In World War I Stout served with the U. S. Navy. Before joining the Nighthawks, he played with Leo R. Davis's Orchestra, in Kansas City. According to his obituary in the Fond du Lac *Commonwealth Reporter*, he played also with the Arch Adrian Orchestra, and operated the Stout Music Center, on East First Street, and later on Forest Avenue. In good Nighthawk fashion, he was a Mason. The Fond du Lac obituary says that he and his wife Florence moved to St. Augustine, Fla., about sixteen years before his death, but information in the *St. Augustine Record's* obituary suggests they moved there about 1960 and then, a year before Stout's death, moved to the tiny community of Riverdale, a few miles southwest of St. Augustine. While mowing his lawn, he

Having eaten nothing all day, Joe and Harold Thiell (whom Joe called "Poot"), enjoy cookies, 23 May 1926, at depot in Raub, Indiana. (Courtesy Special Collections, Kansas City [Mo.] Public Library.)

was injured by his mower and died at Flagler Hospital, Sunday, 21 July 1968, at age 69. He was survived by his widow and two brothers, Ridge and Irv, both of Fremont, Ohio. The Fond du Lac obituary says that Stout's body was cremated, but the St. Augustine paper's obituary says he was buried in the St. Augustine National Cemetery. His widow Florence later lived in South Daytona, Fla.

Harold P.(K?) Thiell played reeds with Coon-Sanders. He was probably with the band longer than any other person except Coonie and Joe, though in the spring and summer of 1923 he was playing with D. Ambert Haley's Fairyland Orchestra. The reason for this brief absence from the Nighthawks isn't clear, but it caused him to miss the trip to Oklahoma City in the summer of 1923. According to Rex Downing, reminiscing in the 1970s, sometime after the breakup of the Nighthawks, Thiell went to Orlando, Fla., where he taught and played in a symphonic orchestra. Correspondence in the Harvey Rettberg Collection shows that by 1960 he and his wife were operating Thiells' Blueberry Lane, Route 1, North Judson, Ind. In a letter of 20 September 1960, he told Harvey Rettberg that he (Thiell) had been quite ill and in the hospital from 24 July to August 29, and his handwriting showed that he was still shaky. "As soon as I feel better, I'm going to try and find something to keep me busy during the winter," he told Rettberg, adding, "About all there is to do here in the winter is to shovel snow, and boy that ain't for me." His wife died about 1961, and Thiell then returned to Joplin, Mo., where he married a high school sweetheart. He died of cancer in the late 1960s. (Joplin Library's Doris Flaker finds, in newspaper files there, one Harold *K.* Thiell, who married Corinne Burress, of Joplin. The author is uncertain that this is the same person as the Coon-Sanders reed player. A daughter was born to them on 29 June 1931, in Carthage, Mo.)

John Thiell, Harold's brother from Joplin, Mo. He played reeds with Coon-Sanders. In the spring and summer of 1923, Harold left and played with D. Ambert Haley's Fairyland Orchestra in Kansas City. At that time, Harold's brother John was hired to fill the vacancy. After the band returned from Oklahoma City, John remained with the Nighthawks, and Harold was rehired to provide a third saxophone.

Max Winslow and his wife Tillie were closely associated with Joe and Madeline Sanders in New York City, 1931-1932. He spent over thirty years in music publishing and was, starting in 1919, a partner in Irving Berlin, Inc., where eventually he became vice president. In the golden era of vaudeville, he was regarded as perhaps the best exploiter of popular songs. But when radio became popular, his dislike of that medium caused him to quit in 1933 and go to Hollywood, where at Columbia Pictures he was a producer working with Harry Cohn. He died on 8 June 1942, at the age of 59, at the Cedars of Lebanon Hospital. His death was the result of a stroke brought on by diabetes. He was buried in the Garden of Memory Mausoleum, Forest Lawn Cemetery, Glendale.

Tillie (Mrs. Max) Winslow, was a friend of Joe and Madeline Sanders' during their six months in New York City, 1931–1932, and friend also of Sime Silverman's, founder of *Variety*. She and her husband left New York in 1933, and after her husband's death in 1942, she remained in Hollywood, where she died 19 January 1962.

APPENDIX C

Coon-Sanders' Schedule of Road Tours

1919?

Tulsa, Oklahoma, to play at a private party given by oilman Earl Sinclair. The engagement was aborted by Earl's brother Harry F., who, for a joke, spirited the band off to New York City by train. The date is conjectural, for Sanders says merely that it occurred shortly after the band's organization, when it had but five members. Aside from Joe and Coonie, a third member was perhaps Harold Thiell, but the remaining two are unknown.

1923

June 11–Aug. 12: Oklahoma City, Okla., at the Spring Lake Pavilion, and, in addition,
June 24–Aug. 12: Oklahoma City's Criterion Theater.

1924

Late spring: On the way to a summer's engagement at the Lincoln Tavern, Morton Grove, Ill., the band spent a week at the Missouri Theater, St. Louis, starting on May 4; then played brief engagements at La Salle and Marseilles, Ill.
Summer: At Lincoln Tavern, Morton Grove, Ill.
Road tour Aug. 29–about Sept. 30: (dates are approximate) 29 Aug., Elkhart, Ind.; 30, Kankakee, Ill.; 31, Decatur, Ill.; 1 Sept., Centralia, Ill.; 2, Terre Haute, Ind.; 3-4, Herrin, Ill.; 5, Springfield, Ill.; 6-12, Milwaukee, Wisc.; 13, Joliet, Ill.; 14, Dubuque, Iowa; 15, Sioux City, Iowa; 16, Grand Island, Neb.; 17, Lincoln, Neb.; 18, Ft. Dodge, Iowa; 19, Cedar Rapids, Iowa; 20, La Salle, Ill.; 21, Peoria, Ill.; 22, Cairo, Ill.; 23, Marion Ill.; 24, Terre Haute, Ind.; 25, Aurora, Ill.; 26, Champaign, Ill.; 27, Anderson, Ind.; 28, South Bend, Ind.; 29, Columbus, Ohio.

1925

April 12–July 4: Davenport, Waterloo, Mason City, and Sioux City, Iowa; Lincoln,

Neb.; Des Moines and Cedar Rapids, Iowa; La Salle, Ill.; Omaha, Neb. (2 days); Rockford, Peoria, and Monmouth, Ill.; Burlington, Iowa; Milwaukee, Wisc.; Minneapolis, Minn. (5 days); Anderson and Indianapolis, Ind.; Lexington, Ky.; Cincinnati, Ohio, (2 days); Kokomo, Terre Haute, and Silver Lake, Ind.; Kalamazoo, Detroit, Port Huron, and Battle Creek, Mich.; South Bend, Ind.; Champaign and Pontiac, Ill.; Vincennes, Ind.; Nashville, Knoxville, and Johnson City, Tenn.; Lexington, Ky.; Cincinnati, Bucyrus, Coshocton, and Columbus, Ohio; Indianapolis, Ind.; Marseilles, Oregon, Quincy, Benid, Herrin, and Cairo, Ill.; Jackson, Tenn.; Carmi, Ill.; Owensboro, Ky.; New Albany, Ind.; Cincinnati, Ohio; Kentland and Elkhart, Ind.; Bucyrus, Akron, and Hamilton, Ohio; Richmond, Ind.; Cleveland, Ohio; Oil City, Jeannette, Carrolltown, and Philipsburg, Pa.

July 8 (?)–Aug. 9: Atlantic City, N. J., Young's Million Dollar Pier.

Aug. 10–about Sept. 7: Philipsburg, Uniontown, Oakmont, and Franklin, Pa.; Dayton, Ohio; Anderson, Ind.; and in Ill., Lincoln, Decatur, Spring Valley, Sterling, Bloomington, and, on 23 Aug., Lewistown.; followed by a short vacation.

Sept. 14–about Sept. 30: Joplin, Mo.; Independence, Kan.; Tulsa, Okla.; Dallas, Houston, and Galveston, Texas; Shreveport, La.; El Dorado, Texarkana, and Little Rock, Ark.; Indianapolis and Lafayette, Ind.; Streator and Sterling, Ill.; and Garrett, Ind.

1926

April: 4, Anderson, Ind.; 5, Vincennes, Ind.; 6, Evansville, Ind.; 7, Terre Haute, Ind.; 8 Dayton, Ohio; 10–11, Cincinnati, Ohio; 12 Huntington, W. Va.; 13 Williamson, W. Va.; 14, Chillicothe, Ohio; 15, Toledo, Ohio; 16, Detroit, Mich.; 17, Battle Creek, Mich.; 18, Streator, Ill.; 19, Galena, Ill.; 20, La Crosse, Wisc.; 21, Davenport, Iowa; 22, Cedar Rapids, Iowa; 23, Chicago, Ill.; 24–30, Milwaukee, Wisc.

May: 1, Racine, Wisc.; 2, Marseilles, Ill.; 3, Bloomington, Ill.; 4–5, Columbus, Ohio; 6, Portsmouth, Ohio; 7, Richmond, Ind.; 8, Terre Haute, Ind.; 9, Miller, Ind.; 10, Manitowoc, Wisc.; 11, Wausau, Wisc.; 12, Marshfield, Wisc.; 13, Norrie, Wisc.; 14, Iron Mountain, Mich.; 15, Milwaukee, Wisc.; 16, Appleton, Wisc.; 17, Ludington, Mich.; 18, Traverse City, Mich.; 19, Cadillac, Mich.; 20, Grand Rapids, Mich.; 21, Ann Arbor, Mich.; 22, Battle Creek, Mich.; 23, Silver Lake, Ind.; 24, Canton, Ohio; 25, Toledo, Ohio; 26, Akron, Ohio; 27, Chillicothe, Ohio; 28, Huntington, W. Va.; 29, Richmond, Ind.; 30, Anderson, Ind.; 31, Indianapolis, Ind.

June: 1, Lexington, Ky.; 2, Bowling Green, Ky.; 3, Nashville, Tenn.; 4–7, Atlanta, Ga.; 8, Louisville, Ky.; 9, Evansville, Ind.; 10-11, Champaign, Ill.; 12-13, Miller, Ind.; 14, Elkhart, Ind.; 15, Waukegan, Ill.; 16, Joliet, Ill.; 17, Marion, Ohio; 18, Lima, Ohio; 19-25, St. Louis, Mo.; 26, Columbus, Ohio; 27–(July 3), Cleveland, Ohio.

July: (June 27)–July 3, Cleveland, Ohio; 4–5, Vermilion, Ohio; 6, Toledo, Ohio; 7, Elkhart, Ind.; 8, Jackson, Mich.; 9–11, Detroit, Mich.; 12, Osceola, Ind.; 13, Huntington, Ind.; 14, Oaklandon, Ind.; 15, Marion, Ind.; 16, Canton, Ohio; 17, Uhrichsville, Ohio; 18, Buckeye Lake, Ohio; 19–24, Pittsburgh, Pa.; 25, Buffalo, N. Y.; 26, Franklin, Pa.; 27, Johnsonburg, Pa.; 28, Carrolltown, Pa.; 29, Keyser, W. Va.; 30, Connellsville, Pa.; 31, Vermilion, Ohio.

August: 1, Huntington, Ind.; 2–3, Toledo, Ohio; 4, Vincennes, Ind.; 5–7, Arcola, Ill.; 8, La Salle, Ill.; 9, Morrison, Ill.; 10, Springfield, Ill.; 11, Herrin, Ill.; 12, Uniontown, Ky.; 13, Madisonville, Ky.; 14, Vincennes, Ind.; 15, Mt. Carmel, Ill.; 16–31, vacation.

September: 1, Mendota, Ill.; 2, Cedar Rapids, Iowa; 3–9, Omaha, Neb.; 10, Havelock, Neb.[*]; 11, Norfolk, Neb.; 12, Sioux City, Iowa; 13, Sheldon, Iowa; 14, Sibley, Iowa; 15,

---

[*]*The Nebraska State Historical Society tells me that Havelock is now part of Lincoln.*

Lamberton, Minn.; 16, Albert Lea, Minn.; 17, Dennison, Iowa; 18, Fort Dodge, Iowa; 19, Dubuque, Iowa; 20, Waukegan, Ill.; 21, Green Bay, Wisc.; 22–24, vacation.

1927

March: 31, Cedar Rapids, Iowa

April: 1–7, Omaha, Neb.; 8, Columbia, Mo.; 9–15, St. Louis, Mo.; 16, Cedar Rapids, Iowa; 17, Davenport, Iowa; 18, Spring Valley (La Salle?), Ill.; 19, Springfield, Ill.; 20, Joliet, Ill.; 21, Galena, Ill.; 22–23, Chicago, Ill.; 24–27, Ft. Wayne, Ind.; 28, Warren, Ohio; 29, Erie, Pa.; 30, Dayton, Ohio.

May: 1–28, Cincinnati, Ohio; 29, Marion, Ohio; 30 —(June 4), Pittsburgh, Pa.

June: (May 30)–June 4, Pittsburgh, Pa.; 5, Sandusky, Ohio; 6, Warren, Ohio; 7, Connellsville, Pa.; 8, Altoona, Pa.; 9, Mahanoy City, Pa.; 10, Springfield, Mass.; 11, Buzzards Bay, Mass.; 12, Boston, Mass.; 13, Waltham, Mass.; 14, Lowell, Mass.; 15, Lawrence, Mass.; 16, Salem, Mass.; 17, Taunton, Mass.; 18, Salem, Mass.; 19, traveling; 20, Butler, Pa.; 21, Oberlin, Ohio; 22, E. Liverpool, Ohio; 23, Batavia, N. Y.; 24, Canton, Ohio; 25, Coloma, Mich.; 26, Anderson, Ind.; 27–(July 17), Cincinnati, Ohio.

July: (June 27)–17, Cincinnati, Ohio; 18, Toledo, Ohio; 19, Norvell, Mich.; 20, Battle Creek, Mich.; 21, Mineral Point, Wisc.; 22, Lone Tree, Iowa; 23, Sring Valley, Ill.; 24, Aurora, Ill.; 25–27, Joliet, Ill.; 28–30, Ft. Wayne, Ind.; 31–(Aug. 6), Indianapolis, Ind.

August: (July 31)–Aug. 6, Indianapolis, Ind.; 7, Huntington, Ind.; 8, Lafayette, Ind.; 9, Vincennes, Ind.; 10–31, vacation.

September: 1, Mineral Point, Wisc.; 2, Galena, Ill.; 3, Elgin, Ill.; 4, Putnam, Mich.; 5, Fremont, Ohio; 6, Toledo, Ohio; 7, Wawasee, Ind.; 8, Putnam, Mich.; 9, Connellsville, Pa.; 10, Canton, Ohio; 11, Marion, Ohio; 12, Lansing, Mich.; 13, open date; 14, Grand Rapids, Mich.; 15, Chicago, Ill. (Trianon); 16, Chicago, Ill. (Aragon); 17–18, Herrin, Ill.; 19, Memphis, Tenn.; 20, Nashville, Tenn.; 21, Chattanooga, Tenn.; 22, Louisville, Ky.; 23, Huntington, W. Va.; 24, Uhrichsville, Ohio; 25–26, Huntington, W. Va.; 27, Hinton, W. Va.; 28, Williamson, W. Va.; 29, Portsmouth, Ohio; 30, Zanesville, Ohio.

October: 1, Charleston, W. Va.; 2–5, Lafayette, Ind.; 6, Evansville, Ind.; 7–13, vacation; 15–(Dec. 3), St. Louis, Mo.

December: (Oct. 15)–Dec. 3, St. Louis, Mo.; 4–8, vacation; 9–23, Kansas City, Mo.; 24–25, vacation; 26, Elgin, Ill.; 27, Ft. Dodge, Iowa; 28, Sioux City, Iowa; 29 Cedar Rapids, Iowa; 30, Des Moines, Iowa; 31, Chicago, Ill.

1928

April: 12, Battle Creek, Mich.; 13, Detroit, Mich.; 17, Green Bay, Wisc.; 18, La Crosse, Wisc.; 19, Cedar Rapids, Iowa; 27, Chicago, Ill. (Merry Gardens).

May: 10, Putnam, Mich.; 11, South Bend, Ind. ; 12–13,* Gambier, Ohio.

1929

February: 8, Ann Arbor, Mich.

March: 15, Chicago, Ill. (Edgewater Beach).

April: 2, Peoria, Ill.; 25, Gary, Ind.; 26, Bloomington, Ind.

---

*Sanders' records have no mention of South Bend but show the band in Gambier, Ohio, on the eleventh and twelfth. A contemporary newspaper and campus document, however, clearly show that the Nighthawks were on Notre Dame campus for the Senior Ball on May 11.

Opposite page: No bigheads here. Coonie and Joe, Cadillac, Michigan, 19 May 1926. (Courtesy Special Collections, Kansas City [Mo.] Public Library.)

1930

March: 28, Champaign, Ill.

April: 3, Waukegan, Ill.; 4, Madison, Wisc.; 10, Davenport, Iowa; 11, Iowa City, Iowa; 16, Evanston, Ill.; 23, Milwaukee, Wisc.; 24, St. Louis, Mo.; 25, Lafayette, Ind.

May: 1, Chicago, Ill. (Midland Club); 2, Chicago, Ill. (Mount Carmel); 8, Grand Rapids, Mich.; 9, South Bend, Ind.

December: 1, Grand Rapids, Mich.; 2, Chicago, Ill.; 3, Galena, Ill.; 4, Cedar Rapids, Iowa; 5–6, Champaign, Ill.; 7, Waukegan, Ill.; 8, Bloomington, Ill.; 9, Chicago, Ill.; 10, Chattanooga, Tenn.; 11–12, Nashville, Tenn.; 13, Terre Haute, Ind.; 14, Chicago, Ill.; 15, Kalamazoo, Mich.; 16, Chicago, Ill.; 17, Sheboygan, Wisc.; 18, Appleton, Wisc.; 19, Eau Claire, Wisc.; 20–21, Chicago, Ill.; 22, Detroit, Mich.; 23, Chicago, Ill.; 24, Indianapolis, Ind.; 25, Chicago, Ill. (Griffiths Party); 26–28, Kansas City, Mo.; 29, Springfield, Ill.; 30, Chicago, Ill.; 31, Milwaukee, Wisc.

1931

February: 11, St. Paul, Minn.; 12, Wausau, Wisc.; 13, Milwaukee, Wisc.; 25, Davenport, Iowa; 26, Cedar Rapids, Iowa.

April: 9, Wheeling, W. Va.; 10, Beaver Falls, Pa.; 16, Youngstown, Ohio; 17, Cleveland, Ohio; 23, Peoria, Ill.; 24, Indianapolis, Ind.; 29, Mendota, Ill.; 30, La Salle, Ill.

May: 7, Grafton, Wisc.; 8, Chicago, Ill., (Drake Hotel); 13, Bloomington, Ill.; 15, Milwaukee, Wisc.; 16–31, Chicago, Ill. (Aragon & Trianon).

June: 2, Pittsburgh, Pa.; 3, York, Pa.; 4, Mahanoy City, Pa.; 5–10, Lexington, Va.; 11, Wilkes-Barre, Pa.; 12, Johnson City, N.Y.; 13, Hershey, Pa.; 15, Olean, N.Y.; 16, Union City, Pa.

July: 18–31, Denver, Colo.

August: 3 or 4 (?), Bloomington, Ill.; 4 or 5 (?), Chicago, Ill.; 6, Toledo, Ohio; 7, Columbus, Ohio; 8, Dayton, Ohio; 9, Hudson Lake, Ind.; 10 (break); 11, Saginaw, Mich.; 12, Coloma, Mich.; 13, Chicago, Ill. (Trianon); 14, Sun Prairie, Wisc.; 15–16, Hartford, Wisc.; 17, Maquoketa, Iowa; 18, Decatur, Ill.; 19, Mounds, Ill.; 20, Fairgrounds Casino, Memphis, Tenn.; 21, Little Rock, Ark.; 22, Monroe, La.; 24–(14 September), New Orleans, La.

September: (Aug. 24)–14, New Orleans, La.; 16–29, Milwaukee, Wisc.; 30, Waukegan, Ill.

October: 1, Springfield, Ohio; 2, Franklin, Pa.; 3, Olean, N. Y.

October 7–(26 April 1932): Terrace Room, Hotel New Yorker, New York, N.Y.

1932

(October 7)–26 March 1932: Terrace Room, Hotel New Yorker, New York, N.Y.

March: 27–April 1, Detroit, Mich. (Detroit dates approximate.) Then returned to Chicago for an extended engagement at the Hotel Sherman's College Inn, during which time Coon became ill and died.

APPENDIX D

Songs Composed by Joe Sanders and Carleton Coon

It would be next to impossible to compile a list of all of Joe Sanders' musical compositions. He said in later years that he had written hundreds, so the following list is certainly not comprehensive. As for the years of composition or copyright, I've had to guess on several, indicate uncertainty on others, and even leave a few others blank. I found some of these titles mentioned in newspaper clippings in Sanders' scrapbooks, but whoever affixed those clippings to the pages rarely gave the source or the date. Though the published score of "Nighthawk Blues" carries no copyright date, the first mention I've seen of the song was on page 6B of the *Kansas City Star*, of 10 December 1922. That several listeners wired that they had enjoyed hearing the number previous to that date indicates that it was composed almost immediately after the first Nighthawk broadcast. Harvey Rettberg is the source of some of the following items; he, in turn, cites such other sources as Clyde Hahn, Murray O'Connor, and Charles Green. Most of these titles, however, are fairly well authenticated in Joe Sanders' papers at the Kansas City Public Library. Joe wrote a number of pieces that are engaging and that deserve much better than the near-oblivion they seem to occupy.

"Anything Your Little Heart Desires" (Chicago: Milton Weil, 1936).

"Autumn 1923," for Kansas City's Second Fall Fashion Pageant; Joe wrote the music, and Milton M. Feld the lyrics.

"Because You Said 'I Love You'" (Chicago: Grossman-Lewis, 1929), with Arthur Sizemore and Bernie Grossman.

"Believe Me," so listed by ASCAP's on-line database.

"Beloved" (New York: Irving Berlin, 1928), words and music with Gus Kahn.

"Billie" (New York: Jack Mills, 1922), with George D. Lott.

"Blazin'" (1926).

"Blue Moonlight" (New York: Ager, Yellen & Bornstein, 1941), with Milton Ager.

"Brainstorm — An Erratic Blues" (Chicago: Forster, 1927), instrumental.

"Daniel Boone" (Chicago: Hubert J. Braun, 1937).

"Debutante Waltz" (1914), perhaps Joe's first composition.

"Do You Miss Me?" (New York: Crawford, 1935), with Bernie Grossman.

"Dreaming of Tomorrow" (New York: Robbins-Engel, 1925), with Bennie Davis.

"Embers" (New York: Robbins, 1931), piano instrumental.

"Geisha Girl."

"Got a Great Big Date with a Little Bitty Girl" (San Francisco: Villa Moret, 1929).

"Half Way to Dawn" (1935).

"Hallucinations" (1927), instrumental.

"Happiness," with Thomas G. Devine.

"Harold Teen" (New York: Irving Berlin, 1929).

"Hi-Diddle-Diddle," by C.A. Koon and Hal Keidel (New York: Feist, 1926).

"High Fever" (Chicago: Ted Brown, 1926), with Charlie Harrison.

"Hindu Dream Man" (New York: Leo Feist, 1921?).

"The House Isn't Home Without You," uncertain date but post–Nighthawks.

"I Can Still Remember" (New York: Remick, 1927).

"I Found a Rose in the Snow" (1935).

"I Want to Go Home" (New York: Remick, 1932).

"I Want You" (1921?).

"I'll Always Remember You." Harvey Rettberg cites Charles Green as saying there was such a song.

"I'll Never Forget I Love You" (New York: Shapiro, Bernstein, 1935).

"I'm a Man about Town (That's about to Settle Down)" (1930), with Charles Newman.

"In the Hills of Old Missouri" (New York: Remick, 1932).

"In the Loft of the Little Red Barn." Harvey Rettberg cites Charles Green as saying there was such a song.

"Inhibition" (New York: Robbins, 1931), piano instrumental.

"Intangibility" (New York: Robbins, 1931), piano instrumental.

"Kick In" (1918), composed in support of Fourth Liberty Loan in Kansas City, Mo.

"Lazy Waters" (Chicago: Milton Weil, 1926), with Gus Kahn.

"Let's Not Forget" (1919), by Sanders and Coon, for Kansas City's Liberty Memorial campaign.

"A Little Bird Told Me So" (New York: Robbins-Engel, 1926), with Bennie Davis.

"Little Feller" (New York: Robbins, 1929).

"Little Orphan Annie" (New York: Irving Berlin, 1928), with Gus Kahn.

"Lonesome (I Wonder If You're Lonesome Too),"about 1928.

"Louder and Funnier" (1927?). Harvey Rettberg cites Clyde Hahn as saying this was a Sanders song.

"Martha" (Kansas City, Mo.: J. W. Jenkins Sons, 1922).

"Maybe It's You" (New York: Remick, 1925), with Bennie Davis.

"My Dear" (New York: Feist, 1929), with Gus Kahn.

"My Paradise" (New York: Irving Berlin, 1931).

"Nighthawk Blues" (1922, but apparently published by Sanders and the *Kansas City Star* in Kansas City, 1923 — Harvey Rettberg believes 1924).

"Nighty Night" (Chicago: Frank Clark, 1926), with Paul Ash.

"Old Legion Buddy of Mine" (1921), by both Sanders and Coon, on occasion of the American Legion's convention, in Kansas City.

"Over the Rim of the Sun" (Nashville: Milene, 1951).

"Patrick Shay" (1917 or 1918).

"Peruvian Nights" (1923?).

"Plantation Grill Blues" (c. 1920). Lyrics and music by Sanders and Coon; mentioned briefly in Plantation Grill ad among miscellaneous materials in the Joe Sanders Collection at the Kansas City Public Library.

"Please Let It Rain for Easter." Of uncertain publication but cited by Harvey Rettberg.

"Right Next Door to Love" (1934), with Bernie Grossman.

"Roodles" (1927?). Cited by Harvey Rettberg but without publication data.

"Sadie, That Yiddisher Vamp" (1921?), with Carleton Coon.

"Save the Grease" (1944). Written to encourage civilian effort in World War II.

"She Loves Me Just the Same" (New York: Feist, 1930), with J. Paul Fogarty and Rudy Vallee.

"Sittin' and Whittlin'" (1928).

"Sittin' Around" (New York: Feist, 1926), with Gus Kahn.

"Slue-Foot" (San Francisco: Villa Moret, 1927), with Al Lewis.

"Snuggles," (1921?), words by Coon — according to unidentified clipping, Sanders Collection.

"Somebody from Home" (1934).

"Somehow" (1923?).

"Southology" (New York: Robbins, 1931), piano instrumental.

"Sparks." Uncertain date; Sanders discusses it in a 1961 interview with Harvey Rettberg and says that he composed this instrumental "mood," along with several others, in late 1920s.

"Sweetheart Trail" (Chicago: Milton Weil, 1930), with Charles Newman and Charlie Crafts.

"A Swingeroo." Uncertain publication data, but Harvey Rettberg cites Charles Green as voucher for its existence.

"Take Me" (New York: Santly Bros., 1930).

"Tennessee Lazy" (1929).

"That Was Destiny" (New York: Feist, 1930), with Gus Kahn.

"There's No One Just Like You" (1919?) Accepted for publication Feb. 1923 by Sam Fox, Cleveland, Ohio.

"Time Out for Love" (Chicago: Forster, 1936).

"Tune In on My Heart" (Hollywood, Calif.: L. Wolfe Gilbert, 1937), with L. Wolfe Gilbert.

"Twinkle Toes." Of uncertain date but Harvey Rettberg cites Charles Green as to its existence.

"Until Yesterday" (New York: Harms, 1928), with Benny Davis.

"The Wail" (1926?)

"Waltzing." Of uncertain date but Harvey Rettberg cites Clyde Hahn as evidence for it.

"Way Down in th Deep, Low South," by C.A. Coon, uncertain date but played on *Maytag Frolics*, on radio, 17 January 1929.

"We Love Us" (New York: Feist, 1930), with Lee Moore.

"What a Girl! What a Night!" (New York: Feist, 1928).

"What Have I Done?" (1930).

"What Were All the Wild, Wild Women Like?" (1920?).

"Why Can't a Fellow like Me Get a Girlie Like You?" Of uncertain date but Harvey Rettberg vouches for its existence.

Bibliography

Abbreviations Used in This Bibliography

JLSC refers to the Joe L. Sanders Collection, at the Kansas City (Mo.) Public Library's Special Collection, and HRC refers to the Harvey Clark Rettberg Collection, now in the hands of the author but to be donated to the Kansas City Public Library.

Private and Archival Collections

Claude F. Anderson, who was married to Floyd Estep's sister from 1935 until her death in January 1982, has very kindly donated a number of Estep family photos and records.

The Auburn-Cord-Duesenberg Museum, Auburn, Ind. This well-operated and fascinating museum has many beautiful specimens of its three pretigious vehicles. The museum has also many audio-visual materials and other items for sale to the public. John Emery and Gregg Buttermore give efficient and cordial help to those interested in the museum's archives and exhibits.

The late Johnny Coon, son of Carleton A. Coon, Sr. His conversations with the author, personal mementos, and tapes of reminiscences he made about his father and the Nighthawks, have been some of the most important sources for this history. The tapes will be turned over to the Kansas City Public Library.

The Kansas City (Mo.) Public Library's Special Collections owns the Joe L. Sanders Collection. The author enjoyed working there on several occasions and is indebted to the several members of the staff for their competent and cordial assitance, especially that given by Sara J. Nyman. I thank also Mary Beveridge, Manager of Special Collections, for permission to use various photographs in the Sanders collection and to quote several of Joe Sanders' lyrics. The Sanders Collection is abbreviated in footnotes as JLSC.

Willis Morrisette's valuable tape recordings of annual meetings of the New Nighthawk Fan Club, Huntington, W. Va., as well as his conversations with the author, both in person and by telephone, have been of great value.

Harvey Clark Rettberg, the dean of Nighthawk enthusiasts and author of several articles on the Nighthawks, was an important mover in my undertaking this history. His collection of jazz materials, temporarily in the author's possession, will be donated to the Kansas City Public Library after the completion of this book. The Harvey Rettberg Collection is designated in footnotes as HRC.

Periodicals Examined

Accelerator. Auburn Automobile Company, Auburn, Ind.
Akron (Ohio) *Beacon Journal*
Albert Lea, Minn., *Evening Tribune.*
Anderson (Ind.) *Herald.*
Appleton (Wisc.) *Post-Crescent.*
Atlanta (Ga.) *Journal.*
Auburn Cord Duesenberg Newsletter. Auburn Cord Duesenberg Museum, Auburn, Ind.
Aurora (Ill.) *Daily Beacon.*
Battle Creek, Mich., *Enquirer and Evening News.*
Bowling Green, Ky., *Park City Daily News.*
Buffalo, N.Y., *Courier-Express.*
Buffalo (N.Y.) *News.*
Buffalo (N.Y.) *Times.*
Cadillac (Mich.) *Evening News.*
Chattanooga (Tenn.) *News.*
Chattanooga (Tenn.) *Times.*
Chillicothe, Ohio, *Scioto Gazette.*
Cleveland (Ohio) *Plain Dealer.*
Cleveland (Ohio) *Press.*
Columbus (Ohio) *Citizen.*
Columbus (Ohio) *Dispatch.*
Columbus *Ohio State Journal.*
Davenport (Iowa) *Daily Times.*
Davenport (Iowa) *Democrat.*
Dayton (Ohio) *Daily News.*
Denison (Iowa) *Bulletin.*
Erie Daily Times, Union City, Pa.
Ft. Dodge, Iowa, *Messenger and Chronicle.*
Fort Wayne (Ind.) *Journal Gazette.*
Fort Wayne, Ind., *News Sentinel.*
Franklin, Pa., *News-Herald.*
Galena (Ill.) *Daily Gazette.*
Huntington (Ind.) *Herald.*
Huntington, W. Va., *Herald-Dispatch.*
Indianapolis (Ind.) *Star.*
Iowa City, Iowa, *Daily Iowan.*
Iowa City (Iowa) *Press Citizen.*
Jackson (Mich.) *Citizen Patriot.*
Jazz Notes. Indianapolis, Ind., Jazz Club.
Johnsonburg (Pa.) *Press.*
Joliet (Ill.) *Evening Herald-News.*
Kansas City (Mo.) *Star.*
Kansas City (Mo.) *Times.*
Keyser, W. Va., *Mineral Daily News.*
La Crosse (Wisc.) *Tribune.*
Lafayette (Ind.) *Journal and Courier.*
Lima (Ohio) *News and Times-Democrat.*
Lowell (Mass.) *Sun.*
Madison, Wisc., *Capital Times Green.*
Marion (Ind.) *Daily Chronicle.*
Marshfield (Wisc.) *Daily News.*
Memphis, Tenn., *Commercial Appeal.*
Meridian (Miss.) *Star.*
Milwaukee (Wisc.) *Journal.*
Milwaukee (Wisc.) *Sentinel.*
Mississippi Rag. Minneapolis, Minn.
Monroe (La.) *News-Star.*
Nashville *Tennessean.*
New Orleans (La.) *Item.*
New Orleans (La.) *States.*
New York Times.
Northwestern University's *Daily Northwestern.*
Notre Dame Scholastic.
Oklahoma City *Daily Oklahoman.*
Omaha (Neb.) *World Herald.*
Pittsburgh (Pa.) *Press.*
Portsmouth (Ohio) *Daily Times.*
Portsmouth (Ohio) *Morning Sun.*
Quincy (Ill.) *Whig Journal.*
Radio Digest.
Richmond (Ind.) *Item.*
St. Louis (Mo.) *Post-Dispatch.*
St. Louis University, *Varsity Breeze.*
Saturday Review.
Second Line.
South Bend (Ind.) *News-Times.*
Springfield, Ill., *Illinois State Journal.*
Traverse City, Mich., *Record-Eagle.*
Variety. New York, N.Y.
Vermilion (Ohio) *News.*
Vincennes (Ind.) *Morning Commercial.*
Vincennes (Ind.) *Sun.*
Virginia Military Institute, *Cadet.*
Waltham (Mass.) *News-Tribune.*
Warren (Ohio) *Daily Tribune.*
Washington and Lee University, *Ring-tum Phi.*
Youngstown (Ohio) *Vindicator.*

Articles in Periodicals

"Actors Fear Theater Reform." *Kansas City Star*, 30 January 1920.
"Advertising on the Radio." *Variety*, 18 March 1925, p. 41.
"Alaska Joins 'Hawks.'" *Kansas City Star*, 25 March 1923, p. 13A.

"Another Chicken Farm Bill." *Kansas City Star*, 27 February 1923.
"As 12th Street Says It." *Kansas City Star*, 16 April 1922, p. 19A.
"As We Go Dancing Around." *Kansas City Star*, 26 November 1922, p. 1E.
"Atlantic City Full of Bands in Cabaret." *Variety*, 8 July 1925, p. 47.
"Bad Radio Tongue Slips." *Variety*, 11 February 1931, pp. 1, 12.
"Ban on Shimmy Shiver." *Kansas City Star*, 2 February 1919.
"Band Reviews: Coon-Sanders Orchestra." *Variety*, 12 August 1925, p. 35.
"Bandit Fighter Still a 'Nighthawk.'" *Kansas City Star*, 7 March 1923, p. 1.
"Bands!" *Variety*, 31 December 1924, p. 26-B.
"Bands as Big Business." *Variety*, 9 September 1925, p. 5.
"Band's Scale of Prices for 1-Nighters." *Variety*, 5 May 1926, p. 25.
"Bands Shuffled." *Variety*, 13 May 1931, p. 92.
"Bands Will Even Cut for That Reno Cure." *Variety*, 20 May 1931, p. 1.
"Beer Is Licking Liquor." *Variety*, 11 August 1931, pp. 1, 43.
"Benson Losing Out in Chicago." *Variety*, 8 April 1925, p. 43.
"Biese Released." *Variety*, 13 May 1925, p. 15.
"Big Amplifiers Await Dance." *Kansas City Star*, 29 December 1922, p. 2.
"Big Time's About Face on Radio." *Variety*, 4 March 1925, p. 4.
Binyon, Claude. "Inaccurate Biographies: Will Rogers." *Variety*, 21 January 1931, p. 49.
"Bits from the Midnight Radio Frolic." *Kansas City Star*, 30 July 1922, p. 15A.
"'Black Bottom' Dance Described." *Variety*, 15 September 1926, p. 28.
"Blackhawk." *Variety*, 6 October 1931, p. 96.
"Blames Jazz for Crime. Love of Good Times Causes Youth's Downfall, Colorado Warden Warns." *Kansas City Star*, 21 January 1922.
"Booze — More or Less." *Variety*, 31 December 1924, p. 8.
"Booze Was Easy to Find." *Kansas City Star*, 3 February 1923.
"Cabaret Reviews: Blackhawk Cafe." *Variety*, 6 October 1926, p. 87.
"Canal Zone Enjoys WDAF." *Kansas City Star*, 6 February 1923, p. 1.
"Charleston — Death Dance." *Variety*, 8 July 1925, pp. 1, 8.
"'Charleston' Rules." *Variety*, 3 February 1926, p. 47.
"Charleston Taboo in Iowa." *Variety*, 12 August 1925, p. 37.
"Chatter in the Loop; Rival Musicians." *Variety*, 8 August 1928, p. 41.
"Cheap Road House Parties Ruined Chicago's Night Clubs." *Variety*, 11 May 1927, pp. 1, 53.
"Chi Cafe Men's Fortunes Gone." *Variety*, 24 August 1927, p. 56.
"Chi Cafes Moving to Low Rent Residence Areas." *Variety*, 26 September 1928, p. 57.
"Chi Network Status Reversed Overnite as WMAQ Goes NBC; CBS Minus 100% Outlet in Chi." *Variety*, 1 September 1931, pp. 59, 60.
"Chi. Off 'Charleston.'" *Variety*, 13 May 1925, p. 15.
"Chicago Remains Main Center for Divorce Actions Despite 10,000 Suits Awaiting Trial." *Variety*, 26 September 1928, p. 29.
"Chicago Stations in Letter-Getting Row." *Variety*, 15 December 1926, p. 44.
"Chicago Stations Stop All Dance Music." *Variety*, 7 March 1928, p. 56.
"Chicago's Civic Loop-Carnival Includes 6 Name Bands for Street Dancing — Lots of Acts." *Variety*, 13 May 1931, pp. 75, 95.
"Chicago's Music Corp. Going After Local Biz." *Variety*, 29 April 1925, p. 39.
"Chi's Fading Nite Life." *Variety*, 23 May 1928, p. 64.
"Chiseling and Hooey Theme of Coon-Sanders' Hot Letter." *Variety*, 4 February 1931, p. 80.
"City's Dress Suit Ready." *Kansas City Star*, 28 October 1921.
Clark, A. G. "The Tuning Troubles of Messrs. Gallagher and Shean." *Radio Broadcast*, May 1923, p. 28.
"Comes a Jazz Bandwagon." *Kansas City Star*, 24 January 1922.
"A Concert Every Night." *Kansas City Star*, 5 March 1922.
"Concerts at 'Midnight'; Coon-Sanders Orchestra Will Play for the Star's Audience." *Kansas City Star*, 3 December 1922, p. 14A.
"Coon-Sanders Break Rule to Play New York." *Variety*, 14 July 1931, p. 49.
"Coon-Sanders May Find Out about Pash Femmes." *Variety*, 20 May 1931, p. 139.
"Coon-Sanders, Nationally Popular Radio Orchestra, Has Gone Auburn." *The Accelerator*, pub. by Auburn Automobile Company, Auburn, Ind., June 1931, p. 3.
"Coon-Sanders on Tour Did $11,000 in 14 Days." *Variety*, 28 April 1926, p. 81.
"Coon-Sanders Sasses NBC." *Variety*, 15 April 1931, p. 3.
"Coon-Sanders to Leave." *Kansas City Star*, 27 May 1923, p. 2B
"Cut-In Penalties for Adjustment at Society Meeting." *Variety*, 8 April 1931, p. 67.
"Cut-Ins with Results." *Variety*, 8 April 1931, p. 67.
"Denver Sanders Booking." *Variety*, 21 July 1931, p. 59.

"Dial Trouble Will Pass." *Kansas City Star*, 19 June 1922.

"Disc Reviews: Coon-Sanders." *Variety*, 26 April 1932, p. 53.

"Enemies of Jazz Speak." *Kansas City Star*, 10 February 1922, p. 7.

"Enter the Jazz Waltz; Dancers Find a Way Around a Ban." *Kansas City Star*, 9 October 1921.

"Epidemic Loss 8 Million [Dollars]." *Kansas City Star*, 1 February 1919.

Farlow, James W. "A Fool and His Car Are Soon Busted." *Kansas City Star*, 1 February 1920.

Faulkner, Roy H. "Faulkner Speaking." *The Accelerator*, August 1928, p. 5.

"A Film Explains Radio." *Kansas City Star*, 28 February 1923, p. 3.

"The Flapper and the Flopper." *Kansas City Star*, 16 April 1922, p. 1D.

"$4,000,000 from Radio." *Variety*, 19 April 1932, p. 61.

"Fox Trot on Ganz's Program; Miss Millar Finds the Conductor Is a Brave Man." *Kansas City Star*, 7 November 1921.

"Fritz Hanlein to Leave." *Kansas City Star*, 10 June 1923, p. 2B.

"Fun for the Nighthawks." *Kansas City Star*, 2 December 1923, p. 3B.

"Gas Lamps Flicker Out." *Kansas City Star*, 7 January 1923.

"Gasoline Is Up a Cent; the New Price at Filling Stations is 22.2 Cents." *Kansas City Star*, 10 April 1922.

"Gets WDAF Far at Sea." *Kansas City Star*, 1 March 1923, p. 1.

Gilchrest, Charles J. "Popular Radio Favorites Recall Old Times as Interviewer Tours Studio." *Chicago Daily News*, 20 April 1932, newspaper clipping in box 15, folder 1, JLSC.

"The Great God Jazz Bows Before Its Successor." *Kansas City Star*, 15 March 1922, p. 13. Reprinted from St. Louis *Globe Democrat*.

Green, Abel. "Abel's Comment." *Variety*, 17 December 1924, p. 41; 24 December 1924, p. 36; 7 January 1925, p. 40.

_____. "Battle for Name Bands." *Variety*, 23 June 1931, p. 57.

"'Guilty' Verdict on Dance." *Kansas City Star*, 24 January 1922, p. 5.

Hahn, Clyde. "The Story of the Coon-Sanders Original Nighthawks Club (...and How It Grew — or, It Went This-away!)." *Jazz Notes* (vol. VI, no. 1 ns), pp. 8–15.

Harrington, Bob. "Tales of Coon-Sanders." *The Mississippi Rag*, April 1991, pp. 10–14.

"Have We Lost Control of Civilization Forces?" *Kansas City Star*, 5 July 1922, p. 18.

"'Hawks' on Land and Sea." *Kansas City Star*, 28 January 1923, p. 2B.

"Hays Ban on Horizontal Clinches; Up-and-Up Okay If on Up-and-Up." *Variety*, 4 March 1931, p. 5.

"Hear WDAF in Subway." *Kansas City Star*, 24 January 1923, p. 1.

"Hello, Sucker!" *Variety*, 13 August 1924, p. 30.

"Hi-Diddle-Diddle," ad for Carleton A. Coon and Hal Keidel's song, with score. *Variety*, 19 May 1926, p. 53.

"'Hip Booze' Makes Chi's Night Life Look Dismal." *Variety*, 14 July 1926, p. 1.

"Holiday Parties Two Nights." *Kansas City Star*, 26 December 1922, p. 1.

"Hollywood Gardens (with Abe Lyman)." *Variety*, 14 July 1931, p. 52.

"Initial on Garter Latest Nutty Fad." *Variety*, 25 March 1926, p. 13.

"Inside Stuff — Radio." *Variety*, 29 September 1931, p. 50.

"Is Traffic Cop Doomed?" *Kansas City Star*, 21 January 1922.

"It Was a Jazzy Occasion; Cake Eater Flapper Carnival at Electric Park Drew 18,000 Persons." *Kansas City Star*, 27 June 1922.

"A Jazz Ban in Schools." *Kansas City Star*, 10 September 1922.

"Jazz Like Booze Problem." *Kansas City Star*, 11 February 1922, p. 2.

"Jazz Now in the Council." *Kansas City Star*, 5 March 1922, p. 4A.

"Jazz Pioneer Is at Pantages." *Kansas City Star*, 3 January 1923, p. 3.

"Jazz Tunes with Meals Called Bad for Digestion." *Milwaukee* (Wisc.) *Journal*, 24 September 1931, p. 2 ["Green Sheet"].

Johnson, Dennis A. "The Happy-Go-Lucky Sounds of Coon-Sanders Nighthawks." *The Mississippi Rag* (January 1974), pp. 7–9.

Karberg, Karl. "Coon-Sanders Band 'Sent' the Young Folks in '20s." Madison, Wisc., *Capital Times Green* (15 April 1961), p. 1.

Kay, Lambdin. "Famed Coon-Sanders Nighthawks Will Play for Noon Concert Monday." *Atlanta* (Ga.) *Journal*, 6 June 1926, WSB section, p. 1.

"Klan Leader Travels in Arsenal." *Variety*, 24 July 1924, pp. 1, 5.

Laird, Landon. "About Town." *Kansas City Times*, 20 May 1965, p. 15D.

Lait, Jack. "Ballyhooed Hullabaloo; Dayton, Tenn., Full of Scribes and Riff Raff." *Variety*, 15 July 1925, pp. 1, 7.

_____. "Night Life of the World: Chicago." *Variety*, 7 October 1925, pp. 5, 60.

"The Late Bird Got This Worm." *Kansas City Star*, 13 December 1922, p. 1.

"Leader of the Nighthawk Orchestra." *Kansas City Star*, 25 February 1923, p. 13A.

"'A Lease' on the Air Asked; Radio Company Needs a 'Clear Track' for Program." *Kansas City Star*, 6 February 1922.

"Leo Fitzpatrick at WJR; 'Merry Old Chief' Moves." *Variety*, 30 September 1925, p. 45.

"Listen In with the Shaves." *Kansas City Star*, 22 February 1922, p. 1.

"Longer Wave to WDAF." *Kansas City Star*, 18 October 1922.

Lowry, Helen Bullitt. "New York Is Taking the Gymnastics Out of Jazz." *Kansas City Star*, 28 February 1922, p. 11. Reprinted from *New York Times*.

"The Man Who Tamed Jazz." *Kansas City Star*, 7 October 1923.

"Many Bands, but They Must Be Good." *Variety*, 6 August 1924, p. 37.

"M.C.A. Man Waved Flag to Stop Train." *Variety*, 20 October 1926, p. 101.

"MCA Nat'l Advertiser After $2,994,000 Year." *Variety*, 11 February 1931, p. 73.

"A Midnight Radio Frolic." *Kansas City Star*, 31 December 1922, p. 9A.

"Mimicry and Tunes Galore." *Variety*, 1 October 1924, p. 29.

Montague, James J. "The Flapper to the Bar." *Kansas City Star*, 13 April 1922, p. 15.

"Movies to Explain Radio." *Kansas City Star*, 22 February 1923, p. 1.

"Music Is Worth $200,000 a Year from Radio." *Variety*, 25 February 1931, p. 62.

"A Music Test for City." *Kansas City Star*, 16 November 1921.

"Musical Comedy by Radio." *Kansas City Star*, 9 July 1922, p. 2B.

"N.O. Clubs and Unions," *Variety*, 1 September 1931, p. 60.

"'Name' Bandsmen Favor Columbia in Chi as NBC Pushes Studio Bands over Midwest for Commercial Jobs." *Variety*, 21 January 1931, p. 67.

"NBC MCA Band Get-Together Hot and Cold." *Variety*, 17 November 1931, p. 61.

"NBC-MCA Conferences in Chi Move to N.Y." *Variety*, 10 November 1931, p. 60.

"New Orleans Jazz—Station WWL, New Orleans." *Jazz Notes*. Feb.-March 1961, pp. 5–8.

"A New [Traffic] Signal in Penn Valley." *Kansas City Star*, 16 October 1922, p. 4.

"New Sound Panatrope." *Variety*, 19 August 1925, p. 42.

"New Voices Wanted by Ether Patrons; Chi Radio Stations Offering Pay." *Variety*, 18 March 1925, p. 4.

"Next [Radio] Concert Wednesday." *Kansas City Star*, 17 February 1922, p. 1.

"Nighthawk Brood Grows." *Kansas City Star*, 17 December 1922, p. 2B.

"'Nighthawk' Charter to 'Ted' Lewis." *Kansas City Star*, 4 February 1923, p. 8A.

"A Nighthawk Is 'Lost.'" *Kansas City Star*, 18 December 1922, p. 1.

"Nighthawk Movies Next Week." *Kansas City Star*, 18 February 1923, p. 14A.

"The Nighthawk Movies Today." *Kansas City Star*, 25 February 1923, p. 12A.

"Nighthawk Rites by WSB." *Kansas City Star*, 6 February 1923, p. 4.

"'The Nighthawks' Add 450." *Kansas City Star*, 9 January 1923, p. 22.

"'Nighthawks' Defy Sleep." *Kansas City Star*, 10 December 1922, p. 6B.

"'Nighthawks' in Air Again." *Kansas City Star*, 12 December 1922, p. 8.

"Nighthawks in Birmingham." *Kansas City Star*, 28 December 1922, p. 1. Reprinted from Birmingham *Age Herald*. The title referred to the Nighthawks' being heard by radio in Birmingham.

"'Nighthawks' in Isle of Pines." *Kansas City Star*, 14 December 1922, p. 1.

"Nighthawks in Mexico Now." *Kansas City Star*, 2 January 1923, p. 1.

"'Nighthawks' in Oil City." *Kansas City Star*, 14 January 1923, p. 8A. Reprinted from the *Oil City* (Pa.) *Derrick*.

"Nighthawks into Hawaii." *Kansas City Star*, 18 March 1923, p. 19A.

"'The Nighthawks' into Movies." *Kansas City Star*, 11 February 1923, p.16A.

"Nighthawks Use Telegrams." *Kansas City Star*, 3 January 1923, p. 1.

"Nighthawks Visit Here." *Kansas City Star*, 7 January 1923, p. 15A.

"No Radio Remote Control in Chicago, Rules Local Union." *Variety*, 25 January 1928, pp. 1, 70.

"Not Exactly." *Kansas City Star*, 21 April 1922, p. 30.

"Now Hawaii Listens In." *Kansas City Star*, 20 December 1922, p. 1.

"Olsen, Bernie and Waring as Lure for Gamblers, Sez Chi Reformer." *Variety*, 27 May 1931, p. 100.

"Orchestra Bookers Being Forced Out of Business by Radio Doing Its Own Booking of Orchestras." *Variety*, 27 May 1931, p. 99.

"Orchestra Booking Co. in Non-Musical Bldg." *Variety*, 12 May 1926, p. 48.

"'Orphan Annie' Adopted." *Variety*, 1 April 1931, p. 57.

"Other Nations Hear WDAF; 'Nighthawk' Dance Frolics Bring Applause from Canada and Mexico." *Kansas City Star*, 9 December 1922, p. 1.

"Phoney and Good Liquor." *Variety*, 30 September 1925, pp. 1, 10.

"Picture Shows to 'Tune In.'" *Kansas City Star*, 22 February 1922, p. 1.

"A Pitfall of Broadcasting." *Kansas City Star*, 15 April 1922, p. 13A.

"Plays Alone for Nation." *Kansas City Star*, 21 January 1923, p. 15A.

"Police Ready for Crooks." *Kansas City Star*, 29 October 1921.

"Poor, Poor Radio!" *Variety*, 25 November 1925, p. 19.

Popper, Joe. "America's Band." *Kansas City Star* (magazine), 9 July 1989, 8–10, 23, 26–28.

"Radio!" *Variety*, 10 December 1924, p. 16.

"Radio Advertising's Cost." *Variety*, 25 March 1925, pp. 1, 40–41.

"Radio Bands Fading Fast." *Variety*, 8 April 1931, p. 67.

"Radio Club Covers Globe." *Kansas City Star*, 24 December 1922, p. 2B.

"The Radio Conference Opens." *Kansas City Star*, 20 March 1923, p. 8.

"Radio Exhibit This Week." *Kansas City Star*, 14 January 1923, p. 8A.

"Radio Interest Wanes 90%; Fan Letters Few; Wires, Too." *Variety*, 21 October 1925, p. 39.

"Radio Is Commercial Performance." *Variety*, 15 April 1925, p. 38.

"Radio Nighthawks." *Kansas City Star*, 8 April 1923, p. 12A.

"Radio Reports: 'Harold Teen.'" *Variety*, 11 March 1931, p. 66.

"'A Radio Shop' Raided." *Kansas City Star*, 8 December 1922, p. 20.

"Radio Stars for Prom." St. Louis University *Varsity Breeze*, 26 March 1930, pp. 1, 3, 8.

"Radio—the 'Sponger.'" *Variety*, 31 December 1924, pp. 7, 136.

"Radio Unites Lost Brothers." *Kansas City Star*, 12 February 1923, p. 1.

"Radio Wires to Big Hall." *Kansas City Star*, 21 February 1922, p. 1.

"Radio's Biggest Music Plug, Theme Songs, Devoted Mostly to Non-Selling Old Numbers." *Variety*, 17 November 1931, p. 61.

"Radio's Effect on Theatre." *Variety*, 17 November 1926, pp. 1, 44, 47.

"Radio's Lone Advantage for Music Is Quick Decision over New Songs." *Variety*, 17 November 1931, p. 60.

"'The Raunch' Dance." *Variety*, 31 March 1926, p. 4.

"The Ravings of a Radio Maniac." *Kansas City Star*, 5 March 1922, p. 10.

"Ready for Midnight Frolic." *Kansas City Star*, 21 June 1922.

"A Real Jazz Disease." *Kansas City Star*, 27 May 1922, p. 16. Reprinted from *Chicago News*.

Rettberg, Harvey Clark. "Coon-Sanders (A Study of Nostalgia)," Part 2. *The Second Line* (March-April, 1962), pp. 9–11.

_____. "Discography of Coon-Sanders Nighthawks." *Jazz Notes*, vol. VI, no. 1 ns (no date), pp. 6–8.

Rohe, Margaret. "1920 Clothes Not for the Buxom Maid." *Kansas City Star*, 8 March 1920.

Ryan, Quin A. "Coon Sanders." *College Humor*, April 1930, pp. 46–47, 108.

"Salome Hawks Have Trouble." *Kansas City Star*, 25 March 1923, p. 13A.

Samuel, O. M. "Nighthawks and Farmers." *Variety*, 11 March 1925, p. 45.

Sanders, Joseph LaCeil. "The Coon-Sanders Story [part I]." *Jazz Notes* (Feb./Mar. 1961), pp. 2–5.

_____."The Coon-Sanders Story (Part II)." *Jazz Notes* (vol. VI, no. 1 ns [n.d.]), pp. 1–5.

"Sees Menace in Jazz; Modern Music Demoralizing to Girls, Preacher Asserts; Exciting, Neurotic Strains Break Down Barriers of Restraint and Effect a Throwback to the Primitive, He Says." *Kansas City Star*, 29 December 1921.

"Shall Kansas City Go Forward?" *Kansas City Star*, 16 November 1921.

"Shimme Caused Her Fall." *Kansas City Star*, 5 September 1921.

Shultz, Herb. "The Dancing World of Coon-Sanders." *Saturday Review*, 14 May 1966, pp. 57, 78.

"16,000 Beer Flats in Chicago Grab Customers from Cafes." *Variety*, 28 March 1928, pp. 1, 57.

"69 Mags and 67 Plays Labeled Fit for Censoring by Wilson." *Variety*, 23 February 1927, p. 37.

"Slower Tempos Mark New Era in Dance Music." *Milwaukee* (Wisc.) *Journal*, 27 September 1931, p. 9 [sports sec.].

"Small Bands in East Face Summer Panic." *Variety*, 18 February 1931, p. 69.

"Society's 1st Cut-In Violation Charges Are against Robbins, Turk, Ahlert." *Variety*, 3 November 1931, p. 59.

"Solos by Air Tonight." *Kansas City Star*, 17 March 1922, p. 2.

"Some of the Methods of Dancing the Welfare Board Frowns On." *Kansas City Star*, 4 October 1923, p. 3.

"Song Sold for a 'Song.'" *Kansas City Star*, 23 September 1922, p. 18.

"Special Radio License Sets Precedent for Hotel Band." *Variety*, 19 November 1924, p. 32.

"The Stage and Stage People." *Kansas City Star*, 2 July 1922, p. 6D.

"The Star's New Radio Set." *Kansas City Star*, 7 May 1922.

"Start War on Sissyism." *Kansas City Star*, 16 February 1922.

"Stein Turns Offers." *Variety*, 15 July 1925, p. 37.

"Stein's Summer Bookings." *Variety*, 9 March 1927, p. 45.

Steward, Anne. "Cooney [sic] and Joe Hard Workers." *Radio Digest,* April 1930, pp. 24, 106.

"Stoppage of Remote Control Goes into Effect in Chicago." *Variety*, 22 February 1928, p. 53.

"A Street Tests Drivers." *Kansas City Star*, 19 October 1922.

"The Streets Ran Booze." *Kansas City Star*, 23 February 1922.

"Suburban Gardens (New Orleans)." *Variety*, 22 September 1931, p. 61.

"Sue for Dance Hall Permit." *Kansas City Star*, 8 February 1922.

"The Symphony by Radio." *Kansas City Star*, 20 February 1922, p. 1.

"Ted Lewis into Nighthawks." *Kansas City Star*, 30 January 1923, p. 11.

"Tests for Loud Speaker." *Kansas City Star*, 31 December 1922, p. 9A.

"Texas Guinan is Getting $1,000 and Worth It." *Variety*, 13 August 1924, p. 37.

"Them Were Real Ducks." *Kansas City Star*, 15 April 1922, p. 13A.

"There Is Jazz — and Jazz." *Kansas City Star*, 15 March 1922, p. 1.

"They Took the Cake." *Kansas City Star*, 28 June 1922, p. 10.

"They're All Radio 'Fans.'" *Kansas City Star*, 17 January 1922, p. 1.

"3 Chicago Stations Stop All Dance Music." *Variety*, 7 March 1927, p. 56.

"Throwing Bouquets," MCA ad giving several clients and their testimonials. *Variety*, 16 June 1926, p. 56.

"Touring Bands Next Season." *Variety*, 14 July 1931, p. 49.

"Tune in at 360 Tonight." *Kansas City Star*, 4 March 1922.

"Varied Music to 'Nighthawk.'" *Kansas City Star*, 28 February 1923, p. 2.

"Victor's New Process." *Variety*, 13 May 1925, p. 41.

"'The Voice of the South' and the 'Chief' Meet." *Kansas City Star*, 11 February 1923, p. 17A.

Wald, Jerry. "Not on the Air." *Jazz Notes*, Feb. and Mar. 1961, pp. 8–10.

"A War on Jazz Music." *Kansas City Star*, 8 January 1922, p. 8A.

"Wayburn Claims His 'Charleston' First." *Variety*, 9 December 1925, p. 4.

"WDAF Entertains Canal Zone." *Kansas City Star*, 8 March 1923, p. 1.

"WDAF in Latin America." *Kansas City Star*, 31 January 1923, p. 2.

"WDAF in the Odd Places." *Kansas City Star*, 2 February 1923, p. 1.

"WDAF One Year Old." *Kansas City Star*, 3 June 1923, p. 2B.

"W.D.A.F. Tests to Start." *Kansas City Star*, 28 May 1922.

"WDAF, the Star's Set Arriving." *Kansas City Star*, 24 May 1922, p. 6.

"WDAF to Open Monday." *Kansas City Star*, 31 May 1922, p. 19.

"WDAF Tomorrow Night." *Kansas City Star*, 4 June 1922, p. 1.

"WDAF Will Talk Tonight." *Kansas City Star*, 5 June 1922, p. 1.

"WDAF's Radio Waves Penetrate the Antipodes." *Kansas City Star*, 15 February 1923, p. 1.

Webb, Elida. "'Charleston' Accidental Discovery." *Variety*, 9 December 1925, p. 4.

"A Week of Features." *Kansas City Star,* 4 February 1923, p. 8A.

"What Others Think of WDAF." *Kansas City Star*, 10 December 1922, p. 2B.

"WHB in 12-Hour Program." *Kansas City Star*, 31 January 1923, p. 2.

"Whisky Now $155 a Case." *Kansas City Star*, 25 January 1922, p. 4.

"White Collar Idle Turning to Taxis, Bring New Type Drivers to B'way." *Variety*, 26 January 1932, p. 1.

"'Who Owns the Air?' Asks WGES in Page Ads in Chicago." *Variety*, 8 December 1926, p. 52.

"Will Talk to Whole Nation." *Kansas City Star*, 15 April 1922.

"Winchell with Lucky Strike Hour and Only Ad Double on Radio." *Variety*, 3 November 1931, p. 57.

"Wireless from the Star." *Kansas City Star*, 15 February 1922, p. 1.

"WKY Is to Present Coon Saunder's [sic] Fun." Oklahoma City *Daily Oklahoman*, 22 June 1923.

"A Woman Driver Ahead." *Kansas City Star*, 1 February 1920.

"Worst Floods Since 1904 Raging." Oklahoma City *Daily Oklahoman*, 10 June 1923.

"You Mustn't Say That." *Variety*, 17 November 1931, p. 31.

Books, Recordings, and Other Sources

Allen, Fred. *Fred Allen Looks at Life; Comedy Highlights from His Greatest Radio Shows.* Bagdad phonograph recording album S-6969. N.p.: Bagdad Records, n.d. (c1971).

_____. *Much Ado about Me.* Boston; Toronto: Little, Brown and Company, 1956.

Allen, Frederick Lewis. *Only Yesterday: An Informal History of the Nineteen-Twenties.* New York: Harper & Brothers, 1931.

American National Biography, 24 vols. New York: Oxford University Press, 1999.
The ASCAP Biographical Dictionary of Composers, Authors and Publishers. 1966 ed. compiled and edited by Lynn Farnol Group, Inc. New York: The American Society of Composers, Authors and Publishers, 1966.
The Baseball Encyclopedia: The Complete and Definitive Record of Major League Baseball. 9th ed. New York: Macmillan, 1993.
Bierce, Ambrose. *The Collected Writings of Ambrose Bierce*. New York: Citadel Press, 1946.
Bode, Carl. *Mencken*. Carbondale and Edwardsville: Southern Illinois University Press, 1969.
Bohle, Bruce. *The Home Book of American Quotations*. New York: Dodd, Mead & Co., 1967.
Carlton [sic] *Coon–Joe Sanders Original Nighthawk Orchestra*, 3 vols., BR 144, BR 145, BR 146. Brighton, Mich.: Broadway Records, 1987–1989.
Clarke, Donald, ed. *The Penguin Encyclopedia of Popular Music*. New York: Viking Penguin, 1989.
Coon, John Allyn. Several conversations with author 18–20 January 1995, Auburn, Ala., including one taped on 19 January. Also, two tapes made solo for author's use, Prairie Village, Kan., January 1995. Coon also, just before his death, made six tapes solo and left them with Steve and Sherry Drummond, who have very kindly allowed the author to use them.
Coon-Sanders' Original Nighthawk Orchestra, vol. 3, compact disc MB 113. N.p.: The Old Masters, n.d.
Date Book for Season 1927–1928, Joe Sanders' pocket book for gigs and personal notes, issued by The Billboard, Cincinnati, Ohio; box 11, JLSC.
DeLong, Thomas A. *Frank Munn: A Biodiscography of the Golden Voice of Radio*. Southport, Conn.: Sasco Associates, 1993.
_____. *The Mighty Music Box: The Golden Age of Musical Radio*. Los Angeles: Amber Crest Books, 1980.
_____. *Pops: Paul Whiteman, King of Jazz*. Piscataway, N. J.: New Century Publishers, 1983.
_____. *Radio Stars: An Illustrated Biographical Dictionary of 953 Performers, 1920 through 1960*. Jefferson, N.C.: McFarland, 1996.
Dunning, John. *On the Air: The Encyclopedia of Old-Time Radio*. New York: Oxford University Press, 1998.
Ellmann, Richard. *Oscar Wilde*. New York: Vintage Books, 1988.
Encyclopaedia Britannica, 1965 ed. S.v. "Chicago," by Bessie Louise Pierce.

_____, 1965 ed. S.v. "Motion Pictures," by Arthur Knight.
Fisher, James. "Guinan, Texas," *American National Biography*. 24 vols. New York: Oxford University Press, 1999, IX: 712–713.
Friedel, Meryl. "Too Many Friends for Joe," unpaged extract , box 15, folder 2, JLSC.
Goldman, Eric F. *Rendezvous with Destiny: A History of Modern American Reform*. New York: Vintage Books, 1956.
Goldsmith, Alfred N., and Austin C. Lescarboura. *This Thing Called Broadcasting: A Simple Tale of an Idea, an Experiment, a Mighty Industry, a Daily Habit, and a Basic Influence in Our Modern Civilization*. New York: Henry Holt, 1930.
Gordon, Lois, and Alan Gordon. *American Chronicle: Six Decades in American Life, 1920–1980*. New York: Atheneum, 1987.
Gottlieb, Robert, and Robert Kimball. *Reading Lyrics*. New York: Pantheon Books, 2000.
Grandorge, Richard (comp.). *Jazz Records, A–Z, 1897–1931, Index*. Hatch End, Middlesex, England: the Compiler, 1963. Index to Brian Rust's two volumes, *Jazz records, A–Z, 1897–1931* and *Jazz Records A–Z, 1932–1942*.
Hark! The Years!: A Recorded Scrapbook of Famous Personalities and Historical Events from Two Centuries! Phonograph recording S 282, narrated by Fredric March. N.p.: Capitol Records, n.d. [1954?].
Hobson, Fred C. *Mencken: A Life*. New York: Random House, 1994.
I Can Hear It Now: 1919–1949, Columbia Masterworks recording ML 4261, narrated by Edward R. Murrow. New York: Columbia Records, 196?. [vol. 1] ML 4095 (1933–1945), [vol. 2] ML 4261 (1945–1949), and [vol. 3] ML 4340 (1919–1932); boxed set orginally issued as separate discs.
Keats, John. *You Might as Well Live; The Life and Times of Dorothy Parker*. New York: Simon and Schuster, 1970.
Kramer, Karl. Chapters 4 and 8 of unpublished history of the Music Corporation of America, HRC.
Larkin, Colin, ed. *The Guinness Encyclopedia of Popular Music*, 4 volumes. Enfield, Middlesex, England: Guinness Publishing, 1992.
Laurie, Joe, Jr. *Vaudeville: From the Honky-tonks to the Palace*. New York: Henry Holt, 1953.
Lombardo, Guy. *Auld Acquaintance*. Garden City, N.Y.: Doubleday, 1975.
McDougal, Dennis. *The Last Mogul: Lew Wasserman, MCA, and the Hidden History of Hollywood*. N.p.: Da Capo Press, 2001.
Mencken, Henry L. *H. L. Mencken, the American Scene: A Reader*. Ed. by Huntington Cairns. New York: Knopf, 1965.

_____. *A Mencken Chrestomathy*. New York: Alfred A. Knopf, 1949.

_____. *On Politics: A Carnival of Buncombe*. Ed. by Malcolm Moos. Baltimore: The Johns Hopkins University Press, 1996.

_____. *Thirty-five Years of Newspaper Work: A Memoir by H. L. Mencken*. Ed. by Fred Hobson, Vincent Fitzpatrick, and Bradford Jacobs. Baltimore; London: Johns Hopkins University Press, 1994.

Mizener, Arthur. *The Far Side of Paradise: A Biography of F. Scott Fitzgerald*. Boston: Houghton Mifflin, 1965.

Mordden, Ethan. *That Jazz!: An Ideosyncratic Social History of the American Twenties*. New York: Putnam's, 1978.

Music of the 1920s and 1930s, phonograph record 734712. N.p.: American Heritage, n.d.

Nash, Jay Robert. *Almanac of World Crime*. New York: Bonanza Books, 1981.

The Original Coon-Sanders Nighthawk Orchestra, 1927–1932, vol. 2., phonograph record TOM-33. N.p.: The Old Masters, n.d.

Originals/Musical Comedy/1909–1935, phonograph record LPV-560. New York: RCA, 1968.

Paper, Lewis J. *Empire: William S. Paley and the Making of CBS*. New York: St. Martin's Press, 1987.

Pearson, Hesketh. *Oscar Wilde: His Life and Wit*. New York: Harper & Brothers, 1946.

Porter, David L. (ed.). *Biographical Dictionary of American Sports: Football*. New York: Greenwood Press, 1987.

"Radio's Aces," the Coon-Sanders Nighthawks, phonograph record LPV-511, "Vintage Series." N.p.: Radio Corporation of America, 1965.

Rettberg, Harvey Clark. Conversation, part of it taped, with author, Pickens, S. C., 19 November 1993, as well as on other occasions, once in person and several by telephone.

Rust, Brian A. L. *The American Dance Band Discography, 1917–1942*, 2 vols. New Rochelle, N.Y.: Arlington House, 1975.

_____. *Jazz Records, 1897–1931*. 2 ed. Hatch End, Middlesex, England: Brian Rust, 1962.

_____. *Jazz Records, 1932–1942*. N.p.: n.p., n.d.

Sanders, Joseph LaCeil. "Brainstorm." "An erratic blues." Chicago: Forster Music Publisher, 1927. Music score "[a]rranged and recorded by the composer." Xerox copy in author's possession.

_____. "Join Coon-Sanders and See America," scrapbook A, box 6.1, folder 1, JLSC.

_____. Taped interview by Harvey C. Rettberg, 17 July 1961, Kansas City, Mo.

Sanders, Madeline Esther Baldwin. Manuscript journal during part of year 1931, JLSC.

Schiedt, Duncan P. *The Jazz State of Indiana*. Pittsboro, Ind.: Duncan P. Schiedt, 1977.

Schroeder, Dan. "Coon-Sanders Kansas City Nighthawks," typescript in HRC.

Shapiro, Nat (ed.). *Popular Music: An Annotated Index of American Popular Songs*, vol. 4: *1930–1939*. New York: Adrian Press, 1968.

Sifakis, Carl. *The Encyclopedia of American Crime*. New York: Smithmark, 1992.

Simon, George T. *The Big Bands*. New York: Macmillan, 1967.

Skretvedt, Randy. Liner notes to accompany *Coon-Sanders Original Nighthawk Orchestra*, vol. 3, compact disc MB 113. N.p.: The Old Masters, n.d.

Slide, Anthony. *The Vaudevillians: A Dictionary of Vaudeville Performers*. Westport, Conn.: Arlington House, 1981.

Smith, Gene. *When the Cheering Stopped: The Last Years of Woodrow Wilson*. New York: William Morrow, 1964.

Spaeth, Sigmund. *A History of Popular Music in America*. New York: Random House, 1948.

Stevenson, Elizabeth. *Babbits and Bohemians: The American 1920s*. New York: Macmillan Company, 1967.

Sudhalter, Richard M., and Philip R. Evans. *Bix, Man & Legend*. New Rochelle, N.Y.: Arlington House, 1974.

Sullivan, Mark. *Our Times, 1900–1925*. 6 volumes. Vol. 1: *The Turn of the Century*; Vol. 2: *America Finding Herself*; Vol. 3: *Pre-War America*; Vol. 4: *The War Begins, 1909–1914*; Vol. 5: *Over Here, 1914–1918*; Vol. 6: *The Twenties*. New York: Charles Scribner's, 1927–1935.

They Stopped the Show! Phonograph recording 2290. N.p.: Audio Rarities, n.d. [1957?].

Tormé, Mel. *It Wasn't All Velvet*. [New York]: Viking Penguin, 1988.

Variety Obituaries, 1905–1992. (14 volumes) New York, London: Garland Publishing, Inc., 1988–1994.

The Voices of the 20th Century, phonograph record CRL 57308, produced by Bud Greenspan, narrated by Henry Fonda. New York: Coral Records, n.d. (1960s).

Voss Diary 1926, Joe Sanders' pocket datebook for gigs and personal notes, box 11, JLSC.

White, T. H. *The Age of Scandal: An Excursion through a Minor Period*. New York: G. P. Putnam's Sons, 1950.

Wonderful Nonsense: Fun Songs of the Roaring Twenties, compact disc TT503 CD. Los Angeles: Take Two Records, 1999.

Ziegfeld Follies, phonograph record VM 107. New York: Veritas Records, 1967.

Index

*Numbers in **bold** refer to photographs.*

Aaronson's (Irving) Commanders 153, 178
Abercrombie and Fitch, Chicago 255
The Accelerator, Auburn Auto Co. 244
Actors Equity Association 48
Acuff, Roy 325
Adams, Cory 127, **132**, **138**
Adamson, Nell 76–78
Adkins, Harry 42
Adrian, Mo. 326
Adrian (Arch) Orchestra 331
Advertisements in Kansas City newspapers 30–32
Aeolian Hall, New York, N.Y. 55
"After Every Party" (song) 109
"After You've Gone" (C-S record) 228
"Aggravatin' Papa" (song) 109
Ahlert, Fred E. 268
Aines Dairy Baseball Team, Kansas City, Mo. 63
"Ain't You, Baby?" (C-S record) 228
Akron, Ohio 151
Akst, Harry 35
Alabama Polytechnic Institute *see* Auburn University
Alamo Cafe, Chicago 127
Alaska 108
Albion, Mich. 173
"The Alcoholic Blues" (song) 35
Alden, Mary 80
Aldridge, Vic 198–199
Alhambra Theater, Milwaukee, Wisc. 132

All Star Dance Orchestra proposed 291
Allen, Fred 125
Allen, Ida B. 108–109
Allen Theater, Cleveland, Ohio 177
Allen's Red Tame Cherry (beverage) 6
"Alone at Last" (C-S record) 155
"Alone in the Rain" (C-S record) 228
Altoona, Pa. 200
American Federation of Musicians 160, 264
American Foundation for the Blind 331
American Institute of Homeopathy 108
American Legion 1921 convention 45, 68
American Quartette 13
American Society of Composers, Authors and Publishers (ASCAP) 137–138, 241, 268, 269
American Society of Newspaper Editors 114
Amos 'n' Andy (radio serial) 9, 232, 240
Amsterdam, Morey 325
"And Especially You" (C-S record) 227
Anderson, Claude F. (Pop Estep's son-in-law) 326
Anderson, Ind. 135, 148, 157, 166
Andre, Pierre 222

Ann Arbor, Mich. 171
Antelope, Cal. 152
Appleton, Wisc. 171
"April Showers" (song) 89
Ararat Temple, Kansas City, Mo. 41
Arbuckle, Roscoe "Fatty" 70, 80
Arcadia Peacock Orchestra, St. Louis 330
Arctic (ship) 95
Arctic Dairy products 31
Arkansas Theater, Little Rock 257
Arlen, Michael 190
Arms, Charles S. 291
Armstrong, Louis 261, 262
Arnaud's Restaurant, New Orleans 263
Arnheim, Gus 275–278
Arnold, Dr. C. A. 43
Around the Clock with the Debutantes (musical program) 18
Arrow Collars 30
Artz, Charles 94
Ash, Paul 238
Asheville, N.C. 291
Ashland Cinema, Kansas City, Mo. 72–73
Association for Research in Ophthalmology 331
Association Park, Kansas City, Mo. 62
Astaire, Adele and Fred 269
Athaneum, Kansas City, Mo. 30, 51
Athletic Park Pavilion, Richmond, Ind. 170, 174

353

Atlanta, Ga. 33, 103, 139, 174–175
Atlanta [Ga.] *Journal* 98, 174–175
Atlantic City, N.J. 145–146, 150, 151, 153–156, 157, 158, 253, 272
Auburn, Ala. 2
Auburn Automobile Co. 157, 208, 243–247, 256, 265, 279
Auburn-Cord distributor, Denver, Colo. 253–254
Auburn, Ind. 243–246, 256
Auburn University 233
"Aunt Hagar's Children's Blues" (song) 75
Aurora, Ill. 135, 196, 202
Aurora, Ill. *Daily Beacon* 196, 202
Automobile Club, Kansas City, Mo. 97
Autry, Gene 326
"Autumn 1923" (JLS song) 112
Avon Comedy Four (quartet) 13

Babbitt, Harry 293
"Baby Blue Eyes" (song) 101
"Baby Face" (song) 153
Baer, Abel 32
Bailhe (Gaston) and the Strand Orchestra 197
Baillie Island, Arctic Ocean 95
Bainbridge, Mary 13
Baker, Belle 266
Baker, Josephine 152
Bakersfield, Calif. 294, 330
Baldwin, Herbert 42, 76–78
Baldwin, Madeline Esther *see* Sanders, Madeline Esther
Baldwin pianos 13
Baltimore (Md.) *Evening Sun* 25
Baltimore Hotel, Kansas City, Mo. 38, 39, 42, 68, 75, 111
The Band Wagon (musical) 269, 280
Bankhead, Tallulah 125
Bara, Theda 47
Barataria, La. 262
Bargy's (Roy) Orchestra 210
Barnes, Pat 221
"Barney Google" (song) 88
Barris, Harry 278
Barrows, Dr. A. F. 92
Barstow, Calif. 94
Basie, William "Count" 43
Batavia, N.Y. 202
Baton Rouge, La. 264
Battle Creek, Mich. 149, 168, 171, 173, 184, 211
Battle Creek, Mich. *Moon-Journal* 211
Baxter's (Phil) Orchestra 207, 209, 223, 327
Bayes, Nora 166
Beardstown, Ill. 93
Beatty, Adm. David (Lord) 45, 68

"Because You Said 'I Love You'" (JLS song and record) 227
Beckham, Tom 71, 111, 112, 113, 324
Beechnut Cigarettes 31
Beethoven, Ludwig van, JLS plays 12
Beiderbecke, Bix 215, 269
Bell, Ben C. and Silpha 94
Bell, James *see* Sell, James
Bell, Paul 42
Bellman, F. W. 232
"Beloved" (JLS song) 153, 188, 224
Belton, Mo. 10–11, 16, 62, 63, 74–75, 330
Benedict, Oliver 42
Benid, Ill. 150
Benitz, Prof. W. L. 149
Benny, Jack 39
Benson, Edgar 121, 123, 164, 196
Bentzell, P. M. 232
Berlin, Irving 18, 35, 55, 57, 153, 176
Bernie's (Ben) Orchestra 142, 145, 212, 227, 237, 238, 253, 268, 286, 288, 296
"The Best Things in Life Are Free" (song) 89
Bestor's (Don) Orchestra 142, 150
Beuder, Bert 75
Bevensee, Lyle 42
Bierce, Ambrose 25
Biese (Paul) Orchestra 124, 142, 145, 147
"Billie" (JLS song) 102
Birge, David (Dewey Birge's son) 3
Birge, Henry Dewey 3, 113, **114**, 117, 118, **122**, **132**, **136**, **138**, 145, 324–325
Birge, Sara (Dewey Birge's wife) **114**
Birger, Charles 130
Birmingham, George 65
Birmingham, Ala. 330
Birmingham (Ala.) *Age-Herald* 50, 91
The Bismarck, Chicago 142
Black, E. R. 42
black bottom (dance) 40, 188–189
"Black Sox" Scandal (baseball) 22
Blackhawk Hotel, Davenport, Iowa 168
Blackhawk Restaurant, Chicago 8, 163–164, 184–190, 204, 210–215, 221, 222, 227–234, 236, 242, 270, 292
Blackouts (revue) 326
Blair, Donald 271
Blake, Eubie 152

Blasco Ibañez, Vicente 29
"Blazin'" (JLS composition and record) 187, 215
Bliss Cafeteria, Kansas City, Mo. 40
Blood and Sand (book) 29
Bloom, Rep. Sol 140–141
Bloomington, Ill. 157, 256
Bloomington, Ind. 233
Bloom's (Ike) Nightclub, Chicago 126
Blue Crescent Entertainers 75
Blue Goose Cafe, Kansas City, Mo. 12–13, 40
Blue Hills Club, Kansas City, Mo. 97
Blue Network (radio) 292
Blue Ridge Inn, Kansas City, Mo. 40
Blue River's contamination, Kansas City, Mo. 79
"Blue Room" (song) 89
Bluehill pimento cheese (ad) 31
Blyth, Ann 293
Boice Voice Shop, Kansas City, Mo. 41
Boice's Novelty Orchestra 41
Boitard, Susanne 24
Bombs in mail (1919) 22
Bond, Ford 274
bones (rhythm instrument) 7
Bonner, Helen 235
Booher's Drug Stores, Kansas City, Mo. 31
Book-Cadillac Hotel, Detroit 285
bootlegging *see* individual mobsters; prohibition
Bordoni, Irene 266
Borge, Victor 293
Borglum, Gutzon 175, 255
Bornzstein, Ben 273
Boston, Mass. 94, 200, 201, 262
Boston Boulevard Bridge, Kansas City, Mo. 97
Boston Red Sox 57
Boswell, Mary 148
Botts, C. D. 85
Boulard, Garry 260
Boyd, W. C. 95
Boyd, William 277
Boyer, J. F. 128
Bradbury, J. W. 94
Bradley, Jack 76–78
"Brainstorm" (JLS instrumental and C-S record) 187, 190
Braniff, Paul 105, 106
Bransohn, Morris 42
Branson, Mo. 111
Braun, Dorothy 153
Bren, Louise 257
Brice, Fannie 39, 278, 279
"Bright Eyes" (C-S recording) 141
Bringing Up Father (comic strip) 32

Index

Britton, Nan 177
Brooklyn, N.Y. 98
Brown, Bobby 137
Brown, Tom 41
Brown Brothers Saxophone Sextette 41
"Brown Eyes" (C-S recording) 141
Brownwood, Texas 94
Bruce, Thomas F. 98–99, 100–101
Brunswick Recording Laboratories, New York 154
Buck, Verne 127
Bucyrus, Ohio 150
Buffalo, N.Y. 119, 178
Buffalo Hart, Ill. 193–194
Builder's Club Minstrel Show, Kansas City, Mo. 13
Bullitt, William Marshall 64
Burgess, H. M. 161
Burgess Dramatic Co. 14, 62
Burlington, Iowa 147
Burning Sands (film) 81
Burress, Corinne 332
Burtnett's (Earl) Orchestra 242
Burton, Mayor Harry B. 33
Bush, Paul 42
Busse's (Henry) Buzzards 155
Butler, Orville 231
Butler, Pa. 202
Buttrick, L. E. 106
Buzzards Bay, Mass. 200, 201
Byerly, W. E. 94

Cadillac, Mich. 171, 172
Cadillac, Mich. *Evening News* 172–173
Cady, Steve 98
Café de la Louisiana, Kansas City, Mo. 40
Cairo, Ill. 134, **137**, 150
Cake-eater Candy (ad) 31
"cake eaters" 27, 28, 29
California Nighthawks 154
Calloway's (Cab) Orchestra 270, 280
Camden, N.J. 154–155, 195
Camel Cigarettes 276
Cameron, Barton 291
Cammack, I. I. 43–44, 52
Camp Bowie, Texas 16, 45, 293
Camp Bowie Jazz Hounds 18, 19–20
Camp Funston, Kansas 20
Camp Travis, Texas 113
Campbell (Johnnie) Society Orchestra 42
Candler, Asa G. 175
Caniff, Milton 212–213, **296**
"Can't Help Lovin' That Man" (song) 89
Canton, Ohio 202
Cantor, Eddie 38–39, 69, 265, 266

Capone, Al 214–215, 217, 220, 228–230
Carmel, Ill. 151
Carney, Don 239
"Carolina in the Morning" (song) 153
Carrollton, Ill. 193
Carrolltown, Pa. 181
Carter's Little Liver Pills (ad) 32
Carthage, Mo. 332
Cascarets (ad) 32
Castle Farm, Cincinnati, Ohio 167
Castoria (ad) 32
Cedar Rapids, Iowa 134, 147, 168, 183, 191, 210, 211
Central Park, New York 283
Centralia, Ill. 129, 131
Centralia, Okla. 9
Chadwick, H. W. 232
Chalis, Beth 154
Chama, N.Mex. 94
Champaign, Ill. 34, 135, 150, 166
Chaplin, Charles 101
Chaplin, Sydney 101
Chapman's (Jack) Chaquette Saxophone Band 42
Chapman's (Jack) Orchestra 196
Chaquette's (Emil) Kansas City Club Orchestra 42, 66, 111
Charles, Ralph 206, **207**
Charleston (dance) 40, 132, 151–153, 188–189
Charleston, S.C. 152
Charleston, W.Va. 206
Charlotte, N.C. 330
Chase, Bill 13
Chase, W. J. 14
Chattanooga, Tenn. 205
Chattanooga News 205
Chattanooga Times 205
Chautauqua Circuit 13, 14, 33–34, 62
Chesterfield Cigarettes (ad) 31
Chestnut, Ill. 193
Chevalier, Maurice 278
Chez Paris, Chicago 127
Chez Pierre, Chicago 227
Chicago, Ill. 22, 29, 37, 52, 53, 74, 94, 95, 103, 108, 113, 116–119, 120, 122, 124, 135–139, 153, 159, 160–164, 168, 185, 188, 189, 196, 202, 203, 204, 206, 210–211, 213–214, 217, 219, 220, 225–230, 236–238, 241, 247–248, 249, 250, 253, 257, 261, 265, 266, 269, 270, 271, 275, 277, 278, 282, 284–289, 293
Chicago American 287
Chicago, Burlington & Quincy Railroad 168–169
Chicago Coliseum 153
Chicago Cubs 241

Chicago Daily News 237, 287
Chicago Evening American 137
Chicago *Herald-Examiner* 153
Chicago Federation of Musicians 160, 214
Chicago night life 126, 135–136
Chicago Tribune 137, 214, 217, 224
Chicago's Hotel Stevens 196
Chicago's South Shore Country Club 196
"chicken dinner farms," Kansas City, Mo. 38
"Chili Blues" (record) 203
Chillicothe, Ohio 167
Chillicothe, Ohio, *Scioto Gazette* 168
"A Chinese Laundry" (skit) 101
"Chiquita Bill" 100
Chocolate Dandies (show) 152
Christian Science Church *see* Church of Christ Scientist
Christmas, F. M. 94
Church of Christ Scientist (and Coon family) 7, 201, 288
Churchill, Winston Leonard Spencer 115
Cicero, Ind. 9
cigarette ads 31
Cincinnati, Ohio 140, 148, 150, 151, 167, 197–200, 202, 280
Cincinnati *Enquirer* 198
Cincinnati Post 103–104
Cincinnati Reds (baseball team) 62
Cincinnati *Times-Star* 200
Cinderella Ballroom, New York 138
Citro's Cafe, Chicago 127
Claney, Howard 276–277
Clark, A. G. 73–74
Clark, Bobby 273
Clark, Dorothy 152
Clark, Frank Haben 137
Clark, W. A. 94
Clarke, Phil, Jr. 291
Cleveland, Grover 45
Cleveland, Ohio 22, 119, 177–178, 182, 218
Cleveland [Ohio] *News* 177
Cleveland [Ohio] *Plain Dealer* 177
Cleveland [Ohio] *Press* 178
Cline, Claude 178
Cliquot Club Eskimos 162, 197
Clopton, Margaret 235
Clown Cigarettes 31
Club Forest, New Orleans 259, 260–261, 263–264
Club Moritz, New York 61
Cobb, Tyrus Raymond "Ty" 57
Coca-Cola 7
Cocoanut Grove, Los Angeles 276

Cohan, George M. 16
"Cohen Buys a Wireless Set" (phonograph record) 49
"Cohen on the Telephone" (phonograph record) 49
Cohn, Irving 88
Cole, Alice 27
Coliseum Rink, Kansas City, Mo. 45
College Humor (periodical) 182, 194–195
College Inn, Hotel Sherman, Chicago 122, 127, 142, 286, 288
The Collegians 14
"Collegiate" (song) 89
"Collegiate Sam" (song) 162
Collins, J. W. 93
Collins, L. C. 96
Collins, Ted 212
Collins and Harlan (singing duo) 80
Coloma, Mich. 202, 257
Colorado State Penitentiary 53
Columbia, Mo. 191, 192
Columbia, Tenn. 205
Columbia Broadcasting System (CBS) 206, 228, 237–238, 240, 265, 268, 274, 286
Columbia Phonograph Broadcasting System *see* Columbia Broadcasting System
Columbia Phonograph Co. 65, 68
Columbia Pictures 333
Columbo, Russ 262, 266
Columbus, Ohio 135, 150, 166, 176, 256
Confrey, Edward E. "Zez" 55, 176, 232
Congress Hotel, Chicago 126, 127, 132, 135–143, 145, 154, 159–164, 223, 237, 256
Conn Band Instrument Co. (sponsored C-S) 79, 107, 128, 169–170, 191
Connellsville, Pa. 205
Connie's, New York 272, 280
Connor, John 233
Conrad's (Coonie) Orchestra 124
Convention Hall, Kansas City, Mo. 33, 97, 111
Cook, Phil 240
Cook County Hospital, Chicago 121
"cookie-pusher" 28
Coolidge, Calvin 45, 110, 114–115, 118, 139–140
Coon, Carleton Allyn, Jr. 241, 255, 288, 289
Coon, Carleton Allyn, Sr. 2, 66–67, 71–72, 102, 109, 134, 136–138, 144, 146, 162, 164–165, 167, 170–172, 191–192, 199, 208, 210, 219, 221–222, 225–226, 246, 271, 326, 336; advises Paley about CBS 206; alleged American Indian ancestry 9; and *Amos 'n' Andy* 9; and Jean Harlow 270; and Newman Theater 79–103, 112–117; as a drinker 5, 36, 242, 266, 281–282, 286; at Book-Cadillac Hotel, Detroit 285; buys office safe 58; "candidate" for U.S. vice president 285–286; composer 45, 64, 188; concern for "shut-ins" 93; cruise on Lake Michigan 170–171; C-S engagement in Dec. 1927 in Kansas City 207–209; drives to Morton Grove, Ill. 117–120; early bands 7–8; early life 6–7; education and marriage 7; engagement at St. Louis's Hotel Chase and Loew's State Theater 206–207; first broadcast 74–75; *Florsheim Shoe Frolic* 234, 236, 239–240; *Florsheim Sunday Radio "Feeture"* 240–241; forms Shut-In Club on WGN 222; friendship with baseball celebrities 241–242; friendships 8, 123, 142, 203, 212; help with Arctic expedition 95; helps JLS get out of Army 20; helps organize C-S Band 57–58, 63; his pranks 69–70; ill while in New England 200–201; illness and death 286–290; illness and rumor of kidnapping 228–230, 287; in a tornado 193–195; in Atlanta 174–175; in Denver 253–254; in First World War 8; in New Orleans 258–264; in Oklahoma City 1923, 105–106; increasing personal problems 242, 255–256, 266, 281–282; meets JLS and plans band 8, 19; Mel Tormé 230–231; "Mister Galagher and Mister Shean" 86–89; negotiates with James Caesar Petrillo 160; new Cord auto 244, 246; New York's Hotel New Yorker 265–285; 1931 road tour 250–265; on first road tour (1924) 128–135; physical and personal description 5–9; posthumously proposed for All Star Dance Orchestra 291; refuses Stein's offer to invest some of Coon's money 142; return to Chicago 285–286; song "Hi-Diddle-Diddle" 175, 188; start of Nighthawk programs 83–86; takes family to Mount Rushmore and Yellowstone Park 255; tiff with NBC 239–240; views on popular dance music 133–134; Walter Winchell show 275–279; *see also* Coon-Sanders Nighthawks; Coon-Sanders Novelty Orchestra
Coon, Claude (CAC's father) 6
Coon, Corona (CAC's half-sister) 6
Coon, "Dada" (CAC's paternal grandmother) 7
Coon, Eula Jenkins (CAC's wife) 7, 112, 120, **170**, 229–230, 265, 270, 272, 273, 274, 281, 287, 292, 331
Coon, Gertrude (CAC's half-sister) 6
Coon, Henrietta "Nettie" Jacks (CAC's mother) 6
Coon, John Allyn 2–3, 5–8, 36, 42, 69, 82, 112, 123, 142, 155, 159, 160, **174**, 175, 179, **180**, 203, 205, 212–215, 223, 228–229, 241–242, 255–256, 267, 270, 281, 282, 287, 288, 291–292, 325, **326**
Coon (John) Theatrical Agency 325
Coon, Maxine (John A. Coon's wife) 325
Coon, Nancy (CAC's daughter) 7, 8–9, 287, 288
Coon, Virginia "Jennie" (CAC's daughter) 7
Coon-Sanders Nighthawks 102–103, 106–109, 114, 117, 121–122, 128, 130–132, 136, 140–141, 146, 148, 164–165, 167, 169, 174–177, 179–181, 183–184, 191–193, 196–199, 208–210, 216, 218–219, 221–222, 225–226, 245–246, 248, 322–323, 326; and Al Capone 214–215, 228–230; and Mel Tormé 230–231; at Atlantic City, N.J. 151, 153–156; at Book-Cadillac Hotel, Detroit 285; at Congress Hotel's Balloon Room 126, 135–143, 159–164; band catered to college engagements 135; band members insured for half-million dollars 196, 202; band starts at Blackhawk Restaurant 163, 184–190; contracts with MCA and others 143–145, 170, 191, 222; 1925 road tour 143–159; C-S at Blackhawk popular with celebrities 212, 213; C-S crazy antics 223–224; C-S first to play on radio on a schedule? 104; C-S sponsorship by several companies 79, 107, 128, 166, 169, 187–188, 211, 225, 234, 236, 240–241; C-S tiff with

NBC; encounter with a tornado 193–195; engagement at St. Louis's Hotel Chase and Loew's State Theater 206–207; engagement in Dec. 1927 in Kansas City 207–209; excursion on Lake Michigan 170–171; fifth and last season (1930–1931) at Blackhawk 236–242; first anniversary on WDAF 113; first broadcast from Plantation Grill 84; first real road tour (1924) 127–135; *Florsheim Shoe Frolic* 234, 236, 239–240; formation of Music Corporation of America 122–124; fourth season (1929–1930) at Blackhawk 227–234; Griffiths' Christmas party **216**, 236; in Atlanta, Ga. 174–175; in Cincinnati 197–200; in Cleveland, Ohio 177–178; in Denver 253–254; in Fort Wayne, Ind. 197; in MCA-NBC wrangle 237–238; in Milwaukee 169; in New England 200–202; in New Orleans 260–264; in Omaha, Nebr. 183, 191–192; JLS composes "College Medley" 187, 188; JLS composes theme song 85–86; Joe and Coonie's singing 101, 211; mock Nighthawk broadcast 101; "My Paradise" the theme song of C-S 268; New York's Hotel New Yorker 265–285; Newman Theater topical skits 82, 101, 102, **103**; Nighthawk logo adopted 85, **86**; Nighthawk-Lombardo competition 217–221; 1923 trip to Oklahoma City 104–111; 1926 road tour 163–185; 1927 road tour 190–210; 1931 road tour 250–265; Notre Dame 1925 Senior Ball 149–150; offer from New York's Palace Theater refused 138–139; on *Maytag Frolics* 231–232; origin of name "Nighthawks" 84; personnel changes 157–158; personnel disharmony 110–111; phonograph records made 116, 141, 155–156, 162, 190, 195, 203, 209, 215, 217; "Pop" Estep leaves band 223–224; program's great and widespread popularity 85–86, 90–104; *Radio Digest* picks C-S as first band in popularity 162; "Radio's Aces" 103; records at Victor in Camden 155–156, 195; relations with Auburn Auto Co. 243–247; return to Chicago 285–286; rivalry with Lombardo's orchestra 188; Roth cancels C-S in fall 1927 at Blackhawk 204–205; Second Fall Fashion Pageant 111–112; second season at Congress Hotel 161–164; spend December 1931 on the road 236–237; starts at Congress Hotel 135–138; summer of 1929 at The Dells 226–227; third season (1928–1929) at Blackhawk 221–225; "tie-in" charge against C-S 268; to Lincoln Tavern 117–120; typical ticket for C-S program **158**; Walter Winchell show 275–279; *see also* individual band members

Coon-Sanders Novelty Orchestra (pre– Nighthawks) 22, 34, 36, 37, 38, 39, 41, 42, 49; a "singing" orchestra 63, 81; and Al Jolson 66–68; and politics 68; approached by WDAF 83–84; band "kidnapped" in Oklahoma 58–61; band and booking agency formed 57–58; charitable events 65; in KC theaters 63, 66–68, 79–82; 1921 American Legion convention 68; on radio 74–76, 79, 81; playing and singing described 68–69; records for Columbia 65; skits at Newman Theater 79–103, 112–117; sometimes called Regal Novelty Orchestra 65; to Muehlebach Hotel's Trianon Cafe (or Room) 63–64

Cooper, Harry 43
Cooperative Club of Manhattan, Kans. 72
Copping, Harry 94
Corbin, "Uncle Dan" 113
Cord, Errett Lobban 246
Cornell University 233
Cornland, Ill. 193–194
Correll, Charles *see* Amos 'n' Andy
Coshocton, Ohio 150
Costa, A. F. 91–92
Cotton Club, New York 273, 280, 284
Coughlin, Rev. Charles E. 327
Country Club, Mission Hills, Kansas City, Mo. 97
The County Fair (film) 66
Coward, Noel 151
Crabtree, Charlie 193
Craddocks (Kansas City baseball team) 62
Craig Co. Okla. 9
Crawford, Helen and Jesse 266, 273, 279, 284
Crawford, Jack 142

Crawford, Joan 112
Crawford's (Jack) Slaves of Music 176
"Crazy Rhythm" (song) 52
Crazy to Marry (film) 80
Crême Elcaya (ad) 31
Crillon Cafe, Chicago 127
criminal elements 124, 129–131
Criterion Theater, Oklahoma City 106, 107, 108, 110
Croft, Sterling 42
Crooks, Noah 36
Crosby, Bing 213, 215, 262, 266, 268, 278
Crosby, Everett 213, 266
Crosley Radio Corp. 140
Crowley, Jim 135, 149
Crumit, Frank 35
"Cryin' for the Carolines" (song) 257
Crystal Beach, Ont. 178
Crystal Gardens, Vermilion, Ohio 178
"Cuban Love Song" (song) 278
Culp (Louis) and the Continental Concert Orchestra 124
Cummins, Bernie 127
Cunningham, Frank 37
Curry, George P. 93
Curth, Frederick J. 39, 63
"cut-ins" 243
"Cutie" (song) 75

Dallas, Texas 158
Damrosch, Walter 52, 56
"Dance and Grow Thin" (song) 27
dancing 40–41, 151–153, 188–189, 190
Daniels, Bebe 80
Daniels, Glenn 42
Dansford's (Danny) Orchestra 170
"Darby Hicks" (fictitious personage of C-S) 69–70, 232
"The Darktown Strutters' Ball" (song and C-S record) 228, 257
Darrow, Clarence 119, 151
Davenport, Iowa 62, 103, 145, 147, 168, 192, 234
Davenport, Iowa, *Daily Times* 145
Davis, Benny 153, 156, 266, 272
Davis, Bette 330
Davis, George 178
Davis, John W. 118
Davis (Leo R.) Orchestra 42, 76, 81, 328
Davis (Meyer) Orchestra 125–126, 140
Dayton, Ohio 157, 167, 256
Dayton, Tenn. 151, 156
Death Valley, Calif. 94

Index

Deauville Dance Hall, Chicago 127
Debs, Eugene V. 47
"The Debutante Waltz" early JLS composition 13
Decatur, Ill. 129, 131, 157, 257
"Deep Elm" (song) 155
"Deep Henderson" (C-S record) 163
Deep River Orchestra 42
De Feo, John 42
De Forest, Lee 154
Delander, Lois 202
Delco-Frigidaire National Convention 167
The Dells, Morton Grove, Ill. 127, 142, **215–219**, 224, 226–228, 234, 236, 339
De Long, Thomas A. 212
De Luca, Giuseppe 199
De Mille, Cecil B. 47
Deming Hotel, Terre Haute, Ind. 170
Democratic Party 24, 30
Dempsey, Jack 24, 109, 112
Denby, Edwin N. 118
Denison, Iowa 184
Denison [Iowa] Bulletin 184
Denni, Mr. and Mrs. Lucien 13
Denny's (Harry) Collegians 149
Denocenzo, Tony 75
Densmore Hotel, Kansas City, Mo., JLS in recital at 13
Denver, Colo. 253–254, 331
Denvir, Robert 234
De Palma, Ralph 150
De Paulo, Peter 150
The Depression 236, 236, 238, 280–281
"Desert Jazz" (C-S skit) 81
"Desires" (song) 108
Des Moines, Iowa 147, 152, 210
De Soto Hotel, Galena, Ill. 168
Desser, Paul 42
Detroit, Mich. 103, 148–149, 168, 211, 284, 285
Detroit Convention Hall 285
Detroit Free Press 285
Detroit News 74
Deveney's Orchestra 41, 42
Dever, William E. 119
Diamond, Jack 273
Diaz, Gen. Armando Vittorio 68
Dix (ship) 95–96
Dixieland Jazz Band 124
Dodson, Mo. 47
Doering, W. F. "Whitey" 130–131
Doheny, Edward L. 61, 118
Donaldson, Walter 153
Donnally, Ruth 137
Donovan, Walter 267
"Don't Be a Fool, You Fool" (C-S record) 162
Doric Theater, Kansas City, Mo. 45, 66–67, 79

Dornberger, Charles 142
D'Orsay, Fifi 278
Dorsey, Jimmy 215
"Down Where the Sun Goes Down" (C-S record) 215
Downey, Morton 266
Downing, A. R. (Rex's grandfather) 325
Downing, Maybelle (Mrs. Rex) 273, 279
Downing, Rex 2, 158–159, 163, **165**, **167**, **174**, 187, **193**, 198, **199**, 203, 204, 215, 217, **221**, **222**, **225**, 229, 235, 244–245, 246–247, **248**, 258, 273, 276, 278, 279, 288, 291, 294, **322**, 325–**326**
"Dreaming of Tomorrow" (C-S record) 156
Drummond, Dorothy 325
Drummond, Sherry and Steve 3
Dubuque, Iowa 96, 132, 168–169, 184, **322**
Duckett, Robert M. 93
Duke Yellman's Dance Orchestra 39
Dunn, James 277
Durham, E. R. 43
Durracott, W. H. 91
"Dusky Stevedore" (C-S record) 217
Dutton, Gilbert 42, 79
Dvořák, Antonin, JLS plays 12

East Dubuque, Ill. 168, **322**
East Is East (film) 101
East Liverpool, Ohio 202
Easterner (ship) 95
Eaton, Ohio 327
Ed, Carl 224
Edelweiss Winter Garden, Chicago 14
Edgar and His Champion Colored Orchestra 124
Edgewater Beach, Chicago 127, 142, 212, 225, 241
Edgewater Night Club, Monroe, La. 258
Edgewood, "chicken dinner farm," Kansas City, Mo. 38
Edison, Thomas Alva 154, 155
Edom, Rosemary 235
Edwards, Wilbur "Eddie" 267
Egyptian Serenaders 134, 142, 176
Ehlers, Marie 52
Ehrnmann, Walter 13, 14
Eichstaedt, Dr. John J. 287
Eighteenth Amendment 57
El Capitan Theater, Hollywood, Calif. 326
El Dorado, Ark. 158
El Rigoletto (restaurant) Kansas City, Mo. 40
"Electric Girl" (song) 109

Electric Park, Kansas City, Mo. 40, 58, 76
Electric Theater, Kansas City, Kans. 7, 14
Electric Theater, Kansas City, Mo. 79
Elgin, Ill. 205, 210
Elkhart, Ind. 127–128
Ellington's (Duke) Orchestra 296
Elms Hotel Orchestra 76
Elon College, N.C. 204
"Embers" (JLS instrumental) 240, 283
Emory University 175
Emporia, Kans. 79
Enid, Okla. 98
Epstein, Al 217
Erdman, Elmer 42
Erie, Pa. 253
Erie Cafe, Chicago 127
Estep, Floyd Eugene 2, 42, 58, 59, 65, 105, 158, 159, 160, **161**, **165**, **167**, **174**, **199**, 203, **221**, **222**, 224, **225**, 244, **248**, 288, 294, **322**, 326, 328
Estep, Frank M. "Pop" 42, 71, 79, 101, **102**, 105, 106, **109**, 111, 112, 117, 118, **122**, 128, **130**, **132**, 135, **138**, **146**, 154, 156, 159, 164–165, **167**, **174**, 175–176, **179**, **181**, **199**, 201, 203, 214, 223–224, **322**, **323**, 325, **326**–327, **328**
Estep, Lulu M. (Pop's wife) 327, **328**
Estep, Mildred Alline Heinze (Floyd's wife) 326
Etting, Ruth 197
Evanston (Ill.) Hotel 120
Evansville, Ind. 166
"Everybody's Doin' It" (song) 40
"Everybody's Overdoin' It" (song) 40
"Everyone I Know Loves You" (song) 13
"Everything Is Hotsy-Totsy Now" (C-S record) 156
"Everything's Gonna Be All Right" (C-S record) 163
"An Experiment in Modern Music" (concert) 55

Factor, Jake "the Barber" 127, 217
Factor, Jerome 217
Fairbanks, Douglas, Sr. 52
Fall, Albert B. 61
Fall, Shorty 136–137
Fall Fashion Pageant, Kansas City, Mo. 111–112
"Farewell Blues" (song) 108
Farris, Dolores 76–78
"Fate" (song) 98
Fatima Cigarettes 31
Faulkner, Roy H. 157, 203, 243–246, 256–257, 265

Favorite Cigarettes 31
Fay, Larry 61
Faye, Julia 80
Federal Building, Kansas City, Mo. 79
Federal Farm Loan Act (1916) 64
Federal Radio Conference 327
Feist, Leo 163, 188, 224
Feld, Milton M. 112
Fellers, Guy 91
Fenlon, Prof. Paul 149
Fenton, Carl 41
Feri, Prof. B. 41
Fields, Dorothy 266
Files, Ada Belle 45
Finley, Milo 39, 42
Finucane, William A. 43
Fiorito, Ted 127, 237, 241
Firpo, Luis 109, 112
Fisher, Bob 250, 251, 252, 273
Fisher, Eleanor 251, 252, **271**, 273
Fisher, Larry 329
Fitzgerald, F. Scott 22
Fitzgerald, Murray 42
Fitzpatrick, John and Edna 112
Fitzpatrick, Leo J. ("Merry Old Chief") 84–85, 90–91, **92**, 95, 98, 99, 103, 113, 174, 285, 327
Five-Minute Club, Chicago, Ill. 29
Flaker, Doris 332
"Flamin' Mamie" (C-S record) 162, 201
Fleming, Judge Edward J. 68
"The Flippity Flop" (C-S record) 227
Florsheim, Harold 239–240, 241
Florsheim Shoe Co. 225, 240
Florsheim Shoe Frolic 234, 236, 239–240, 242, 248
Florsheim Sunday Radio "Feeture" 240–241, 242, 248
Foch, Marshal Ferdinand 45, 68
Foley, Red 325
Fond du Lac, Wisc. 331
Fond du Lac, Wisc. *Commonwealth Reporter* 331
Fontenelle Hotel, Omaha, Nebr. 183
"For de Lawd's Sake Play a Waltz" (song) 52
Forbstein, Leo F. 39, 63, 80
Forbstein, Louis 38, 42, 78, 111
Forbstein's Royal Orchestra, Kansas City, Mo. 63
Ford, Medora 251
Ford's (Jack) Arcadia Peacock Orchestra 163
Forget-It Club, Kansas City, Mo. 68
Forster Music Publishing 279
Fort Dodge, Iowa 132–134, 210
Fort Dodge, Iowa, *Messenger* 133–134

Fort Scott, Kans. 45
Fort Wayne, Ind. 197, 203
Fort Wayne, Ind. *Journal-Gazette* 203
Fort Worth, Texas 16, 19, 103
Forty Minutes of Music (radio program) 74
Forum Cafeterias, Kansas City, Mo. 40, 112
Fosdick, Marion 13
"Four Horsemen" (Notre Dame) 135, 149
Fourth Liberty Loan 16
Fouts, Benjamin W. 90
Fowler-Jones Coal Co. Kansas City, Mo. 13
Foy, Bryan 86–87
Foy, Eddie 86
Franklin, Pa. 156, 181, 265
Frazier, O. E. 93
Freeman's Funeral Home, Kansas City, Mo. 288
Fremont, Ohio 205, 331
Frey, Fran 89
Frey, Hugo 54
Friar's Inn, Chicago 126, 127, 189
Frick, Henry 201
Friedel, Meryl 292
Friend, Cliff 32
Fritzel's (Mike) Nightclub, Chicago 126
Frolics Cafe, Chicago 127, 227
Fry's (Charlie) Orchestra 151, 154
Fuller, Earl 53
Fuller, Laurence 171–173
Fuller Brush Co. 240
Funk, J. P. 94

Galena, Ill. 168
Galena, Ill. *Daily Gazette* 201, 205
Galena Public Library, Galena, Ill. 168
Gallagher and Shean (comic duo) 73–74, 86–87, 151
Galli-Curci, Amelita 56
Galligan, Sheriff 134
Galveston, Texas 158
Gambier, Ohio 211
Gannon, T. A. 232
Ganz, Rudolph 54
Ganz, William 42
Garber's (Jan) Orchestra 200, 213–214, 237, 238
Garland, Charles 187, 211
Garrett, Ind. 158
Garrett, Lloyd 80
Garrick Inn, Chicago 126
Garvin, William M. 94
Gary, Ind. 225
Gay, Byron 89
Gay, Perry 42
Gayety Theater, Kansas City, Mo. 13, 39, 66, 79

Gayety Theater Building, Kansas City, Mo. 8, 58
Gem City Business College, Quincy, Ill. 112, 113
General Electric 74, 154
General Federation of Women's Clubs (on jazz) 22
General Hospital, Kansas City, Mo. 93
Genevans (orchestra) 127
Gentlemen Prefer Blondes 190
George Institute of Technology (Ga. Tech) 174–175
"Georgia on My Mind" (song) 257
Geraldine Company 275
Geren, Pardue "Duca" 262
Gershwin, George 56
Gigli, Benjamino 199
Gilchrest, Charles J. 95
Gilchrist, William Fuller 326
Gilham, Art "Whispering Pianist" 175, 197
Gilkison, S. V. 101
Gillespie, Marcella 75
Gillis Opera House, Kansas City, Mo. 39
Gin Isle, Minneapolis 147–148
Gingham Inn, Chicago 127
The Girl from Frisco (musical starring JLS) 13
"Give Her a Kiss for Me" (C-S record) 268
Globe Theater, Kansas City, Mo. 39, 98
Gloucester, Mass. 201
Gluck, Alma 56
Godfrey, Arthur 212
Golden Pumpkin, Chicago 142
Goldkette, Jean 232, 269
Goldman, George 207
"Good Morning, Mr. Zip-Zip-Zip" (song) 19
"Goodbye, Broadway, Hello, France" (song) 153
Goodheart, William R. 124, 164 (note) 186, 220, 271, 284, 327
Goodheart's (Billy) and the Illinois Collegians 124
Goodman, Benny 9, 204, 329
Gordon, Jeanne 199
Gordon & Koppel (business) 27
Gosden, Freeman F. *see Amos 'n' Andy*
"Got a Great Big Date with a Little Bitty Girl" (JLS song and record) 224, 227
Grace Hospital, Kansas City, Mo. 16
Gradle, Dr. Harry 121
Grafonola Shop, Kansas City, Mo. 41, 66
Granada Cafe, Chicago 127, 219
Grand Avenue Methodist Temple, Kansas City, Mo. 11

Grand Hotel, Anderson, Ind. 166
Grand Rapids, Mich. 171, 236
Grand Rapids, Nebr. 132
Grand Terrace Cafe, Chicago 213, 229
Grand Theater, Chicago 238
Grand Theater, Kansas City, Mo. 39
Grange Hall, Antelope, Cal. 152
Gray, Harold 212
Gray's (Charles) Campbell Society Orchestra 42, 328
Great White Way Orchestra 89
Green, Abel 125, 141, 147
Green Bay, Wisc. 184, 211
The Green Hat (play) 190
Green Lantern, Anderson, Ind. 166
Green (William R.) Orchestra 76
Greenfield, Mass. 200
Greenlee, Chuck 233
Greensboro, N.C. 204
Greenville, Miss. 93
Greenwich Village, New York City 283
Greenwich Village Follies (revue) 98
Griffith, Bob 233
Griffiths, George W. **216**, 236
"The Grizzly Bear" (song) 52
Grogan, S. A. 94
Grosch, David 11
Guinan, Mary Louise Cecilia "Texas" 61–62
Guthrie, Okla. 106
Guyon's Paradise, Chicago 126
Guy's (Red) Orchestra 258

Hackett, Marty 266
Hahn, Clyde 2, 203–204, 281, 287, 291, 293–294, 325
Haid, Bill 145, **146**, 163, **164**, **165**, **167**, 203, 327
Haid (Bill) and His Thieves of Sleep 327
Haid, Doll 148
Hair Groom (product) 30
Hairgrove, E. L. 43
Hairgrove, F. L. 43
Haley's (D. Ambert) Fairyland Orchestra 42, 58, 65, 105, 113
Hall, "Dick Wick" 99–100
Hall, Roy 94
Hall, Willie 43
Hall-Mills murder case 80
Halliburton, Cliff W. 293
"Hallucinations" (JLS instrumental and record) 187, 209, 217
Hamilton, Paul 217
Hamilton College 233
Hamm, Freddy 18
Hammontree Orchestra 76
Hamp's (Johnny) Orchestra 237, 238

Hancock, John 201
Handler, Al 127
Hanes Clothes (ad) 30
Hanlein, Fritz 42, 101
"Happiness Boys" (radio team) 49, 88
"Happy Days Are Here Again" (song) 276
Hardin, J. W. 42
Harding, T. Swann 265
Harding, Warren G. 24, 25, 72, 97, 108, 110, 177, 200
Hardy, Harold Lewis 193
Hare, Sam 127, 215–217, 226–227
"Harlem Madness" (C-S record) 228
Harlow, Harold E. 42
Harlow, Jean 270, 278
Harmony Boys, Kansas City, Mo. 104
Harms, T. B. 141
Harold Teen (comic strip and radio show) 224
"Harold Teen" (JLS song) 224, 231, 232
Harrington, Bob 201–202, 215, 325
Harris, Frank 42
Harris, Sam 18
Harris, Waldo E. 92
Harrisburg, Ark. 222, 325
Hart, William S. 278
Hartford, Wisc. 257
Hartwitt, Fritz 42
Hastings, Nebr. 325
Hathaway Motor Co. Kansas City, Mo. 46
Hawaii 91, 95
Hawaiian Quintet 63
Hawley, O. F. 93
Hayes, Grace 261, 264
Hayes, Thamon 43
Hayman, Joe 49
Hays, Will H. 199
Heifetz, Jascha 56
Held, John, Jr. 189
Hellinger, Mark 266
Henderson's (Fletcher) Orchestra 250
Hendrix, Clyde 65, **66**, 75
Henrotin Memorial Hospital, Chicago 286–287
Henry Grady Hotel, Atlanta, Ga. 174
Herbert, Victor 45, 56
Herbert Tareyton London Cigarettes 31
"Here Comes My Ball and Chain" (song and C-S record) 225, 257
"Here Comes the Hot Tamale Man" (C-S record) 163
Here Goes the Bride (play) 273
Hermitage Hotel, Knoxville, Tenn. 150

Herrin, Ill. 34, 129–131, 133, 150, 205
Herrin (Ill.) Public Library 129
Herron, Clarence 76–78
Hershey, Pa. 250
Hess, Edwin 175
Hiawatha, Utah 93
"Hi-Diddle-Diddle" (CAC composition) 175, 188
Hibbe, Dr. (CAC's dentist) 286
Hickman, Art 41
"Hicks, Darby" *see* "Darby Hicks"
Higgins, H. W. 93
"High Fever" (JLS composition) 187, 190
"High Up on a Hilltop" (record) 203
Highland Radio Supply, Kansas City, Mo. 100
Highland Rose Garden, Quincy, Ill. 150
Hill, Fred 139
Hill, W. A. 14
Hillcrest Club, Kansas City, Mo. 97
"Hindu Dream Man" (phonograph record) 65
"Hindustan" (song) 279
Hines, Earl "Fatha" 213
Hinton, Joe 206
Hinton, W.Va. 206
Hitchcock, W. L. 94
Hitchler, Owen 18
Hitz, Ralph 274, 280, 284
Hoffman (Earl) Orchestra 127
Hoffman (Mel) Orchestra 42
Hofmann, Josef Casimir 21, 54
Hollywood, Calif. 53, 70, 112, 292
Hollywood Canteen, Los Angeles 330
Hollywood Club, New York 272
Hollywood Gardens, New York 253
Holm, Celeste 293
Holmes, Rev. John Haynes 119
Home Run Cigarettes 31
"Hong Kong Dream Girl" (C-S record) 156
Hoosier Athletic Club, Indianapolis, Ind. 148
Hoover, Herbert Clark 50, 252, 285, 327
Hope, Bob 329
Hoppe, Willie 286
Hopper, De Wolf 14, 153
Hoquiam, Wash. American Legion Post 16, 275
Horowitz, Willie 267
"Horses" (song) 89
"horse's neck" (euphemism) 89
Hosford, J. W. and Roy R. 93
Hotel New Yorker, New York 261, 264, 265, 267–285

Hotel Oliver, South Bend, Ind. 135
Houchin, Matilda and L. E. 93
Houdini, Harry 82
House, Rev. Wade 205–206
"The House Isn't Home Without You" (JLS song) 282
Houston, Texas 158
How Ya Gonna Keep 'Em Down on the Farm?" (song) 57
Howard, Mack 257, 264, 265, 270, 271, 272, 273, 280
Howard, Willie and Eugene 111
Howe, Ed 26
Hoxie, Charles A. 154
Hoyne, Maclay 185
Huckett, Edwin 42
Hudson-Essex Motors 187–188, 211
Hudson Lake, Ind. 256
Huff, Jack 117, 120, 122, 127
Hughes, Charles Evans 64
"Hula Lou" (song) 118
Huntington, Ind. 178
Huntington, W.Va. 3, 167, 173, 206, 294, 325
Huntington, W.Va. *Herald-Dispatch* 167
Hutchison, Ed 154

"I Ain't Got Nobody" (C-S record) 202, 206
"I Can't Realize" (C-S record) 155
"I Don't Want to Get Well" (song) 15, 16
"I Know You're Lying" (song and C-S record) 267
"I Love Me" (song) 108
"I Love Louisa" (song) 277
"I Love My Wife but Oh, You Kid!" (song) 94
"I Love You" (song) 147
"I Married the Bootlegger's Daughter" (song) 35
"I May Be Dreaming" (song) 279
"I Need Lovin'" (C-S record) 190
"I Want to Go Home" (JLS song and C-S record) 267–268, 281
"I'd Rather Be Alone" (C-S record) 163
"I'd Rather Two-Step Than Waltz, Bill" (song) 40
Idle Hour Pavilion, Huntington, Ind. 178
"If He Can Fight Like He Can Love, Good Night, Germany!" (song) 19
"If I Meet the Guy Who Made This Country Dry" (song) 35
"I'll Say She Does" (song) 19
"I'll See You in C-U-B-A" (song) 35
"I'll See You in My Dreams" (song) 153

"I'll See You Later in Slumberland" (song) 279
Illinois, and Ku Klux Klan 21. 34
Illinois Vigilance Association 53
"I'm Always Chasing Rainbows" (song) 57
"I'm Bringing a Red Red Rose" (song) 153
"I'm Gonna Charleston Back to Charleston" (C-S record) 155
The Impossible Mrs. Bellew (film) 101
"Improvisations" (JLS instrumentals) 240
"In Flanders Fields" (poem) 64
"In the Hills of Old Missouri" (JLS song) 282
Independence, Kans. 158
Independence, Mo. 79
"Indian Cradle Song" (C-S record) 215
Indiana, and Ku Klux Klan 21, 34
Indianapolis, Ind. 54, 148, 150, 158, 330
Indianapolis Raceway (1925) 150
influenza epidemic 16, 24
Inge, William 325
"Inhibition" (JLS instrumental) 240, 283
Insomnia Club (C-S radio club) 139, 168, 183
Inspirators (orchestra) 127
"Intangibility" (JLS instrumental) 240, 283
Interstate Cafe, Kansas City, Mo. 40
Iowa, and Ku Klux Klan 34
Iowa City, Iowa **130, 135, 138,** 202
Iron Mountain, Mich. 171
"Is She My Girl Friend?" (C-S record) 209
Isbell, Harold 162
Isis Theater, Kansas City, Mo. 63
Isle of Youth (formerly Isle of Pines) Cuba 92
"It Ain't Gonna Rain No Mo'" (song) 118
"It Had to Be You" (song) 153
It Wasn't All Velvet (book) 230–231
"It Will Never Be Dry Down in Havana" (song) 35

Jack o'Lantern, Kansas City, Mo. 104
Jackson, Bee 152
Jackson, Hal 94
Jackson, Mich. 184
Jackson, Miss. 258, 264
Jackson, Tenn. 151
Jackson Co. Mo. 24
Jackson County Home 65
Jacobs, Ferdy 111, 112, 327–328

Jacobson and Ray (guitar artists) 137
Jacques, Gen. Baron 68
Jaeger, F. E. 94
"Jamaica ginger" 37
Janis, Elsie 52
jargon on streets 28–29
Jarman, John J. "Lop" 288, 328
jazz 22, 40–41, 48, 51–56
Jazz Age 22, 25
"Jazz Must Go" (article) 52
"The Jazzing Fool" (song) 76
Jefferson, Thomas 251
Jefferson Barracks, Mo. CAC stationed at 8
Jenkins, Allan (CAC's brother-in-law) 288
Jenkins, Jack (CAC's brother-in-law) 288
Jenkins, Wayne (CAC's brother-in-law) 288
Jenkins' Sons, J. W. Music Co. 12, 41, 73, 75
Jerome, M. K. 35
Jessel, George 153, 199
"Jig Time" (song) 278, 287
"Jimmy" (song) 75
"Jing-a-Ling-a-Ling" (C-S recording) 141
Johns, Harold 42
Johns' (Brooke) Oklahoma Collegians 178
Johnson, H. 15
Johnson, Henrietta (CAC's mother-in-law) 287
Johnson, Myron 42
Johnson, Dr. Samuel 189
Johnson City, N.Y. 250
Johnsonburg, Pa. 181
Johnston, Bob 233
Johnston, E. J. 253–254
Johnston City, Ill. 130
Johnstown, Pa. 202
Joliet, Ill. 132, 196, 202
Jolson, Al 66–68, 101, 148, 153, 269
Jones, Ada 81
Jones (Billy) and Hare (Ernie) 49, 88
Jones, Dale 3, 294
Jones (Ev) and His Merry Makers 178
Jones, "Hell Roaring" 94
Jones, Josephine 235
Jones, Paul 91
Jones, Robert Tyre "Bobby" 57
Jones's (Isham) Orchestra 41, 79, 127, 139, 253
Joplin, Mo. 111, 158, 332
Jordan, Mont. 94
Jost, Rep. Henry L. 112
The Joy-Casters—Grab a Little Rainbow (C-S radio club) 200
Joyce, Isabell 149

Joyce, Peggy Hopkins 33, 277
Judson, Arthur 206
"June Night" (song) 120
Jung Hotel, New Orleans 260
Jurgens Lotion 278
"Just a Little Love Song" 75

Kaelin (Kaeling?) Eddie 42
Kaffir, Leo 274
Kahn, Art 163
Kahn, Gus 153, 188, 224, 282
Kalamazoo, Mich. 148
Kamman, Bodo 42
Kane, Vincent J. 275
Kaney, Sen **221**, 234, 239
Kankakee, Ill. 129
Kansas City, Kans. 7, 8, 44, 52, 93
Kansas City, Mo. 11–20 (*passim*); autos popular 46–47; band spends Christmas 1931 in 236–237; Brother Roy drives Joe's Cord back home 249; Carleton Coon's funeral 288–290; dance bands 41–43; dancing 40–44, 55; Eula Coon remains in 120, 139, 157, 158, 174, 182–183, 187, 203; Eula Coon returns from New York 281; fads and styles 25–32; gasoline and oil 46; jazz and jazz musicians 22, 36, 38, 41–44, 48, 51–56; music, vaudeville, cinema, and drama 21–22, 38–39, 54; new dial telephones 78; new street lights 97; Nighthawks' engagement Dec. 1927 207–209, 223, 225; 1921 American Legion convention 45, 68; postwar description 21; Prohibition 34–38; racing cars 45–46; radio in 42, 49–51, 71–104; reaction to a changing society 47–48, 70–71; restaurants 39–40; rumor of C. A. Coon's "kidnapping" 228–230; Sanderses at KC briefly in summer 1931, 253, 254–255, 260, 264, 265; traffic problems 69, 81; "uglies" 79; Union Station's popularity 38; wry view of romance and marriage 32–33
Kansas City (Mo.) Athletic Club 62
Kansas City Blues (baseball team) 12, 62, 330
Kansas City (Mo.) Board of Public Welfare 43, 44
Kansas City, Clay County & St. Joseph trolley 47
Kansas City (Mo.) Club 97
Kansas City Florist Club Orchestra 76
Kansas City (Mo.) Grand Opera Company 11
Kansas City (Mo.) Merchants Assoc. 111–112
Kansas City (Mo.) Oratorio Society 11
Kansas City (Mo.) *Post* 74, 75, 208–209
Kansas City (Mo.) Public Library, Special Collections 3, 79
Kansas City [Mo.] *Star* 6, 22, 24, 27–30, 33, 35–36, 37, 38, 41, 42, 44, 45, 48, 49, 50, 52, 53, 55, 63–64, 69, 72–75, 78, 81, 90, 91, 92, 96, 97, 98, 112, 113, 209, 228–230, 287, 288
Kansas City [Mo.] *Star-Times* 79
Kansas City (Mo.) Symphony Association 54
Kansas City (Mo.) Telephone Co. 97
Kansas City (Mo.) Union Station 38, 97, 207–209
Kansas City Veterans Hospital 293
Kansas City White Sox (ball team) 63
Kansas City (Mo.) William R. Nelson Post, American Legion 327
Karberg, Paul F. 257, 293, 326
Karcher's (Frank) Egyptian Serenaders 124
Karzas, Andrew 126
Kassel's (Art) Orchestra 238, 291
Katz, Al 266
Kaufman, H. L. 127, 163
Kaufman, Irving 31, 81
Kay, Lambdin 98, 174–175
Keach, Kelvin 274
"Keep the Home Fires Burning" (song) 22
"Keeping Out of Mischief Now" (song and C-S record) 267
Keet, Joe 267, 272
Keidel, Hal 188
Keith-Albee Circuit 14, 34, 125
Keith Komedy Karnivals 34
Kekoa, R. 95
Kellogg, "Squint Eye" 100
Kelly Stables, Chicago 127
Kemmerer, Wyo. 94
Kemper, James D. 51, 76–78
Kemp's (Hal) Orchestra 292
Kendrick's (Ben) Orchestra 42, 76, 83
Kennaway, Inc. (booking agency) 274
Kenny, Nick 266
Kentland, Ind. 151
Kessel, Harry 98
Key West, Fla. 278
Keyser, W.Va. 181–182
Keyser's (Kay) Orchestra 293
"Kick In" (JLS song) 16
Kick In (play) 101
Kieckhoffer, Augie 286
Kilauea Volcano 91
King, Eddie 269
King, Hal 75
King Cotton Serenaders 204
King (Wayne) Orchestra 237, 275, 291, 329
Kingly Shirts (C-S sponsor) 166
Kipling, Rudyard 26
"Kiss Me by Wireless" (song) 73
"Kitten on the Keys" (instrumental) 55, 176
Klantauqua 33–34
Klein, Emanuel K. "Manny" 279
KMOX, St. Louis, Mo. 234
Knapp, Evalyn 112
Knapp, Orville 42, **71**, 111, 112, 117, 118, **122**, **128**, **132**, **134**, **136**, **138**, **144**, **146**, 154, 157, 158, **164**, 328
"Knights and Ladies of the Bath" (C-S radio club) 222, 283, 286
Knights of Columbus, JLS sings for 13
Knights of Pythias Armory, Keyser, W.Va. 181
Knights of the Flaming Circle 112, 129
Knox, Col. Frank 237
Knoxville, Tenn. 150
Knutsen, Erling 42, 101
Kohlman, Elmer "Crab" 70, 101, **102**, 105, 110, 111
Kokomo, Ind. 148
Konop, Dean T. J. 149
Kornheiser, Phil 163
Kose, Woody 235–236
Kramer, Karl 122, 123, 126–127, 142, 143, 164, 185, 190, 191, 204–205, 211, 219, 220, 266, 284, 328
Krebs, Elmer 70, **221**, **222**, 224, **225**, 231, 244, **248**, 267, 291, 328
Kreigh's Restaurant, Belton, Mo. 75
Kreiser, Lillian 11
Kreisler, Fritz 56
Kremer, Ray 199
Ku Klux Klan 21, 33–34, 112, 118, 129, 156
Kuhn, Eddie 42, 74, 104, 329
Kummer, Marion 277
KYW, Chicago 136–138, 139, 167, 178, 237

La Boheme, Chicago 127
La Crosse, Wisc. 168, 211
La Crosse [Wisc.] *Tribune* 211
"Lady Be Good" (song) 89
Ladies' Home Journal 52–53
Lafayette, Ind. 158, 203
Lafitte, Jean 262
La Forge, Dr. A. W. 108

La Guardia, Fiorello H. 35
Laird, Landon 87
Lait, Jack 126
Lake Klinger, Mich. 256, 265
Lake Taneycomo, Mo. 111, 226, 253
Lakeshore Athletic Club, Chicago 229
Lakeside Park, Denver, Colo. 253, **254**
Lakeville, Ohio 173
Landis, Cullen 80
Landrum, Carl 329
Landry's (Art) Orchestra 111, 147
Lane, Numa 42
Las Vegas, Nev. 329
La Salle, Ill. 119, 134, 147, 192
Laska, Edward 35
Lasky, Jesse 87–88
"The Last, Long Mile" (song) 15
Lauder, Sir Harry 39
Laughlin, George 149
Laval, Pierre 272
Lawless, Ed T. 285
Lawrence, Gertrude 163
Lawrence, Mass. 200
laxative ads 31–32
Layden, Elmer 135, 149
"Lazy" (song) 120
"Lazy Waters" (C-S recording) 141
Leake, Harry J. 92
Leake, Dr. J. P. 24
"Learning" (phonograph record) 65
Lee, Thomas B. (Christian Science reader) 288
Lehigh University 233
Lemare, Jules 278
Lenexa, Kans. 325
Lenge, Michelino Angelo 39
Leon Springs, Texas 113
Leonard, Harlan 43
Le Roux, Robert A. 275
Le Seur, Lucille Fay see Crawford, Joan
"Let's Not Forget" (JLS-CAC song) 64
Leu, Gladys 69, 329
Levine, E. E. 90
Lewis, David N. 166
Lewis, J. A. 13
Lewis, Joe E. 215
Lewis, Sinclair 8
Lewis, Ted 2, 41, 54, 68, 98, 168, 197, 213, 227
Lewistown, Ill. 157
Lexington, Ky. 148, 150
Lexington, Mo. 6
Lexington, Va. 250
Liberty Inn, Chicago 127
Liberty Memorial Campaign (1919) Kansas City, Mo. 64
Liberty Theater, Cleveland, Ohio 14

Liberty Theater, Kansas City, Mo. 39, 63
Lieb, Tom 232
Lighter, Sam 76–78
Lilac Time (film) 201
Lincoln, Ill. 157
Lincoln, Nebr. 113–114, 132, 147
Lincoln Park, Oklahoma City 105–106
Lincoln Tavern, Morton Grove, Ill. 117–120, 122, 123, 127, 142, 292
Lindbergh, Charles A. 199–200, 275
Linder, Hank 105, 127, **130**, **131**, **132**, **138**, 157, 166, 174, **322**
Lindy's, New York 273, 279, 280
Lingham, Dorothy 271
Linick, Art 137
Linwood Methodist Episcopal Church, Kansas City, Mo. 11, 13
Liszt, Franz, JLS plays 12
Lithicum, Joe 146
Little, Little Jack 240
"A Little Music from King Tut's Tomb" (C-S skit) 102
Little Orphan Annie (comic strip) 212
"Little Orphan Annie" (JLS song and C-S record) 153, 212, 224
Little Rock, Ark. 158, 159, 257–258, 325
Litton (Henry C.) Clothing, Chicago 215
"Livery Stable Blues" (music) 55
Livingston, Joseph L. "Fud" 279
"Lo and Behold" (song and C-S record) 267
Loami, Ill. 193
Lockhart, Mr. 58–60
Loew's Empress Theater, Kansas City, Mo. 39
Lombardo, Carmen 205, 266, 291
Lombardo, Victor 291
Lombardo's (Guy) Royal Canadians 2, 124, 145, 204–205, 217–221, 266, 268, 269
London, England 95
Lone Tree, Iowa 202
"Lonesome (I Wonder if You're Lonesome, Too)" (JLS song) 240
"Lonesome Mama Blues" (music) 73
Long, Huey Pierce 260
"Long Boy" (song) 16
"Look for the Silver Lining" (song) 89
Loos, Anita 190
Lopez, Vincent 6, 41, 117, 125, 145, 200, 202. 260, 261, 266, 285
Los Angeles, Calif. 276, 277, 294, 326, 331

Los Angeles (Calif.) Research Laboratories 90
"Louder and Funnier" (JLS song and C-S record) 209
"Louise, You Tease" (C-S record) 162
Louisiana, Mo. 256
Louisiana Rhythm Kings (i.e., Coon-Sanders) 217
Louisville, Ky. 93, 175, 205
"Love Everlasting" (song) 277
Lovendahl, Yalmar "Axle Flooey" 156, 157, **331**
"Lovin' Sam" (song) 101
Lowe-Campbells (Kansas City baseball team) 62
Lowell, Mass. 200
Lowell [Mass.] *Sun* 201
Lown, Bert 266
Lowry, Helen Hullitt 55
Lucas's (Jon) Band 154
Lucia di Lammermoor 76
Lucky Strike Cigarettes 31, 274, 275, 276, 278, 286
Lucky Strike Dance Hour 275–276
Ludington, Mich. 170–171
Luper, Del 204
Lyman's (Abe) Orchestra 176, 253, 260, 262, 266, 284, 329
Lymar Hotel, Herrin, Ill. 129
Lyons Motor Co. Kansas City, Mo. 46
Lytell, Jimmy 279

MacDowell, Edward, JLS plays 12, 13
Macfadden, Benarr 189, 206
Mack, Roy 40, 76
Mack, Willard 101
MacMillan, D. B. (explorer) 95
Madden, Rosaline 235
Madison Square Garden, New York, N.Y. 118, 153, 280
Madisonville, Ky. 182
Maeterlinc, Georgette Leblanc 97
magazines see periodicals
Mahanoy City, Pa. 200, 250
Mainstreet Theater, Kansas City, Mo. 69
"Making a Jazz Band" (C-S skit) 80
Maloney, Julia 235
"Mamma Loves Papa" (music) 32, 55
Mammoth Oil Co. 59–61
Manchester, Ohio 184
"Mandalay" (song) 120
Manhattan, Kans. 7
Manitowoc, Wisc. 170, 171
Manning, Frank 42
Maquoketa, Iowa 257
"March of Time" (song) 278
"Margie" (song) 153

Marion, Ill. 130, 134
Marion, Ohio 177, 200, **331**
Mark Strand Theater, New York, N.Y. 138
Marks's (Frank B.) Orchestra 42, 76
Marlo, George 282
Marseilles, Ill. 119, 150
Marshall, Mich. 173
Marshfield, Wisc. 171
"Martha" (JLS song) 75, 79
Martha's Vineyard, Mass. 91
Marvin, Johnny 81
Marx Brothers 39
Masar, Steve 234
"Masculine Women, Feminine Men" (song) 31
Mason City, Iowa 147
Masonic Building, Chicago 176–177
masonry, in Chicago 9, 176–177, 213
Mattoon, Ill. 131–132, **131–134**
Maxfield, Harry 217
Maxwell, Billy 58
May Day riots (1919) 22
Mayaguez, P. R. 94
Mayo, Dr. Charles Horace 6 (and note)
Mayo, Dr. William James 6 (note)
Maytag Corporation 231
Maytag Frolics 231–232
Maywood Theater, Kansas City, Mo. 63
McAdoo, William Gibbs 64, 118
McCallum, Angus 50
McClure, John 42
McCormack, John 21, 56, 155
McCourt, Frank 14
McCrae, John (poet) 64
McCue Sisters (singers, dancers) 261
McCullough, Paul 273
McCurdy Hotel, Evansville, Ind. 166
McDougal, Dennis 123, 218–220, 229
McDowell, Bill 205
McElwain, George B. 95–96
McGee, Jay 161
McGinnis, Kenneth 50
McGinnis, O. E. 50
McGurn, Jack "Machine Gun" 215
McKee, Alex 233
McKinney, J. H. 96
McLean, Edward B. 118
McLean, Evelyn Walsh 118
McLean, Harley "Hal" 65, **66**, 75, 101, **102**, 105, 111, 329
McMeachin, Bob 293
McMeachin, Jim 293
McMeachin, Pauline 293

McPartland, Jimmy 204
McQueen, George 261, 329
McReynolds, Rex 94, 95
McVicker's Theater, Chicago 137
"Me and My Shadow" (song) 98
Meadow Lake Club, Kansas City, Mo. 97
Meadows, Lee 199
Melia, Bill 283
Mellin, Bobby 286
Mellin (George) and His Royal Syncopators 139
Mellon, Andrew W. 24
"Memories" (song) 153
Memphis, Tenn. 96, 205, 257, 264, 325
Memphis Five 124
Mencken, Henry Louis 25, 78, 151, 189–190
Mendota, Ill. 183, 236
Menkes, Sallie 137
Meredith, F. H. 93
Merry Gardens, Chicago 126, 211
Merry Go Round, Chicago 127
Merwin, Mo. 113
Messiah (oratorio) 88
Mexican Gulf Oil Co. Tampico 94
Mexico City, Mex. 94, 95
Meyer, Mary Jane Sanders 3
Mianos Jazz Band, Kansas City, Mo. **59**
Midnight Frolic (musical program) 18
"The Midnight Rounders" (skit) 69
Milburn Club, Kansas City, Mo. 97
Miles City, Mont. 94
Millar, Anna 54
Miller, Bessie 52
Miller, Donald C. 149
Miller, Glenn 204
Miller, Janet K. (JLS's great-niece) 3, 9, 79
Miller, Kelly 94
Miller's (Ray) Band 142, 184–185
Milton, Tommy 46
Milwaukee, Wisc. 132, 147, 169, 171, 182, 234, 237, 264–265, 267, 328
Milwaukee Journal 169, 265
"Mine, All Mine" (C-S record) 209
Mineral Point, Wisc. 204
Minneapolis, Minn. 98, 103, 147, 223
Minneapolis *Argus* 94
Minnehaha Falls, Minn. 148
Mintz, Herby 137
Minute Circle, Kansas City, Mo. 13
Miss Buckeye (airplane) 206, **207**
Mississippi River 96, 147, 147–148

Missouri Jazz Hounds *see* Camp Bowie Jazz Hounds
Missouri Theater, St. Louis, Mo. 118
Mr. and Mrs. (comic strip) 32
"Mister Gallagher and Mister Shean" (song) 73–74, 86–88, 101, 110, 113
"Mister Gallagher and Mister Shean in Egypt" (skit) 86
"Mr. Radio Man" (record) 49
Mitchell, Douglas Edward 2
"Moanin' for You" (C-S record) 228
Mohr, Halsey K. 35
Mole, Irving Milfred "Miff" 279, 329
Monaco and Leslie (song writers) 31
Monks, Johnny and Rhoda 251
Monmouth, Ill. 147
Monroe, La. 257–258
Monroe, La. *News-Star* 258
Montague, James J. 26
Monticello Apartments, Oklahoma City 106
Montmartre, Chicago 127
"Moon Dear" (C-S record) 162
"Moonlight and You" (C-S record) 141
Moonlight Novelty Orchestra 42
Moore, Franklyn 260
Moran, George "Bugs" 217, 228–229
Moran and Mack (comedy team) 69, 197
Morath, Max 16
Moreman's Orchestra, Kansas City, Mo. 63
Morgan, Marion 293
Mori's Cabaret, New York, N.Y. 152
Morrisette, Willis 294
Morton, Roy 76–78
Morton Grove, Ill. 117, 215, 226, 236
Moten, Bennie 43, 296
Motion Picture Herald 286
Motion Picture Producers and Distributors of America 199
Moulin Rouge, Chicago 127, 189
Mounds, Ill. 257
Mt. Carmel, Ill. 182
Mt. Moriah Cemetery, Kansas City, Mo. **289–290**, 291
Mt. Pulaski, Ill. 193
Mount Rushmore, S.Dak. 175, 255
Mountain, Billy 42
Mountain, John 76–78
Mudd, Dorothy 235
Muehlebach Hotel 7, 37, 39, 63–64, 69–70, 74, 97, 98, 101, 108, 113, 117, 139, 174, 223

Mulhollon, Verne 95
Muntsch, Wilhelmina 235
Murphy, Georgia 13
Murphy, Sam 42
Murray, Billy 81
Murray, Ken 326
Murrell, L. C. 93
Murrow, Edward R. 110
Music Corporation of America 122–124, 126, 127, 139, 141–142, 143, 145, 147, 158, 161, 164, 166, 168, 169, 170, 176–177, 184–185, 190, 191, 203, 204, 205, 211, 217–221, 229, 236–238, 240, 242, 250, 253, 257, 265, 269, 271, 274, 276, 284, 285, 292, 293, 296, 327, 328, 330–331
"Music in the Moonlight" (C-S record) 228
Music Weavers Band 154
Muskogee, Okla. 62, 330
Musolino, Louis and Mary M. 112
Musolino, Nicholas L. 2, 42, 69, 71, 78, 105, 112–113, 117, 118, **122**, 128, **130, 132, 136, 138**, 146, 150, 154, 156, 157, 158, **159**, 164, 325, 329
Musolino, Rudy (son of Nicholas M.) 329
Mutt and Jeff (comic strip) 5, 156
"My Baby Knows How" (C-S record) 190
"My Best Gal" (C-S recording) 141
"My Daddy's Dreamtime Lullaby" (song) 116, 132
"My Paradise" (C-S theme song) 268, 278, 281, 284
"My Sunday Girl" (song) 162
"My Suppressed Desire" (C-S record) 225

Nagel, Conrad 80
Nane, Pete 7
Napoleon, Phil 279, 329
Nash, Jay Robert 215
Nashville, Tenn. 150, 174, 205
National Broadcasting Co. (NBC) 206, 234, 237, 239, 240, 274, 275, 276, 278, 325
National Broadcasting Co.'s Artist Bureau 237, 274, 276
National Music Managers Association 124–125
Natural Bridge, Va. 251, 252
Nauet, Joe 94
NBC Symphony Orchestra 329
Neah Bay, Wash. 96
"needle beer" 37
Neibauer, Eddie 142
Nelson, Jack 275, 278
Nesbitt, Evelyn 153–154
New Albany, Ind. 151

New Bedford, Mass. 200, 201
New Casino, Kansas City, Mo. 41, 42
New Coon-Sanders Nighthawks Fan Club 2–3, 203–204, 293–294, 325
New Diamond Theater, Kansas City, Mo. 63
New Orleans, La. 54, 258–264
New Orleans Item 261
New Orleans *Times-Picayune* 261
New Orleans States 261
New York, N.Y. 22, 26, 48, 55, 60–61, 68, 119, 124, 138–139, 140, 145, 151, 152, 153–154, 162, 163, 168, 169, 177, 200, 206, 220, 237, 238, 239, 246, 253, 265–285
New York *Daily Mirror* 276
New York *Daily News* 276
New York Evening Graphic 189, 206
New York Hippodrome 117
"New York Is Taking the Gymnastics Out of Jazz" (article) 55
New York Polo Grounds 149
New York Times 27
New Yorker (magazine) 51
New Yorker Hotel *see* Hotel New Yorker
Newark, N.J. 41, 74
Newman Concert Orchestra of Forty 39, 63
Newman Theater, Kansas City, Mo. 39, 63, 76, 80, 81, 82, 98, 100, 101–102, 104, 108, 111, 112, 117
"News and Gossip of the Hotel Muehlebach" 64
Niagara Falls, N.Y. 174, 178–179, **180**
Nicaragua 95
Nice People (film) 80
Nichols, Red 279, 329
"The Night Before Christmas" (C-S skit) 82, 101
"Night Riders" (C-S club) 275, 283
"Nighthawk Blues" (JLS song) 2, 69, **70**, 85–86, 101, 108, 109, 113, 116, 132, 175, 278, 281
"The Nighthawk March" (music) 98
Nighthawks *see* Coon-Sanders Nighthawks
"The Nightingale Love Song" (song) 13
"Nighty Night" (JLS song) 183, 187
Niles, Mich. 144, **146, 148**
"No One Just Like You" (JLS song) 80, 102
Nordberg, Arthur 329

Nordberg, Carl "Swede" 65, **66**, 75, 101, **102**, 105, **107, 109**, 110, 111, 329
Nordberg, Harold 42, 232
Norfleet, Robert 42, 65, **66**, 69, 75, 105
Norrie, Wisc. 171
North American Aircraft Corp. 330
North Carolina State, Raleigh 204
North Judson, Ind. 332
Northwestern Broadcasting System 237
Northwestern University 234
Northwestern University's Associated Fraternities 219
Notre Dame Scholastic 150
Notre Dame University *see* University of Notre Dame
Nowata, Okla. 94
Nutty Club (C-S device) 186, 187, 211

Oak Ridge Park Pavilion, Cadillac, Mich. 172–173
Oakmont, Pa. 156
Oberlin, Ohio 202
O'Day, Molly 277
Odessa, Mo. 117–118
O'Farrell, Buck 112
Office of War Information 327
"Oh! You Have No Idea" (C-S record) 215
O'Hare (Husk) Casino Club Ensemble 139, 237
Ohrman, Clare and Harold Van 253, 280
Oil City, Penn. 91
Okeh (phonograph records) 43
Oklahoma, Klan in 21, 33, 112
Oklahoma City 95, 104–111
Oklahoma City Country Club 107
Oklahoma City *Daily Oklahoman* 105, 108, 110
"Ol' Man River" (record) 203
"Old Legion Buddy of Mine" (JLS-CAC song) 45
"Old Man River" (song) 89
Olds, Maury 203
Olean, N.Y. 250, 251, 265, 273
Oliver Hotel, South Bend, Ind. 149
Oliver's (King) Jazz Band 124
Olmstead, Rev. Edwin B. 11
Olsen (George) Orchestra 89, 145, 202, 227, 268, 271, 296
Omaha, Nebr. 62, 147, 182, 191, 330
Omaha, Nebr. *Bee* 183, 191
Omaha, Nebr. *Evening World* 192
Omaha, Nebr. *World Herald* 183

"On Revival Day" (song and C-S record) 267
1-2-3 Club, New Orleans 260
O'Neill, Nebr. 99
Onset, Mass. 201
Oregon, Ill. 150
"Oriental Love Dreams" (song) 116, 132
Original Dixieland Jazz Band 54
Original Kentucky Nighthawks 154
Orlando, Fla. 332
Orlando, Okla. 326
Orpheum Circuit 142, 329
Orpheum Theater, Kansas City, Mo. 39
Orpheum Theater, Nashville, Tenn. 150
Orpheus Quartet 13, 113
Orr, H. A. 93
Orr, Tom 94
Oshawa, Ont. 94
Osterman, Jack 61
"Ostrich Walk" (song) p. 109
Our Times (book by Mark Sullivan) 40, 51–52
"Over There" (song) 16
Owens, Bobby 13
Owensboro, Ky. 151

Paderewski, Ignace 21
Page, Oran P. "Hot Lips" 43
Page, Walter 43
Palace Theater, Cleveland, Ohio 29
Palace Theater, New York 139, 272
Palais de la Rue, Chicago 127
Paley, William A. (drummer) 228, 286, 288, 329
Paley, William S. 206, 228, 237, 286
Palmer, A. Mitchell 47
Palmer, Bee 153, 154
Palmer House, Chicago 215, **216**, 236
Palmesana, Phil 42
Panatrope, electrical recording system 154
Panico, Louis 291
Pantages Theater, Kansas City, Mo. 53, 207–209
Pantages Vaudeville Circuit 329
Paramount film executives in Kansas City 87
Paramount Theater, New York 273
Paris, France 41, 57
Parker, Vera 94
Parker, Virginia 93
Parrish, George 42, 78
Parrish, Lawrence 42
pas ma la (dance) 189
Paseo, Kansas City, Mo. 97

Passaic, N.J. 95
"Patrick Shay" (JLS song) 15
Pattison, Pat 267, 288, 330
Paul Talking Machine Shop, Kansas City, Mo. 66
Payne's (Art) Orchestra 124
Peace, Harold 284
Pearson, Ted 234
Pease, Harry 15
Peerless Quartette 13
Peking Cafe, Kansas City, Mo. 40, 75
Pendergast, Tom 68
Pennsylvania Hotel, New York 265, 269
Pennsylvania State Forestry School 204
Pennsylvania State University 204, 233
Penny, O. W. 283
Peoria, Ill. 134, 147, 225
Pepsodent Co. 240
Pere Marquette 21 (ship) 170–171
Perfect, Rose 273
periodicals threatened by Congress 189–190
Pershing, Gen. John J. 16, 45
Pershing Palace, Chicago 127, 142
Pershing Road, Kansas City, Mo. 97
Peters, C. 42
Petrillo, James Caesar 160, 214
Phelps's (Bert) Royal Garden Orchestra 76, 83
Philadelphia, Pa. 156
Philipsburg, Pa. 151, 156
Phillips, Prof. Charles 149
Phillips, Ed 91
Phoenix, Ariz. 100, 327
phonofilm, electrical recording process 154
phonograph recording 154–155
Piantadosi, George 282
Pickens, S.C. 2
Pickett (Wilbur) and His Melody Men 197
Pickford, Mary 52
Pickwick Club, Boston 152
Piedmont Cigarettes 31
Pike (Louis A.) and the Music Masters 197
The Pilgrim (film) 101
Pitcairn Island 95
Pitchfork Club — Hey! Hey! (C-S radio club) 198, 205
Pittsburgh, Pa. 74, 156, 200, 249, 250
Pittsburgh Pirates (baseball team) 62, 330
Plantation Grill, Hotel Muehlebach 37, 39, 42, 74, 83, 91, 95, 111
Plantation Orchestra 104
"Play, Gypsies, Dance Gypsies" (song) 89

Pleasant Garden, N.C. 293
Point Barrow, Alaska 95
Pollock's (Ben) Orchestra 204–205
Polo Grounds, New York 112
Pompeiian Room, Hotel Baltimore, Kansas City, Mo. 38, 39, 68
Pompeiian Terrace Players, Hotel Baltimore, Kansas City, Mo. 38, 42, 111
Pontiac, Ill. 150
Pope (Bob) and His Hotel Charlotte Orchestra 330
Pope, Robert 42, 105, 163, **165**, **174**, 179, **193**, **199**, 215, **221**, **222**, 225, 236, 244, **248**, 258, 288, **322**, **323**, **326**, 330
Popper, Joe 6, 69, 142, 242
Port Huron, Mich. 149
Porter, Cole 31, 125
Portland, Ore. 93
Portsmouth, Ohio 94, 169, 206
Portsmouth [Ohio] *Daily Times* 169, 206
Portsmouth (Ohio) *Morning Sun* 169
Postum (beverage) 31
Prairie Village, Kans. 2, 325
"Pray, Children, Pray" (song) 278
The President's Daughter (book) 177
Preston, Edward H. 90
Preston, James H. 90
"A Pretty Girl Is Like a Melody" (song) 57
Priests of Pallas Festival, Kansas City, Mo. 44–45
Pritchard Hotel, Huntington, W.Va. 167
The Private Life of Helen of Troy (film) 32
Produce Merchants Baseball Team, Kansas City, Mo. 63
prohibition and scofflaws 22, 34–38, 57, 93, 118–119, 124, 147, 149, 178–181, 185, 189, 205–206, 227, 281
Purcell, H. W. 89
Purdue University 233, 236
Purviance, Edna 101
Pusatari, Sam 42
Pushtart, Sam 42
Putnam, Mich. 205, 211
PWX (Havana, Cuba) 139

Quillen, J. W. 149
Quincy, Ill. 112, 150, 329
Quincy, Ill. *Daily Herald* 150
Quincy, Ill. *Whig-Journal* 150
Quinlan, Jack 207–208
Quodbach, Al 217–220

Rachmaninoff, Sergei 21, 56
radio 1, 42, 48, 49–51, 53, 71–79, 95, 98–99, 101, 114, 124–125, 136–138, 139–141, 146–147, 162, 174–175, 190, 214, 238–239, 268–269, 275–279; *see also* Columbia Broadcasting System; National Broadcasting Co.
Radio Corporation of America 124
Radio Digest (magazine) 62, 162, 265, 291
Radio Digest Illustrated (magazine) 49
Radio Orchestra 42
"Radio Shop" (gambling den) 50
Radio Supply Co., Kansas City, Mo. 73
Rainbo Gardens, Chicago 117, 227
Raleigh, N.C. 93, 204
Rapid City, S. D. 255
Rappe, Virginia 80
Raub, Ind. **177**
raunch (dance) 151
Raven Club, Kansas City, Mo. 58
RCA Victor *see* Victor Talking Machine Co
"Ready for the River" (C-S record) 215
Reagan, Pres. Ronald 331
Reardon, Joe W. 42
Reardon, William 152
Rector's Restaurant, New York 53–54
"Red Hot Mama" (recording) 2, 116, 132
"Red Necks" 259–260
Reddish, Bert 94
Reed, Helen 12
Reed, Sen. James Alexander 8, 112
Reed, Novus 12, 13, 14
Regal Novelty Orchestra *see* Coon-Sanders Novelty Orchestra
Regent Theater, Kansas City, Mo. 63
Regina, Sask. 91
Reid, Wallace 80
Reiner, Fritz 329
"Remember" (song) 89, 153
"Remembering" (song) 120
Remick, Jerome H. & Co. 140
Remick and Witmark, Publishers 282
Renault, Francis 154
Rendezvous, Chicago 127
Rendezvous Cafe, New York 138
Reno, Nev. 161
Research to Prevent Blindness, New York 331
Reser, Harry 162, 291
Rettberg, Harvey Clark 1, 2, 188, 203–204, 212–213, 224, 241, 267, 268, 269, 281, 282, 287, 293–294, **295**, 332
Rettberg, Hilda 294, **295**
Revere, Paul 201
Revue Productions (MCA) 330–331
Reynolds' (Ross) Orchestra 176
Reynoldsville, Penn. 94
Rhapsody in Blue (music) 56
Rhyne, Hal 199
Rhythm Boys 215, 278
Rice, Grantland 149
Rich, Freddie 266
Richman, Harry 266, 271
Richmond, Ind. 166, 169–170, 174
Richmond, Mo. 113
Richolson, Jean 148, 157
Richolson, Joe 2, **71**, 112, 117, 118, 122, **130**, **131**, **132**, **133**, **134**, **136**, **138**, 146, 154, 157, **164**, **165**, 167, **174**, **197**, **199**, 203, **221**, **222**, **225**, 227, 236, 244, 288, 292, 294, **322**, **326**, 330, 331
Rickard, Earl 221
Ridley, R. H. 95
Ridpath Co. 14
Rigoletto (opera) 76
Riesenweber's Cafe, New York 54
Riley, Earl 42
Riley, Jack 7, 19, 42
Riley-Ehrhart Orchestra 42, 76
Riley's Dance Orchestra 39
Rinker, Al 278
Rip Van Winkle's, New York 61
Ripley's "Believe It or Not" 62–63
Ritz Brothers, comedy team 215
Riverdale, Fla. 331
Riverton, Ill. 193
Robbins, Jack 273
Robbins Music Publishers 268
Robinson's Shoe Co., Kansas City, Mo. 30, 73
Robison, Willard 42
Robison's (Willard) Deep River Orchestra 328
Rochester, Minn. 6
Rock City, N.Y. 252
Rockford, Ill. 147
Rockford, Mickey 265
Rockne, Knute 149, 203, 232, 253
Roe, J. W. 232
Roesch, R. E. 95
Roesner's (Walt) Stage Band, Capitol Theater, New York 329
Rogers, H. E. 35
Rogers, Will 89, 156, 167
Rohe, Margaret 27
"Roll 'Em, Girls" (song) 27
"Roodles" (C-S record) 202, 206
Rooney, Mickey 293
Roosevelt, Franklin D. 8, 64, 237, 279, 285
Roosevelt, Theodore 16
Roosevelt Hotel, New Orleans 260
Roosevelt Hotel, New York 269
"Rose of the Rio Grande" (song) 108
Roseland, La. 259–260
Roseland Ballroom, New York 138
Ross, Betsy (home) 156
Ross, David 274
"Rosy Posy" (song) 75
Roth, Lillian 266
Roth, Otto 163, 164, 186, 187, 204, 211, 236, 237, 242–243
Rothafel, Samuel L. "Roxy" 78
"Round My Heart" (C-S record) 267
Roxy Theater, New York, N.Y. 31, 78
Royal Dance Palais, Galena, Ill. 168
Royal Plantation Grill Syncopators 111
Royal Theater, Kansas City, Mo. 39, 78
Rubinoff, Dave 266
Ruby, Harry 35
Runge's Music Store, Richmond, Ind. 169–170
Runnin' Wild (revue) 152
Rush Medical College 120–121
Rushing, Jimmy 43
Russ Lyon Realty Corp., Phoenix, Ariz. 327
Russell, Jane 293
Russo, M. A. 101
Russo, Michael 42
Russo's (Danny) Oriole Orchestra 127
Rust, Brian 141, 163, 202, 203, 224, 225, 327, 328, 330
Ruth, George Herman "Babe" 57, 205
Ryan, Quin A. 182, 221, 222
Ryan, William 173, 211

Sacco (Nicola) and Vanzetti (Bartolomeo) 47
Sackett, Sally 251
Sacramento, Cal. 152
"Sadie, That Yiddisher Vamp" (JLS song) 68
"Safety First" (song) 13
Saginaw, Mich. 14, 257
St. Augustine, Fla. 294, 331
St. Augustine [Fla.] *Record* 331
St. Francisville, La. 92
St. Louis, Mo. 54, 75–76, 103, 117–118, 119, 130, 163, 182, 192, 206–207, 234
St. Louis *Globe-Democrat* 118
St. Louis *Post Dispatch* 75–76
St. Louis Street Cemetery, New Orleans 263–264

St. Louis University 234–236
St. Luke's Episcopal Church, Chicago 29
St. Mary's of the Woods School, Terre Haute, Ind. 148
St. Valentine's Day Massacre 229
Salary averages in early 20s 24
Salem, Mass. 200, 201
Sale, Chic 153
Salome, Ariz. 100
Salter, Carl S. 94
Sammons, Col. Cleveland 18
Samoa 137
Sampson, Gov. (Ky.) Flem D. 283–284
Samuel, O. M. 139–140
Samuels, Rae 68
San Pedro, Calif. 94
Sande, Earl 277
Sanders, Gertrude "Trudy" (JLS's second wife) 290, 293
Sanders, Helena Soice (JLS's mother) 9, 10, death 16
Sanders, Isaac (JLS's grandfather) 9
Sanders, John (b. 1702) 9
Sanders, Joseph Harrison (JLS's father) 9, 10, 16, 209, 225
Sanders, Joseph La Ceil 2, 5, 10, 12, 14, 17, 23, 60, 102, 107, 122, 128, 132–134, 137–138, 146, 157, 162, 164–165, 167, 174, 177, 180–181, 192, 196, 198–199, 208, 210, 219, 221–222, 225–226, 247, 249, 252, 263, 295, 322–323, 326, 331, 336; advises Paley about CBS 206; ancestry 9; and Newman Theater 79–103, 112–117; as a drinker 5, 36; as composer, arranger, skit writer 13, 15–16, 35, 45, 64, 68, 80, 85–86, 102, 112, 120, 187, 202, 224, 240–241; ASCAP member 241; at Book-Cadillac Hotel, Detroit 285; at Niagara Falls 178–179; at Oklahoma City 104–110; attitude toward "plugging" others' songs 163; band's "in" jokes 69–70; baseball 14, 16, 62–63; becomes a Mason 232; brief, last leg of road tour 265; buys house in Kansas City 217; "candidate" for U.S. presidency 285–286; composes "Nighthawk Blues" 85–86; continues road tour in early August 1931, 256; Coon's "kidnapping" 228–230; Coon's sickness and death 286–290; C-S engagement in Dec. 1927 in Kansas City 207–209; drives to Morton Grove, Ill. 117–120; dubious about Blackhawk job 186–187; early life and education 9–12; early musical studies and activities 13–16, 40; encounter with the "Red Necks" 259–260; engagement at St. Louis's Hotel Chase and Loew's State Theater 206–207; final road tour summer 1931, 250–265; first broadcast 74–75; *Florsheim Shoe Frolic* 234, 236, 239–240; *Florsheim Sunday Radio "Feeture"* 240–241; goes to Hollywood to work in film industry but forms another band 292–293; goes with Madeline to Canada 203; great fan of rail travel 166, 168–169; helps organize C-S Band 57–58, 63; hires Floyd Estep and Downing 158–159; ill with flu while in New England 200–201; in a tornado 193–195; in Army 16–20, 23; in Atlanta 174–175; in Denver 253–254; in New Orleans 258–264; in 1934 backs out of deal to return to Blackhawk but tries to continue Nighthawks 292; incidental composing and jottings 173; Joe ill with flu 211–212; last years in Kansas City 293; later financial relations with Eula Coon 292; later relations with MCA 142–143; low morale and concern for Coon's personal problems 255, 266–267, 279, 281–284; marries 79; meets CAC 8, 19; meets Mel Tormé 230–231; "Mister Gallagher and Mister Shean" 86–88; move to apartment in New York 280; negotiations with Quaker Oats 240; New York's Hotel New Yorker 265–285; on band's first road tour (1924) 127–135; opinion of "Pop" Estep 224; physical and personal description 6; plays for Texas City disaster benefit in 1947 and retires in 1953, 292–293; proposed for All Star Dance Orchestra 291; refuses Stein's offer to invest 142; relations with Auburn Auburn Auto Co. 157, 160, 203, 243–247; return to Chicago 285–286; risks injury as carpenter 196; start of Nighthawk programs 83–86; tiff with NBC 239–240; views on popular dance music 133–134; visited by Harvey and Hilda Rettberg 294; Walter Winchell shows 275–279; *see also* Coon-Sanders Nighthawks; Coon-Sanders Novelty Orchestra

Sanders, Lavinia Pickerill (JLS's grandmother) 9
Sanders, Madeline Esther Baldwin (JLS's first wife) 79, 107, 109, 111, 120, 148, 150, **157**, 161, 173, **196**, 198, 203, **208**, 211, **226**, 249, 253, 255, 257–262, 263–264, 265, 270–274, 279–280, 283, 284, 285, 288, 289, 290, 292, 293, 330
Sanders, Mary (JLS's sister-in-law) 249, 330
Sanders, Priscilla 293
Sanders, Roy Garvin (JLS's brother) 9–10, 12, 16, 62, 249, 263, 330
Sandusky, Ohio 200
Sanella, Andy 275
Santa Marta, Colombia 283
Sarnia, Ont. 149
Satterlee Electric Co. Kansas City, Mo. 73
Saturday Evening Post 238
Savannah, Ga. 52
Savoy Theater, Fort Worth, Texas 19
Scanlan, Walter 81
Schenck, Joe *see* Van and Schenck
Schenectady, N.Y. 74
Schenkelberger, Dr. (Joe's physician) 211
Scholl, Dr. William Mathias 270
Schreiber, Taft 161
Schribman, Cy 201
Schroeder, Dan 222, 225, 270, 281, 285
Schroeder Hotel, Milwaukee 264–265
Schubert, Franz, JLS plays 12
Schueing, Ed 266
Schultz, Charlie 137
Schumann Choral Club, Kansas City, Mo. 11
Scientific American (magazine) 100
Scopes evolution trial 151, 156
Searles, Nancy Coon (CAC's daughter) 294
Seattle Harmony Kings 124
Secret of Suzanne (opera) 30
Selby, Jimmie 63–64
Sell (Bell?) James 42
Sellinger, Henry 217, 221
Shanley, Claire 253
Shannon, Joe 68
Shaughnessy, Florence 235
Shaw, Mrs. Frederic C. 288
Shayne, Al 154
The Sheik (film) 47
"The Sheik of Araby" (song) 75
Shell, George 251
Shelton, W. L. 73
Shepard, John 94

Sherman Hotel, Chicago 120, 196, 286, 289
Sherwin-Williams 237
"She's a Mean Job" (song) 68
Shields, Roy 325
shimmy (dance) 40–41, 43, 152
"S-h-i-n-e" (song) 120
Shores, Alice 235
"Show Me the Way" (C-S recording) 141
Shreveport, La. 158
Shubert Theater, Kansas City, Mo. 39, 69, 98, 111
Shuffle Along (show) 151
Shutt, Arthur 279
Sibley, Iowa 183
Sigworth, Ralph 91
Silver, Frank 88
Silver Lake, Ind. 148, 177
"Silver Moon" (record) 203
Silver Slipper, Chicago 127
Silverberg, Seymore 76–78
Silverman, Sime 333
Silverstone, Harry 65, **66**, 75
Simmons, William J. 33
Simon, George T. 204, 220–221, 292, 328
Simpson, Russell 80
Sinclair, Earl 58
Sinclair, Harry F. 59–61, 118
"Sing a New Song" (song and C-S record) 267
Singer, Jean 232
Singin' the Blues (musical) 272
"Singin' the Blues" (song) 278
Sioux City, Iowa 93, 132, 147, 183–184, 210
Sioux City [Iowa] *Journal* 183
Sissle, Noble 152
"Sittin' and Whittlin'" (JLS song) 231
"Sittin' Around" (C-S record) 162, 163
Skinner, Frank 279
Skinner, Otis 29
Skinner, Thomas 95
"Skinner's Sock" (C-S record) 217
Skretvedt, Randy 217
Skylark Gasoline 31
"Sleepy Time Gal" (song) 163
Slide, Anthony 61
"Sluefoot" (JLS song and record) 187, 209, 257
Smalle, Ed 81
Smartt, Polk 205
Smeck, Roy 199
"Smilin' Skies" (C-S record) 225
Smith, Alfred E. 118, 285
Smith, B. Howard 76–78
Smith, Dr. (JLS's physician) 253
Smith, E. A. 166
Smith, Rev. Gypsy 205–206
Smith (Harl) and His Orchestra 327

Smith, Helen 288
Smith, Jess W. 104
Smith, Kate 212, 266
Smith, Z. I. 42
Snuffy Smith (comic strip) 88
Sobol, Louis 266
Society Clothes (C-S sponsor) 166
Soddy, Prof. Frederick 48
Soice, John (JLS's great-grandfather) 9
Soice, Mary Steffenhaugen (JLS's great-grandmother) 9
"Some Little Bird" (C-S record) 65–66, 68
"Some of These Days" (C-S record) 141
"Somebody from Home" (JLS song) 282
song composing, arranging in 1920s 143
Sooner Serenaders Orchestra 110
South Bend, Ind. 120, 135, 149, 203, 211, 212
South Bend [Ind.] *News-Times* 149, 212
South Daytona Beach, Fla. 332
"Southology" (JLS instrumental) 240, 283
Spaeth, Sigmund 88, 89, 268
"Spain" (song) 120
"Sparks" (JLS instrumental) 241
Specht's (Paul) Orchestra 124
Speck, Lt. Cyrus Q. 18, 20
Spiegel, F. R. 94
Spielman, Lewis 226
Spivak, Charlie 204
Spring Lake Pavilion, Oklahoma City 105, 106, 108, 110
Spring Valley, Ill. 157, 193
Springer, "Tonto Bill" 100
Springfield, Ill. 132, 193–195, 237, 256
Springfield *Illinois State Journal* 132, 194
Springfield, Mass. 200
Springfield, Ohio 265
Spur Cigarettes 31
Stacks, Tom 162, 197
Stafford, Kans. 9
Stalling's Orchestra, Kansas City, Mo. 63
Standard Hotel, La Crosse, Wis. 168
Stanley, Aileen 81
Stanley, King 232
Starke, Pauline 80
Starved Rock, Ill. 265
Statler Hotel, Buffalo, N.Y. 178
"Stay Out of the South" (C-S record) 209
Steadman, Richard 73
Steed (Howard) and His Seven Syncopating Soldiers 329

Steele, H. W. 101
Stein, Doris 288, 330
Stein, Jules Caesar 120–124, 127, 141–142, 143, 145, 154, 164, 166, 170, 176–177, 184–185, **186**, 188, 203, 204, 218–220, 229, 236, 238, 242, 253, 256, 265, 269, 274, 276, 285, 288, 291, 292, 293, 330–331
Stein (Jules) Eye Institute 331
Stein, William 121, 217–218
Sterling, Ill. 157, 158
Steubenville, Ohio 94
Steve Canyon (comic strip) 212–213, **296**
Stevens, Ralph 42
Stevens Hotel, Chicago 219
Stevenson Elizabeth 24
Steward, Anne 62, 265
Stewart, Rev. George H. 29
Stinson-Wheeler Orchestra 76
Stinson's (Ray) Orchestra 42, 113
Stokowski, Leopold 56
Stoller, Nate 231 (note)
Stone, "Doggy" 251
Stone Mountain, Atlanta 175
Stookey, Eula Coon *see* Coon, Eula Jenkins
Stool, Joe 267
"Stories" (song) 80
Stout, Charles Russell "Russ" 1, 2, 42, 163, **174**, **193**, **199**, 217, **221**, **222**, **225**, 244, **245**, 246, 247, **248**, 273, 288, 294, **322**, **326**, 331–332
Stout, Florence "Sis" (Russ's wife) 217, 246–247, 273, 331–332
Stout, Irv (Russ's brother) 332
Stout, Ridge (Russ's brother) 332
Stout Music Center, Fond du Lac, Wisc. 331
Stovin, H. M. 91
Strahan, H. P. 43
Straight's (Charley) Orchestra 127, 163, 232, 329
Stravinsky, Igor 56
Streeter, Ill. 158, 168
Stroupe, Brooks Y. 232
Stuhldreher, Harry 135, 149
"Stumbling" (song) 76
Suburban Gardens, New Orleans 260–261, 262, 264
Sullivan, Helen 75
Sullivan, Mark 40, 51, 88, 89
Summers & Son, Portsmouth, Ohio 206
"Sun Dodgers," Chicago (radio program) 103
Sun Prairie, Wisc. 257
Sunday, Rev. Billy 33, 205–206
"Sunny Disposish" (song) 89
Sunset, S.C. 293
Surf Hotel, Chicago 120
Swain, Mack 101

Swanson, Gloria 101, 278, 279
Sweeney Radio Station Orchestra 42, 78–79
Sweeney School of Auto-Tractor-Aviation, Kansas City, Mo. 49, 74–75, 78–79
"Sweepin' the Clouds Away" (C-S record) 228
"Sweet and Lovely" (song) 278
Swift Company 240
"Swingin' Down the Lane" (song) 89, 109
Swope Park, Kansas City, Mo. 97
Syracuse, N.Y. 119
Syrup of Figs (product) 32

Taft, William Howard 64
"'Tain't So, Honey, 'Tain't So" (record) 203
"Take Me" (JLS song and record) 228
Tall, Sam 43
Talley, Marion 199
Talmadge, Constance 101
Talman, Woods 251
Tammen, Harry H. 61–62
Tampico, Mexico 90
Taney Co., Mo. 111
tango (dance) 40, 43
Tanguay, Eva 39
Tannen, Julius 286
Taunton, Mass. 200
Taylor, Floyd 42
Taylor, William Desmond 70–71
Tchaikovsky, Peter Ilyitch 89
Teagarden, Charlie 204
Teagarden, Jack 204, 215
Teapot Dome oil scandals 61, 104, 118
Tearney's (Al) Town Club, Chicago 185
"Teasin'" (song) 75
Telephone Building, Kansas City, Mo. 79
The Temple, Mt. Moriah Cemetery, Kansas City, Mo. **289–290**
Templeton's Harmony Cafeteria, Kansas City, Mo. 40
"Tennessee Lazy" (JLS composition) 187, 203
Terrace Room, Hotel New Yorker, New York 265, 266, 267, 270, 278, 284
Terre Haute, Ind. 129, 138, 148, 166, 170
Terry, William Harold 241–242
Terry and the Pirates (comic strip) 212
Texarkana, Ark. 158
Texas, Klan in 33
"That's All There Is" (C-S record) 156

"That's How I Feel About You" (C-S record) 225
Thaw, Harry K. 153–154
Thayer, Kans. 9
theater organs 98–99, 101, 137, 192, 273
theme songs of bands 268
"There's a Light in the Window" (JLS song) 282
"There's a Long, Long Trail" (song) 22
"There's No One Just Like You" (song) 116, 132
"There's Sunlight in Your Eyes" (song) 76
"They Were All out of Step but Jim" (song) 15
Thiell, Harold P. (K?) 2, 42, 65, **66, 71,** 75, 101, 104–105, 111, 112, 117, 118, **122,** 127–128, 129, 131–132, **133, 136, 138, 146,** 154, 157, 159, **164, 165, 167,** 177, 179, 188, **199,** 203, **221, 222, 225,** 244, **248,** 281, **288,** 294, **322, 323, 326, 332**
Thiell, John 71, **102,** 104–105, 106, **108,** 111, 112, 117, 118, **122,** 128, **130, 132, 136, 138, 146,** 154, 157, 159, **164, 165, 167, 199,** 203, 205, **221, 222, 225,** 244, **248,** 288, **322, 326, 332–333**
Thomas, Ira 130
Thompson, William Hale 119
Three Hundred Club, New York 61
"Three O'Clock in the Morning" (song) 75, 98
"tie-ins" 268
Tiger Club, Kansas City, Mo. 58
Tilden, William Tatem, II 57
Tisdale, Virginia 11
Tobias, Harry 278
Tokyo, Japan, earthquake 111
Toledo, Ohio 168, 205, 256
"Too Bad" (C-S record) 162
"Too Busy" (C-S record) 215
"Toot, Toot, Tootsie" (song) 153
Tormé, Melvin Howard "Mel" 230–231
tornadoes 193–195, 207
Torrey, Ted 252
Touhy, Roger 124
Town Club, Chicago 189
Tracey, William 35
Traverse City, Mich. 171–173
Traverse City, Mich. *Record-Eagle* 172
Traynor, Pie 198
"Treasure" (record) 65
Tremaine, Paul 42, 78
Triangle Music Co. New York 102
Trianon, Chicago 127
Trianon, Terre Haute, Ind. 166

Trianon Ensemble 42, 101
Trianon Room, Hotel Muehlebach 38, 63
"True Blue Lou" (C-S record) 227
Truman, Harry S 8, 45, 79, 279
Tucker, Sophie 278
Tucson, Ariz. 94
Tufts, Sonny 293
Tulsa, Okla. 58, 105, 106, 158, 330
"Tuning Troubles of Messrs. Gallagher and Shean" 73–74
Turk, Roy 268
Turner (J. C.) and the Southern Serenaders 124
Turner, Rand 251
Turner, Reginald 291
Twelfth Street Theater, Kansas City, Mo. 79–80
Twin Lakes Pavilion, Fort Dodge, Iowa 132–134
"Twisting the Dials" (phonograph recording) 49
"Two Time Dan" (song) 109
Tynan, Thomas 53
Tyrone, Pa. 156
"Ty-tee" (song) 75

Uniformed Firemen's Association of Greater New York, Local 94, 275
Union City, Pa. 250, 253
Union Depot Hotel, Vincennes, Ind. 166, 182
Uniontown, Pa. 156, **162**
University City Studios 331
University of Arkansas 233
University of Chicago 120
University of Detroit 149
University of Illinois 233, 234
University of Indiana 225
University of Iowa 234
University of Kansas 62, 235, 267, 287, 330
University of Kansas Alumni Association 8
University of Massachusetts 233
University of Michigan 225
University of Notre Dame 135, 149, 212, 236
University of Vienna 121
University of Wisconsin 234
Urichsville, Ohio 184
U.S. Coast Guard 37
U.S. Dept. of Commerce 49, 99, 146–147
U.S. Dept. of Justice and MCA 331
U.S. Four (quartet) 13–14, 257
U.S. Internal Revenue Service 36, 229
U.S.S. *Oklahoma* 94
U.S.S. *Yarborough* 96

Valentino, Rudolph 28, 31, 47, 228
Valentino Inn, Chicago 127
Vallee (Rudy) and His Connecticut Yankees 213, 236, 262, 266, 269
Vallejo, Calif. 278
Van, Gus *see* Van and Schenck
Van and Schenck (vaudeville team) 15, 27, 63, 81, 285
Van Dyke, Henry 43–44
Van Nuys, Calif. 146
Vancouver, B.C. 278
Vanderbilt University 233
Vanity Fair, Chicago 142
Variety, New York 34, 61–62, 100, 116, 119, 120, 124, 125, 135, 136, 138, 139, 140, 141, 143, 145–146, 147, 154, 155, 163, 168, 170, 176, 180–181, 187, 188, 189, 224, 227, 238, 239, 242, 243, 247, 253, 260–261, 265, 268–269, 274, 275, 280–281, 287, 292, 327, 328, 333
Varsity Breeze (St. Louis University) 234–236
vaudeville's decline in popularity 125, 269
Velva, N.Dak. 94
Vendeloo, N. Van 101
Venetian Gardens, Chicago 219–220
Verdi, Giuseppe, JLS plays 12, 13
Verdigris River 105
Vermilion, Ohio 178
Vermilion [Ohio] *News* 178
Via Radio (film) 100
Via Wireless (film) 100
Vicksburg, Miss. 94, 258
Victor Talking Machine Co. 2, 43, 65, 116, 141, 145, 154–155, 190, 203, 209, 215, 226–228, 267–268, 269, 293
Vieux Carré, New Orleans 262–263
Vigo County Public Library, Terre Haute, Ind. 166
Vincennes, Ind. 150, 166, 182, 203
Vincennes [Ind.] *Sun* 182
Vintage Series (RCA) 1965 issuance of C-S records 2
Virginia Military Institute 250
Virginia Military Institute *Cadet* 250–251
Virginia Ramblers (band) 124
Vista, Calif. **328**
Vivaudou's Mavis Talcum Powder 31
Vocalian Records 217
Vocco, Rocco 265, 266, 267
Voigt, L. L. Jr. 233
Vollet, Margaret 235
Volstead, Andrew 119

Von Tilzer, Albert 35
Von Tilzer, Harry 35
Vortex (play) 151

"Wabash Blues" (C-S record) 209
Wagner, Charles 42, 79
"The Wail" (JLS composition and C-S record) 187, 209
Wailuku, Maui, Hawaii 91
Wainwright, Alaska 95
Wakeful Order of the Midnight Sons (C-S club) 139
Wald's (Jerry) Orchestra 9, 266, 284, 293
Walder, Woody 43
Waldorf-Astoria Hotel, New York 273
Walker, James J. "Jimmie" 279
Wall Street Bombing (1920) 22
Walsh, Sen. Thomas J. 61, 118
Walter, Bruno 329
Waltham, Mass. 200
Walton, Gov. J. C. 112
Ware, Professor 11
Waring, Tom 153, 156
Waring's (Fred) Pennsylvanians 111, 153, 156, 178, 212, 227, 288, 296
Warm Springs, Ga. 2
Warner Brothers Vitaphone 199
Warner Hotel, Chillicothe, Ohio 167
Warren Sisters 12
Washburn, Mel 274
Washington, George 251
Washington and Lee University 250
Washington, D.C. 104, 126, 139, 140, 152, 156
Waterloo, Iowa 147
Watkins, Elizabeth 251
Watkins, Frankie 75
Watson, M. V. 43
Watts, Calif. 93
Waukegan, Ill. 234, 265
Wausau, Wisc. 171
Wawasee, Ind. 205
"Way Down in the Deep, Low South" (CAC song) 231
Wayburn, Ned 152
WBBM, Chicago 186, 190, 211, 214, 217–218, 237, 238, 286, 287
WCFL, Chicago 214
WDAF, Kansas City, Mo. 39, 42, 49, 50, 51, 70, 75–79, 80, 81, 82, 83–104, 113, 114, 239
"We Don't Want the Bacon" (song) 16
"We Love Us" (JLS song and record) 228
"Weary Blues" (song) 108
WEAU, Sioux City, Iowa 183
Webb, Elida 151

Webster, Ben 43
Weems's (Ted) Orchestra 2, 142, 176, 236, 237, 296
Weihe, Karl 18
Weiner, Ark. 325–326
Weiss, Karl 260
Weiss, Seymour 260
Welch, Rev. Casimir J. 69
Welsh, J. Remington 137
Welty's (Glenn) Orchestra 124
WENR, Chicago 214
Wentworth Military Academy 7, 287, 325
Werner, Edward 42
Werner, Glen 42, 78
Werner's Orchestra, Kansas City, Mo. 63
West, Mae 169
West, Thomas, Lord De la Warr (JLS's ancestor) 9
Westcott Hotel, Richmond, Ind. 170, 174
Western Baseball Association 62, 330
Western Radio Company, Kansas City, Mo. 71–74
Western Vaudeville Managers' Association 14
Westinghouse Electric and Manufacturing Co. Pittsburgh, Pa. 74
Westphal (Frank) and His Columbians 145
Westport High School, Kansas City, Mo. 11, 12, 62
Westport High School Herald 12
Wetherbee, Scoop 136–137
WGAR, Cleveland, Ohio 327
WGN, Chicago 190, 204, 214, 217, 221, 239
WGR, Buffalo, N.Y. 327
WHAD, Milwaukee 169
"What a Girl! What a Night!" (JLS song and C-S record) 224, 225, 231, 257
"What a Life!" (song and C-S record) 267
"What Is Love Without a Quarrel?" (song) 13
"What Were All the Wild Wild Women Like?" (JLS song) 35
"What'll I Do?" (song) 89
"What'll We Do on a Saturday Night When the Town Goes Dry?" (song) 35
WHB, of Sweeney School, Kansas City, Mo. 42, 49, 50, 78–79, 97
"When Lights Are Low" (song) 120
"When the Moon Shines on the Moonshine" (song) 41
"When You're Smiling" (C-S record) 217
"Where the Blue of the Night

Meets the Gold of the Day" (song) 268
Whip-o (product) 31
White (Bob) and His Hollywood Gang 124
White, Stanford 153–154
White City Ballroom, Chicago 126
White City Gardens, "chicken dinner farm" 38
White City Park, Herrin, Ill. 129
White River, Mo. 111
Whiteman, Paul 2, 41, 49, 55, 104, 106, 143, 145, 153, 168, 212, 213, 215, 237, 239, 241, 268, 296, 329
Whiting, Richard 89
Whittier School, Kansas City, Mo. 43
"Who (Stole My Heart Away)?" (song) 89
"Who Takes Care of the Caretaker's Daughter, While the Caretaker's Busy Taking Care?" (song) 88
Who Wouldn't Be Jealous of You?" (C-S record) 225
"Who Wouldn't Love You?" (C-S record) 156
Whoopee (musical and film) 265
"Who's Your Little Whoozis?" (song) 277
"Why Don't My Dreams Come True?" (song) 116, 132
Wichita, Kans. 329
Wickersham, George W. 64
Wickey, Rose 43
Wiggs, Earl 280
Wilcox, Harry 147–148
Wilde, Oscar 178 (note) 291
Wilder, Lewis Suydam 233
Wilkes-Barre, Pa. 250
Wilkinson, Dudley "Bud" 166, **174**, **175**, 266, 272
Wilkinson, S. W. 91
Willard, Jess 109
William Jewell College 14, 62, 330
Williams, Bert 41
Williams, Cathy Birge (Dewey Birge's granddaughter) 3

Williams, Charles E. 94
Williams, Rev. Elmer L. 227
Williams, Frank 93
Williams, Harry "Happy" 69, 75, 101, **102**, 105, **109**, 111
Williams (Ralph) Orchestra 190
Williams, Roger 201
Williams, Ted 42
Williamson, W.Va. 167, 206
Williamson Co. Ill. 112, 129, 131
Willis, Polly 137
Wilson, Walter "Uncle Bob" 137
Wilson, Woodrow 57, 64
Winans, Patti 232
Winchell, Walter 266, 272, 275–279
Winnipeg, Man. 91
Winslow, Max 274, 333
Winslow, Tillie (Mrs. Max) 273, 274, 333
Winter, Arthur Ogden 42
Winter Gardens, La Crosse, Wisc. 168
Winton Theater, Cleveland, Ohio 14
Wisconsin Hotel, Milwaukee 169
Wisconsin Roof, Milwaukee 147
Wisconsin Theater, Milwaukee 169
Witmark Trio 75
WJJD, Chicago 238
WJR, Detroit 327
WJZ, New York 138
WKY, Oklahoma City 106
WMAQ, Chicago 214, 237
WMCA, New York 274
WNRC, Greensboro, N.C. 204
The Woman with Four Faces (film) 108
Women's Christian Temperance Union 223–224
The Wonder Bar (musical) 269
Wonders, Ralph 266
Wood, Walter 13
"The World Is Waiting for the Sunrise" (song) 57, 108
World Theater, Omaha, Nebr. **183**
World War (First) 8–13, 15–20
Worley, Sam 98
"Would You Rather Be a Colonel with an Eagle on Your Shoulder or a Private with a Chicken on Your Knee?" (song) 19
Wright, Glenn 198
Wright, Hoyt 166
Wright (Jack) and the Nomads of Syncopation 124
Wright, Lamar 43
Wrigley Field, Chicago 242
Wrigley's Chewing Gum 31
WRW, of *Kansas City Post* 74
WSB, Atlanta 98, 174–175
Wunderlich's, The Music Center, Kansas City, Mo. 13
Wurlitzer's (Rudolph) Music Store, Kansas City, Mo. 208

Yankton, S. D. 98
Yarrow, Rev. Philip 53
Yellman's (Duke) Orchestra 39, 42, 73, 76–78, 83
"Yes, Sir, That's My Baby" (C-S record) 155–156
"Yes, We Have No Bananas" (song) 55, 88, 89, 108
Yip, Yip, Yaphank (musical) 18
York, Pa. 250
"You Don't Need the Wine to Have a Wonderful Time" (song) 35
"You Tell Her, I Stutter" (song) 113
Young (Ernie) Music Corporation 38, 52, 122, 124, 143–144
Young, S. Glenn 34, 130
Young's Million-Dollar Pier, Atlantic City, N.J. 145–146, 150, 151, 153–156
Youngstown, Ohio 242
Youngstown [Ohio] *Vindicator* 242
"You're Driving Me Crazy" (song) 230–231
"You're the Top" (song) 31

Zanesville, Ohio 206, **207**
Zelaya, Alfonzo 54
Zelston, Bob 222
Ziegfeld, Florenz 57, 87, 166
Ziegfeld Follies 57, 87, 166 (note), 265, 271
Zukor, Adolph 87–88

www.ingramcontent.com/pod-product-compliance
Lightning Source LLC
Chambersburg PA
CBHW081534300426
44116CB00015B/2632